The David & Charles Book of Castles

Drawings and plans by Richard Maguire

DAVID & CHARLES
Newton Abbot   London   North Pomfret (Vt)

The David & Charles Book of

Castles

Plantagenet Somerset Fry

British Library Cataloguing in Publication Data

Fry, Plantagenet Somerset
    David & Charles book of castles.
    1. Castles — Great Britain
    I. Title
    728.8'1'0941   NA7745
    ISBN 0 7153 7976 3

Typeset by Bookmag, Inverness
and printed in Great Britain by Alden Press for
David & Charles (Publishers) Limited
Brunel House Newton Abbot Devon

Published in the United States of America by
David & Charles Inc
North Pomfret   Vermont 05053   USA

Contents

Acknowledgements

In the Bibliography I have acknowledged the very considerable help afforded my research assistants and myself by many government departments, university and city libraries, local authorities and private organizations. Here, I want to thank individual people who worked with me on this most absorbing project, one which I have long wanted to undertake but which could not be done alone. In particular, my grateful thanks are due to Geoffrey Kelly and Richard Slaughter, of the University of East Anglia, who helped prodigiously with the examination of so many journals, chronicles and documents of England and Wales, and Charlotte Sellar who searched so many records in Scotland. I also received considerable assistance from J. G. Davidson and his colleagues at Scotland's Ordnance Survey in Edinburgh, from the chief librarian and her colleagues at Ware Public Library, and from Staff of the University Library at Cambridge. I had much encouragement and guidance from Stuart Rigold, who, sadly, died suddenly in the summer of 1980. I owe a debt to Dr Ronald McGregor, lately Director of Map Studies, University of Edinburgh, for considerable help and specialist guidance over the castles of Scotland. Among those who have made available information on particular castles I want to acknowledge the enthusiastic help and support of Philip Mayes, Pamela Judkin, Richard van Ryl, John Whitehead and Helen Bailey.

To Wendy Galletti my gratitude for a sterling job deciphering my scribble, often typing quantities of text at very short notice, and to my wife Fiona, as always, my gratitude for reading the text critically and making numerous valuable suggestions.

Whatever virtues this work has, they are enormously enhanced by the fine drawings and plans, all sensitively prepared by the artist Richard Maguire. The plans are understandably simple and factual but these drawings are works of art, and I owe a great debt to him.

Book editors generally get ignored in acknowledgements, but in this case, I should like to pay tribute to Anthony Lambert of David & Charles for his skill and patience in making this book ready for publishing.

Finally, I must thank the President, John Morrison, and Fellows of Wolfson College, Cambridge, who by electing me a visiting senior member have provided me with a most stimulating and comfortable environment in which to write a great part of this book.

PLANTAGENET SOMERSET FRY
Wattisfield, Suffolk 1980

Introduction

Why another book on castles? The reader may well ask. What is there left to say that has not already been written in the seemingly endless succession of books on the subject? And indeed, apart from details of recent excavations at several castle sites — and one can reckon that there will be about a dozen interesting discoveries every ten years — the subject may *seem* to have been all but exhausted. And yet it has not.

Throughout western Europe there is a growing interest in castles, their architecture, the economics of building them, their roles in medieval society, their influence on events, their influence on each other. There is even a learned journal devoted to 'castellology', called *Château Gaillard*, which is named after the famous French castle of that name, built by Richard the Lion Heart on a rock overlooking the Seine. And there are the books and monographs that continue to appear. These may be divided into two kinds: the academic studies, all of which are essential reading for anyone interested in castles beyond the point of an afternoon out visiting one; and the more popular surveys which attempt to encapsulate in one volume the complex subject of castles and what people used them for. There will always be a need for both kinds. I believe there is also room for a fresh look at castles which bridges the gap between the serious study and the popular survey, that projects in perhaps simpler terms the latest thinking about castles based upon the most recent investigations. And there is room for a one-volume gazetteer of the castles of Great Britain, whether they be extensive palatial stone buildings or long-neglected earth mounds with or without stone remnants.

There is a tendency in popular studies of castles to perpetuate some of the theories and assumptions of earlier works. One can, for example, still read of the notion that there was a tidy progression in the development of medieval castle-building. Square great towers (wrongly called keeps) were followed by polygonal great towers

7

which in turn advanced to cylindrical great towers. Yet this view has been disposed of for some time (see chapter 4). Another oft-repeated contention is that the role of the castle declined because of the introduction of gunpowder and artillery, but this overlooks the long period (more than three centuries) after this innovation during which castles remained for most of the time manifestly important. It also ascribes to early artillery an effectiveness that it certainly did not possess. Several medieval castles withstood months of intermittent artillery attack during the Civil War (notably Raglan and Donnington) and are still standing to prove it. These and other assumptions merit discussion, for alternative views add greatly to the overall fascination of castles and their development.

The first third of this book is directed towards an understanding of castle design and building, of the materials used, and of the role castles played in medieval society. It proposes no new theories and it reveals few startling discoveries. But the most interesting research results of recent years are discussed in some detail.

The first part is followed by the Gazetteer which is arranged in alphabetical order, first in England, then Wales and lastly Scotland. It contains a full list of over a thousand castles and sites that have any significance. It is comprehensive within the limits of the definition of a castle which is given on p.9, and it covers a building period of about 600 years, from 1066 to about 1650. The Gazetteer is probably the first of its kind to deal with the castles in all three countries in one volume. Excluded are the later seventeenth- and eighteenth-century baronial houses in Scotland, which might have afforded some protection against siege but which were not normally designed for that purpose. Likewise, English and Welsh great houses which are (or were) called 'castle' but which were not fortified are omitted.

This is a source book of information about castles and castle sites, the result of visiting several hundred sites over the past few years and of studying the considerable literature on the subject, from the earliest medieval texts (in translation) to the most recently published books and papers. In several instances I have been able to examine and discuss findings yet to be written up, and it is a privilege to be allowed to include digests of these. Within the compass of the book it is not possible to include everything, but there is enough to whet the appetite of castle enthusiasts to take up the search for more, to join the ranks of those many painstaking and enthusiastic local historians and archaeologists who have done so much for castle history, without whose work no book like this could be written.

1
What is a Castle?

Buildings are generally designed and constructed for a single purpose. The cathedral, the house, the factory, the office block, the barn, the hotel, the theatre — even the lighthouse, the prison and the public convenience — each is designed basically to fulfil one function. Looking back in history it was the same: the temple, the villa, the arena, the pyramid, the palace, they were single-purpose buildings. The exception was the castle. From the beginning, when it appeared as a structure in the years following the break-up of the empire of Charlemagne and the resulting collapse of the authority of central government in western Europe in the ninth century, the castle was built for two separate but interdependent purposes. It was a home for its owner, where he could shelter his family and dependants and entertain his guests, and at the same time a structure strong enough to keep unwanted people out and from which he could sally forth to attack his neighbouring or more distant enemies or rivals. In short, it was a properly fortified residence. And since the castle was introduced at a time when society was becoming dominated by the mounted knight in armour and by his superiors — the lords, counts, dukes and kings, in ascending order — whom he served and to whom he owed allegiance, we should add the word 'military' to our definition. Thus, the castle was a properly fortified military residence, which is as exact a definition as can be given.

The stereotyped idea of a castle is generally one of a palatial complex of many towers, great and small, some clustered together, others standing alone; thick, tall, battlemented walls interspersed with numerous turrets and a huge gatehouse or two; drawbridges with screeching chains; a vast dining hall; dark corridors; grim dungeons where prisoners eked out their days in a losing battle with rats, hunger and diseases; a chapel and a courtyard; and a plethora of portcullises and heavily iron-studded gates at every point where men came in or went out. This is the familiar picture, fostered by the

imaginations of some medieval artists, Victorian illustrators and twentieth-century cinema set designers. True, there are some very large castles in Britain that once had most of these features, like Warwick, Caerphilly, London, Caernarvon, Leeds (Kent), and Alnwick.

The great majority of castles, however, were much less complex and glamorous than that. The timber castle at Ardres in Flanders, built in c.1117, seems palatial from its near-contemporary description (p.34) but we must allow for exaggeration. We have also to allow for the fact that palatial castles were extremely expensive to build and that very few people throughout the Middle Ages could afford them. And yet each castle, however complex or however simple, was an intensely individual structure, reflecting the mixture of basic military needs for defensive and offensive capability with the more personal residential demands of the owner, and it is this, perhaps more than anything else, that makes castles so fascinating.

Our definition embraces many thousands of castles, in a great variety of shapes and sizes, which, during a period of 6–700 years, appeared all over western Europe (as well as those in eastern Europe and the Levant). More than 2,000 of them were built in the British Isles and all were of two fundamental designs — the fortified great tower and the fortified enclosure, and in numerous instances, combinations of the two. These design types and their variations are discussed in chapter 4, but we should identify the two basic forms. The great tower, *magna turris* as it is called in medieval documents, is the right phrase for that vertical structure, generally though not always taller than its maximum width, which is nowadays commonly called a 'keep'. Keep is a misleading word: it was not used in English literature until the later half of the sixteenth century, and it will not be used in this book, except with one particular type of castle, the shell keep (p.52). The great tower was a fortified house, with two, three, four or five storeys. It was square, rectangular, cylindrical, polygonal, or D-ended in plan. It had thick walls, battlemented parapets at the top, well-protected entrances, narrow windows (though there were exceptions) and generally, though not always, stood on a sloping plinth. It was built of wood, stone, or sometimes both, or later of brick. If it was made of wood, it was almost certainly part of a motte castle (see chapter 3). If it was stone or brick, it stood inside a surrounding wall with a gateway and with or without turrets along the wall.

It was extremely rare for a great tower not to be inside a walled enclosure of some kind, whereas the fortified enclosure was often constructed as a complete castle without having a great tower. In these instances, and they were many and varied, the quarters that would otherwise be in a great tower were disposed in alternative buildings inside the enclosure, such as a chapel, dining hall, chambers and guardrooms, which would be ranged together or separately along the inside of the wall or free-standing in the courtyard. Some castles with great towers would also have additional buildings in the enclosure. Enclosure castles were provided with a gateway or a larger version of the gateway, a gatehouse which in some cases were as big as a great tower (cf. Tonbridge, Dunstanburgh, Baconsthorpe). Although the great tower inside an enclosure was the last line of defence under siege, since defenders of the castle retired to it once they had been dislodged from the parapets on the wall, it should not be thought that enclosure castles without great towers were not capable of offering stout resistance. Many indeed were provided with specially strong towers or turrets along the wall, each of which could be fought for, inch by inch, tower by tower, before surrender. Two excellent examples of such enclosure castles are Framlingham and Conwy (qq.v).

It used to be thought that the first castles were all built of wood, either on mounds of earth (motte castles) or on more level ground, and that stone castles followed as a form of improvement and as more permanent structures. Stone castles were certainly longer lasting, but it is now clear that castles of wood and castles of stone were built at the same time, in Britain and in Europe, though in Britain the great majority of the two hundred or so castles built between 1066 and about 1100 were wooden. What largely determined the choice of material was how quickly the castle was needed and what was available locally. Wooden castles in Britain (whose characteristics are described in chapter 3) were often built of oak. In the eleventh century this tree was plentiful and widely distributed, and of its many species, green oak was especially suitable for buildings. Green oak was easy to work, and if cut down after about thirty years growth, it was ready to be made into planks and posts to be cut and shaped without a lot of trimming and wastage.

Stone castles were generally built from the nearest supply of stone, and in Britain, as in Europe, the geological map provides a fascinating variety of types of rock which produce stone for building (see p.65). Among the most instantly recognizable types of stone for castle building are flint, red sandstone, yellow sandstone, carstone,

Barnack and granite. A fine limestone produced at Caen in Normandy was also used in several British castles, though it was an expensive operation bringing it across the Channel to the site. Later in the fourteenth century and the fifteenth century, some castles were built of brick, which was often made locally. Brick may seem too soft a material to use for fortification, but this is not so and it will be noted that one or two brick-built castles were involved in sieges or attacked with guns (such as Caister).

The castle was the product of feudalism, the system whereby a lord and his vassals had a contract, the former to provide protection and to lease land to the latter in return for services of one kind or another, in particular military service. In the chaos that followed the break-up of central government in the countries of western Europe in the ninth century, accelerated as it was by Viking invasions, there emerged a new unit of society, the estate or domain, which was controlled by a king, a lord, or the church, and which became a self-reliant and self-sufficient community. The estate was based on land, not as a mere possession so much as a food-producing unit. The controllers retained some of the land for themselves and employed people to work on it, generally under conditions of slavery; the remainder was leased to tenants to work for themselves in return for payment in kind, that is, a proportion of the produce. Some controllers, particularly the kings, owned several estates, some bordering on each other and others scattered, and they employed people to manage them and collect the produce from the fields. Because it was so difficult to move goods about the countryside in those times, controllers found it more satisfactory to visit their estates and live off their produce for short periods rather than have everything brought to a central point. Where controllers were kings (rulers of large areas) or powerful counts (like the counts of Anjou), they were generally accompanied on these visits by a retinue of officials to assist with the variety of business that had to be dealt with, such as the administration of justice, taxation and estate matters. As Maurice Keen put it, government became peripatetic (in *The Pelican History of Mediaeval Europe*). But in doing so, it yielded its authority to a considerable extent to the lords at the next level in the social structure, for they had the advantage of permanent residence in their domains. They had their own domain laws and were responsible for maintaining order in their territories. They swore allegiance to the king or to their senior counts but they often ignored their authority. William, Duke of Normandy, for example, was so powerful that his

13

overlord, the king of France, was afraid of him. The lords became petty kings in their domains and had private armies to defend them against the attacks of neighbours and rivals. But private armies had to be paid for, fed, clothed and equipped, and lords expected their tenants who were, after all, protected by the armies, to contribute to these expenses. Gradually, tenants surrendered many rights and freedoms as the price of continued security. In effect they, and in due course their children after them, came to be bound to the land for their lives. For the lords the system was useful for continuity in the working of the estates.

There was another class of men, neither great lords nor tenants: they were the professional fighting men. They were bound to the king or the lords by oaths of loyalty to fight for them, usually on horseback, to assist them in any enterprises they might undertake. In return they were protected by the king or lords in the latters' courts, they were given help to maintain their horses, equipment, weapons and armour, and they might be granted land to run as income-producing farms or allotted the revenues of existing estates. These vassals, as they were called, were very important members of the communities. Sometimes they were appointed as local governors by the king, and later as governors of greater regions, counties as they were known (from the Latin *comes*), who collected taxes, presided over local courts and led local levies of troops in the war. They were called upon to protect their neighbourhoods when these were threatened by invasion, particularly during the long years of the Viking raids in western Europe (c.780–c.1020, and even afterwards). Very gradually, a new kind of aristocracy developed, a military caste, and it was strengthened when it became hereditary. When a vassal died his son took over. He became the king's man, as the saying went, with an oath of fealty to the king, promising to serve faithfully for life. In return he was given a fee (Latin, *feudum*), that is, the rights and revenues that his father had enjoyed. It is from this that the term feudal is derived. The feudal system was not, however, foolproof, and vassals could not always be depended upon to keep their oaths of loyalty. They could be won over by other more powerful lords ready to give them a better deal. Or they could rebel in order to set themselves up as great lords. They were the men with the weapons, the horses and the training for war; the initiative was generally on their side. Only a powerful king, duke or count could control his vassals, and some of them even failed to do this effectively. The warring between lords and vassals, and also between lords and their superiors, was to become a more or less permanent feature of the European scene for nearly half a millennium, from the beginning of the eleventh century right through to the mid-fifteenth. This warfare was sometimes waged in the open, that is, pitched battles between mounted knights and foot-soldiery on both sides, but it was more often waged round the power base of the lord, his properly fortified military residence. This brings us back to the castle to whose definition we must now add one final phrase. The castle was the properly fortified military residence of a lord, and by lord we include king, duke, count and certain kinds of knight. A lord required a fortified residence for his own and his family's comfort and protection, to shelter his dependants in time of war and to provide barracks for his knights and their horses, together with the blacksmiths, armourers, carpenters and other needed craftsmen. He also required headquarters from which to administer his estates, and here the nature and size of the castle played a vital role. The castle dominated the landscape. It was the visual expression of his authority over the land he controlled. His tenants and their workers could feel some security under the shadow of the building, as it were, and some of his potential enemies might be overawed by it, or at least, encouraged to think twice before attacking it. The extent of the lord's control, moreover, could be measured by how far he and his knights could ride to battle, fight and return to the castle in one operation, thought to have averaged about ten miles each way. In other words, he who held the castle controlled the land around it. The principal objective of a lord at war was not only to keep things that way but also to take the castle of his enemy, if he could, for that would greatly increase his power and wealth, since he would also win the lands that went with it — subject, of course, to the permission of his overlord that he might enjoy his prize.

The possession of castles, therefore, was as crucial to maintaining power as having a well-disciplined private army of armoured knights. This was recognized by most of the kings, dukes and counts in the tenth and eleventh centuries (and later too) and by no one more so than Fulk Nerra, Count of Anjou from 987 to 1040. He riveted his hold upon Anjou by building at least thirteen castles (which can be named, p.19) and probably several more. And in Fulk's last years, William, Duke of Normandy, then in his teens, studied the lesson of building and acquiring castles as strategic weapons which he was to employ so effectively in his later campaigns to dominate his duchy and, later still, England.

2

Castles in Europe

Castles were not a British invention. They had evolved in western Europe as an integral part of the development of feudalism at least two centuries before William, Duke of Normandy, landed on the south coast of England in September 1066. When castles did finally come to Britain, they were grafted onto the landscape by force. They were entirely European structures and to the English, then the Welsh, and finally the Scots and the Irish, they were strange, foreign and terrifying. A study of British castles must therefore include a quick look at western European castles of the tenth and eleventh centuries.

The castle in Europe was then a properly fortified military residence for a lord (or king). In many instances, its role went beyond our basic definition. In what is now Switzerland, some castles acted as toll stations for mountain passes; in France, some were military arsenals; in Italy, they could be repositories for holy relics, and, in Germany, they might be watch-towers. Or they could be any of these things in all these and other countries. But whatever function they performed, castles were the most important secular buildings in medieval western Europe. Apart from ordinary homes, they were probably the most numerous, too. Authoritative estimates range from over 10,000 in Germany, as many in France, several thousand in Spain, about 1,000 in what is now Belgium and, as we have seen, eventually well over 2,000 in Britain and Ireland. The map on p.29 relates solely to motte castles in Britain between about 1066 and sometime in the thirteenth century. It would have been hard to travel for ten miles in most districts without seeing one.

The earliest fortifications in these times were enclosures surrounded by ditches and earthwork ramparts, with wooden buildings inside. They were derived from Roman forts and camps of several centuries before, and in the late eighth and most of the ninth century in western Europe these enclosures were chiefly defensive. They

16

were often built in a hurry, to escape the Viking raids or to protect communities threatened by marauding robbers and brigands. As the Viking raids became more numerous and wide-ranging, the need for fortifications increased. This coincided with the growth of the feudal idea of society. Small areas of land were coming under the control of powerful lords (and larger areas under greater lords, or kings) which they ruled from fortified enclosures and, in due course, castles. In time, castles became symbols of their authority as well as practical signs of it.

Castles evolved from these community-protecting fortified enclosures into more personal residences intended chiefly for housing lords, their families and most necessary dependants, such as servants, armed knights and perhaps bodyguards. William Anderson, in *Castles of Europe*, has suggested a possible evolution, from investigations at the Husterknupp, a fortified site on the River Erft in western Germany, as follows. An assemblage of buildings for domestic use, with stables for horses and stores for weapons, was surrounded by a tall and thick wooden palisade (a). Sometimes sites

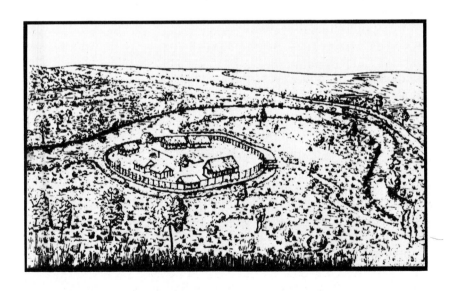

were chosen in a loop of a river or stream. The lord and his dependants lived within, safe — or at least safer — from attacks by Vikings, marauders or greedy neighbours. As the power of the lord grew, because of the increasing need for a protector, he began to separate himself from his dependants, who were becoming more

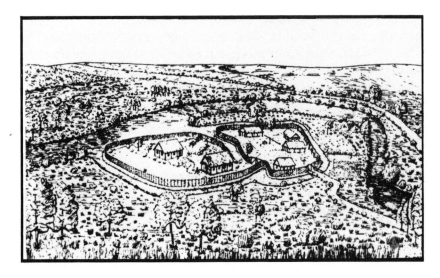

firmly bound to him. This is shown by a change in castle design. The enclosure split into two, with palisading round both halves, the lord's half being on slightly higher ground (b). The new form then evolved into the motte-and-bailey castle in which the lord's quarters were piled one on top of the other inside a wooden tower (c). Stage (a) was the general pattern in the late eighth, ninth and perhaps into the tenth century; stage (b) was raised in the tenth and stage (c) probably dates from the mid-eleventh century. It seems likely that many western European castles followed this sort of pattern, but in time

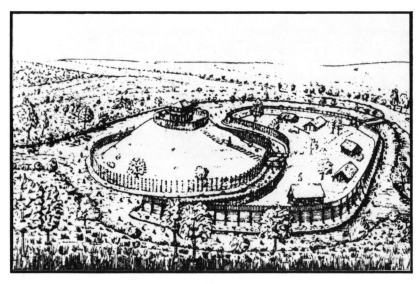

the last stage, a real castle according to our definition, probably began to be built from scratch in the late tenth or early eleventh century, particularly in France, where it was used as an offensive weapon in the imposition of feudalism. By this time, many towers in stage (c) were built of stone and not wood. Certainly, when the Conqueror came to England in 1066 he knew all about the construction of stage (c) castles in both materials, and the Bayeux Tapestry depicts several examples of wooden castles already raised in Normandy by him or with his permission, or by his adversaries. It also portrays the first motte-and-bailey castle he built in England, on the shore at Hastings.

Motte-and-bailey castles are explained more fully in the next chapter. We turn now to the earliest stone castles in western Europe. It is not possible to say which were the first to be built, but among them were some of the tenth-century castles in France. One was Peyrepertuse, erected on a mountain ridge in the Pyrenees. Another was a structure, part of the Château du Coudray, at Chinon, near Tours. Another was Rouen, put up in the late tenth century. A fourth was Doué-la-Fontaine, in Anjou, built by Theobald, Count of Blois, in the mid-tenth century. This rectangular stone tower is now considered to be the earliest stone great tower built as a fortress-residence in France (actually, it was an improvement on an even earlier single-storeyed hall). And at the Chillon Castle complex, at the extreme east of Lake Geneva in Switzerland, the tower of Alinge is datable to about 1000.

The castle at Doué-la-Fontaine was dated less than ten years ago. Before that, the rectangular great tower at Langéais, a two-storeyed fortified hall on raised ground, built sometime between 1000 and 1020, was for a long time taken to be the oldest stone castle in France. It was built by Fulk Nerra, Count of Anjou, who had inherited a realm whose land was rich and fertile and over which he intended to rule with absolute authority, and which he aimed to expand at the expense of his neighbours. He was a warrior with a perfectly foul temper and is said to have been the founder not only of the great race of Plantagenet, but also of the furious and volatile disposition of practically every member of it. Nominally, Fulk was a vassal of the king of France, but in reality he was more powerful than his suzerain. His policy was to win land and construct a great castle upon it, from which to police the land. Thirteen castles are known to have been raised during his rule: Château Gontier (c.1007), Durtal, Baugé, Montlévrier, Passavant, Montreuil-Bellay (c.1020), Faye-la-

19

Vineuse, Montcontour, Mirebeau (c.1005), Langéais (c.1010), Montrésor, Sainte-Maure and Chaumont. There are believed to have been several others, including Trèves, Montbazon and Montfaucon (c.1025).

Many of these Angevin castles were added to in succeeding centuries. Langéais had new structures put up beside it, and in the fifteenth century these were demolished, except for the original great tower. In their first stages, some of the castles consisted only of a stone great tower with wooden palisading round the enclosure in which they stood. Others were variations of the motte-and-bailey castle. Wooden great towers were, for the most part, every bit as effective defensive/offensive fortresses as stone towers. The great castle of Ardres, fortress of the counts of Guisnes, was a wooden castle in the early 1100s. A description has survived (chapter 3).

Langéais Castle, on a spur beside the River Loire, is interesting for several reasons. It has features that figure in some later castles in France and Britain, though we do not mean by this that the builders of the latter were necessarily influenced by it. Basically, it was an oblong tower, about 55ft by about 23ft, and two storeys high, with walls about 10ft thick, more like a hall than a tower. (Chepstow great

Langéais, near Tours

20

tower in Wales, started c.1067-71, was over twice as long as it was broad — 100ft by 40ft — looked rather like a hall and was perched on a spur of land beside the River Wye.) But the military purpose of Langéais was clearly shown by its extremely limited window space, its pilaster buttresses along the outside walls and its entrance, a plain round arch situated at first-floor level and so less easy to break into. The walls were made from unusually small stone blocks, set in regular courses.

During the first decades of the eleventh century, Fulk advanced the development of the feudal system in Anjou, putting into practice its military aspects better than any of his neighbours. His conquests made him rich, which enabled him to spend freely on stone for his castles. His restless and aggressive nature and his fiery temper kept his subjects in a perpetual state of fear and insecurity. He bequeathed to his son Geoffrey II (1040–60) a formidable county and a legacy of planned military enterprises, many of which the son was able to fulfil, notably the reduction of the city of Tours. Fulk and Geoffrey, perhaps more than any others, developed the military and aggressive role of the castle, since they used them as offensive weapons. One has the impression that they did not sit behind castle walls resisting siege, but rather stormed out of the gates, fought battles in the field and marched on to besiege other castles. They were the greatest castle-builders of their time in Europe, but they were not the only ones. Their castles were being studied and imitated, and in the end improved upon, by the Normans.

The Normans originated from Viking settlers in north-west France. Under their leader Rollo they established a colony around the mouth of the Seine, with a capital at Rouen, in the early 900s. Rollo was obliged to acknowledge Charles the Simple, King of France, as his overlord, but the Viking raids of the previous century had so fragmented France that royal authority was impossible to enforce. Rollo and his successors, first counts of Rouen and later dukes of Normandy, built up their power base over the years through the medium of feudalism and by the use of castles. Wooden castles were built in Rollo's time (not on mounds of earth but simple palisaded enclosures), but his grandson Richard I (942–96) introduced stone castles, notably at Rouen where, sometime in the 970s or 980s, he built a fortress-palace that contained a great tower of stone. At Ivry, near Evreux, his half-brother Ralph held a castle which the early twelfth-century chronicler Ordericus Vitalis described as huge and strongly fortified. According to another chronicler, it was sited on top of a hill overlooking the town. Ordericus added that the builder was put to death after finishing the work, so that he could not repeat his skills on behalf of anyone else! Other castles built in Normandy between about 1000 and the 1030s included Falaise, Cherbourg, Tillières and Cherrueix. Falaise, probably the place where William, Duke of Normandy, was conceived and born of a love affair between his father, known as Robert the Devil, and Arlette, a tanner's daughter, received a great tower in the time of William. It was rebuilt by his youngest son, Henry I, sometime in the early 1100s, and is said to have influenced the design of Norwich's great tower (q.v).

The dukes of Normandy encountered the same difficulties in maintaining their authority as other dukes and counts. The vassal lords they appointed to police the various sub-divisions of land could not always be relied upon to keep their oaths of loyalty. In times of danger from outside, particularly from Anjou or even from the kings of France, or of civil war, vassals sometimes forgot their feudal obligations and pursued private quarrels, besieging each other's castles and even building new ones to add to their power. Technically they were not allowed to build a castle without leave from their dukes; control of castle-building had been instituted as early as the mid-ninth century when Charles the Bald (823–77), King of France, banned the construction of fortifications without royal permission and had, in 864, actually ordered 'castles and fortifications and enclosures' raised without leave to be demolished. The rule was upheld in Normandy but 'illegal' (sometimes known as adulterine) castles were built, nonetheless, and by the time of the death of Robert, Duke of Normandy, in 1035, there were almost as many castles in private hands as those which belonged to the duke or to a lord loyal to him. At Robert's death the position was aggravated because he had named his bastard son William, not yet ten years old, as his heir. William was not acceptable to many of the duke's vassals and there was a fresh flurry of castle-building (mostly of small castles) without permission. 'They raised earthwork enclosures throughout many districts and built themselves very safe castles', was how the chronicler William of Jumièges (who died c.1090) put it.

For ten years the Duchy of Normandy was in a state of anarchy. Then, in 1047, William, barely twenty years old but already hardened by his war-ridden environment, met and crushed a coalition of vassals at the Battle of Val-des-Dunes. This was a battle in the open, and he triumphed through the superior skill and horsemanship of his loyal armed knights and by his leadership. In the same year he began the siege of the castle at Brionne and, the next year, brought it down. These two events were not the end of his troubles, but they did mark the end of the period of anarchy, a fact which was decisively confirmed when William ordered the destruction of many of the adulterine castles.

For the next eighteen years, William warred incessantly to stabilize his duchy. He fought against his own vassals, against Anjou and even against the Vikings, notwithstanding that he was of Viking descent himself. He fought in the open field, he besieged and took his enemy's castles, and according to the records, he won every battle and every castle he invested. By 1065 he had become the foremost warrior and one of the most experienced castle-builders in Europe. He had developed feudalism in Normandy to such an extent that all his knights were bound to give him up to forty days' service each year, which more or less guaranteed him a standing army in battle order throughout the year. Most of his lords had sworn oaths of allegiance to him (they had by now stopped worrying about whether he was legitimate or not) and few were prepared to break them. His long run of success and his gifts of leadership won him a respect offered to few men in those times.

But the Viking spirit was essentially restless, adventurous and warlike. William, his male relatives and his lords were unable to settle down and enjoy what they had. They felt an irresistible urge to move on, seek new lands to conquer and bring under the Norman concept of feudalism, and in the middle of the eleventh century, they fanned outwards from Normandy, south into Italy under Robert Guiscard and north-west into England under William himself. William picked a quarrel with Harold II, king of the English, who had refused to continue the pro-Norman policies of his predecessor Edward the Confessor (who surrounded himself with Norman lords for friends), and in 1066 he embarked upon the only successful invasion of England to have taken place in the thousand years following the time of Ethelred II, the Unready. In return for their military assistance in the form of men, arms, horses and money, William offered his land-hungry lords large areas of England in which to settle and construct new feudal lordships, once the Anglo-Saxons had been overcome and dispossessed.

William planned the invasion with consummate skill and carried it out with remarkable daring. Using a force of hardly more than 6,000 men, he launched his attack against a nation of more than one million people. His weapons were the mailed knight on horseback and the motte-and-bailey castle. He intended to impose upon England a revised form of feudalism which had as its principal obligation the allegiance of every man in the kingdom to the king first, and to his immediate overlord, or superior tenant, a tardy second. It would be easier to enforce this revision in a newly conquered land, and the danger of over-mighty lords threatening to break up the new order could be greatly reduced by allotting to the lords their lands in separated estates. If they wanted to rebel, they would not be able to assemble all their knights and troops without running the gauntlet of crossing king's land, or lands belonging to other lords whose support, or even acquiescence, could not necessarily be counted upon. William had rebellions on his hands in Normandy now and again during the remainder of his rule (1066–87) but, except for those led by Waltheof and Hereward, both of whom were Anglo-Saxons who refused to recognize the Norman Conquest, there were no rebellions in England. Under a strong king, William's system worked. It was greatly facilitated by his keeping control of all castles built by himself or by permission. This was the beginning of the system of licensing castles in England, though it was not formalized until the thirteenth century. Castles acted not only as offensive structures in the consolidation of William's conquest and settlement; they were also administrative centres for the king and his lords in the business of getting the feudal system to work in preliminary years. For either use they had to be built in a hurry, and it is easier to understand the nature of castle-building if it is remembered that the great majority of castles were raised under great pressure. The very first, the wooden castle at Hastings (q.v.) was probably built inside a fortnight. It had to be, for when William landed nearby at the end of September 1066, his adversary, Harold II, was marching hotfoot down from his recent victory against Harald Hardraada, King of Norway, at Stamford Bridge in Yorkshire and would reach the Sussex shore within that time.

3
Motte Castles in Britain

William the Conqueror and his Norman lords and knights built the first castles in Britain expressly as military stronghold-cum-residences from which to police their newly conquered lands. They built them of stone (with or without timber) and of earth and timber, and the majority of the earliest castles were of this latter type. These consisted of a huge flat-topped mound of earth (motte) surmounted with a tall wooden tower, with an irregularly shaped enclosure (bailey) at one side of the tower (or in some cases surrounding it), the whole encircled by a deep ditch. The top of the motte and the perimeter of the bailey were enclosed by timber palisading. These castles, which for convenience we will henceforth call motte castles, were erected in their hundreds between 1066 and about 1200 (and a few even later). The most prominent remains of a great many of

them, the mottes, can still be seen throughout England and Wales, and here and there in Scotland. They are as a rule instantly recognizable. A few examples which can be seen unadorned in towns or villages include Thetford (Norfolk), Pleshey (Essex), Hawick (Borders), and in the countryside at Hallaton (Leicestershire) and Hen Domen (Powys). There are also many more, bearing the remains of later stonework additions, such as Carisbrooke (Isle of Wight), Clifford's Tower (York) and the two mottes at Lewes (Sussex).

At the time of the Conquest there were numerous motte castles in western Europe, as well as a sizeable number and variety of stone castles (to which we have referred). They complemented the military force that was part and parcel of the feudal system of society. The system was not then operating in Britain. In Scotland and Wales society was to some degree clannish and neither country had strong central government. In England, the Anglo-Saxons were more united, but they had no need for instruments of military repression such as armies of mailed and mounted knights or exclusive fortresses, and there were no castles. The three castles in Herefordshire — Ewias Harold, Hereford and Richard's Castle — suggested in the *Anglo-Saxon Chronicle* and believed by later historians to have been built by Norman friends of Edward the Confessor in the 1050s, cannot be substantiated. Such experience as the Anglo-Saxons had of defensive earthworks and fortifications was confined to their *burhs*, towns that were strengthened with walls and ramparts, in which whole communities sought protection from the raids of the Vikings.

When the Conqueror arrived on the shore at Hastings, late in September 1066, one of his first acts was to have a motte castle built on the spot. It is possible that the wooden components had been pre-fabricated in Normandy and brought over in one or two of his invasion transports (there is evidence of tower pre-fabrication in the twelfth century). But whether that was so or not, the castle went up with great speed. The construction work was done largely by Anglo-Saxons pressed into service as diggers, as graphically shown on the Bayeux Tapestry, and this *before* the great battle, which was to be fought on 14 October. It was a sign of things to come.

The Anglo-Saxon army was overwhelmed and the king, Harold II, slain. Even if Harold had had a castle nearby, it would probably not have made any difference to the outcome. But the fact that there were no castles anywhere in England did have a decisive effect upon

Building the motte castle at Hastings, as depicted on the Bayeux Tapestry. The castle was raised on the shore *before* the battle which William of Normandy won so resoundingly

Anglo-Saxon resistance to the conquerors. Ordericus Vitalis reckoned that they did not stand a chance against the Norman knights. William's conquest was certainly swift and thorough. By the end of 1066 he had been crowned King of England at Westminster Abbey, work had been started on two, possibly three, motte castles in London, and the Anglo-Saxon earthworks at Dover had been reconstructed. Work had probably begun on several other motte castles as well, including Wallingford and Winchester.

In the next twenty years the Conqueror built, or gave his lords leave to erect, nearly a hundred motte castles upon the landscape of England. By 1100, his successor, William Rufus, and his lords, had pushed the number over 200, and these included many in east and south Wales. Probably twice as many again were raised and in use by about 1150, and this does not include the first stone castles that were being built on a smaller numerical scale. Motte castles had also begun to be erected in Scotland by Norman associates of the kings of Scotland, Edgar, Alexander I and David I. It is worth considering these figures and what they meant to the native inhabitants of Britain.

Until the first of the stone great towers were completed in the last years of the eleventh century and the first cathedrals and abbeys went up, these motte castles were the biggest buildings ever seen in this country since Roman times. Many of them, particularly those in East

27

Anglia, could be seen from great distances. They dwarfed the houses nearby: the smallest mottes were at least 100ft across the base, though the average was much greater, at between 200 and 250ft (as at Ongar, Pleshey, Lewes, Berkhamsted, York *et al*). With their wooden towers, motte castles were anything from about 70ft to about 120ft tall (Thetford may have been 140ft). The top of the motte at Berkhamsted was large enough to contain several houses, on whichThomas Becket, later Archbishop of Canterbury, spent money in 1157–8. More than a hundred houses were demolished in Norwich to make room for the motte castle put up in the early part of the Conqueror's reign. To many of the simpler town and country folk in England, motte castles were objects of terror. But they were meant to be, for the conquerors had them built to frighten the Anglo-Saxons into submission and keep them subjugated. To emphasize the point, the Normans compelled the Anglo-Saxons to do most of the building work.

The keynotes of William's invasion and conquest were speed and ruthlessness, which of course create terror. They were the equivalent of Nazi *Blitzkrieg* methods. Motte castles were wanted in a hurry. Some were actually completed for occupation purposes inside a fortnight (Hastings, York, Dover). But this was only possible by deploying — employing implies payment for the work — large gangs of men, and William had a vast pool of labour to draw upon in England. Before the Conquest, English kings had a right, called *burh-bot*, to direct workers from their normal jobs into building fortifications for the *burhs*. The men were helping to protect themselves and their compatriots, and they probably received pay. The Conqueror, on the other hand, was forcing men to work on private fortresses which were, with bitter irony, being raised in order to suppress them. According to the first volume of *The History of the King's Works*, 'Burh-bot became castelwerke'. Labour gangs were rounded up from the nearest towns and, where necessary, from further afield. To build a motte castle at Ely (now visible as Cherry Hill) William took men from Bedfordshire and Huntingdonshire as well as from Cambridgeshire. He also expropriated land from the Abbot of Ely for the site.

It has been suggested that William had a preconceived overall strategic plan for castle-building in England. This is unlikely, for he could not have known the geography well enough. Moreover, an overall plan was not necessary. His army of mail-clad mounted knights, supported by archers of high skill, was the most formidable

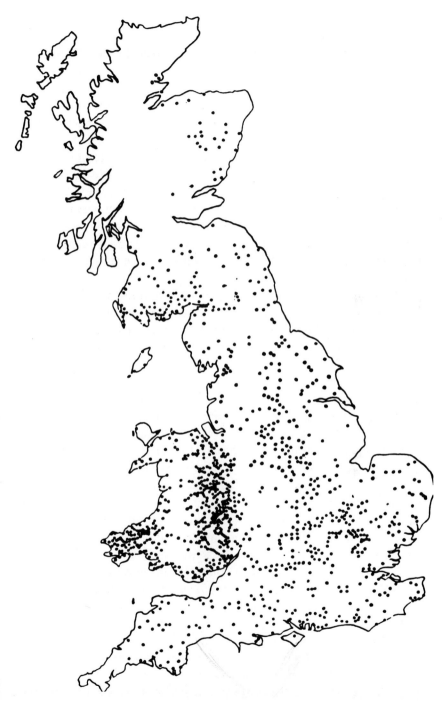

The distribution of motte castles in Great Britain (after D. F. Renn)

in western Europe. Even the king of France, the overlord of Normandy, was afraid of them. William was confident that he would be able to establish his bridgehead in Sussex, take the English by surprise and win in any confrontation with the forces of the English king. So it happened, and with his army of only 6,000 men he swiftly overran a nation of over a million people. He could afford to work out the castle-building programme as he went along. It would follow certain tactical requirements.

William divided the programme into two spheres. He would build a number of castles himself with Anglo-Saxon labour directed by Norman captains, at sites at or near key points in England. He would also allow his followers to build castles in those pockets of land he had decided to award them for their part in his victory. They too would use Anglo-Saxon labour. But their castles were to be held only with his specific permission: what he gave he could always take away. Practically every castle built in his reign, and in that of Rufus, was sited on or near the important routes of communication across the country. They were near river crossings (Hereford, Cambridge, Bedford, Shrewsbury); they guarded harbours (Dover, Newcastle, Rochester); they protected the coasts from foreign attack (Bramber, Arundel, Lewes); they were bult on elevated land to dominate extensive areas of countryside (Carisbrooke, Ely, Windsor), or to overawe towns (York, Lincoln, Winchester, Norwich). They were always near a water supply of some kind. The need for them was often dictated at short notice. Ely Castle, for example, was erected to deal with the last embers of resistance to Norman rule following the surrender of Hereward the Wake. Durham Castle was built to house a garrison for the Bishop of Durham to call out in the event of invasion from Scotland, which the king expected following his recent expedition across the River Forth.

In general, motte castles conformed more or less to a basic plan. The motte stood astride or next to an edge of the bailey. There were, however, many variations of the plan. In some cases the motte was inside the bailey, as at Montacute (Somerset) and Oxford. At Lewes and Lincoln there were two mottes astride the edges of one bailey. At Windsor there were two baileys, one each side of the motte, and one at lower level than the other — still the basic plan today. Mottes and baileys were constructed in a variety of shapes. Mottes ranged in height from about 25-30ft (Hawick) to over 80ft (Thetford). The size of a bailey might be anything from two to ten acres or so, but would generally be such that it could be covered at all points within bowshot

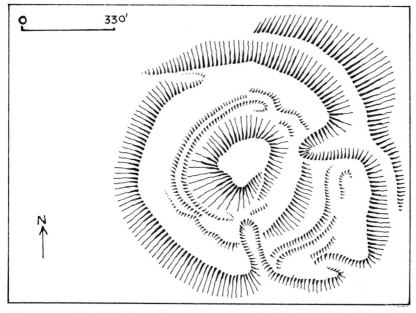

Montacute: plan of the eleventh-century motte castle (after Ella S. Armitage). The high oval motte is still visible today

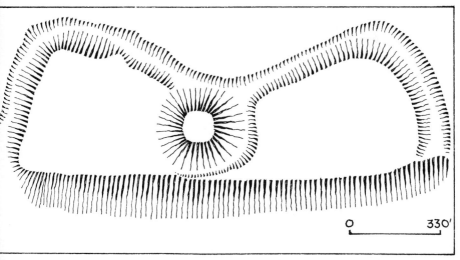

Windsor: ground plan of the original motte castle as it was in the Conqueror's time, long before the splendid buildings were raised

31

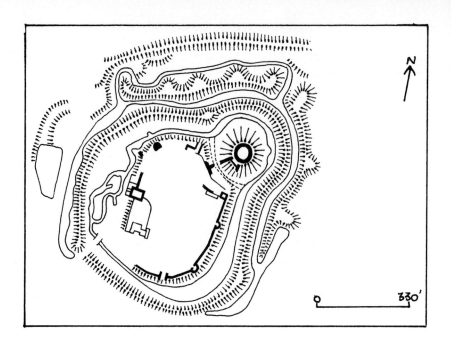

Berkhamsted: the dark lines indicate the remaining masonry, including foundations

Skipsea: the motte was separated from the bailey by marshes

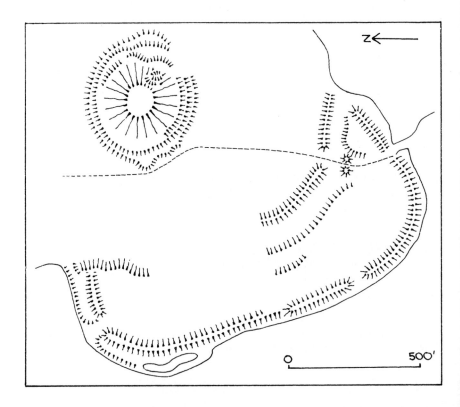

from the tower. Indeed, each castle was a unique structure; no two of the several hundreds erected were exactly alike. A few years ago, D. F. Renn classified motte-and-bailey types for quick identification, as follows:

Mottes: 3 main base shapes — round, oval, angular

Baileys: 6 basic plans — circular, oval, triangular, quadrilateral, lobed, polygonal

He also classified the four main relationships of mottes to baileys: central, with separate ditch round the motte base (Montacute); internal, without ditch (Oxford); peripheral, that is, motte astride the line of the bailey bank (Berkhamsted); and external (Skipsea, Yorkshire).

The construction of a motte castle followed much the same procedure everywhere, depending upon the geography of the site. Some mottes were adapted from natural hill or rock structures. Others were raised artificially by excavating earth from a notional ring on level ground and heaping it upwards inside the ring, which in turn became roughly a V-shaped ditch. If the ditch was to be water-holding, known as a wet ditch, the depth below the water line would not be more than a few feet. Mud and water make good obstacles in themselves. Generally, more earth and other materials were needed than were thrown up from the scooping, and they would have to be brought from elsewhere. Materials included stones (flint and rock), gravel, chalk, clay, loam and sand. Some mottes were built on top of existing earthworks, burial mounds and even buildings. One of the motte castles at York was raised over a crouched burial ground (in which corpses were buried in a foetal position); and Thetford was erected over part of an Iron Age hill-fort. Cambridge was put up on an Anglo-Saxon graveyard. The two mottes at Lewes contained squarish blocks of chalk and these may have come from earlier buildings. Lincoln and Norwich were raised on the remains of demolished streets.

The digging gangs, probably containing a hundred or more labourers, closely supervised by armed Norman soldiers, worked all day. At this rate an average motte could be raised within two to three weeks (York took eight days). The timberwork and the bailey probably needed another month or so. When the motte was complete the top was flattened down, and in some instances covered with a kind of hardcore of stone and earth. A palisade of timber planks with sharpened points was malleted into the top around its perimeter, reaching about 7–8ft high. Some planks were cut to provide slits for observation and for firing bows. And in the centre of the motte a large wooden tower was built.

The tower was the focal point of the castle. It acted as a watch-tower, not only over the area around the castle but also over the bailey itself, in case of revolt in the garrison. It is thought that Anglo-Saxons were recruited to strengthen garrisons where there were not enough Norman troops, and subject people employed by their conquerors can seldom be relied upon for long. As the flat top of the motte was likely to become a fighting platform in time of siege, the tower was in some cases raised on thick wooden stilts, in order to give more freedom of movement to defenders. This was the case at Abinger Castle (q.v.) in Surrey, whose tower post-holes were discovered during a fine piece of archaeological work there in 1949–50. Posts would have had to be sunk very deep in order to keep the tower upright in high winds. A tower was blown down from one of the mottes in York in 1228.

The tower was the last line of defence in time of siege, when those of the garrison that had managed to retreat to the top of the motte withdrew inside and shut the door against the besiegers. It was also intended to be a residence for the castle owner. This raises an interesting point: were these towers fit to be occupied for more than a few days or weeks at a time? A description of that at the motte castle of Ardres in Flanders, built about 1117, suggests it was almost palatial: 'The first storey was on the surface of the ground where were cellars and granaries . . . In the storey above were the dwelling and common living rooms of the residents, in which were larders, the rooms of the bakers and butlers, and the great chamber in which the lord and his wife slept. Adjoining this was a private room, the dormitory of the waiting maids and children. In the inner part of the great chamber was a certain private room, where . . . they used to have a fire . . . In the upper storey of the house were garret rooms . . . High up on the east side of the house, in a convenient place, was the chapel, which was made like unto the tabernacle of Solomon in its ceiling and painting . . .' This was written towards the end of the twelfth century (translated early this century) by a writer who was familiar with the building. On the other hand, nothing like this kind of accommodation could have fitted inside the tower of, say, Abinger, which we know to have been not more than 12ft square and probably not more than 40ft tall. Since the earlier motte castles in

England and Wales were designed chiefly to play a military role as a base from which Norman troops could police a district, their towers would have been much simpler than that at Ardres. They had the same accommodation as that of an ordinary grange or manor-house of the time, that is, kitchen and stores at one end, main dining/living room in the centre and owner's sleeping quarters at the other end. Turn this horizontal accommodation vertically on to the kitchen end and you arrive at a tower, three storeys high, with the rooms in the same order, bedroom at the top. That could be fitted into a tower like Abinger.

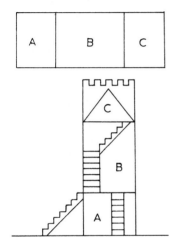

How the plan of a Norman horizontal hall-house was turned up on end to make a vertical great tower. A=kitchen/store; B=great hall; C=solar

Quarters for horses, cattle and other livestock, workshops for blacksmith and armourer, even perhaps a small chapel, all these would have been erected in the bailey, itself well protected by a high palisade all round the edge. Outside this was a ditch as deep and wide as the motte ditch, and wet wherever water could be let in from local springs, river or stream, or in some cases from the sea. Access from the bailey to the motte was by bridge or causeway over the separating ditch, or if there was no separating ditch, through a simple gateway, and then up a flight of steps to the gate in the palisade at the summit of the motte. The motte which can still be seen at Hawick has been provided with a modern step-way that conveys a life-like idea of a medieval flight of steps.

Like their stone successors, motte castles had an offensive/defensive role, and kings and lords knew very well that there was a good chance they would be put to the test of siege. A motte castle's wooden parts were naturally vulnerable to fire, though it should not be forgotten that thick planks of timber take much longer to burn to the point of collapse than walls of lath and plaster. Castle owners guarded against possible attempts during sieges to burn down their bailey walls and motte towers by draping them with wet hides or regularly splashing them with buckets of water. This was easier to do in the bailey which was near water level if it was surrounded by a wet ditch, but the tower was further away. Contemporary writers often refer to individual castles being burned down. The towers were probably destroyed by fire started by flaming bolts from bows or from siege catapults by men on the other side of the bailey bank. But if the besiegers were unable to get the woodwork alight then they would attack the motte directly.

Standing at the base of the great motte at Thetford today, it is difficult to imagine how any medieval army could successfully besiege the tower on the summit. Beneath a top layer of chalk rubble, the mound was earth. One morning of heavy rain would render the sides like an ice rink, sheer and unscaleable. Unless the timber flight of steps, which rose at 45° to a height of 80ft, could be captured the besiegers would have had to crawl up the slippery sides, yard by yard, hammering wooden stakes into the earth and using these to tie ropes with which to hoist themselves up, one stake at a time — a sitting target for the garrison on top, which could pelt them with all manner of missiles, especially the sharp, cutting and very heavy flintstones with which the Thetford terrain bristles. Many attackers would be pushed down or would slither into the castle's huge moat, so it was necessary to start out with a force of several times the size of the castle garrison (which would probably be between 50 and 100).

Other ways open to the investing army were to try to cut off supplies to the garrison, especially water, and starve them into surrender, or to bring up siege engines like mangonels and trebuchets (chapter 6) and assault the motte wall and tower with a heavy barrage of big stone balls. But these engines would not have been available before the middle of the twelfth century. Even if the assailants succeeded in capturing the steps and breaking into the palisade gateway, that would involve the greater part of the force, which would leave the rear part of the motte uncovered and so allow defenders to abandon the tower, let themselves down on ropes to the ground and slink off to rafts and boats waiting on the River Ouse nearby, and so escape.

Motte castles were built in considerable numbers, generally

without leave, by the various barons and knights who used the unsettled days of the reign of Stephen (1135–54) as an opportunity to settle old scores, indulge in territorial aggrandizement and generally earn the well-used soubriquet 'the turbulent baronage'. The *Anglo-Saxon Chronicle* bemoaned the state of the country thus: 'For every great man built him castles and held them against the king; and they filled the whole land with these castles. They sorely burdened the unhappy people of the country with forced labour on the castles; and when the castles were built, they filled them with devils and wicked men.' When Henry II (Plantagenet) became king in 1154, he brought some order to England with speed and vigour. One of his policies was to demolish as many of these adulterine castles as he could, as well as many of those that had been licensed. The first years of his reign saw the destruction of several hundred. More were pulled down after the failure of a revolt in 1173–4, organized against the king by his son, Prince Henry, and supported by many powerful barons. One castle to go was Thetford.

Motte castles continued to be built right into the thirteenth century, though the number diminished. The first stone castles, meanwhile, had been going up in England and Wales since about 1070–80. Many of them were stonework fortifications or buildings grafted on to motte castles, notably Farnham, Berkeley, Berkhamsted, Guildford, Totnes, Bristol and Newcastle. One or two mottes 'received' stone towers, with disastrous results later on. The great tower on Duffus motte (Grampian) split and one wall slid down the slope. It is still there, leaning over perilously near the bottom. The builders at Guildford Castle were not so trusting of the earthwork in the motte. Their great tower was erected half on and half off the slope, and it was the same at Clun in Shropshire. The extent to which a motte castle could be converted to stone was limited, however, and in the next chapter it will become clear that most stone castles in Britain were built from scratch, even if in some instances they occupied motte castle sites.

4

The First Stone Castles

The Normans imposed an alien ruling class upon English society, dominating the countryside with their motte castles. The speed with which they were erected, the overpowering heights which many of them reached and the huge numbers of them built, were all decisive psychological factors in the Norman success. Motte castles were also extremely useful buildings and served well for a variety of purposes beyond the fortress-residence role, such as watch-towers, administrative centres, garrisons for military police and even prisons. But as in Normandy, Anjou and elsewhere in Europe, the new feudalism was not maintained solely by the use of motte castles. The Normans intended their dominion in England to be permanent, and their ruthless, practical genius required expression in something more durable than mounds of earth topped with buildings of timber. So they grafted their experience of stone castle-building upon the landscape of England, and within ten years or so of the Conquest the first stone castles were under construction. We know for certain of the beginnings of the White Tower of London (c.1078–80), of Colchester (at much the same time) and of Chepstow (c.1067-71). Work also began at Pevensey, Rochester, Eynsford, Peveril, Brough and others a few years after 1080.

What kind of stone castles did the Normans build in England and in those parts of Wales they overran and settled? It is tempting to slot them into neat categories over and above the two fundamental types we mentioned in chapter 1, namely, the fortified great tower and the fortified enclosure. But it really cannot be done. Very few castles were built in one operation (however long it took) and without later additions, alterations or improvements. Many had several building periods, spread over two, three or even four centuries, which would have meant that their categories changed probably as many times. Let us look at some of the earliest. In London in about 1078–80 (there is considerable disagreement as to the foundation date),

William I started a huge, rectangular great tower (118ft by 107ft) with an apsidal extension at one end, which eventually rose to a height of 90ft. This was the White Tower. At Colchester, probably a year or two before, he authorized an even larger rectangular great tower (151ft by 110ft) of much the same height, also with an apsidal extension. At Chepstow, beside the River Wye, William allowed one of his principal lords, William FitzOsbern, to construct an oblong tower which was probably meant to be a hall but which was to be fortified (and later enlarged). This was between 1067–71. At Rochester, possibly just before William's death, and certainly within a year or two of it, work began on a stonework enclosure near the River Medway, within which, later in the 1120s, a rectangular great tower 113ft tall (125ft with its corner turrets) was to be raised. In 1088 William's son, William Rufus, authorized the erection of a walled enclosure at Eynsford in Kent which was never to have a great tower at all. Rufus also allowed an enclosure to be built at Brough in Westmorland, whilst the Peveril family had been granted leave to build at Peveril in Derbyshire sometime in the 1080s. And at Richmond in Yorkshire, in a superbly commanding position over the valley of the Swale, Alan the Red, who held the estate from 1071 to 1089, was given leave to start on his castle; before he died nearly the whole triangular enclosure of stone and a two-storeyed hall (Scolland's Hall), integrated in its south-east corner, had been built. Each of these structures was different from the next, even at these early stages. The differences were to become more marked as additions and improvements were made. The White Tower at London, for example, became the central feature of an extensive and complex stone castle of concentric walls with towers and turrets and gates, while Colchester great tower remained almost in isolation, surrounded only by existing Roman and freshly dug Norman earthworks, some of which were later replaced by stone walling with towers and gates. Colchester never grew into the kind of complex that the Tower of London became.

It is easy to see that we cannot classify Norman stone castles meaningfully. Each was a unique structure, the brain-child of a master mason who tailored it to the chosen site. In these early castle-building days, these masons were improvisers, practical men who learned their craft by experience and who did not have the architectural disciplines often ascribed to them. There were no manuals for them to study, so far as we know, and no contemporary plans have been found. As a rule masons were locally hired craftsmen

Chepstow

who visited one or two castles nearby and learned something from them, but who in the end did what the country builder does today, that is, discussed the overall idea with his client, made a number of suggestions to fit his requirements, probably pointed out what could *not* be done, and then got on with the job.

Later in the twelfth century, named masons working on royal castles appear in official records like the Pipe Rolls, though generally the entries relate to what they were paid. It is interesting to find some masons working on several castles, for that is evidence of their experience, suggesting they could be among the most practised master masons in the castle-building business. But it is too early for them to have become the kind of sophisticated military architects we

A fourteenth-century drawing of Gloucester great tower from the *King's Works*

shall encounter in the later thirteenth century, like Master James of St George, whose design skills were triumphantly displayed in the Edwardian castles in Wales and the Savoyard castles in east France, west Switzerland and north-west Italy. Experienced as the eleventh- and twelfth-century masons were, they built castles for their employers to on-the-spot site assessments and requirements. In the 1170s, for example, Richard of Wolviston worked at Norham and at Bowes, and possibly at Durham, too, but despite some similarities Norham great tower and Bowes great tower were not the result of a master plan adjustable to both sites. The differences were too great.

As the eleventh century gave way to the twelfth, other stone castles began to go up in many more parts of England, notably Ludlow,

Norwich, Canterbury, and more were started in the first decades of the 1100s by, or with the permission of, Henry I and Stephen, the best known of which (not in chronological order) were Hedingham, Portchester (inside a Roman fort), Corfe, Ogmore, Bramber, Castle Rising, New Buckenham, Goodrich, Carisbrooke, Kenilworth and two that have since vanished, Bristol and Gloucester. Most of these castles had a great tower as the central feature, the home of the lord (or in the case of a royal castle, of the king's governor or castellan), in which he and his family and closest associates and dependants lived, to which they retired in time of siege, accompanied by anyone else within the castle walls, especially if the gates or the walls were successfully breached. It is appropriate now to look at great towers.

In chapter 1, the categories of great towers were listed as rectangular, square, polygonal, cylindrical and D-ended. To these should be added triangular, like Beaucaire on the Rhône in France, though none of this type was built in Britain. The first stone great towers in England were mostly but not all rectilinear (that is, rectangular or square). They can be classified in four categories:

1. Rectangular where the height was greater than the longer horizontal dimension (Rochester and Hedingham).
2. Rectangular where the height was less than the longer horizontal dimension (Norwich, Castle Rising).
3. Square where the height was greater than the width (Appleby, Guildford).
4. Cuboid, notably Dover (95ft tall, 96ft by 98ft), Bamburgh.

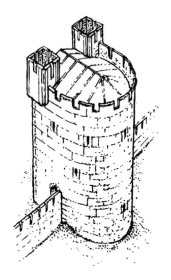

A D-shaped great tower set in the enclosure curtain wall, as at Helmsley

Norman pilaster buttresses on corners and mid-wall, as at Rochester great tower

Rectilinear great towers have thick walls, generally at least 10–12ft, thicker at the corners, and in some cases, such as Dover, as much as 20ft. Walls were built of rubble and mortar and faced with better quality masonry, or built straight from cut stone blocks whose outer surfaces were smoothed and squared. They rose from a splayed (or battered) plinth (but occasionally, as at Richmond and Goodrich, there was no battered plinth), which provided defenders with an oblique surface on which to throw down missiles from the battlements at the top, or through slits in the wooden hoarding or holes in stone machicolation, confident that these would bounce into the faces of besiegers. Many towers incorporated shallow pilaster buttresses along the outer wall faces and at corners for strengthening. In some later castles, a latrine shaft was incorporated in the pilaster buttress. Some corner buttresses were so proud of the wall line that they are more rightly known as buttress turrets, such as at Kenilworth. The corners of some rectilinear great towers were reinforced with fine-cut ashlar quoins keyed into the otherwise rubble coursing of the walls, as at Colchester, Guildford and many more. At Middleham you can see a good example not only of rubble masonry walls faced with better quality stonework (where the latter has come away in some places, probably taken for another later building) but also how the quoins were keyed into the masonry at the corners. Norwich great tower was restored in the nineteenth century more or less to resemble its original apearance in the twelfth, and this provides a good idea of the high quality of stonework of which Norman castle-builders were capable.

Walls generally contained a variety of small rooms, such as chambers, garderobes (latrines whose exits issued out on to the wall exterior or down a shaft to emerge at or near ground level into the surrounding ditch — Orford is a good example), devotional chapels, guardrooms, stores, small kitchens and bedrooms. The great tower walls at Castle Sween in Argyll, however, contained very few chambers. At Hedingham, and at other great towers, the upper level

(left) Part of a projecting garderobe above the southern ditch at Harlech, built by Master James of St George. It is similar to a pair of his design at the castle of La Batiaz, near Saillon in Switzerland; (above) Garderobe shoots opening in the batter (splayed plinth) of a great tower. These are based on Orford

of the two-storeyed great hall has a mural passage all the way round, like the triforium of an abbey or cathedral, which passes through the window bays at that level and joins up at the spiral staircase in the north-west corner turret. In many great towers the well is situated in one of the corner turrets, and as in the case of Dover, the well-head was raised to the floors above the basement, serving each floor. Window openings in great tower walls were generally small on the outside, though splayed on the inner walls to let in more light and to help funnel smoke out from interior fires. The distribution of windows and loopholes (thin apertures of varying shapes through which arrows could be shot outwards with some protection from retaliation — see drawing below) was often irregular, and there were fewer at lower level than on high. Many of the two-storeyed great halls in these towers had no windows except at top level, with only loopholes at lower levels, or perhaps nothing at all. Great towers with particularly scant window provision include Brough, Brougham, Guildford, Middleham, Newcastle, Richmond and the cylindrical Conisbrough, but there are great towers with a generous window area at Corfe, Rochester and Scarborough.

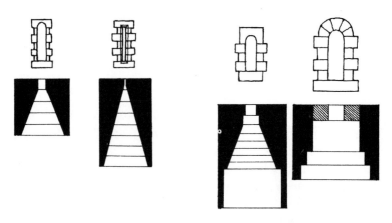

The two figures on the left show windows in the basement storey of (a) Chepstow great tower and (b) Skenfrith. The two on the right show the elevation and plan of window openings at (c) Colchester Great Hall and (d) Canterbury (reconstructed from ruins)

As a rule there was only one point of entry to a great tower, namely, through a doorway generally placed at first-floor level, which was reached by a flight or flights of steps. In most great towers the steps were wholly or certainly in part covered by a special structure built over them against the wall. This was the forebuilding, and among those that have survived are some of interesting design, notably Castle Rising which has a decidedly ecclesiastical look with its blind arcading, Newcastle which is two-storeyed, has two turrets that are battlemented and occupies the whole of the east wall width, Dover which wraps right round the corner of the great tower, and Rochester which is four-storeyed. Forebuildings were often keyed into the wall, especially if they were constructed at the same time, but sometimes one would be added as an afterthought and was more of a 'lean-to', as at Hedingham where it has since disappeared. The line of the roof of the forebuilding can be seen on the wall, and it does not appear to have been keyed in. Indeed, the entrance door to the great tower was protected by its own portcullis. Some forebuildings, including Dover and Rochester, contained a chapel at one level, generally over the level of the doorway into the tower, and in the case of Dover there were two chapels.

The newel stair was one way to build a spiral staircase in stone. This is how it was done at Colchester great tower

Storeys of great towers were reached by staircases whose arrangement varied from castle to castle. Most great towers had spiral staircases built into the corner turrets, rising clockwise or anti-clockwise, continuously in one corner all the way up or, in some instances, rising at alternate corners floor by floor, compelling besiegers who had broken in to fight their way across each floor before being able to get to the next. Some towers had straight flights of stairs, as at Richmond and Bamburgh.

It will be seen that the interior features of great towers were often planned with care and thought to take into account the dual fortress/residence role, and to allow for the fact that in time of siege the complement of people inside might be swelled several times over. It was said of Coucy great tower in France that 1,000 people could be accommodated in such circumstances. Most towers were divided internally down the middle or a little off-centre (like Rochester and Duffield) with a cross-wall, sometimes at every floor level. This cross-wall might be a solid wall, a huge flying arch, an arcade of arches or wide pillars and spaces. It served several purposes: it strengthened the tower; it enabled floor joists and beams to be cut to about half the length that would be required to extend the entire tower width and so reduced the need to find huge trees for long timbers; and it provided an additional obstacle for besiegers who had broken in and were fighting their way gradually up the tower (as at Rochester in 1216), though a flying arch would be no obstacle.

Coucy, France. The great tower (cross-section by Viollet-le-Duc) rose to over 180ft. Note the use of buttresses rising to arches on each storey

The arcaded cross-wall at Rochester great tower. The well shaft rises up the centre turret

Polygonal towers or turrets placed in enclosing walls or as part of gatehouses are quite common in Britain. The Romans had employed this shape, but polygonal great towers are rare. They have been described by some authorities as a development — indeed, an improvement — upon rectilinear great towers, but of course they are not. None of those that have survived appears to provide any advantages not offered by rectilinear great towers, except possibly that the inherent weakness of the latter, namely, that any of their four corners could be undermined and brought down to allow insurgents to crawl through gaps produced in the masonry, is partially obviated by the fact that obtuse angles are more difficult to dislodge than right angles. None incorporates the variety of rooms in their walls that one finds in so many rectilinear great towers. Only Orford Castle in Suffolk whose design is multangular (polygonal with three equidistantly placed square-plan buttress turrets in the circumference — see plan on p.272) offers sizeable accommodation in the walls and buttresses. Orford is a unique structure with no parallel in Britain and therefore in no sense any kind of 'transitional' great tower, whatever that phrase may mean. Two possible reasons for building polygonal great towers, such as Odiham, Chilham or Tickhill (qq.v.), have been conjectured. One is that the builders intended them to be completely cylindrical but ran into difficulties in construction. This is disposed of by the fact that builders had for sometime been erecting both church and castle cylindrical towers. The other and perhaps more acceptable explanation is that they were the personal preference, for unspecified reasons, of the owner — in the case of Odiham, King John. Certainly, the hexagonal great tower built at Raglan (much later, in the fifteenth century, q.v.) was the choice of the owner, Sir William ap Thomas, and his son, Sir William Herbert, who made the six-sided shape a feature of other parts of the castle including the gatehouse, the Closet tower, the kitchen tower and the end of the Long Gallery.

If the polygonal great tower was not a tidy or logical step in the development of great tower design, nor was the cylindrical great tower the next stage after that. It has been a long-held view that cylindrical great towers were superior to rectilinear great towers, and certainly they had some advantages over the latter: they were more difficult to undermine; large round stones and other missiles hurled at them by catapults, trebuchets, mangonels and other siege artillery tended to bounce off unless the hits were dead on; men defending then had all-round vision over besiegers; and they were easier and

A drawing by John Norden, c.1600, of Orford Castle as it appeared to him. Only the multangular tower remains today

thus cheaper to build because they did not need ashlar quoin-reinforced corners. But a number of other points need also to be considered. The chronological progression theory, namely, that cylindrical great towers did not appear in Britain until the rectangular great tower had been established but found wanting, does not hold. Firstly, rectilinear great towers continued to be built for nearly four centuries (the Hastings Tower at Ashby de la Zouch, c.1470) and so cannot be said to have been outdated. Secondly, the earliest cylindrical great tower in Britain so far datable with any precision is that at New Buckenham in Norfolk (q.v.). This was built in the 1140s, at the same sort of time as the early and uncompromisingly rectilinear great towers of Hedingham, Norwich and Rising. Indeed, it was built for the same man as Rising, namely, William d' Albini, Earl of Sussex, who married the widow of Henry I. Additionally, two of the earliest great towers in Britain, London and Colchester, had rounded (apsidal) extensions at one end.

50

Numerous round church towers (particularly in East Anglia) were raised before square-plan church towers. And there were many cylindrical great towers built in France in the eleventh century concurrently with rectangular ones. Fourthly, comparatively few cylindrical great towers were ever built in Britain, which does not say much for their 'superiority'. Finally, cylindrical great towers had some positive disadvantages as well. One was that while the entrance to a rectilinear great tower was protected by a forebuilding, cylindrical great towers had no such coverage (with the exception of Barnard, q.v.). Forebuildings acted as additional fighting platforms for defenders in time of siege, as well as cover for the steps into the tower, and such a feature will have been missed in the cylindrical great towers. Conisbrough, a cylindrical structure, had only a simple flight of steps up to the entrance. Defenders trying to get in during a siege were totally exposed to everything that their attackers could hurl at them.

It is clear that cylindrical great towers, like polygonal great towers, were styles of buildings concurrent with rectilinear towers. The decision whether to build square or polygonal or round depended upon factors such as the type of stone material available, whether ashlar quoins and dressing could be afforded, how quickly the tower was needed and so forth. Clearly, too, there was an element of what was fashionable, and everybody knows that what is fashionable is by no means necessarily an improvement on what has gone before. The tower was to be the owner's home as well as his fortress and if he was wealthy or influential he would wish to impress: a rectilinear great tower was on the whole more imposing than a cylinder tower, though Pembroke is a massively impressive exception, as Bothwell in Scotland must have been before it was severely damaged.

There is one final point. A number of the great towers in the Welsh Border castles, like Bronllys, Longtown, Tretower (inside a shell keep) and Skenfrith (qq.v.), all raised in the last years of the twelfth and first years of the thirteenth century, are cylindrical, while the towers in the Border district between England and Scotland, built in the thirteenth and fourteenth centuries, are rectilinear, notably Aydon, Belsay, Chipchase and Prudhoe (qq.v.). Clearly we are confronted with examples of regional preference.

We have looked in some detail at the nature of great towers of the years c.1070–c.1200, since they predominated in castle works of the period. Every one of them, except Bowes in Yorkshire (built between 1171 and 1187), is part of a castle containing other buildings. Normally, these consisted of an enclosing curtain wall with mural towers or turrets, a gateway or larger gatehouse, and other buildings set up inside the enclosure, leaning against the curtain or standing free. Orford, for example, now consisting only of its multangular great tower, was once a substantial stone enclosure with wall towers and gatehouse surrounding the great tower. Pembroke great tower stands inside an inner enclosure that is part of a larger enclosure, with various other structures in the curtain and standing free. The castle owner could not get everything into a great tower, certainly not his horses and cattle which were best protected inside the enclosure. If the great tower was to be a residence and a last line of defence, it needed additional protection, so a high and thick enclosing wall was built with a walkway and parapet around the top, mural towers (square, round or polygonal) and a gatehouse for covering every angle and area of the wall. The art of keeping besiegers away from great towers was to build as many obstacles as possible between them and the tower, compelling them to fight for each one, be it ditch or rampart, turret or gatehouse, in the hope that these would either drag out the siege long enough for a relieving force to raise it, or that so many besiegers would be killed or wounded before the time came for the final assault on the tower that it might be abandoned.

Another type of castle built in Britain from the earlier half of the twelfth century, and mainly in that century, too, was the shell keep castle. This is the term used to describe a motte castle that, later in its history, has had the wooden parts wholly or partly converted to stonework. The palisade round the flattened top of the motte was removed and a stone wall erected. The wall was given a gateway. In some cases, wing walls were built down the motte slopes to meet the bailey wall which was also converted to stone. This is well demonstrated at Pickering and Berkhamsted. Inside the stone enclosure at the top — the shell keep — one of two plans was followed. Either, as at Restormel, a series of buildings was put round the inside of the wall, using it as the fourth side, or, as at Launceston and Tretower, a central tower was built to contain similar quarters but stacked one on top of the other. The tower was often a cylindrical one, but not always so (Farnham and Totnes were rectangular). The outer wall of the shell was topped with a battlemented parapet which was reached by steps, sometimes sited next to the gateway.

There were many variations of the shell keep castle. At Berkeley (p.187) and Farnham the motte was revetted with stonework; at

Farnham the foundations of a rectangular great tower, about 50ft square with thick walls, were found near the top inside the shell keep which had substantial rectangular buttresses. At Carisbrooke, Cardiff and Castle Acre the shell keep was polygonal; at Acre the motte was recently excavated and found to contain the lower parts of a seemingly massive rectangular great tower, perhaps on the scale of Norwich; at Restormel there was a courtyard inside the compartmented shell; and at Rothesay in Bute, Scotland, one of the only shell keeps in Scotland, round towers were added to the circumference of the shell for extra protection, and later a large gatehouse was built that had the appearance of a great tower. Other shell keep gateways were substantial; Restormel's was two-storeyed and presented a formidable challenge to the besieger.

If we stick to the two basic stone castle types, the shell keep castle properly belongs to the fortified enclosure type. We are also left with a considerable number of other castles built during the Middle Ages, and these must be included with the enclosure type as well.

The fortified stone enclosure was a fortress capable of offering resistance to attackers or intruders and of providing a satisfactory residence for a lord and his dependants in a variety of buildings assembled inside. Numerous enclosures, sometimes — and not very helpfully — called castles of *enceinte*, or ringworks, were built over a long period, from the earliest in the times of William I and II, including parts of Eynsford, parts of Richmond before the great tower, embracing Framlingham, c.1200, Beeston, c.1225, Barnwell, c.1265, the sophisticated Conwy, 1280s and Caernarvon, c.1283–c.1323 (which for all its magnificence is only an enclosure with flanking towers), and continuing through the fourteenth century to Bolton, c.1379, and Bodiam, c.1386 and even to Thornbury, c.1510, possibly the last major castle of the medieval kind to be built in Britain.

Some enclosures were built round a bailey of a motte castle previously having a wooden palisade wall, or on a new site on low or high ground, or even adapting an earlier site of something else, such as a Roman fort or an Anglo-Saxon *burh*. Some enclosures, like Eynsford, began with a simple stone wall built in a ring, inside which various buildings were raised, in stone or wood, at the same time or later. Most enclosures were fortified outside by ditching and ramparts. The ditch was sometimes a wet one, that is, supplied with water generally to a level deeper than a man's height, provided from nearby springs, a lake or a river, or in a few cases, the sea. Some

ditches were dry, in which case they might be lined with clay or with stone slabs, though the recently discovered ditch thus lined at Bedford was probably wet. Many enclosures were further fortified at the time of construction, or later, by building towers or turrets, cylindrical, square, D-ended or polygonal, in the walling, either as an integral part or 'tacked on'. Some were complete towers, some were open-backed (like Framlingham). The towers were inserted along the circumference or at the extremities where two stretches of wall met, as at Inverlochy. Some were raised standing free from the wall. Some enclosures, like Eynsford, had no towers or turrets, except a gateway or gate-tower, and relied upon their position, the walling thickness, and the ditch and rampart defences outside. The walling is generally called the curtain wall because it hangs, so to speak, between the towers. A quick look at Framlingham from any angle with its thirteen rectilinear flanking towers and gateway (in most cases several feet taller than the high curtain), shows the curtain effect very well. Curtains were usually battlemented and had a parapet along the inside near the top reached by ascending a tower or, more rarely, an outside staircase.

In the Middle Ages there were at least two criteria by which a castle was judged to be fortified. In early Norman times, when permission was given to build a castle, it meant that the structure, wooden or stone, was allowed to be surrounded wholly or partly by ditching and ramparts where the distance from the bottom of the ditch to the top of the rampart was equal to the distance an average digger could throw a spadeful of earth (from a ditch base to a rampart top) in one go, that is, about 25–30ft. Later, licences were granted to build 'in stone and lime' and to 'crenellate', that is , construct along the top of the curtain and round the tops of towers, battlements of merlons (solid projections) and crenels, or embrasures (gaps in between). Numerous licences to crenellate were granted by the kings over the centuries, and these are generally indicated in the Gazetteer where known.

Enclosures become increasingly interesting as they acquire improvements or alterations. The enclosure at Rochester developed into a castle with one of the biggest rectangular great towers in

---

(opposite) Bolton: the south-east tower, and adjacent to it the arch into the gatehouse

Britain (besieged and taken in 1216, an event documented, see chapter 6). The enclosure at Ludlow was begun in the very late eleventh century and over succeeding centuries acquired a unique range of buildings including a gatehouse whose entrance was subsequently blocked up to make the building a great tower (see also Dunstanburgh). The enclosure at Caernarvon was built in two main stages and became one of the most sophisticated defensive structures in Europe (one gateway had five portcullises in series). The enclosures at Goodrich were built up over the thirteenth and fourteenth centuries, long after the original great tower had been erected on the rocky outcrop overlooking the Wye. There were many smaller enclosure castles of varying shapes and construction, each different from the next, and they are included in the Gazetteer. All of them fulfil the dual role of the castle and enjoyed, or endured, a variety of fortunes.

5
Building Castles

In chapter 3 we saw that motte castles could be erected in a few weeks. Stone castle construction, however, was a very different matter and generally took years, despite the fact that most stone castles were wanted in a hurry. D. F. Renn estimated that the annual building rate on a great tower was about 10ft of elevation, allowing for weather, stopping work in winter or if funds ran out. Scarborough, some 90ft tall, took ten years (1158–68). This 10ft average applies to great towers. In the same period, work on other parts of the castle may have been done simultaneously, such as constructing the curtain with towers (if any), raising the gateway or gatehouse and so forth. At Orford, for example, it is thought that the whole castle, great tower and surrounding enclosure with its smaller (rectangular?) towers and gate went up in seven/eight years. The time may seem lengthy, but the medieval builder had no mechanical aids except the pulley-wheel crane and the wheelbarrow, and stone cutting and dressing had to be done by hand.

Every stone castle posed a veritable catalogue of problems, some of which had to be dealt with in advance and which could not be solved merely by riding roughshod over the feelings of local people. Early in the Norman occupation, the conqueror-lords steam-rollered their way through towns and countryside to clear sites for castles and pressed Anglo-Saxons into forced labour. But in the time of Henry I, who introduced a new spirit of co-operation between Norman and Anglo-Saxon (setting an example by marrying the daughter of an Anglo-Saxon princess), proper formalities were observed. Some sites were paid for, some were exchanged, and there are even instances of compensation being paid for intrusion upon neighbouring land, such as at Gloucester. It is interesting to look at the problems, for it is still a matter of some wonder how well the medieval builder coped with them, particularly in the construction of the great tower type of castle.

A medieval picture of building a wall (redrawn by R. Maguire)

Some stone great tower castles were superimposed upon motte castles because the site had proved advantageous. Others were built on new sites, generally selected for their strategic position *vis-à-vis* the lands of neighbours as well as suitability for controlling their own lands, and for their nearness to water sources. There were other important questions for the builders to consider. Could stone be quarried on the site, or nearby, and was it suitable or too soft? If not, where was the nearest quarry? Did it belong to the king or the Church? Most quarries were royal or ecclesiastical property. How much would it cost to use on a contract hire basis? Where was the nearest waterway for transporting the stone and other materials? Water transport was much cheaper than land cartage; and it was quicker. Many of the best quarries, like Barnack in Northamptonshire, were close to navigable rivers. How easy would it be to find enough masons and assistants to extract stone (by hammering iron wedges into the layers in the stone beds) and to cut by saw or split the lumps into appropriate shapes and sizes, and to dress (smooth) them? What sort of rubble was available nearby? Were there any Roman remains, like tiles and brick segments? At Colchester great tower, both brick and dressed stones were taken from the extensive ruins of the old Roman town at Camulodunum and used in the masonry, and can be seen in many parts of the tower, notably in some of the steps of the great stairs. The owner and builder of a castle also considered whether they wanted to obtain a supply of the cream-yellow limestone quarried at Caen in Normandy, generally reckoned the best of its kind, to make the ashlar quoins and other features like arch heads, keystones, window mullions and lintels, loopholes and battlement tops.

While masons were attending to the stone supply problems, carpenters and joiners were worrying about timber availability. Was there a source close to the site and were the trees big enough to produce the lengths of beam and plank? In some cases owners contracted to buy the wood from a supplier; in others they would buy a stretch of forest with the appropriate trees. Oak in one or other of its many species was preferred. Wood was also needed for burning to make charcoal for blacksmiths.

There were other materials wanted in quantity; lead for the tower roofs and water pipes; iron for a multitude of requirements; sand and lime for mortar (cement). All had to be acquired and transported to the site. Details of this kind today would be skilfully estimated down to the last nail, and the operations supervised by one or other of a building team of architect, quantity surveyor, consulting engineer and services engineer, but in those times there were no such disciplines. Estimating had to be guesswork.

Once the material supply problem was satisfactorily in hand, the building gangs were recruited, or pressed into service, generally from the immediate neighbourhood, though in the case of the castles of Edward I in Wales, the authorities found they had to recruit from English counties, from Norfolk to Devonshire, because they could not expect to depend upon loyal service from the Welsh whom they had just overcome. In early Norman days men were not generally paid, but as Norman and Anglo-Saxon began to edge towards a more balanced relationship, castle owners started to pay wages. Pay was not standard, except in so far as it was low everywhere. In the late thirteenth century we read of diggers, carpenters and masons being offered bonuses for good work — and docked wages for absenteeism — but these were the country men recruited for work on the Edwardian castles in Wales. A site supervisor, *custos operationum*, at Builth could earn 12d a day in 1277 and a master mason 7½d a day in 1278. Piecework was also done; at Flint, in 1280, masons were paid 1d or 1¼d per stone for cutting and dressing. Diggers were paid 3d a day at Rhuddlan. At Deal in 1539, a number of labourers on the site of the coastal fort being built at the order of Henry VIII struck because of low wages: they were only paid 6d — and some even 5d — a day. The differentials of the thirteenth century seem much the same as today; the head of a building team on a large project would expect to earn about 3½ to 4 times the basic wage (without overtime) of the builder's labourer.

Work on a castle site began with a careful scrutiny of the ground. If it was an existing motte site, the owner would have known about its earth content, whether there was rock or not. It it was a new site, this would have to be discovered. The presence of rock meant that possibly the great tower could be built on rock foundations. If so, the rock was flattened by gangs of men chipping it away with iron cold chisels, and the plinth of the tower was laid down. If the ground was soft, deep trenches were cut, a yard or two wider than the intended thickness of wall, and filled with an assortment of rubble, stone and timber — a kind of hardcore — which was rammed down. The plinth was laid on these foundations. In many great towers, plinths were battered, that is, they sloped outwards and downwards for structural strength and for ricochetting missiles, but some led straight downwards, like Richmond. Then the first levels of wall were put together above the plinth. In some castles the walls consisted of an inner 'skin' of an aggregate of rubble, old brick, pebbles and almost anything else hard, held together by a tough mortar of sand and lime which set hard as rock, sometimes prepared by creating a trough of wooden planks between which the aggregate was poured. The method may have been learned by the Normans from the Saracen castle-builders in Spain of the tenth century who used *tapia,* a mix of pebbles and cement poured between boards and left to dry in the sun. A fine example of a castle built of this material is at Banos de la Encina. The aggregate skin was generally clad, in England, with an outer skin of dressed stone, and the corners of the towers were set with quoins of dressed stone which tied in with both skins. In some castles, such as Rochester, the walls were all rubble (Rochester was Kentish ragstone), with corners of ashlar. At Middleham great tower you can see stretches along the wall faces that are stripped of the outer skin, and parts of the corners where the quoins have disappeared, leaving the inner rubble skin exposed. At Baconsthorpe, the quoins in the corners of the great flint-built rectangular gatehouse were deliberately taken out to provide stone for a later building nearby.

As the first courses of wall went up, scaffolding became necessary to continue the work. Long poles held together with rope were erected anchored here and there with horizontal poles, called put-logs, let into the masonry already built. These put-logs slotted into put-log holes, and many great towers (notably Hedingham) today bear the patterns of rows of put-log holes. In most cases they were horizontal lines. A more sophisticated system was used during the building of some of the Edwardian Welsh castles of the late thirteenth century, where helicoidal, or inclined, scaffold paths, about 35–40 degrees from the horizontal, supported ramps for hauling or winching materials, notably at Harlech gatehouse. This system appears to have been a speciality of Master James of St George, the Savoyard master-mason, and it was not widely used elsewhere. Whether the ramp for a wheelbarrow was more efficient than the pulley wheel and basket is a moot point.

Great tower walls rose in a vertical straight line (though at Oxford the walls tapered inwards with offsets spaced out in the height) either solid or hollow with passages here and there, and in the greatest of the towers, chambers and staircases, until they reached the desired height, whereupon they were topped with the wall-walk and parapet and given the outer protective battlements. Many towers had corners which were in effect corner turrets, and these rose higher than the four walls with their battlements. Corner turrets contained the spiral staircases and also rooms, and they acted as buttresses. Some great towers had one corner turret of slightly greater dimensions than the other three.

When the walls were completed they might be coated with plaster and whitewashed, or whitewashed directly on the stonework. Occasionally, the plastering was made to look like coursing of large stone blocks (as may be seen on many Georgian or nineteenth-century town buildings), by means of thin lines etched into the wet plasterwork. The great tower at London is called the White Tower because of the whitewashing it received in the thirteenth century. Whitewashing was not simply decorative; indeed, with the smoke and dirt given out by fires and from slops thrown out of windows and loops, it would not have remained clean for long. It was a preservative for the stone, and it is also held that medieval builders thought it helped to fireproof the castle.

The building operations we have outlined applied to great towers. They were much the same for gatehouses and gatehouse-towers, chapels and halls. Put-log holes can be seen in many smaller curtain wall towers and in gatehouses, such as at Tonbridge. In some of the

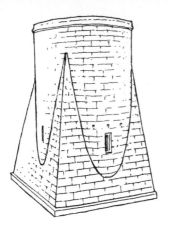

A cylindrical tower rising from a spur base. This type of tower fortification first appears in British castles in the late twelfth century

Edwardian castles, the put-log holes are also in helicoidal pattern on the smaller towers and gatehouses. At Goodrich the three early fourteenth-century cylindrical towers in the inner quadrangle enclosure stand on a square base with spurs up the tower sides, an alternative to a battered plinth. This type of support was particularly appropriate for structures on sheer cliff faces, like the Constable's Gate at Dover.

Since castles were residences as well as fortresses, we should not be surprised to find them having many domestic features. Internally, many had fireplaces, some of considerable decorative attractiveness and elaboration, from the simple thirteenth-century sloping ashlar

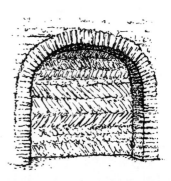

(left) A wall fireplace in the King's Gate at Caernarvon; (right) A fireplace in Colchester's great tower. Note the Norman herringbone masonry. Colchester has some of the best examples of this type of masonry courses. Another example is at Tamworth

hood on corbels and columns at Tretower great tower to the massive 20ft wide pillar-supported hood at the great hall at Linlithgow. Windows in great towers and halls are endlessly fascinating in variety. Loopholes (arrowslits) are likewise varied. We have mentioned the chapels in the forebuilding at Dover. At Castle Rising the chapel is next to the great chamber, at its east end. At Conisbrough the chapel, hexagonal in plan, projects into one of the wedge-shaped buttresses. At Colchester and the White Tower of London, the chapels are in the apsidal ends in the east wall. Numerous great towers had kitchens in the wall thicknesses, or in the basement, or at the top — perhaps a better place, so that the cooking smells could get out without affecting the occupants. At Orford there were two kitchens, at ground- and first-floor level.

What did all this castle building cost? A great deal of work has been done on the costing of building works on castles in the Middle Ages, particularly those in royal hands, and the costs to private owners other than kings must have been much the same. Expenditure for many royal castles is well documented, and sums looked at in relation to the total income of the kings in a year are startling. Translated into modern equivalents, as far as they can be reliably, they appear even larger. We may take the position over the period c.1155–1215, namely, the reigns of Henry II and his sons Richard I and John. It is reckoned that the king's annual income from taxes and rents was not much more than £10,000. In today's terms that would be about £2½m. It is also estimated that none of his lords was worth more than about one-twelfth of that £10,000, and that the average knight could live comfortably on £20 a year.

If the king's annual income was about £10,000, then from the evidence in the Pipe Rolls of the Exchequer, he seems to have spent a significant percentage of it on castle works, from new structures like Orford, to new parts at Dover, Newcastle and so forth, to repairs and upkeep on many others. *The History of the King's Works* considers the outlay on castles to have been the biggest single item of expenditure in all three reigns. Orford cost about £1,400 in seven years, Dover had nearly £7,000 spent on it in nine, Newcastle cost £1,000 in ten years and Bowes £600 in seventeen years. *King's Works* estimates that about £780 a year was spent on castles by the crown throughout the period 1155–1215, or a total of over £46,000 — in today's terms, £11½ million, which is about 7–8 per cent of the total income the crown received over the sixty-year period. Interestingly, while Henry II spent some £21,000 on about ninety castles, the great

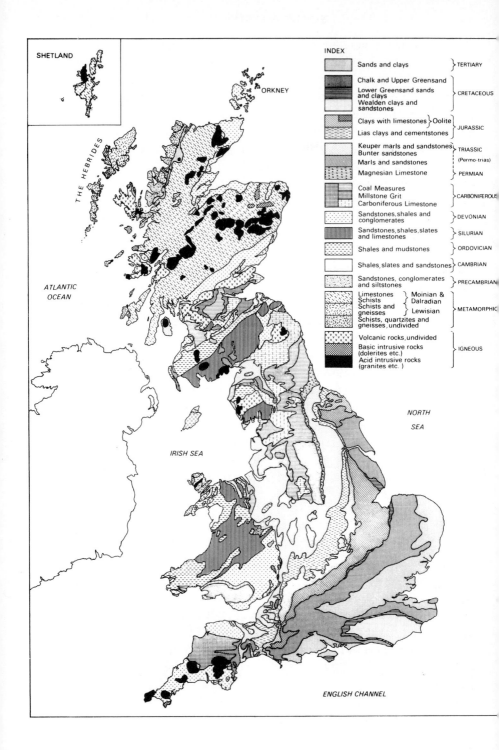

SHETLAND

ORKNEY

THE HEBRIDES

ATLANTIC
OCEAN

NORTH

SEA

IRISH SEA

ENGLISH CHANNEL

INDEX

Sands and clays	}	TERTIARY
Chalk and Upper Greensand		
Lower Greensand sands and clays	}	CRETACEOUS
Wealden clays and sandstones		
Clays with limestones } Oolite	}	JURASSIC
Lias clays and cementstones		
Keuper marls and sandstones	}	TRIASSIC
Bunter sandstones		
Marls and sandstones		(Permo-trias)
Magnesian Limestone	}	PERMIAN
Coal Measures		
Millstone Grit	}	CARBONIFEROUS
Carboniferous Limestone		
Sandstones, shales and conglomerates	}	DEVONIAN
Sandstones, shales, slates and limestones	}	SILURIAN
Shales and mudstones	}	ORDOVICIAN
Shales, slates and sandstones	}	CAMBRIAN
Sandstones, conglomerates and siltstones	}	PRECAMBRIAN
Limestones	Moinian & Dalradian	
Schists		
Schists and gneisses	Lewisian	METAMORPHIC
Schists, quartzites and gneisses, undivided		
Volcanic rocks, undivided		
Basic intrusive rocks (dolerites etc.)	}	IGNEOUS
Acid intrusive rocks (granites etc.)		

majority of the expenses were on less than thirty castles. In John's reign, £17,000 was spent in fifteen years, the lion's share being on only ten castles: over £500 on Hanley, Horston, Lancaster and Norham; over £1,000 on Corfe, Dover, Kenilworth, Knaresborough and Odiham (his polygonal great tower castle); and over £2,000 on Scarborough. A graph of his expenditure over the fifteen years would show an acceleration towards the latter end, in both new works and repairs, and this has been taken as an indication of the growing tension between him and his feudal lords at home and growing danger of invasion from abroad (Dover, Southampton and other castles in south-east England receiving the main attention).

If we turn now to the expenditure of the three Edwards (I, II, III) in Wales from 1277 to 1330, the figures for which many writers on castles quote with relish, the sums involved are centred on ten new castles (Aberystwyth, Beaumaris, Builth, Caernarvon, Conwy, Flint, Harlech, Hope, Rhuddlan and Ruthin) with renovations to three Welsh-originated castles (Castell y Bere, Criccieth and Dolwyddelan). Aberystwyth (£3,885), Beaumaris (£14,444), Builth (£1,666), Caernarvon (£19,892), Conwy (£14,248), Flint (£8,951), Harlech (£6,224) and Rhuddlan (£9,292) give an idea of the sort of money the kings were laying out. These sums are the minimum, as they do not include absolutely everything, but they are near enough for us to stand back in some wonder, more so when it is learned that some of the castles began to decay almost before they were finished, that Beaumaris and Caernarvon took more than a quarter of a century to complete, that Beaumaris was never involved in any warlike event, and that the whole programme stretched the royal resources to the limit.

The geological map (opposite).
The quality and suitability of stone in Britain for building castles varied from one region to another. East Anglia is almost stoneless and the scarcity was overcome by using flint — form of chalcedonic silica originating from the Chalk formation (Castle Acre, New Buckenham), and septaria — nodular concretionary masses of clayey limestone occurring in the London clay (Colchester, Orford). Central England on the other hand has a great belt of limestone stretching from Dorset in a broad 'S' through the Cotswolds to Lincolnshire and into Yorkshire, and limestone was widely used for castles. Among the best-known types were Barnack (Cambridge), Weldon (Rockingham), Ancaster (Belvoir) and Portland (Southampton). Another type of limestone is carboniferous, a grey stone with good weathering properties (Chepstow, Rhuddlan, Caernarvon). Sandstone is a rock type that occurs in England, Wales and Scotland and yields an excellent freestone for building (Edinburgh, Goodrich [old red], Durham, Appleby, Bridgnorth). Many castles were built with local rubble but dressed with ashlar blocks, such as limestone from Caen in Normandy (Dover, Portchester).

6
Sieges: Attack and Defence

In the last chapter we looked at the construction of stone castle buildings. The emphasis was on the builders providing those amenities which they and their employers agreed could be included within the confines of the site, the availability of materials and the cash limits. There was one more factor of crucial importance. What were they going to do to the buildings to help keep intruders out, to make it difficult for a siege to succeed, and at the same time enable troops within to sally forth on to the offensive with the minimum of difficulty? It is appropriate to look first at the means with which besiegers could break into a castle and eventually compel its garrison to surrender.

In the Middle Ages, besieging a castle was not as a rule a sudden or surprise operation. The king, or lord, who set out against the castle of a rebel, or a rival, announced his intentions, sometimes by letter demanding the surrender of the castle on pain of having a barrage of artillery hurled at it, sometimes by sending a delegation under the safe conduct of a white flag to make his demands to representatives sent out of the castle to 'parley', that is, discuss the matter. Occasionally, the king, or lord, would arrive outside the castle walls himself and have a herald or crier call out for surrender. If no surrender was forthcoming — and medieval lords were fearless and impetuous men who loved a fight, who placed the honour of throwing down a challenge and of accepting one very high on the list of virtues — then both sides withdrew to prepare for siege.

The besieging army will generally have arrived in the neighbourhood of the castle with its siege equipment ready, its ammunition accumulated and stacked up. In the case of the siege of Bedford in 1224, Henry III issued the order for surrender, heard that it was rejected, and had very quickly to gather up his men and munitions from all over the country to prosecute the assault. How should a besieging army attack and what siege equipment did it employ?

66

Assuming the castle about to be besieged was a fortified great tower inside a fortified enclosure with flanking towers and a gatehouse, the principal points of attack were the gatehouse, with its wooden gates that could be set alight and burned or more simply battered down; the walls, which could be either broken through by battering or holes made in them by means of undermining the foundations, or which could be scaled by ladders or whose parapets could be fought for and captured by means of belfries filled with fighting men; and the great tower, which could be invaded once a

A thirteenth-century picture of a siege (redrawn by R. Maguire)

corner had been successfully undermined by sappers and a way through to the interior opened up. In addition, the inside of the enclosure and the top of the great tower could be subjected to barrages of missiles of one kind and another from several kinds of siege engine positioned outside and some distance away. Barrages would reduce the numbers of effective defenders within the enclosure and would help to demoralize the garrison generally. They would also damage the walls of the great tower. The weaponry available to besiegers, certainly by the eleventh century in Europe and by the close of that century in Britain, were the battering ram, the *terebra*, the *ballista*, the mangonel — and a little later, an improvement on the mangonel, the trebuchet. In addition, attackers had a variety of mobile protective shields and platforms such as the penthouse, the 'cat', the mantlet and the belfry. And they had scaling ladders as well.

The ram was a long pole with an iron-cased head. It was suspended from ropes or chains within a wooden-framed structure on wheels and covered on its sides, known as a penthouse. It was wheeled up to the wall and driven against it again and again. To do so it was necessary first to fill in the ditch in front of the castle curtain to make a bridge, and all manner of things were used to close that trench, including on a few occasions corpses of humans and animals. To protect the men operating the ram in their wooden framework, a gabled structure was fitted over the frame, called a *testudo*. The *terebra* was a smaller pole with a sharp iron point, and it was used to pick holes in the masonry of the lowest parts of the walls, and this, too, was covered with a smaller penthouse, sometimes known as a 'cat' or a 'sow'. The *ballista* was a special device for firing iron shafts and javelins. It was much like a huge crossbow and was remarkably accurate. It was meant for picking off individual defenders along the walls. The mangonel, and its successor, the trebuchet, were engines for discharging stone balls or metal balls, or rotting animal carcases or even lumps of the deadly Greek fire, lobbing them over the top of

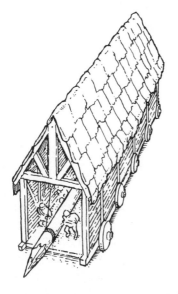

A battering ram being operated under the protection of a penthouse, or cat

the wall. The mangonel worked on the principle of torsion. A pivoted arm ending in a cup (or a sling) was held by a twist of ropes that stretched between posts. The arm was pulled down against the torsion and the missile put into the cup. When it was released, the arm swung up and over, hurling its projectile in a trajectory to take it over the enemy wall. Mangonels were often sited some way from the walls, behind a rapidly heaped up earth rampart. The trebuchet worked on the principle of the unequal counterpoise arm. A pivoted arm ending in a cup or sling was counterbalanced at the other end by a weight greater than the missile. The counterweight could be slid along to adjust the swing. When let go, the weight swung down and brought the cup up and over, discharging the missile generally with greater force than a mangonel, and with more accuracy because its range could be adjusted by sliding the counterweight along the arm. Trebuchets appeared in western Europe in the late twelfth century.

The principal missiles were stone balls, sometimes quickly fashioned by masons on site (as at Bedford, and a pile of stone balls can be seen at Pevensey). These were very effective against masonry if they scored direct hits. Greek fire, the liquid akin to the napalm of of the twentieth century, made from a type of naphtha and used since its discovery by the Egyptian chemist Callinikos in c.650 AD, was more devastating. It is known to have been used by Edward I at the siege of Stirling in 1297. Rotting carcases of animals were expected to spread germs among the defenders, though their effectiveness was more probably limited to producing temporary nausea among those immediately disarrayed when the carcases landed on the ground and split open, disgorging everything in a disgusting mess.

The belfry was a movable timber tower on wheels, several storeys tall, with step ladders between floors. It carried besiegers on each floor. On the top floor a drawbridge hinged so that when the belfry was hauled up to a castle wall, the flap could be lowered to provide a platform for the men inside to surge forward on to the wall walk and engage the defenders in hand-to-hand fighting. As the first ranks of the besiegers ran across the platform, other men clambered up the belfry ladders to support them. A belfry was easy to build, for it consisted of tree trunks that did not have to be stripped or planed. Those used in Philip Augustus' siege of Château Gaillard in 1204 were constructed of trees cut down and their branches removed. Occasionally, a belfry was used to move a small siege engine close to the walls. Henry I built his belfries several feet taller than the walls of Pontaudemer Castle when he laid siege to it in 1123, so that archers

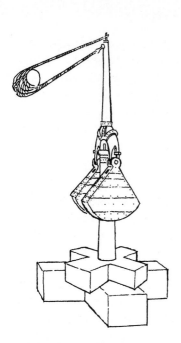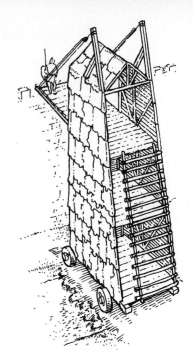

(left) A trebuchet in full swing; (right) A belfry dragged close to a castle wall. The side of the top storey is let down to allow troops to rush to the wall-head. Belfries were also called siege-towers

and stone throwers could direct their fire down into the enclosure.

The other protective structure used for a variety of exposed and dangerous tasks was the mantlet, a sloping screen made of timber or wickerwork panels on wheels. One of the activities of a mantlet was to protect a gang of men approaching a castle's wooden gates in the gatehouse to set them on fire with burning tow arrow tips. Another was to protect miners chipping away at the foundations of a curtain wall or the wall of a flanking tower to cut open a hole which could then be propped up with logs. These were burned and when they collapsed, the masonry (hopefully) came down with the charred timber. This was successfully done at Château Gaillard: it was also done at Rochester before the attack on the great tower, in 1215.

Mining was undertaken during many sieges in Britain. Three examples of interest are Rochester (1215), Dover (1216) and Dryslwyn (1287). In the war between King John and those of his barons who had obliged him to set his seal upon Magna Carta in 1215, which we will hereafter call the Magna Carta war (it was fought because the king refused, rightly, to stick to the terms extracted from him by illegal pressure), some of the barons' supporters seized

Rochester. The king demanded its return but the constable refused. He had several hundred troops in the castle precincts and they took up defensive positions, ready to resist the king's inevitable assault. It came unexpectedly soon — within days John had broken into the city and positioned an array of siege engines on and around the original eleventh-century motte and had begun a preliminary barrage of fire from the siege engines against the bailey wall in the south before attacking the great tower itself. Part of the bailey wall was probably brought down by miners, for this type of siege engineering was an especial favourite with the king. Then John, already determined to undermine the great tower, ordered 'as many picks as you are able' to be sent to him by the sheriffs of Canterbury, and prepared to excavate. The south bailey wall yielded and the defenders withdrew into the great tower, their last refuge. A mine shaft was dug and a tunnel driven towards the tower's south-west corner. A few weeks later, after a daily barrage from siege engines which pounded the tower walls, the sappers arrived underneath the corner foundations. Beams and props were set up as a temporary support frame, and the king sent an urgent call to his justiciar, Hubert de Burgh, ordering him to despatch 'with all speed forty of the fattest pigs of the sort least good for eating, to bring fire to the tower'. The pigs were brought, killed and their corpses crammed into the tunnel within the support frame. The pigs' bodies were set alight and burned steadily for some hours, unaffected by the lack of oxygen in the tunnel. Suddenly, the supports gave way and, jarred by the continuing barrage against the masonry, the corner gave way, leaving a huge gaping hole into the tower basement. The king's men rushed in, chased the defenders behind the cross-wall and fought them, floor by floor, through the great tower until surrender. The siege had taken nearly two months.

A few months later, Dover Castle, held by Hubert de Burgh, was besieged by Prince Louis of France, whom the Magna Carta barons had invited to England to lead them against King John. (The reward was the English throne, but in offering it, the barons succeeded in generating more support for King John than they had reckoned — but that is another story.) Louis ordered from France a huge siege engine which was nicknamed Malvoisin, or Bad Neighbour. He also decided to try to break into Dover by means of tunnelling. A mine was dug in the direction of the gatehouse and emerged under its eastern tower. The props were put up and fired, and the tower collapsed. But the resourceful de Burgh and a handful of men-at-arms rushed to the gaping hole left open and frantically

Dover, perhaps the greatest castle in the British Isles, was begun in the reign of Henry II

plugged it with timber beams, wedging them down with other planks. They fought off the attack valiantly, until the French prince called off the siege with the news of King John's death at Newark.

At Dryslwyn, near Llandeilo in Carmarthenshire, in 1287, when forces of Edward I were besieging the castle held by a rebel Welsh cousin of Llywelyn the Last, Lord Stafford and a detachment of men crawled along a tunnel dug by sappers leading up to the floor of one of the castle towers. As they edged forward, however, there was a landslip and masses of earth fell down, asphyxiating the young peer and his fellows. This was the kind of disaster all tunnellers have dreaded, including would-be escaping prisoners from German prison camps during World War II.

There is no doubt that in siege operations the attackers had the lion's share of the advantage — certainly in the first two centuries of castle history in Britain. Naturally, when designing and building castles, the works supervisors considered the defensive fortifications above everything else, but they were limited in what they could provide against attack. The answer to stone balls hurled by mangonels or trebuchets at curtain or tower walls was thicker masonry. Ten to twelve feet of well-mortared blocks or tightly compacted rubble with cement (with or without ashlar dressing) could normally withstand even the largest stone ball which the best trebuchet was capable of hurling, and many towers (but rather fewer curtains) had 10–12ft thick walls, some more substantial than that (such as Dover, 20ft and Duffield, 18ft) and of course thicker walls took longer to yield to battering rams or *terebrae*. But the problem of warding off missiles sent over the tops of walls could only be solved by raising the heights of the walls. Framlingham has a 40ft tall curtain which was higher than average. But higher walls could be overcome by improving the range and trajectory of siege engines, and better mangonels were produced. The trebuchet was introduced, quite possibly for this purpose. The answer lay rather in arranging things so that the besieger could not get close enough to give his siege engines their maximum fire power (see chapter 7).

We have seen that a regular technique for bringing down walls was to undermine them. How could a gang of enemy sappers be prevented from tunnelling through to the foundations of a great tower? One answer was provided at Kenilworth, where the corner buttress turrets were made excessively thick, almost twice as thick as the tower walls in between. Another answer was to dig a very deep and wide moat round the tower, which could not be tunnelled through, but that meant taking up a large amount of otherwise valuable space inside the enclosure. A third was to sink a

Mineshaft: sappers about to set fire to a series of props in a mine tunnel under the corner of a great tower. This is how the corner of Rochester great tower was brought down in 1215–16

Steps cut in the rock in the mine tunnel at St Andrews

countermine. Here, the defender, having detected or guessed the direction in which the attacking miners were tunnelling, bored down through the basement floor, or through the open ground outside the tower, in the opposite direction, hopefully to meet somewhere along the way underground. This happened at St Andrews in 1546, though the tunnels met at a point underground where one was about 6ft above the other — and this was in the rock on which the castle stood. You can crawl along the two tunnels today and see the join, stepping from the higher tunnel to the lower by means of an iron ladder. The St Andrews' tunnels, incidentally, dispose of the theory that castles built on rock foundations could not be undermined by tunnelling.

Other devices for fighting off besiegers and their armoury were beams with forked heads to deflect battering rams, poles with forked

St Andrews: mine and countermine

74

heads to push scaling ladders away from the walls and sacks stuffed with feathers, wool and rope ends lowered down from the parapet to deaden the blows of a battering ram.

There were several features that builders could incorporate in castles for defending them. One was hoarding, or brattices. This was a wooden gallery around the top part of a curtain wall or tower wall supported on horizontal posts let into the masonry. The gallery was protected on its outer side with timber panelling, with slits for observation, and provided with a timber sloping roof. The floor, also of timber, was slatted to allow defenders to drop missiles or liquids on to attackers. To prevent the timber being set alight, wet hides were hung on the front walls and draped over the sloping roof. Hoarding was vulnerable to stones, however, and a few carefully aimed balls could smash a hole in it, breaking the continuity of the structure and causing it to collapse. In later centuries, this wooden hoarding was incorporated in a stone form and called machicolation (see Glossary). Another feature, more specifically to deal with attackers' attempts to fire the gates, was the inclusion in the ceiling of the passage in the gateway or gatehouse of a series of holes which were situated in the floor of the room over the passage. Generally called murder-holes, because it is commonly said that they were used for pouring boiling liquids or molten lead on to attackers who had managed to get through the gates, they were more probably used for

(left) Medieval timber hoarding at the wall-head. This type of defence preceded stone machicolation (after Viollet-le-Duc); (right) Section of the ceiling of the gateway at Deal showing the murder-holes used for spying and possibly for water in case of fire

pouring cold water on to wooden gates that had been set alight.

Perhaps the two most famous defensive features of a castle, however, were the drawbridge and the portcullises. The drawbridge worked like a see-saw, pivoting in the centre with heavy weights at one end. When the catches were released, the weights pulled one end down and the bridge part, which straddled the moat, swung upright across the gates of the entrance to the gateway passage. Alternatively,

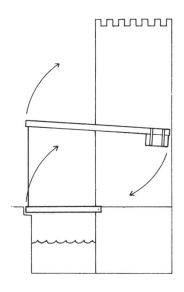

Probably the earliest type of mechanical drawbridge. The top beam pivots in the centre, and is weighted at one end, inside the tower. When that end is lowered, the other end (outside) rises, lifting by means of chains the outer end of the platform across the moat in front of the gate

the bridge was lifted and lowered by chains which were turned inside the gatehouse. The portcullis was a grille of wood or iron, or wood lined with iron on its outer faces. It was set in deep grooves (see photograph of grooves at Caerlaverock Castle) and was raised or lowered by chains on a winch system operated in a room above the chamber or passage whenever the portcullis was required. Some castles were provided with many portcullises: at Caernarvon the King's Gate alone had six. It is not hard to imagine the palaver associated with admitting someone who had a bona fide invitation to visit the castle.

Nearly all castles had a parapet along the top of the curtain wall, round the flanking towers (if there were any) and the gatehouse. The top of the great tower was invariably battlemented. Indeed, as we have seen, what determined whether a stone fortress/residence was fortified was the existence of battlements, or crenellation. When Bedford Castle was partially demolished after the 1224 siege, Henry

(left) Caerlaverock: the port-cullis groove in the great gatehouse

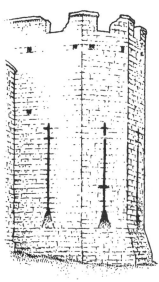

(left) The inside of the shell keep and great tower at Bedford, c.1224-5. It is an adaptation of the drawing that appears in the contemporary manuscript of Matthew Paris's *Chronica Majora*; (right) Fish-tail arrow slits at Grey Mare's Tail Tower on the east wall of Warkworth's inner bailey

III ordered that the bailey walls should be reduced in height and not have any battlements. Castles were also provided with arrow slits, or loopholes, in many parts of the buildings, at all levels. These were narrow openings, usually vertical, splayed inwards to give the archer room to shoot without fear of retaliation. There was a variety of arrow slit shapes, and a tour of several castles will generally give an interesting range of local preferences, from the simple vertical loop, anything from one to three yards long and 1½–4in wide (see those at Brougham, Dover, Newcastle), to loops with round holes at top,

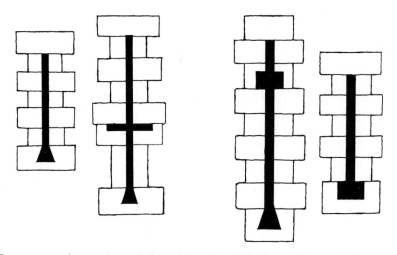

Some types of arrow loop; (left to right) Skenfrith (fish-tail bottom), Trematon (crosslet with fish-tail bottom), Manorbier (top crosslet with fish-tail bottom) and Pembroke (slit with rectangular oillet)

middle and bottom (Trematon), loops with horizontal cross loop in the middle (Berkeley), loops with holes at top and bottom and at each end of horizontal cross loop (Kenilworth), and loops with one vertical and two horizontal cross loops. Arrowslits are often found in walls near corners of towers where there is a spiral staircase or a platform for archers, in the merlons of the battlements, in wall chambers and even where one of the wedge-shaped buttresses at Conisbrough joins with the cylindrical wall of the great tower. At Dover, the Avranches Tower in the outer curtain, a polygonal flanking tower perched on a cliff edge, bristles with rows of arrow slits behind which are fighting galleries.

7

Better Defence Systems

In his attempt to build a castle from which he could be sure to exclude all unwanted people, a castle owner naturally aimed at making his castle impregnable. This is a term used at some time or other to describe many interesting and sophisticated military fortress-residences that in fact did fall to siege or stratagem. Château Gaillard, for example, one of the most famous castles of European military architectural history, was built at great speed (1195–8) but no less skill and sophistication by Richard Coeur de Lion, and was claimed to be impregnable. Basically, it was a great tower placed at the extreme end of a rock spur high over the River Seine near Les Andelys covering the approach to Rouen, the capital of Normandy, defended by a series of obstacles aimed at frustrating all attempts to capture it. The plan shows better than any description how Richard and his engineers confidently expected to be able to deflect any assault. One point to note about the inner bailey curtain is that a large segment of it consisted of a series of 'closely set, bellying' towers of solid stone aimed to offer the maximum flanking, 'giving the impression . . . of a gigantic jelly mould' (W. Anderson). The tower itself was cylindrical on one side (the cliff side) and tailed into a pointed 'beak' projection on the inner bailey side, and had machicolation round the top.

Despite its position and the defences — natural rock cliff, deep and wide ditches, banks, thick walls and so forth — the castle was successfully besieged by Philip Augustus, King of France, in 1203–4. After several months of assault it fell, chiefly through expert and effective undermining operations. Miners got under the outer bailey wall and across the ditch. Then one soldier got into the middle bailey through the drain of a garderobe and into the chapel where he hauled several colleagues up through the window. The defenders fled behind the safety, as they thought, of the inner bailey, but the French successfully undermined its 'jelly-mould' wall at a point

79

under a stone bridge to the gateway, and forced the defenders to surrender because they could not effectively escape down the sheer rock face with impunity. The great tower was not even assaulted.

It has been said that the capture of Château Gaillard shocked all Europe, but it is more likely that the shock was the news soon afterwards that Normandy had fallen to the French. But the castle was certainly a prestige symbol: Richard built it as a direct challenge to Philip Augustus on the basis of 'Here I am: come and get me.'

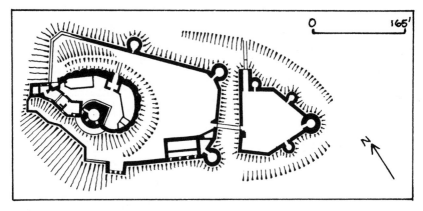

Château Gaillard (after Anderson): the miners dug underneath the cylindrical tower at extreme right, and eventually got into the inner part of the castle at the south east. Note the 'beellying out' of the inner curtain wall (at left)

Château Gaillard does not seem to have been as advanced as is often claimed. With its last line of defence at the top of the peak, the avenues of escape for beleaguered defenders were strictly limited. This does seem a look backwards in design, especially when one considers Dover which had started to become concentric with its great tower central in the plan, nearly fifteen years earlier (c.1185–9). The odds were against the defenders at Gaillard from the start if they ended up in a corner from which they could not escape.

In the thirteenth and fourteenth century, the offensive/defensive role of British castles appears to have become more pronounced, and this was a step towards achieving that elusive 'impregnability'. One of two lines of defence turned over to the offensive would have a better chance of keeping people out of a castle than starting on the defensive from the outer ramparts inwards. This may have been the thinking behind the growing practice of building an outer ring of fortifications around an inner fortress (of tower encircled by curtain, or of curtain with flanking towers), and indeed of adding a third 'ring' outside that, which is the principle of concentric fortification.

The idea stemmed from Byzantium and the Near East. The walls of Constantinople built by Theodosius between 410–47 were raised on the following plan: an inner wall about 40ft tall and an outer wall about 30ft tall were erected parallel, separated by about 15ft. Each wall had protruding towers at regular intervals. In front of this composition was a moat bridged only at the points where the five main gates were situated. There was a parapet between the walls which could only be reached by staircases inside the towers, which themselves were massively built to support the weight of artillery such as machines for hurling big stones and for discharging Greek fire. The higher wall provided scope for a line of archers to fire their arrows over the heads of another line of archers along the lower wall. This also enabled offensive troops from the lower wall to descend and go out through passages into the foreground and thence into the battlefield, while being covered by the higher wall archers. There is something in the fact that between the 400s and 1204 (the disastrous year when the Crusaders of the Fourth Crusade attacked the great

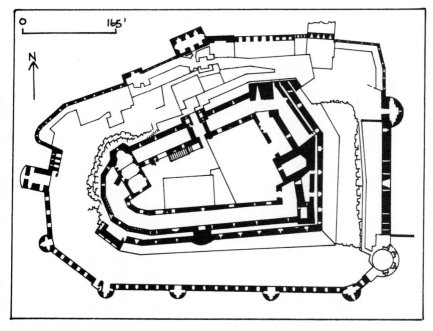

Krak des Chevaliers, Syria: ground plan of this mainly twelfth- and thirteenth-century Crusader Castle. It will readily be seen as a fine concentric plan (after Muller-Wiener, via Anderson)

81

city), no one had succeeded in breaching these walls.

The lessons of Constantinople's seeming impregnability were grafted by the Crusaders on to a number of castles that they built between about 1100 and about 1300 in the Near East, notably those in Syria at Sahyun, Markab and the much-mentioned and possibly overpraised Krak des Chevaliers (see plan on p.81). The Krak was begun at the end of the eleventh century and became fully concentric in the late twelfth, and until 1271 it resisted attack successfully. The principles of concentric design were applied throughout Europe, and reached Britain probably through returning Crusader knights, possibly soon after the Second Crusade (1147–9). It is difficult to resist the wish to believe that Henry II, one of the greatest castle-builders, worked out the concentric idea for himself and was not influenced by the Near East when he ordered the works at

Krak des Chevaliers: a model of the famous Crusader castle in Syria. The Krak was constructed in the twelfth century as a thick curtain with flanking towers and gate, surrounded later by a twelfth/thirteenth-century high curtain with towers, to form a concentric plan. The Krak resisted sieges in two centuries.

Dover. There, the great tower was surrounded by an inner curtain with flanking towers and gateways, and that was surrounded by a substantial section of outer curtain also with flanking towers, and with steep, scarped cliffs outside. This work was completed by Henry's death in 1189. Dover was probably the first castle in Britain to become concentric, although it was a concentricity from improvement, not from scratch. The Tower of London began to receive its concentric form in the reign of Henry III, but it was not until the 1270s that the first concentric castle was built in Britain from new, and then it was in Wales and not England — the remarkable Caerphilly, still regarded by some authorities as the greatest castle in the British Isles.

The concentric principle in Britain, as far as entirely new castles were concerned, was embodied in an inner quadrangle of high curtain walls and flanking towers (generally cylindrical) at the four corners. Two opposite walls were usually dominated by huge twin-towered gatehouses, although in some castles there was only one. Encircling the inner quadrangle was a second quadrangle, lower

in height but with towers along the perimeter, or not, as in the cases of Harlech and Caerphilly. The distance between the quadrangles was only a matter of yards and this allowed the defenders on the battlemented inner quadrangle walls to fire over the heads of their fellows who were raking the assailants from the lower quadrangle walls. The lower defenders could also go over to the offensive and sally forth to attack a besieging army, confident that the inner defence could take care of itself. This was the plan at Caerphilly, which was surrounded entirely by an artificial moat and lake complex (see chapter 8). It was also the plan at Harlech, built in the period 1283–90 and sited high on a rock above what was the estuary of the Dwyryd River, though the outer lower wall was only a few feet above the ground and contained no flanking towers. At Caerphilly, too, the lower outer wall was only a few feet tall with no towers. And it was the plan, triumphantly displayed at Beaumaris, built between 1295 and 1330, but never completed. Other concentric castles raised in the later thirteenth century and early fourteenth century were Rhuddlan and Kidwelly in Wales and Caerlaverock in Scotland. The appearance of the concentric castle in thirteenth-century Britain is often described as the apogee of military fortification in medieval Britain. So it was, but only a handful of new concentric castles were built and an equally small number of other castles were improved to concentric 'status'. It was an extremely expensive undertaking, and only the crown and the very richest nobles could afford it. And yet castles were still required and they still needed to be as capture-proof as possible.

In the late twelfth century another feature was introduced to the castle scene, the gatehouse. Previously, gateways to enclosure castles were simple and small, like the single tower pierced by a passage, with a chamber over it, at Exeter (c.1068) or the hardly complicated version of the same at Framlingham (c.1200). Then, at Dover, we see the beginning of a larger idea, a pair of flanking towers placed one each side of the entrance to the inner bailey by a doorway through the curtain wall, near enough for both to cover the entrance (King's Gate and also at the opposite end of the inner bailey, Palace Gate). These towers are rectangular. The idea develops a little later into the gateway in which the towers are closer together to form an integral

(opposite) Lewes: the barbican which leads to the gatehouse. Originally built in the early fourteenth century, it has been restored. Note the fine courses of knapped flint

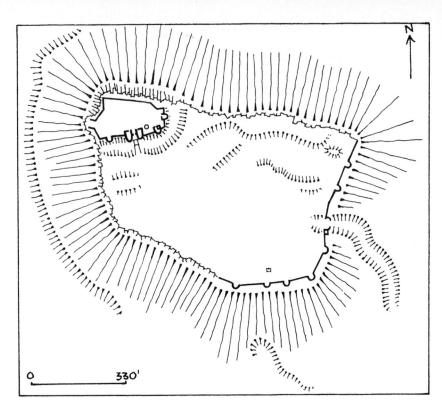

Beeston (after Ridgway)

structure where they are joined by a roofed passage over the arch which they protect, and which contains residential accommodation, such as at Beeston (c.1220–30), Rockingham (1280–90), lit on the exterior only by arrow slits, St Briavels (1292–3), Llanstephan (c.1280) and Skipton. The idea is still further enlarged at Tonbridge (c.1275), at the great Edwardian castles of Harlech, Flint and Beaumaris, and the de Clare castle, Caerphilly, where the structures are so vast that we can call them gatehouse-towers or great gatehouse-towers (but not keep gatehouses), and which have gates, machicolation (in some cases), portcullises, murder-holes, draw-bridges, and suites of sumptuous accommodation. Tonbridge, for example, has what was described in *Archaeologia Cantiana* as a noble apartment in the upper storey measuring 52ft by 28ft by 15ft high. By this time the gatehouses had often become the central point of the castle and the strongest features, like Tonbridge and Dunstanburgh (c.1313–25). They drew the main attention of the attackers in the same way as did the great towers. Some were cylindrical towered, but many were square or polygonal.

In the fourteenth century and afterwards, some gatehouse-towers were converted into great towers by blocking up the entrances and building alternative ways into the enclosure. This happened at Dunstanburgh, Ludlow, Llanstephan and several others. It was partly as a result of the inconvenience endured by people using the gatehouse as a residence within the castle. The heavy and complicated machinery needed to operate several portcullises and a drawbridge took up a lot of space in the gatehouse. At Harlech, for example, a portcullis actually operated from a chapel, while at Tonbridge and Dunstanburgh the great hall was sited on the second floor, at some inconvenience. At Tonbridge, too, the noise of gate and portcullis closing must have been frightful: two portcullises were provided, one at each end of the entrance, plus a pair of gates and portcullises over entrances to the side lodges and even to wall-walks.

A good many castles had large gatehouses and some of them were unusually elaborate. At Denbigh, the gatehouse is the star feature of the formidable enclosure castle with curtain wall and flanking polygonal and cylindrical towers. It consisted of three large polygonal towers, each over 40ft across, clustered in a triangle. The order of obstacle to an intruder was first to cross the drawbridge covering the approach to the entrance passage which was flanked by two of the towers and joined across the top of the passage. Then he had to get through an outer portcullis and gate and an inner portcullis and another gate, running the gauntlet of murder-holes in the passage ceiling. Once through, he entered a roughly octagonal chamber with vaulted roof and ahead was the third tower, bigger than the others and joined to them on the sides of the octagonal chamber by thick-walled linking buildings. At the right of the chamber was a passage into the main courtyard of the castle, but this was protected by yet another portcullis, while passage to it was observed through spy-holes in the walls.

To make it more difficult, and certainly more hazardous, for assailants to head for the gatehouse, many castles were given an arrangement of walls projecting outwards from the gatehouse, sometimes at right angles, sometimes at more acute angles and rounded on the way, which terminated in another gateway with, or without towers, guarded by a portcullis and perhaps another drawbridge. This was the barbican, or outwork, which was generally unroofed. There was a wall-walk along each of the walls protected by a battlemented parapet. Defenders could stand along the parapets and shower them with arrows and missiles.

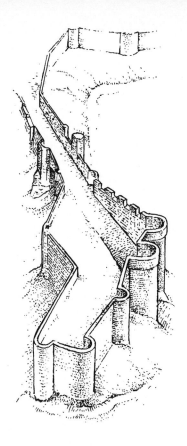

A barbican adjoining a gate-house. This is based on Scarborough

Barbicans appear first in later twelfth-century castles, the one at Dover being among the earliest. They were simple structures for the most part, though the barbican built at Goodrich in the early fourteenth century was quite elaborate, ending in a half-moon tower-like structure with walls several feet thick, and with a gateway at right angles to the gate passage that led into the half-moon from another side. Interesting barbicans can still be seen at Warwick, Conwy, Chepstow and Sandal, and at Lewes is one of the finest of many surviving barbicans in Britain.

It might seem to the twentieth-century castle enthusiast that the castle had reached the point of impregnability. But medieval military builders were not so sanguine and they continued to look for ways to improve defences, such as higher walls, greater distances between outer walls and the ditches and banks outside, and more towers along the curtains. They also developed the employment of water defences, using natural sources, diverting rivers, manufacturing dams and creating artificial lakes, at which we look briefly in the next chapter.

8
Water Defences

The earliest castle-builders of Europe appreciated the value of surrounding castles with wet ditches, that is, moats which were more or less permanently supplied with water from springs or nearby rivers. The motte castle at the Husterknupp (see chapter 2) in western Germany had been developed from a fortified farmstead lying in marshy ground, and by stage c was almost completely surrounded by water which was provided by what appears to have been a natural and gradual rise in the water level of the district. Many of the first motte castles in Britain were sited on river banks or near rivers, or on land which had natural springs. Berkhamsted motte castle was almost totally surrounded by water from its first years, fed by springs. Skipsea motte castle was sited in a mere which separated the motte from its bailey. Clavering, one of the very earliest Norman castles, had moats fed by the River Stort. And Rothesay, one of the very few shell keeps in Scotland, stood like an island in a surrounding moat fed by a stream from a nearby loch. And a good many castles have ditches today that are dry and tidily sown with grass but which were wet in their active military-residential role, for the Normans and early Plantagenets (and the lords whom they allowed to build castles) generally provided their greater fortresses with wet moats most of, if not all, the way round.

Two major castles in Britain which may be classified as water-castles or lake-fortresses (along with their other classifications) are Kenilworth in Warwickshire and Caerphilly in Wales. In both cases the use of extensive areas of water was deliberately integrated into the overall plans as a major defensive feature, and they were worked out according to the topography of the sites.

Caerphilly has already been mentioned in relation to its concentric form. Its water defences were additional fortifications, and they rested principally upon the creation of two large lakes. The south lake with its moats encircling three sides of the inner fortress was fed from a stream of the Nant-y-Gledyr. To the north of the inner fortress was raised a scarped bank curved at its two ends. The western end leads into a Hornwork, or separate earthwork island, revetted with stone and encircled by the water from the south lake. The east end joins at right angles to a stone platform (the north platform) raised above water level and screened with a curtain wall and polygonal towers and a gatehouse at the north end. This arrangement formed a north lake whose levels could be controlled by sluices. In the same straight line, but veering slightly to the south-east, a south platform was erected with a curtain and a close row of projecting buttresses. This contained tunnels and sluices that regulated the flow of water from the south lake behind into the ditches in front. Between the two fortified platforms is a third 'hook-shaped' platform with curtain but no towers or buttresses (the central platform), at the northern end of which is the main entrance to the castle, and this entrance gate joins with the north platform. The 950ft-long continuous platform was in the nature of a vast barbican, acting as a huge dam. The inner fortress is thus an island site, protected on all sides by lakes whose levels could be controlled by the defenders.

At Kenilworth, the original castle of the twelfth century was a polygonal enclosure whose ends led into a massive rectangular great tower of mid-twelfth-century construction, and in King John's reign, was circled by an outer enclosure with flanking towers and many pilaster buttresses. His son, Henry III, granted Kenilworth to his brother-in-law, Simon de Montfort, who was almost certainly responsible for the elaborate water defences which were to figure so dramatically in the great siege of Kenilworth in 1266. Basically, the castle of Simon de Montfort was artificially surrounded by water from springs south of the castle flowing into the low ground around it by means of a 400ft-long mole, or dam, topped by a double wall with gatehouse at each end, projecting from the south-east of the outer curtain. In effect, the 'island' site stood in a large lake, called the Great Mere, which covered the south and west sides and fed a moat round the north and north-east sides leading into a lower mere on the east side, north of the mole.

During the siege, which was conducted by Prince Edward, Henry's eldest son, against supporters of Simon de Montfort (who had fought the king and lost at Evesham in 1265), barges were brought by road from Chester in order to launch a water-borne assault on the castle from the Great Mere. The attack was beaten off

Bodiam Castle built by Sir Edward Dalyngrygge showing the formidable twin-rectilinear towered gatehouse

by the defenders, probably by a combination of missiles from siege engines in the castle enclosure and concentrated fire from archers along the south wall which had been erected by King John.

There were many other castles with important water defences, and among them was Bodiam in Sussex. Bodiam Castle was built in one complete operation in the 1380s in a huge rectangular lake artificially created and fed by the River Rother. The water defences are interesting. In front of the main gatehouse to the north is a causeway out to a second gate and thence to an octagonal island platform in the lake. Today, this is connected to the north bank of the 'mainland' by a second causeway probably built in the seventeenth century. In the 1380s, however, no second causeway was provided at that point. Instead, there was a long bridge from the octagon westwards to the west bank. An intruding force, therefore, had to expose its flank to everything that the defenders wanted to hurl at it, including fire through the gatehouse gun-ports. The rear postern had a bridge projecting across the southern part of the lake to a harbour specially cut in the River Rother which in the fourteenth century was navigable at that point.

Kirby Muxloe, built by Lord Hastings (who also built the Hastings great tower at Ashby de la Zouch), was another castle with special water arrangements for the moat. An artificial lake was constructed in 1480 for this fortified manor house which superseded (on the site) an older but unfortified manor. The work was supervised by one Davy Bell. He received pay, recorded in the accounts of the building work that have survived. These also include entries regarding payments to men to stay up all night to watch the level of the lake which was fed by a local brook, to see that it did not rise too high up the ramparts or up the sides of the castle. It is interesting to speculate what these 'dykers' could have done if the water had gone over the top. The lake received its water from a tributary of the brook. A stonework dam was built a little lower down over the brook. When the brook was low, the water went under the dam through a hollowed oak log which could be plugged at the brook end, to maintain enough water for the lake. A kind of wooden grille was placed in the tributary to trap solid matter floating in it. Where the brook and the tributary join, there was another dam with a sluice underneath which could also be blocked off with a plug. The outlet sluice of the lake (at the opposite end) had decayed so much when work was done to clear the lake (in 1913) that it had to be repaired to allow the lake to be emptied.

It is not likely that Hastings ever thought a widened lake was enough to defeat any attempt to take his castle, for he also had a considerable number of gun-ports built into the towers and the gatehouse at low level, to cover every possible angle of attack. Likewise, Sir John Fastolf, who built Caister Castle near Great Yarmouth as a structure surrounded by two lakes connected by a causeway, did not rely entirely upon water defences. Caister had gun-ports, notably in its very tall great tower, at several levels. Professor Allen Brown in *English Castles* cites the repulse of an attack by French raiders in 1458, 'when "many gonnes" were "shotte"'.

Moats were of course effective obstacles against besiegers, whether dry or filled with water, and the greater part of the thousand or so castles in the Gazetteer in this book were provided with ditching and ramparts of some kind. It is pleasing to record that some which were originally wet moats but which dried up over the centuries, have been cleared out and refilled in the present century, as at Berkhamsted, to reveal the castles more in their medieval state. The presence of a drawbridge does not always indicate a wet moat, for it was necessary to be able to bridge a dry moat as well. And a stone-lined ditch does not necessarily indicate a dry moat; Bedford Castle had a stone-lined moat which appears from recent excavations to have led directly into the river, and so must have been part-filled if not wholly filled with water. Wet moats made undermining walls of towers or gatehouses behind them practically impossible, but there was nothing to stop an attacking army getting across the moat to the stretch between it and the walls (called the berm) and under cover of a penthouse boring underneath the foundations of a wall. Medieval castle owners probably echoed the belief in the effectiveness of a moat that Shakespeare puts into the last soliloquy of John of Gaunt (*Richard II*, II. i.), when he says: 'This precious stone set in the silver sea, which serves it in the office of a wall, or as a moat defensive to a house . . . '

9
Edwardian Castles in Wales

When we come to the remarkable structures erected in Wales in the late thirteenth century by Edward I, or by powerful lords with his permission, as part of his invasion, conquest and suppression of Wales in the years 1277–83 and thereafter, we may be tempted to accept the notion that they represent the apogee of military architecture in Britain. But that is to suggest that everything which came before was but a lead-up to these castles and everything that followed was in the nature of a decline. There is a case for believing otherwise, for they are more properly outside the general stream of British castle history. These castles ought to be viewed for what they are, what they were built for, and what happened to them.

Their plans and construction were part of a single, exclusive programme initiated by Edward to make short shrift of the Welsh in a vigorous campaign and to impose his dominion over them. Wales was to be absorbed. The programme began and virtually ended with him. It was not repeated by him in his attempts to conquer Scotland (if Caerlaverock was intended to be a castle on the Welsh scale, it was a lone one, and not part of any programme — and there is argument as to how much of it was Edwardian-inspired in any case). It was not imitated by any succeeding monarch in Britain: the only comparison that could be advanced is the programme of coastal fortification initiated by Henry VIII in the invasion scare of 1538–43 (see chapter 15) and these fortresses were entirely defensive structures. Within half a century some of the Welsh castles were in a state of decay and requiring considerable attention.

The Edwardian programme was gigantic by the standards of the time, and it involved men, materials and money on an unprecedented scale. Ten new castles were to be built, at Aberystwyth, Beaumaris, Builth, Caernarvon, Conwy, Flint, Harlech, Hope, Rhuddlan and Ruthin. The majority were to be major works, in some cases associated with town fortifications. Work was also to be

The impressment of workmen for the King's Works in north Wales, 1282-3

undertaken on four new 'lordship' castles, Chirk, Denbigh, Hawarden and Holt, on three originally Welsh-built but captured castles, Castell-y-Bere, Criccieth and Dolwyddelan. We shall be looking at the figures applying to the first ten; details of the work on the others will be found in the Gazetteer.

The vast programme was to cost nearly £80,000 in the years 1277–1304, approximately £16 million in today's terms, and another £15,000 (£3 million) were spent between 1304 and 1330. It involved a major exercise in recruitment and impressment of labour from all over England. The map at p.95 reproduced from the *History of the King's Works* vol I, shows the areas from which craftsmen and labourers were drafted to Wales for these works, via two gathering points, Bristol and Chester. In round figures about 150 masons, 400 carpenters, 1,000 diggers and 8,000 woodcutters for clearing, were raised by one means or another in the year 1282–3. Most counties contributed, from Norfolk to Hampshire, Northumberland to Warwickshire. Those who assembled at Bristol were taken by ship to the south Wales coast and then travelled to the site at Aberystwyth. At Beaumaris, 3,500 or so men were employed on the castle in the summer of 1295 — a figure equal to about 15 per cent of the total number of men employed in trade or commerce in London at the time. At Harlech, 1,000 men were at work in 1286.

Although the craftsmen and workers were paid, they were also conscripted, that is, they were drafted for the jobs. In Professor Allen Brown's phrase, 'this was direction of labour'. And the military was employed to guard contingents of men travelling to Chester and Bristol. One batch of men coming from Yorkshire to work at Flint and Rhuddlan was guarded by sergeants who were paid 7½d a day in case the men should abscond. Bonuses were paid for fast work, in kind rather than cash, but wages were docked for absenteeism.

The purpose of the castles was to terrify the Welsh into submission, to frighten those already defeated so that they would not rise, and to provide the Welsh with a permanent reminder of who was master of their land. Stage One, from 1277–82 was to include new castles at Rhuddlan, Flint and Aberystwyth, and renovations at Builth. It is thought that the scale of the works at Flint and Rhuddlan (where the River Clwyd was diverted more than two miles off course so that there would be uninterrupted access to and from the sea) alarmed the Welsh in north Wales enough to initiate the 1282 campaign in which they were finally crushed and their great prince,

Llywelyn the Last (1246–82) killed. This victory prompted Edward I to embark on Stage Two of his programme — Caernarvon, Conwy, Harlech, Beaumaris, Hope and Ruthin.

The sites of the Edwardian castles were well chosen. They were not all new sites: there had been a motte castle at Caernarvon and a stone structure at Builth. All except Builth were by or very close to the sea which guaranteed access, and which meant that they could all be supplied with men, weapons and food if they were attacked by Welsh forces from the landward side, as happened at Caernarvon in 1294–5.

Of the new works, four were concentric, built so from scratch: Aberystwyth and Rhuddlan (lozenge-shaped plan), Harlech (slightly rhomboidal) and Beaumaris (almost square). Conwy and Caernarvon were curtain enclosures with flanking towers and gatehouse, like Framlingham in concept but vastly more sophisticated. Flint was an enclosure with corner towers and a huge cylindrical great tower outside the south-east corner separated by a moat; in fact, like a motte-and-bailey castle in plan. Hope and Ruthin were enclosures with towers, etc, and Builth a motte castle with later shell keep (or possibly great tower: the documents of the time say *magna turris*).

The programme may well have been ignored in most parts of England (except the homes of the men drafted to Wales) to whom Wales was a distant land of men speaking a foreign tongue, but it was real enough to the men of Wales, and on several occasions they rose to attack the structures as they went up, pulling them down or burning them. Notably, Caernarvon was severely damaged in 1294 and 1295 by Prince Madog ap Llywelyn.

Edward's programme required a master mind to superintend the works involved. The king was a ruler with grandiose ideas not only of uniting the component parts of Britain into one kingdom, but also of ensuring that future generations should forever see monuments to his power. He chose one of the foremost castle-builders of western Europe, Master James of St George, who may be regarded as combining the abilities and functions of master mason, designer and military engineer. Magister Jacobus Ingeniator or Magister Jacobus Le Mazun appears first in British records in 1277–8. He had been working on castles in Savoy, in particular at Yverdon, Chillon and Saillon, and appears in records in Turin as Magistri Jacobi Cementarii and Jaquetto de Sancto Jorio (George). Dr A.J. Taylor examined Saillon Castle in the 1950s and found architectural parallels with Harlech and Conwy. He also examined the castle at St

Georges d'Esperanche in the Viennois, south-east of Lyon, and found parallels with the plan of Conwy and details comparable with Harlech. One was a garderobe shaft at St Georges which was almost the same as the one beside the north-west tower at Harlech. Master James, therefore, arrived in Wales fully experienced as a castle designer, mason and engineer, and was appointed Master of the King's Works probably in 1282, for which he was to receive 3 shillings a day, plus a pension of 1s 6d a day for his wife, who gloried in the name of Ambrosia, should she survive him. It is clear that he more than pleased his employer, for preferments of one kind and another followed, and he seems to have been on the royal payroll up to his death in c.1309. For example, he was appointed Constable at Harlech, 1290–3, was granted an estate in 1295, and worked for Edward from 1298 to 1305 in Scotland on several fortification projects, particularly Linlithgow, and possibly Caerlaverock.

The age of the specialist military architect-engineer had arrived in Britain at this time. Men like Master James and his colleague, Master Robert of Beverley (who made the Tower of London concentric, fortified Goodrich and improved Windsor and Rochester) and no doubt others of whom we lack details so far, were in a different category from those builders of the twelfth century whom we met in chapter 4. These thirteenth-century men had benefited from the important rediscovery of Greek sciences, in particular geometry, and this enabled them to visit a site and assess its possibilities, envisage a structure thereon as a whole and say what was possible and what was not. That is not to say that their buildings were without mistakes: they erred, like their predecessors — and like their colleagues on the cathedrals (Ely, York, Peterborough *et al*) — and often had to change direction as the work went on. It is thought that mason-engineers made wooden models of the structures they proposed to build (some were made as presents for royal children) and they may also have committed schemes to paper, though such plans have not survived for castles. They worked with the leaders of the other disciplines, such as master carpenters and probably ironsmiths, in a team, and did not interfere with them. It is unlikely that they exerted the supervisory role that architects today take for granted.

The Edwardian castles are described under their entries in the Gazetteer, but one or two points may be mentioned here, that are common to many of them. We have seen, in the chapter on the first stone castles, that few castles were built and finished in one operation or series of operations. Among the few are some of these Welsh castles: Aberystwyth (1277–89), Harlech (1283–90), Rhuddlan (1277–82), Flint (1277–85), Conwy (1283–9), Caernarvon (1283–1327) and Beaumaris (1295–c.1330, unfinished). They were planned and constructed as single and enormous units. Nothing of importance was added as an afterthought and no major rebuilding was done to improve the fortification. Four of them were built after the conquest and absorption of Wales and so were not aggressively offensive structures so much as administrative centres, police headquarters as it were, terror weapons, buildings from which to emerge only in time of civilian disturbance. They were lived in, not by monarchs or their families (except in rare circumstances and for extremely short periods), but by constables and officials, and so they differ somewhat from the private military fortress-residence role of other castles. Additionally, five of them were built in association with towns which were fortified with walls and turrets at the same time, in the hope that castle and town would work together to make the new order in Wales function as smoothly as possible. They have been compared with *bastides*, a type of town built by lords in southern France to protect their feudal borders, when the townsfolk were expected to contribute to the lord's purse and help defend his interests in return for mercantile privileges. In a subtle way the arrangement in Wales was to create pockets of loyal, or at least passive, people among a population that was hostile. And architecturally, of course, the castles have several features in common, notably (except for Flint) the great gatehouse which was a substitute for the great tower. The gatehouse in the Edwardian and lordship castles reached high sophistication in defensiveness as well as strength in construction. At Rhuddlan and Beaumaris, Master James incorporated two massive gatehouses at opposite ends of the inner enclosure. And at Denbigh, a lordship castle, the great gatehouse was one of the most elaborate of its kind anywhere in Europe, as we have seen in chapter 7.

Readers may by now have wondered where the massive and splendid concentric castle at Caerphilly fits into this picture of works in Wales. It was not a royal castle, though it belonged to a man who had exceptional wealth and wielded considerable power, Gilbert de Clare, Lord of Glamorgan, a semi-independent province about a quarter of the size of Wales. Caerphilly was started by de Clare in 1268. What gave him the idea of building Caerphilly on the concentric plan, and much like the later Harlech and Beaumaris as it turned out? And what influence, if any, did his plan have on Master James of St George? It is possible we may have the answer before the end of the present century, but for the moment the questions remain open.

This chapter is primarily concerned with the Edwardian fortresses of the late thirteenth century, but it should not be thought that the Welsh were unable to build their own castles or find a use for fortification. They felt the heavy hand of the Normans only a few years after the Conquest of 1066, but unlike the Anglo-Saxons they determined to maintain resistance for as long as possible. They were helped by their natural geography: the Normans were at first more interested in the low-lying territories of Wales. The Welsh, therefore, were able to learn about castle-building and to put it into practice.

Soon after the Conquest, three powerful, bullying, war-happy robber-barons, Hugh d'Avranches, Lord of Chester, Roger of Montgomery, Lord of the Lands of Shropshire, and William FitzOsbern, Earl of Hereford and Master of the Wye Valley, launched a three-pronged invasion of Wales, taking the difficulties of Offa's Dyke, the Brecon Hills and the Black Mountains in their stride and establishing a firm foothold in a substantial part of the ancient land of the Cymru. Motte castles were raised with astonishing swiftness over wide areas, at Clifford, Monmouth, Chepstow, Montgomery, Deganwy, Radnor, Brecon, Cardiff and many more. By the end of the eleventh century, the Normans were settled in the west the south and some of the north-east, leaving only the centre and mountainous north-west in Welsh hands. And they had started to build in stone at Chepstow and elsewhere.

The Welsh were taken aback by the Norman invasion and their brutal and grandiose military engineering, and at first made only sporadic attempts to fight back. Newly erected Norman mottes were besieged and sometimes taken, building works in stone were interrupted by lightning raids of Welsh warriors who pulled down the walls and set fire to the wooden parts, as at Cardiff, Laugharne and Llandovery (where the castle was said to have been seized before the mortar had dried between the stone blocks). Then, in the middle of the twelfth century, the Welsh recovered their poise and their national spirit was rekindled under strong leaders like Owain Gwynedd and Llewelyn the Great. Their attacks on Norman castles and towns were stepped up, they were better organized and on the whole more successful in their outcome. Henry II had tried but failed to reassert English power in the south-east and west, and the Welsh had taken the fullest advantage of the difficulties between his son, John, and his grandson Henry III, and their factious barons, which resulted in civil wars in both reigns. The Welsh did not have the technical capacity to assault the tough, well-built fortresses still in English hands, like Chepstow, Cilgerran and Pembroke, but they could and did build castles of their own, especially in the north.

Castell-y-Bere, near Dolgellau, under the slopes of Cadair Idris, had an irregular curtain with towers, one of them a sizeable rectangular tower, and the castle was able to withstand siege. Dolbadarn, an unusual boomerang-shaped enclosure with a large cylindrical great tower, is 40ft high today, and had other towers and buildings in which Llywelyn the Last is said to have imprisoned a brother, Owain. Dolwyddelan, the birthplace of Llywelyn the Great, was a three-storeyed rectangular great tower with an entrance protected by one of the few forebuildings put up by Welsh masons. Criccieth, a triangular enclosure on a mound over the sea, had two rectangular towers. There were others, such as Dolforwyn in Montgomeryshire and Ewloe in Flintshire, both built as acts of defiance of the English by Llywelyn the Last.

But these castles were mostly sited on rocky outcrops in mountainous countryside, and they were intended much more for the defensive purposes of the princes struggling for independence or playing military 'hide-and-seek' with the English. When the conquest of Wales was completed (in the 1280s) by Edward I and English rule established in fact as well as in law, some of these Welsh structures were allowed to decay, if not actually encouraged to fall down. Dolbadarn was stripped of its timber for the new Caernarvon Castle and others were used as quarries for their stone. Others were remodelled for English use, as we have seen.

10

Life in a Medieval Castle

Although a castle was a private fortified military residence belonging to a king or a lord, there could often be a good many people living or staying in it. In time of peace it was the owner's home or in the case of kings and some great lords, one of many homes. He would generally be accompanied by his wife and children, and perhaps one or two aged relatives, and would be attended by a staff of people, clerks, servants, grooms and craftsmen. He might have important guests, and they would have their families and servants. And in the case of a lord owner, he might be favoured with a visit from the king which as a rule meant that the royal family would be accompanied by a retinue of servants and bodyguards, many of whom would fetch up at the host castle some days in advance to ensure that everything was properly prepared for the royal visit. The castle had, therefore, to be able to cater for the needs not only of the owner, his family and immediate servants, but also for substantial and short-notice increases in occupants. It is as well to understand this when wandering over the remains of castles, for many of them appear to be too small to have accommodated more than a dozen or two people in any comfort.

In time of war, that is, siege or preparation for expected siege, more people would be brought into a castle than normal. Lords were not as a rule heads of communities and they tended to keep themselves and their families to themselves, but when a hostile army was approaching they would be moved by policy if not by sympathy to invite local villagers, farmworkers and others into the greater security offered by their castles. Those invited would be expected to bring with them as much as they could in the way of food and armaments (if they owned any), for once a siege had begun, supplies from outside were usually cut off. But castles sited by the sea or on estuaries could receive supplies by ship. Castle owners sometimes remembered to get in enough stores for emergencies, as at Lancaster in 1215 and Bedford in 1224, but there was not often much time for an owner to stock up for a prolonged siege because it was obviously not possible to determine how long a siege would last. Nor was it easy to find supplies locally if the owner of the castle was in open rebellion against the king. To supply such a man would probably result in an arrest for high treason when the siege was over.

The great majority of British castles occupied a defensive area of not more than about 50,000 sq ft, frequently much less. This was enough space for temporary huts and tents for surplus guests, though that depended to some extent upon the layout of the castle, but the more permanent stone buildings like great towers, gatehouse-towers, halls and so forth, were not designed to accommodate more than an owner, his household and a reasonable guest retinue. (But Coucy great tower in France was said to be able to accommodate about 1,000 people under siege.) Additional buildings were erected in numerous castles later on in their history, as part of the structure, because their owners had become more prosperous, but it was always expensive to build in stone.

Whatever the number of people in a castle at one time, the routine from daybreak to dusk remained much the same at the end of the Middle Ages as it had been at the beginning of the Norman occupation of England. The principal apartment in a castle was the great hall. This might be a separate structure as at Winchester or the main part of a great tower, generally taking up two storeys without an intervening floor, as at Hedingham and many others. Here, the owner and his wife occupied one end of it as a bedroom, curtained off from the rest of the hall, or in better castles partitioned off in stone or timber, the walls perhaps being decorated with paintings or hung with tapestries. This partitioned area was the solar. The lord rose at daybreak and dressed himself, or allowed a young son of a neighbouring or friendly lord, who was learning to become a squire or a knight, to help. The other occupants of the tower slept on benches or straw along the walls, and they joined the lord for the first meal, for in a medieval castle lords and household lived together and this precluded most of the ordinary privacies we now take for granted.

The lord and his family and a few chosen guests sat at a top table which stretched across one end of the hall. This was generally a solid rectangular table that might not be moved much from its position for as long as it survived. A second and perhaps a third table of the trestle kind was put up at right angles in the centre, to form a 'T', and this

The Great Hall of Winchester Castle

arm was occupied by the rest of the household. There they waited to be served. The first meal, however, was little more than bread and ale, or wine for the lord if it could be obtained. Once this was over, the tables were cleared, the trestles removed and the great hall became an administration office. Here, the business of the day — financial and legal, complaints, petitions, grants — was discussed, rents paid, disputes brought for arbitration, sometimes even courts held. If it were in time of siege, this period was reduced to a minimum or abandoned altogether, for the life of those in the castle had to be given over to resisting the assault by all means available. In time of peace, once the business was done, the lord could go down to the bailey yard to look at the horses, talk to the knights, squires and soldiers, watch them and the archers and crossbowmen practising their skills, and in the years after the introduction of firearms, to study the techniques of loading and manoeuvring artillery pieces. James II of Scotland was too fond of guns: during the siege of Roxburgh Castle in 1460 he got too close to a rudimentary cannon aimed at the castle; it blew up and killed him.

The main meal of the day was lunch and this was prepared for the lord by about midday, sometimes earlier, for the day had begun long before our twentieth-century 7.30–8.30am start. It was a much more elaborate meal. The trestles were brought out again, throne-like chairs were provided for the lord and his wife at top table, while everybody else sat on benches. The movable chair with a back was late in reaching England, though it had been in use in Wales probably since the tenth century. Tables were given cloths, each place had a special mat, and bread rolls were set down beside them. Lord and family had silver and earthenware utensils, the household had cruder pottery, horn or wood. In some castles the food was cooked in a kitchen in the tower, on the same level (perhaps in a mural chamber) as the top storey which enabled the fumes to rise without affecting those in the castle, or in the lower levels. There was a chance that cooked food arrived hot. In others, the kitchens were part of separate buildings outside so the food had to be brought across the enclosure from the kitchens to the great hall, where it arrived tepid and unappetising. (At Chequers in Buckinghamshire, the Prime Minister's official country home, a similar arrangement applied, with similar results, as late as about 1910.)

The menu for a medieval lunch embraced meat, boiled or roasted, or more exotic fowl like pigeon or heron or partridge. Medieval man did not have potatoes, but his vegetables were much the same as ours and he enjoyed salads and herbs. There was butter and cheese, bread and fruits. And there was wine, perhaps from Gascony or Burgundy, and ale from local small breweries or even brewed in the castle. And in case anyone wanted it, water from the castle well.

The only implements on the tables were knives. Diners hacked pieces off meat joints which might be roasted on a spit over a fire in the hall (whose smoke went up the chimney if there was one but into the hall itself if there was not), and they ate it with their fingers. Alternatively, they had meat or fish (according to the day of the week) put into bread baps or flat cakes and brought in to them. Meat and fowl bones were thrown to the floor which was often covered with rushes or straw. These were changed regularly but dogs wandered about the rushes looking for scraps. We may look at a simple menu regularly enjoyed by the Percys, perhaps at Alnwick, in the fourteenth century: 'For my lord and lady a loaf of bread in trenchers [cut in slices and used as plates], a quart of beer or a quart of wine, two pieces of salt fish, herring or sprats.' While the business of eating and drinking was going on, the lord and his guests might be 'gladded with lutes and harps . . . mirth of song and of instruments of music . . . '. Henry III once organised a tremendous banquet at Gloucester for friends: 5,000 chickens, 1,100 partridge, hares and rabbits, 10,000 eels, 36 swans, 34 peacocks and 90 boars were laid in. Kings paid a lot of attention to their food and the cooking of it. King John had new kitchens built at Ludgershall early in the thirteenth century, specifying that they had to have ovens capable of accommodating two or three whole oxen for roasting at one go. At Hertford, in the 1430s, the arrangements included a private kitchen for the king, a scullery, a saucery, a buttery and a storehouse for the king's fish.

Men and women must eat, and they must also get rid of waste products. How did the castle occupant manage? Castle towers and halls contained garderobes or latrines. These were no modern water closets but small mural chambers with a simple hole in the floor or in a stone platform raised two feet or so from the ground, which connected with a drain shaft built into the wall thickness, or in a special pilaster on the outer wall. These led down to the moat at the bottom or into cesspools. Sometimes there were arrangements to flush the effluent away but these were not as a rule so elaborate or so carefully planned as at many of the contemporary abbeys, notably Fountains in Yorkshire. Despite efforts to site them discreetly at the end of a narrow passage in a wall reached via a right or left hand turn, it is not hard to imagine how the malodorousness of these garderobes offended. Some could be flushed by water from conduits from the tower water supply (as at Caernarvon and Dover) but most were dealt with by servants with buckets. Some garderobes were so noisome that the kings objected strongly. Henry III complained about the garderobes at Marlborough and the Tower of London, and once ordered one to be resited even if it cost £100. At Winchester, however, a garderobe had a ventilation shaft, and at Middleham a special turret with three floors of garderobes was built, cut off from the main great tower.

After his midday meal, the lord and his friends would probably go hunting or take some other vigorous exercise, riding perhaps, or even taking part in the military drills and practices in the bailey. Men hunted deer and boar through the forests, none more so than many of the kings, especially the Conqueror, who set aside huge tracts of forest land for his exclusive use, and his son, William Rufus, who was accidentally shot while out hunting in the New Forest. Men also enjoyed hawking with hooded falcons. While they were out, the household servants attended to various domestic chores, got ready the meal that the lord and guests would eat when they returned and prepared some food for the next day. The hunters would return in the early evening and perhaps want to bathe. This they did in wooden tubs, behind curtains, with warm water brought to them. Then the last meal of the day followed, lighter than the midday meal. They might wander into the castle garden if it was a warm summer evening and the castle had one. At Arundel, Henry II was especially attached to the garden outside his royal apartments. At Edzell Castle in Scotland there was one of the best gardens in Europe.

In the Middle Ages religion played a far greater part in men's lives than today. The Normans, for example, were on the whole a brutal, temperamental and aggressive race of people who acted in an unchristian-like manner for the greater part of their lives. And yet their belief in God and in the possibility of a happy afterlife was dominant, and it was reflected in their cathedral and church building, the way many of them left their money to religious foundations, and in their habit of seeking remission for their sins by funding good works. We should not be surprised, therefore, to find that most castles in England and Wales had a chapel, and some had two, and that there was usually a resident chaplain on the lord's household staff. Each morning mass would be taken by the chaplain for the lord and his household. Some of the chapels in castles that

(*above*) Spofforth: a clean example of a vaulted chamber; (*opposite*)
Warkworth: the Chapel, facing the Altar

have survived seem more like small churches, notably the Chapel of
St John in the Tower of London.

We have laid some stress upon the fact that a castle was a lord's
home. But of the hundreds of castles that remain in one condition or
another, scattered about the countryside of Britain, there are very
few that give one any feeling that they could have been comfortable
places to live in. Perhaps indeed they were not so. And yet for feudal
lords there was no alternative to living in buildings of this kind. They
lived in an era of warfare, between nations, between lords, between
kings and rebel lords, and they had perforce to organize their lives
around a permanent capability for defending themselves. A feudal
lord might inhabit a castle for a lifetime without actually undergoing
a siege or even being threatened, but how could he know he would
never be attacked? His building, therefore, had to be a combination
of fortress and residence, and generally it had to be fortress first.
That meant sacrificing much in the way of softer surroundings.
There were wooden floors in great towers, but builders often
inserted vaulted stone ceilings to cut down the danger from
spreading fire. Staircases had to be stone, and the almost incessant
tramp of people up and down them must have been very noisy.
Doors were heavy and doubtless creaked and squeaked on their

hinges, and one can imagine a tower reverberating right through with the bang of the main door where the forebuilding joined the tower proper. Then, lords kept prisoners for various reasons. Some were held with freedom to walk about under careful watch and slept probably as comfortably as a lord's guest or servant. Others were treated much more harshly. They were confined in ground-floor chambers with only an arrow slit as a window, or in oubliettes, dungeons reached only through an opening in the ceiling, where they were likely to be forgotten (hence the name of the cell). Even the hardest of captors could not have remained totally unmoved by the cries of prisoners thus incarcerated.

Lambert of Ardres' description of the castle of Arnold, Lord of Ardres (see chapter 3), may be weighed against the following extract from the *Anglo-Saxon Chronicle* in the entry for 1137:

> For every great man built him castles and held them against the king; and they filled the whole land with these castles. They sorely burdened the unhappy people of the country with forced labour on the castles; and when the castles were built, they filled them with devils and wicked men. By night and by day they seized those whom they believed to have any wealth . . . they put them into prison and tortured them with unspeakable tortures . . . they hung them up by the feet and smoked them with foul smoke. They strung them up by the thumbs, or by the head . . . they tied knotted cords round their heads and twisted it till it entered the brain. They put them in dungeons wherein were adders and snakes and toads. Some they put into a 'crucethus' that is to say, into a short, narrow, shallow chest into which they put sharp stones; and they crushed the man in it until they had broken every bone in his body. In many of the castles were certain instruments of torture so heavy that two or three men had enough to do to carry one. It was made in this way: a weight was fastened to a beam which was attached to a sharp iron put round the man's throat and neck so that he could move in no direction, and could neither sit, nor lie, nor sleep, but had to bear the whole weight of the iron. Many thousands they starved to death. (Translated by G. Garmonsway)

In case anyone thinks of this extract as the exaggerated fantasy of a medieval chronicler with a grudge, let him consider the pit prisons in many Scottish tower-houses of the fifteenth and sixteenth centuries.

In time, lords moved out of their great towers and into more spacious building ranges inside the castle walls, and with that improvement in their environment the quality of life advanced. But as soon as there was danger from an enemy assault, or in times of civil war in the land, lords and their household had to be prepared to go back into the stronger towers (or gatehouse-towers) and rough it

110

once more. There was a step forward in comfortable living when the Bodiam-type of quadrangular fortified manor-house began to be built in the fourteenth century, while in the fifteenth century, more attention still was paid to the residential aspects in the construction of new castles and the improvement of old. At Raglan, begun c.1431, the inner area was divided into two parts, the Pitched Stone Court and the Fountain Court, which looked like the square of a medieval city. There were terraces, open staircases, long buildings with handsome doors and mullioned, stained glass windows, the whole surrounded by a powerfully fortified enclosure with very thick outer wall, corner and median towers, and protected by ditching and a substantial hexagonal great tower in its own enclosure and ditch.

Today, some castles built in medieval times but later enlarged and modernized are serving as residences of the highest luxury and sophistication, notably Windsor, Alnwick, parts of the Tower of London, parts of Dover, and much smaller ones like Penhow, while the owner of Borthwick has made the gaunt, grim, cavernous castle superbly comfortable without altering its medieval construction. But comfort was not the preoccupation of medieval castle-builders on the whole, and we should not take it for granted in their works, but only be gratified when we find it. Owners were moving towards a better balance between military needs and residential comfort in the fifteenth century, but this coincided with the growth in the building of purely residential houses and mansions which are outside the scope of this book.

(overleaf) Raglan: the gatehouse and (right) the Closet Tower. An excellent example of machicolation round the tower tops

111

11

The Fortified Manor House

While Edward I was squandering a sizeable percentage of the royal revenues on his grandiose castle-building schemes in Wales, other lesser men continued to build or improve castles in England, generally with the king's permission. They were doing so with motives different from their ancestors of the Conqueror's time, and without the pressures that afflicted society during the 'nineteen long winters' of Stephen's reign. Feudalism was not quite dead but it was dying. Men no longer built castles to dominate their lands and frighten the populace: they wanted grand homes with room to spread, to house the possessions they won in wars abroad, bought with money they inherited or made out of better usage of their lands, in particular sheep-rearing and wool production. They still needed protection from enemies, they still feared the possibility of invasion from France, or from Scotland, and so they continued to fortify their homes. But it was no longer acceptable to live in a tall tower and share it with family and dependants and servants. It was uncivilized to dine in a room at the corner of which the tower's main staircase was exposed, its users clattering their way up and down. And it was quite intolerable to live in a gatehouse whose portcullis or drawbridge machinery ground its creaking wheels and shafts round and round at the back of the chapel during prayers.

From about the last quarter of the thirteenth century, many of the new castles to be built began to look different from their predecessors. Principally, they appeared to combine the military function with the residential needs in a single integrated structural form. In doing so, the residential character gradually assumed greater importance as the need for military fortification lessened (though it did not by any means disappear). This does not mark a decline in the medieval castle, if we adhere to our original definition of a properly fortified private military residence. Castles continued to be built for at least another two centuries in England and Wales, and longer still in Scotland (see chapter 14). Furthermore, some of them were to be as strong as many of the fortresses of the twelfth and thirteenth centuries, like Bodiam (late fourteenth century), Bolton (late fourteenth century), the improvements at Warwick (late fourteenth and early fifteenth century), Ashby de la Zouch great tower (late fifteenth century). What did decline was the feudal system that created and fostered castles. Feudalism began to break down in the fourteenth century through a number of causes. The Black Death of 1349–50 ravaged Europe and England, and in England carried off about a third of the population, the majority of the dead being the tenant and serf classes. This radically changed the labour position and struck at the roots of the lord-tenant relationship. The wars in France carried off numbers of nobles and their sons and led to confusions of feudal loyalties: more and more tenants were drawn into the spheres of influence of fewer and fewer lords, and the system could not work at all. And the growing need for men on the land reduced the number available for armies abroad, with the result that lords had to employ mercenaries of whatever nationality they could find, and pay them. Some accepted land, but more wanted money, at a time when money in the form of minted coin was circulating much more widely than before.

More than a hundred new castles of one kind or another were built in England and Wales between Beaumaris (1295–c.1330) and Thornbury (c.1510–20). One kind widely preferred was the fortified manor house. These were very different from one another in numerous characteristics, bearing in every case the unique and individual whims and preferences of the owner. But they all had features in common as well. They were often quadrangular, which was not a new idea, for quadrangular plans had been followed in the twelfth century at Old Sherborne, Windsor and others. They had substantial corner towers, gatehouse on one side, postern on the opposite side, and additional towers or turrets in between the corner towers. The towers and gatehouses were often three-storeyed, or even four-storeyed, but the apartment ranges in between were generally two-storeyed. They stood in lakes or were surrounded by vast moats. In some cases the apartments set aside for the owner were cut off from the rest of the apartments, by walls without doorways, separate staircases, or other complicated devices. The received reason for these precautions is that owners were not willing to trust their retainers (who increasingly were mercenaries and so would desert or rebel at the drop of a ducat). But this is perhaps to exaggerate the number of mercenaries a lord might have in his private army, and also to overdraw the lack of principles in mercenaries as a class.

A typical quadrangular fortress was Bodiam. A licence to build it was granted in 1385 to Sir Edward Dalyngrygge, a knight who had fought in the wars in France. The licence permitted him to strengthen 'with a wall of stone and lime, and crenellate and construct and make into a castle his manor of Bodyham, near the sea, . . . for the defence of the adjacent country and resistance to our enemies . . . '. At the time there was serious danger of invasion of Kent and Sussex from the French. The plan of Bodiam was a range of apartments round the inside of a square, with round corner towers, gatehouse with square turrets and additional square plan turrets mid-wall. The outer walls were from 6-8ft thick, the building was two storeys high, though the towers and gatehouse rose to three storeys. The outer walls contained very few windows and were equipped with loops and gun-ports. The gatehouse and the postern

A basement chamber with ribbed vaulting, based on Chepstow

gate were machicolated round the parapets. The apartments on the south and east sides and for half the north side (to the gatehouse) formed a complete residential suite of chapel, pantry, kitchen, solar, chamber and hall. Much the same accommodation is provided in the remaining apartments on the west and half of the north sides. The two suites were not connected, and the smaller range (west and north-west) was not connected to the gatehouse. The castle well was sited in the south-west round corner tower, in the main accommodation suite. The south-east round corner tower had a vaulted ceiling in the basement. These arrangements have led some historians to regard the separation of the suites as a deliberate scheme to frustrate possible rebellion and attack on the owner by the retainers (who occupied the smaller range). The well was, for example, kept in the lord's part so that it could not be poisoned. But it seems more likely that the separation was in order to frustrate attack from besiegers or intruders from outside, in just the same way as a great tower in an older castle provided an ultimate refuge for defenders once the gatehouse and/or flanking towers round the enclosure had fallen. If Dalyngrygge, for example, was attacked from outside in one suite, he could quite easily transfer to the other suite by going out of one door into the courtyard and into another.

Bodiam was a good example of a fortified manor house. There were several others of the fourteenth century, notably Bolton in Yorkshire, built at much the same time, Maxstoke built in the 1340s and Shirburn in Oxfordshire, c.1380. Most of them were sited in fine lakes which provided excellent defence. The water defences at Bodiam are described in chapter 8.

Some of the fortified manor houses of the fifteenth century look less military than residential, especially when they are built of brick and not stone, like Tattershall in Lincolnshire (c.1430–c.1450), Caister in Norfolk (1432–c.1446) and Herstmonceux in Sussex (c.1440). But in many features they were still formidable enough. They were built to impress and to overawe, as well as to accommodate, and undoubtedly to provide shelter in time of civil disturbance too. Herstmonceux was certainly built to repel raiders from France — it has seventeen towers and turrets, arrow slits and gun-ports, and some of the machicolation was real — while by any standards Tattershall's 110ft-tall tower was a powerfully defensive structure. From the fifteenth century on, it was not unusual for large mansions to be built with castellar features, such as turrets, gatehouses and so forth. Some were given false machicolation, that is, the machicolation around the parapet looked genuine from a distance but was not. The machicolation over the gate at Oxburgh was genuine.

The fifteenth century saw the origination of several new castles of strength in England and Wales. They were built by rich and powerful men who were favoured by the kings and granted leave to construct them not so much as war bases, but as manifestations of the financial and territorial wealth of their owners. Possibly, some of them were raised in a spirit of competition with one another, or with

Tattershall: the great tower rises to more than 100ft, and is built of brick

towns and cities which had for a long time been growing in strength and independence through commercial enterprise. They were certainly solid evidence of wealth and power. Caister was built by Sir John Fastolf, a knight who made his fortune in the wars in France, Tattershall by Ralph Cromwell, a grasping and very able politician who rose to be Treasurer of England (1433–43) with all the perquisites that that entailed, Raglan (with a hexagonal great tower in stone) by an ambitious father-and-son team, Sir William ap Thomas and Sir William Herbert, the fifteenth-century equivalents of property and business tycoons, and of course the stone great tower of Lord Hastings at Ashby de la Zouch, another political parvenu who became in turn mighty, over-mighty and was suddenly executed. These and others of the period give some substance to the phrase quoted for the first time by Sir Edward Coke in 1623 and since oft-repeated, 'a man's house is his castle' — in more usual form today, 'an Englishman's home is his castle', an indication that the military-first and residential-second roles were being reversed.

12
Gunpowder and Firearms

The decline in the use of castles as fortress-residences was due to changes in medieval and post-medieval society. Castles ceased to be needed, and as men began to build beautiful houses, castles were on the whole not even wanted unless they could be modernized, and this generally could be done only at the expense of their military defensiveness. The decline was not the result of the discovery of gunpowder or the consequent development of firearms. Gunpowder had been known to, and used by, the Chinese for centuries. It was introduced in Europe by the independent discovery of its manufacture in c.1250 by Roger Bacon (c.1214–90), the English-born scientific experimentalist and philosopher. It may be presumed he did not try to hide his work. The first suggestion that it may have been used in castle siege warfare is in the time of Edward I at his siege of Stirling Castle in 1304. This was a major operation by the English King, and it involved assembling for assault purposes catapults, mangonels and trebuchets, some of them so huge that they had to be constructed specially for the job, and which were given names like 'The Parson', 'The Vicar' and the famous 'War-wolf'.

The siege, which is thought to have been superintended by Master James of St George (by then an old man of nearly seventy), is mentioned in medieval accounts, and in one there is an order by the king for a supply of sulphur and saltpetre to be sent up from York. To what use these two constituents of gunpowder were put we do not know, but since charcoal, the third constituent, would have been obtainable near the castle, we may infer some explosive device. One account states that fire was hurled into the castle, but this could have been Greek fire (see chapter 6). For more tangible evidence of any form of gun we have to wait until the 1320s when, in a manuscript now at Christ Church, Oxford, there appears a picture of a rudimentary cannon. This shows a table on which lies a huge, presumably iron, bulb-shaped vessel with narrow neck and wide mouth, and it is discharging a bolt, or heavy arrow. An operator stands to the right behind the bulb, holding what looks like a long bar which may be red hot, to ignite the gunpowder. The arrow head is hard up against a pillar of an entrance into a battlemented tower. The implication is obvious: it is a type of gun or cannon. The word 'gun', or 'gonne' as it occasionally appears in contemporary manuscripts, is probably derived from mangonel.

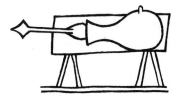

A drawing of a cannon, taken from the earliest known picture of this firearm, c.1327

The picture probably represents the earliest type of cannon, and it may be one used by Edward III in about 1327 in his first clash with the Scots. A later historian, John Barbour (c.1316–96), refers to 'crakys of wer', the Lowland Scottish phrase for cannon or gun, used by Edward in this war. It is also said that cannon was used at Crécy in 1346. These early guns were probably still discharging bolts and not shot. Progress towards a useful type of cannon was in fact very slow. Up to the middle of the fourteenth century, guns had to be breech-loaded. They were no more effective than cross-bows or

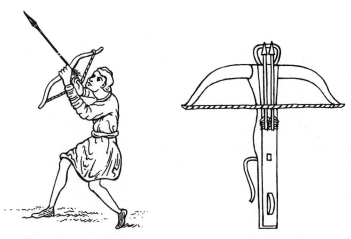

(left) A medieval archer shooting with a shortbow; (right) A crossbow

long-bows and much less accurate. Barrels had to be cleaned after every firing, which meant time had to be allowed for the barrel to cool down. That could be up to an hour. Guns were difficult and costly to make, and to move around. They were easily captured by a defending force that sallied out of a castle to attack besiegers. Many cannons blew up in the faces of those firing them, as much the result of faulty manufacture of the gun as of clumsy handling of the gunpowder charge. James II of Scotland (1437–60), an enlightened monarch and one perhaps too deeply interested in pyrotechnics, 'did stand near the gunners when the artillery discharged [at the siege of Roxburgh Castle]: his thigh bone was dung in two with the piece of a misformed gun that brake in shooting, by which he was stricken to the ground and died hastily . . .' (quoted from the *Historie and Cronicles of Scotland* by Robert Lindsay of Pitscottie).

A copy of a medieval sketch of a handgun in operation

The principal value of early cannons was more psychological than destructive. Opponents may at first have been demoralized by gunfire, and there were instances when surrender followed the first shot or two. The garrison at Berwick yielded to Henry IV's first gun shots in a siege in 1405. The same happened at Devizes Castle 240 odd years later in the Civil War. Certainly, opponents' horses would have been thoroughly frightened and would have bolted. On the other hand, there is a record of two cannons firing over 400 shots at the siege of Ypres, in 1383, and not one person being injured. But the longer term potential of gunpowder and guns must have been appreciated, for military engineers clearly determined to press on with the dangerous and expensive business of developing them.

In the fifteenth century new types of gun and improvements to existing types emerged. Among these were hand-guns, though the earliest of these were cumbersome and manifestly awkward to use (see picture). Engineers also discovered that the muzzle velocity of a gun would be increased if the bore was reduced. Cannons were made smaller. One experiment was a number of small hand-guns clustered together and fixed to a carriage, with charges in each barrel. These would be lit by the swift movement of a taper across every touchhole. Cannons were also made with longer barrels. In the middle of the century we see the introduction of very large guns, on the whole better made than their predecessors, though they were still pretty unsafe for their users. The great Ottoman sultan, Mohammed II, who captured Constantinople by siege in 1453 and thus altered the course of European history, used the largest cannon the world had hitherto seen. Its barrel was 26ft long and it could fire a ball weighing about 650lb a distance of over a mile. But this barrel took well over an hour to cool down after discharging one shot. Its value was morale breaking. Two years later, there appeared in Scotland at the siege of Threave Castle, the famous 'Mons Meg', an 'iron murderer' which can still be seen at Edinburgh Castle. The cannon is about 13ft long, and it was manufactured from long, flat hammered iron bars girded by hoops, the normal way to make gun barrels at the time. The barrel bore was 20in, and if properly loaded and charged with about 105lb of powder and set at an angle of about 15 degrees, it could fire an iron ball over 1,400yd. Mons Meg was made in Flanders, probably at Malines, which was rendered as Mollance in Scottish dialect (from which Munce or Mons). Meg is short for Marjory or Margaret, a name sometimes given to guns. Mons Meg exploded in 1680 when used to fire a salute for the birthday of James, Duke of York, (brother of Charles II), and later James II (VII of Scotland). The gun was left unrepaired until 1829.

The first gun made in Britain was probably one fabricated in 1474 for James III (1460–88). An early instance of Scottish home-produced guns in use at a siege was at Dumbarton in 1489, when the next king, James IV (1488–1513), successfully brought the castle's owner, Lord Darnley, to his knees. The king also employed Mons Meg at this siege. The first English gun does not appear to have been made before the time of Henry VIII, who acquired a special interest in ordnance. By this time, there had been significant improvements in gun-making, not least gun barrels of non-ferrous metals like brass. These could be cast instead of made in strips. By the 1530s guns were being made in sizes and in ranges: a culverin was a cannon that normally fired a ball from 15-18lb weight a distance of between 1 and 1½ miles, though hand-culverines of much shorter range, using smaller shot, are also mentioned. A saker was smaller than a culverin and fired a 6lb-ball up to about a mile. A demi-cannon shot balls weighing 27-32lb. A falcon was a very small cannon that fired a

2lb-shot about a mile, and a falconet was even smaller, shooting a 1lb-ball rather less. These guns were usually mounted on two wheels, except for the hand-guns. Of course, there were others, and the names given above were sometimes applied to guns of different size and range.

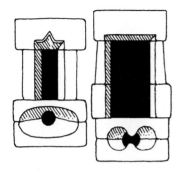

Scottish castle gunports: Muness (two different types of ornamental shot-hole, the right hand having a dumbbell port at bottom)

Guns could be mobilized to attack castles. As the ranges were far greater than those of mangonels and trebuchets (which are believed to have discharged missiles over little more than 500 or so yards), they could be positioned much further away from the castle, out of range of any retaliatory fire, until the first defenders began to use guns in response. Guns inside castles were positioned at ground level

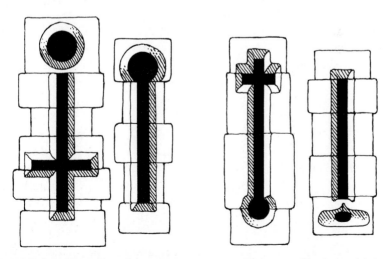

Scottish castle gunports: (left to right) Ravenscraig (inverted keyhole with large opening), (crosslet with separated port at bottom), Tullycairn (inverted key hole with top crosslet) and Leslie (slit with wide-mouth port)

inside inner or outer baileys, or on platforms at wall-walk level, or on the tops of towers, or even on turrets specially built for them (notably, the coastal fortresses). Guns at ground level could be elevated high enough to shoot over the wall top, though the exercise was a hazardous one. Guns on wall tops could be dipped to fire outwards into the thick of a besieging army, but that was also dangerous — and superfluous if the ball had rolled out of the barrel before the charge was fired.

Artillery was seldom a dominating weapon in British castle sieges until the seventeenth century. Bamburgh was besieged in 1464 by the great 'Kingmaker', Richard Neville, Earl of Warwick, when he used two enormous cannons like Mons Meg, and the castle was almost battered into surrender. But this was an unusual occurrence. Machiavelli (1469–1527), the wily, Florentine statesman and author of *The Prince* (a manual of dictatorship, no less), had no time for gunpowder artillery and said as much in the 1520s. Fauchet, writing in the 1600s, stated that cannons were used only by cowardly people.

Claypotts: a formidable looking gun-port opening beside the doorway into the tower-house

Claypotts: a vaulted chamber in the tower-house, showing the splayed embrasures leading to the gun-ports

But used they were, though it is clear that their value in sieges was hotly debated. Crossbows and longbows were still widely in use at this time: James V of Scotland (1513–42) is known to have preferred the bow to the gun.

So far as castle designers were concerned, few alterations were made in any castles before the mid-fifteenth century in response to artillery. In England and Wales, the main and one of the only adjustments was the insertion of gun-loops, or gun-ports. Existing arrow slits were altered to cater for hand-guns or very small culverins. At Bodiam, for example, the oillets (round openings out of the bottom end of straight arrow slits) were adapted for hand-guns. At some other castles, such as Kirby Muxloe, a round opening was inserted, spaced apart, below an arrow slit. At many castles, special gun-ports were built in, as at Raglan and Caister. These were splayed on both horizontal sides or all round, outside and sometimes internally too, that is, the openings converged inwards from both faces of the wall, creating an 'X' in plan. This allowed the maximum sweep from side to side for the guns. But many castles did not have gun-ports, notably three big fortresses built in Scotland in the first half of the fifteenth century — Borthwick, Comlongon and Elphinstone.

But while it may seem that a certain indifference to artillery existed

Ravenscraig: looking up at the southern face of the north-western tower of this artillery castle

among many castle owners in Britain, there was another side of the coin. At Ravenscraig in Fife, Scotland, there was built the first castle specifically designed for defence by firearms. This interesting structure was begun in the spring of 1460 by the advanced-thinking James II for his wife, Mary of Gueldres, only a few months before his untimely death at the siege of Roxburgh on 3 August. The castle is positioned on a prominent and exposed rocky site jutting into Kirkcaldy Bay. The rock rises as sheer cliff on the west side to about 70ft above the beach and falls away to the east in steep terraces. A wide natural gully divides the site from the mainland, and this was artificially extended. The front of the castle facing the northern landward end of the promontory consists of a range of buildings with a well-fortified entrance passage in the middle, at ground floor. At each end of the range was a huge D-plan tower with walls 10–14ft thick, both projecting into the ditch. The west tower is still four storeys tall plus garret but without its roof, and has a vaulted basement which was at the same level as the ground floor of the centre range whose chambers and passages are also vaulted. The towers were given keyhole gun-ports, some of them designed to accommodate falconets (very small cannons). The central range had a second-storey artillery platform with a parapet in front, and this parapet contained wide-mouth openings for small guns. The eastern tower, three-storeyed with round front projecting into the ditch, has its basement storey and half the first storey below the level of the ground floor of the central range, the top of the top storey being in line with the central range's ceiling. Each tower had a well. The outer wall of the western tower stands sheer on a slope down to the beach.

The western tower is in reality a great tower, fortified and residential, and it was occupied for a time by Mary of Gueldres. Each storey had mural chambers as well as main centre rooms, with garderobes. There were kitchens and other offices in a detached range behind the tower towards the end of the promontory. The whole front of the castle presented a most formidable array of gun-ports through which, if provoked, the garrison could have discharged the most murderous fire. Its position on the shore meant that if besieged, a garrison could hold out for a very long time because it could be supplied from the sea (cf. Tantallon).

Another castle in Scotland that almost bristles with gun-ports is Noltland, on Westray in the Orkneys. This is a Z-plan castle whose end towers are square plan upon a central rectangular block. The exterior wall surfaces of the castle are equipped with over 70 gun-ports at several levels and of two kinds — rectangular and unsplayed, and oval with splays. S.H. Cruden described it as 'an astonishing parade of ranks of gun-ports'.

In the sixteenth century the majority of new Scottish tower-houses were given gun-ports at various levels. Designers were fond of inserting them at or near entrances (Claypotts and Tolquhon are interesting examples). Older castle buildings were adapted to take gun-ports, such as at Caerlaverock. And the artillery-fortification of tower-houses and other forms of castle in Scotland continued into the seventeenth century, and in a few cases into the eighteenth. Corgarff in Aberdeenshire began as a rectangular tower-house of the mid-sixteenth century. In 1746–7 it was occupied by Hanoverian

Noltland, on the Orkney island of Westray, is one of the earliest Z-plan castles

troops as a base for policing the area after the collapse of the Second Jacobite Rising at Culloden in 1746. The tower was then surrounded by a star-shaped curtain wall with numerous gun-ports, of tall vertical shape, intended for muskets.

Perhaps the damage done to Borthwick Castle in Midlothian by the artillery of Cromwell in 1650 demonstrates as well as anything the limited influence of guns in castle warfare. Today the east wall of the massive tower contains a large gash in the 15ft-thick masonry (which has been partly patched up). The owner, Lord Borthwick, surrendered rather than have further damage done, but it is clear that Cromwell would have been hard put to reduce the tower to a heap of stones (as is implied in his threat contained in a surviving letter to Borthwick and quoted on p.393).

13
Border Castles

If the need for castles began to diminish generally in England and Wales in the fourteenth century, there was one area where, on the contrary, it grew. That was the border district between England and Scotland, which was for centuries, after the Scots won their War of Independence under Robert Bruce, the scene of warfare, looting, destruction of crops, farms and houses by raiders on both sides. It was also the scene for many better organized invasions, counter-invasions and 'punitive' expeditions employing armies, siege-engines (where needed) and the other paraphernalia of medieval warfare. Principally we are concerned here with great castles, and smaller fortified tower-houses, known as peles (but we are not including the smaller fortified more horizontal houses known as bastles) on the English side in Northumberland whose northern boundaries make up about three quarters of the whole Border. There are more than 200 of them, though not all are of medieval origin. (Bastles were two- or less frequently three-storeyed, generally with only slits for ventilation and light, the ground floor reserved for livestock which were brought inside during trouble, the first floor given to accommodating the owner and his family, and others to whom he might offer refuge.)

The word pele comes from the Latin *palus*, a stake, which was used in the building of a palisade round a tower. Pele-towers probably began as wooden towers, like motte castles. They were generally three-storeyed with substantial walls, small and few windows (see Vicar's Pele, Corbridge), though the visitor will find two- and four-storeyed peles. Nearly all the peles and bastles are of fourteenth century or later date. Some were built on the remains of older castles, including motte castle sites.

The third fortified structure in Northumberland is the castle proper, and both principal types — great tower with enclosure and enclosure with flanking towers, gatehouse, etc — are found. Some

Bamburgh: the south-west aspect. The great tower stands just behind the curtain wall

were begun soon after the Norman conquest. Bamburgh was started on a rocky hill beside the sea during the Conqueror's reign by Robert de Mowbray, Earl of Northumberland. It was captured after an interesting siege by William Rufus in 1095, in which, as the *Anglo-Saxon Chronicle* puts it, 'he ordered a castle to be built in front of Bamburgh and called it in his language Malueisin [Malvoisin]', which in English means 'Evil Neighbour'. This second castle was really a siege-castle, which was probably a substantial belfry. Bamburgh remained a royal castle into Stephen's reign, passed to Henry, Earl of Huntingdon, son of David I, King of Scotland, was recovered in 1157 by Henry II and was a royal castle thereafter into the seventeenth century. In the 1160s, or possibly earlier but there is no certainty about this, the first work was carried out on building its great tower, which eventually became almost cuboid (like Carlisle and Dover), 69ft x 61ft by an estimated 60ft tall, greatly rebuilt much later. The possibility of the earlier date for starting the tower —

c.1140s — relies on comparing it with that at Carlisle, built by Henry of Huntingdon's father, and it is certainly an interesting idea that two key great towers used on and off for centuries by the English against the Scots should have been partly the work of the Scots.

Other great castles of Northumberland begun in the eleventh or twelfth centuries, to which we may add some in Durham and Cumberland, were Alnwick (c.1100), Carlisle (c.1092), Durham (c.1072), Norham (c.1120), Newcastle upon Tyne (c.1080), Prudhoe (c.1170s) and Warkworth (c.1140), and these were to be added to in subsequent centuries, so that some like Alnwick ended up by being palatial as well as military. In the thirteenth to fifteenth centuries several medium-sized castles were raised, including Aydon, Belsay, Bothal, Bywell, Chillingham, Chipchase, Edlingham, Etal, Ford (all in Northumberland), Cockermouth in Cumberland, Raby in Durham and Sizergh in Westmorland (see entries in Gazetteer). Some of these began as towers, great or pele, and were subsequently enlarged.

There is an interesting point about the small peles of Northumberland and Cumberland; they were diminutive and were only effective against the kind of small-scale though tiresome raiding carried out by the Scots, and of course the Scots had their own small tower-houses as protection against equally irritating English raiding. And yet the peles were modelled on great towers and were in a sense miniature versions of them. The parapet at the Vicar's Pele at Corbridge was no less in proportion to the size of the rest of the tower than Newcastle's. Many of the larger towers had additional bartizans and turrets, and some had machicolation as well, as at Featherstone and Chipchase.

A bartizan, or roundel, at the end of a tower wall. Bartizans are generally found on castles in Scotland, but a few were featured in English castles

Why was there this emphasis on vertical building in Northumberland? The answer is that the great tower, the tower-house and the pele are all examples of a horizontal residence being up-ended and fortified for security reasons. Even when in the later fourteenth and fifteenth centuries there was more prosperity and more people were able to build themselves fine residences, there was always the need to fortify and protect against marauders. It is also possible that there was some influence from the Scottish preference for building upwards rather than sideways, manifest not only in their numerous tower-houses great and small, but also in many of their private homes and in towns one would expect normally to be out of danger. The pele-tower was the least complicated and least expensive way for a landowner to provide himself with a private residence incorporating military, that is, defensive and offensive, characteristics. Many pele-towers even dispensed with stone stairs, and merely had a wooden step ladder leading from the higher level to the ground, which could be lifted out of reach of raiders at a moment's notice. Some pele-towers have no doorway or staircase inside between the ground floor and the quarters above. Some ground-floor chambers were vaulted to prevent fire. Peles were very often built with as much thought as their greater counterparts.

It has been said that the essential military character of many northern towers and pele-towers is the reason for not displaying any great variety of layout, decorative effect or architectural interest,

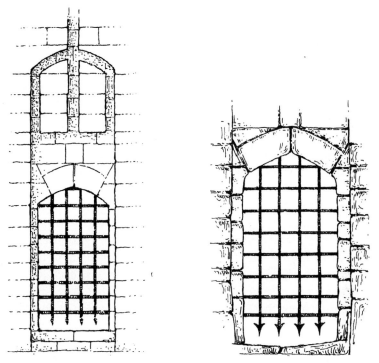

Two examples of yetts; The one on the left has a recess above for the mechanism of the drawbridge in front

such as one finds in the greater castles and fortified houses of the rest of England of the same period. This view is not really tenable. A closer look at any six Northumberland or Cumberland towers would reveal many details of individual character in one that are not repeated in the other five, which of course is part of the fascination of castles in general — each one is different somewhere. Chipchase Tower, for example, has four storeys, with turrets on the four corners, each rising from corbelled courses, with a short projecting wing at the south-east end up the whole height. The entrance to the tower was in this wing at first-floor level, and it was defended by a portcullis. The top storey was a great chamber or hall, with an adjacent kitchen screened off at one time. The chapel is in the wall masonry on the third floor. Edlingham Tower once had a forebuilding on the west wall which has now disappeared. Vicar's Pele, Corbridge, has its entrance on the ground floor and this was defended by an iron yett. It has straight flights of stairs in the wall thickness, and bold parapets round the top. The tower is roofed with a gable. Cocklaw Tower had a postern opening from the main chamber at second-floor level, about 18ft from the ground. This was accessible only by ladder or rope.

Many Northumberland peles were surrounded by a simple enclosing stone wall called a barmkin. As a rule the barmkin was not fortified by any flanking towers or gatehouse, and the gateway was little more than a break in the masonry, or an arched doorway. The barmkin was intended for penning livestock in time of trouble. Presumably, the prime animals were shepherded into the ground-floor area of the tower, where a tower had such an area allotted. This was not normally the case with the greater towers.

There were exceptions to the vertical building preference. Haughton Castle was more a fortified hall-house, of two storeys at first, but with a later addition of another two floors with turrets at the top corners. Aydon was a substantial rectilinear block in cruciform plan, two storeys high, with four main room areas on each floor. The higher floor was reached by means of an external open staircase.

Watching over these smaller castles and towers in the Border country, as it were, stood the great castles — Alnwick, Bamburgh, Carlisle, Durham, Norham, Newcastle, Prudhoe and Warkworth. Owned and improved over the years by the Crown or by powerful magnates like the Percys, they were among the greatest fortresses in the land. Two of them, Carlisle and Norham, had particularly tempestuous histories.

Carlisle is a great tower inside a triangular curtain with buttresses and gatehouse attached to a larger bailey also enclosed on all but one side by a stone curtain wall with flanking towers. The last side was a long stretch of man-cut ditch and bank. It began as an earthwork castle erected by William II in c.1092. It was taken by the Scottish king, David I, in the 1140s and he started the stone great tower. Carlisle was returned to Henry II in 1157. Besieged by William the

Carlisle: the great tower which has been much altered. There was a forebuilding on the east wall. The north wall (facing the viewer in the picture) contains the well, in the centre pilaster

Lion, King of Scotland, in 1174 with a huge army, it held out for three months. It was successfully besieged and taken by Alexander II, King of Scotland, in 1216. Returned to Henry III a year later, it was in a sorry state after Alexander's attentions, and it continued to decay. Then in 1285–90, Edward I rescued the castle and greatly improved it. Carlisle was besieged by Robert Bruce soon after his victory at Bannockburn in 1314, using catapults for hurling large stones, and then trying to assault it from on high with a belfry, but this became stuck in the mud on the far side of the moat. The castle was besieged twice by the Scots in Richard II's reign, but it did not fall. And it was besieged again in the Civil War by Leslie, the Scottish general and ally of the English Parliamentary cause. The garrison is said to have been reduced to eating rats, linseed meal and dogs.

Norham, at the north-east end of the Border, has a great tower inside a roughly D-shaped inner enclosure of stone (whose north-east and south-east sides form two sides of the great tower), with a deep moat round the enclosure. This is situated in the north corner of a much larger outer stone enclosure with flanking towers of various shapes, D-ended, square and even one with a pointed edge, and with a gatehouse. This outer enclosure is also surrounded by a moat and bank. The great tower was the first stone building, 84ft x 60ft, eventually reaching to about 90ft tall, with walls from 11–14ft thick. It was raised between 1160 and 1174. Norham was besieged in 1214 by Alexander II of Scotland for six weeks but without success. Robert Bruce tried three times (1318, 1319 and 1322) to take Norham by siege, using the latest siege engines (which were presumably new developments of the trebuchet). He failed each time, but in 1327 he was successful. It was returned to England under the ensuing peace treaty. For more than a century Norham remained unassaulted and the castle was gradually repaired and enlarged. Then, during the Wars of the Roses, Norham, held by the

Norham, near Berwick, was founded c.1120 by Bishop Flambard

Yorkists for a time, was besieged in 1463 by the Lancastrians. It was relieved by the great 'Kingmaker', Richard Neville, Earl of Warwick, the foremost Yorkist general. But in 1464 the garrison defected to the Lancastrians. The next major siege was in 1513, by James IV, King of Scotland, in the short war with England. James used the famous cannon Mons Meg and others and smashed down large masses of the great tower and the castle walls, barbican and other towers. The state of the great tower today is largely the result of that particular battering. The garrison surrendered, but it was of no value to James for he and the flower of his nobles and knights were cut down and killed at the grievous Battle of Flodden. Afterwards, Norham was returned again to English hands.

14

Castles in Scotland

The development of Scottish castles follows much the same pattern in the earlier Middle Ages as those in England and Wales. The Normans had imposed castles upon the English landscape by force, and had also built them in those parts of Wales which they took over, notably the Welsh Marches and border districts. And Edward I and his lords planted more castles in the remaining free parts of Wales as they overcame them in the last decades of the thirteenth century. In Scotland, castles were introduced not by force but by choice, by those kings who were influenced by Norman ideas, and by Norman lords whom the kings welcomed into Scotland and to whom they gave lands (in many cases with permission to build castles). The kings were in effect implementing the introduction of feudalism into parts of Scotland, predominantly into the Lowlands and up the north-east to Moray and Nairn. The first castles in Scotland, therefore, were motte castles, and between about 1100 and about 1250 more than two hundred were raised. The most notable remains today are those at Duffus (Grampian), Mote of Urr (Dumfries and Galloway), Bass of Inverurie and Doune of Invernochty (Grampian), Hawick (Borders), Dunsceath (Highland), some of which later received stonework. These castles were constructed in the same way as the English motte castles and played much the same role, for while the kings of Scotland and their lords were 'feudalists', their subjects were not so receptive to the new order and had, therefore, to learn. Scottish castles had additional roles, to act as fortresses for the defence of the country against attack from England (a very real and continuous danger) and also against continued Viking incursions up to the middle of the thirteenth century.

Motte castles were raised in south-west Scotland in some quantity, as the map in chapter 3 indicates. They were also built north of the Forth in a north-easterly sweep from the Clyde, up the fertile Midland Valley into Aberdeenshire, Morayshire and Nairnshire.

Bass of Inverurie: an aerial view of this late twelfth-century motte

The Bass of Inverurie was raised c.1180 and rose to at least 60ft tall before its wooden tower was built upon the summit. It is a handsome monument today, although its top has no buildings. At Hawick, the motte was much smaller, and probably supported no more than a watch-tower. Today, it has a flight of steps up the slope which gives a good idea of how the summit would have been approached in its time of use as a castle. (The stone steps up the motte to the quatrefoil stone great tower at Clifford's in York give a similar impression.) At Duffus, near Elgin, the motte, built in about 1150, was given a rectangular stone great tower upon a splayed plinth, with a projection on the east wall containing a straight flight of stairs and acting as a kind of forebuilding. This tower was built in about 1300. At a later (unknown) date, the north-west corner fractured away from the rest of the tower and slid down the motte, coming to rest in the position it is today. The Mote of Annan, raised in the early twelfth century, was 50ft tall and separated from its bailey by a deep ditch. The motte at Selkirk was developed upon a natural mound in the early 1100s and also had a wide and deep ditch around it.

As in England and Wales, stone castles began to be built in Scotland at much the same time as the earth-and-timber motte castles. Probably the earliest (for none has yet established an earlier claim) was Castle Sween. This interesting structure remains to a substantial extent what it was when erected on the shore of Loch

Sween in South Knapdale, Strathclyde. It is a quadrilateral stone enclosure, the two shorter sides parallel, the longer two not so. The walls are about 7ft thick and as tall as 40ft for much of their perimeter. The south wall has a small entrance with a rounded arch. The walls have pilaster buttresses mid-wall and clasping the corners, and no windows. There is a sea gate on the west wall. Inside the enclosure is an open straight flight of stairs against the wall just to the east of the entrance. This rose to the wall-walk behind the parapet, and in doing so traversed over the entrance passage. Against the north wall were built two smaller towers, one square and one cylindrical, at later dates. There are remains of apartments ranged against the enclosure wall inside. S.H. Cruden suggests Sween was a great tower, not an enclosure. We retain an open mind on the matter. The date of the castle cannot be given precisely, but it is reckoned to be late eleventh or early twelfth century, which suggests a structure put up under Norman influence (probably by permission of one of the Scottish kings), and this is supported by the pilaster buttresses, a Norman feature.

If Sween was the first stone castle in Scotland (in the sense in which we use the term) others were soon to follow, and they emerged in the main patterns with which we are already familiar in England and Wales: the great tower, the curtain enclosure with, or without, flanking towers, and the shell keep. Sween's successors include the enclosure types Kiessimul (twelfth/thirteenth century) on the Isle of Barra in the Outer Hebrides, Mingary (thirteenth-century beginnings) in Ardnamurchan peninsula, Highland, Dunstaffnage (early thirteenth-century beginnings) in Strathclyde, Tioram (early thirteenth-century beginnings) in Moidart, Highland and Skipness (thirteenth-century beginnings) in Kintyre, Strathclyde.

Kiessimul rises almost sheer out of the water, as it were, for it straddles a small island off Barra. It is a stone enclosure upon island rock foundations. The plan should be seen rather than described (see p.446). The walls of the curtain are 5-7ft thick and battlemented. The square-plan tower in the south-to-south-west line of wall rises from a splayed plinth (which is suggestive of Norman influence) and was built probably in the late twelfth century, before the curtain, which is early thirteenth century. There is a straight staircase along the northern wall outside, which crosses the original entrance in the basement. The tower rises to four storeys and was battlemented at the top. Mingary is less nondescript in plan: it is an irregular hexagonal enclosure with walls 6ft thick, between 30 and 40ft tall today, with an entrance at the north-west opening to the ditch protecting the north side, and a sea gate at the south leading to the sea in the Sound of Mull, which is reached by steps cut in the rocks. The section of wall that braces the north-west corner of the curtain is thickened on both sides of the entrance, and this thickening incorporates a stairway rising over the entrance and leading to the wall-walk.

Dunstaffnage is described more fully under its Gazetteer entry. Tioram stands on a rock promontory jutting into Loch Moidart, and is cut off at high tide. Its plan is an irregular pentagon, and the walls, still nearly their original height, reached to about 30ft, and are 8ft thick for the most part. There are several remains of battlements jumbled among later repaired stonework. A rectangular great tower was raised within the enclosure later in the thirteenth century. Many more of these simpler enclosure castles were built in the twelfth and thirteenth centuries, with individual variations: Roy in Highland, with a square projecting tower on one angle; Kinclaven in Tayside, with projecting corner towers (now vanished); and Kincardine, with ranges of buildings against three sides.

Enclosure castles of greater elaboration and dating to the thirteenth century include Kildrummy in Grampian, Dirleton in Lothian, and Inverlochy in Highland. Dated to about 1270–80, Inverlochy is an almost square-plan curtain enclosure, with walls nearly 10ft thick and 30ft tall. On each corner is a cylindrical tower. The north-west tower is somewhat larger than the other three and is provided with a slightly curving staircase in the wall thickness to each floor from ground upwards. The other towers have similar flights. The north-west tower had ingenious arrangements for allowing defenders to retire from the curtain parapet wall-walk if under assault, to prevent them being followed into the tower itself and also to avoid intrusion into the tower from the curtain parapet on the other side.
the other side.

The other kind of castle, the shell keep — which is in its way a form of enclosure castle, but is put into a separate class because it is always built on a motte summit — is a rarity in Scotland. The best known is Rothesay, in Bute. Rothesay's shell curtain wall is almost circular, and it was raised probably in the late twelfth century on a flat-topped motte of earlier date (first half of twelfth century). The wall is about 9ft thick and in many parts as tall as 30ft. The motte was surrounded by a deep wet moat. Around the shell were built four equidistantly placed cylindrical towers of some strength, on

Peel of Lumphanan: an aerial view

spreading bases, and they were taller than the shell. They are still there, but damaged, two of them greatly. There is some doubt whether the towers were built at the same time as the shell, or just before the siege of Rothesay by the Vikings in 1230 or after that. Two other mottes that received shell keeps are the great Peel of Lumphanan (Grampian) and the Doune of Invernochty. Neither has much more to show today than low stretches of walling. The Peel has been the subject of recent excavations over several years and these are not yet completed. The motte appears to have been part natural, part artificial. The Doune has a little more surviving stonework than the Peel. It is a huge motte with a summit area of 250ft by 120ft, which is over 60ft tall from the ground level of the motte. Both mottes had extensive earthworks with relatively sophisticated water defences.

These castle patterns take us to the end of the thirteenth century. Two outstanding castles remain to be mentioned: Bothwell in Strathclyde, a great tower castle which is attached to a powerfully defended curtain wall enclosure with flanking towers and twin-towered gatehouse, like Flint Castle in some respects; and Caerlaverock, a triangular plan high-walled enclosure castle with large corner towers and a huge twin-cylindrical towered gatehouse, unlike any castle this side of the English Channel or North Sea. We

142

may single out one or two of their more vital features. Bothwell has been described as 'among the foremost secular structures of the Middle Ages in Scotland', and its cylindrical great tower (of which only one half remains standing) has been called 'the grandest and most accomplished piece of medieval secular architecture in Scotland' (Simpson). The second comment seems a trifle exaggerated, when such monuments as Borthwick Castle or Stirling Castle's great hall are considered, but there is no doubt that the great tower must have created a sensation when it was completed. Some 80ft tall, 65ft in diameter, with 15ft thick walls, it had four storeys, the lower two vaulted, and some rooms, passages and even garderobe chambers in the wall thicknesses were also vaulted. Built of a gentle hued red freestone ashlar, the great tower — or donjon as it is generally known in Bothwell's case — was intended to be a fortress-residence, as its accommodation (storage basement, owner's hall, garrison's quarters and lord's private quarters at the top) and its fortifications (thick walls, fighting deck at top, separate wide moat)

Bothwell: an aerial view of this splendid ruin. Note the surviving half of the great tower (or donjon)

attest. The castle was slighted by the Scots after their great victory at Bannockburn in 1314, as a result of Robert Bruce's policy of neutralizing castles once held by the English in the War of Independence, where they were likely to be strategically valuable to the English again in the event of renewed hostilities. It was captured by Edward III during his campaign against the Scots in 1336 and partly repaired for English use, but was retaken by the Scots in 1337 and again dismantled. These two slightings have made the history of the buildings, certainly in the fourteenth century, difficult to determine. It is of interest to mention that Bothwell's donjon bore resemblances to the massive cylindrical great tower at Coucy in France, now demolished (in 1916; see also Kildrummy). Coucy Castle had been built by Enguerrand de Coucy in the period 1225–40 and Enguerrand's daughter Marie married Alexander II of Scotland (1214–49).

The dating of Caerlaverock is problematic. The better argument is for c.1280–90, which means it was Scottish-built as a fortress with which to protect the north Solway coast and its hinterland against English attack. The alternative suggestion is c.1290-1300, built by Edward I once he had taken control of Scotland after the fall of Balliol and intended as a bridgehead for English forces to advance into south-west Scotland in the event of trouble. But Caerlaverock was besieged in 1300 by the old English king and captured, an event celebrated in a ballad by the scholar, Walter of Exeter, an extract of whose description of the castle is quoted in the Gazetteer entry. There is no record of it having been taken from the English by the Scots earlier, and so on balance we may attribute its construction to the Scots and to the period before the Edwardian aggression. The dominating feature of Caerlaverock is its massive twin-cylindrical towered gatehouse standing on a rock outcrop in low, marsh-girt land. It became a gatehouse tower later in its history, but even in the first building stage it must have been an imposing structure (and in much-damaged state today it is impressive), with tall, narrow entrance passage overwhelmed by the two flanking towers which were bridged by a vaulted hall approachable only from a staircase behind in the courtyard. The gatehouse admittedly bears resemblances to some of those built in the great Welsh castles—Beaumaris, Rhuddlan and Caerphilly, the first two of which were the work of Master James of St George. But this is not necessarily evidence that he had any hand in the Caerlaverock work, as has been mooted. Moreover, twin-cylindrical towered gatehouses were, by c.1280, already fairly common in Europe (cf. Angers, Carcassonne, Avila) and were being erected in castles throughout England and Wales, in one form or another.

The fourteenth century saw the emergence of the peculiarly Scottish castle, the tower-house. It was a basic form of tower that was over the next three centuries to be developed with many interesting variations, and probably about seven hundred of them were to be raised in nearly every part of Scotland. From the early 1300s, the Scots chose to build vertically, and the first tower-houses were extremely well put together. The survival of so many tower-houses, albeit in most cases their walls only, testifies to this high constructional skill. Tower-houses completely dominated Scottish castle-building. Castles like Kildrummy and Bothwell were no longer built, but this by no means implies that the need for fortified residences had diminished. On the contrary, it was to become more pressing. The fact that the War of Independence had been won and King Robert I (Bruce) later recognized (posthumously) by the Pope as king of the independent kingdom of Scotland, did not remove the English threat. Nor did the check to English ambitions materially affect Scotland's feudal organization. And there were other reasons for continuing to raise fortress-residences. The lords in the Highlands, the clan chiefs, continued to menace the kingdom's stability and order. The lords of Galloway retained considerable independence. The Douglases, who dominated large tracts of southern Scotland, were reluctant to make a bid for the Scottish throne, but at the same time did not like the Stewart succession of 1371, and for nearly a century did what they could to subvert it. But the continuing need for kings and lords to protect themselves, their families and dependants and to watch over their lands was gradually leavened with a growing desire for more comfortable living. This became more apparent in Scottish tower-houses of the fifteenth and sixteenth centuries, and in many cases they became almost palatial, yet without losing their defensibility.

Numerous tower-houses were given walls many feet thick: the average was 6–7ft, which is about six times the average thickness of house walls today. The towers had battlemented parapets (like Drum) or parapets protected by toughened corbelled turrets on the corners overlooking them, or both. Some parapets projected outwards, proudly supported by corbelling (Old Dundas). Many were surrounded at the time, or later, by stone curtains which in Scotland are known as barmkins, and these were often tall.

Tower-houses were also surrounded by ditches and banks, the moats sometimes fed from nearby streams or rivers, with drawbridges across leading to and from gateways. From the last decades of the fifteenth century a few tower-houses began to be equipped with gun-ports for small cannons and other artillery. But great towers like those at Borthwick, Comlongon, Drum, Elphinstone, Hallforest and Threave did not have them. After about 1500, tower-houses were equipped with a variety of loops for smaller guns, oillets at the bottom of the loops, wide-mouth ports, fan-tail openings and so forth, inserted in new structures and in earlier buildings alike.

Most early tower-houses had the entrance on the first floor, reached by stone staircase or wooden stairway, or even a simple ladder, their basements having no access to the first floor except by means of a single hatch in the ceiling. Most entrances were protected by an iron yett, an open-work grille of interlacing iron bars that acted like a portcullis. Some could be raised and lowered, others swung open and shut on hinges. Chambers with spy-holes were built into wall thicknesses from which to look out into great halls, some of them in fireplace flues (such as Elphinstone). Walls were fitted with channels, one end of which issuing secretly into a chamber, the other opening into a second room, perhaps on another floor, enabling an eavesdropper to hear what was going on in the room at the other end, a medieval form of 'bugging'. These were called luggies, and there were luggies at Affleck, Elphinstone and many others.

Considerable attention was also given to staircases in Scottish tower-houses and many were constructed with some ingenuity. The earlier towers had spirals in one corner in the wall thickness, though some had straight mural flights. They were not designed so much for the easy use of the owner as to deter intruders. The flights did not always all go up the same corner, which meant that intruders and occupants had to cross the floor to reach another flight, as in some English great towers. In some castles, flights crossed over other flights. In others, spiral flights led from ground to the parapet without opening into intervening floors, which were reached by a second set of flights nearby but not easily seen. Some tower-houses had straight flights as well as spirals, such as Elphinstone. Some had false storeys and unexpected changes of floor levels to baffle intruders.

The desire for more residential space and accommodation (kitchens, servants' rooms, guest rooms and so forth) was met with similar attention and ingenuity of design. Plain rectangular tower-houses like Crichton (the earliest building), Comlongon, Cumbrae, Drum, Elphinstone, Hallforest, Loch Leven and Threave, and many more, built over the years c.1300 to c.1450 (Drum was a little before 1300), were well provided with chambers, closets and stairs within the wall thicknesses. Before the end of the fourteenth century the first rectangular tower-houses with extending wings had been built, erected as one unit. These were the L-plan tower-houses — a rectangular tower-house block with a short wing, usually of square plan, projecting from one side, generally one of the longer sides. These wings are sometimes called jambs, but we shall continue to use the term wing. The purpose of the wing was to incorporate private apartments and stairs that could be separate from the main block whose storeys generally consisted of one main large room, or hall, in some cases screened off near one end, in others more solidly walled off. Let us look briefly at Affleck in Angus, built soon after the middle of the fifteenth century.

At Affleck the wing contains five storeys to the main block's four: in the main block are cellars, common hall, owner's hall and solar; in the wing are three flights of spiral stairs, upwards from ground level, which came to an end at the third storey: then a mezzanine chamber (at the same level as the upper half of the owner's hall in the main block), and at the top a vaulted private chapel (or oratory). The solar is reached by another spiral stair from the owner's hall in a different corner, making the chapel accessible only from the solar. The mezzanine chamber is attainable only by a mural flight of stairs from the lower level of the owner's hall. Off the mezzanine is a garderobe. The wing also enabled Affleck's tower to have a well-protected entrance at ground floor (which was additionally more convenient from a residential viewpoint). The angle, called the re-entrant, could easily be defended by covering fire from both main block and wing. Later, many L-plan towers had gun-ports inserted adjacent to the entrance. This re-entrant door arrangement was a feature of most L-plan tower-houses.

Most of the fourteenth- and fifteenth-century tower-houses, L-plan and plain, were not large and not the sort of size we came to expect in twelfth-century English great towers. They averaged between 30 and 40ft, square or rectangular, rising to 40–60ft tall (with some large exceptions). Each was an individual structure built by a master mason in charge of a gang of craftsmen, stonemasons, carpenters, ironsmiths, plasterers, glaziers, diggers and (doubtless) apprentices and men-of-all-work. The tower-houses were not built from sets of drawings obtained from a central Ministry of Fortification and Building, or a Department of Works, though some castles for the kings were built under the aegis of a governmental organization of royal works. Tower-houses were put up on well-chosen sites and tailored to fit them by men who had building in their blood, masons who undoubtedly worked on neighbouring castles and took ideas from one to the next, enlarging their experience and increasing their ingenuity as they went, like the Bell family of masons in Aberdeenshire in the latter half of the sixteenth century. To an extent, their designs will have been governed by the amount of money available to pay for works. Licences to build often spelled out the basic fortifications allowed, which were regarded as the standard equipment, as it were: walls, ditches, iron gates, and parapets and turrets at the top of the tower. Loops and gun-ports were not specified, but presumably were embraced in the general phrasing along the lines 'warlike apparatus necessary for its defence', quoted by S.H. Cruden.

Two tower-houses of the end of the period perhaps represent the apogee of the tower-house in its simple but nonetheless formidable

Borthwick: one of the most magnificent great towers in Britain. Note the bombardment damage sustained from Cromwell's artillery during the Civil War

shape. They are Borthwick in Lothian and Comlongon in Dumfries and Galloway, and are among the strongest castles ever built in Scotland. Borthwick, begun in 1430 by the first Lord Borthwick, is a rectangular tower-house with two wings off one longer wall (the space between being very small). The horizontal dimensions are 75ft by 68ft, and the massive tower rises to over 100ft tall. The walls are 10–14ft thick, except for the two short facing inner sides of the wings. The tower is a labyrinth of staircases, passages and wall chambers, some of considerable spaciousness. It was enclosed by a barmkin with a large cylindrical tower at the south-west corner and a gatehouse, probably of early sixteenth-century construction. Comlongon, seat of the earls of Mansfield (still), is a massive square-plan tower-house of c.1440, whose thick walls are honeycombed with chambers, garderobes, stairs and, at ground level, dungeons, as at Elphinstone. The basement is vaulted, and the great hall has two fireplaces: the second fireplace (in a recess) acted as a cooking range for the kitchen in the recess, which would have been screened off.

We have seen that, apart from the castles in the Border counties of England, particularly Northumberland and Cumberland, the military uses of English and Welsh castles came to an end in the early sixteenth century (to be revived in the Civil War, 1642–6, and for a few years after). It was not the case in Scotland — indeed, their military role became more important. The sixteenth century in Scotland saw the gradual watering down of the Auld Alliance with France, which coincided with growing aggression on the part of England. Three times in a generation Scottish armies were badly defeated by the English, at Flodden Field (1513) where James IV and the flower of his nobles were slain, Solway Moss (1542), news of which hastened James V's death a few days later, and Pinkie (1547), together with many lesser but still damaging skirmishes and invasions, including the notorious 'rough wooing' of 1544–6, when Edinburgh was burnt. Internal conditions were not helped by the fact that three times in the century the kingdom passed from a dead or deposed monarch to a successor in infancy: James V succeeded James IV in 1513, aged one; Mary, Queen of Scots succeeded James V in 1542, aged one week; James VI succeeded Mary, Queen of Scots, aged one. Years of minority rule, when one faction after another jockeyed, intrigued and even murdered to gain power, recreated the sort of anarchy England had endured in Stephen's reign, and this entailed lords fortifying castles and attacking those of their rivals. Little wonder that in so uncertain and dangerous an age, leading men, and lesser lairds and rich merchants too, chose to shut themselves in strong, tall, ill-lit fortresses of stone, at a time when their contemporaries in England were building themselves horizontal residences chiefly of brick, with tall, wide windows and without a gun-port to be seen anywhere. Building activity slowed down in the decades after the disaster of Flodden, but a fresh impetus came with the troubles of the time of Mary, Queen of Scots.

In Scotland, gunpowder was monopolized by the Crown, though the system did not always succeed in preventing factious lords obtaining and using it. Ravenscraig in Fife was the first castle in Scotland — indeed, in Britain — to be designed specifically for systematic defence by guns (see chapter 12 and in Gazetteer). It was commissioned by the pyrotechnic enthusiast, James II, in 1460. By that time, an artillery wall had already been added to Threave Castle, not by the king but by the Douglas family which owned it. But cannon was not regarded as a major war weapon until the sixteenth century, by which time a variety of smaller guns, including hand-guns, had come into use, and the Crown was unable to exercise much control over possession and employment of them. This is reflected in the appearance of small gun-ports in a variety of styles in numerous castles: the inverted keyhole at Affleck and others, the loop with crosslet at top and oillet at bottom (Towie Barclay and others), the dumb-bell (Rowallan), the wide-mouth port (inserted later at Caerlaverock, built in new at Noltland, Claypotts, *inter alia*) and at Tolquhon two rows of three ports beside the gateway.

The sixteenth century also witnessed new shapes of tower-houses, notably the stepped L-plan, the Z-plan and the rectangular tower with various wings added to its sides. The stepped L-plan was an L-plan with an additional square (or occasionally semi-cylindrical) wing in the re-entrant, housing the entrance and a staircase, as at Craigievar; at Greenknowe Tower the step was a semi-cylindrical turret. The tower with wings added haphazardly round the sides varied individually every time: Elcho has a square tower on the south-west corner, a smaller square tower on the north-west corner and a cylindrical tower on the north-east corner, with a fourth tower, cylindrical with staircase, on the north wall. McLellans has two steps in the re-entrant and a square tower on the south-west corner, with separate spiral staircase.

The Z-plan castle was a unique style of fortified residence. A rectangular tower block was augmented with two wing towers, at diagonally opposite ends of the block. Each wing, equipped with gun-ports and/or shot-holes, covered two faces of the block, which in turn, similarly equipped, could cover the wings, so that it was impossible to attack the castle from any direction without coming into the field of fire. The wing towers were square in plan (Noltland, Glenbuchat) or cylindrical (Claypotts, Kilcoy), or one of each (Tolquhon — a modified Z-plan, and Midmar). The first Z-plan was built late in the fifteenth century but the period usually associated with them is the second half of the sixteenth and early years of the seventeenth. Sixty-five Z-plan castles were built in Scotland, a good many of which have survived. Two of the most interesting are Claypotts, with its wide-mouth gun-ports, one inserted right by the entrance, at chest level, and Noltland, with over seventy gun-ports, arranged in tiers along every wall round the whole castle.

The two most famous castles in Scotland are Edinburgh and Stirling. Both stand on mighty basalt rock mounds, nearly 300ft high above the ground below (Edinburgh, 270ft, Stirling 250ft), dominating the countryside around them for miles, each visible from the other on a clear day. Their strategic positions speak for themselves. Stirling in particular guards the principal routes into the Highlands. Both have today an extensive range of buildings clumped together on their summits, in Stirling's case dating from the fifteenth century, and in Edinburgh's a chapel dating from the early twelfth century, a tower of the fourteenth century, and the rest also dating from the fifteenth century. They were always royal fortresses, even in the days of timber and earth: Edinburgh was the fortified residence of Malcolm III Ceanmor, and Stirling the fortified residence of Malcolm's son, Alexander I, who died there in 1124. And, of course, Edinburgh Castle is guardian of Scotland's capital, and has been ever since the city was officially established as capital by James III. Neither of them falls into any of the castle types we have outlined. They are royal palace-fortresses which have assumed their present form over a long period, due to special requirements, many of them over and above military needs. They have had lavished on them the finest skills available to Scotland at the times concerned, notably the great hall at Stirling (built by James III's favourite, the courtier and architect, Robert Cochrane, who was hanged at Lauder Brig by Archibald 'Bell-the-Cat' Douglas, Earl of Angus, in 1482).

Two more palace-fortresses may be considered alongside Edinburgh and Stirling, and they are Falkland and Linlithgow. Falkland, owned by Her Majesty the Queen and administered by the National Trust of Scotland, was begun by James II and considerably extended

Linlithgow: the great hall, or Lyon Chalmer. The fireplace spans almost the whole breadth of the hall

by James IV and V, so that it became a courtyard castle with a tower-house-cum-gateway flanked by two huge cylindrical towers with battlemented parapets. Linlithgow, now roofless, but with most of its walls standing, is a splendid quadrangular castle building (of fourteenth- to seventeenth-century work) one of whose principal features is the great hall on the eastern range, with walls about 10ft thick, sandwiched between two massive corner towers, and containing at its southern end what has been described as the finest fireplace of its kind in Scotland.

In the seventeenth century new structures were built, some of them castles in the right sense, such as Craigievar (stepped L-plan, 1625–6), Coxton (rectangular tower-house, 1644) and Leslie (stepped L-plan, 1661). Many others were magnificent-looking mansions, in some cases built round earlier more military structures, like Cawdor, a practice already followed in the previous century, as at Glamis, Crathes, Midmar, Tolquhon and Aberdour, among others. Some of these mansions were highly ornamented, with tall, pointed turrets, rows of oriel windows, false machicolations, excessive and non-military battlementing, mansion-type windows, ornate entrance arches and window voussoirs, pediments and so forth. They certainly adorn the building scene of Scotland and enhance towns and countryside alike, but they are not fortified residences. 'This house was not a Tower . . . and had neither Fosse nor Barmkin-wall about it, nor Battling, but was only an ordinary house . . .' The quotation is taken from a summary of a legal case of 1630, and it is an appropriate comment on these ornate mansions, as well as a pertinent definition of a castle in Scotland.

15

Coastal Forts in England and Wales

Throughout the Middle Ages, the east and south coasts of England (and to a lesser extent the remaining coastline of England and that of Wales) were always in danger of sudden raids by pirates or by expeditions from hostile countries in western Europe, notably France. More serious invasions, which would entail securing a bridgehead on the coast before advancing inland, were also considered from time to time, on some political or military pretext or other, though the magnitude of the operation involved in crossing the sea with a fleet of ships filled with men and their arms, siege equipment and other supplies was not as a rule underestimated. William the Conqueror achieved his successful invasion and conquest by the adroit manner in which he chose to cross to and land in Sussex at a time when he knew that the bulk of Harold II's military forces were fully occupied nearly three hundred miles north in Yorkshire dealing with an invasion by the Viking ruler of Norway, Hardraada, together with the fact that there were no coastal fortifications in the south to oppose him. Once he had beaten Harold and his forces at Hastings, William protected his position by fortifications at Dover and Pevensey (he had already built Hastings motte castle). Dover Castle was obviously a key fortress, the gateway into England, and the royal family spent considerable sums on expanding and strengthening it over the centuries that followed.

Whatever the dangers of invasion, however, no programme of coastal fortification as such was embarked upon by Norman or Plantagenet kings. There were of course the Cinque Port towns, whose walls were fortified by royal order, and other towns like Southampton received walls with flanking towers. Towards the end of the fourteenth century, when the successes of Edward III in the 100 Years War with France had faded into remembrances of past glory and given way to a renewed initiative by France, some castles were built near, if not on, the coast, such as Bodiam in Sussex, by private individuals with royal permission, and sometimes encouragement. These were conceived as fortresses for beating off French or other European attack on the coast or meeting an invading army that had landed successfully and driving it back to the sea. They were also fortress-residences for their mighty owners. Possibly some contribution may have been made by the kings. But it was not till the late fifteenth century that we see the beginning of real co-operation between the Government and an owner in constructing (or improving) a castle on the coast, fortifying it so that artillery could be used and also resisted.

One of the earliest examples was at Dartmouth in Devonshire where the owner was in fact the town council. Built chiefly between 1481 and 1495, it was the most advanced fortification in England at

The cylindrical end of the tower of Dartmouth. The large openings in the curved parapet were originally the top embrasures. The landward side of the parapet was later raised to provide protection against attack from behind, and fresh embrasures inserted above the originals. In the distance (at left) is the renovated tower of Kingswear Castle, a smaller fort built contemporaneously (c.1491–c.1502) to cover the other shore of the Dart estuary. It is now a house

the time and the first English castle to be specifically designed for firearms. (Ravenscraig in Fife was the first Scottish castle for firearms, c.1460–63.) Dartmouth was built around the remains of an older fortress raised with the encouragement of Edward III in the late fourteenth century, and the town, which had already received a grant of £30 from customs revenue for protecting it, had this enlarged by another £30 by Edward IV in 1481 for a period of five years, as a compensation to the town which had 'begun to make a strong tower and bulwark of stone and lime adjoining the castle . . . they shall . . . repair and keep it garnished with guns and artillery and other ordnance . . . '. Henry VII increased the £30 grant to £40 a year for maintenance, and this figure was paid for the next three and a half centuries. Dartmouth was given enough specially designed gun-ports for guns to cover the Dart Estuary from every angle of attack, in a tower in which the positioning of the guns rendered them offensive as well as defensive. Sited near the water level, the gun-ports were rectangular openings in the walls and these could be closed by shutters, like those seen in paintings of wooden warships. The ports were splayed inside 'to allow a degree of traverse without increasing the size of the "port" itself'. A few years later, a companion fortress was built on the east side of the estuary at Kingswear, just south of Comerock, with a square-plan tower having similar gun-port arrangements.

The new works at Dartmouth were followed by small blockhouses along the coast of Dorset, Devonshire and Cornwall, constructed to carry guns, some of them being added to coastal town walls, such as Lyme Regis, Swanage, Falmouth, Fowey and Pendennis.

The first systematic programme of coastal fortification in Britain (since the forts of the Saxon Shore of the Roman occupation) was initiated by Henry VIII in the late 1530s. In the early 1530s the king, determined to marry Anne Boleyn but unable to get a divorce from Katherine of Aragon to do so, broke with the Church at Rome, rejecting Papal authority over the Church of England and Wales, had his marriage annulled by the pliant Archbishop Cranmer, and in 1533 married Anne Boleyn. This not unexpectedly brought coals of fire upon his head from Europe. France and the Holy Roman Empire, currently at loggerheads, were persuaded by the Papacy to bury their differences and unite to bring Henry to heel and, by a treaty in 1538, they agreed to make moves to restore Papal authority in England. Henry decided to anticipate invasion as far as he could by defending the coastline with new structures at strategic points and by sending the navy to sea to scour the waters of the Channel and keep watch. The building programme was ambitious and it aimed to erect a blockhouse or bulwark at every haven and landing place, from Hull to Milford Haven in Pembrokehsire. The ambitions were not all achieved, but between 1538–9 and the mid-1540s a very impressive accumulation of major fortresses, smaller blockhouses and improvements to existing buildings had been more or less completed. They included the castles of Deal, Hurst, Walmer, St Mawes, Portland, Pendennis, Sandown, Sandgate, Calshot, Camber and Southsea, and a number of blockhouses such as Brownsea, Tilbury, Gravesend, Harwich and Dale & Angle in Pembrokeshire.

Among the first to be built were what came to be called 'The Three Castles which keep the Downs', because of the name of the quiet waters between them and the Goodwin Sands. They were, north to south and each a mile apart from the next, Sandown, Deal and Walmer. Deal was the biggest, six-foil in plan with six large cylinder bastions clustered round a taller, central cylindrical tower. Walmer was quatrefoil round a central tower. Sandown was similar, but it has almost disappeared beneath the sea. Interestingly, a clear picture of Sandown was taken over a century ago, showing it almost as it had

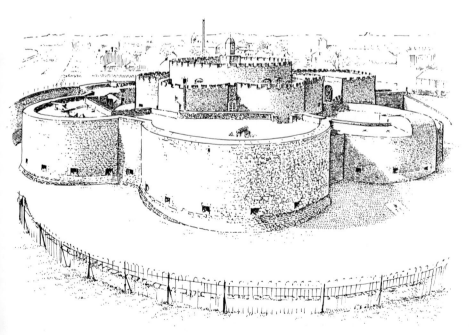

Deal is the largest of the coastal fortresses built by Henry VIII

A nineteenth-century photograph of Sandown coastal fort of Henry VIII's time, taken before the fort was destroyed by sea erosion

been in its heyday. Work began on the three in the spring of 1539, when masons and quarrymen prepared the stone blocks and carpenters and woodcutters put up the scaffolding. By the beginning of summer 1539, about 500 more workers were drafted in, and these included brickmakers and carpenters, for the castles were built of both stone and brick. By then about 1,400 men were at work on all three. As the time factor was crucial, materials had to be obtained from the nearest local sources and much stone was removed from the recently dissolved monasteries in the neighbourhood, such as the Carmelite Friary at Sandwich. This is evidenced by the presence of quantities of Caen stone in the masonry. Since the castles had brickwork as well, nearby kilns were used to make bricks and tiles.

The earliest of these coastal fortresses were designed specifically to consist of projecting gun-towers and bastions, squat, cylindrical or semi-cylindrical with broad sloping or rounded parapets, which provided frontal and flanking fire from their guns. Some had extra tiers of guns. The bastions were to cluster round the larger, taller central tower and they were to be surrounded by moats and in some cases, like Walmer and Hurst, outer curtain walling. Hurst's bastions were clustered round a multangular central tower. The idea derived from a manual of fortification by the great German artist, Dürer, and it may have been adapted here by the weird Bohemian engineer, Stefan von Haschenperg, who was certainly employed at Sandgate Castle in the early 1540s. He was sacked by the king for extravagance and lewdness — a considerable irony coming as it did from Henry VIII, probably the most spendthrift of all English kings. Haschenperg also designed the earthwork bulwarks which linked the three castles of the Downs.

The various coastal castles of this programme are in the Gazetteer, but we may look at Walmer in some detail. Walmer was smaller than Deal. It has four substantial cylinder bastions clustered round the central cylinder tower which was separated from them by a narrow courtyard. Guns were mounted on the top of the central tower and there were two tiers of gun-ports in the bastions which were enclosed by a moat. This was crossed by a causeway. The causeway led to a drawbridge in front of the castle entrance. The entrance passage contained eight murder-holes in the vaulted ceiling, in front of the portcullis and heavy door at the rear of the passage. The interior has been greatly altered because it is the official residence of the Lord Warden of the Cinque Ports.

In order to finish the work as quickly as possible, some of the work-force was pressed into service, as had been the case with many of the Edwardian Castles in Wales (see chapter 9). Some of the men may have been the ringleaders of a strike at Deal Castle in June 1539 for better pay. Skilled workers were getting 7d or 8d a day, but ordinary labourers received only 5d. Some of the latter stopped work and demanded an extra penny a day. The overseer of the project was Sir Edward Ryngley, formerly comptroller of the royal fortifications at Calais, and he met the strikers' demand head-on. As he wrote, 'after I had spoken with them I caused them to return to work, as Robert Lorde who was present at Deal can inform . . . I have sent the 9 first beginners, 5 to Canterbury Castle and 4 to Sandwich Gaol.'

The two coastal forts in Cornwall, Pendennis and St Mawes, are also of great interest. They sit one each side of Carrick Roads, the inlet coming in from Falmouth Bay and leading eventually as far as Truro. Pendennis was started in late 1539 and St Mawes in the next spring. Both were completed by 1543. Pendennis, on the western side of the Roads, high up on a promontory, was a squat, cylindrical tower enclosed in a symmetrical, multangular curtain. St Mawes, on the east side, is sheltered by a hill. A writer of the time of Elizabeth I put it: 'St Mawes lieth lower and better to annoy shipping, but Pendennis standeth higher and stronger to defend itself.' Pendennis was considerably enlarged with a multangular enclosure with star-pointed bastions (six of them) at the very end of the sixteenth century after the defeat of the Spanish Armada which, incidentally, was the beginning of new dangers for Cornwall rather than the end of

St Mawes coastal fort from the west. Note the royal arms on the west bastion wall, with an inscription in Latin coined by Leland

them. Spanish raiders attacked many ports in Cornwall for several years after the defeat, and it was this that prompted the parsimonious queen to spend some money on Pendennis and others. St Mawes, whose history is a relatively dull one (even in the Civil War it surrendered without firing a shot in defence), was well armed: a survey of ordnance in 1609 lists two sakers and an iron minion, a culverin and six demi-culverins of iron and one of brass on the bastions, two culverins and a brass saker in the courtyards. This is much the same stock of guns as were held at Walmer, but at Walmer there was an extra gun, an 8in cannon that was said to be able to discharge shot for a distance of two miles.

The huge enterprise set in train by Henry VIII occupied many people for several years. The expected invasion did not occur, however, and it is possible that the fortress programme and the speed with which it was carried out made some impression upon the military chiefs of the Catholic powers. But if there was no invasion, there were raids, and one on the Isle of Wight in 1545 was accompanied by an assault on Southsea, near Portsmouth. This was beaten off in three days. The king decided to continue with the programme, and in that year Yarmouth Castle on the Isle of Wight was begun, together with one at Sandown on the south-east side.

The larger Henrician coastal fortresses are called castles, though they were not private military residences in the same sense as medieval castles. They were equipped with accommodation for their governors, or castellans as they would have been known in earlier days, and this was installed in the central great tower. To that extent they conformed to the definition of a fortified residence, but the difference lies in the role of the residential aspect which was secondary to that of the military role. Coastal fortresses were not homes. They were defensive/offensive buildings in which it was possible for a number of people (generally pre-arranged) to live for a term of service.

But if their role was not exactly that of the medieval castle, coastal castles nonetheless deserve inclusion in any summary of British castles. The same cannot be said of structures like Martello towers, and these are not part of our summary.

16

The End of the Castle

Castles were medieval structures, an integral part of the medieval scene. They had a clear cut role — fortress-residences for kings and lords. When the need for this role began to diminish as medieval society changed, castles were adapted to new roles, allowed to decay or were pulled down and the materials used for constructing new buildings or repairing old ones. Many castles were converted as they stood into more comfortable residences by their owners or sold to new owners to do the same. In some cases the alterations were integrated into the existing structure: ranges of domestic buildings were erected against the inside of walls of enclosures, ornate fireplaces were built into walling in towers or halls, and windows were enlarged (which of course weakened the walls). In other instances, new free-standing buildings, not associated with the castle as it were, arose within their precincts, such as at Compton and many others. Of the hundreds of castles of one kind and another built in Britain in the Middle Ages and surviving into the sixteenth century, few continued to look as they had in their military heyday. Owners still called them castles, even put in ashlar gun-ports or musket loops, but perhaps — in England and Wales at all events — they did not really envisage their homes ever playing the medieval role again. (It was different in Scotland, as we saw in chapter 14.)

The decline of the military role in England and Wales was due to a great extent to the sensible legislation of Henry VII who, soon after his defeat of Richard III at Bosworth in 1485, virtually took over the nation's facilities for manufacturing gunpowder and by statute forbade the maintenance of private armies (see Hedingham Castle). This stopped great lords indulging in private wars, using cannon and hand-guns, and brought siege warfare to an end in England and Wales for a century and a half.

Over the sixteenth and early seventeenth centuries, castles were to be little more than quaint and picturesque relics of a bygone society.

In quite a few instances owners patched them up and attempted to maintain them. Perhaps they even let visitors tramp round them. But in far more numerous cases owners allowed their castles to decay. They became objects of interest to travellers and antiquarians who commented upon them, generally deploring the deterioration and harking back to their better days. The foremost was John Leland (c.1506–52), the London-born antiquary. He spent six years (1536–42) making a detailed tour of England and Wales examining, amongst other things, castles, and he wrote numerous descriptions and comments that are of great interest and value to castle historians.

The Crown had been far the biggest owner of castles throughout the Middle Ages. When Henry VII won the throne at Bosworth he came into about forty castles, including Carisbrooke, Carlisle, Dover, London, Nottingham, Portchester, Scarborough and Windsor. As he also took over the Principality of Wales he acquired a further string from Conwy to Cardigan, including the great Edwardian fortresses; and as Duke of Lancaster (by virtue of being the heir to the House of Lancaster through his mother Margaret Beaufort) he could add another collection, notably Bolingbroke, Hertford, Kenilworth, Lancaster, Leicester, Pevensey, Pickering, Pontefract, Tickhill and Tutbury. He even obtained the Duchy of York castles of Conisbrough, Sandal and the Neville ('Kingmaker') castles of Middleham, Warwick and Barnard. And he was owner of Richmond. During his reign he acquired even more: Pembroke, Cardiff, Newport (Monmouthshire) and Tonbridge (then one of the greatest castles in England).

It is not necessary to enlarge upon the Crown's further acquisitions in the time of his son Henry VIII or of his grandchildren Edward VI, Mary I and Elizabeth I. Clearly, the Crown had far more fortresses than it could possibly need or want, and to keep them all in good, or even indifferent, repair for whatever purpose would have been a crushing drain upon the royal funds. What mattered was that practically all the major fortresses in England and Wales were out of private hands and so constituted no danger to the peace of the realm. There was some need for those fortresses on the Border between England and Scotland and the royal accounts contain details of expenditure on several, some of it high, some of it niggardly (the penny-pinching Elizabeth I refused absolutely to help Hunsdon to repair the very important castle of Norham). These castles included Wark, Berwick, Carlisle (where the twelfth-century great tower was altered to take sixteenth-century guns), Bewcastle (Cumberland)

and Harbottle. The Crown maintained a handful for a variety of more peaceful reasons, notably Pontefract 'to prevent the Ruynes of a Monument of such antiquity and goodly building' (cited in *The The History of the King's Works*, vol. 3, p.289). Chester was a centre of local government, and Tutbury was a royal hunting lodge. And of course the Crown maintained London, Windsor, Dover, Portchester and Carisbrooke for defence and for royal palace purposes. Interestingly, Fotheringay in Northamptonshire was meant to be one that received attention. Leland found it in good condition: it was given a face-lift in 1566 for a visit by Elizabeth I (painting railway stations in the present century has this among many precedents). But when Fotheringay was selected as the location for the trial and eventual execution of Mary, Queen of Scots, in 1586–7, the great part of it was in poor shape. The walls were low enough to jump over, and the outer gatehouse had decayed to the point of uselessness. Would an attempt to rescue Mary have been successful?

In 1609 the state of the royal and Duchy of Lancaster castles was reviewed by the Exchequer. More than sixty 'of his Majestie's decayed castells' were described as decayed, very ruinous or utterly decayed. Among those described as utterly decayed were Beaumaris, Aberystwyth, Conwy, Caernarvon, Ruthin and Rhuddlan. Some of the others in the list were labelled 'utterly ruinated and serve for noe use'. One has to remember that these buildings were examined by agents of the king (James I), presumably to see whether any, and if so which, were suitable for him to occupy or stay at, and that 'decayed' might mean not much more than that windows were broken, damp was coming in, dry rot had eaten at some timbers and so forth.

Quite suddenly, in 1642, castles came into their own again for what was to be their last flourish, their fighting finish as Professor Douglas Simpson called it. The king, Charles I, and Parliament went to war to determine once and for all who was the sovereign power, the monarch or the people through its elected representatives in the Commons. The king had unwisely left London and raised his standard at Nottingham, abandoning the capital with its vast wealth in the hands of Parliament. We are not concerned with the main progress of the war, since that was fought army-against-army in open battles. But while the leaders on both sides fielded armies of several thousands each in an attempt to win decisive victories, there were many much smaller and highly localised campaigns going on concurrently, in which the old castles of England and Wales played the central role. Soon after the outbreak of the war, both Royalists and Parliamentarians in all parts of the countryside took them over and repaired them. In many cases the disrepair was so extensive that only parts were rebuilt, parts that could be fortified without much difficulty and which would perhaps stand siege for a time. On the Royalist side, many of the Crown castles and those belonging to lords and knights who were loyal to the king's cause were put into a state of defence and garrisoned. Each was allotted a number of men, between fifty and three hundred, presumably according to size and to strategic importance. Geographically, the countryside could be said to have been divided into two parts, so far as the respective sides in the Civil War are concerned: the king drew his support from the west, from Wales and from the north; Parliament was dominant in the east and south. But these areas were not exclusive to one side or the other, and every county had its share of supporters of both. If a Royalist castle was garrisoned by the king's men, Parliamentary supporters attacked it, and vice versa. Both sides lived on the produce of the neighbouring countryside; they plundered the locality if they could not get supplies by asking or by purchasing. On the whole the Royalists behaved marginally worse than the Parliamentarians. They were fighting private wars, sometimes oblivious of what was going on elsewhere, conscious only of doing their bit for their 'party'. This is one of the reasons why we read of many castle sieges going on long after the great battles of Marston Moor and Naseby had been fought and the issue decided. Many castles were besieged and captured more than once, alternating between king and Parliament. Sometimes a siege took only a day or two to produce surrender, such as at Nunney or Devizes; others lasted several months, like Raglan, Denbigh, Pendennis, or well over a year, like Pontefract and Donnington.

When the principal Civil War battles had been fought and Parliament triumphed, the victors decided it was time to reduce the Royalist-held castles. Some had been held for years, effectively locking up many men in garrisons that would have been better employed in battle for the king. Once he had lost the war, he advised garrisons to make what terms they could with threatening Parliamentary armies, though secretly he hoped that as many as possible would hold out and so obstruct the victorious Parliamentarians in the exercise of their new power.

Accounts of several Civil War sieges of castles have survived and they make fascinating reading. One of the longest sieges was that of Donnington Castle in Berkshire, from July 1644 to April 1646.

The rectangular-plan gatehouse tower with twin cylindrical towers flanking the entrance is all that remains of Donnington, Berkshire.

Donnington was appropriated by Charles I. In the autumn of 1643 the king appointed Colonel John Boys commander of a garrison consisting of about two hundred infantry, twenty-five horse, and four cannon. Boys promptly fortified the castle with a series of earthworks, intended chiefly to separate the building from would-be attackers. The principal work was a star-shaped outwork of pointed bulwarks surrounding the stone curtain enclosure with its six flanking towers and its massive eastern gatehouse. Then he waited. The castle commanded a fine view over the London to Bath Road near Newbury and was thus of considerable strategic value, for it threatened enemy forces attempting to get to London from the West.

In July 1644, Parliament sent a force of some 3,000 men under Lt. Gen. Middleton to besiege and take the castle. A formal demand to surrender was sent in to Boys. He replied curtly that he proposed to hold on to the castle. So Middleton began the assault, using scaling ladders. This was a disaster. It cost him about a tenth of his force killed or wounded and he did not get the castle. Sometime in September a fresh force under a new commander, Horton, renewed the assault, this time using artillery set up on rising ground just outside Newbury. For twelve days the cannon thundered across the gently rolling Berkshire hills round Speen and Hamstead Marshall. Three of Donnington's towers were smashed down and great gashes were torn in the curtain. Boys was again invited to surrender, and again he refused. The next month, yet another Parliamentary force attacked, using artillery, and it is recorded that over a thousand shots were fired, causing much damage. Still Boys refused to yield. Then news arrived that the king was on his way to relieve the garrison, and as they did not know the size of the king's force, the Parliamentarians backed away.

The king reached the gallant and exhausted garrison and re-provisioned it. No doubt every man present cheered when Charles knighted their commander for his leadership and courage. Soon afterwards, the second Battle of Newbury was fought and ended in stalemate, the Royalists managing to extricate themselves in good order. The battle was followed by yet another siege of Donnington. The Parliamentary commander, Sir William Waller, demanded surrender. Again Boys refused. Waller threatened to leave not one stone upon another, but Boys replied that he would fight for the land on which they stood. Besiegers then poisoned one of the castle wells, then regretted it and warned the garrison not to use it. Boys sent a troop of men out to clean the well, and they retrieved a bag of poison.

167

In November the garrison was relieved a second time by the king. By this time four towers had gone. There was a respite during the winter, which Boys used to strengthen the earthworks. By March he was ready to withstand siege again. But the Civil War was almost over. Charles I had lost. Parliament once again demanded surrender but before yielding, Boys sent envoys to the king to ask for instructions. The king told him to shift for himself and to get the best terms he could. After a parley with the Parliamentary forces, Boys finally surrendered, on 1 April 1646, some twenty months after the first demand.

The siege of Donnington may seem to have been an inordinately prolonged business, but this kind of story was enacted at several other sieges, notably at Denbigh, Raglan and Corfe. Pontefract, then one of the most majestic castles in northern England, was besieged three times. Cromwell himself almost despaired of getting the Pontefract garrison to yield. He described it as one of the strongest inland garrisons, well watered, difficult to undermine because every important part of the castle stood on rock. Pontefract fell in the third siege, from mid-1648 to March 1649 and Parliament decided to demolish it. The success of this can be judged by the meagre remains visible today of what was one of the most foremost castles of the Middle Ages.

It was not enough to reduce castles in Royalist hands. Parliament was determined to break them up and render them permanently incapable of being used for military purposes again. This process was known as 'slighting' and it was generally carried out with great thoroughness. The idea was not new: Robert Bruce had followed a similar policy in Scotland after his successful campaign to drive out the English. Many castles in England and Wales were ordered by Parliament to be slighted, mostly those that had been held at some time or other during the war by the Royalists. The demolition of Raglan in the summer of 1647 was begun with vigour, but no matter how hard the teams worked, they were unable to destroy it. An account of the slighting was written towards the end of the seventeenth century. In it the writer said that 'The Great Tower [the Yellow Tower of Gwent], after tedious battering the top thereof with pickaxes, was undermined, the weight of it propped with the timber whilst the two sides of the six were cut through: the timber being burned it fell down in a lump . . . After the surrender the country people were summoned into a rendezvous with pickaxes, spades, and shovels to draw the mote [moat] in the hope of wealth . . .' (quoted from *Raglan Castle* by A.J. Taylor).

The subsequent history of the many hundreds of castles in England and Wales has been enormously varied. Many have disappeared in town development schemes or under roads, railway stations, electricity power stations, and other public civil engineering works. Many have been left gradually to decay. Many that had deteriorated badly have been carefully restored, some by private owners, but the majority by the Department of the Environment (formerly the Ministry of Public Building and Works) without whose efforts it would not be possible to provide a fair picture of the castles of Britain. Many, like Berkeley, Chirk and Blair are lived in by descendants of their medieval owners. Some were used as quarries for building materials for later, more peaceful structures. Some, like Winchester and Leicester, are still used today for assizes. Some were until recently used as prisons. The Tower of London is used for military purposes, as well as being opened for visitors. Dover was used for similar purposes until 1958. Windsor is still a royal residence: indeed since early Norman times it has not been anything else, though it was of course fortified. It has had more spent on it than any other castle in the kingdom.

Gazetteer

Introduction to Gazetteer

There are over 1,050 entries in the Gazetteer. They represent the great bulk (though not all) of the castles and castle sites in England, Wales and Scotland. Included are as many known sites as possible of castles, whether of earth and timber, or stone, or brick, raised between 1066 and c.1500 in England and Wales (together with the Henry VIII coastal forts) and of over 500 in Scotland from the late eleventh century to the beginning of the seventeenth. I have attempted to include not only every one that has figured as important in the history of England, Wales and Scotland, but also those that have little or no recorded history but which have something of interest for the enthusiast or which have significant building details. It is probably the most extensive gazetteer of castles in Britain ever assembled in one volume. Yet, in compiling this gazetteer — as in putting together lists, say, of famous people or artefacts or places — one can never satisfy everyone. Something will be left out: it may even be a glaring omission. If this has happened with this book, it will have been inadvertent and will hopefully be brought to our attention. If it is not inadvertent, then the reason may lie in the fact that the castle is not in our view a castle within the definition given in chapter 1. I have chosen buildings or traces of buildings that conform or once conformed to our definition, and every one in the list has, or once had at least one of the characteristics — thick walls, ditching, battlementing, arrow-loops, gun-ports, portcullises — or a combination of these fortifications.

A word should be said about how the Gazetteer entries are planned. Where possible the remains of what can be seen today have been outlined, but because of space limits it has been necessary to highlight some parts remaining and overlook others. For the same reason, the historical details and personalities associated with the castles have been kept to a minimum. This is a source book of information which can be used as a pointer to further study of any

172

particular castle or any aspect of design or fortification. It is a gazetteer of buildings which, in the majority of cases, can be seen and explored, and the building details seem to me to be more important. The reader who wants to pursue the historical side can do so without difficulty by searching among documents and publications (see Bibliography). Those more interested in the buildings, or earthworks, may like to follow a simple suggestion. The entries have been prepared in such a way that it should be possible to take a piece of paper and draw out a rough plan (in about 140 cases, the basic plan is drawn out accurately and reproduced in the book). From the plan it should be possible to get an idea of what ground the buildings cover, or covered, and armed with this the site can be explored. Castles in the care of the Department of Environment, or Welsh Office, or Scottish Development Department, are described in great detail in special blue covered handbooks, each of which has a comprehensive site plan. These books are normally obtainable on the site or from HMSO bookshops or any of the HMSO agencies in the UK.

Of the 1,050 or so castles listed, quite a few have very little to see; they are no more than mounds or stretches of ditch and bank or gutted shells of unsafe masonry. Some are interesting, nonetheless, because of what they once were or the position they occupied, or because of some important association. Several hundred are marked with one dagger, or two daggers: one means that the castle is worth visiting if you are in the neighbourhood; two daggers mean that the castle is, in my view, worth a special expedition. These marks have been allotted only to castles that are easily accessible. Many of those which are privately owned and to which visitors are not admitted would otherwise have one or two daggers. Those which are accessible but which have no daggers should not necessarily be ignored. The choice of castles that merit daggers is a personal one and it was based upon the degree to which they illustrate the many aspects of castle-building discussed in the preceding chapters. In some instances it was also based upon their siting. For example, Cambridge Castle has very little except its original mound, and yet if you climb to the summit and look down it is immediately clear what a commanding position it once had over the river, the town and the countryside below.

It is sometimes easier to read about castles than to visit them. Although the great majority are in ruins, one cannot always just scramble over them and explore the remains. Hundreds are in private ownership and the owners quite naturally cherish them, even if the remains amount (as many do) to little more than straggling heaps of stone dotted about overgrown earthworks. Some are not open to visitors. Rather more *are* open, though the owners do not all advertise the fact. Some admit visitors on a regular basis, some on occasional days, and some will admit visitors at special request. Some owners change their arrangements at relatively short notice. Their castle may have become unsafe and it has to be closed for restoration work. Unfortunately, castles also get vandalized and owners decline to keep them open unless they can personally supervise the visiting or employ a custodian. Some owners decide to take more of the castle into their own use and close parts to the public. It is therefore best in every case where a castle is privately owned to check with the owner first before setting out to visit it. If it is listed in the *AA Guide to Stately Homes, Castles & Gardens*, or the *ABC Historic Houses, Castles and Gardens*, the visiting arrangements may be relied upon, but even these most useful annual reference works advise that details are accurate only at the time of going to press, for that is all they can do.

Apart from the privately owned castles, there are several hundred in the care of public organizations, and these are more easily accessible. Nearly 200 are in the care of the Department of Environment (for England), the Welsh Office or the Scottish Development Department. As a general rule, these castles are open either throughout the year during hours of daylight (approximately) or on a regular basis. Some are freely accessible all the time. They have been looked after, often extensively restored and made attractive with such care and skill as to put the nation forever in the Government's debt.

Many castles are in the care of local authorities, who maintain them in good repair, and in some instances have landscaped them. Some of these are freely accessible. For others it is necessary to obtain a key or find the keeper. A small number of castles are National Trust (England and Wales) or National Trust for Scotland property. These are generally open during normal National Trust hours. Many castles are listed in telephone directories. Local authority information offices, and the English, Welsh and Scottish tourist boards' main and branch offices and outposts have details of visiting hours of most castles in their areas, and of telephone numbers of many private owners as well.

Throughout the Gazetteer the entries are marked with the Ordnance Survey Grid Reference number, which should help to locate them. Many are also given a code letter, or abbreviation, to indicate their accessibility:

A   freely accessible because in public parkland, churchyard, open space, beside road, lake, river, etc.

O   open to the public at regular times, or by application. Advisable to check first.

C   not normally open to visitors. In some cases, castles in this category can be seen in some form from the road.

P   privately owned. These may sometimes be open. Advisable to apply or to check in advance.

DoE   Castles in England in the care of the Department of Environment. Open.

WO   Castles in Wales in the care of the Welsh Office. Open.

SDD   Castles in Scotland in the care of the Scottish Development Department. Open.

NT   National Trust (England & Wales).

NTS   National Trust for Scotland.

These codings were as correct as possible at the time of going to press. I shall be glad to hear of any changes that have occurred since.

England

ABINGER Nr Guildford, Surrey
(TQ 114460) A
A motte castle built in c.1100, this was the subject of extensive excavations in 1947–9, under the direction of Dr Brian Hope Taylor. They revealed post-holes of a wooden tower and also of the surrounding palisade, and of a horizontally placed bridge from the motte to the bailey, across a wet moat that was filled by a local spring. It is thought the first structures on the motte were dismantled in the mid-twelfth century and the castle remodelled. The motte top was heightened and a small square-plan tower built on the new top. The post-holes of the tower indicate that the tower may have stood on stilts, as it were, to provide a fighting platform underneath the tower ground floor. Posts went into the ground to 4ft deep or more, which suggest a tall tower. A gap in the circumference of palisade posts is believed to indicate the gateway at the south-west. The motte is near Abinger Church.

ACTON BURNELL Shropshire   †
(SJ 534019) DOE
Acton Burnell is known as a castle, but it was really a manor house whose builder, Robert Burnell, Chancellor of England and Bishop of Bath and Wells, obtained a licence to fortify in the 1280s. It is a huge two-storeyed rectangular tower-hall, now roofless, with smaller (13ft sq) towers on the corners, with a projecting block between the two west towers. It was built of local red sandstone and is more like a palace than a castle although the parapets are battlemented. Yet with walls only a few feet thick and with so much window space, Acton Burnell does not give one much feeling of security.

ALBERBURY Nr Shrewsbury, Shropshire   (SJ 358144) A
A small thirteenth-century stone enclosure castle, polygonal in plan, containing a rectangular great tower with thick walls, now in ruins.

ALDFORD Nr Chester, Cheshire
(SJ 419596) C
A motte castle was built at Aldford in the twelfth century. Walling erected on the summit of the motte was discovered in recent excavations. Some fragments of stonework round the bailey survive. The castle overlooked a ford across the Dee.

ALDINGBOURNE Nr Arundel, Sussex
(SU 923048) A
One of the castles in Britain (cf. Lydford) where the lowest storey of the stone great tower was enclosed, as it were, inside a mound of earth. The mound can be seen. The tower was square in plan, with a small forebuilding at the south-west. It was built of limestone and flint, quarried locally, with dressings of Caen ashlar. Aldingbourne was erected in the mid-twelfth century, but is now fragmentary.

ALDINGHAM Lancashire
(SD 278698)
An earthwork enclosure about 120ft square was converted into a motte castle by filling in and raising the height of the enclosure. A further bailey was added. This is unusual: motte castles were generally built from scratch using natural mounds or rising ground or by creating artificial mounds on virgin sites. In the twelfth century the motte seems to have been heightened, which suggests that the first tower was dismantled and a new one built (this happened at

176

Abinger). There was a tradition that Aldingham was abandoned for another castle nearby, namely, Gleaston. Excavations in 1968 revealed no remains that can be dated later than the thirteenth century.

ALLINGTON Nr Maidstone, Kent †
(TQ 752579) O
Today's Allington Castle is an extensive twentieth-century renovation by Sir Martin Conway (later Lord Conway of Allington) of a late thirteenth-century quadrangular structure with square and round towers on corners and mid-wall. The latter had been raised by Stephen of Penchester, under a licence granted by Edward I in 1281, beside the remains of an earlier Norman motte castle of the eleventh century. Allington Castle is sited on the west bank of the Medway River. Some Norman stonework has survived opposite the motte, in the form of some walling in herringbone pattern, which leads into a much later stretch of wall and which may have been part of the bailey wall after its conversion from timber to stone.

Considerable alterations were carried out in the late fifteenth century, converting it to a grander Tudor mansion with large windows, a long gallery, new kitchens and other accommodation ranges. The castle was burned down c.1600 and the remains patched up for use as a farmhouse. This was bought by Sir Martin Conway at the beginning of the present century. It became a Carmelite nunnery in 1951.

ALNWICK Northumberland †
(NU 187137) O
The splendid palatial residence at Alnwick with its towers, gatehouses and high curtain with battlements is the result of centuries of building. Alnwick began as a motte castle of the eleventh century, and in the early twelfth century a polygonal stone shell keep was raised on the summit. Stone walling was added to the bailey, and in 1138 the castle was described as a very well fortified one.

Alnwick: much of this castle is restored work of the fourteenth century with later buildings added to improve the residential role. Outside the walls, only traces of which are of the twelfth century, William the Lion, King of Scotland, was captured during an attempt to take the castle by siege in 1174

William the Lion, King of Scotland, besieged it in 1172 and again in 1174, but on the second occasion a relieving army surprised him and his principal lords and knights as they rested a while from the fighting and captured them. The castle remained a powerful Border fortress throughout the thirteenth century.

Early in the fourteenth century Alnwick was bought from the Bishop of Durham by Henry Percy, ancestor of the great earls of Northumberland, who then began a major improvement programme. Percy rebuilt the shell keep by making it a larger enclosure with seven semi-circular towers round it, in a form that has led it to be called a clustered donjon. The great curtain wall round the central tower was strengthened with several flanking towers, square, rectangular, D-ended and cylindrical. The inner tower and the outer curtain received huge gatehouses and a great barbican. The greater part of the work was done by Percy, his son, grandson and great-grandson, and in magnificence it was hardly less impressive than contemporary royal works at Windsor.

In the fifteenth century, Alnwick was often in the front line of war. Headquarters of the Percys who rebelled against Henry IV in 1404–5, it was besieged and taken by that king. It was attacked during the Wars of the Roses. Subsequently, it began to decay, until in the eighteenth century the 1st Duke of Northumberland rebuilt it, employing Robert Adam as architect. The result was not felicitous and it was swept away in the nineteenth century by Anthony Salvin who restored it to its external medieval appearance.

ALTON Staffordshire
(SK 074425) O
A castle was built on a rocky precipice in the time of Henry II. The slopes provided defence to most sides, but a ditch has been found cut into the rock. There are traces of masonry indicating a curtain wall.

ALMONDBURY West Yorkshire
(SE 152140) A
Remains of a twelfth-century motte castle raised upon the site of an Iron Age hill-fort were found in excavations earlier this century.

AMBERLEY Nr Pulborough, Sussex
(TQ 027132) Gardens open
Today, Amberley Castle is a much restored structure occupied as a home. It appears to have begun as a stonework enclosure with high curtain walls, towers, hall and gateway, erected in the fourteenth century following a licence to build dated 1377. It was a fortress residence for the bishops of Chichester. The hall is in ruins, the gateway has been restored and there are stretches of high curtain wall.

ANCROFT Nr Berwick-on-Tweed, Northumberland (NV 043437) A
Described in the 1540s as a 'little fortress', this interesting tower was constructed in the thirteenth century as an integral part of Ancroft Church, a twelfth-century chapel raised by Holy Island monks. It is three-storeyed above the lower storey of the nave, about 22ft by 26ft, with a spiral staircase in one corner. The small windows are set in thick walls.

ANSTEY Hertfordshire
(TL 404330) A
Anstey was a motte castle of the late eleventh or early twelfth century. The surviving motte is a low one, about 30ft high, and was surrounded by a wet moat of varying width. The motte top is almost ¼ acre in area and may have contained more buildings than just a tall wooden tower. The castle was strengthened during the Magna Carta war (1215–16) by an opponent of King John.

APPLEBY Cumbria   †
(NY 685200) O
Beginning as a motte castle, probably of early twelfth century construction, Appleby became an enclosure castle with a sandstone rubble curtain around the bottom of the motte, inside which was built a square-plan great tower, in about 1170. The great tower rises to about 80ft and has four storeys. The first floor is reached by a spiral staircase in the south-east corner and the remaining floors by the continuation of this, together with a second staircase in the south-west corner. Unusually for a square great tower, the entrance is not protected by any forebuilding. The castle was surrounded on all sides by moats except for the side that abuts on to the River Eden.

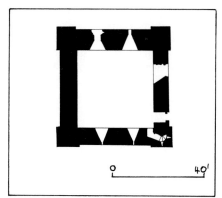

Appleby: plan of ground floor of great tower

left, Appleby: the great tower

Appleby was held for Henry II from 1173–9 and again for the royal family from 1190–1203. During the first period it was attacked by William the Lion, King of Scotland, and the constable surrendered without putting up a fight. In 1203 King John granted the castle to Richard de Vipont. Some improvements were carried out in the thirteenth century. The gatehouse in the eastern wall is fifteenth century.

ARDLEY Oxfordshire
(SP 539273) A
An oval enclosure with a shallow ditch in Ardley Wood. There are traces of Norman masonry. It has been conjectured that it was an adulterine castle of Stephen's reign, demolished after 1154 at the orders of Henry II.

ARMATHWAITE Cumbria
(NY 506459) O
Armathwaite is a four-storeyed pele-tower of the fifteenth century, overlooking the Eden River and not far from the Carlisle to Penrith road which was used frequently by the Scots in Border raids.

ARUNDEL Sussex †
(TQ 019074) O
Arundel Castle is nearly 900 years old, and has been owned by the dukes of Norfolk for more than half that time. We are concerned with the castle only up to the sixteenth century.

It began as a substantial motte castle, whose motte was 60–70ft tall, with elevated bailey on each side (a layout similar to that of Windsor Castle), raised on a spur overlooking the Arun River. This was probably built c.1088. About a century later the motte received a shell keep with ashlar pilaster buttresses and a battlemented parapet, which was approached through a rounded arch, later replaced by a gate-tower constructed against the shell wall, next to the arch which was filled in. A wing wall of stone led down the motte slope on one side to a small turret from which a stone curtain continued round the top of the bank of one of the baileys and into the other. This work was mainly of 1176–89, and the king, Henry II, spent about £330 on the curtain, a chapel, a chamber and work on the shell keep which he may have begun at an earlier date. Henry also made a garden for himself, probably the

179

earliest royal garden in an English castle.

From the thirteenth century onwards, the castle was held for the most part by the earls of Arundel, and later the dukes of Norfolk, and the late medieval structures that emerged were their work.

ASCOT d'OILLY Oxfordshire
(SP 304191) A

Ascot d'Oilly is an interesting castle, consisting of raised ground surrounded by broad ditching. The mound was piled in stages against the lower walls of a great tower as the masonry went up (cf. Aldingbourne). Only traces of the tower remain, and they indicate that it was about 35ft square, with walls 8ft thick. The tower was demolished, probably in 1175–6, and this could have been at the order of Henry II following his suppression of the serious revolt led by his eldest son, Prince Henry, who was backed by many barons.

ASHBY DE LA ZOUCH   ††
Leicestershire   (SK 363167) DOE

Ashby was a Norman hall of twelfth-century beginnings. Over three centuries it was extended to become a fair sized manor house. In 1464 it was granted by Edward IV to William, Lord Hastings, his Lord Chamberlain, and Hastings, having risen rapidly to a high position on the Yorkist side in the Wars of the Roses, decided to convert the manor into a castle. In 1474 Edward gave him the necessary licence, which covered his property at Kirby Muxloe as well (q.v.).

The principal building of Hastings' time was his new great tower (Hastings' Tower). This formidable structure was a fortress-cum-residence of the old kind. It originally reached about 90ft to its semi-octagonal angle turrets. It is rectangular in plan, about 47ft by 41ft, with a rectangular extension on the north-east side. The main tower was four-storeyed, but there were seven floors in the extension. The tower walls are nearly 9ft thick on the ground floor, which has no windows and only a small door once protected by a portcullis. To provide the owner with a separate water supply that was safe from being tampered with, a special well was sunk in the north wall, despite the existence of two other wells outside. There was an underground passage from the

basement of the tower along to the kitchen building to the west. The tower was placed on the periphery of the castle and not in the centre. This enabled the owners to have a view of the other occupants of the castle.

The most interesting feature of the great tower is that it was rectangular in an age when it is believed in some quarters, that rectangular towers had long since given way to cylindrical towers (see chapter 4). In fact, rectangular towers never gave way to those of other shapes.

ASHLEY Hampshire
(SU 385308) A

South of the church are the remnants of an enclosure castle of earthworks, inside which are foundation traces of stonework building. This was approximately rectangular, with a cylindrical turret, of probably late twelfth/early thirteenth century.

ASHTON KEYNES Wiltshire
(SU 049943)

An earthwork enclosure which had a dry-stone wall along the ramparts. It was probably raised in the time of Stephen.

ASLOCKTON Nottinghamshire
(SK 744402) A

A rectangular earthwork enclosure whose moat was fed from a nearby stream, with a low motte, about 16ft high. Nothing of its history is known. Some earthworks remain.

AYDON Nr Corbridge,   †
Northumberland   (NZ 001663) DOE

Aydon Castle began as a private residence of the late thirteenth century. It was probably built by Robert de Raymes as a two-storeyed home with the solar, dining hall and kitchen on the higher floor. These were reached by an outside staircase. The house had hardly been completed when Raymes felt compelled to fortify it with battlements (he obtained a licence in the first years of the fourteenth century) because of the increasingly unsettled conditions in Northumberland that followed Edward I's illegal assumption of the throne of Scotland and his invasions of Scotland. Raymes then surrounded the house with 'a wall of stone and lime against the king's enemies, the Scots', and this had towers and a deep ditch outside.

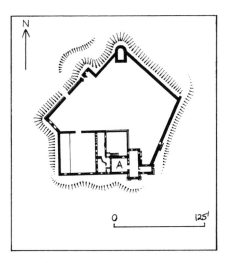

Aydon: A = position of great hall

BACONSTHORPE Nr Holt, Norfolk †
(TG 122382) DOE

Without bothering to obtain a licence, the Heydons, an aggressive, self-seeking middle-class Norfolk family of the fifteenth century, constructed a quadrangular manor house at Baconsthorpe and fortified it. A deep ditch was excavated round the north, west and south sides and the east side was protected by a lake which fed the ditch. In the middle of the south wall the Heydons erected a substantial three-storeyed rectangular gatehouse largely of flint, faced on the outside with the best East Anglian knapped flintwork, with ashlar quoins. The quadrangle was completed later in the century and it contained several flanking towers, square and cylindrical, and a range of long rooms on the east side. The gatehouse was approached by a drawbridge over the moat. An outer gatehouse was added, some 50 yards away to the south.

John Heydon I, who built the inner gatehouse, was a tough and quarrelsome magnate who survived the dangerous sport of backing first one side, then the other in the Wars of the Roses (1455–85). Today, the castle is in ruins, but is well worth a visit.

The precautions were not entirely effective: the Scots captured Aydon Castle in 1315, and took it again in 1346. It was recovered later in the fourteenth century, and remained in private ownership until 1975. Substantial parts of the original work survive.

Baconsthorpe: the gatehouse and part of the moat. Note that the ashlar quoins have been removed from the corners of the building, leaving the flint walling standing. The stones were used to construct a barn nearby, sometime in the sixteenth century

BAKEWELL Derbyshire
(SK 221688)

There was a motte castle at Bakewell in the twelfth century. It may have been one of those raised illegally in the time of King Stephen. The motte appears to have been added to an earlier rubble-built ramparted enclosure, possibly square in plan. It was for a long time believed that Bakewell was a *burh* of the time of Edward the Elder (900–24), Alfred the Great's son, but this was disproved by Ella Armitage (*Early Norman Castles of the British Isles* p. 47).

BAMBURGH Northumberland ††
(NU 184350) O

Bamburgh stands on a 150ft-tall rock face on the wind-swept Northumbria coast, one side sheer with the cliff to the shore. Its remaining structures, the residue of a powerful medieval castle, are but the last in a line of fortified buildings on the site. Iron Age men, Romans, Anglo-Saxons, even Vikings had built fortifications there. And in 1095, whatever shape the structure was, it was besieged by William II using a siege castle (a temporary structure like a belfry) nicknamed Malvoisin — Evil Neighbour — and taken from its holder, Robert de Mowbray. Thereafter, except for a few years, Bamburgh was a royal castle up to the seventeenth century.

The building history of Bamburgh is problematic. The principal structure is the great tower which from a distance looks like Dover's. But it is not like it (except that it is almost cuboid) and it is much smaller: the measurements are 69ft by 61ft by 65ft tall. It has been drastically altered. It has proud clasping buttresses on the corners and also along the walls, and it has a spiral stair serving all floors in the northern corner. The basement is vaulted and the entrance is at ground-floor level. There is a straight flight of stairs in the wall thickness at ground level.

There are some remains of a curtain wall enclosing the castle, with cylindrical and square towers, and there is a gatehouse at the east. Again, much of this bears alterations and repairs of later periods. The stonework may possibly have been initiated when the castle was held by Henry, Earl of Huntingdon, a son of David I of Scotland. This was during the chaotic years of Stephen of

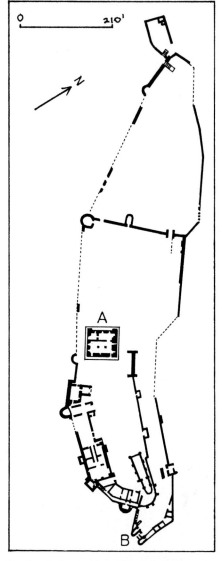

Bamburgh: from a plan of the castle drawn at the end of the nineteenth century, A=great tower; B=great gate

England, a time when Henry's father captured Carlisle Castle and started work on its great tower (q.v.). The attribution of Bamburgh's great tower to Henry II between c.1160 and c.1170 may relate to continuation of works already begun.

Considerable sums were spent on repairs

by King John and King Henry III, and to a lesser extent by Edward III. It was held on behalf of the Lancastrians in the Wars of the Roses and was besieged twice, in 1462 and 1464. On the second occasion, when the assault was directed by Richard Neville, Earl of Warwick, the great 'Kingmaker', the castle fell after the walls were pounded with artillery. It deteriorated still further until it was rehabilitated by two owners between the mid-eighteenth and early twentieth centuries.

BAMPTON Nr Tiverton, Devon
(SS 959225) A
The remains of a motte castle beside the River Batham have been found here. Bampton was a motte castle probably of the twelfth century. It may have been held against King Stephen.

BAMPTON Oxfordshire
(SP 310031)
A motte castle was raised at Bampton by Queen Matilda during the reign of Stephen, in about 1142 — the year she escaped from Oxford Castle allegedly in only a nightgown. Bampton was taken by Stephen and later destroyed.

BANBURY Oxfordshire
(SP 454404) A
There is practically nothing to see of Banbury Castle, but it is included because its original formation has been carefully calculated by recent excavation. Some of the houses in Castle Street were repaired in the mid-seventeenth century using stone blocks which were part of the castle's masonry. Fragments have been found of towers and wall.

The castle was built in the early twelfth century by the Bishop of Lincoln, though it was of a more domestic than military character. In the reign of King John, the castle was strengthened (1201–7, according to Pipe Rolls). Then, sometime later in the thirteenth century (or possibly early fourteenth), it was remodelled into a concentric plan, the inner enclosure being a rectangle with one side angled outwards and the outer enclosure a rectangle. Both curtains were surrounded by ditches and both had corner towers and interval towers.

BARNARD CASTLE Durham   †
(NZ 049165) DOE
Barnard occupies a commanding position overlooking the Tees. Beginning as a small fortified enclosure of the late eleventh or early twelfth century, and belonging to the Baliol family, it developed over several stages into a considerable 6½-acre roughly oblong enclosure (thirteenth and fourteenth centuries). This was divided into four baileys, or wards: the inner ward inside the smaller stone walled enclosure, the middle ward to the south, the Town ward to the east, and the outer ward which is about equal to the other three together and most of which is bounded by sheer cliff.

The most interesting feature of Barnard is its cylindrical great tower, which is perched

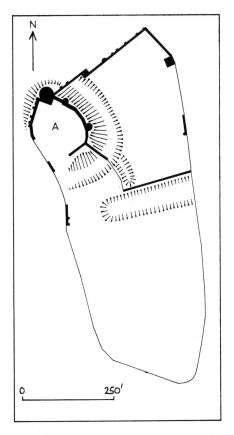

Barnard Castle: note in north-west corner the cylindrical great tower with a forebuilding. A=inner ward

183

at the north-west of the inner ward astride the curtain. Known as the Round Tower, and built of sandstone blocks which contrast with the rougher masonry of the curtain, it is about 36ft across and 40ft tall, with a battered plinth, though it was taller in its heyday. There are signs that the tower, of early thirteenth-century construction, was raised on the ruins of an even earlier structure. The Round Tower is unusual for having a forebuilding. To the south-west of the tower and projecting from a narrow range of rooms beside it are the remains of a one-storey thirteenth-century great hall.

Barnard was besieged by Alexander II, King of Scotland, in 1216. It was still held by the Baliols, though for a long time the possession was contested with the bishops of Durham. A descendant of these Baliols was John, who became King of Scotland in 1292. When he was deposed in 1296, Barnard passed to the Durham bishop, but it was granted in c.1300 by Edward I to the Earl of Warwick. It was held for a time by Richard, Duke of Gloucester (later Richard III), through his wife who was the daughter of Richard Neville, Earl of Warwick (the 'Kingmaker'). A white boar (Gloucester's emblem) is carved on a window soffit in the west wall of the inner bailey. Excavations are in progress.

BARNSTAPLE Devon
(SS 557332) A

William the Conqueror had considerable trouble in Devon in the first years of his new order in England: Devonians did not accept the Conquest without a fight. A motte castle was built here in William's reign by one of his followers, Judhael, who was probably responsible for the clearance of twenty-three houses on the site to make room for it (Domesday Book). A cylindrical shell keep was built round the motte top early in the twelfth century and further improvements were made later in the same century. The motte remains.

BARNWELL Nr Oundle,
Northamptonshire   (TL 049853)

There are traces of a possibly twelfth-century motte castle beside the thirteenth-century building that is Barnwell Castle. The stone structure was started c.1265 and

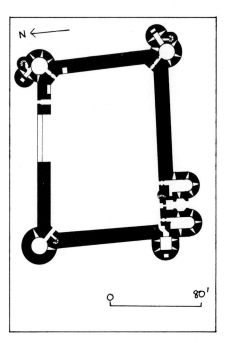

Barnwell (after Simpson): note the cluster of turrets in the north and east corners of the enclosure

is quadrangular, with cylinder towers on the north-east, north-west and south-west corners. On the south-east corner is a twin-towered gatehouse, whose exterior ends are D-ended. The quadrangle walls are of military dimensions: 30ft tall and over 12ft thick. The two northern towers have the unusual feature of their staircases being inside another adjacent round turret, whilst a third turret, also adjacent, contained the garderobes, providing an irregular trilobe plan for each tower. The castle is a ruin and is open only on certain days.

BARWICK-IN-ELMET West Yorkshire
(SE 398375)

A motte castle of the twelfth century contains some stone walling. It was raised in the reign of Stephen, and may have been an adulterine castle.

BASING Hampshire
(SU 663526) C

Basing is famous for the role it played in the Civil War. In that time it was a fortified

184

house which was defended valiantly for three years by the Marquess of Winchester, its owner, on behalf of the King. The house stood on the remains of a much earlier structure, an earthwork enclosure with bailey, which had stone additions of the thirteenth and fourteenth centuries. There have been excavations recently, but so far these have not yet clarified the early history of the castle.

BEAUDESERT Warwickshire
(SP 157662) A

An earthwork enclosure, with a flat-topped oval motte, dating probably from the twelfth century. Stonework has been found in the enclosure but it is too scanty to suggest any definite shape of castle that may have been built there.

BEDFORD †
(TL 053497) A

Bedford began as a motte castle of the late eleventh century, near the Ouse which flows through the town. Sometime late in Henry I's reign or early in Stephen's, the castle received important stonework. This included a shell keep on the motte. At the same time, or later, a cylindrical great tower was raised inside. There is a thirteenth-century drawing of these two structures in a manuscript of Matthew Paris's *Chronica Majora* (now at Corpus Christi College, Cambridge), which describes the great siege of 1224. The castle was enlarged to a rectangular stone curtain enclosure with towers, the south wall of which bordered the river and contained a wall-tower acting as a water-gate. Recent excavations revealed several features. One was part of the moat along the inner bailey to the west of the motte. This moat was lined with stone. It is thought that the motte was surrounded by a stone-lined ditch. Other stretches of ditch along the sides of the outer bailey, at west and east, have also been revealed. To the west of the motte are the foundations of a Norman rectangular hall. The motte was lowered by digging out the top layers after the 1224 siege, and the remainder of the castle was destroyed at the command of Henry III.

A description of the siege was written by Matthew Paris, and another appears in the *Dunstable Chronicle*. The castle was held by Faulkes de Bréauté, an aggressive and powerful lord who had taken prisoner one of three Dunstable justices who had imposed fines upon him in their court. The King, Henry III, ordered the release of the justice, Henry de Braibroc, but de Bréauté refused. Instead, he left the castle in the care of his brother William while he went westwards to Wales for support. The King thereupon decided to besiege Bedford Castle. Requisitions were sent out to many parts of the country for supplies: men and arms were ordered from Dorset and Cumberland; 25,000 quarrels came from the royal arsenal at Corfe Castle; carpenters trudged across the countryside from Windsor; ropes, picks and men to operate them came from Cambridge and Northampton; quarrymen came in from various parts of Bedfordshire to make the stone balls for the siege engines. By 20 June, the King was ready to begin siege operations. Engines placed round the outer bailey of the castle opened fire. This was vigorously returned by the defenders.

The barbican fell first. Then the engines succeeded in breaching the walls of the outer bailey. The defenders withdrew inside the inner bailey and into the shell keep with its tower. Henry ordered wooden belfries to be moved towards the inner bailey and archers showered arrows into the bailey while miners began to dig a tunnel under the wall of the bailey. They emerged successfully inside and troops followed through the tunnel, and after hand-to-hand fighting in the bailey captured it. The King now ordered the great tower to be undermined, and after several days' hard digging, the foundations of the great tower were reached and the wooden props erected and then fired. The earth of the motte gave way and the great tower split asunder. This was the signal for the defenders and their wives to surrender.

The King had the ringleaders, some twenty-four or so men, hanged, and he ordered the castle to be de-fortified. The remaining walls were reduced in height. Faulkes returned to see his brother hanging in the castle grounds, and he threw himself on the King's mercy. He was spared.

If the great tower was cylindrical, its collapse as a result of undermining is a cogent argument against the received superiority of cylindrical towers to rectangular towers. The motte can be seen.

BEESTON Cheshire ††
(SJ 537593) DOE

The sandstone crag at Beeston is about 500ft above sea level at the top, and it commands one of the gaps in the hill range around Chester on the south and east. In the early years of the thirteenth century the land belonged to the enormously powerful and independent Ranulf, Earl of Chester, who in about 1220 began to build Beeston Castle. He died in 1232 and his son died in 1237, whereupon the castle passed to the Crown, in the person of Henry III, who enlarged it, using it as a prison for captives in border wars with Wales. In the first years of the fourteenth century, when Edward, Prince of Wales (later Edward II), took an interest in the castle, major new works were undertaken, including heightening three towers in the inner bailey, and inserting a drawbridge and an extensive wall before the bridge. Beeston was nearly finished by the end of Edward II's reign (1327). The names of some of the masons and carpenters who worked there in the 1300s are documented: Master Robert, a carpenter, who also worked at Chester, Scarborough and Windsor in his time, received 6d a day.

The castle consisted of a strongly fortified upper enclosure with flanking D-ended towers and a substantial gatehouse, opening southwards into the lower bailey. The curtain round the tower bailey had seven towers, all cylindrical, and an easterly gatehouse. Ridgway commented: 'Full use was made of the natural defences afforded by the nature of the site.' Tall, strong walls were not needed on the north or west sides of the crag. Beeston was maintained in good repair throughout the fourteenth and for part of the fifteenth centuries, but in Henry VIII's reign Leland described it as ruinous.

It has many interesting features: one is that the well was cut into the sandstone crag to a depth of about 370ft, a prodigious feat. (see also Bolingbroke Castle.)

BELSAY Northumberland
(NZ 085786) C

Belsay is on the western side of the main road from Newcastle upon Tyne to Jedburgh in Scotland. Built in the mid-fourteenth century, it began as a substantial rectangular tower of about 70ft in height to the top of the tallest bartizan, with three storeys, approximately 55ft by 47ft, and with walls 9ft thick. The tower is an imposing structure. It has four bartizans in the top storey, each of them battlemented and machicolated, as is the rest of the parapet. On the top storey a brattice of stonework projects to cover the entrance door lower down, which is between two projecting wings. The tower has several unusual features. The roof of the spiral staircase is partly vaulted; the largest room at ground level has pointed tunnel vaulting and was used as a kitchen. A mansion was added to the castle in the seventeenth century. The tower may have been built by the same masons who built Chipchase and Cartington (qq.v.), as all three have the same masons' marks.

BELVOIR Leicestershire
(SK 820337) Stately home open

Many centuries before the great stately home of the earls and dukes of Rutland was erected here, a motte castle was built on a natural mound by Robert de Todeni (or Todnei) sometime before 1089. Whatever structures were raised afterwards, and these are thought to have included a shell keep, the castle was destroyed by King John. There was some rebuilding, but so much alteration has been done by owners in medieval times, by earls of Rutland in the sixteenth and seventeenth centuries and by dukes of Rutland in the nineteenth, that it bears no resemblance to its original shape.

BENEFIELD Northamptonshire
(SP 987884)

A rectangular moated enclosure site once contained a castle in the twelfth century, and this was confiscated by John c.1208.

BENINGTON Hertfordshire
(TL 296236) O

Benington was raised as a motte castle early in the twelfth century. It is encircled by a wide and deep dry moat. Sometime in the mid-twelfth century a small stone tower was erected on the motte, nearly square in plan, about 45ft by 41ft, with walls 7–8ft thick, the masonry of flint rubble and ashlar dressings. In about 1176 Henry II ordered the tower to be demolished — the Pipe Rolls record payment for 100 picks for the job — but Benington is mentioned in the last years of the century and again in about 1212. One additionally interesting feature at Benington is that on one side there is a depression with two ponds and traces of a dam. This suggests that the depression could have been flooded for defence purposes, as at Saltwood in Kent (q.v.).

BERKELEY Gloucestershire †
(ST 685989) O
A motte castle was raised here on rising ground overlooking the plains between the Severn and the Cotswolds, probably by William FitzOsbern, one of the Conqueror's commanders at Hastings, who led the invasion of south Wales by the Normans. In the mid-twelfth century the castle became the property of Robert Fitzhardinge, a supporter of Henry II. He received permission to build a castle of stone. The motte was then sliced vertically and trimmed to make it more cylindrical, whereupon the sides were revetted in red sandstone with buttresses, and the stonework continued upwards above the top of the motte. This shell keep enclosing a motte is about 62ft tall. It has three small semi-cylindrical turrets in the stonework. A forebuilding was constructed on the wall line between two of the turrets. One of the turrets contains a prison cell in which Edward II is said to have been confined before being murdered in another part of the castle 'with a hoote brooche put thro the secrete place posteriale' — the gruesomely appropriate end for a medieval homosexual.

The bailey in which this unusual shell keep stood was surrounded by a stonework curtain which makes the inner ward. There was a range of buildings inside, which have been replaced by later structures, many of them of fourteenth-century work.

The castle is still in the hands of direct descendants of the Fitzhardinges, the Berkeley family.

BERKHAMSTED Hertfordshire ††
(SP 996083) DOE
One excellent way to see at a quick glance

what a typical motte castle looked like (without its wooden tower and palisading) in the eleventh century is to visit Berkhamsted Castle. And there is a bonus because you can also see how motte castles were converted to stone. Enough of the stone curtain round the bailey is standing and there are also traces of the shell keep on the motte summit that replaced the wooden palisade round the wooden tower (see also Pickering). A further bonus is provided in the restoration of the double moat around the whole castle.

Berkhamsted motte castle belonged to the Conqueror's half-brother Robert of Mortain and is mentioned in Domesday Book. The motte was built to about 45ft tall, flattened to produce an oval top of about 60ft across. The bailey, oblong and about 450ft by about 300ft, is joined to a segment of the motte base. Both motte and bailey were (and are) surrounded by a wet moat, giving the appearance of a castle standing in a lake. Outside the moat is a rampart, which in turn was almost completely encircled by another moat. This produced a concentric castle plan, though it is not likely that the outer earthworks were raised or the outer moat dug before the thirteenth century, and Berkhamsted is not reckoned among the concentric castles.

The castle received its first stonework in the twelfth century, when it belonged to the Crown but was held by various lessees. One was Thomas Becket (later the martyr Archbishop of Canterbury) who held it from about 1155–65 and who spent money on 'the king's houses on the motte', which means buildings. It is thought that he raised the shell keep, some 60ft in diameter, where the wooden palisade stood, and the curtain round the bailey. Both are twelfth-century masonry in flint and rubble with ashlar dressings. Further improvements were made by later lessees — and after 1200 directly by King John — including wing walls up the south slope of the motte from the bailey and round towers along the bailey curtain.

In 1216 Berkhamsted was besieged by Prince Louis of France who may have built the bastion-shaped earth projections in the outermost rampart beyond the northern edge of the outer moat. If so, he would have used them as platforms for siege artillery.

187

The castle fell after a continuous barrage by day for about a fortnight. After John's death, his widow Isabella was allowed to live at the castle and some further works were done. Then in 1227 Henry III gave it to his brother Richard, Duke of Cornwall, who resided there quite often over the next forty years or so. He may have built a three-storeyed tower along the western part of the curtain: some foundations of a square tower have been identified. There is also thought to have been a tower inside the shell on the motte, mentioned in a survey of 1327.

In the fourteenth century the castle was given to Edward I's wife, who held it from c.1300 to 1317, and it was then occupied by Edward II's wife until 1326 and up to 1336 by her son John of Eltham. The Black Prince was the next holder. In 1360 Berkhamsted was used as a place of honourable confinement for King John of France who had been captured at the Battle of Poitiers (1356).

BERRY POMEROY Nr Torquay, †
Devon (SX 839623) O
Berry Pomeroy is on a wooded hill near the River Dart. It is a quadrangular fortified house with an unusual gatehouse whose towers are polygonal. Grooves for the portcullis can still be seen. Over the gateway there is a guardroom, with several loopholes, and this is divided by a wall supported by pillars and almost rounded arches. Berry Pomeroy was probably begun in the twelfth century and later enlarged. The castle became the property of Edward Seymour, Duke of Somerset, who was Lord Protector for part of the reign of the boy king Edward VI (1547–53). Somerset did an extraordinary thing at Berry Pomeroy. He started to build inside the quadrangle a new Tudor mansion which was completed in Elizabeth I's time. The mansion is totally out of keeping with the medieval ruins around it.

BERWICK-UPON-TWEED †
Northumberland (NT 994535) DOE
Berwick Castle and Town Fortifications stand on rising ground between the east bank of the mouth of the Tweed and the North Sea. We are concerned only with the castle which was begun in the twelfth century and of which the only remains are a west curtain wall with three cylindrical flanking towers.

The castle represented a very small part of the area of the fortified town, positioned in its north-west corner. The north-west to south-west wall still standing reaches the edge of the River Tweed. At that point there is the ruin of a cylindrical gun-tower of the fifteenth century. The wall leading down the bluff to the gun-tower is called the White Wall. The last and steepest part of it is stepped like a roof step gable, and behind it is an incredibly steep and long flight of stairs known as Breakneck Stairs. At the top of the bluff are the remains of another cylindrical gun-tower. Berwick Castle was originally an irregular quadrilateral with cylindrical and polygonal flanking towers.

BEWCASTLE Cumbria
(NY 566747) Open by appointment
This was an enclosure castle of uncertain origin. The remains include a small gate-tower on the west side.

BICKLEIGH Nr Tiverton, Devon †
(SS 937068) O
A Norman motte castle of the late eleventh or early twelfth century was dismantled in the mid-twelfth. Sometime in the period a small stone chapel was built inside the bailey and it is still standing. In the fifteenth century the powerful Courtenay family raised a fortified quadrangular mansion on the site, incorporating some of the earlier buildings. An interesting gatehouse of the fourteenth century, which has earlier (Norman) bases to the imposts of the vaulted entry, two rooms on either side opening into the arch, a great hall stretching across the top of the arch at first-floor level, and at one time had a second-storey, which was destroyed.

BIGGLESWADE Bedfordshire
(TL 184445) A
A recent survey by aerial photography revealed at Biggleswade the remains of a motte castle with double ditch and a single one about the bailey. Both are curiously segmented with what appear to have been baulks across the ditching (see *Bedfordshire Archaeological Journal* Vol III, pp. 15-18).

BISHOP'S CASTLE Nr Clun, Shropshire (SO 323891) A

This was a motte castle, probably of the twelfth century. A shell keep was constructed at a later date, and fragments of stonework down the slope of the motte suggest that there was a wall connecting the shell to a curtain round the bailey. Fragments can be seen near the Castle Hotel.

BISHOP'S STORTFORD †
Hertfordshire (TL 490215) O

This is sometimes known also as Waytemore Castle. Remains of the castle stand beside Bridge Street. It began as a motte castle. A rectangular great tower was built on the motte top early in the twelfth century. The northern end of the tower was slightly curved outwards. In the north-east and south-east corners were sunken chambers. The castle was improved in King John's reign, and a licence to crenellate was granted sometime in the mid-1300s, which seems oddly late in the day considering its history. The castle was used as a local gaol in the seventeenth century. Remains of the tower and the chambers can still be seen on the summit which is surrounded by flint rubble walling.

BISHOP'S WALTHAM Hampshire (SU 552173) DOE

This was a fortified palace begun by Henry of Blois, brother to King Stephen, and Bishop of Winchester from 1129–47. The palace buildings were ranged round a quadrangle. One was a square tower of three storeys, another was a gatehouse. Possibly the earliest structure was the twelfth-century apsidal chapel that has a Romanesque crypt.

BITCHFIELD Nr Belsay, Northumberland (NZ 091771) C

Like Belsay Castle, this tower has had a mansion built beside one of its walls. The tower, rectangular in plan, is three-storeyed, about 31ft by about 23ft. Each storey contained one main room, with a staircase leading to the next. On the first floor a garderobe was inserted in one corner. The tower walls are about 4ft thick along three sides and over 6ft along the north side on the ground floor. The tower has been restored.

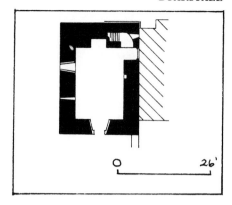

Bitchfield: plan of ground floor of tower. Hatched part = east portion of later house adjoining

BLENKINSOP Nr Haltwhistle, Northumberland (NY 665645)

Blenkinsop is named after its builder, Thomas, who in 1349 was granted a licence to fortify a tower-house. It was square, with 7ft-thick walls, a ditch on two sides and a stream along the third. Some masonry from Hadrian's Wall appears to have been used in the stonework. The castle was later absorbed in rebuilding work of the 1880s.

BLETCHINGLEY Surrey (TQ 323506) C

An early enclosure of earthworks was fortified by the addition of a rectangular tower, with walls about 5ft thick, late in the twelfth century. The castle was associated with Thomas Becket, the martyr Archbishop of Canterbury, and it was held for a time by the powerful de Clare family (see Caerphilly). Bletchingley was besieged and taken by royal forces in the wars between Henry III and some of his barons in the 1260s: 5ft walls were not well able to withstand much bombardment with stone shot from trebuchets or mangonels in the mid-thirteenth century. The castle was destroyed but some earthworks remain.

BOARSTALL Buckinghamshire (SP 624143) NT   not open at present

A fortified manor house of the late fourteenth century which was remodelled much later. It has an interesting gatehouse remaining from its medieval beginnings. Boarstall

189

was licensed in 1312, and was a quadrangular-plan building. It was garrisoned during the Civil War by Parliament, captured by Royalists and retaken by Parliament.

BODIAM Sussex   ††
(TQ 785256) NT

Bodiam Castle stands near the River Rother where it forms the boundary between Kent and Sussex. It was built by a veteran of Edward III's wars in France, a knight with the picturesque name of Sir Edward Dalyngrygge. He was granted a licence to fortify his house against invasion from France, then a real danger, for the nearby Cinque Port of Rye had been sacked by the French only a few years earlier.

Dalyngrygge took his licence as one to start building afresh, and he put up his stone castle a little way from the site of his manor house. He raised a symmetrical quadrangular castle and created an artificial lake round it by letting the river into a rectangle of marshy ground (see chapter 9). The four corners of the quadrangle were fortified with substantial four-storeyed cylindrical towers, the east and west walls having square interval towers and the south wall a square postern. The north front has a formidable twin-rectilinear towered gatehouse. These towers were later provided with gun-ports for covering fire all round the castle by adapting arrow loops (the fortifications are elaborated on p. 91).

Bodiam's defences were never severely

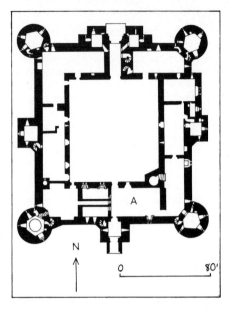

Bodiam: ground-floor plan. A=Lord's hall

tested: the castle was half-heartedly attacked in 1484; and in the Civil War a Parliamentary army threatened it with bombardment which produced an immediate surrender by the garrison. Thereafter, Bodiam deteriorated until in 1917 a new owner, the Earl Curzon (once Viceroy of India) rescued it and restored its outside elevations to their medieval appearance.

Bodiam: machicolations over the rear entrance

(above) Bolingbroke: an aerial view of the remains of the interesting polygonal enclosure with cylindrical (and one polygonal) flanking towers, erected in the 1220s by Ranulf, Earl of Chester, builder of Beeston in Cheshire. Only the footings remain, but excavations are in progress which may provide additional detail

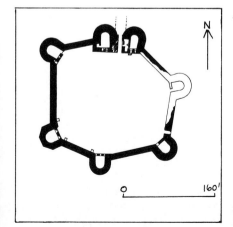

Bolingbroke: plan

BOLINGBROKE Lincolnshire   †
(TF 349649) DOE

Ranulf, Earl of Chester, a powerful baron of the early thirteenth century, with lands in many parts of England, built two major castles in the 1220s. One was Beeston in Cheshire, the other was Bolingbroke in Lincolnshire. Of Beeston there are considerable remains; of Bolingbroke, practically none. But we have an account from the seventeenth century, and recent excavations described in *Mediaeval Archaeology* have revealed some of its foundations. The layout appears to have been as follows: an irregular hexagonal curtained enclosure of stone with substantial and thick walled semi-cylindrical (almost D-ended) towers on four angles; on the fifth the tower was semi-cylindrical but its base was semi-octagonal and there was a twin-semi-cylindrical towered gatehouse on the north-east angle. The seventeenth-century description speaks of the castle lying in a square, the area within the walls being about 1½ acres. It had four strong forts. The gatehouse was a strong, uniform building.

Bolingbroke became the property of the Earl of Lancaster in 1311 and passed eventually to John of Gaunt, Duke of Lancaster, fourth son of Edward III, when

191

he married Blanche of Lancaster in 1359. Henry Bolingbroke, later Henry IV (1399–1413) was born at the castle. Works costing more than £1,000 were carried out at the castle during the reigns of Henry IV and of his son, Henry V (1413–22), and also later in the sixteenth century.

The castle was held for the king in the Civil War, though by that time it had decayed considerably, and the only part of it capable of being defended was the gatehouse. It was besieged by Parliament for several days and then the garrison surrendered. It was thereupon slighted. Remains of three of the towers were visible, according to a map of 1718, but today the foundations recently excavated are the only traces to be seen.

BOLSOVER Derbyshire †
(SK 471707) DOE
An enclosure castle with an outer bailey, whose stone enclosure resembled that of Eynsford in Kent, the original Bolsover was built in the twelfth century. It received a great tower of stone c. 1173–4. More domestic buildings were added in the thirteenth century. Then it was allowed to deteriorate after Edward I and his successors leased the buildings to people not interested in fortification, and by the seventeenth century it was ruinous.

It was obtained by Charles Cavendish, one of the flamboyant and ambitious sons of Bess of Hardwick who began to build Chatsworth. Cavendish decided to rebuild Bolsover in the medieval style, but with palatial accommodation inside. His work was chiefly the 'Little Castle', which resembled a late medieval tower-house with battlements and corner turrets, though it was not a properly fortified residence. The castle was taken by the Parliamentarians in the Civil War and slighted. But it survived and was renovated.

BOLTON Nr Leyburn, North †
Yorkshire (SE 034918) O
High on the north slope of Wensleydale stands the considerable fortified manor house of Bolton Castle. Granted a licence in 1379, Lord Scrope, Richard II's Chancellor, had already begun to build a formidable quadrangle with substantial rectangular

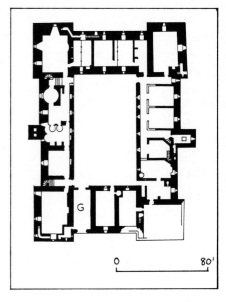

Bolton: plan of ground floor. G = gatehouse

corner towers. The builder was John Lewyn, a noted master mason who also worked at Raby, Bywell and Dunstanburgh, and the building contract for the work has survived. It was constructed from local stone, with quoins and arches in freestone from Greets Quarry a little further away. The owner's quarters were separated from those of his retainers. All doorways into the inner buildings from the courtyard were filled with portcullises. The only entrance to the castle in Scrope's time was a gatehouse in the eastern wing, protected by the south-east tower which at ground level contained a guardhouse. The vaulted passage in the gatehouse was covered at each end by a portcullis.

Bolton was held by one of the Scropes for the king in the Civil War, and it was besieged for over a year (1644–5) by Parliament before the garrison surrendered.

BOTHAL Northumberland
(NZ 240866) C
Bothal Castle stands by the River Wansbeck, not far from Morpeth. Thought but not yet proved to have begun as a motte castle of Norman times, Bothal was a fourteenth-century manor house which was

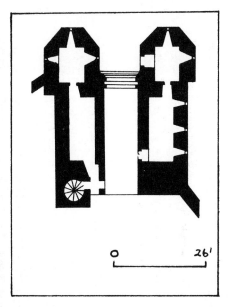

Bothal: plan of ground floor of gatehouse-tower

fortified by its owner by licence in the 1340s. The castle at one time consisted of a walled enclosure with towers and buildings. The main feature was, and still is, a splendid square gatehouse-tower. This has twin turrets with semi-octagonal front ends flanking the entrance which is a passage with a vaulted roof in which are murder-holes and portcullis grooves. On the gatehouse first floor is the great chamber, or hall, which was considerably embellished in later centuries. A survey of the 1570s recorded that Bothal was notable for 'fair gardens and orchards, wherein grow all kinds of herbs and flowers, and fine apples, plums of all kind, pears, nuttes, wardens, cherries . . .'.

BOURN Cambridgeshire
(TL 322562) C

Bourn was an earthwork enclosure with wooden buildings and was erected in the last years of the reign of the Conqueror. It was demolished in the time of Henry III, and Bourn Hall was built across part of the site. The original castle was held by the Picot family, one of whom was sheriff of Cambridgeshire and is mentioned in Domesday Book.

BOURNE Lincolnshire
(TF 095199) A

A motte castle of unusual plan was built here. The mound stood inside a bailey surrounded by a ditch and further encircled by another ditch, in concentric plan. It appears to have been raised in the later part of the twelfth century. Stonework was added in the thirteenth century, including a great tower and a gatehouse, but there is no masonry to be seen.

BOWES Durham †
(NY 992135) DOE

This is one of Henry II's great tower castles. It was built in a corner of an old Roman fort overlooking the Yorkshire approach to the Stainforth Pass between the years 1170 and 1187. The recorded cost of about £600 may not represent the full cost, for the great tower, at 82ft by 60ft and probably reaching about 70ft, was a massive structure for its time, with pilaster buttresses at the corners and in the wall centres and with walls about 11ft thick. It had mural chambers, vaulted passages in the walls, an off-centre cross-wall with the larger sector possibly divided by a second cross-wall, and a forebuilding on the east wall (now vanished).

Bowes great tower is remarkable in that it appears to have been constructed on its own, with no buildings around it. It was built chiefly as a defence against Scottish raids. The tower is now ruinous.

BRAMBER Nr Steyning, Sussex †
(TQ 185107) NT

This castle began as a motte inside a D-shaped bailey beside the River Adur, probably in the 1070s. The bailey itself is on a natural knoll which was flattened, and the motte was raised to about 40ft in height in the middle. It was constructed of chalk, mixed with clay and flints. The bailey, surrounded at first with a wooden palisade, was in the early twelfth century given a stone curtain of flint and pebble. A square-plan gatehouse was inserted in the curtain, about 38ft by 40ft, pierced by an entrance. Later in the century the entrance was blocked so that the gatehouse could be given another storey and thus converted to a gatehouse-tower. An alternative entrance to the castle was provided by a gateway in the curtain nearby.

Recent excavations have revealed the existence of buildings inside the curtain in the neighbourhood of the gateway, that the curtain appears to have had more than one period of construction, and a number of other slightly confusing features that will in time be clarified with further work. Bramber's chapel was not erected inside the bailey but in a separate enclosure, surrounded by ditching, just south of the gatehouse-tower.

Only fragments remain of the buildings.

BRAMPTON BRYAN Hereford & Worcester (SO 370726) C

This fortress belonged to the Harley family. It has been considerably altered and extended, and the original form obscured. Brampton was a motte castle of the (?) early twelfth century which received in the fourteenth century a curtain with towers and a square-plan gatehouse with a long barbican projecting outwards. This gatehouse can be detected in the present structure.

BRANCEPETH Durham (NZ 223377) C

Brancepeth Castle is largely a nineteenth-century restoration round the remains of a fourteenth-century castle that belonged to the Nevilles. The Neville castle followed an even earlier Norman building.

BRANDON Nr Wolston, Warwickshire (SP 408759)

An earthwork enclosure of the early twelfth century whose ditches were provided with water from the River Avon by means of sluices. In the thirteenth century (c.1226), a great tower of unusual shape was added, which was rectangular with the centres of its two longer walls indented, providing a plan of an 'H'. The indents were blank arches, each 5ft deep. The tower was held for Henry III during his war with Simon de Montfort and the barons, 1264–5. Some earthworks and some stone fragments remain.

BREDWARDINE Hereford & Worcester (SO 335444) A

Traces of the stone walls of a rectangular great tower, about 78ft by about 45ft, are on a platform here beside the River Wye. The castle is thought to have been built in the second half of the twelfth century.

BRIDGNORTH Shropshire †
(SO 717927) O

An enclosure castle on the narrow ridge of rock in Bridgnorth beside the River Severn, it was first mentioned in 1102. But its principal feature, a square great tower, was not built until the reign of Henry II who had taken the castle from the Mortimers (supporters of Stephen) in 1155. The great tower, of which only some ruined walls remain, is of cut and dressed sandstone, with pilaster buttresses. It leans about 10 degrees off the vertical. There was a forebuilding, which has gone. The castle was severely damaged during the Civil War.

BRIDGWATER Somerset
(ST 302378) A

William de Briwerre was licensed to build a castle at Bridgwater in c.1200. It appears to have been a rectangular enclosure. There is part of a water-gate beside the River Parrett in the town. During the Civil War Bridgwater Castle was fortified by the Royalists but, nevertheless, fell to the Parliamentarians.

BRIGHTWELL Berkshire
(SU 578908) A

The mound of a motte castle of the early twelfth century can be seen near the village church.

BRIMPSFIELD Gloucestershire
(SO 941148) A

There are some fragments on the site of a thirteenth-century castle here. The shape has not been determined.

BRINKLOW Warwickshire
(SP 438796) A

A motte castle was raised at Brinklow in the early twelfth century. The motte was about 40ft high. The bailey, surrounded by ditch and ramparts, was cut in two by another ditch with ramparts.

BRISTOL Avon
(ST 594732) A

There is very little to see of the ancient castle of Bristol. A motte castle was raised on land between the Avon and the Frome, probably in the reign of the Conqueror. In King Stephen's reign, Bristol received a rectangular great tower said to have been about 90ft by 75ft and perhaps about 70ft tall (cf. Canterbury, to which it has been compared: *King's Works*). This great tower was described in the thirteenth century (in Robert of Gloucester's Chronicle) as the flower of English great towers. It had four corner turrets, one higher than the other three. Parts of the foundations were exposed in 1948 but no coherent plan could be deduced. Excavations of 1951 revealed traces of a substantial curtain wall, and work of the late 1960s produced evidence of a gateway and some tunnelling. The city wall at one time abutted the castle at each end of its west side.

The castle was taken over by Henry II after the 1173–4 revolt led by his eldest son, and it remained in Crown hands up to the 1650s when, already in a state of decay, it was destroyed.

BROMWICH West Midlands
(SP 158904)
A motte castle of unknown date was excavated here in 1968–9. Evidence of timber plank lining of the motte was uncovered.

BRONSIL Hereford & Worcester
(SO 749372)
A few remains of a fortified quadrangular manor house, with corner and mid-wall towers, have been dated to the fifteenth century. The castle was surrounded by a moat.

BROUGH Cumbria   †
(NY 791141) DOE
Brough stands on a steep and prominent escarpment overlooking the south bank of the Swindale Beck, in one corner of the remains of a rectangular Roman fort. The first work was a roughly triangular enclosure of stone begun late in the eleventh century, making Brough one of the earliest castles in Britain to have stonework. There are several building periods. Part of the original curtain on the north side has characteristic Norman herringbone masonry. The castle belonged to the de Morvilles until it was surrendered to Henry II in 1173, when it was soon afterwards attacked by William the Lion, King of Scotland. The Scottish King captured Brough after a hard

fight. But he was himself captured by the English under the walls of Alnwick Castle later in 1174, and Brough was returned to Henry II who granted it to Theobald de Valoires. He erected a rectangular great tower upon the remains of a previous tower in the west angle of the enclosure in the wall circumference which had been destroyed in William the Lion's siege. The newer tower, about 55ft by about 40ft, was four-storeyed, built of sandstone dressed rubble, with pilaster buttresses on the angles and centrally in the north and south walls. It was restored much later on, in the seventeenth century, by Anne Clifford, Countess of Dorset, Pembroke and Montgomery (owner also of Brougham, q.v.). One of her works was the cylindrical tower in the south-east corner, called Clifford's Tower.

BROUGHAM Nr Penrith, Cumbria   †
(NY 537290) DOE
A roughly quadrilateral enclosure on the south bank of the River Eamont, Brougham received stonework in the time of Henry II, probably about 1170. One of the first buildings was a substantial square great tower built of sandstone rubble, having ashlar dressings. The tower has pilaster angle buttresses on north, west and south walls, and on the east wall is a forebuilding. The tower appears to have been erected in two stages, the first three storeys followed by a top storey whose stonework is of better quality than the earlier work. Other buildings were added in later periods, the last being by the aged Anne Clifford, Countess of Dorset, Pembroke and Montgomery, who had enormous wealth and was owner also of Appleby and Brough castles. Anne Clifford restored all three castles to make them habitable, and she died in Brougham Castle in 1678 at the (then) great age of almost ninety.

BROUGHTON Oxfordshire   †
(SP 418382) O
Broughton is substantially a sixteenth-century country house surrounded by a broad wet moat, with some fourteenth-century military remains such as towers and battlements. The moat used to be crossed by a causeway into a barbican. During the early part of the Civil War, the castle was used for

Brougham: the great tower complex

clandestine meetings of opponents of Charles I. When the Royalists won the first major battle of the war at nearby Edgehill, they raced on to Broughton and captured it.

BRYN AMLWG Shropshire
(SO 167846) C
Some remains of stone walling round an enclosure castle of the twelfth and thirteenth centuries, which had towers and a gatehouse, are to be found on this privately owned site.

BUCKDEN Cambridgeshire
(TL 192677) C
Buckden was for many years a residential palace, used by bishops of Lincoln, including the famous Robert Grosseteste (1190–1252), who may have built a hall on the site. In the late fifteenth century, considerable building works were undertaken, including a brick gatehouse, a rebuilt hall and chapel, and a great tower within the assemblage of other buildings, all surrounded by a moat and a stone curtain round the grounds, altering the palace into a castle by virtue of its fortifications.

BUCKINGHAM
(SP 695337) A
There was a motte castle on the north side of the Ouse in Buckingham, and it was sited in a loop in the river which acted as the bailey. It may have been a castle held by the Giffard family. The site has been covered by a church, for which the motte would have had

to be levelled, and so we do not know the original height of the motte. Stone foundations were discovered in excavations on the motte site.

BUNGAY Suffolk   †
(TM 336896) A
A motte castle erected in a loop of the Waveney at Bungay may date from the early twelfth century. The motte has been levelled. The castle was held by the Bigods who were powerful in East Anglia. Hugh Bigod, Earl of Norfolk, at first a supporter of Stephen in the king's war with his cousin Matilda, changed sides. In 1154 he still held Bungay, but in 1157 Henry II confiscated it, restoring it to the earl c.1164. Bigod then converted the castle to stone. The levelled motte received a substantial great tower of flint faced with sandstone, 70ft square, rising, it is estimated, to about 90ft, with walls 18ft thick. Only foundations up to the level of ground-floor loops remain. The great tower which had a cross-wall, and a staircase in the north wall, was given a forebuilding over an entrance on the south wall. One dramatic discovery in the excavations of the early 1930s was an uncompleted mining gallery dug under the south-west corner of the great tower. This may have been dug when, after Bigod had joined Henry II's eldest son, Prince Henry, in his unsuccessful 1173–4 revolt, the king confiscated Bungay (among other estates) and began to demolish the great tower. The demolition was stayed on payment of a

196

ransom, but the great tower decayed and was finally pulled down. It appears that it was later restored in some form. In the 1290s, Roger Bigod, descendant of Earl Hugh, was granted permission to rebuild Bungay. He built a multangular curtain enclosure (somewhat similar in concept to Framlingham, which had been erected by Hugh Bigod's son), but without flanking towers. In the west of the curtain is a pair of twin-cylindrical tower ends flanking an entrance. These are the remains of a gatehouse, and there is argument as to whether this is the work of the 1290s or of a much earlier date. Parts of the curtain and the gatehouse remain.

In the eighteenth century, it appears that a narrow house was built between the cylindrical tower ends. The drawbridge pit was found underneath the foundations of this house (demolished in the nineteenth century).

BURGH Suffolk
(TG 475046) DOE
This is the site of one of the famous forts of the Saxon Shore built by the Roman occupying forces in Britain along the east coast in the third century AD. It was called Gariannonum. In early Norman times a small motte castle was raised in one corner of the fort quadrangle. The mound was levelled in 1839, but the ditch that separated the mound from the bailey has been identified by aerial photography.

BURLEY Leicestershire
(SK 894119) A
Excavation of a motte castle of late eleventh-early twelfth-century origin was carried out in the 1930s.

BURTON-IN-LONSDALE North
Yorkshire (SD 649721) A
A motte castle with two baileys, probably of the early twelfth-century. It is first mentioned in 1129, though the estate is noted in Domesday Book as belonging to the king. The motte was constructed of sand coated with clay. The bases of the ditches were paved with stones of varying sizes (cf. Bedford). The castle's history from the early twelfth century to the early fourteenth century is unknown, but in 1322 it was confiscated from the Mowbrays who held it in opposition to Edward II. The mound is visible.

BURWELL Nr Cambridge,
Cambridgeshire (TL 587661) A
A rectangular banked platform enclosed by a wide moat, this castle was excavated in the 1930s and found to have been raised on the site of a late Roman-British structure. The castle was built in the time of King Stephen, possibly ordered by the king himself. The diggings revealed stonework remains of a curtain wall and a gatehouse of square plan with buttresses angled at 45° on the two corners projecting into the ditch. The walls were made of local clunch, but it is clear the castle was not completed.

It appears that in c.1142–4, the king ordered castles to be built to deal with his principal adversary, Geoffrey de Mandeville. The latter was killed in 1144 and this may explain why the castle was never finished. There are some fragments near the church.

BUTTERCRAMBE Nr York, North
Yorkshire (SE 533584) O
William de Stuteville, who held Knaresborough Castle from about 1173 to 1203, was granted a licence to fortify a castle at Buttercrambe in c.1200. The castle was probably a motte castle, though the remains have been greatly disfigured by later building work. If it was a motte castle, the date makes it a late example of the kind. Motte castles were still 'thrown up' when a fortress was needed quickly for some purpose in the thirteenth century, and of course with their wooden towers they made excellent watchtowers. The motte is still visible.

BYTHAM Nr Bourne, Lincolnshire †
(SK 992186) A
On a hill overlooking the village of Little Bytham stands the mound of the motte castle built possibly before 1086 and certainly by 1140. The earthworks contain traces of stonework, though not enough to say anything about the form which it took.

BYWELL Northumberland
(NZ 049618) C
The main feature of Bywell was its huge gatehouse-tower (today, the only substan-

tial remainder of the castle). Built in the 1430s by the Nevilles, Bywell backed on to the River Tyne. The gatehouse is a three-storeyed structure about 60ft wide and 38ft deep. A 10ft arch and passage lead through the centre of the ground floor whose main rooms on either side are vaulted. Bywell gatehouse has an unusual style of machicolation on the battlements: there is a short stretch directly over the central arch, and on the tower corners are the remains of octagonal turrets that are machicolated. The entrance was protected by a portcullis. At the back of the passage is an entrance to a staircase to the floors above and this was protected by a substantial iron gate.

CAINHOE Nr Clophill, Bedfordshire   †
(TL 097374) A
An earthwork castle of the late eleventh or early twelfth century, with a motte and three baileys well protected by ditches. Stonework was added but as yet the nature of the castle in its final form is not known. Some excavations were undertaken in 1972–3.

CAISTER Nr Yarmouth, Norfolk   ††
(TG 504123) O
Caister Castle was built between 1432 and 1446 by a self-made adventurer and knight, Sir John Fastolf, who acquired a fortune after many years of distinguished military service. The building work is particularly interesting because many details of the materials, labour and costs have survived. One of these was a note of an attempt by one mason, Henry Wood, to overcharge for his work.

Caister was built of locally made brick, probably from clay on the banks of the Bure about a mile away. The castle has a double enclosure in the form of two quadrangles surrounded entirely by water. The outer quadrangle was linked to the inner by a drawbridge, and was itself approached from outside by another drawbridge, on its north side. The inner quadrangle contained the main living quarters. The principal feature of the castle, however, was, and still is, the very tall, slim cylindrical great tower, 90ft with five storeys of residential accommodation, but equipped with machicolated para-

Cainhoe: an aerial view of motte-and-bailey remains

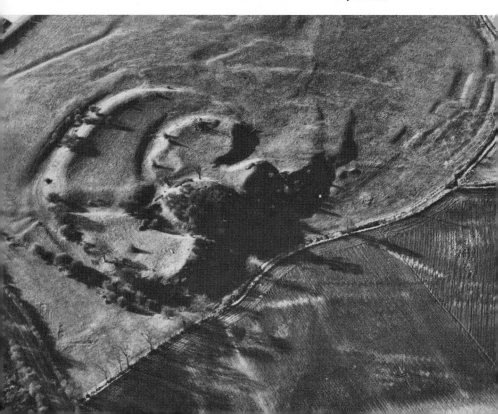

Caister

pet, gun-ports at several levels, and constructed of walls 4ft thick. Adjacent to the cylindrical tower is a hexagonal turret running from ground level up to a little higher than the top of the tower. The top of the turret is pierced with gun-ports on each facet, for hand-guns. These were employed on at least two occasions, one of them in 1458, against French raiders. (See R. Allen Brown, *English Castles*, p. 140.)

The castle is an interesting example of water-castle (see chapter 9). Caister was occupied for a time by the well-known Norfolk family Paston, whose letters of the fifteenth century have survived to give a remarkable view of country life of the period.

CAISTOR Lincolnshire
(TA 116012) A
A mound near the church is possibly the remnant of a motte castle of the Anarchy (c.1140).

CALLALY Nr Whittingham,
Northumberland   (NU 051099) O
The present mansion at Callaly stands near the site of a motte castle raised in the twelfth century. A pele-tower was built in the fifteenth century and this forms part of the mansion which is seventeenth century with

nineteenth-century improvements. The pele was 42ft by 39ft and rose to three storeys.

CALSHOT Nr Fawley, Hampshire
(SU 488025) DOE
This is one of Henry VIII's coastal castles. It was built in 1538–40 with stone used from Beaulieu Abbey and intended to guard the approaches to Southampton Water. The tower is cylindrical with windows splayed outwards and stands on a polygonal base platform.

CAMBER Sussex
(TQ 922184) DOE
Camber was one of the coastal fortresses erected by Henry VIII in the period 1538–44, but it was not an entirely new structure. There had been an earlier circular tower-fort at Camber, begun probably in the 1480s, and added to in the period 1511–14, and this was incorporated in what became an octagonal-plan castle with a semi-circular bastion on each alternate angle towards the cardinal points, inside which was the circular tower. The tower was 65ft in diameter, with walls 11ft thick, and the bastions, also with 11ft-thick walls, were built of brick inside with an ashlar surface. It is ruinous. Recent excavations have revealed aspects of its earlier history.

Cambridge: the motte, now in front of the Cambridgeshire County Council building. A remarkably commanding view of the city can be seen from the top

CAMBRIDGE †
(TL 446592) A

There is a very fine mound right in front of the Shire Hall in Castle Street, Cambridge. This is the sole remnant, except for earthworks, of a once important medieval castle here. The motte was raised in c.1068, and twenty-seven houses were demolished to make room for it. The earthworks were of partly Norman, partly Roman construction adapted by the Normans, and there were some later ones erected by Edward I.

Sometime, probably in the late twelfth century, the castle received its first stonework. There is a record of a charge of £41 for transporting stone, lime and sand for Cambridge Castle in c.1190. Thereafter, work on the castle was desultory.

Then in the years 1283–99 major works were undertaken by Edward I 'to make Cambridge one of the strongest castles in England'(*King's Works*). They included a stone curtain, with gatehouse, barbican, cylindrical angle towers, a great tower on the motte, and a hall. These works amounted to £2,630. Then the king appears to have lost interest.

In the fourteenth century the castle was 'raided' for stone to build colleges. By 1600 only a gatehouse was left complete, and it was in use as a prison. The castle was refortified during the Civil War, but slighted afterwards.

CANTERBURY Kent †
(TR 145574) Open on application

An early motte castle raised before 1086, Canterbury was a royal castle throughout its history, except that it appears to have been granted in 1227 to Hubert de Burgh for his lifetime. It received a substantial great tower, on a sloping plinth, about 90ft by 75ft, of which only the lower part survives, but which the authors of the *King's Works* estimate probably reached 75–80ft tall, with an appearance not unlike that of Domfront in Normandy, built by Henry I. Various dates for the tower have been suggested: late eleventh century, *temp.* Henry I, and even early Henry II; but it remains unsettled. The great tower was built of flint rubble with dressings of Caen stone and sandstone. It has pilaster buttresses on the angles and mid-wall, and had two cross-walls inside. It

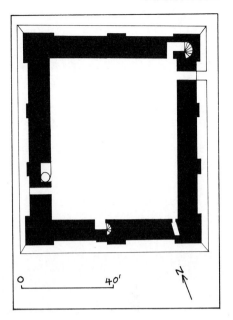

Canterbury: ground-floor plan of great tower (after *King's Works*)

had two spiral staircases, one in the east corner and one on the south-west wall in the section of wall supported by the mid-wall pilaster buttress. Foundations of a forebuilding along the north-west wall were found recently. And excavations in 1975–6 revealed fragments of the great tower buried in the castle ditch which had been located for the first time.

The castle had gates, barbican, bridge, chapel and other buildings, chiefly of late twelfth- and thirteenth-century work. In 1380 a new gate with towers was built as part of a general move to improve the fortifications of many south-east counties' castles.

CARISBROOKE Isle of Wight †
(SZ 486877) DOE

A very early Norman motte castle raised in c.1070. The motte, built of chalk and flint, rose to over 60ft. It was erected beside a bailey which was a raised platform of earth surrounded by ditching. By 1136, the motte castle had been almost completely converted to stone, with an irregular polygonal shell keep built of squared rubble on the mound. A rectangular-plan stone curtain

Carisbrooke: the polygonal shell keep on the motte

round the raised bailey has flanking square turrets on south-west and south-east corners (converted in the 1580s into star-pointed gun-turrets for coastal defence). The shell keep has a buttress on the north side. It was once taller than it is at present, though the floor of the parapet walkway remains, and to the north is the well sunk to some 160ft. The north stretch of curtain wall ascends the motte to the shell and protects a flight of steps into the gateway on the west side of the shell. On the west side of the curtain is a twin-cylindrical turreted gatehouse with parapet machicolation over the central chevron-head arched entrance. The gatehouse is basically c.1335, with some later additions, and has grooves for three portcullises. The doors to the entrance are at least five centuries old.

The bailey inside the curtain has received a variety of buildings, erected against the inside wall and free-standing, sufficient for the castle to be a residence of some elaboration. Some of the buildings are in ruins, others have been restored and are used, including one as a museum. This has among its exhibits an eighteenth-century cot which had been in the family of Commander P.K. LL. Fry, OBE (father of the author) since the 1790s.

The castle was besieged in 1377 by a French commando force, but the garrison held out. Carisbrooke is also famous for acting as the place of confinement of Charles I for a period after the Civil War.

CARLISLE Cumbria ††
(NY 397563) DOE
The earliest structure at Carlisle was a wooden palisaded enclosure on the high bluff overlooking the River Eden. This was raised by William Rufus in 1092, in approximately triangular plan. Henry I is recorded as having ordered a 'castle and towers' to be raised to fortify the city in 1122, but what buildings followed this order is not clear, except for walling round the city, and those may well have been of wood. Carlisle was surrendered to David I, King of Scotland, by Stephen in 1136. Some time

202

between 1136 and 1174 the massive great tower was built, but whether by David I who held Carlisle until 1153, or his successor Malcolm IV, or Henry II of England who recovered it in 1157, we do not know. The chronicler, Jordan Fantosme, refers to it as 'the great old tower', when writing about William the Lion besieging Carlisle in 1173–4. The dimensions were 67ft by 60ft, and 65ft high, approximately cuboid, like Dover, though this was coincidental. The great tower has been substantially altered over the years, but some features remain, such as the clasping pilaster buttresses on the corners. There was a forebuilding of ashlar in Norman style, which contained a straight staircase to the first-floor entrance. The alterations are considerable and are summarized in the Department of Environment's booklet on Carlisle Castle.

Note the inner enclosure, whose north-east wall is deep buttressed, with a four-teenth-century gatehouse at its south-eastern end, the Captain's Tower in the west wall and the shallow buttresses on the south-eastern wall. The inner enclosure occupies the north-eastern corner of the much larger outer enclosure whose curtain wall has several flanking towers. The history of Carlisle has been a long and stormy one.

CARLTON Nr Louth, Lincolnshire (TF 395836) A
A motte and some ditching survive from a (?) twelfth-century motte castle built here by the Bardolph family. The mound remains.

CARTINGTON Nr Rothbury, Northumberland (NU 039045) A
Early in the fifteenth century a tall rec-tangular tower was built under the shadow of the Rothbury hills. It was about 41ft by about 31ft, with 6ft-thick walls. The tower was part of a quadrangle of buildings which were greatly altered in later years, and the original ruins are partly obscured.

CARY Nr Wincanton, Somerset (ST 641322) A
There are remains of the foundations of a substantial great tower at Castle Cary, which had been built of rubble with ashlar facing. The tower, almost square in plan, was about 78ft wide, and appears to have been enclosed

within banks and moat, some of the banks being of later date. The great tower had a cross-wall. Dating is difficult, but there is mention of the castle in the time of Stephen. The tower may be of Henry II's time.

CASTLE ACRE Nr Swaffham, †† Norfolk (TF 819152) DOE
Castle Acre has been the subject of some interesting excavations in the past decade. It began as a Norman motte castle in c. 1080, or perhaps earlier, raised by the de Warennes, earls of Surrey. The earthworks were later to be considerably extended, incorporating a village, and they can still be seen from various high points at Castle Acre village today. The mound was low and it received its first stonework sometime before the end of the eleventh-century, when a hall-tower was built on it. It is unlikely that the hall was intended to be a fortified building. The lower courses of this have survived. Before the end of the century, the excavations suggest, a simple stonework gatehouse was erected in the perimeter of the wooden palisade round the motte.

The hall-tower was about 72ft square, with a cross-wall, and a door in the south wall. Sometime in the early decades of the twelfth century, the castle was streng-thened. The motte was enclosed by a polygonal-plan flint rubble curtain wall, raised upon heightened ramparts. Curtain walling was raised round the bailey leading down to the River Nar, and the level of the bailey was raised in places. There are foundations of buildings in this bailey that have yet to be more closely examined, according to the workers on the site in 1979. The hall-tower also received some attention. Interestingly, the tower walls were thick-ened inside: the evidence for this is instantly apparent. What was happening? The Ancient Monuments Inspectorate of the DOE considers that the hall-tower was being transformed into a fortified great tower. Then, probably about 1150, the work was halted, the southern half of the tower was pulled down, but work was continued on the northern half. How far we do not yet know, nor do we know the final appearance of the northern half. The curtain wall was also heightened in places, and so was the rampart on which it stood. The

Castle Acre: an aerial view of the castle showing in particular the interesting finds inside the shell wall on the mound. The various stages of construction of what is thought to have been a great tower can be followed by reference to the Gazetteer entry

gatehouse was strengthened.

The DOE has suggested that the northern half of the hall-tower, now a ruin about 10ft tall, was a great tower in the manner of Castle Rising or Norwich. This is difficult to sustain: the dimensions of the existing remains are not right for structures of this sophistication. The excavations are continuing, and more information may emerge to revise the suggestion.

CASTLE COMBE Wiltshire
(ST 837777) C
There are some remains of a medieval castle behind the manor house to the north of Castle Combe village. The castle began as a cluster of earthwork and timber enclosures with ditching, probably during the twelfth

century. Some of the enclosure walling was converted to stone and some free-standing buildings were erected, including a great tower.

CASTLE RISING   ††
Nr King's Lynn, Norfolk
(TF 666246) DOE
Castle Rising stands in an enormous area of man-made ditches and banks (about 12 acres), which are in a fine state of preservation. They give the visitor an excellent idea of major Norman defensive earthwork fortifications. The inner bailey, sandwiched between two smaller outer baileys, contains two buildings: the foundations of a Norman chapel of the eleventh century, which was raised before the great tower which is dated

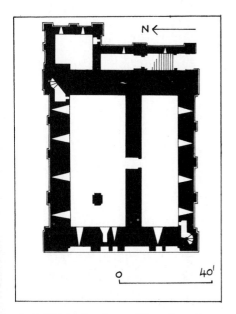

Castle Rising: plan of ground floor of great tower

A mural gallery at the higher level of a two-storey great hall in a great tower, based on Castle Rising

c.1138–40. Perched on the top of the inner bank of the inner bailey are the remains of the gatehouse, a rectangular tower pierced by an entrance passage with a room over, built at much the same time as the great tower.

The great tower is among the most interesting in eastern England; it is also in very good repair. It is a squat, rectangular great tower whose horizontal dimensions at 78½ft by 68½ft, are greater than the height which reaches to 50ft today, and was several feet higher when it had its parapet and tops to the corner turrets. The corner turrets are clasped by pilaster buttresses and there are three more shallow pilaster buttresses along each of three of the four sides. The fourth side has a forebuilding (with its own clasping corner pilaster buttreses) rising to the same height as the great tower. This is reached by a two-flight staircase behind a stout wall adjoining the forebuilding. The stairs begin to rise just behind a round Norman arch with corbelled frieze which is on the south front at the east end of the tower. Note the blind arch decoration of the higher level of the protecting wall.

The great tower has an off-centre cross-wall all the way up. Both side walls and cross-wall have chambers and passages. The tower is built of rubble courses with ashlar facings, some of it Barnack stone from Northamptonshire. The rubble contains local carstone. Comparison of the tower with Norwich has been suggested, but the visitor may judge for himself. The remains of the great tower at Castle Acre, now beginning to emerge in excavation, have also been suggested as being of a tower similar to Castle Rising, but we think this unlikely.

Built by William d'Albini, Earl of Sussex, Castle Rising was for some thirty years the home of Isabella, mother of Edward III. She was sent there by her son after he broke up the conspiracy between her and her lover, Roger Mortimer, but there is no evidence that her time at Rising was a confinement.

CASTLETHORPE Hanslope, Buckinghamshire (SP 798446) A
This was a motte castle with two baileys, and it was raised in the twelfth century. The castle was besieged and destroyed in 1215–16 by Faulkes de Bréauté who captured Bedford Castle in 1215. In 1292 William Beauchamp was granted a licence to crenellate a wall that he built round a house and garden that appear to have stood on or near the motte castle site. Some traces remain of the earthworks.

Castle Rising: the forebuilding of the great tower. Note the decorative treatment, especially the blind arcading

CAUS Shropshire
(SJ 337078) P
An eleventh-century motte castle covering about six acres, Caus received a shell keep on the motte in the twelfth century and a rectangular curtain round the inner bailey. The curtain had cylindrical towers on the corners. The stonework was protected by extensive earthworks, including double ditching. The castle was demolished during the Civil War, and there are few remains today.

CAWOOD North Yorkshire
(SE 573376) C
An ecclesiastical fortified residence was built here in the fourteenth century. The gatehouse survives amid some farm buildings now on the site.

CHALGRAVE Nr Toddington,
Bedfordshire   (TL 009274) A
Chalgrave was a motte castle of twelfth-century beginnings, whose motte once buttressed a square wooden building, possibly a tower. The tower was dismantled and the motte was enlarged. Part of the bank round the bailey was faced with stone.

CHARLTON Nr The Wrekin,
Shropshire   (SJ 597112) P
There are some fragments of earthworks of a thirteenth- and fourteenth-century castle on this site.

CHARTLEY Stowe, Staffordshire
(SK 010285) P
A motte castle with two baileys (created by a ditch that divided one bailey), which had a cylindrical tower on the summit. The tower had a small projecting lobe. Around the inner bailey was raised a rectangular-plan curtain along two adjacent sides, with semi-cylindrical turrets. The stonework is probably thirteenth century.

CHENEY LONGVILLE Shropshire
(SO 417847) C
The remains of a moated castle of quadrangular plan round a courtyard, built in c.1394 (the licence was granted in that year), are associated with a much later house on the site.

CHESTER   †
(SJ 404657) DOE
The Conqueror raised a motte castle here, with inner and outer bailey, just outside the site of the old Roman town, in 1069–70. For a time it was leased to the earls of Chester but it is not possible to say much about its first century and a half. There are remains of what is considered a twelfth-century square tower on the motte. In 1237 the castle came into royal ownership, and an extensive improvement programme began soon afterwards. This was the start of the major stonework, which was partly new work and partly rebuilding of earlier work of stone and wood. Henry III raised the outer bailey curtain with a tower and rebuilt the great hall. Edward I rebuilt the outer gatehouse and put up new domestic buildings. The inner gatehouse, leading into the inner bailey, is probably of the same period. Repairs and small improvements were carried out on a regular basis over the years up to the close of the fifteenth century.

Chester was besieged during the Civil War.

A plan of the castle appears on p. 208.

CHICHESTER Sussex
(SU 863051) O
A very early motte castle was built by the site of the north gate of Roman Chichester by Roger de Montgomery, one of the Conqueror's principal lords and commanders, in c.1066–7. In time the castle passed to the Albini family (cf. Castle Rising); Philip d'Aubigny (Albini), one owner of the castle, was ordered to demolish it by King John, but he evidently ignored the command for he was told again to demolish it by John's son Henry III in 1217. The castle was destroyed a few years afterwards and a Grey Friars priory built on the site of the bailey. There are earthwork remains.

CHILHAM Nr Canterbury, Kent
(TR 066535)
Chilham was a great tower castle inside a curtained enclosure surrounded by a ditch, a conventional plan for the twelfth-century. The great tower was of polygonal shape (octagonal, with one side projecting into a turret to contain the spiral staircase). The tower was built of Kentish ragstone and dressed with ashlar quoins on the corners.

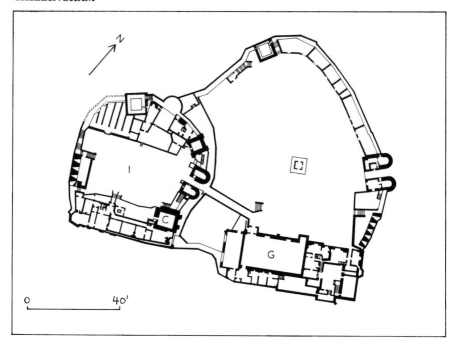

Chester in the eighteenth century. Ground plan dated 1769. C=Caesar's Tower; G=great hall; I=inner bailey

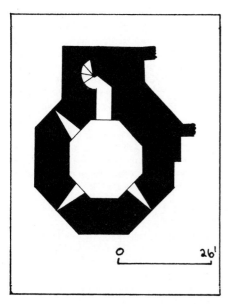

Chilham: ground floor of great tower, with forebuilding c.1171–5

The period of construction was between c.1171 and 1175, during which time over £400 was spent by Henry II who had taken it over as a royal fortress (cf. Tickhill, Odiham, Orford). The great tower has been partly restored, but is not open. It can, however, be seen from the gardens.

CHILLINGHAM Northumberland
(NV 070249) C
In 1344 a licence to fortify and crenellate his family mansion at Chillingham was granted to Thomas Heton. The structure seems to have been a quadrangle with corner towers. It has been extensively rebuilt.

CHIPCHASE Nr Haughton,
Northumberland   (NY 882757) C
Chipchase Castle is today an imposing structure on the western bank of the North Tyne. The fortified part is principally the fourteenth-century rectangular tower, 51ft by 34ft, which is at one end of the later Jacobean mansion. The tower is 50ft tall and

208

has machicolated cylindrical turrets on the angles reaching to another 10ft, with machicolation along the walls between. The entrance was guarded by an oak portcullis which is still *in situ*. The tower is four-storeyed and the parapet, battlement and turret area forms a fifth.

CHRISTCHURCH Hampshire   †
(SZ 160927) DOE
A motte castle was raised here in c.1100 by Richard de Redvers, cousin of Henry I. The motte received a rectangular great tower, about 50ft by 45ft, with walls 9ft thick. It was three storeys high, built of Freshwater limestone and local ironstone with ashlar dressings of Purbeck, Binstead and other stones. The great tower has not been dated beyond a presumption that it is c.1300. Beside a stream in the castle bailey there are the remains of a rectangular Norman hall of mid-twelfth-century construction. The south-east corner has a projection right into the stream and contains garderobes. The hall has angle and mid-wall buttresses. The ground floor was lit by short arrow loops in the stream-side wall and one other. Note the chimney emerging from the fireplace and the chevron-moulded rounded heads to the windows on the first-floor level on the stream side.

CHURCH STRETTON Shropshire
(SO 448926) A
Also called Brockhurst Castle. A motte castle overlooking the terrain between Shrewsbury and Ludlow, protected by natural hills. Stonework curtain walling was found in recent excavations.

CLARE Suffolk
(TL 772452) O
Clare Castle began as a motte of the late eleventh century. It had two baileys (in one of which the nineteenth-century railway station was erected). A polygonal shell keep was built round the motte top sometime in the twelfth century, possibly by the de Clare family whose descendants became powerful in south Wales in the thirteenth century and built Caerphilly. Traces of a wall down the motte slope from the shell to join up with the curtain round one bailey have been found. Some remains are visible in Clare Park.

CLAVERING Nr Newport, Essex
(TL 471320) A
Although it is now generally accepted that no castles, not even motte castles, were built in England before 1066, the enclosure at Clavering was for a long time considered to have been a structure raised by a Norman lord at the encouragement of Edward the Confessor. The moat round the enclosure was fed by the River Stort which may have driven a watermill nearby.

CLAXTON Nr Norwich, Norfolk   †
(TG 335038) O
This fourteenth-century enclosure castle, whose remains today consist of a long stretch of wall with six flanking towers, was licensed in 1333. On the north side of the south face are traces of a hall, with staircases and upper rooms. The ruins stand inside an area which is part surrounded by a moat.

CLEOBURY Cleobury Mortimer,
Shropshire   (SO 681761) A
Earthworks beside the river here are possibly the remains of an early twelfth-century castle which is recorded as having been pulled down (?) by Henry II in 1155.

CLIFFORD Hereford & Worcester
(SO 243457) P
There are indications of three castles in this area. One was a simple motte castle near Old Castleton (SO 283457), probably the one mentioned in Domesday Book and thought to have been built in c.1070. The second was another motte castle known locally as Newton Tump (SO 293441). The third, at Grid Reference SO 243457, near the church, was a motte castle on earthworks about 3½ acres in area. This was given a polygonal enclosure of local sandstone with five round towers, two of them flanking a gate, and a hall building, in the thirteenth century. The castle was held by the Clifford family and later passed to the Mortimers. Substantial remains have survived.

CLIFFORD'S TOWER York   ††
(SE 605515) DOE
This is a fascinating castle. A motte raised in 1069–70 on the north side of the Ouse, built of marl and clay in layers, with gravel and stones above and with layers of timber,

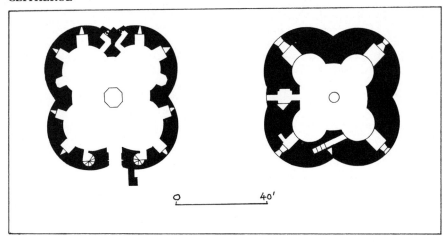

Left.Clifford's Tower in York, which is quatrefoil in plan and was built between 1245 and 1270, has been compared with the great tower at Étampes (ground plan on right). Étampes was built between 1130 and 1150

supported a timber great tower. It was burnt down during the anti-Jewish riots in York c.1190, and rebuilt, which involved raising the height of the motte to the present height (60ft). Then in 1228 the second tower was blown down in a severe gale. In 1245 Henry III ordered the rebuilding of the castle and over the next twenty-five years a curtain with several towers and two gateways were raised round the bailey, while on the motte was built an unusual great tower, now called Clifford's Tower, of magnesian limestone in fine cut and dressed blocks. (It was known as the King's Tower until the end of the sixteenth century.) The plan of the tower is quatrefoil, in some respects similar to the great tower of Étampes, some 30 miles south of Paris, which was built c.1140. A fore-building was inserted at Clifford's between the in-turning arcs of two adjoining 'foils'. The timber joists of the ground/first floor were supported by corbels in the inner wall masonry (a few can still be seen). A portcullis was inserted in the inside archway to the exit. There was a chapel over the entrance passage. These works cost about £2,600, in money of the time.

CLITHEROE Lancashire †
(SD 742416) O
A motte castle built on a natural rock

outcrop was given a square great tower, about 35ft wide, of limestone rubble dressed with ashlar. The tower corners have pilaster buttresses. The stonework is probably twelfth century, and the tower is among the smallest of the great towers. It has no garderobe and no fireplace, and the thick walls contain no useful chambers, leaving the core of the tower incapable of providing comfortable quarters. The castle belonged to the de Lacy family, but in 1399 it became Crown property. At some time the tower was surrounded by a curtain wall.

CLUN Shropshire †
(SO 298809) A
The castle at Clun began as a substantial motte castle with two baileys, close to the junction of the rivers Clun and Usk. The motte was joined to the baileys by cause-ways. In the twelfth century the top of the motte was surrounded with a stone curtain of irregular shape, with a twin-turreted gateway. Down the north slope of the motte a rectangular great tower, some 80ft tall, was erected (c.1160), half on, half off, with its base at ground level. The great tower has buttressed corners and three storeys with basement, the top three provided with windows (see Guildford). The tower, though derelict, is still upright.

210

Clifford's Tower: an aerial view of the quatrefoil great tower on the motte

COCKERMOUTH Cumbria
(NY 123309) O

Cockermouth was built in the thirteenth century on a site by the junction of the rivers Cocker and Derwent, which gave it water defences for most of its flanks. It was an enclosure castle with curtains and towers, and an inner gatehouse. Considerable modifications, including an outer gatehouse and barbican, were made in the fourteenth century. Some of these were ordered by Edward III who held the castle for a period. Part of the earlier stonework is present among the later buildings.

COCKLEPARK TOWER Nr Morpeth,
Northumberland   (NZ 202910)

An interesting three-storeyed tower-house of the fifteenth century which has one end with corners embellished with machicolated bartizans at the wallhead, and machicolations between. The tower-house was later extended by a domestic building on one end. The castle was occupied and in use up to a few years ago, but it is now unsafe.

COCKLAW TOWER Nr Hexham,
Northumberland   (NY 939712)

This rectangular tower is an interesting, large pele-tower, three storeys tall, each storey containing one main room. One wall was thick enough to accommodate several chambers and the spiral staircase. Cocklaw was built in the early fifteenth century. It has been well preserved.

COLCHESTER Essex   ††
(TL 998254) O

Colchester great tower was one of the first to be built in England (c.1075–80), after a serious raid on the town by the Danes, and it is by far the largest great tower in Great Britain. In plan the tower is much the same as that of the White Tower of London, notably with its apsidal extension on the east wall. Indeed, the similarities in the two plans have led some historians to think that both were designed and built under the direction of the same man, Bishop Gundulf of Rochester. The great tower was built partly over the remains of a *podium* of a Roman temple dedicated to the Emperor Claudius (41-54), for Colchester had been a Roman city.

The dimensions of Colchester were 151½ft (north-south), 110ft (east-west) and about 90ft high, with the corner turrets rising to 105-110ft. The corner turrets project from the walls in a more pronounced manner than the White Tower, and they contain both staircases and chambers. The tower walls are about 12½ft thick at the base

211

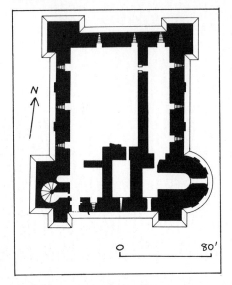

Colchester: ground plan of great tower

(and so slightly thinner than London), leading down into a battered plinth where they widen out to 17½ft. The tower well in the south-west is 5ft wide and over 40ft deep, and is lined with septaria (see p.64). The tower was built of Roman brick and dressed stone mostly quarried from the Roman ruins nearby, together with septaria lumps and Kentish ragstone. The dressed stone is said to have been Barnack or Reigate, with some ashlar from Caen. One interesting feature is the clear outline of battlements in the masonry at first-floor level, subsequently built on as the tower was continued upwards. This is thought to have been because it was required to be defended at short notice, and the work level so far reached was hurriedly crenellated.

The tower was four-storeyed, but the top two storeys were pulled down in 1683 when the castle was sold to one John Wheeley for demolition. Evidently he abandoned the massive undertaking after reaching the bottom of the third floor. Today the great tower houses an excellent museum.

COMPTON Nr Paignton, Devon   †
(SX 865648) NT
A fourteenth-century fortified manor house which belonged to the Gilbert family. It was fortified as a precaution against 'commando' raids which the French launched frequently upon the south Devon coast in the later years of the century. Towards the end of the sixteenth century Compton was owned by Sir Humphrey Gilbert, founder of the English colony in Newfoundland. It has been radically altered since, but retains some original stonework.

CONISBROUGH Nr Doncaster,   ††
South Yorkshire   (SK 515989) DOE
Conisbrough stands on a natural mound which was given counter scarp banks to provide a wide and deep moat that almost surrounds the castle. The castle was built in the period c.1174–c.1190 by Hamelin Plantagenet, illegitimate half brother of Henry II. It is a great tower castle enclosed in a curtain wall (which was 35ft tall and 7ft thick), with flanking solid half cylindrical towers and a gatehouse with projecting barbican in front (of which there are a few remains). The barbican led out from the gatehouse, angled twice to the right, and then turned left downwards to the twin towered gate half-way down the mound, the gate having a drawbridge across the moat.

The principal feature of the castle is the uniquely shaped great tower (unique, that

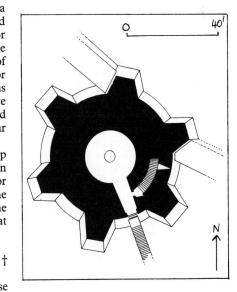

Conisbrough: ground-floor plan of great tower. The outside staircase is not the original

212

Conisbrough: the great tower behind the curtain

is, in the UK, for there is a similar shaped tower in France). Built of limestone ashlar, the tower is basically cylindrical, but with six wedge-shaped buttresses placed equidistantly round the outer wall of the cylinder. Both cylinder and buttresses stand on a splayed plinth, and rise to 95ft tall, though the buttresses originally rose higher, to over 100ft. Only one buttress, the south-east, has accommodation of any size, a six-sided chapel. Two have water cisterns and two had space in the top where they emerged above the cylindrical wall for shelter leading to staircases. Otherwise, the stairs are in the wall thickness. There are fireplaces, hand basins and garderobes in the walls. The tower is notable for its scarcity of window openings and arrow loops.

The great tower had the disadvantage affecting most cylindrical towers, namely, that the entrance was not protected by a forebuilding. Entry was via a flight of steps (not those at present in position) into a simple doorway.

The castle was not put to the test of siege.

COOLING Kent
(TR 755760) P

A castle was built at Cooling in the 1380s to protect the approaches to the Thames from foreign raids. Sited near the Cliffe Marshes, Cooling was a double quadrangular castle with cylindrical corner turrets. Its building works were well documented. Yevele, the celebrated fourteenth-century architect/master mason, worked there. The gatehouse, which survives today in remarkable condition, was built under the direction of William Sharnall. Cooling was attacked and taken by Sir Thomas Wyatt in 1554 during his rebellion against Mary I (Bloody Mary), which he led in protest against her plans to marry Philip II of Spain.

CORBRIDGE VICAR'S PELE †
Northumberland   (NY 987644) O

The Vicar's Pele is one of the simpler Northumberland pele-towers and was built in c.1300. It is called Vicar's Pele because it was the vicarage for the church next door. It is three storeys high, with one room to each storey, and is built largely of stone taken

213

Corfe: a particularly interesting view of Corfe which shows very clearly the plan of the castle as represented on p. 215. The 'Gloriette' of King John is to the right of the much-ruined great tower, towards the top of the picture

from the Roman fortress at Corstopitum nearby. The vicar's study/bedroom was on the top floor, reached by a staircase in the wall, and its windows were screened by battlemented parapets. The ground-floor entrance was through a thick, wooden door lined with iron grating.

CORFE Dorset   ††
(SY 958823) O

Corfe Castle was King John's favourite fortress and he graced it with a remarkable 'Gloriette', a block of apartments next to the great tower. These were the best appointed quarters in any castle in England at the time, c.1200–5. A fine arch survives among the

remains. It is sad that in their efforts to render Corfe unfit for military use after the Civil War, the demolition gangs of the Parliamentarians proved over-zealous and virtually destroyed what must have been one of the most fascinating castles ever built in England.

Corfe began as a motte castle of the 1080s, erected on a steep hill. The outline of the castle precincts at this early period, viz. an ear-shaped plan, remained much the same for most of its history. The changes that did follow were mainly additions of stone buildings and walls. The castle had received its first stonework by the end of the eleventh century: a small hall with some herringbone

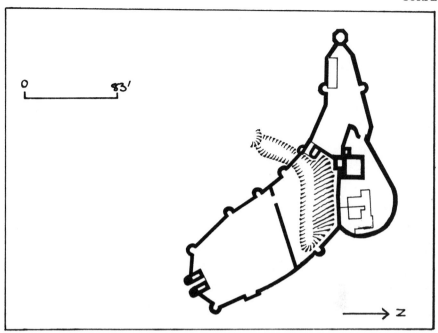

Corfe: plan of Corfe (after RCHM) as it was c.1285. GL = King John's 'Gloriette'; GT=great tower

masonry on the south and pilaster buttresses on the west situated towards the western tip (now fragmented); and a rough coursed rubble curtain wall round a high point on the north, roughly pear shaped, the taper to the west. This enclosure became and remained the inner bailey. In the reign of Henry I an almost square great tower was built in the inner bailey, along its south wall. This is a ruin today. It rose three storeys, with a cross-wall, was built of ashlar and had pilaster buttresses along the walls and beside, but not wrapped round, the corners. It also had blind arcading between them, reminiscent of Norwich but not necessarily designed or built by the same engineers: the idea of such features was in circulation at the time. Corfe, incidentally, is one of the castles whose great tower is referred to as a great tower several times in contemporary records; two instances are in the reigns of Edward I and Elizabeth I. The great tower received a forebuilding soon afterwards, but probably not before the siege of 1139 when, according to the *Gesta Stephani*, the castle was one of the strongest in all England.

In the early thirteenth century King John lavished over £1,400 on Corfe, including the 'Gloriette', the curtain (with octagonal projecting tower on the extreme western tip) around the west bailey and the deep ditch and bank which divide the south-east outer bailey from the remainder of the castle. The outer bailey also received some, if not all, of its stone curtain and flanking towers. Henry III completed the curtain and put in the south-east gatehouse (finished by his son, Edward I), and also the inner gatehouse from the bridge, across the ditch of King John, into the inner bailey. Corfe was used by Henry III (and other kings) as an arsenal as well as a fortress-residence. In 1224, some 25,000 bolts were ordered from Corfe by the king for his siege of Bedford Castle (q.v.). Edward I completed the curtain round the outer bailey (south-east) and raised the height of the great tower by an extra storey, besides heightening the cross-wall (*medium murum turris*). Thereafter, Corfe was maintained rather than improved, but in the late 1370s a fresh tower, thought to have been five storeys tall, was raised near the

215

'Gloriette' of King John, but it has disappeared, apart from the cellar.

Henry VII's mother, Margaret Beaufort, had Tudor windows put in the great tower and elsewhere. Elizabeth I sold it to Sir Christopher Hatton for nearly £5,000 in 1572, just under five centuries from the date of its original construction. Corfe had also been used as a royal prison, on and off, for nearly 400 years. The castle was besieged in 1646 by Parliament, and it fell as a result of betrayal, not enforced surrender. In March of that year it was blown up by gunpowder and undermining. Two-thirds of the great tower were destroyed.

COTHERSTONE Durham
(NZ 015200) A

A motte castle of the twelfth century which received stonework. Remains of the mound are to the north of the village.

COTTINGHAM Nr Beverley,
Humberside (TA 041330) P

A motte castle whose motte was square at the top was built here in the twelfth century. In c.1200 King John granted William de Stuteville, the holder (who also held Knaresborough and Buttercrambe) a licence to fortify the site. How this was carried out is not clear, but it may have been by means of a tower on the motte. In the fourteenth century the site was transformed when a licence was granted to fortify a manor house. The mound survives.

COUPLAND Nr Millfield,
Northumberland (NT 936312) P

Coupland Castle, about two miles from Millfield, is an L-plan tower of the late sixteenth century. The tower is three-storeyed, with the entrance staircase in the 'L' extension which is actually taller than the main tower, It has been restored and extended.

COVENTRY West Midlands
(SP 336788)

A rectangular enclosure castle with surrounding ditchwork (part of which was excavated a few years ago). This was originally a priory, but it was taken by Robert Marmion during the Anarchy of Stephen and converted to a fortress 'with pits and trenches'. Marmion is said to have been killed when his horse stumbled and jerked him into one of his trenches. The castle was dismantled by Stephen in c.1147, but in Henry II's time it was repaired.

CRASTER Nr Dunstanburgh,
Northumberland
(NU 256197) Open by application

Craster is a few miles south of Dunstanburgh. The pele-tower, built probably in the first years of the fifteenth century, is now part of a mansion. It has two storeys above the ground-floor part which is vaulted. Craster Tower has been considerably altered, and has Gothic-style windows.

CRESSWELL Nr Druridge Bay,
Northumberland (NZ 293933) P

The tower at Cresswell is a fine rectangular building with one corner bearing a turret at the top. Cresswell was built in the thirteenth century and is still in good repair.

CREWKERNE Somerset
(ST 421107) A

A mound at Crewkerne, known as Castle Hill, may have been a Norman motte castle. Excavations revealed some (?) twelfth-century pottery which has been taken to Taunton Museum.

CROFT Leominster, Hereford & †
Worcester (SO 449655) NT

Croft Castle is a fourteenth-century quadrangular-plan castle, but with the north end off the right angle by about 10 degrees. The quadrangle has cylindrical towers on the corners and one rectangular flanking tower mid-wall on the north side. The north-west tower is in its original form, but the other towers have been altered. The old castle has been considerably modified to make it a more sumptuous residence, with a pair of semi-octagonal turrets flanking a one-storey gate turret of rectangular plan on the east wall. The gate leads into the hall, behind which is the open courtyard. This work is among the extensive improvements done in the eighteenth century.

The castle is named after the family that has owned it, with an interval of about 150 years, since its construction. It was a rendezvous for Yorkist leaders during the Wars of the Roses.

CROMWELL'S CASTLE Tresco
Island, Isles of Scilly
(SV 882159) DOE
This was a coastal fort built by Oliver
Cromwell in c.1650, about 600ft from the
Edward VI coastal fort, called King Charles'
Castle (q.v.). It is a tall cylindrical tower
with walls over 12ft thick, whose entrance
was a doorway high up the south side
attainable only by a staircase which wound
round the tower. The upper storey is pierced
with gun-ports.

CUCKNEY Nottinghamshire
(SK 566714) A
A motte castle probably raised in the time of
the Anarchy (1135–54), it is also known as
Castle Hill. The mound can be seen near the
Church. It is thought to have been an
adulterine castle.

DACRE Cumbria
(NY 461266) P
At Dacre there is a very fine pele-tower,
which is still occupied. It was erected in the
fourteenth century and given two wings,
much in the Scottish tower-house manner.
One of the wings has the staircase. Dacre
was altered in the late seventeenth century.

DARTMOUTH Devon   †
(SX 887503) DOE
The earliest surviving English coastal fortress specifically built to carry guns, Dartmouth was well sited on a rocky promontory
on the west bank of the Dart Estuary, about
a mile south-east of the town. Built by the
corporation of the town in the period
1481–c.1495, it was tailored to fit the site, as
can be seen in the plan. Basically, it is a
square tower on the rock edge over the sea,
buttressed on the northern side by a
cylindrical tower, though internally the two
towers are one structure. Both towers are
battlemented, and all the walls are well
provided with gun-ports, particularly at
lower levels. There are well-crenellated gun
platforms stretching out on both sides.

The corporation was granted an annual
sum of £30 by Edward IV to 'repair and keep
it garnished with guns . . .' and this was
increased to £40 in 1486 by Henry VII. The
masons building the castle in the 1480s were
paid 7d a day, and labourers 5d, more or less
the same as those at Deal, sixty years later,

Dartmouth: ground-floor plan

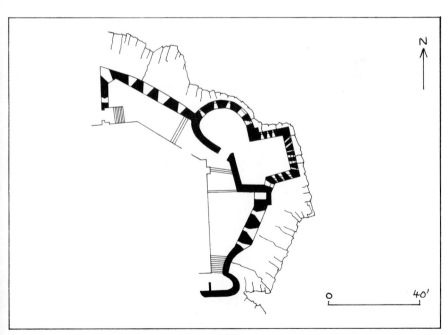

which makes the strike at Deal easier to understand. Some of the stone for the construction was brought from Charleton, near Kingsbridge.

Many additions and alterations were carried out in the sixteenth and seventeenth centuries. The castle was captured after a siege of one month by Prince Maurice on behalf of Charles I during the Civil War and held by a garrison of about 500 men for three years, until it was stormed by Sir Thomas Fairfax for Parliament in 1646 and forced to surrender.

DEAL Kent   ††
(TR 378521)
Deal is the largest of the coastal fortresses built by Henry VIII over the period 1538–43 in anticipation of invasion from Europe because of his break with the Church of Rome. It is one of the most remarkable and satisfying military structures to be seen in England. Sixfoil in plan, robust and formidable in construction, well sited down on the Kent coast sands, and in very good condition, Deal has much to offer the castle enthusiast.

In Deal's plan, six squat bastions surround a central great tower, cylindrical, taller than the bastions, with an outer ring of six larger bastions, each of which is protected by a wide and deep ditch. The tops of the outer and the inner bastions and the central tower are all battlemented, and the flat roofs' mounted cannons and guns of varying sizes and ranges covered extremely effectively every inch around the castle within the ranges. The curved walls of the bastions and the tower were also liberally provided with gun-ports lower down. This outward defence capability was doubled up inside. Once through the entrance arch, intruders were threatened by several murder-holes in the ceiling. In front of them was a pair of enormously heavy wooden doors, massively studded with iron bolt-heads. If the doors were broken open, a cannon in the back wall of the hall faced the intruders. Even if they passed that, they could not reach the central great tower without running the gauntlet of cannon, gun and musket fire all the way round the inner courtyard, from every possible angle.

The central tower itself was very well

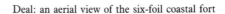

Deal: an aerial view of the six-foil coastal fort

protected, but so many modifications have been carried out on it over the centuries for one reason or another that it is not possible today to see all of the defence mechanisms, in particular, those at ground-floor level. Access to the first floor, for example, was by stairs in the centre. These stairs were double. One flight started opposite the entrance to the tower and went up to the first storey. The other began on the opposite side and went up to the roof over the tower. Yet both used the same newel.

The building of Deal has been mentioned already in chapter 16 on coastal fortresses. Deal was besieged after the Civil War in 1648, when it was held by Royalists, but surrendered after it had been 'much torn and spoiled with the granadoes'.

DEDDINGTON Oxfordshire
(SP 471316) DOE
Deddington Castle began as an earthwork double enclosure of the twelfth century that accumulated stone buildings inside over the years. There is very little to see today. Excavations revealed parts of a stone curtain and the base of a small rectangular tower, of the mid-twelfth century, erected on a mound, both within the inner enclosure. There are also remains of a hall of about 1160 and a chapel of the thirteenth century (some of the stained glass was found).

Piers Gaveston, the homosexual favourite of Edward II, was confined here for a while after his arrest by Thomas, Earl of Lancaster, in 1312 and before his execution.

DEVIZES Wiltshire †
(SU 002613) P
Devizes Castle began late in the eleventh century as an enclosure on a natural promontory, with two baileys. It appears to have been a formidable castle even in the early twelfth century, for the *Gesta Stephani* refers to its 'impregnable fortifications'. But scarcely anything of this fortress now remains. Suggestions have been made that it had an inner enclosure with curtain wall with towers, probably rectilinear, enclosing a great tower and an aisled hall; this enclosure was reached by a gatehouse from an outer bailey which was enclosed by a stone curtain with towers and gatehouse. Henry II acquired it in c.1157 and used it as

an official prison, though he spent no money on it. Much work was done by Henry III who continued its use as a prison for 'distinguished' captives, including, for a short while, his counsellor, Hubert de Burgh for some unspecified misdemeanour, and who also raised residential accommodation for his own use.

The castle was demolished at the end of the Civil War, in 1646, though a few parts remain standing. One of these, a tower, was offered to the author as a small residence, of three storeys, in the 1960s for £5,000. The castellated building upon the old site is nothing to do with the original castle.

DONINGTON Leicestershire .
(SK 448276)
An earthwork enclosure of the early twelfth century, Donington was held by the de Lacy family (see also Clitheroe) and probably had stonework by the time of King John. The castle was attacked during the Magna Carta war (1215–16). It passed in 1311 to Thomas, Earl of Lancaster, Edward II's cousin, and eventually became Crown property. The stone buildings probably included a rectangular hall (Leics. Arch. Soc. Trs. xxxii, p. 53). The remains have been absorbed by Donington House.

DONNINGTON Nr Newbury, ††
Berkshire (SU 461694) DOE
Although this enclosure castle with added gatehouse-tower was built in the fourteenth century, its greatest days were during the Civil War when the garrison defending it on behalf of Charles I held out for nearly two years against Parliamentary besieging forces (see p.167).

The castle stood on a high spur (over 400ft) over the old London–Bath road. The enclosure was a rectangle with six flanking towers (four cylindrical and two square), inside which were ranges of buildings using the enclosure wall as outside walls. The west end wall was polygonal, while along the eastern wall was the opening into the gatehouse inner part, protected by a portcullis, the grooves of which are still visible. The gatehouse was the principal feature and is now the sole remnant of the original fourteenth-century castle, for which a licence to crenellate was granted in 1386 to

Richard de Abberbury, chamberlain to Richard II's queen, Anne of Bohemia.

The gatehouse is a rectangular-plan tower with twin cylindrical towers flanking the entrance, the whole tower on a splayed plinth. It is about 65ft tall and resembles that at Saltwood in Kent, built at much the same time. It has three storeys, the two towers having four levels. The gatehouse is lit by slim loops in the towers but by windows over the entrance arch. A barbican projected in front of the entrance.

In the 1640s, the castle was surrounded by a remarkable five-star pointed defensive earthwork, which was reinforced with timber. Each of the five points was a bastion with a gun emplacement covering all flanks.

DORCHESTER Dorset
(SY 690908)

In medieval Dorchester there was a castle, probably of motte and bailey construction, in the north part where the later prison was built near Sheep Lane. There are no remains of the castle, though some pillar bases were said to have been found in the eighteenth century that suggest the one-time existence of a hall. The castle was fortified during the troubles of Stephen's reign. For a time it was held by Henry II and exchequer records show several sums of money spent on it over about a century.

DORSTONE Hereford & Worcester
(SO 312416) A

A motte castle of the late eleventh/early twelfth century which survived into the thirteenth century without conversion to stone. The mound is over 20ft high.

DOVER Kent ††
(TR 326416) DOE

Considering all its splendid features, its great military interest, its strategically important site and its long history of occupation and use, Dover has to be the greatest of all the hundreds of castles in the British Isles, not excepting the Tower of London.

Dover has everything. It is concentric, and began to be so nearly a century before any other British concentric fortress, new or adapted. The great tower, an almost 100ft cube, with walls from 17–21ft thick all round and big enough to contain many sizeable chambers, is the most massive in Britain. The great tower's forebuilding, three-towered over three flights of stairs and wrapped round both edges of one corner and along one whole wall, is more substantial than any other. The castle's inner curtain

Dover: an aerial view of the 'Gateway to England', amply demonstrating the strong position and the complex defensive arrangements of the foremost castle in Britain

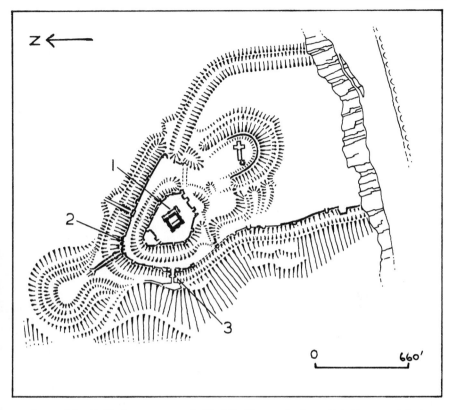

Dover (after DoE): 1=great tower; 2=Norfolk Towers; 3=Constable's Tower and Gate

wall has fourteen flanking towers (including gate-towers), while the outer curtain, which enwraps the inner at the north end and continues southwards right to the cliff's edge on the sea, creates an outer bailey of several acres. The outer curtain has over twenty towers of varying shapes — square, D-ended, polygonal, rectangular, beaked — among which are gate-towers including the huge Constable's Gate which is perhaps the most elaborate gateway in any British castle.

This astonishing structure sprawls across the whole natural mound known as Castle Hill. In the middle of the outer bailey stand the ruins of a Roman pharos, or lighthouse, a clear sign of the strategic value of the site to the Roman forces of occupation. When the Conqueror defeated Harold II at Hastings, he headed not for London, capital of his new kingdom, but for its 'Gateway', Dover,

where the Anglo-Saxons had already raised a *burh*. There, William improved the fortifications by erecting a motte-and-bailey, it is recorded, in only eight days.

But the incredible layout of stonework that is now Dover really began with Henry II, builder of many castles, who appointed as his master mason Mauricius Ingeniator (Maurice the engineer) who had already built the great tower at Newcastle upon Tyne where he was known in the lower rank of Mauricius Caementarius (Maurice the builder). Between 1180 and 1189, Dover great tower, the whole inner curtain with its towers and part of the outer curtain were all constructed. King John extended the latter, erecting several towers and the north gateway (incorporated in what is now called the Norfolk Towers). Between them, Henry and John spent over £8,000 (or more than a million in today's terms).

221

In 1216 there was a set-back. The king's agreement to the Magna Carta had been followed by civil war in which the barons asked Louis, son of the French king, to come and take the English throne. He arrived in England and without wasting much time, besieged Dover, which was held by John's staunch friend, Hubert de Burgh. Louis went straight for the king's newly completed north gateway and captured the barbican. Sappers, meanwhile, dug a tunnel under the gate and successfully brought part of its eastern tower crashing down. Hubert de Burgh and a handful of troops rushed to the gaping hole and plugged it with huge timber beams, wedging them down with other planks. They fought off the attackers who withdrew. Almost at once, news arrived that John had died at Newark, and had been succeeded by his son Henry. Louis thereupon called off the attack and the castle was saved.

Among the considerable building works done at Dover in Henry III's time was a quick but substantial repair to his father's gatehouse: the damaged eastern tower was rebuilt solid. The entrance was blocked by the insertion of a third (solid) beaked bastion. This is the cluster of three towers that make up the Norfolk Towers. A big round tower was raised in the ditch in front, and beyond that a new outwork of earth. The outer curtain was finished, along with the rest of its towers, and the great Constable's Gate was constructed (see below), which became the residence of the castle's guardian. Dover was now complete, concentric and perhaps at last impregnable.

The great tower, 95ft tall on a splayed plinth, and almost square (98ft by 96ft) excluding the forebuilding, is built of Kentish ragstone, dressed with Caen stone, the two colours presenting a pleasing contrast. Each corner has a pronounced corner buttress turret, and there are equally pronounced pilaster buttresses mid-wall all round. The wall thickness of the tower diminishes from 21ft at ground level to 17ft at the top. There is a cross-wall nearly 7ft thick all the way up. The tower has four storeys, a basement, first floor and second floor which is in fact two storeys tall with the upper level containing a mural gallery, like Hedingham (*inter alia*). The main entrance

to the tower is at this second storey by means of the elaborate stairs, doors and landings in the wrap-around forebuilding of north-east and north. The forebuilding contains a chapel. The storeys in the great tower are connected by spiral staircases, in north and south corner turrets. The well arrangements are interesting. There is a vaulted room on the second floor (in the wall thickness) which is a well chamber. The well head comes up to this chamber and at one time provided direct water supply through pipes to the double storey and elsewhere. Remains of lead piping can be seen today near the well head. The well itself is lined with Caen ashlar downwards for about 170ft and continues thereafter for another 70ft through natural chalk.

The Constable Gate is a remarkable structure. It was built into the outer curtain (at west) early in Henry III's time, and was a development upon a simpler tower at that point erected during John's reign. It consists of a cluster of different sized, rounded towers, the cluster curving outwards, set high above the ditch in front, dominating all angles of approach. The fronts of the rounded towers have spur bases dropping right down into the ditch. The central projection is a pair of cylindrical towers flanking the entrance passage, joined across the top. The rear parts of the cluster contain residential quarters for the castle's constable and his household, together with guard-rooms and fighting platforms. The central gatehouse was guarded by a drawbridge which bridged the ditch between the gate front and the barbican on the other side. The passage through the complex had portcullis and doors. The Constable's Gate became the principal entrance after the siege of 1216, when the damaged gateway was repaired.

Much of this great medieval building work remains, but it has been altered over the centuries as the need to fortify Dover Harbour has from time to time become urgent. If it was 'the Key to England' in the thirteenth century, it is hardly less so today.

DRIFFIELD Humberside
(TA 035585) A
A twelfth-century motte castle was built here at what came to be called Moot Hill. Excavations were undertaken in 1975.

DUDLEY West Midlands
(SO 947907) O

A motte castle with oval bailey mentioned in 1086 (Domesday Book) was destroyed in 1175. It stood in a magnificent position on a levelled hill just outside and over 100ft above the town. It was owned by Gervase de Paynel, who supported the revolt of Prince Henry against his father, Henry II, in 1173–4, and de Paynel paid for backing the wrong side by losing his castle. The castle site lay desolate until the middle of the thirteenth century when a descendant, Roger de Somery, began to rebuild. He was granted a licence in 1265 but died in 1272 before the new works were anything like completed. These were carried on by his son, John, who made himself loathed in the neighbourhood for the dishonest and bullying means by which he raised money to pay for them.

John de Somery's work included an interesting great tower upon the old motte, rectangular in plan but with cylindrical turrets on the four corners. Dudley's great tower rose two storeys, and part of the tower remains. The work also included a tall enclosing curtain wall, about 8ft thick, and a substantial square-plan gatehouse which incorporates fragments of the castle's original gateway of the twelfth century.

Later in the fourteenth century, a chapel, a hall and other domestic buildings were erected round the inside of the curtain, and the gatehouse was reinforced with a twin-cylindrical flanking towered barbican front which is now in ruins.

Dudley was taken over by the Dudley family in the reign of Henry VIII, and much of the dwelling part remodelled by John Dudley, Viscount Lisle and later Duke of Northumberland, who was Protector of the Realm during the last two years of the reign of Edward VI. The castle was garrisoned by Royalists during the Civil War. It was captured by Parliamentary forces in 1645, and the great tower was partly demolished by order in 1646.

DUFFIELD Derbyshire   †
(SK 344441) O

Duffield great tower was once one of the largest of the fortress residences in England: today it is scarcely more than an outline of

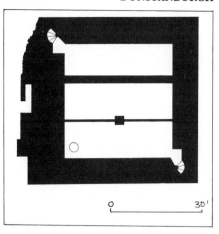

Duffield (after D.F. Renn): this is a plan of the remaining foundations of the great tower

foundations on a site, which cannot really give an idea of its magnitude. The great tower was built in the 1160s–70s on the mound of an earlier motte castle by the de Ferrers family. The tower was 95ft by 93ft, with walls about 15ft thick, and it is estimated that it reached as high as 120ft, putting it (if this was so) superior to Dover. The tower was divided unequally by a thick cross-wall and the larger half by what may have been a pair of arcades. In the largest part was the castle well, sunk through shale to about 80ft. There had also been a forebuilding on the western end and spiral staircases in both east and west walls.

The remains of the tower show signs of having been subjected to great heat, suggesting it may have been burned. It is known that it was demolished after 1266 when it was taken from the de Ferrers family by forces of Henry III.

DUNHAM MASSEY Cheshire
(SJ 750878) P

A motte stands in the grounds of Dunham New Park. It may be the castle of Hamo de Masci in the twelfth century.

DUNSTANBURGH Nr Craster,   †
Northumberland   (NU 258220) DOE

Dunstanburgh occupies about 9 acres high on the cliffs above the sea. It was a stonework enclosure whose main feature was the huge gatehouse-tower at the extreme southern

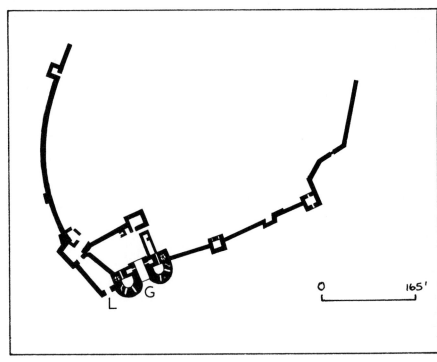

(above) Dunstanburgh: the gatehouse-tower. There was a forebuilding in front of the entrance arch, added when John of Gaunt converted the gatehouse into a great tower

(left) Dunstanburgh (after Graham). G = gatehouse converted to great tower. L = later entrance

end. The enclosure had flanking towers and turrets of rectilinear shape. The first works were erected in the early fourteenth century and consisted of the entire enclosing wall, about 6–7ft thick, but 10ft thick for a stretch leading north-eastwards out of the gatehouse into the small Constable's Tower. They also included the massive gatehouse, now in ruinous condition. This consisted of two D-ended towers flanking an arch entranced passageway. In front of part of the gatehouse was a ditch cut in the rock, and a barbican projected towards it, though the ditch was not completed. The entrance was protected by a portcullis. The gatehouse was three storeys high but the cylindrical towers

were two storeys taller. The gatehouse-tower had a great hall on the second floor, with tall, mullioned and transomed windows at each end.

All this work was carried out by Thomas, Earl of Lancaster, cousin of Edward II, whom he opposed because of the king's mis-government and his unfelicitous choice of friends. Lancaster was defeated at Boroughbridge in 1322 and executed at his castle at Pontefract. Dunstanburgh passed in due course to John of Gaunt, Duke of Lancaster, fourth son of Edward III. It was John who closed up the entrance to the gatehouse with a stone wall and a forebuilding in front (now disappeared) and turned it into a residential great tower, building an alternative gateway with barbican 100ft or so along the curtain wall in a north-westerly direction. His works were carried out in the 1370s and 1380s.

Dunstanburgh was besieged during the Wars of the Roses when much damage was done to the fabric by the cannons, particularly those of Richard Neville, Earl of Warwick, the leading Yorkist general. It is now in ruins.

DUNSTER Nr Minehead, Somerset
(SS 991434)
The present imposing fortified manor house known as Dunster Castle is a replacement of an earlier Norman earthwork castle which may be the same as that of Torre mentioned in the Domesday Book. There are no remains of the earlier work except for a mound, scarped out of a natural hill, and we do not know if it ever received stonework. The castle of today began as a fortified manor house in the fourteenth century. It came into the possession of the Luttrell family, famous for the *Luttrell Psalter* in the British Museum (which has so many revealing pictures of everyday life in four-teenth- and fifteenth-century England), and which has owned the castle ever since. It was besieged during the Civil War when its governor surrendered it to Parliament in 1646. It was restored by Salvin in the nineteenth century.

DURHAM †
(NZ 274423) O
Originally a motte castle, raised against a cliff in a loop of the Wear, probably by the Conqueror in c.1072, and granted to the Bishop of Durham. The motte was built up from layers of sand and earth. Its wooden tower rested on four posts, 'one post at each strong corner', according to a modern rendering of a twelfth-century description by Laurence, the Prior of Durham (cf. Abinger). In the early twelfth century a shell keep of sandstone in roughly octagonal plan was erected on the motte around the wooden tower which may have been retained for some time afterwards. This was destroyed in 1340 and rebuilt. In the banked and ditched bailey, partly curtained, domestic struc-tures were raised over the years, one of the earliest being a chapel whose crypt — still in wonderful condition — has six pillars with carved capitals. Other buildings include a range to the north, a great hall (rebuilt) and a gatehouse. In c.1494–1500 the Bishop of Durham restructured the kitchen which is huge.

The castle was a bishop's palace rather than a fortress, although it was always kept in a state of defensibility. The castle walls were connected with the walls of the City of Durham, and thus the whole peninsula was surrounded by the Wear, with the cathedral included. The castle is now part of Durham University. The Lower Hall is entered through an elaborate doorway of three orders, possibly the finest example of late Romanesque architecture in Britain.

DYMOCK Gloucestershire
(SO 711293) A
Traces of a motte castle, probably of the twelfth century, have been found here in the village. It is known as Castle Tump.

EARDISLEY Hereford & Worcester
(SO 311491) A
This was a rectangular enclosure with a motte. The bailey was surrounded by a moat fed by a stream. It may have been built late in the eleventh century at the time of the Norman advance into Wales. The castle is mentioned in the reigns of Henry II and John, but there is little further information.

EATON SOCON Cambridgeshire
(TL 173588) A
Erected beside the Ouse, this Norman double enclosure for which Saxon houses were destroyed (according to excavations of 1962–3) was surrounded with moats filled with water from a diversion of the river, which also operated a watermill. There have been several investigations into its early history, but the origins are still uncertain. The Beauchamp family held the castle in 1156, but before that it was a fortress in the possession of the de Mandevilles. The emergency excavations of 1962–3 suggest it was an adulterine castle in Mandeville's hands during the troubled times of Stephen's reign. Some earthworks remain.

ECCLESHALL Staffordshire
(SJ 827295) P
Eccleshall began as an enclosure and was surrounded by a moat fed by the River Stow. Stonework was added, principally a curtain wall with polygonal flanking turrets, and there was also a stone bridge across one arm of the moat. In c.1200 Bishop Muschamp of Lichfield had been granted a licence to fortify his house, and the stonework may be part of these works. There are some remains of later stonework, including a tower and some walling.

EDLINGHAM Nr Alnwick, †
Northumberland (NU 116092) A
The ruins of Edlingham Castle, originally
built c.1400, show it to have been an
enclosure castle with a tower outside the
walls. The tower, about 40ft square, has
elongated buttresses, placed obliquely on its
corners, and it had cylindrical bartizans at
the top. The tower was three-storeyed, with
the first floor vaulted, and a spiral stairway
encased in a special projection on the west
wall where there was also an adjacent
forebuilding (since vanished). Note an
interesting fireplace on the south wall of the
second floor.

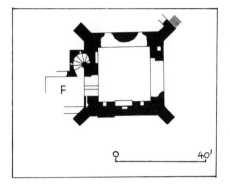

Edlingham: ground plan of great tower.
F=traces of forebuilding

EGREMONT Cumbria
(NY 010105) P
A motte castle of the twelfth century created
by scarping a natural mound, which is
outside the present structure. This received
stone walls and a gatehouse later in the
century, or perhaps early in the thirteenth.
The gatehouse was faced with ashlar and was
inserted in the curtain wall. Some of the
curtain has herringbone masonry. There
were other buildings in the enclosure. The
mound and some stonework remain.

ELLESMERE Shropshire
(SJ 403347) A
A motte castle of the late eleventh century,
possibly built by Roger de Montgomery
who led the Norman invasion into central
Wales. The castle was given to the Peverels
by Henry I but taken back by Henry II in
1154 who granted it to his brother-in-law

David, son of Owain Gwynedd, Prince of
Wales, in about 1177. The castle alternated
between the English and Welsh crowns up
to the 1240s and then passed to the le Strange
family. The site is open as a bowling green.

ELMLEY Hereford & Worcester
(SO 979403) O
There is very little left of this late eleventh-
century earthwork castle which received
stone additions in the twelfth and possibly
the thirteenth centuries. The earthworks
consist of ditching and banking of irregular
plan. There are remains of a stone rectangular structure with a projection that suggest a
great tower with forebuilding. This may
have been of the late twelfth century. There
are also remains of a curtain wall. The ruins
are in Elmley Castle Park, near Pershore,
whose bridge on the outskirts is thought to
contain stone taken from the old castle.

ELSDON Northumberland †
(NY 939935)
An interesting and well-preserved motte
castle of the late eleventh century, the motte
is separated from the bailey by a deep ditch.
The motte is about 30ft above the bailey, one
side of which is itself some 60ft above the
water level of the burn at Elsdon. The other
three sides of the bailey were protected by
ditches. It is thought that Elsdon Castle was
abandoned in c.1156.

ELY Cambridgeshire
(TL 541799) A
Cherry Hill mound is probably the remnant
of the very early motte castle raised by the
Conqueror in c.1070 during his campaign
against Hereward the Wake. It may have
been the same castle at Ely that was fortified
by Bishop Nigel, during the reign of
Stephen, who also built a fort of lime and
stone nearer to the site of the cathedral (Lib
Eliensis). There is believed to have been a
windmill on Cherry Hill in the thirteenth
century.

EMBLETON TOWER Northumberland
(NU 231224)
There is some uncertainty about the date of
this tower-house, and the building period is
given as c.1330-40 and as the end of the
fourteenth century. The tower-house has

Etal: an arch to the gatehouse from inside the enclosure

two vaulted chambers in the basement. It was modified much later when a vicarage was built on to one side.

ETAL Nr Ford, Northumberland   †
(NT 925394) A
The castle at Etal was built on a roughly quadrangular plan, with a rectangular great tower (about 46ft by 32ft), half in and half out of the north-west corner of the enclosure (cf. West Tower at Dolbadarn in North Wales). The great tower was four-storeyed with one large room to each floor, and the ground-floor room was vaulted. The east wall had a projecting forebuilding with a portcullis. At the south-east corner of the enclosure was the castle's gatehouse, a large square-plan building, about 36ft square, with projections on the east entrance on either side of the vaulted passage into the courtyard, protected by a portcullis and a gate. The enclosure wall was about 3ft thick, running from the south-west of the gatehouse to another smaller rectangular tower in the south-west corner, but only stretches of it survive.

Etal Castle was captured in 1513 by James IV of Scotland a few days before the Battle of Flodden Field nearby, where he, with a dozen of his highest and boldest nobles, were to lose their lives. The castle had been licensed in 1341.

It is in a ruinous state.

EWIAS HAROLD Nr Pontrilas,   †
Hereford & Worcester (SO 385287) A
This is one of the castles claimed as pre-Conquest built. Certainly, the Normans did build mansions or enclosures in England before 1066, generally at the encouragement of Edward the Confessor, but they were not fortified in the strict sense, nor were they of a military nature. There is a reference in the *Anglo-Saxon Chronicle* for 1052 to Pentecost's Castle which is identified with the pre-Conquest enclosure at Ewias Harold. In the Domesday Book there is a reference to Castellum Ewias which William FitzOsbern *refirmaverat*, that is, had strengthened or reinforced. By 1086 Ewias had become a motte castle, and its motte was 50ft tall. At one time the motte was believed to have received a shell keep of stone, about 90ft in diameter, built sometime in the twelfth century. Today, only earthworks remain.

EXETER Devon †
(SX 921930) O

Soon after the Conquest, William I went westwards towards Dorset, Devon and Cornwall. Arriving at Exeter in 1067, he was met by considerable opposition. The defenders assembled within the old Roman walls, which the Conqueror is supposed to have breached by means of undermining. In the northern corner of the walls, William raised a castle of earth and timber. The following year a simple single-tower gateway was built (which still stands as a good example of an early stone gate-tower).

Exeter Castle was in royal hands from Henry II's time to 1348. During that time many additions were made — towers, walls, extensive ditches (parts of which were discovered in recent excavations), hall and great chamber. Only the gateway remains, along with fragments of wall.

EYE Suffolk †
(TM 148738) O

Eye Castle was a motte castle raised during the Conqueror's reign, and it is mentioned in Domesday Book. It was built by William Malet, and the mound is about 50ft tall.

There is flint rubble masonry on the motte slopes, which is medieval, and it is part of the walling that would probably have connected with a bailey curtain. There are several references to work done on repairs and on strengthening (such as heightening the walls) in the Pipe Rolls of Henry II and Richard I. The bailey was about 2 acres and a local study revealed that the castle well was in the bailey. The mound and some stone fragments remain.

EYNSFORD Kent ††
(TQ 542658) DOE

One of the earliest examples of a stone enclosure castle in England, Eynsford's order of building periods was as follows: a low platform of earth was raised artificially beside the River Darent, a wooden tower about 36ft square was erected upon it, and in about 1088 the platform was enclosed by a 6ft-thick curtain of coursed flint rubble up to about 20ft. This walling was carried on up to about 30ft tall in c.1100. The level of the platform was adjusted and associated earthworks were carried out, including a moat along the east and south sides of the platform.

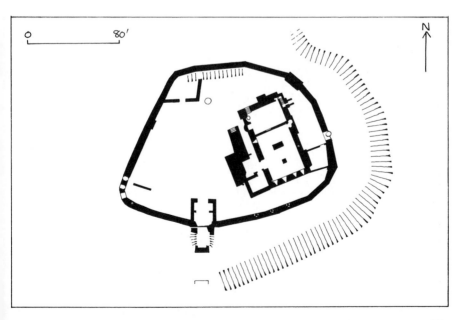

Eynsford: ground plan. The enclosure curtain is c.1100. The buildings inside are chiefly twelfth century, with some of the thirteenth

229

The enclosure received stone buildings, for the most part free-standing, in the twelfth century. The principal building was a rectangular hall with solar, and with undercroft below, and this was erected across the site of the wooden tower. It had a forebuilding of some complexity. The hall is now only as high as its undercroft. A stone gate-tower was added at the same time, which is estimated to have been c.1130. This gate-tower, now in ruins, is on the south side, and it led to a bridge across the moat. The bridge was timber built, and its construction and operation (part of it appears to have been movable) have recently been the subject of considerable research.

FARINGDON Oxfordshire
(SU 297957) A
An earthwork enclosure castle was built here by Robert, Earl of Gloucester, during the Anarchy of Stephen's reign, in c.1144, and it was destroyed by the king a year or two later. There is a mound known locally as the 'Clump', which may be the original earthworks. Skeletons lying tangled and on top of each other were found in diggings in 1935, which suggest a siege. Stones found may have been reinforcement of the motte.

FARLEIGH HUNGERFORD   †
Nr Trowbridge, Somerset
(ST 801577) DOE
This is a fourteenth-century double courtyard castle protected by a moat, walls and towers. Sir Thomas Hungerford, Speaker of the House of Commons and a man of great wealth, built it between c.1370–83. He appears to have been granted a pardon in 1383 for failing to obtain a licence to crenellate it. The site is one of strength, backing at the north on a deep dyke, with natural scarps to east and west. The castle began as a quadrangular enclosure with cylindrical towers on the corners and a substantial gateway of D-ended towers flanking an entrance. Inside, an extensive range of buildings of a domestic character was erected — indeed there was a greater area devoted to buildings than to open courtyard. It is suggested that these were grafted upon the remains of an earlier castle that had been destroyed in the mid-fourteenth century, which was connected

with the chapel of St Leonard outside (and which Hungerford rebuilt).

Hungerford's son, Walter, enlarged the castle to take in the chapel and did so by building a polygonal enclosure curtain with a flanking cylindrical tower and two gateways (east and west). Walter Hungerford surrounded the newer works with a moat extension along the southern end. He also put a masonry dam and sluice in the original western ditch to control the water flow from a large pond, thus creating a kind of 'water-castle'.

FARNHAM Surrey   ††
(SU 839474) DOE
Farnham is an interesting variant on the normal motte castle. Looking at the inner part, the shell keep as it is called, the visitor sees a mound enclosed within a many-sided shell of stonework, with a shallow gatehouse and four rectangular-plan buttress turrets which originally rose higher and contained windows. On the summit of the mound (today almost the same height as the shell wall) is a large 51ft square stone platform which is in fact a flange on top of a 37ft square stone substructure extending down the middle of the mound to ground level. This contains a well shaft. The structure and its flange supported a square great tower (evidently of stone) about which little is known. Whatever it was, and whether it had been finished, it was pulled down by Henry II's order in 1155. The earth may have been heaped up round the substructure afterwards, to make a mound in much the same way as was done at Ascot d'Oilly, Wareham, Totnes and South Mymms, or the substructure may have been sunk into an already established motte, which was about 30ft tall.

Farnham belonged to the Bishop of Winchester, Henry of Blois, brother of King Stephen, and when he left England to go to France after the death of his brother in 1154, the new king, Henry II, seized the castle and had it slighted. It was rebuilt, possibly by Henry of Blois, but in a different form. The mound was encircled closely by a substantial shell wall up to about 10ft thick, rising considerably higher than the 30ft of the mound, with the gatehouse and the buttress turrets built in. Garderobe chutes were inserted in the wall, and buildings were

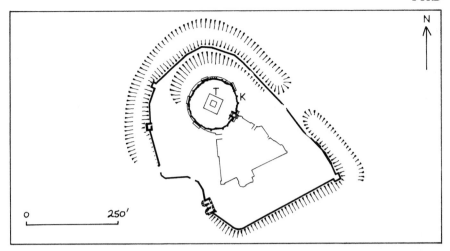

Farnham: plan of castle of several periods. Centre: late twelfth-century shell keep (K) revets mound on which earlier (c.1138) square great tower (T) was raised, with basement within the earth of mound

ranged round its inside. The space between the wall and the slopes of the mound were filled in later (thirteenth century). The whole structure was fortified by the erection of an outer curtain wall (much of which still remains), which had square-plan flanking turrets, and a twin-semi-octagonal towered gatehouse on the west side. The gatehouse is probably thirteenth century. The curtain has been extensively repaired, in many places in brick.

From about the 1280s right up to the seventeenth century, the castle was extended within the outer curtain, but these structures were of a domestic nature and the castle itself ceased really to have any defensive significance. Farnham was attacked during the Civil War and was then slighted by Parliament. It continued to be a residence of the bishops of Winchester after an interval of about twenty years.

FEATHERSTONE Nr Haltwhistle, Northumberland (NY 674610) O

The present mansion at Featherstone, built in the seventeenth century, incorporates some much earlier stone building, including a very fine arch of the late twelfth century and a handsome square pele-tower which has an arm to make it L-plan. The tower was erected in about 1330 by Thomas de Featherstonehaugh. It has the distinct feature of rising in three stages which are marked with sloping offsets. At the top the corners are crowned with bartizans.

FOLKESTONE Kent (TR 214380) A

This was an enclosure castle at the end of a natural mound protected on three sides by sheer cliff and on the fourth by a deep ditch and bank. There was an outer bailey, also with ditches. In the enclosure a well was sunk to some 85ft deep. Rubble masonry has been found which may have been part of a stone structure on the site, possibly of the early twelfth century. Traces remain on Castle Hill.

FORD Nr Etal, Northumberland † (NT 944375) O

Ford Castle was built for defence against Scottish raids into Northumberland. A licence to crenellate his home was granted in 1338 to William Heron, who built a quadrangle with towers on the four corners. The towers were different in size, two of them were square, one nearly square and one rectangular. The strongest was the north-west tower, which came to be called the King James Tower, and that has survived.

Ford was captured by the Scots in 1385 and dismantled by them. Evidently, there was enough structure left to make it worthwhile restoring, for by the beginning of the sixteenth century it had been rebuilt and refortified. But in 1513 Ford was taken by James IV of Scotland a few days before the Battle of Flodden (see Etal Castle). The eighteenth-century mansion grafted upon the old remains has largely obscured the original work, except for the King James Tower.

FOTHERINGAY Northamptonshire
(TL 061930) P
Almost certainly, Fotheringay's greatest claim to fame is that it was the scene of the execution of Mary, Queen of Scots, in 1587. By that time it was more of a manor house and was not fortified. Indeed, it was said that some of the walls were low enough to jump over. But Fotheringay began as a Norman motte castle on the north side of the Nene, with no ditch between motte and its bailey. An investigation recorded in 1975 (RCHM) suggested that some masonry near the river may have come from the motte, which indicates a building or a wing wall. Mentioned early in the thirteenth century, the

castle was held by William the Marshal, Earl of Pembroke and also by Ranulf, Earl of Chester (builder of Beeston and Bolingbroke). Interestingly, the castle had been used for prisoners from Scotland several times. There is very little left to see.

FOULDRY Morecambe Bay, Lancashire
(SD 233636) A
Known also as Piel Castle, Fouldry sits on an island in Morecambe Bay. In the 1320s a concentric castle was built here, consisting of a great tower inside an inner bailey, surrounded by an outer ward, with broad ditches and thick stone walling. The great tower is square in plan, 60ft wide, and rose to about 50ft, having pilaster buttresses on the corners. Much of the building was restored in the mid-nineteenth century.

FRAMLINGHAM Suffolk   ††
(TM 287637) DOE
Framlingham Castle was built between c.1189 and c.1200 by Roger Bigod, Earl of Norfolk, on the site of an earlier timberwork castle raised by his grandfather in c.1102. This earlier castle had been destroyed on the orders of Henry II in 1175, but part of the hall survived and was built into the curtain

Ford: the King James Tower is on the left

Framlingham: an aerial view. Note the open backs to most of the flanking towers

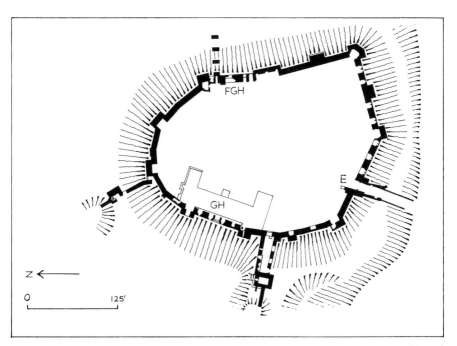

Framlingham: E = entrance through gate-tower; GH = site of second great hall FGH = position of first great hall (c.1160)

233

wall enclosure which has twelve rectangular flanking towers and a gateway. The enclosure is a simple enough structure at first sight, and it is an excellent early example of this type of castle. But the walls are about 44ft tall and 8ft thick, and the flanking towers rise about another 20ft, which would have presented quite an obstacle to a besieging army. Added to that, the structure stands on a mound surrounded by extensive wide and deep ditching with high counterscarp banking. A nearby stream was dammed to provide water for part of the ditching. The castle was besieged, however, in 1216 and taken on behalf of King John, but there is no evidence of major siege damage, which may suggest that the Bigod defenders (Roger Bigod was a supporter of the Magna Carta barons) gave in without much of a fight.

The enclosure was provided with additional buildings inside. Ten of the flanking towers were open-backed, which means they were of entirely military purpose: in time of war temporary backs of timber would be erected above the wall-walk level, making each tower top a separate and integral fighting unit approachable only from the wall-walk. A great hall built by the Bigods on the west wall has disappeared into the masonry of a poor house built there in the seventeenth century.

FRAMPTON Lincolnshire
(TA 327391) A
Remains of a rectangular moated enclosure here may be of the castle mentioned in c.1216.

FRODSHAM Cheshire
(SJ 514775) P
In the eighteenth-century Castle Park House at Frodsham are traces of the earlier (Norman) castle, though it is not possible to suggest a clear plan. There are indications that a tower was built on the high ground.

GIDLEIGH Nr Chagford, Devon
(SX 671884) A
Remains of a (?) Norman tower, about 22ft by 13ft are to be detected on this site.

GILLING Nr Helmsley, North
Yorkshire (SE 611768) P
The ground floor of a square tower-house built by the de Etton family in the mid-fourteenth century is incorporated in the later (sixteenth-century) tower block built by Sir William Fairfax. The block was remodelled in the eighteenth century. There is a possibility that the original tower was raised on an earthwork of eleventh-century origin. Gilling Manor belonged to Alan the Red who built Richmond Castle.

GLEASTON Nr Furness Abbey,
Cumbria (SD 261715) P
Gleaston was a simple quadrangle castle with corner turrets, built in c.1330. The walls were 9ft thick and built of crudely dressed limestone rubble blocks. There were some red sandstone dressings. There was a larger tower in the north-west corner, about 90ft by 50ft, at the highest point of the castle site. The castle was dismantled in 1458. This may have been a by-product of the Wars of the Roses (1455–85), but under what or whose insistence we do not know.

GLOUCESTER
Although there is nothing to see of Gloucester Castle, it is included because of some interesting aspects of its history that survive in medieval documents. One of these is a simple but revealing sketch of the great tower, drawn in the fourteenth century. Gloucester began as a motte castle of the Conqueror's reign (sixteen houses were demolished to make way for its site, according to Domesday). It was enlarged by William Rufus (eight more houses were cleared away) and further extended by Henry I and Henry II. Henry I built the great tower in c.1112, which may have looked like the drawing on p.42. According to Leland, who saw it in the 1540s, the great tower was 'high'. Interestingly, it is one actually described in another medieval document as *magna turris* (in an Exchequer record of 1328). Considerable repairs and some improvements were carried out by Henry III (including a bridge across the River Severn leading to a barbican in the outer wall). Gloucester was besieged twice in the war between Henry and Simon de Montfort between 1264–5. Further works were done in the reigns of Edwards I, II and III and also in the fifteenth century.

234

GODARD'S Kent
(TQ 808582) A
A twelfth-century enclosure castle of flint masonry. Fragments of the gatehouse survive, together with portions of curtain wall.

GOODRICH Ross-on-Wye, ††
Hereford & Worcester (SO 579199) O
Goodrich Castle is sited on a high rocky spur over the right bank of the River Wye, commanding a crossing of the river. It is protected partly by a natural steep slope and valley, and partly by a moat cut out of the rock. The first stone building at Goodrich is mid-twelfth century, a square great tower built upon the site of an earlier undetermined castle which was probably wooden. The great tower is constructed of pink local sandstone ashlar, with clasping pilaster buttresses all the way up the corners and about two-thirds up the centre of the tower's walls. There is a doorway into the basement, with a chevron headed arch, and above that another doorway into the first floor, with a round-headed arch, supported upon moulded side pillars. This has been partly blocked up and has a later window. The first-floor entrance was probably reached by an outside stair, for there is no evidence of a forebuilding. The tower has three storeys, reached by spiral staircase in the north-west angle. It is over 60ft tall today, and probably rose originally to nearer 70ft including battlements.

The tower stood on its own for a time, enclosed perhaps by a timber palisade, but there is no certainty about this. Then, in the very late thirteenth century, Goodrich, by then held by the de Valence family, was given a very substantial renovation. It was converted into a formidable quadrangle castle with massive cylindrical towers on three corners, and a vast gatehouse-tower on the fourth (north-east) corner. The cylindrical towers were raised on square bases with spurs that clamped the towers to the rock base upon which they stood. This feature can be seen very well today. The south-west tower contains traces of foundations of an earlier tower of unknown date. Inside the quadrangle some elaborate apartments were built, including a great hall (65ft by 27ft), a solar abutting on to the north-west tower and kitchens. The north-

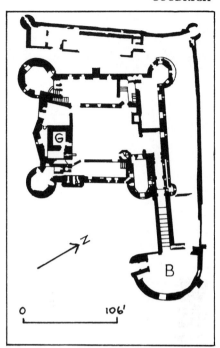

Goodrich: plan of castle of several periods. G=great tower of twelfth century, enclosed by late thirteenth-/early fourteenth-century quadrangle with towers; B=barbican of fourteenth century (like Lion Tower at Tower of London, now disappeared)

east corner tower was erected as a gatehouse, coupled with a chapel. This tower is not in good condition. The chapel has an apsidal east end. Extending from the gatehouse is a sloping causeway and bridge which crosses over the moat, leading downwards for about 40ft into a half-moon barbican whose exit is at right angles, facing south. The outer wall of the barbican curves round into the outer enclosing wall of the castle which continues around the north and east sides. The barbican arrangement is similar to one built at much the same time at the Tower of London.

Goodrich was slighted after the Civil War.

(overleaf) Goodrich: the view from the south. The great tower (centre) appears squashed against the much later curtain walling. The south-east tower (right) is a good example of a spur-based tower

235

GREAT CANFIELD Nr Dunmow,
Essex (TL 595179) A
A substantial motte castle was raised here by
the de Vere family which in the 1130s–1140s
also built Hedingham great tower. The
moats round the inner and outer baileys
were fed from a diversion from the River
Roding, which appears to have been regulated by a dam system. The only dating
known is early thirteenth century. (See also
Pleshey and Ongar.)

GREYSTOKE Cumbria
(NY 435309) P
The Greystoke family was granted a licence
to crenellate their home, a pele-tower in
Cumberland, in 1353. Little of this remains,
for there have been many additions to the
tower to make it into a mansion.

GROBY Leicestershire
(SK 525076)
A motte castle, possibly of the eleventh
century, was given stone buildings in the
twelfth. The rubble from these was much
later heaped over the remains of a tower
which may have been a great tower. The
castle was destroyed in the 1170s after the
rebellion of Prince Henry against his father
Henry II (1173–4). The site has disappeared
under roadworks (Med. Arch. VIII, p.235).

GUILDFORD Surrey †
(SU 999495) Great tower open
Guildford Castle has an almost square great
tower, of Bargate rubble, flint and chalk
courses. Note that some courses are set in
herringbone. This was built in the mid-
twelfth century upon the side of an earlier
motte. The reason for setting the great tower
to one side of the motte was in order to use
part of the natural rock (from which the
original motte was created) as foundation.
There are also remains of a contemporary
gateway and fragments of the curtain wall.
   The castle was used as the county gaol for
nearly 400 years (c.1200–1600). In 1381 it
was a clearing house for prisoners taken
during the disturbances caused by the
Peasants' Revolt, but so many were brought
to Guildford that half of them were transferred to Lewes and Arundel.

HADLEIGH †
Nr Leigh on Sea, Essex
(TQ 810860) DOE
This was a thirteenth-century creation,
begun by Hubert de Burgh, the celebrated
minister of John and the young Henry III. It
was a polygonal curtain enclosure. Edward
III took much interest in Hadleigh and
lavished considerable sums in converting it
to an extensive castle with several drum
towers, and a large cylindrical tower that
covered the north-west entrance to the
enclosure. Domestic buildings included a
great hall, a chapel and suites for the king
and the queen. The majority of his works
were done between 1361–70 and cost over
£2,300. The castle was intended to play both
military and domestic roles: the substantial
towers support the former. There are many
references to domestic expenditure and to
visits by the kings to Hadleigh in Exchequer
records. The remains to be seen today are
chiefly of the Edward III period.

HALLATON Leicestershire †
(SP 780967) A
A very interesting motte castle, whose motte
area occupied hardly less space (630ft in
circumference at the base) than its inner
bailey. Excavations a century ago revealed
some of the lumber assembled at the base of
the motte, and this included tree trunks
bearing axe marks, boulders and clay
lumps (*Early Norman Castles*, p.88).

HALTON Nr Frodsham, Cheshire
(SJ 537820) P
A late twelfth-century stone enclosure castle
on a rock site with several flanking towers,
including a twin-towered gatehouse (probably thirteenth century). The curtain walls
were 20–30ft tall, some of them standing
today. There was also a rectangular hall
building in the enclosure. The castle has
been obscured by later buildings.

HALTON Nr Aydon, Northumberland
(NY 997678) P
The tower at Halton was erected in the
fourteenth century. It adjoins a much later
mansion. The castle is near the remains of a
Roman fort whose stones were employed in
the tower's construction. The tower is
rectangular, about 31ft by 24ft, and is

four-storeyed, with cylindrical bartizans at the tops of the four corners, not unlike the arrangement at Chipchase Castle.

HANLEY Hereford & Worcester
(SO 837415) A

Hanley was built by King John between 1207–12, possibly on the site of an earlier rectangular moated enclosure. The castle commanded the high road from Worcester to Upton upon Severn. From 1216, Hanley was held for about a century by the powerful de Clares (see Tonbridge and Caerphilly). A description of 1416 indicated the existence of several stone towers, a palisade (presumably wooden) and a chapel. Nash, the eighteenth-century historian of Worcestershire, stated that Hanley contained, *inter alia*, a great tower in the north-west corner. Nothing remains, however, except the quadrangular moated site.

HARBOTTLE Nr Rothbury,
Northumberland (NT 932048) P

Harbottle began as a motte castle on the north bank of the River Coquet, with the motte astride the southern curve of the bailey. It was raised in about 1157 by Robert de Umfraville at the request of Henry II, presumably as a fortress to protect that part of Northumberland from the Scots. Part of the bailey wall was of stone, with a stone gateway and a turret towards the north. On the motte a rectangular tower was raised, though it is now much ruined. Gun-ports were added at a later date. In 1515, Margaret, the widowed queen of James IV of Scotland, and also sister of Henry VIII of England, was banished by the Regent, the Duke of Albany. She fled to Harbottle and towards the end of the year gave birth to a daughter there, who later became the mother of Lord Darnley, second husband of Mary, Queen of Scots. Margaret's second husband was the Earl of Angus, father of the child.

HARTSHILL Warwickshire
(SP 325942) O

A motte castle which later received a stone curtain round its bailey. There is a Tudor period timber-framed house in the bailey.

HASTINGS Sussex
(TQ 822095) O

Three castles were raised in England by the Conqueror before or immediately after the Battle of Hastings — Pevensey (September 1066), Hastings (before the battle, October 1066) and Dover (in October, a few days after the battle). Hastings was a motte castle raised near the shore by his troops and by local labour pressed into service, and is recorded on the Bayeux Tapestry (scene 52-3). It is possible that the wooden tower was assembled on the site from parts shipped over from Normandy after prefabrication there. The bolts and other iron parts were transported, it is suggested, in casks. Hastings received a stone great tower in the twelfth century, which has completely disappeared, its site eroded by the sea. It may not have been upon the site of the motte castle. Lengths of eleventh- and twelfth-century walling and a thirteenth-century gatehouse remain (*King's Works*).

HAUGHLEY Suffolk †
(TM 025624) A

The motte at Haughley Castle is one of the largest surviving mottes in Britain. At 80ft tall and about 80ft in diameter at the top, it is the equal of Thetford. The motte is not so readily visible today as Thetford's, chiefly because the village of Haughley is on rising ground. The inner bailey of the castle measured about 390ft by about 300ft, and the rampart round the encircling ditch is about 16ft high in some places. Recent studies suggest that the outer bailey enclosed Haughley Church and much of the village, in the same manner as at Castle Acre. There are stonework remains on the motte that may be from a shell keep raised there. The castle was dismantled in c.1173, during Henry II's war against his eldest son — as was Thetford.

HAUGHTON Nr Humshaugh,
Northumberland (NY 918729) P

Today, Haughton is an imposing mansion, part medieval tower-house, part nineteenth-century house, on the west side of the North Tyne. Probably begun in the late fourteenth century, it became a substantial castle based upon a narrow rectangular great tower with square corner turrets and an extra turret in the centre of the front wall at roof level. The tower was enclosed by a curtain, some of which remains.

HEDINGHAM Essex ††
(TL 787359) O

This is one of the most famous Norman great towers in England. It is still privately owned but is open to visitors. The castle began in the late eleventh or early twelfth century as an earthwork and timber fortress held by the de Veres, one of whom became 1st Earl of Oxford in 1141. Sometime late in the reign of Henry I or early in Stephen's time, the great tower was built on the flat raised platform which had formerly held the wooden castle. Built of Barnack oolite ashlar facing on rubble, the tower today stands to over 73ft tall, with two corner turrets extending for another 20ft. It is rectangular in plan, 62ft by 55ft, on a splayed plinth with flat pilaster buttresses on the angles and mid-wall. The tower has four storeys (or five, taking the second (great hall) storey as two). The entrance is at first storey and its round-headed arch has chevron moulding. A forebuilding was added at a later date. This has disappeared, except for founda-

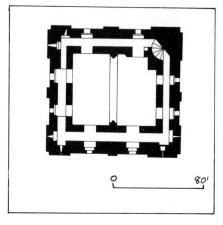

Hedingham: plan of gallery level of second floor. Note overall gallery running round all four sides of great tower

tions, leaving only a flight of stairs, not all of which are original. The creasings where the forebuilding roof joined the west wall can be seen. The entrance had a portcullis.

The tower walls are between 10–12ft thick. They are filled at every storey with chambers and passages. On the upper level of the great hall double storey, a wall passage runs right round through all the window bays, whose windows provided extra light into what was otherwise a dark hall. The windows at this level are paired. There is one staircase, a spiral, all the way up the north-west corner. The cross-walls, at first and second storey levels, take the form of flying arches, the arch on the double storey rising at its centre to over 20ft. The tower, well built and on the whole well appointed so far as accommodation is concerned, contained no chapel or kitchen. There is evidence of other buildings outside, including a hall and a chapel.

Hedingham Castle was on several occasions involved in warfare or drama. Robert de Vere, one of the barons who compelled King John to consent to Magna Carta, was besieged in his castle in the ensuing Magna Carta war, and forced to surrender by the king. In 1918, the great tower was severely damaged by a fire which destroyed the interior woodwork, and the present woodwork is replacement.

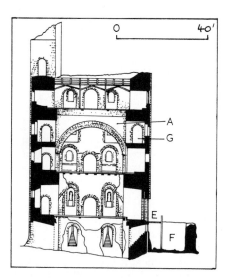

Hedingham: section through elevation of great tower (after W.D. Simpson). A=flying arch cross wall on second-floor level; F = remains of forebuilding; G = gallery of second floor

Hedingham Castle

The outer surface of the great tower contains several orderly rows of put-log holes, used for the horizontal posts of the building scaffolding.

HELMSLEY North Yorkshire   ††
(SE 611836) DOE
What strikes the visitor perhaps most forcefully about this late twelfth-century stone enclosure castle with great tower is the huge earthwork ditch-and-bank defence system. Simple enough as a quadrangle inside another quadrangle, the castle was in fact extremely well defended. The ditches are in the main over 30ft deep. There may have been an earlier wooden castle on the site to which part, if not all, the earthworks relate. A thick curtain wall with D-end and

round flanking towers was raised along the edge of the platform in the inner quadrangle. On the north-east of the wall was inserted c. 1200 a D-ended rectangular great tower which originally rose three storeys (the gable line of its first height can be seen) but later (c. 1300) two further storeys were added plus turrets on the square corners facing the inside of the quadrangle. It is possible that the rounded apsidal end which faces outwards over the scarping was added in stage two of the building of the tower. Several other buildings (some of them sixteenth-century) were erected in the enclosure. A substantial western tower (rectangular) of c. 1200 remains. The south-east inner gateway led out to a barbican and to a second gateway. The area between the two gateways was enclosed inside a smaller stone enclosure with turrets, built between the mid- and late thirteenth century.

The heightening of the great tower in the fourteenth century demonstrates the continuing value of great towers. Too much of it has been destroyed to work out its internal accommodation which after 1300 would have included much residential space. Note the exposed 'stalk' of the spiral staircase in the damaged turret.

HEREFORD

(SO 509395) A

Hereford is one of the castles once said to have been erected by Norman lords in the time of Edward the Confessor (cf. Ewias Harold and Clavering). But as it is now accepted that no castles were built before 1066, Hereford can probably be included among the first batch of motte castles erected by the Normans between 1066 and 1071. It was held by William FitzOsbern, one of the Conqueror's principal lords (and commander of the Norman assault on South Wales in 1067-8). It was a motte castle of which no trace remains, with a bailey, one side of which bordered the River Wye. Leland described the castle in the 1540s as having walls 'high and strong and full of great towers'. He also talks of one great tower encircled by ten semi-circular towers. Excavations in the last decade have revealed a confusion of stoneworks of medieval and

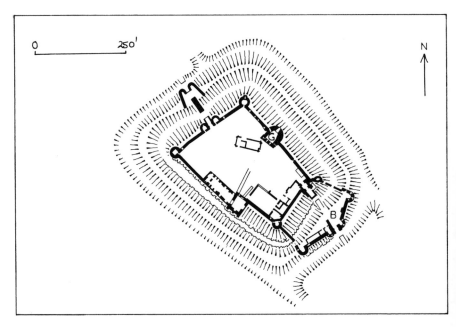

Helmsley: the thick bold lines represent the curtain walls and towers of c. 1200. B = barbican area of thirteenth century; G=great tower. Note the profiles of the ditching

much later origin. Documents certainly record considerable stone works of the thirteenth century, which include a great tower whose form we are not able to determine, but which was sited on the motte. The bailey is now Castle Green.

HERSTMONCEUX Sussex
(TQ 646104) C

Sir Roger Fiennes, a veteran of the wars in France, was granted a licence to build and crenellate Herstmonceux in 1441. It was constructed of brick, in basically quadrangular plan, with greensand stone dressings. It stands in a lake creating a wide moat round it. At each corner is a boldly projecting octagonal tower, and three semi-octagonal turrets project along its north, east and west fronts. On the south front are two turrets in between which is a massive gatehouse, created by a further pair of semi-octagonal turrets flanking a handsome entrance arch, with machicolated battlements all round the top of the structure where the two turrets change from octagonal plan to cylindrical. Behind the parapet

rising from the cylinders, as it were, are two inner cylinder towers, bringing the height of the gatehouse to about 85ft. The entrance arch is recessed and bears long slots for the drawbridge gaffs. Murder-holes are incorporated beneath the arch over the entrance. The gatehouse parapets have cross-arrow loops which are also inserted in the flanking towers themselves. The middle tower on the north front has a postern gate, also recessed for a drawbridge and slotted for the bridge gaffs.

The castle was allowed to decline, and much of the masonry was used to build a house nearby called Herstmonceux Place. But the outer masonry of the castle was carefully restored by two owners in the present century. It is now the official residence of the Astronomer Royal and so is not normally open to visitors.

HERTFORD †
(TL 325125) O

It is likely that Hertford began as a motte castle quite early in the Norman period, for a constable was appointed by the Conqueror.

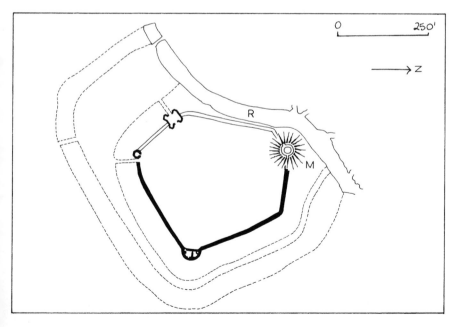

Hertford (after *King's Works*): plan of castle as it is today. The bold line represents remaining walls and towers. R=River Lea; M=mound of original motte castle. Internal buildings omitted

It was sited right by the River Lea which provided the water for its inner and outer moats. Renn thinks a small cylindrical tower about 30ft across may have been built on the motte, which was a low one (about 20ft). The earliest documentary evidence of work on Hertford is 1171–4. This may have included the approximately pentagonal stone curtain that surrounds the inner bailey and joins up with some stone walling up the motte sides. After this there was a lot of activity at Hertford over many years. The curtain acquired towers and an interesting three-storeyed gatehouse which is probably fifteenth century. This gatehouse has been restored. Considerable excavation work has been done at Hertford in recent years (1970s), substantiating the motte-type origins of the castle. (E. Herts. Arch. Soc. Trans.)

HEVER Nr Edenbridge, Kent †
(TQ 477452) O
Hever is basically a quadrangular fortified manor house, with great gatehouse, begun in the 1270s. It sits in a lake rather like Bodiam and Kirby Muxloe. A licence to refortify the manor house was granted in 1340 to the owner, William de Hever. A third fortifying was carried out in c.1380 by Sir John de Cobham. Thereafter, the castle changed hands several times, and in c.1460 it became the property of Henry Boleyn (Lord Mayor of London) who was great-grandfather of Anne Boleyn (second wife of Henry VIII and mother of Elizabeth I). The castle was greatly modified by the Boleyns, and the artificial lake was probably the work of Henry's son, in about 1482. The three-storey gatehouse with square flanking turrets is probably of this date, though it has been altered and renovated. Much restoration was done by William Waldorf Astor in 1903–7, who added a number of Tudor-style houses nearby to form a kind of village for his guests to stay. William Waldorf Astor became 1st Viscount Astor of Hever. The castle is still owned by the Astors.

HINTON WALDRIST Berkshire
(SU 376991)
A motte castle was erected here late in the eleventh century.

HOLGATE Stanton Holgate, Shropshire
(SO 562896) P
Near the church are the remains of a motte castle mentioned in the Domesday Book, thus dating it to at least 1085. The motte summit has traces of masonry in rectangular outline suggesting a tower or hall. There are remains of a round tower in the bailey, and of a thirteenth-century gatehouse. The tower is today part of a farmhouse.

HOLY ISLAND Northumberland
(NY 129416) NT
A coastal fort was built here on the great outcrop of rock called Beblowe Crag, some 6 miles across the sands from Bamburgh. It was put up by the Earl of Hertford (later, Duke of Somerset), brother of Jane Seymour, Henry VIII's third wife. When the king died in 1547, his son by Jane became Edward VI, and Somerset was appointed Lord Protector of the kingdom. During the Protectorate, Somerset expanded the castle to include living accommodation and equipped it with artillery.

The castle was occupied by Parliamentary forces during the Civil War, but thereafter its military importance declined, though it was for some time garrisoned. During the nineteenth century it was used as a base for the Northumberland Artillery Volunteers. Then, at the beginning of the present century Sir Edwin Lutyens restored and converted it into a fine residence.

HOME Hereford & Worcester
(SO 733618) A
Remains of a twelfth-century motte castle can be seen by the stream.

HOPTON Shropshire
(SO 367779) P
Hopton was a motte castle of the twelfth century which received a rectangular great tower on the motte sometime in the (?) thirteenth century. The stonework was surrounded by wet moats. It was captured by Royalists in the Civil War. The great tower still stands.

HORNBY Lancashire
(SD 587687)
A motte castle, with a low motte of about 22ft, held by Roger de Montbegon but seized by King John in 1205.

244

HORSFORD Nr Norwich, Norfolk
(TG 205156) A
A motte with some ditching is all that
remains today of the Norman earthwork
castle built here, possibly soon after the
great motte castle was raised at Norwich in
c.1070.

HORSTON Horsley, Derbyshire
(SK 375432) A
Only fragments of this castle of early
Norman times have survived. It is on a spur
of rock. The principal feature was a
rectangular (?) great tower with ashlar
masonry dressings, standing on a battered
plinth and with pilaster buttress corner
turrets. The great tower was battlemented
in c.1205. Further works were carried out in
Henry III's time, and in 1264 Horston was
captured by the de Ferrers family (of
Duffield Castle fame) who began to dismantle it. Afterwards, Horston was held by
others and repairs were carried out, but by
the sixteenth century it was a ruin.

HULL Humberside
(TA 104287) A
Hull was the northernmost coastal fortress
built by Henry VIII in the period 1538–44
(see chapter 16). It was a rectangular
three-storeyed great tower with a surround-

ing curtain, with two bastions, one on each
side. Each bastion had two curved faces
closing to a point (see plan). A long curtain,
19ft thick, extending from each side of the
castle, led to trefoil-shaped blockhouses,
each made up of three bastions like those
above. The fortress was built from brick
newly made on the spot, and from stone
taken from the recently dissolved monas-
tery-abbey at Meaux. Only traces remain.

HUNTINGDON Cambridgeshire
(TL 240714) A
On his first expedition into the north of
England in 1068–9, the Conqueror built
several motte castles, some on the way up,
others on the return journey. One of the
latter was a two-bailey motte castle on the
north bank of the Ouse at Huntingdon. The
motte is nearly 40ft high. The second bailey
may be of later date than 1068–9. A second
mound was erected a few hundred yards
from the first, in the twelfth century. It has
been suggested this was a siege castle
(RCHM Huntingdonshire). Huntingdon
Castle passed from the Conqueror's niece
Judith to her daughter Matilda who married
David I, King of Scotland, who was also Earl
of Huntingdon. When William the Lion,
King of Scotland, joined the revolt of Prince
Henry, eldest son of Henry II of England, in
1173, he was captured at the siege of

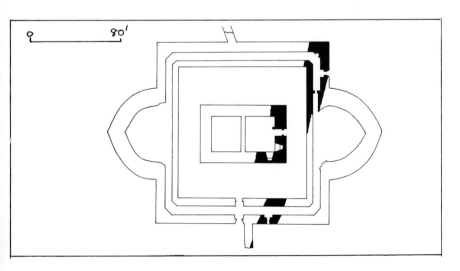

Hull (after DoE): plan of the remains of Hull coastal fort, after excavation

245

Alnwick Castle and forced to make a humiliating peace by Henry II. Huntingdon Castle, William's property by virtue of his being grandson of David I, was besieged and taken. Henry ordered the castle to be demolished, for which iron hooks were employed to dismantle the woodwork palisade, suggesting that part at least of the castle was still wooden. Stone remains have been found.

HUNTINGTON Nr Kington, Hereford & Worcester   (SO 249539) P
A motte castle with two baileys was raised here by the powerful de Bohun family. A stone tower was raised on the motte in the late twelfth century. Some fragments remain.

HURST Nr Milford, Hampshire   †
(SZ 319898) DOE
One of the Henry VIII coastal fortresses built during the 1538–43 invasion scare, it was intended to guard the approach to Southampton Water. It was built of squat semi-cylindrical towers in trefoil shape around a taller central polygonal tower, with obtuse angle curtain walls in between. The castle was not required, however, and it began to deteriorate. But in the eighteenth and nineteenth centuries, Hurst Castle was considerably rebuilt, partly in granite, which to an extent masks the original shape.

In 1648, Charles I, bound for London from the Isle of Wight on his way to trial for treason, was kept at Hurst for a short period.

HUTTONS AMBO York
(SE 763674) A
A rectangular enclosure raised on a spur above the River Derwent, with rampart and ditch. The earliest building was a timber hall, but this was replaced by a stone hall of sandstone rubble on the same site, probably early in the thirteenth century.

HYLTON Nr Sunderland,   †
Tyne & Wear   (NZ 358588) DOE
An imposing ruin, Hylton Castle today consists of the repaired ruin of a substantial gatehouse-tower built by Sir William Hylton between 1395 and 1410. Apart from the

ruins of St Catherine's Chapel nearby, there are no other remaining buildings, and it is difficult to say with certainty what shape the original castle took. It may have been a quadrangular castle of which the gatehouse-tower was the main entrance and the dominating feature.

This gatehouse-tower is interesting. It was a residential building — indeed, its internal appointments indicate that it was the Hylton family's main residence. The ground floor is pierced by an arched passage on the west front, which may at one time have passed right through to the east side. This passage was once protected by a portcullis. The west front is broken by four square-plan buttress turrets, capped with machicolated and battlemented octagonal tops. Between the two centre buttress-turrets the parapet is supported by a segmental arch. The carved figures on the battlements are not original. The façade of the west front has been altered, chiefly in the detail of the window and front arch arrangement. The north and south sides are relatively plain but of fine quality masonry. The east façade has a central projecting rectangular tower, also battlemented.

Inside, the gatehouse-tower, which is now a shell, originally had a ground floor of guardrooms and chambers on both sides of the entrance passage, and the spiral staircase began its upward turn in the south corner of the east block. The staircase rose to the roof. Above ground floor were three further main storeys. In the centre all the way up to the roof was a tall great hall. At each storey level, at either end of the hall, chambers, kitchens (first and second storeys) and other rooms opened off. One chamber was of two storeys.

INKBERROW Hereford & Worcester
(SP 017572)
There was a castle here, erected between 1154 and 1216. Earthwork traces remain.

KENDAL Cumbria
(SD 522924) O
Kendal was an enclosure within earth banking which in the twelfth or early thirteenth century received stone additions. There was a surrounding stone curtain with

Kenilworth: an aerial view

cylindrical corner towers, a hall and a square tower (which may be of the twelfth century). Recent excavations exposed a gatehouse-tower which has a cobbled road through the pierced arch, and traces of a bridge across the moat. It appears that there had also been some form of motte castle on the site.

KENILWORTH Warwickshire ††
(SP 278723) DOE

Professor W. D. Simpson wrote that from a distance Kenilworth Castle looked like a burnt out factory. Certainly, it is not until one is close to the varied assemblage of buildings of red sandstone, for the most part ruinous, that one can see that it is the wreck of a once splendid medieval castle, one of the most formidable in the Midlands.

Kenilworth was granted in c.1120 by Henry I to his chamberlain, William de Clinton. The first structure was a banked enclosure surrounded by a wide ditch, on which was raised a motte castle. Sometime in the middle of the century, a substantial rectangular great tower was erected upon the motte, possibly after levelling the summit. A stonework curtain was raised along the line of the bank (also levelled), but this has almost gone. The great tower, which

stands on a splayed plinth, began as a three-storeyed building including basement, the basement being filled with earth, this being the top of the motte. The two storeys above had one principal room each. The entrance to the tower was by means of a staircase protected by a huge forebuilding on the west side, and the door was at second-storey level. Both great tower and forebuilding were altered by Robert Dudley, Earl of Leicester, in the 1570s. The tower was heightened and the forebuilding gutted and converted into a courtyard.

The castle was appropriated by Henry II in c.1174, and it remained in royal hands until 1253 when Henry III granted it to Simon de Montfort. King John had spent over £1,000 on it, and this included part of the outer stone curtain, the gatehouse and some of the mural towers. Henry III had the royal apartments modernized. It may also have been he who ordered the construction of the formidable water defence system — a dam 'affording a broad causeway across the water to a large outer barbican, to pond back the currents of two streams, flowing respectively past the south and west sides of the raised platform on which the castle stands'. The lake thus formed was more than 100 acres in area. At all events, when in 1266 Henry III came upon the castle to besiege it, held as it was by the son of Simon de Montfort who had rebelled in 1264, he was faced with assaulting a castle completely surrounded by water, at almost every place too wide to allow a mine tunnel to be dug. The siege began in June and it lasted for six months. During this time, the defenders as well as the attackers employed stone throwing siege engines. When the king brought up wooden belfries against the outer walls, young de Montfort smashed them down with stone shot from inside. The attackers replied with their artillery, and one account of the siege refers to stone balls colliding in mid-air and smashing to fragments. The garrison finally surrendered when food ran out and many were starving. The castle had not been taken by siege: even a water-borne assault by boats filled with armed men rowed across the great lake failed.

The castle became the property of John of Gaunt, Duke of Lancaster, in the 1370s, and he remodelled it, converting it from a feudal castle into a palace. He built large domestic ranges to the west and south of the great tower, including a fine great hall, kitchen with three fireplaces and great chamber. Further works of repair and improvement were done in the fifteenth century when it reverted to the Crown (1399). In the sixteenth century, it was the property of Robert Dudley, Earl of Leicester, Queen Elizabeth I's early favourite, whom she nearly married, and he added an interesting range of buildings on the south-east corner of the inner curtain.

KILPECK Hereford & Worcester
(SO 444305) A
Kilpeck is interesting as a motte castle that had several baileys. Remains of a polygonal stone enclosure wall with splayed plinth are on the motte, probably indicating a shell keep. It was built in the 1130s.

KING CHARLES'S CASTLE Tresco Island, Isles of Scilly
(SV 882161) DOE
This coastal fort was first constructed in the time of Edward VI (1547–53). It was a two-storey rectangular structure with one end semi-hexagonal and the other having two tower projections. There are gun-ports in the hexagonal end. During the Civil War the castle was reinforced with a star-shaped earthwork around it, carried out on behalf of Charles I, which probably explains its name. (See Cromwell's Castle.)

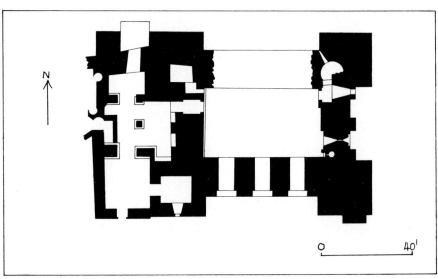

Kenilworth: ground floor of the great tower c.1160–80. Forebuilding at left was converted in Tudor times into a courtyard

KINGERBY Lincolnshire
(TF 056928)
A motte castle inside a rectangular-plan enclosure surrounded by a ditch. The castle was burnt at the beginning of the thirteenth century. In later years a mansion was built by the site.

KINGTON Hereford & Worcester
(SO 291569)
The remnants of an earthwork castle of mound and ditch, of possibly twelfth-century origin, are near the church at Kington. The castle was taken from its holder, Adam de Port, in 1172 by Henry II and remained in royal hands until about 1203 when John gave it to his friend William de Braose.

KINNARD'S FERRY Lincolnshire
(SE 806002)
Also known as Owston Ferry Castle, this is the site of a motte castle of the twelfth century built probably by the Mowbrays. It was dismantled at the orders of Henry II in 1175–6, and this may have been following the rebellion of his son, Prince Henry, in 1173–4.

KIRBY MUXLOE   †
Nr Leicester, Leicestershire
(SK 524046) DOE
Lord Hastings, who built the Hastings great tower at Ashby de la Zouch, began to build this attractive fortified house in brickwork in c.1480. It is interesting that the accounts for the building work have been preserved, although the castle was never completed. Lord Hastings was executed during the works, and after a time his widow could no longer afford to complete them.
The castle was a quadrangular structure with rectangular corner towers, tower projections mid-wall on three walls and on the fourth a substantial gatehouse with semi-octagonal turrets flanking the entrance on the inner as well as the outer face. The castle stood in a wet moat resembling a lake. All that remains today is the gatehouse and one corner tower, still surrounded by a wet moat. It is evident that much of the stonework on the edge of the bank and ditch is of an earlier date, probably fourteenth century, and so the structure of Lord Hastings was raised on the remnants of an earlier building, traces of which are also evident in the present remains.
Received opinion is that Kirby Muxloe was hardly a castle in the sense of being a military residence, but the surviving structures contain several gun-ports of ashlar, strategically built into the brickwork and apparently covering every angle of possible attack. Parts of the wall of the surviving tower are over 10ft thick. And the accounts indicate that the gatehouse was to have machicolation round the parapet.

KIRKOSWALD Cumbria
(NY 560410)
A stone curtain enclosure with towers was built here in the thirteenth century, following the grant of a licence to fortify in c.1201 to Hugh de Morville. A tower remains, along with some scattered masonry. The stone castle may have been erected on an earlier motte site.

KNARESBOROUGH North Yorkshire †
(SE 348569) O
Knaresborough Castle stands on a very high rock overlooking the town and the valley of the Nidd. It began as an enclosure on the rock in the eleventh century. Some time in the twelfth century it received a roughly triangular stone curtain with flanking towers and other buildings inside. One of these was a tower which may have been residential, a great tower. It was in royal hands on and off from the beginning right through to the end of the fifteenth century, and most of the works done on it were carried out by the kings. The most extensive work was in the time of Edward II and Edward III, notably between 1307–50, and the existing remains are chiefly of this period. Edward II had a tower (possibly the suggested great tower) demolished and a brand new rectangular great tower built, about 64ft by 52ft with four storeys. The north wall protruding from the curtain is semi-hexagonal. The tower was built between 1307–12 at a cost of nearly £900. The staircase to the first floor was defended by three gates and three portcullises. The curtain wall is 40ft high in places.

KNEPP Sussex
(TQ 163209) C
A motte castle of the early twelfth century, which received a great tower of sandstone probably in the time of Henry II. The tower was raised on the mound. Some 30ft or so of the structure remains in a ruinous state. The castle is believed to have belonged to the de Braose family.

KNOCKIN Shropshiire
(SJ 334223) P
A motte castle with a low motte, probably of the twelfth century, was reinforced with stone additions. There are traces of curtain wall round part of the bailey. There are no moats but the site lies between two streams that provided natural defences.

LANCASTER †
(SD 473620) O
Lancaster Castle stands on a knoll overlooking the River Lune, with steep west, north and east sides. It may have begun as a motte castle, but early in the twelfth century it received a great tower of stone, about 80ft square, with 10ft-thick walls, which has been extensively restored. It had pilaster buttresses, a cross-wall and spiral staircases. It was surrounded by ditching, much of which has been filled in. Adjoining the great tower was a thirteenth-century rectangular hall along a curtain wall which ends in a cylindrical tower. At right angles to the hall projects a further stretch of curtain at the end of which is another tower, this time rectangular, also of the thirteenth century. When the castle came into the possession of Henry IV, by his right as Duke of Lancaster, in 1399, he began major new works. These have not been specified by documents but must include the handsome and formidable twin-semi-octagonal turreted gatehouse with boldly projecting machicolated and crenellated parapet round the top, and polygonal turrets emerging above the parapet. The gatehouse entrance arch is wide, and had a portcullis. The gatehouse is over

Knaresborough: (left) the masonry blocks reduce in thickness as the courses ascend, in this remnant of a flanking cylindrical turret; (right) part of the rectangular great tower built in the time of Edward II. The polygonal end of the tower overreaching into a ditch can be seen at right

Lancaster: the splendid gatehouse, from a photograph of c.1900. The gatehouse is still in good condition

60ft tall and was built using masonry from decayed other parts of the castle.

The castle was granted to Roger of Poitou by the Conqueror, it was returned to Henry I who granted it to Stephen of Mortain, and then in the ownership of Richard I it was granted to his brother John. It reverted to Richard in 1194 and remained in Crown hands until 1267 when Henry III granted it to his son, Edmund, Earl of Lancaster. That is how it eventually came to Henry IV.

The site is partly occupied as a court-house. Some parts are open at regular times.

LANGLEY Nr Hexham,
Northumberland (NY 835624)
Sometime in the mid-fourteenth century, Thomas de Lucy built Langley great tower, an H-plan structure, four storeys high, with four substantial corner turrets reaching to about 66ft on the arms of the 'H'. It was attacked and severely damaged by Henry IV during his campaign against the Percys and Archbishop Scrope in 1404–5. An early nineteenth-century description notes that the inside of the ruined tower was 'red with marks of fire'. The castle was restored as a home in the 1890s. Note the prominent buttresses. It now houses a restaurant.

LAUNCESTON Cornwall ††
(SX 330846) DOE
A motte castle was raised here early in the Conqueror's reign by his brother, Robert of Mortain. The motte received a shell keep of roughly cylindrical plan early in the thirteenth century, with walls about 10ft thick. This has two stair flights in the masonry to higher levels. Later in the same century a cylindrical tower was raised inside, built of dark-coloured shale, unlike the stonework of the rest of the building on the motte. It has a pointed arch door on the western side. The stonework between the tower and the shell wall was at one time roofed, as it may also have been at Tretower and Sandal. The sides of the top of the motte have been revetted with a stone wall for several feet, sometimes referred to as a mantlet wall. The gateway at the south at bailey level leads to a flight of steps up the motte side.

The great mapmaker, Norden, described the castle as 'this triple crowned mounde' and today the visitor can see exactly what he meant. Very recent excavations exposed the remnants of a substantial stone hall in the bailey, about 60ft by 18ft internally. The hall is thought to have been used as a courtroom rather than for domestic pur-

251

poses. The first work on this hall appears to have been undertaken c.1200–1. The building was raised upon the ruins of earlier structures, mainly two houses, which were of twelfth-century origin.

LAVENDON Buckinghamshire
(SP 917544)

A substantial motte castle was raised at Lavendon, probably in the twelfth century. It had three baileys. The motte was demolished during World War II (Antiq. Jnl. xxxix).

LEEDS Nr Maidstone, Kent
(TQ 836533) O

The first castle on the two-island site in a lake, which is now occupied by the splendid group of buildings originating from Edward I's time and with later additions, was an earthwork enclosure whose wooden palisade was converted to stone and provided with two towers along the perimeter, now vanished. The conversion may have been done in the reign of Stephen, or shortly afterwards. The castle was held for Empress Matilda by Robert of Gloucester in c.1138 but was taken by Stephen at the end of the year. Traces of arches in a vault thought to be Norman were found at the beginning of this century. The castle came into the possession of Edward I in c.1278 when the owner, William of Leybourne, handed it to him in part payment of some debts.

Edward I rebuilt much of the castle as it stood at the beginning of his reign, and enlarged it, providing an outer stone curtain round the edge of the larger island, with cylindrical open-backed flanking towers and a square-plan water-gate on the south-east. The gatehouse at the south-west, a single tower pierced by an arched passage, was improved. It led out via a drawbridge across to a smaller island on which was built the 'Gloriette', a D-plan tower complex containing other buildings, which was extensively altered in Tudor and later times.

The lake in which the two-island site stands was created by damming the River Len. Leeds was besieged by Edward II when Bartholomew of Badlesmere, holding it as a gift of the King, joined a revolt and allowed his castellan to refuse to let the Queen, Isabella, enter it. The King took the castle and hanged the castellan.

Much of what is visible today is of nineteenth-century origination and reconstruction work by the then owner, Charles Wykeham-Martin.

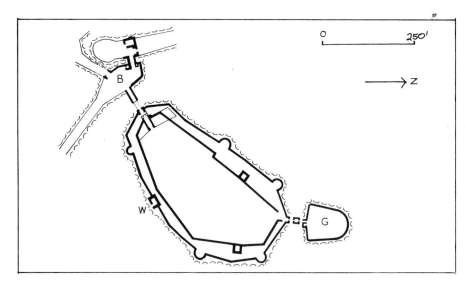

Leeds: ground plan, nineteenth century (after KW). The inner enclosure walls are early thirteenth century. The outer wall, 'Gloriette' (G), water-gate (W) and barbican (B) are of Edward I's reign

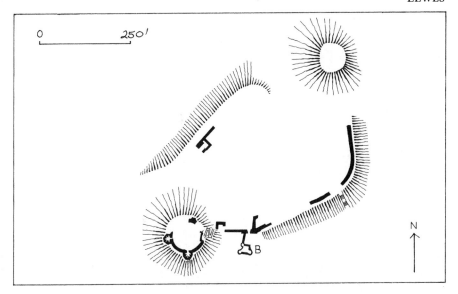

Lewes (after R. Allen Brown): ground plan. Note both mottes. Left-hand motte carried the oval shell with polygonal turrets. The dark lines indicate remaining medieval masonry. The barbican (B) is basically fourteenth century, with restoration of later years

LEICESTER   †
(SK 585040) O

Leicester Castle was a motte castle with inner and outer bailey, probably raised in 1068. The motte was once over 30ft high. Early in the twelfth century the castle received stone buildings, including a hall which remains standing to this day. It was probably built by the 2nd Earl of Leicester, after he succeeded his father in 1118. The 2nd earl's son joined Prince Henry's revolt against Henry II, 1173–4, and had Leicester Castle confiscated and severely damaged for his pains. But the family continued to reside within the castle grounds. It was held for a time by Simon de Montfort, Earl of Leicester, but when he was slain at the Battle of Evesham in 1265, the castle was taken over by Henry III who gave it to one of his sons, Edmund Crouchback, Earl of Lancaster. Eventually it became the property of John of Gaunt, Duke of Lancaster, the biggest landowner in England in the last two decades of the fourteenth century. This was the most splendid period of Leicester Castle's history, by which time its military role had taken a marked second place to its

residential role. It had become an enclosure with buildings round a square court, the most distinguished being the castle hall, oblong with sandstone walls over 4ft thick.

Henry IV and V spent money on constructing new boundary walls, and a gateway, the Turret Gateway, much of which remains.

During the fifteenth century it deteriorated as the fortunes of the House of Lancaster declined. Richard III, the last Yorkist king, stayed there a few days before the Battle of Bosworth on 22 August 1485.

Leland described it in 1536 as 'of small estimation'. It has a later history which is not relevant here. There are some early works to be seen.

LEWES Sussex   †
(TQ 415101) O

Lewes began as one of the few motte castles consisting of two mottes associated with one bailey. Both mottes stand astride the bailey limits. It was raised by Gulielmus de Warenne, the Conqueror's chief justiciar, in c.1069–70, on the edge of the town of

Lincoln: inside the polygonal shell keep on one of the two mounds of the old motte castle. Note the interesting obtuse-angled stones keying two angled walls together

Lewes, and was provided with defensive earthworks and moat. The western motte was largely of compacted chalk blocks. It carried a wooden tower and palisade which were later replaced by a flint rubble walled shell keep of oval plan (some of it of knapped flint set in herringbone facework), about 10ft thick, which was later still given two semi-octagonal towers on splayed plinths along the circumference, possibly in the late thirteenth century. A rectangular building was built on the summit before the shell keep, and traces of this were found at the end of the last century. A curtain wall was raised along side of the bank between the two mottes, but it is incomplete. In the south are the remains of a rectangular gate-tower, and in front of it a magnificent barbican added in the early fourteenth century. Restored, this barbican is one of the best in England: corbelled cylindrical turrets on the corners, machicolated parapet over the central pointed arch, built of close-packed small size knapped flint stones.

The eastern motte, known as Brack Mount, contains traces of a flint shell wall. This mount was also constructed of chalk blocks.

The castle is largely ruined, and parts of the town have spilled over the site. It is, however, an important site with numerous points of interest.

LEYBOURNE Kent
(TQ 688589) P
A circular enclosure with banked ditch and an additional banked area adjacent to it, with masonry remains, are the remnants of a castle here which has been incorporated in a much more modern structure.

LIDGATE Nr Newmarket, Suffolk
(TL 722583) A
This was a rectangular motte with one bailey, and ditch and rampart on the south side. There were two other baileys, one encircled by a wet moat and the other by a dry moat. The motte castle appears to have been given its additional enclosures and buildings 'for manorial requirements'. There is some flint masonry which may be part of a gatehouse.

LINCOLN   ††
(SK 975718) O
Lincoln is one of the handful of motte castles

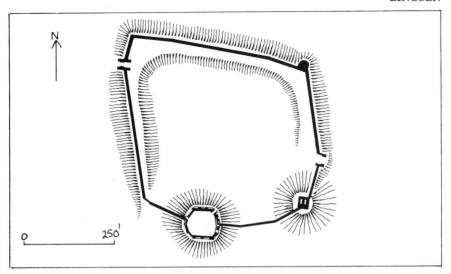

Lincoln: ground plan. Note the two mottes. The larger motte received the polygonal shell keep. Buildings within the enclosure have been omitted

that had two mottes associated with one bailey (Lewes was another). It was started in 1068 on the Conqueror's orders and sited in the south-west of the upper Roman enclosure, where 166 houses were cleared to allow the castle with its earthworks to be built. The site covered 5 acres and overlooks the Witham and the western valley of the Trent. One of the mottes, raised astride the line of the enclosing bailey wall, was adorned, sometime in the twelfth century, with an interesting shell keep, some 20ft tall, fifteen sided, bolstered by pilaster buttresses on the angles, with an entrance projecting out of one of the sides having a fine rounded arch. This is reached by a steep flight of steps which may follow an original flight. There is another entrance at the south end of the shell. Inside the shell some of the stones on the angles are cut and set horizontally as wide angled 'V' shapes, presumably to form a stronger join than several quoins cemented together.

The shell keep, known as the Lucy Tower, has wing walls: one leads in a curve down the motte slope in double thickness with parapet walk and up the slope of the other motte right to the structure on the summit. This wing wall is stepped for some of its length. The other wing wall travels in

the opposite direction from the Lucy Tower right round the castle, interspersed with gateways at west and east. The eastern gateway is a handsome structure, with pointed arch surmounted by two semi-cylindrical turret projections (containing spiral stairs), in between which is 'sandwiched' a chevron-plan wall projection, whose apex is in line vertically with the keystone of the arch. This gateway is a reconstruction of the original and simpler gate, and is of thirteenth-century construction with some later work added.

The second motte carries a square-plan tower structure with a nineteenth-century Observatory Tower. The date of this motte is not certainly known. It has been suggested that Ranulf, Earl of Chester, who held the castle in the 1140s, and who was granted leave to refortify it (with limitations) by Stephen, raised it in the south-east corner in the line of the bailey wall and on it erected a wooden tower, which was later converted to stone. But it has also been mooted that this was the original 1068 motte, and that the Lucy Tower stands on a much later one. The name Lucy stems from Ranulf's mother, Lucy, Countess of Chester, who died c.1136, passing the castle to him. This could date the motte and the shell keep to c.1130 or

255

earlier. There is a reference to a stone curtain at Lincoln Castle in 1115. Perhaps this is the period of the building of the Lucy Tower and second motte.

Today, the castle can be visited, and there is much to see: the Lucy Tower, the eastern gateway, the curtain wall (some of the parapet of which can be walked), the Observatory Tower and Cobb Hall, a small tower on the north-east angle of the curtain.

LLANCILLO Hereford & Worcester
(SO 367256) A

Traces of stone walling can be seen at this motte castle site.

LONGTHORPE TOWER †
Nr Peterborough, Cambridgeshire
(TL 163983) DOE

This is a borderline structure so far as inclusion in a gazetteer of castles is concerned. It began as a square great tower of c. 1300 supported by angled buttresses at the lower part of its height. It is three storeys tall, has walls 6–7ft thick, and is built of small stone rubble with larger quoins. The ground floor is vaulted, but the room inside is not connected to the storeys above which are in fact reached by a passage at first floor from the building next door (which is partly of slightly earlier date). The first floor contains the great chamber, also vaulted, and this has recesses, including a possible garderobe, and a narrow staircase up to the top floor, above which was the roof with a parapet and wall walk.

The tower was raised to protect the owners and their lands from the possibility of French invasion up the River Nene. It is comparable with some of the pele-towers of the northern border counties (see chapter 14).

One particularly notable feature of Longthorpe is the series of remarkable wall paintings in the great chamber. These had been whitewashed, possibly for centuries, but were revealed by cleaning, soon after World War II. The pictures are religious and allegorical.

LONGTOWN Hereford & Worcester †
(SO 321291) A

A motte of some 35ft in height at the corner

of a rectangular double bailey, probably of late eleventh-century construction, was later crowned with a cylindrical great tower of sandstone rubble on a battered plinth. Walling skirts down the motte slope towards a right-angle of curtain wall within the northern half of one bailey. The tower is interesting: its three lobes project slightly (at 120 degrees from each other) from the cylindrical plan, the lobes acting as buttresses. One has a staircase. The tower is probably early thirteenth century. Note the corbelled garderobe shoot halfway up the tower beside one of the lobe buttresses.

LOWER DOWN Lydbury, Shrophire
(SO 336846) P

An early motte castle here is believed to have received a polygonal shell keep in the twelfth century. Only fragments remain.

LUDGERSHALL Wiltshire †
(SU 264513) DOE

An extensive earthwork enclosure beginning in the late eleventh century in which a kind of motte castle was raised. The earthworks consisted of two adjacent double-ditched enclosures with double ramparts. Excavation has revealed a complex series of buildings of several periods:
1 Three phases of timber buildings, of late eleventh and early twelfth century, were found. Some rough brickwork was incorporated with the third phase.
2 An enclosed rectangle of stone and timber buildings of the same period, including a timber tower.
3 A phase in which some of these works were demolished and others preserved, and a great tower of stone was begun, in the mid-twelfth century, but evidently not finished. This was superseded by another larger great tower, with stone steps, which incorporated the smaller tower. This later tower was then pulled down and replaced by a tower set in a rampart with a timber rampart walk, in c. 1200. In the thirteenth century four more phases converted the castle to more of a residence, including a great hall (c. 1244–5), large chambers, one for Prince Edward, son of Henry III, and several ancillary buildings. There were three chapels, all of about the same time. By this time the castle was a hunting lodge for

the king and his sons, and after Henry III's death it passed to his widow. Ludgershall had by then surrendered its military role.

LUDLOW Shropshire †† (SO 508746) O

This is a castle of considerable interest, and some of it is of great antiquity. The site stands upon the top of a rock promontory over 100ft high overlooking the River Teme. Sometime in the last ten to fifteen years of the eleventh century, a stone curtain enclosure was raised in multangular plan, roughly an oval shape, whose north and west abut upon the steep and rocky south bank of the Teme, and whose east and south were protected by a rock-cut dry moat. The curtain, about 10ft thick for most of its length, was provided with a simple stone gateway in the south, which may have been like the Norman gate at Exeter. The curtain was also flanked with two square and two polygonal wall towers along north and west

sides which, according to Professor R. Allen Brown, indicate that the idea of a curtain wall with flanking towers as a form of defence was introduced much earlier into English castles than has previously been accepted. Professor Brown's valuable suggestion is lent some weight by the existence of similarly dated walling having a flanking tower (incorporated in later work) at Rochester, and by flanking towers at Richmond, also of early date.

Ludlow Castle will doubtless have had wooden buildings, but in the early twelfth century an unusual Norman chapel was built, much of which remains today. Modelled, it is thought, upon the Church of the Holy Sepulchre in Jerusalem, it has a circular nave with a battlemented top and a billet-on-chevron moulded round-head arch at the entrance on the west. The chancel has disappeared. The chapel is among the earliest castle chapels in Britain.

Sometime, possibly in the early years of

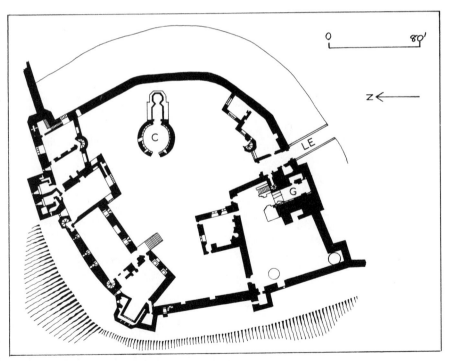

Ludlow: outline ground plan of the castle. The earliest buildings were the round chapel (C), the first gatehouse (G) and the enclosing curtain. The gatehouse was later altered to make a great tower. LE = later entrance

Stephen's reign, the gateway was enlarged into a tower-cum-gateway. Afterwards, that gateway was blocked up (as happened much later to the gatehouse at Dunstanburgh), to make a great tower of nearly square plan. At that time, a fresh entrance was cut into the curtain beside the great tower. In the later fifteenth century the great tower was substantially reduced in size: its northern and parts of its western and eastern walls were demolished and a new wall erected 12ft or so further back.

The other buildings inside the enclosure, including great hall, great chamber, annexes, service rooms, kitchen block are mostly of fourteenth-century construction, altered and in some respects beautified, in the Tudor period.

In 1138, Ludlow, then held by a supporter of Queen Matilda, was besieged by Stephen. One day, he and Prince Henry of Scotland (a son of David I) were walking near the gatehouse when a grappling iron on the end of a rope was let down, its hook catching in the prince's cloak. Gradually, he was lifted off the ground, but with great presence of mind, Stephen grabbed at the rope and cut it with a knife. The prince was saved, but the king did not capture the castle.

LUMLEY Nr Chester-le-Street, Durham
(NZ 288511) C
A quadrangular fortified manor house erected in the 1390s following a licence to crenellate of 1389–90. The holder, Lord Lumley, was a supporter of Richard II who was deposed in 1399. The castle has a quadrangle about 80ft square with substantial square towers at the corners. The towers were topped with octagonal turrets bearing machicolation. The east wing of the quadrangle has an interesting gatehouse.

LYDFORD Devon †
(SX 510848) DOE
This is one of the castles whose great tower was raised before the motte which was subsequently piled up round the tower base. (cf. Aldingbourne in Sussex, Doué la Fontaine, Anjou). The castle is very early: forty houses were destroyed to make room for it soon after the Conquest. The site is in the corner of a previous Anglo-Saxon *burh*.

The square great tower (about 50ft) is on a platform to the east of a sizeable banked bailey, and is of two periods: the lower stonework is of the twelfth century and the top part is of the thirteenth. It was during the works of the thirteenth century that the motte was piled up round the bottom part, blocking up the windows. The tower has a cross-wall. In the east wall are two double-splayed windows, which is an unusual feature.

The great tower decayed, but in the eighteenth century it was patched up and used as a courthouse and prison for the Stannary Court until the last century.

LYDNEY Gloucestershire
(SO 617025) O
In Little Camp, by Lydney Park, the remains of a Norman stone castle were excavated earlier this century. The plan was approximately pentagonal, with uneven sides, with a rectangular tower (50ft by 57ft) of local limestone rubble with squared sandstone facing in one of the corners. Next to the tower was a gateway, also rectilinear in plan. An iron mine was found in the courtyard. The dating is early twelfth century. The surrounding earthworks are all that remain.

LYMPNE Nr Hythe, Kent
(TR 117342) O
A castle was built on the edge of a sheer cliff at Lympne in the 1080s. In the fourteenth century the remains of this early structure, whose form is not known, were replaced by a great hall with a tower at each end. The west tower is D-ended, the east tower, square. Lympne Castle was probably raised as a defence against raids from French naval forces coming across the Channel over which the site commands a splendid view. It is also known as Stutfall Castle.

LYONSHALL Nr Madley, Hereford & Worcester (SO 331563) A
An earthwork enclosure with an additional bailey, the remains of which are near the church. A cylindrical tower was erected on a low platform in the enclosure, probably in the thirteenth century, and the enclosure was surrounded by a stone curtain.

MALMESBURY Wiltshire
(ST 935872)
There was a castle of some kind at Malmesbury, according to several records, but the design is not established. Probably raised during the Anarchy of Stephen's reign, Malmesbury Castle had stonework, some of which may be that absorbed in Castle House on what is now thought to be the site. It was pulled down in 1216 by monks from the abbey, with the king's consent. There are stretches of wall which may be part of the old curtain.

MARISCO Lundy Island
(SS 141437) O
A thirteenth-century rectangular tower inside a curtained enclosure was raised here, using local stone, but the lime and other materials were ferried over the sea from Devon. The name of the castle comes from a family of pirates who used the island as a haven. Some of the outer walls are still standing.

MARLBOROUGH Wiltshire
(SU 183686)
The earliest mention of Marlborough motte castle is 1110, but it could have been raised before that. The remains are in the grounds of the college. Henry II added stone buildings, using quarrels (squared stones) for part of the works. There are accounts also for more than 176,000 shingles which suggest extensive roofing to buildings.

King John was attached to Marlborough Castle, possibly because it was close to the great hunting forest of Savernake. He had new kitchens built, with ovens big enough to allow roasting of two or three whole oxen at one time. He also built the circular shell keep with narrow pilaster buttresses on the motte summit, since vanished. Henry III spent over £2,000, including constructing a tower inside the shell, though it is now not possible to determine its plan. The castle was still garrisoned in the mid-fourteenth century. Today, there is only the motte, over 50ft tall.

MARSHWOOD Dorset
(SY 404977) A
A motte castle of the twelfth century was later improved by the erection of a rectangu-lar great tower on the mound. Some parts of the ground storey masonry remain.

MAXSTOKE Warwickshire
(SP 224891) P
A licence was granted in c.1345 for this quadrangular fortified house with corner polygonal towers and a gatehouse. It was one of the earliest fortified houses of this kind to be built. It has been considerably modified since the fourteenth century. It is sur-rounded by a wide and deep moat.

MEMBURY Nr Ramsbury, Wiltshire
(SU 305745) A
The site of an aerodrome during World War II, Membury was excavated under an emergency scheme (what would be called a rescue project today) in 1941. This revealed a rectangular earthwork inside which were building foundations. A twelfth-century tower was replaced by a thirteenth-century (or later) mansion, and there was a cylind-rical tower in the enclosure rampart work.

MEPPERSHALL Bedfordshire
(TL 132358) A
A motte castle with two baileys in front of it, in series, all ditched and banked, and these are inside a larger rectangular moated enclosure split into segments. The grant of a charter to Meppershall by Stephen has led to the suggestion that the castle may have supplied troops and weapons for the siege of Bedford Castle of 1138.

MERDON Hursley, Hampshire
(SU 421265) A
A circular enclosure with ditch and bank, probably surrounded by a flint built curtain and provided with a gate-tower having walls 7ft thick, and with quoins of clunch (hard chalk). The castle was probably little more than a sparsely fortified manor house of an early date, possibly c.1130–40. Fragments of stonework remain among earthworks.

MIDDLEHAM Nr Leyburn,   ††
North Yorkshire   (SE 128875) DOE
There was a motte castle about a quarter of a mile from the present ruins of the later stone castle at Middleham. This motte dates from about 1086. About a century later (c.1170), Robert Fitzrandolph, descendant of the original owner of Middleham, was granted

Middleham: (above) a view from the south-east; (below) the south side of the great tower. The central turret and the square turret at left (on the west side) are both garderobe towers

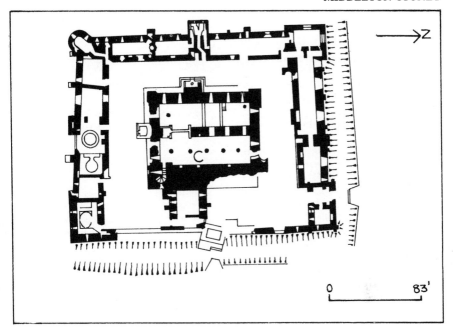

Middleham: ground plan. The great tower is in the centre. The great hall is over the cellars (C). The outer quadrangle is thirteenth and fourteenth century

leave to build a great tower, and a very substantial structure emerged: rectangular, 108ft by 78ft, two-storeyed, about 60ft tall, with walls 10–12ft thick, and with a cross-wall, two garderobe towers, clasping corner buttresses, one larger than the other three, splayed plinth on three sides, built of rubble inside and faced on the exterior with limestone ashlar. Entrance was (as usual with great towers) through a first-storey door, and in this case approached up a long flight of stairs on the east wall of the tower, once protected by a long forebuilding. All this is now in a very ruinous condition.

In the thirteenth century, the great tower was enclosed in a quadrangular curtain with buildings ranged along three sides, including corner towers and gatehouse. A tall chapel was built on to the east side of the great tower, abutting the forebuilding. Further buildings were added in the fourteenth and fifteenth centuries. It was also surrounded by a moat inside a further surrounding wall, with additional ditching and walling round what is presumed to have been a second courtyard to the east.

Middleham came into the possession of the Nevilles, passing to the great Richard, Earl of Warwick, the 'Kingmaker', and thence through his second daughter, Anne, to her husband, Richard, Duke of Gloucester, later Richard III. He and Anne are thought to have loved the castle and enjoyed it as a residence. Its ruinous state today is a consequence of being severely slighted after the Civil War.

MIDDLETON STONEY Nr Bicester, Oxfordshire (SP 534233)
There was a motte castle at Middleton Stoney in the twelfth century, adduced from some pottery of that time discovered in excavations of about thirty years ago. The earliest documentary mentions, however, are of later date, viz. 1215–16, and these include an order from John that the castle should be dismantled. By that time some stonework had been added. The levelling of some of the earthworks suggest that the order to dismantle was in part, if not totally, carried out. The motte has been dated to c.1140.

261

MILEHAM Nr Litcham, Norfolk
(TF 916193) A
A motte castle was raised here in the twelfth century. Later, the motte was given a square great tower of flint rubble, with splayed plinth. The mound remains, bearing some stone fragments.

MISERDEN Gloucestershire
(SO 945092)
A motte castle built in the twelfth century near the river was improved with added stonework. This consisted of a shell keep of probably early thirteenth-century origin. But the castle was left to deteriorate, and by the fourteenth century it appears not to have been worth restoring, for a new manor house was built on the site. Remains are in Miserden Park, open from time to time.

MITFORD Northumberland
(NZ 170855) C
Early motte castles were few and far between in Northumbria, but one was erected at Mitford in the 1100s. The later stonework additions are interesting; the motte top was surrounded with a D-shaped shell keep inside which was a great tower of five sides, rectangular with one side angled outwards. This is possibly the only five-sided great tower in England. The tower basement is vaulted, two rooms of which are barrel vaulted, and the rooms are separated by a cross-wall. The structures stood on a natural mound of local sandstone. There are also some remains of a rough course rubble curtain round one bailey.
   Mitford was confiscated by King John in 1215 from the holder for his part in the Magna Carta war. Two years later, it was besieged by Alexander II, King of Scotland, but not captured.

MOCCAS Hereford & Worcester
(SO 348246)
A motte castle of the twelfth century was superseded by a late thirteenth-century fortified manor house, of which there are no remains.

MONTACUTE Somerset
(ST 493169)
A very early castle built on a site obtained by the holder, Robert de Mortain, by exchang-

ing land with Athelney Abbey in 1069–70. The castle was later given to the priory of Cluniac monks nearby, in c.1104, by Robert's son, and the stonework that had probably been added in the first years of the century was used for building works by the monks. Montacute was a motte castle whose motte was surrounded by a ditch and which stood inside a bailey that was also encircled by ditching (see plan on p. 31).

MONTFICHET Addle Hill, City of London
A motte castle with a tower on a low motte was raised here in 1066–7 by the Conqueror soon after he had been crowned in Westminster Abbey. It was demolished in the thirteenth century.

MORETON CORBET Shropshire †
(SJ 562232) DOE
A sandstone and rubble great tower of diminutive size was built here in c.1200, inside a roughly triangular stone enclosure. Remains of this castle may be seen beside the ruins of the Elizabethan manor house built for Robert Corbet in c.1579. The castle was given a gatehouse, probably in the fourteenth century, and this has been restored.

MORPETH Northumberland
(NZ 200857) O
A motte castle was built on Ha' Hill by the River Wansbeck in the reign of William Rufus who captured it in 1095. Stonework was added in the mid-twelfth century, but whatever type of castle emerged it was destroyed by King John in 1215. Later in the thirteenth century a second castle was built nearby in part of the bailey of the original castle, and a gatehouse (of uncertain date) and some curtain wall remain. The gatehouse was given polygonal bartizans and a fine pointed arch to the entrance passage. In the Civil War, 500 Scots fighting on the Parliamentarian side held out against a siege by Montrose and 2,500 Royalists for three weeks before surrendering.

MOUNTSORREL Leicestershire
(SK 578148) A
Mountsorrel is the site of a huge quarry of pink stone, in use certainly since the time of Elizabeth I and quite probably much longer.

The castle there began as a motte castle on a natural rock overlooking the town and the River Soar. It was held by the earls of Leicester from c.1140 until taken by Henry II after the revolt of his son, Prince Henry, 1173–4. The castle was given stonework, including a tower, hall and chamber. Richard I spent money on Mountsorrel, and John ordered timber from Leicester (about 7 miles off) to build hoarding (in 1215) along its walls. The castle was besieged in 1216–17 and finally dismantled.

MULGRAVE North Yorkshire
(NZ 840117) O
A polygonal-plan curtain enclosure with gateway between two towers encircled a great tower having round angle-turrets and a forebuilding. The castle was begun c.1215, and the great tower was probably work of c.1300. Additions were made in later years. Now in ruins.

MUNCASTER Ravenglass, Cumbria †
(SD 103964) O
A pele-tower of the late thirteenth century is incorporated in the south-west of the present castle at Muncaster. The castle guards an approach to Eskdale and overlooks the anchorage at Ravenglass which was once a busy harbour. The buildings were substantially reconstructed in the 1850s by Anthony Salvin, the well-known Victorian architectural restorer. Muncaster is remarkable for having been in the possession of the same family, the Penningtons, for more than seven centuries.

MYDDLE Nr Shrewsbury, Shropshire
(SJ 469235) C
A fourteenth-century small quadrangular castle with outer bailey was almost completely destroyed in the seventeenth century, reputedly as a result of earth tremors. There are remains of one turret.

NAFFERTON Northumberland
(NZ 072657)
Now known locally as Lonkins, the ruins of a castle also called Nafferton lie near a bridge across the Whittle Dean. The bridge itself is thought to have been built of stone blocks from the castle after it became ruinous.

NAWORTH Cumbria
(NY 560626) C
This castle, built in the early fourteenth century, appears to have been a simple walled quadrilateral enclosure with a great tower in the wall at one end and a gateway at the other. A deep moat was cut on three of the four sides. It is possible that the great tower was the first building. A licence to crenellate had been granted in 1335 to Ranulf de Dacre at a time of hostilities between England and Scotland. The tower has been alluded to as a pele, and it may have been just that. The considerable changes wrought in the buildings since the fourteenth century have obscured much of the castle's original plan. The present appearance is due largely to restoration by Anthony Salvin after a fire in the 1840s. (cf. Norwich.)

NEROCHE Nr Buckland St Mary, †
Somerset (ST 272158) O
Sometimes known as Castle Neroche, this is an unusual structure. It began as an earthwork enclosure on a spur of the Blackdown Hills, in the eleventh century, erected inside a larger and much earlier earthwork ring. Then in the 1100s, the smaller enclosure was rendered into a motte castle by building a 25ft tall motte across it. Neroche was apparently occupied during the troubled days of Stephen's reign. Later in the twelfth century part of the outer ditch was lined with stone, and a shell keep was raised in one corner of the motte.

The eleventh-century castle was probably built by Robert of Mortain, the Conqueror's half brother and holder of Montacute.

NETHER STOWEY Somerset
(ST 187396) A
An early motte castle with two baileys, Nether Stowey was given a substantial rectangular great tower, about 60ft by 50ft, on the motte top which was itself several times larger in area. The great tower had a southern forebuilding and a cross-wall. The date of the tower is probably mid-twelfth century. The castle eventually came into the ownership of the Audley family. There are a few ruins on Castle Hill.

NEWARK Nottinghamshire ††
(SK 796540)

Newark Castle stands on the west bank of the Trent, on a platform raised over an earlier inhabited settlement. The castle has deteriorated so much that it is at present closed to visitors. This is sad because it is a noble ruin, and it is worth going to see it from the road in the town. It began as an earthwork enclosure raised in the 1130s by the Bishop of Lincoln, and it remained a church-owned castle throughout its active existence.

The first stonework was probably added in the time of Stephen. Major works were also carried out in the time of John and Henry III. Approximately rectangular, the castle became a stonework quadrangle, four storeys tall. The corner and mid-wall towers were square and taller than the quadrangle. There is a remnant of a hexagonal (symmetrical) tower of the thirteenth century on the south-west adjacent to an earlier postern. The gatehouse was a square-plan tower of three storeys pierced at ground level by a wide passage approached through a shallow round-headed arch. The present windows are replacements of later date than the original twelfth-century Norman ones. The gatehouse is 45ft by 30ft with walls 8–9ft thick and buttresses on the corners. The front has sloping offset buttresses supporting the lower part of the walls, on either side of the entrance.

Newark was held for King John in the Magna Carta war, and he died there in 1216. It was also held for King Charles I in the Civil War, resisting siege several times, but surrendered in May 1646, whereupon it was slighted by Parliament.

NEW BUCKENHAM Norfolk ††
(TL 084904) O

There are extensive earthworks at New Buckenham embracing part of the present village. The inner and smaller part is a figure of eight site divided by a ditch and with ditching all round. The ditch has been widened. Remains of a thirteenth-century gateway into one of the loops of the 'eight' are reached by a wooden bridge across the ditch, and some fragments are partly buried in a high rampart on one side. In the inner bailey, which is about two acres in area and which is almost totally surrounded by the continuation of the high rampart, 20–30ft tall, is the lower part of a flint rubble cylindrical great tower. This tower is of considerable interest and importance in the story of castles (see p. 50).

The tower is about 65ft in diameter. Its walls are 11–13ft thick (13ft at the base), and it has a cross-wall about 5ft thick. In the basement there is an opening in the

Newark: a view of the northern side of Newark Castle, where it fronts on to the Trent. From a photograph of c.1920

New Buckenham: the stub of the cylindrical great tower built in the 1140s. The entrance was probably reached by a causeway from the bank behind the tower at first-floor level

cross-wall with a rounded doorway with ashlar quoins at the base. There is a rough stonework entrance from which any dressings it may have had have been removed. It may not be the original entrance. The height of the tower is at present about 25ft at the tallest point, and this appears to represent two storeys judging from post-holes in the cross-wall that may be slots for floor crossbeams. It was probably four-storeys, which, with parapet, could have taken it to about 65–70ft. Walking round the remains of the tower one has an immediate feeling of a tower of some size, and one which was built with some care and skill.

Its importance lies in its date, namely c.1140–50. This makes it probably the earliest cylindrical great tower in Britain, ante-dating Conisbrough by thirty years or so, Orford (which is cylindrical inside) by about twenty to twenty-five years and Pembroke by half a century, and helps to discredit the received idea that cylindrical great towers were an advance upon rec-

tangular great towers. Clearly, the two styles were being built concurrently.

There are fragments of flint rubble masonry elsewhere in the inner bailey but as yet these have not been excavated. (Norfolk Arch. xxxii)

NEWCASTLE Tyne & Wear   †† (NZ 253639) O

Sited by the River Tyne where it joins the Lort Burn, Newcastle began as a motte castle in c.1080, with a bank and ditch, on a steep headland. Part of the bank was clay lined. In the late eleventh and early twelfth centuries, the ownership of the northern counties of England was often disputed with Scotland and for a time Newcastle was held by the Scottish kings, notably David I (1124–53). The motte castle was probably demolished to make way for a new stone castle begun by Henry II in c.1168. Works continued for about ten years with a short interruption (1173–4), under the direction of Mauricius Caementarius (Maurice the mason), and in that time a substantial rectangular great tower, 62ft by 56ft, was built, enclosed by a curtain wall with flanking towers, part of which was ashlar faced. This work cost over £1,100, and may have included other buildings, such as the gate on the west side (later destroyed).

The great tower is built of sandstone slabs, on a splayed plinth, has proud clasping angle buttresses, broad buttresses in the centre of east and west walls and narrower ones in north and south. The buttressed corner on the north-west is multangular. The basement storey is vaulted. There are five storeys, one being the upper part of a double height storey with chambers and passages in the walls at the higher level as well as the lower. The walls are 15–18ft thick. The top storey has a mural gallery all round. There is an extensive forebuilding along the east side which has been altered over the centuries. Originally this had three towers, ascending from entrance at ground level to entrance into the great hall at the third-storey level (ground level of the two-storeyed great hall). The tallest tower of the forebuilding contains a chapel, vaulted and with a round-head arch with dog-tooth moulding. The stairs in the forebuilding are broken into three flights with interval landings. At one time there was a third (lower) tower over what is now the pavement in front of the first steps up to the outer arch in the second tower of the forebuilding. The storeys are reached by spiral staircase in the south-east. The great hall was not accessible directly from the spiral stair but via an intermediate straight flight of steps in the wall, which was later abandoned as a means of access. The hall is 30ft by 24ft and is 40ft high with a brick vault roof, a nineteenth-century renovation of an originally lower ceiling. In the north-east corner is a vaulted room containing access to the well, with basin recesses and pipe holes through which water used to be conveyed to other (lower) parts of the tower. The well is nearly 100ft deep, and is ashlar lined.

The curtain enclosure was many sided, was surrounded by ditching and banking and contained postern gates, rectangular flanking towers, and had additional buildings raised against the inside in later years, notably the great hall of c.1210, an aisled

building that was finally demolished in 1809. In 1247–50, the Black Gate was constructed at the north-west of the curtain enclosure. This was a rectangular tower projection from the curtain with central passage piercing the ground floor, and with drawbridge across a pit into a polygonal chamber at the other end of which was an elliptical-plan gate-tower. This was pierced by a passage with gates, portcullis and a drawbridge out front, the whole structure designed to produce flanking fire upon attackers, covering a considerable length of the curtain wall, including a second gate through the curtain.

Newcastle was repaired and remodelled here and there on several occasions in the period from the mid-thirteenth century to mid-fifteenth century, including a major rebuild of the curtain. It was often attacked during hostilities with Scotland, and in the Civil War it was captured.

NEWCASTLE UNDER LYME
Staffordshire   (SJ 845459) A
The River Lyme was effectively dammed to produce a sizeable lake to protect the motte raised here probably in the twelfth century. Remains have been found of a long and narrow building with pilaster buttresses, of the twelfth century. This was a tower that is said to have reached 70ft tall. The mound is visible.

NORHAM Nr Berwick,   ††
Northumberland   (NT 907476) O
Norham stands on the south bank of the Tweed. Its site is protected on north and west by a steep cliff which forms part of the river bank. The east is protected by a ravine and the south sides by an artificially deepened hollow which leads into the river at the south-west. In the north-east corner of this site is a roughly D-shaped inner bailey which is protected on its west and south by an inner ditch leading eastwards into the ravine, and its other two sides are actually along the ravine (east) and the steep part of the river bank (north). In the south-east corner of the inner bailey (which is enclosed by a thick stone curtain, now much ruined), is a massive rectangular great tower, also in ruins. We return to this structure below. Other buildings in the inner bailey include a

Norham

hall with kitchens (north), and at south, a flanking tower with triangular front, called Clapham's Tower, built in 1513 and equipped with gun-ports. The outer bailey is enclosed by a curtain wall, also much ruined, with several flanking towers and two gates, the West Gate and Sheep Gate (at the south), again, both buildings now ruinous. The West Gate leads out to a barbican, and the Sheep Gate once led out to a drawbridge across the outer moat, since replaced by a causeway.

Norham Castle, which for a long time belonged to the bishops of Durham, endured the most punishing treatment over several centuries. Founded by Bishop Flambard in c.1120, it was destroyed by the Scots in the 1140s. It has been an enclosure castle of wood and earth upon a platform attached to an outer bailey with ditches and banks. It was rebuilt in stone in the 1160s at the demand of Henry II, and the bishop employed Richard de Wolviston as mason in charge (see p. 42). This was the time when the great tower was begun.

The castle was held by the King from 1173–89, and again by King John from 1208–16. He may have built Sheep Gate.

Norham stood in the front line for attack by the Scots, and on numerous occasions it was besieged, and even captured. Each time damage was done, with the result that there is evidence of new work and repair work in nearly every generation between the twelfth and the sixteenth centuries. Fully to understand its history and its building story, the DOE guide should be consulted. Despite its ruinous condition, it is well worth a visit.

The great tower is worthy of brief description. It is 84ft by 60ft, reaching 90ft in some parts of the wall which remain standing. Rectangular in plan, the tower began as a three-storey building, two storeys above a vaulted basement. This work was done by the Bishop of Durham between 1158–74. The tower was heightened by two further storeys in the fifteenth century during a major renovation of the whole building. A cross-wall was inserted above the vaulted basement for support of the new works above. This new building was besieged and burned in 1513 by James IV of Scotland who employed artillery, including Mons Meg. The castle surrendered only a few days before the disastrous defeat of the Scots at Flodden Field, at which James was slain.

NORTHALLERTON North Yorkshire
(SE 365940) A

An enclosure castle was built at Northallerton in c.1068 but almost the whole site has been destroyed by nineteenth-century railway works. In c.1160, a motte castle was raised nearby by Bishop Pudsey, and this was employed on behalf of the rebel son of Henry II, Prince Henry, in 1173–4. The King crushed the rebellion, which was a serious one and supported in many parts of England, and Bishop Pudsey's castle was doomed. It was levelled in about 1176. Nearby, the Bishop of Durham fortified a house on Pudsey's castle site and this saw military use during the revolt of the Mowbrays and Archbishop Scrope in the early years of the reign of Henry IV. There are remains of the earthworks.

NORTHAMPTON
(SP 748604) A

There is practically nothing left of this important medieval castle which stood on one of the main roads to the north of England. The first structure was a motte castle, built in the 1080s, on a site from which several Anglo-Saxon houses had been cleared. In c.1110 Henry I took over the castle and enlarged it. Works including a substantial ditch (over 90ft wide and 30ft deep) and rampart (20ft tall) round a large bailey. This was one of those occasions when the Crown paid compensation for encroaching upon another owner's land. By 1164 the castle had a great hall, a gateway, curtain walling and a chapel. Sometime soon afterwards, a great tower was built though it is not possible to say what shape or size it achieved.

Northampton was besieged by the Magna Carta barons' forces using French-built siege artillery, but John relieved the garrison and forced the attackers to withdraw. Evidently major repairs were needed after this engagement. More than £150 was spent on work on the tower. Despite continuing expenditure, however, the castle was not properly defensible by the time of the Barons' War against Henry III, led by Simon de Montfort who used the castle as a headquarters. There was more spent on it over the next century but the castle continued, nonethless, to deteriorate. The remnants were obscured by the erection of a railway over the site in the nineteenth century, and only a fragment or two remains.

NORWICH   †
(TG 232085) O

Even before the Norman Conquest, Norwich was one of the biggest towns in England — and it remained so until at least the eighteenth century. Close to the North Sea coast, it required defence from foreign assault, notably the Vikings. The Conqueror recognized the need to guard Norwich and its neighbourhood, and in 1067 he ordered William FitzOsbern, one of his principal barons, to build a motte castle there, but it remained a royal castle. It was a huge mound, probably the largest ever built in England (though not as tall as Thetford), and it was part a natural protuberance and part artificial. The motte was over 40ft tall, and big enough in area to carry a complete inner enclosure of palisade wall, great tower of timber and other buildings. It is possible the tower was erected on a smaller motte within this summit enclosure. One hundred and thirteen buildings were demolished to make room for the castle.

In 1075 the castle was besieged, and again in 1087–8, on the second occasion by Roger Bigod, a powerful Norman noble in revolt against William II. It remained a royal castle, with a short interval (c.1136), until 1173. Sometime in the reign of Henry I, probably between c.1125–35, the motte received a very substantial great tower. This was 95ft by 90ft and rose to 70ft tall. It was built in somewhat similar style to the King's great tower at Falaise Castle in Normandy of c.1120. The internal arrangements (which were destroyed in later centuries) included a large hall and chamber on the first floor, with garderobes, a chapel and a room for the castellan. The ground floor contained storage chambers, armoury, and (possibly) prison cells. The second floor contained guardrooms and a gallery inside the walls all round. The tower also had a kitchen, one of the earliest built in a great tower in England.

The great tower was built of ashlar blocks of Caen stone facing a flintwork core. The walls had pilaster buttresses, interspersed with tiers of blind external arcading of varying size and punctuated with windows and loops (which were restored in the 1830s by Anthony Salvin). The present battlemented parapet (also of the 1830s) is probably a good reconstruction of the original. Evidently the great tower was built largely by masons released from working on Norwich Cathedral for a period, and presumably stone consigned for the cathedral was also diverted.

The castle was appropriated by Henry II in 1157 from the Count of Mortain, one of Stephen's sons. Work was carried out, which included raising a palisade. During the 1173–4 revolt of Prince Henry against his father (the King), Hugh Bigod, Earl of Norfolk, captured Norwich on behalf of the prince. When the revolt collapsed, Bigod lost nearly all his possessions and captures and Norwich reverted to the King, who spent money on further works. In 1268–70, the wooden wall round the castle was replaced by a stone curtain, at a cost of £500. Twenty years later Edward I spent a similar amount on rebuilding the hall in the great tower, though what kind of deterioration necessitated such expense we do not know. Further excavations are in progress.

NOTTINGHAM †
(SK 569394) O

The present castle at Nottingham has nothing to do with the medieval castle that began as a motte castle in c.1068. The motte was raised on what is now called Castle Rock. Henry II appropriated the castle in the 1150s and spent about £900 on it in the years 1170–5, which may have included a great tower. The castle remained in the Crown's hands for six centuries, during

which time it grew in magnificence until, in the mid-fifteenth century, it filled the land now occupied by the General Hospital and the Castle Rock. Then after the accession of the Tudor monarchy it deteriorated, and it was almost completely destroyed in 1651 at the orders of Cromwell.

In 1617, John Smythson (who designed Bolsover Castle) drew a plan of the castle as it then was, though we do not know how many buildings were standing above their foundations or how much curtain wall was intact. The plan is plate 48 of *King's Works*, ii, and shows the extent of the fortress'. The polygonal tower jutting out of the north-west curve in the curtain was a 'goodly tower', described by Leland as having been erected by Edward IV.

Of the many historical events associated with Nottingham Castle, one is of special interest. The castle was held by Queen Isabella (widow of Edward II whom she and her lover, Roger Mortimer, had put to death in 1327). She and her paramour attempted to hold out against the young Edward III, but by tunnelling through the rock he entered the fortress and arrested the guilty pair. The actual tunnel is said to be that which is today called Mortimer's Hole and which can be inspected by visitors. A gateway into the medieval castle, built in the thirteenth century, has been drastically restored.

NUNNEY Nr Frome, Somerset †
(ST 737457) DOE

The most immediately dramatic feature of Nunney is the huge, gaping hole in the north wall of this high, compact, rectangular tower building with huge corner cylindrical towers. This wall was smashed through by cannon of Oliver Cromwell at first-floor level above the entrance in 1645. The castle was surrendered two days after Cromwell's assault and in due course some of the inside was stripped.

Nunney tower has been described by S.E. Rigold (of DOE) as distinctly French. Certainly there is very little like it in the UK. The towers were the same height as the two walls (north and south) — on the east and west side, the towers are coupled together — and the parapet at the top was machicolated all round. Each tower carried on top a

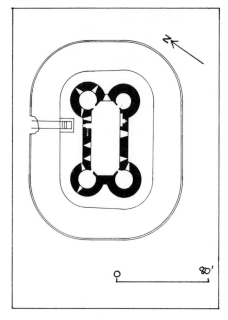

Nunney

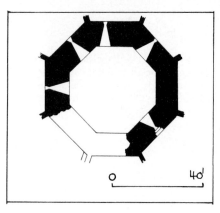

Odiham (after D.F. Renn): ground-floor level of polygonal great tower

smaller diameter cylinder turret. The diameter of the towers was about 27ft, and the height from the straight plinth below to the parapet was 54ft. The tower walls are 5–6ft thick. The lower part of each tower was lit by narrow loops only, as built in the 1370s (the licence to crenellate was granted to Sir John de la Mere in 1373), but some of these were enlarged in the sixteenth century to let in more light. The tower had four storeys, and was entered through a very narrow door. The great hall was on the second floor.

OAKHAM Leicestershire   †
(SK 861090) O
The twelfth-century hall at Oakham is one of the best-preserved examples of a free-standing hall in a Norman castle. It is constructed of ironstone rubble with ashlar dressings, and though it has been repaired, it is a fine example of early medieval hall. The castle began as a motte castle and acquired its first stoneworks in the twelfth century.

ODIHAM Hampshire   †
(SU 726519) A
This was one of King John's favourite

castles. Today, you can see the shell of the polygonal (octagonal) great tower built by him between 1207–12, at a cost of about £1,000. The corners of the great tower had angle buttresses, but there was no forebuilding. Odiham was besieged in 1216, by which time it had part of its enclosure of curtain wall. In 1324–5, major repairs were carried out. After David II, King of Scotland, was captured at the Battle of Neville's Cross in 1346, he spent eleven years in exile in England. Some of this confinement was at Odiham.

OKEHAMPTON Devon   †
(SX 584942) DOE
A motte castle of the Conqueror's reign (probably before 1070) set on the top of a naturally fortified ridge, was greatly extended for a long way down the ridge as buildings round an elongated bailey, in the early fourteenth century. The castle has been compared with German hill-top castles like Staufen and Rothenburg. There are in fact two distinct parts.

The motte first received a square great tower, built of shale rubble and granite with granite dressings, followed by a rectangular block joined to its south-west wall, with an entrance passage between the two in the wall. The tower was given garderobes with slate lining. The second part consisted of a number of buildings beginning below the bottom of a slope down from the tower, such as kitchen, lodgings, solar, hall, guard-

270

rooms, chapel and then a gatehouse leading to a long barbican causeway with its own outer two-storey gate block.

The history of Okehampton was uneventful until 1538 when the then owner, the Marquis of Exeter, was beheaded for alleged high treason and his castle dismantled. The ruins are nonetheless extensive and worth a visit.

OLD SARUM Wiltshire   †
(SU 138327) DOE

An early Iron Age hill-fort at Old Sarum was, long afterwards, taken over by Anglo-Saxons and turned into a *burh*. After 1066, the *burh* was converted by the Normans into a town. The greater part of the very extensive earthworks are of the late eleventh century, though some of them were modifications to much earlier work (possibly Roman or even Iron Age). In c.1078 the Conqueror transferred the Anglo-Saxon bishopric of Sherborne to Old Sarum, and

the earthworks became an enclosure for not only a new cathedral built before the end of the century by Bishop St Osmund, but also a citadel. In the centre of the enclosure an inner ring of earthworks was raised. A circle of ditch banked round the outside surrounded a circular platform of earth, flattened down. Early in the twelfth century, inside the ring to the north, was built a quadrangle of apartments for the bishop, including a long hall, a chapel, a kitchen and a tower. Around the top of the platform a curtain wall of flint rubble was erected, later in the twelfth century, apparently upon the remains of an earlier wall. The flint wall had pilaster buttresses at intervals all round. At the west was a postern tower-and-gate and at the east a main gatehouse was built.

The castle thus formed received several additional buildings in the thirteenth century, including a long rectangular hall at the south-west edge, a bakehouse just to the south of the east gatehouse and some

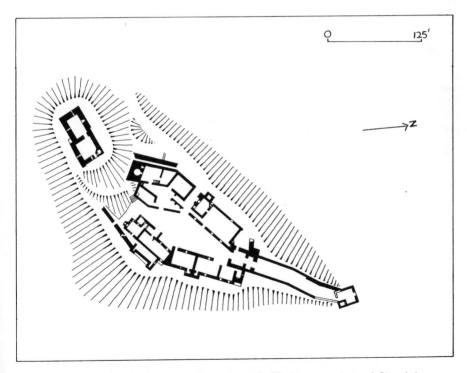

Okehampton: plan showing the rectangular tower on the Norman motte (at top left) and the more domestic buildings of much later date spreading towards the north-east

271

chambers were added to the palace part at the north. In the early 1200s, the see at Old Sarum was moved to Salisbury where a new cathedral was built, in which many of the stones of the earlier cathedral were used. It appears that there was continual friction between the cathedral staff, clerical and lay, and the secular occupants of the castle.

Old Sarum became an administrative centre and headquarters of the sheriff of Wiltshire. Today, the visitor will see much of the earthworks and many foundations and fragments of buildings, including a fine stretch of splayed plinth of the postern tower. Many relics have been recovered and are in Salisbury Museum.

OLD WARDOUR Wardour Park,   †
Tisbury, Wiltshire   (ST 939263) DOE
Old Wardour was built by the 5th Lord Lovel, with a licence to crenellate of 1393. He raised a very unusual structure consisting of a hexagonal-plan range of apartments round a hexagonal courtyard. The range was not a perfect hexagon: the ends of the third and fifth arms joined into an elongated and widened sixth arm in which was recessed the entrance, making the two ends of the sixth arm look like towers. The inner hexagonal yard was perfect and had a central well. Much of this structure remains, though in poor condition.

Additions and alterations were carried out in the 1570s, and in the Civil War Old Wardour was besieged twice, first by Parliamentarian forces in 1643 who captured it, and then again in 1644, this time by the original owner, Lord Arundell, who attempted to undermine the walls.

ONGAR Essex   †
(TL 554031) P but A
A motte-and-bailey built in the early twelfth century by the de Lucy family, Ongar has a substantial motte now 50ft tall and which was probably taller in the early days of its existence. The motte is 230ft in diameter at the base and was surrounded by a wet moat about 50ft wide. A tower of flint rubble was raised on the motte summit, probably in the 1150s, but was pulled down much later, for a structure of brick replaced it. That, too, was demolished. Ongar's motte-and-bailey plan is much like that of Pleshey.

ORFORD Suffolk   ††
(TM 419499) DOE
Orford stands on the Suffolk coast, at one time guarding the harbour which used to be a major port. Today, its only remaining structure is its unique great tower, which is in very fine condition. The castle was built by Henry II between 1165–73, cost £1,413 (plus incidentals not listed in the records) and when finished consisted of an enclosure wall of stone with several rectangular flanking towers and a twin-towered gatehouse around the multangular great tower. Outside the enclosure was a very substantial ditch, with a stone bridge across it, leading from the gatehouse.

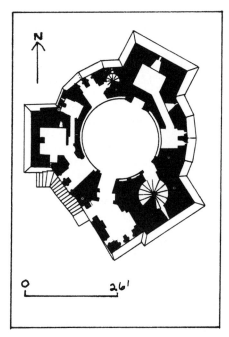

Orford: ground floor of the multangular great tower (c.1165–7)

Orford was part of Henry II's programme of stone castle construction designed to give practical effect to his policy that the king and not the barons should govern the country. He appreciated as much as anyone that he who would control the land must first control the castles on it. In East Anglia there were at the time no castles held by the Crown or royal castellans, but he rectified this by confiscating several, including fortresses belonging to Hugh Bigod, the most powerful magnate in the district. His own work at Orford was swift. The remarkable great tower was up and complete within two years (1165–7). The whole castle was ready in time to deal with the 1173–4 revolt led by his son, Prince Henry. The castle was garrisoned, supplies of all kinds were brought in — according to the records, bacons, cheeses, salt, iron, ropes, tallow and even hand-mills for grinding corn. But attack never came. Instead, Henry used the fortress as a centre for offensive military operations against Bigod who was supporting his rebellious son.

The design of the great tower is unlike anything else in Britain, and it fits into no pattern (few castles do in any case). It is not transitional, as we have shown (pp. 49–50). Basically, the tower is twenty-one sided on the exterior, and cylindrical inside. The twenty-one sides include three equidistantly placed rectangular-plan buttress turrets, the south-east larger than the other two because it is a forebuilding-cum-turret (the turret containing a spiral staircase all the way up). The tower is about 90ft tall, has splayed plinths, rises five storeys (basement and two double storeys), plus a roof level (which had battlemented parapets between the three turrets projecting some 20ft upwards). The buttress turrets contain chambers all the way up: two kitchens, one chapel, a prison cell, closets. Each of the double storeys was a hall of two levels. On the western side, just north of the west turret, in the outer wall face is a fine battery of four round-headed shoots from garderobes in the higher levels of the turret.

The great tower is built of local septaria with oolite dressings and some dressings of Caen stone. It was built upon a virgin site that had no previous earthwork and timber fortification.

Orford was captured in 1216 towards the end of the Magna Carta war, but not seriously harmed. There are records of various sums spent on repairs throughout the rest of the twelfth, the thirteenth and the early fourteenth centuries: Edward III bestowed the castle upon a local lord in c.1336. Thereafter, its history is uneventful. The curtain, towers, and gatehouse gradually decayed and collapsed through neglect. The last stretch of wall fell down in 1841.

OSWESTRY Shropshire
(SJ 290298) A
A motte castle of the late eleventh century was erected by Rainald (or Reginald) de Bailleul (or Baliol), a Norman lord who was an ancestor of King John Baliol of Scotland (1292–6). Stonework was grafted on the motte in the form of a shell wall, sometime in the twelfth century. Only fragments remain.

OXFORD †
(SP 510061) O
Oxford was a private castle built in c.1071 by Robert d'Oilly (see Ascot d'Oilly) with the king's permission. Anglo-Saxon houses were cleared to provide the site, on which was erected what was previously said to have been a motte castle *ab initio*, but which is now considered to have been an enclosure to which a 60ft motte was added later. When the motte was raised, clay was used to encase part of the sides to prevent the gravel slipping down into the ditch. Later, the motte was crowned with stone walling to produce a decagonal concentric shell wall, the inner wall 22ft in diameter, the outer wall 58ft. Before this structure was built (probably mid-twelfth century), an earlier square tower had been raised, of coursed limestone rubble, and this is dated to pre-1100. It is still known today as St George's Tower, and is interesting because it is stepped inwards at several places up its height, and has very few openings of any kind. It has been suggested that it was from St George's Tower that Empress Matilda, the daughter of Henry I, who vied with Stephen for the English throne for the best part of nineteen years (1135–1154), and thus helped to create the state of disorder known as the Anarchy, escaped clad only in a nightgown in 1142.

Money was spent on Oxford Castle by Henry II and John. In 1216 a church was dismantled to provide additional stone for fortifying the castle and to give it a barbican. But by the end of the thirteenth century the castle was in a poor state.

PEMBRIDGE Hereford & Worcester   †
(SO 448193) O

The castle occupies a roughly rectangular site, and was partly surrounded by a wet moat. A cylindrical great tower was built, probably in the early thirteenth century, three storeys tall. Other stone buildings included a two-storeyed gatehouse, a separate hall block, also of two storeys, and a chapel block of three storeys. The castle's history in the Middle Ages is almost unknown. It was held for the King in the Civil War when it was besieged and most of its buildings ruined. The present house, of seventeenth-century origin, stands in the old enclosure, partly on the remains of earlier structures.

PENDENNIS Nr Falmouth, Cornwall ††
(SW 824318) DOE

One of the two new fortresses built in the 1538–43 invasion scare in the reign of Henry VIII (the other was St Mawes), which were sited to protect the Carrick Roads north of Falmouth Bay. Pendennis was raised on high ground on a projection of land on the west coast of the bay. The castle is a squat cylindrical tower enclosed in a symmetrical multangular curtain. It was built to resist attack by enemy raiders or pirate fleets. The much larger enclosure of earthworks and its star-point-bastions were erected in the last years of Elizabeth's reign and the first years of James I's.

The central tower is three-storeyed, about 35ft tall and 56ft in diameter. It is built of granite ashlar with Pentewan freestone used for the carvings. The entrance to the tower is reached by a stone bridge which replaces the original drawbridge over the ditch surrounding the curtain. The portcullis is still in the up position in the gateway. The entrance leads into the first floor, whose room is octagonal and whose walls are about 16ft thick. A spiral stairway leads down to the basement storey and also up to the top storey. There is, too, a separate staircase from inside the gateway part up to the second storey. There are gun-ports on both first and second floors, splayed inwards and outwards to allow a wide swing of the guns, and the gun-ports in the multangular curtain wall were similarly arranged.

Pendennis was held for Charles I in the Civil War. A Parliamentary army under Fairfax drew up outside its walls in March 1646 and demanded surrender. The governor, Colonel John Arundell, replied, 'I will here bury myself before I deliver up this castle to such as fight against his Majesty'. So Parliament besieged it, for five months, until supplies inside ran out. The garrison then came out with colours flying and the trumpets and drums of the band playing.

PENDRAGON Mallerstang, Cumbria
(NY 782026) A

A square great tower built of rubble, with intra-mural passages, and with angle buttressing, was raised inside an enclosure beside the River Eden at Mallerstang at the end of the twelfth century. Its position rendered it vulnerable to attack by raiding Scottish armies and it was burned in 1341. The Royal Commission on Historical Monuments regarded the tower as an early pele-tower, but the dimensions, 64ft square externally, 42ft square inside (at second-floor level), qualify it more as a great tower, similar perhaps to Appleby. The remains stand on raised ground.

PENRITH Cumbria   †
(NY 513299) A

The beginnings of Penrith Castle are obscure. Sometime in the fourteenth century a tower was raised, and at the end of that century a quadrangular castle was built, in plan similar to Bolton, Yorkshire, but without the corner turrets. A licence to crenellate was granted in 1397–9 to William Strickland, later Bishop of Carlisle. Much of the interesting walling remains. The castle was intended to defend Penrith against Scottish raids. It is near the railway station.

PENWORTHAM Lancashire
(SD 524291)

A motte castle posssibly built before 1086, in which the base of the wooden tower descended some 12ft beneath the top of the motte, which was raised round it (cf. South Mymms, Totnes). The castle guarded the estuary of the River Ribble and a ford across it, which lay in the line of the road to the north. Only the mound remains.

274

PETERBOROUGH Cambridgeshire
(TL 195987)
In the Deanery garden stand the remnants of a motte called Tout Hill, with a flat top about 42ft across. It was probably erected in the last years of the eleventh century, before the foundation of the cathedral (cf. Ely).

PEVENSEY Sussex ††
(TQ 645048) DOE
The Romans constructed one of their coastal forts of the Saxon Shore (as they were known) at Pevensey in the third century AD. It was called Anderida. It was an elliptical enclosure with flanking D-ended bastions, unlike the other forts of the same time which were more generally rectilinear. Inside the remains of this fort, William the Conqueror sheltered his forces once they had landed on the Sussex coast at the end of September 1066. Immediately he cut a ditch in front of the remains of the Roman west gate to reinforce the ruins of the old fort which he considered usable, at all events temporarily.

Once the Conqueror had won Hastings and made sure he had at least the south-eastern part of England under his control, he granted Pevensey to his half brother, Robert of Mortain, who raised a castle in the east end of the fort in the shape of a roughly rectangular banked enclosure using a section of the original Roman curtain wall and two bastions on the south-eastern side. The remainder of the Roman enclosure became the outer bailey. This was the first Norman castle raised in England.

Soon afterwards, the first building work in stone began and this included the unusual great tower, started in c.1100, and a postern gate let into the Roman wall at the south-east end. The great tower was a rectangular structure using the east wall as part of one wall and incorporating the Roman bastion. Three more projecting round solid bastions were added much later in the century. D.F. Renn suggests that they could have been used as siege engine platforms for repelling assault: there is evidence that the castle had a siege engine, and a number of rounded stones for use as shot were found in the castle grounds (and can be seen today).

The tower may have been as tall as 80ft and was 55ft by 30ft horizontally and internally. The castle is full of interest, not

least because it was besieged many times, and the visitor is recommended to obtain the DOE booklet by D.F. Renn to expand on this short summary.

PEVERIL Castleton, Derbyshire ††
(SK 150827) DOE
Sometimes known as the Castle of the Peak, Peveril was a very early castle. Raised on a natural, easily defendable and almost inaccessible ridge with two precipitous sides, the first work was a stone curtain along the north side of a triangle, containing herringbone masonry, continued along other sides in the twelfth century. After the 1173–4 revolt of Prince Henry against his father Henry II, the king fortified the castle by adding a 40ft square great tower, 60ft tall. This tower is a simple structure and was not really residential though, of course, people did stay. It had no forebuilding—unusual for a square great tower. The tower was faced with ashlar and cost a little under £200.

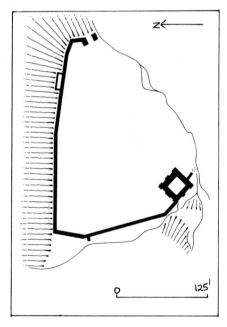

Peveril: the north wall was raised before the end of the eleventh century, and the extension southwards in the early twelfth. The great tower is late twelfth century. Some later buildings are omitted

Peveril is named after its original owners, the Peverel family. William Peverel forfeited it to Henry II in 1155 after he was disgraced, it is said, for having been involved in the murder of the Earl of Chester. The king took a fancy to the site and the great tower was perhaps intended to be a kind of *pied-à-terre* for visits to Derbyshire and the Peak District.

PICKERING North Yorkshire †† (SE 800845) DOE

This was a motte castle of the late eleventh or early twelfth century. The motte stood in its own surrounding ditch and two baileys surrounded that, in two curved halves, one half of later date than the rest, also ditched and banked. Sometime in the mid-twelfth century, a stone curtain was built along the northern bailey bank, ending on one side as a wing wall up to the motte top. It appears that from c.1218–36 work was done on constructing a circular shell keep on the top. A long open stairway leading to a square entrance tower had been put up when the northern bailey wall was erected. Later still, c.1323–6, a second curtain was built, this time along the southern bailey bank, and this had three flanking rectangular towers. Various buildings were raised in the two

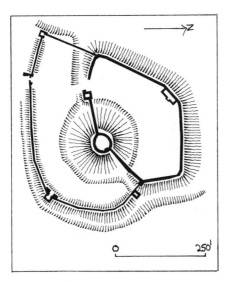

Pickering: the bold lines mark the principal stonework remains

baileys, including a King's Hall of c.1314, a chapel and constable's lodgings in the northern bailey.

The castle was besieged in the Magna Carta war of 1215–16. In 1267 it was granted to Edmund, Earl of Lancaster (Henry III's son) and taken back by the king, in this case Edward II, in 1323. He was fond of Pickering and lavished nearly £1,000 on it between 1323–6, and this included the second (southern bailey) stone curtain and towers. The actual order for this work is preserved in the Public Record Office.

The remains give an excellent illustration of converting a motte castle to a more complex stone castle (cf. Berkhamsted).

PLESHEY Nr Chelmsford, Essex † (TL 666144) O

Pleshey is a figure-of-eight motte castle with a very large outer bailey that now encloses the village of Pleshey. The motte, over 50ft tall, is separated from the inner bailey by a deep ditch which surrounds the motte. There was a rectangular building on the summit, 67ft by 56ft, with buttresses. It was built of flint, and is thought to have been a great tower. Remnants of other stone buildings have been excavated on the castle site, including a chapel (thirteenth or fourteenth century) and round towers. There is today a brick-built bridge from the inner bailey across the ditch to the motte, and this is thought to be fifteenth century. An aerial view of Pleshey today gives a very good idea of what an early Norman motte castle looked like (without its tower and wooden palisades).

PLYMPTON Nr Plymouth, Devon † (SX 544557) A

An interesting motte castle, whose motte is a local view point, with a (now incomplete) cylindrical shell wall on the top, approximately 50ft across. The stonework is mid-twelfth century at the earliest.

PONTEFRACT West Yorkshire †† (SE 460224) O

For much of its active history, Pontefract Castle was the principal royal castle in the north of England. Kings generally stayed there on visits to the north. For some time it was the major royal arsenal in Yorkshire. It

Pontefract: oil painting by Alexander Keirinx, c.1625, in Pontefract Museum

was the place of imprisonment and death (from causes still unknown) of Richard II, and of the imprisonment prior to execution of Thomas, Earl of Lancaster, cousin of Edward II and the principal trouble-maker in that sad monarch's reign. And it was besieged three times between 1644 and 1649, during and after the Civil War. The *History of the King's Works*, vols. i, ii, and iii, give details of considerable expenditure over the centuries on the castle, and record many descriptions of the state of the castle at various times, mostly of a depressing nature, that suggests that the deterioration was usually more than a jump ahead of the willingness or capacity of the Crown to fork out on repairing it.

The castle was demolished with the consent of Parliament in 1649, and a thorough job was done, so that today we are unable to give an accurate reconstruction of its building history. Space limits preclude a detailed discussion of its features, but we can sketch its general shape and discuss the nature of its prime feature, the great tower, since we disagree with received interpretations.

Pontefract began as a motte castle which used a splendidly placed natural rock mound, nearly 40ft high on rising ground, as a base. The slopes of the mound provided considerable natural protection to the site

then and after its development from a simple Norman motte-and-bailey into a many towered enclosure castle. It was started by Ilbert de Lasci (Lacy), a Norman follower of the Conqueror, sometime in the eleventh century.

Stonework was in time added to Pontefract, though we do not know when it was begun, nor what shape it took. Some authorities think that the base of the motte was later encased in stonework, perhaps in the thirteenth century. Other work included converting the oval inner bailey's wooden wall, and possibly the palisading round two outer baileys as well, into stone walls (stretches of the inner bailey wall survive today, notably on the north-west).

The castle was taken in hand c.1311 by Thomas Plantagenet, Earl of Lancaster, and it was from that time that major works began. Over the decades that followed the castle received a variety of flanking towers (chiefly, and interestingly, in square plan), improvements to a gate-tower in the inner bailey wall (which might have had some affinity with that at Denbigh: the twin turrets flanking the entrance were polygonal), the west barbican, some kitchens (notably, the Great Kitchen in the early fifteenth century), the Swillington Tower (named after the steward of the castle in the time of John of Gaunt, owner in the late

277

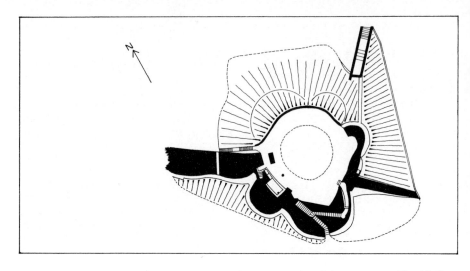

Pontefract: this is a modification of an early twentieth-century plan of the great tower. The thin line arcs inserted at top indicate the approximate position of the two missing lobes, though the radii may well have been different from those suggested. The plan shows clearly that the tower was neither quatrefoil nor trefoil, and that whatever shape it was, there was no symmetry. All this is proved by the aerial photograph

fourteenth century) which was built 1399–1405 on the outside of the castle to the north. Part of the Swillington Tower can be seen today beside the road under the castle hill. And Thomas of Lancaster started work on the great tower which absorbed the previous stonework on the mound, whatever form it had taken. The tower was continued after Lancaster's execution, and may not have been finished until the time of John of Gaunt, who carried out works on Pontefract between 1374–8.

The great tower, or donjon, is today no more than an assortment of stubs of towers a few feet tall, not even forming a complete and enclosed shape. There has been much argument as to its original design and form. S. Toy (1939) claimed it was quatrefoil and even drew a plan. *King's Works* vol. ii (1963), suggests it was trefoil, interpreting a description by Leland and an oil painting attributed to Joos de Momper, c.1620–30, now at Hampton Court. But the Leland description says: 'the Donjon cast ynto 6 roundelles, 3 bigge and 3 smaul, is very fair, and hath a fair spring' (for 'spring' read 'well'). Six roundels do not make a quatrefoil (or quadrilobe) or a trefoil (or trilobe);

even if of different radii, they make a sexfoil (or six lobes). Today, there are four lobes visible, of different sizes and shapes, as indicated on the plan and amplified in the aerial photograph. One of the lobes at least is beaked, and a second has a similar shape. On the north side of the great tower ruins, there is a considerable arc in which there are no lobes — indeed, no stonework at all. We have discussed with the Pontefract Local History Society our suggestion that the empty arc contained two more lobes (at least), for this would fit in with Leland's phrase. One of these may have been larger than the other, and on the plan we suggest outlines of two lobes, their positions but not necessarily their shapes. Clearly, the apparent symmetry of the lobes shown in the Hampton Court picture and also in the almost identical painting in Pontefract Museum now attributed to Alexander Keirinx, c.1625–30, is fanciful. (Pontefract Museum's picture was formerly attributed to Momper as well. Does this mean that the Hampton Court picture is now to be attributed to Keirinx? One is clearly a second version of the other, by the same artist.) It is not borne out by the founda-

278

tions, the stumps of the remaining lobes which are asymmetrical, or the aerial photograph. The tower was probably cylindrical inside, like Conisbrough and Orford, and we suggest it may have been built with its lobes 'bellying out' (cf. Château Gaillard, p.80), which would provide a greater wall surface from which to give maximum cover against assault. Beaking of the lobes would not be unique. It was a feature of the rebuilt Norfolk Towers at Dover Castle. To put it another way, the tower was a cluster of uneven but curvilinear lobes tailored to fit the site, the best the builders could do with the natural rock. In no circumstances could they have been influenced by the symmetrically quatrefoil great tower at York (Clifford's): the problems were quite different. One further point of interest is that the lobes which have survived (to a limited height) appear to have been put together in sections, which were not always keyed together externally. A detailed search by cutting out a segment of masonry might provide a clue as to why this keying was not done.

The great tower rose to three storeys, had bartizans at the top of some lobes and contained a well in the south-west lobe reached by a staircase in the masonry. This well chamber has been suggested as the prison occupied by Richard II between 1399 and his death (c.1402), but this is fanciful. An old description of the castle (which there is no cause to question) mentions six chambers at ground-floor level, five at first-floor level and an unspecified number in the second storey. These chambers were presumably in the lobes and if so, would have opened into a central chamber on each floor, the core of the great tower.

The solution to the problem of Pontefract's great tower may yet be solved completely: a programme of fresh excavation at the castle could be initiated in the near future following some interest shown by the DOE.

PONTESBURY Shropshire
(SJ 401060)
The site of an (?) eleventh-century earthwork enclosure which was surrounded by a ditch and rampart was found to contain footings of sandstone, some 14ft thick, which may have supported a later square great tower. There are not enough details to sketch any history.

Pontefract

PORTCHESTER Hampshire ††
(SU 625046) DOE

This is a really splendid fortress. It is a Norman castle built in the north-west corner of an almost perfect Roman fort of the Saxon Shore, the great majority of which is still standing. The Roman fort is not in the scope of this book. The Norman castle is a quadrangular enclosure with a great tower, the enclosure's north and west sides provided by the old Roman wall and the great tower built into the corner, but standing proud several feet north and west. A moat was cut round the east and south enclosure walls, while the north and west walls were protected by their own 'period' ditches and banks. The south-east walls of the inner enclosure had buildings ranged inside, and a tower and a gateway tower leading across the south moat. The square great tower itself is in very fine condition. It is faced in Caen ashlar and has pilaster buttresses mid-wall and on the corners. There is a forebuilding which appears to have been rebuilt more than once.

The tower is dated about 1120, but it went up two storeys only, and was heightened later. It had a cross-wall right to the top. The dimensions are 56ft square with walls 8ft thick. The ashlar work seems of better quality in the lower part than higher up. The tower has few windows and these are small: there are also rows of very slim arrow loops. The parapet at the top was battlemented.

In 1133 an Augustinian priory was built in the south-east corner of the Roman fort, and the chapel of this remains there. The castle was probably appropriated by Henry II at the beginning of his reign and it remained in royal hands thereafter. It was cared for by some of the kings. Edward I granted it to his mother and later on to his second wife. It was often garrisoned in the later fourteenth century as it was an embarkation point for English armies off to the wars in France, and also as a defence against invasion from the French. It was also used as a prison, in particular in the eighteenth century for French prisoners of war taken in the various wars, such as the Seven Years War.

Portchester

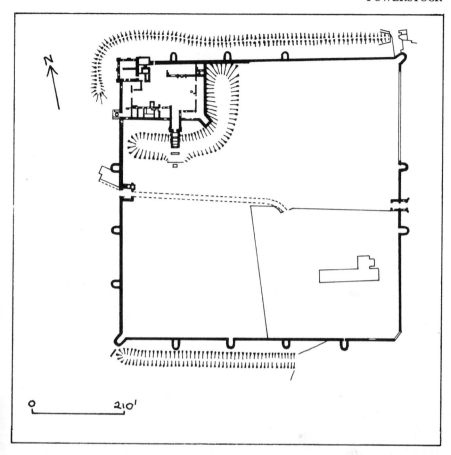

Portchester: ground plan. The Norman great tower (c.1120–30) is in the extreme top left corner. The enclosing walls are chiefly remnants of the Roman coastal fort of the third century AD

PORTLAND Dorset   †
(SY 684743) DOE

A coastal fort of Henry VIII's time during the invasion scare, c.1538–43, Portland stands on the northern shore of the Isle of Portland and guarded Portland Harbour. It was built to face another coastal fort which protected Weymouth Harbour, Sandsfoot, which has nearly vanished. Portland was probably built in 1540 and is in fine condition. It has seventeenth-century additions. The basic sixteenth-century plan was a segment of a circle with the curved outside housing a two-storey gun battery towards the sea. There is an octagonal great tower placed centrally in the rear part of the

segment, enclosed by a turret on each side. The apartments in the tower and the side turrets were for the governor and his staff. At one time the castle could mount thirteen guns. The battery had embrasures for nine guns (five at ground level and four at the upper level). Four more could be accommodated above the great tower.

POWERSTOCK Nr Bridport, Dorset
(SY 522959) A

A twelfth-century motte castle, possibly raised during the Anarchy of Stephen's reign, was taken by Henry Plantagenet, Count of Anjou, who became Henry II in 1154. Some stone buildings were added later, remains of which were still to be seen in the eighteenth century. They may have been put up by King John.

PRESTON Lancashire
(SD 512302) A

This was an early motte castle, erected on the end of a projecting cliff. The castle is thought to have been abandoned as a fortress in the early 1100s, for the site was given by Stephen, Count of Boulogne in c.1123 to monks of the order of Savigny at Furness Abbey, a newly founded monastic congregation which was amalgamated with the Cistercian order later in the century.

PRESTON CAPES Northamptonshire
(SP 576549) A

A motte castle formed from a natural sandstone mound, probably late in the eleventh century. The mound was surrounded on three sides by a ditch. The south side was possibly protected by a masonry wall.

PRUDHOE Northumberland †
(NY 092634) DOE

An extensive castle of Norman origins, improved over the years from early twelfth-century beginnings to the fourteenth, and even later. It began as a motte castle of c.1080s. Then it developed into a roughly figure-of-eight plan enclosure, with the waist not much narrower than the two loops. This is about 3 acres in area, stands on a natural spur on the south bank of the Tyne and is well defended by a deep ravine on the south and east sides, with ditches to south and west. The first structure was an early twelfth-century earthwork. Sometime, probably c.1175 or soon after, a great tower, almost square in plan, 44ft by 41ft, three storeys tall with 10ft-thick walls, and with a forebuilding at the eastern end, was raised in the western part of the enclosure which may have by then been partly given a stone curtain. The great tower is one of the oldest in Northumberland. The gatehouse was also built in the twelfth century. The castle had been unsuccessfully besieged in 1173, and again in 1174, by William the Lion, King of Scotland.

In the thirteenth century a barbican was added on the south side, about 36ft long, which led to a drawbridge across the moat, and a second barbican led from that to the gatehouse. The gatehouse was given a vaulted basement and a chapel on the first floor. This chapel is interesting for its oriel window over the gateway, said to be the earliest oriel window in any castle in northern England, possibly in all England.

Prudhoe became a Percy possession in 1381. Excavations in progress.

PULFORD Cheshire
(SJ 375587)

A motte castle of probably mid-twelfth century is alluded to in a late twelfth-century record. It was sited near the River Alyn.

PULVERBATCH Shropshire
(SJ 423023) A

There are two motte sites here, one at SJ 433016 and the other, which has its bailey, at SJ 423023. The latter may be that mentioned in 1205. It is known locally as Castle Pulverbatch and the earthworks are visible. The former mound is also visible, by Wilderby Hall.

QUATFORD Shropshire †
(SO 738907) A

On a cliff beside the Severn, Roger de Montgomery, one of the Conqueror's principal earls and commanders, built a motte castle sometime between 1066–86. It is mentioned in Domesday Book. Roger de Montgomery used the fortress as a hunting lodge as well as a castle for cowering the neighbourhood. Some stonework was added, but in the early twelfth century the buildings were dismantled and re-erected at Bridgnorth. There are traces of the original motte.

RABY Nr Staindrop, Durham †
(NZ 129217) O

Raby is impressive to look at from the main road, but it has been aptly described by one of Britain's leading castellogists, Professor Allen Brown, as a 'rambling and ill-fortified castle'. It was built by the great baronial family of Neville in the late fourteenth century, as a quadrangular structure with high towers and much lower surrounding curtain wall with crenellations. The licence was granted in 1378. One of the original buildings was the Neville Tower, the entrance gate-tower on the west. The castle evolved over the next two or three generations to become an extensive palatial residence of towers and ranges of apartments clustered round a small courtyard, with a series of stretches of inner curtain, and enclosed completely by an outer curtain with numerous open-backed rectangular flanking towers and a separate gatehouse to the north. The largest tower is Clifford's, about 81ft tall, rectangular, with walls over 10ft thick.

RAYLEIGH Essex †
(TQ 805909) A
A motte castle of the eleventh-century whose motte slopes were revetted with ragstone and flint rubble, one of the very few to receive this treatment. The motte, some 50ft tall, was given a substantial wooden tower on its 70ft diameter summit. Interestingly, the tower was never replaced with a stone tower, and indeed no stone buildings were ever erected at Rayleigh, although the castle was in use right into the middle of the thirteenth century. It was improved by several timber structures and some complex ditch and bank construction. The mound is on the outskirts of the town.

READING Berkshire
(SU 718736)
Traces of a motte castle thought to have been built in the grounds of the abbey in the mid-twelfth century may be the remains of the Reading Castle that is recorded as having been destroyed by Henry II in c.1154.

REDCASTLE Shropshire
(SJ 572296) P
Two rock crests close together were the site of this thirteenth-century curtain wall castle with flanking square and cylindrical towers. There is little to see.

REIGATE Surrey
(TQ 252504) A
Warenne, Earl of Surrey in William II's reign, built a castle at Reigate. It was an enclosure castle with a deep surrounding ditch. Though there are no traces of stonework, it will have been enlarged and improved with stone, since the castle was occupied by Royalists during the Civil War. There is also a record of the castle having been captured in 1264 by Simon de Montfort during the Barons' War against Henry III. It stood on the hill near the railway station.

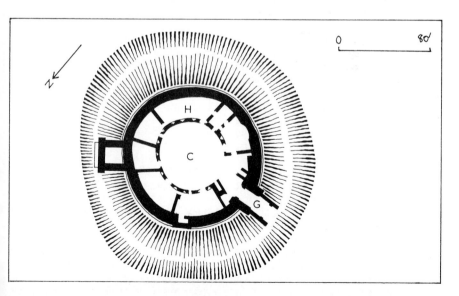

Restormel: plan of shell keep. C = courtyard inside, surrounded by buildings ranged round the 'shell'; H = hall; G = gatetower (the oldest stonework)

Restormel: an aerial view of the oval shell keep on the mound. The gatehouse-tower is beside the staircase

RESTORMEL Lostwithiel,   ††
Cornwall   (SX 104614) DOE
A very fine example of a shell keep castle raised on an earlier motte. The motte was raised in the twelfth century by Baldwin FitzTurstin. The slate and Pentewan stone shell keep, almost completely circular, 125ft across, 8ft thick, was erected in c.1200. The top was crenellated. There was a ring of apartments of stone and wood raised around the inside of the shell, one-storeyed and two-storeyed, ranging over the later part of the thirteenth century. These included kitchen, great hall, solar, and barrack room for retainers. The earliest stone structure was a square-plan tower at the south west, which was a gate tower, c.1100. It presumably sat in the circumference of an otherwise wooden palisade. Another square tower was inserted in the circumference once it had been converted to stone (c.1280s). This was in the east and it was two-storeyed, the top floor containing a chapel. A barbican was added to the south-west gate-tower in the thirteenth century. Holes for the joists of hoarding are sited round the outer wall of the shell just below parapet level. The whole shell and mound were surrounded by a wet moat and high bank outside. Water was brought into the castle by lead pipes. A document of c.1337 mentions the conduits: recent archaeological excavations revealed lead piping. There was also a well dug to some 50ft.

Restormel was acquired by Richard, Earl of Cornwall, a son of Henry III, and it passed to Edmund, Earl of Cornwall. Both were responsible for the various stone walled apartments inside the shell. The Black Prince held the castle from 1337–76.

RICHARD'S CASTLE   †
Hereford & Worcester   (SO 484703) A
This was one of the castles mentioned in the *Anglo-Saxon Chronicle* in an entry some years before the date of the Norman Conquest, but which is now accepted as not having been a fortified residence before 1066. Richard's was a motte castle whose mound and inner bailey stand inside a larger outer bailey fortified by a ditch and rampart. Some time in the twelfth century, thought to be c.1175, a slightly asymmetrical octagonal great tower of sandstone ashlar was built on the 30ft mound. The dimensions were 44ft across, approximately 20ft internally, and

284

with walls up to 12ft thick. Entrance was at first-floor level. Some form of apsidal extension was added to its eastern wall, though its purpose is not clear. A wing wall projected to south.

The original inner bailey palisade was replaced by a stone curtain with turrets, some open backed, and a gate-tower.

Richard's, named after Richard, son of Scrob, a Norman lord and friend of Edward the Confessor, was temporarily held by supporters of Simon de Montfort in his war with Henry III, 1264–5.

RICHMOND North Yorkshire   †† (NZ 174006) DOE

A very interesting castle of the earliest beginnings, formidable looking, dominating Swaledale from a great height, but which never saw military action. The first work at Richmond, on the edge of a very tall cliff over the River Swale, was a triangular curtain forming an enclosure, the south side being the cliff edge. The curtain has thick walling, nearly 10ft in places. The site was granted to Alan the Red in the 1080s, and it was he who started the works. These also included one of the earliest stone halls in England, known as Scolland's Hall, though this may have been raised by his brother after Alan's death in 1089. The gate-tower was also begun in the eleventh century, in the north apex of the triangle. It was probably similar to that at Exeter.

Scolland's Hall may have been preceded only by the hall (which became a great tower later) at Chepstow, in c.1071–5. The name comes from Scolland, Steward to Alan the Red. It is two-storeyed and once had a cross-wall. At its east end is a gateway out of the triangle. Adjoining it on the extension of the curtain is the Gold Hole Tower, containing garderobes; the lower part is eleventh century, the remainder, fourteenth century. The curtain wall contains courses of herringbone masonry. There are square flanking towers on the east stretch of the curtain.

The great tower is the dominant structure at Richmond. It was built as an extension upwards of the original gate-tower and it is possible to see where the new work began. The tower was raised in the mid-twelfth century (c.1150–70), and it reached 100ft

Richmond: an aerial view of the triangular enclosure dominated by the magnificent early twelfth-century great tower

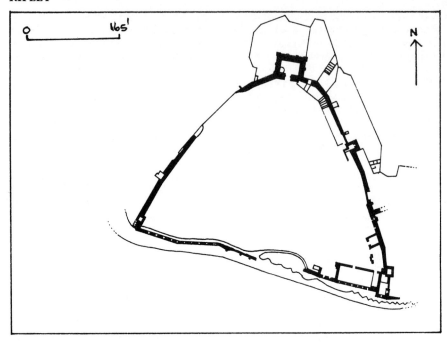

Richmond: the stone curtain and the hall at bottom right are of late eleventh century. The great tower at the top is an early twelfth-century enlargement of a simpler gate-tower of the 1090s

tall, retaining the fine archway of the eleventh-century gateway. This is at ground level. There is another smaller entrance at first floor, not protected by a forebuilding. Some think the original archway was blocked up when the tower was built, and if so it has been opened up again. The tower was built of squared ashlar, but much has been taken away and replaced with rubble masonry. Despite its height, the great tower is four-storeyed, the second floor (third level) open to the roof. Each corner of the tower supports two-storeyed corner turrets. Along the wall-walk behind the battlements you can see the pitch of the original roof of the tower, which has been replaced. The great tower has straight flights of stairs from floor to floor, like Bamburgh. There are also rooms and garderobes in the wall thickness of the tower, which is 10–12ft.

RIPLEY North Yorkshire   †
(SE 283606) O
Today, Ripley Castle is an eighteenth-century mansion incorporating some much

earlier structures of a tower castle. The sole remaining part of military significance is the twin-turreted gatehouse, thought to have been built in c.1418 by an ancestor of the present owners, the Ingilby family.

ROCHESTER Kent   ††
(TQ 742686) O
A castle at Rochester is mentioned in the *Anglo-Saxon Chronicle* entry for 1087–8 and is alluded to in Domesday Book (1086). Presumably that was the motte castle erected in the time of the Conqueror which, when held by his half brother, Odo, Bishop of Bayeux, was besieged by the Conqueror's son, William Rufus, and taken. This castle was probably on what is now Boley Hill (the name may be a rendering of bailey) to the south of the stone buildings now standing.

A stone curtain was raised, probably in 1088, round a levelled platform to the north-east of Boley Hill, following for a stretch some walling from the old Roman town. The curtain was given one, possibly two, rectangular flanking towers on the south-east axis. These have disappeared (though the southern tower built by Edward III, which survives, may incorporate some of its stone). A gateway was inserted on the south side. Round three sides a ditch was cut, and the River Medway provided the defence for the fourth (west) side. This work was begun by Gundulf, Bishop of Rochester, who was also associated with the early stonework at the Tower of London, notably the White Tower. Some of the curtain was heightened later and its line in the south altered.

In c.1127 the great tower was begun, and the work probably took ten to fifteen years. It is today in excellent condition considering its age and that it was besieged twice in the thirteenth century, and is more or less complete except for the roof (two gables), its floors and some of the forebuilding. The great tower, built of Kentish ragstone with Caen ashlar dressings, is 70ft square, rises to 113ft to the battlemented parapet, and its four corner turrets rise to 12ft taller. The tower has pilaster buttresses mid-wall, north-west and south-east, two buttresses along the north-east and one on the south-west — the second disappeared in

1215 when the corner tower collapsed after mining (see below), and clasping pilaster buttresses on three corners, the west and east corners being larger than the north (and presumably the south, too, before the collapse).

The walls are 12ft thick at lower level and 10ft higher up. They stand on a straight plinth. The entrance is at first floor. It is protected by a handsome three-storey (plus basement) forebuilding whose second floor is double, with a mural gallery at the higher level, and above this a chapel. The main tower has a cross-wall all the way up, centrally, and at the second storey (a double storey which has a higher gallery level with a mural passage all the way round through the window bays), the cross-wall becomes pierced by arcading which has survived and is a row of four round-headed arches with chevron moulding. Up through the centre of the cross-wall rises, from the basement, an ashlar-built well shaft which served every floor. The walls are more generously provided with windows than in many great towers of the first half of the twelfth century (see Hedingham, which is sparse). This spread of windows undoubtedly improved

Rochester: the rectangular great tower. The cylindrical corner turret is the replacement for the earlier square turret damaged by undermining in the siege of 1215–16

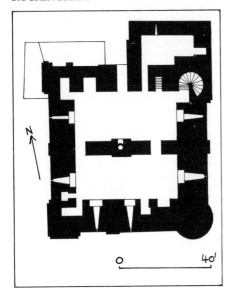

Rochester: ground floor of the great tower

the lighting in the great tower.

In 1215, the castle was besieged by King John (see p. 70). He undermined the south corner turret and it collapsed, allowing his troops to rush in. But even then, they had to fight almost inch by inch for the tower, since the defenders used the cross-wall to great effect to slow the besiegers down. Afterwards, probably about ten years later, the shattered corner was rebuilt in cylindrical shape, solid stone most of the way up, with a cylindrical turret at the top.

The castle was besieged again, this time in 1264, during the war between Henry III and Simon de Montfort, but the great tower was successfully defended by the king's men. It remained in royal hands until the seventeenth century, but despite repairs it had deteriorated, and by the eighteenth century only the great tower and some walling with two towers remained better than ruinous, which is the position today.

ROCKINGHAM Northamptonshire   †
(SP 867913) O
Rockingham is mentioned in Domesday

Book. It was a motte castle built by the Conqueror on a steep hill overlooking the Welland Valley, with two quadrilateral baileys. It seems probable that the early castle had a residential and recreational role rather than a military one. Archbishop Anselm had one of his periodic confrontations with William II here in 1095, which resulted in a trial before the King's court.

The castle was taken over by Henry II in c.1156 and thereafter, over at least two centuries, many new works and repairs were recorded. Among the major features were its twin-cylindrical towered gatehouse, still impressive today, built by Edward I (c.1280–90), and its *magna turris*, as recorded in Exchequer rolls, which is thought to have been more of a shell keep on the motte and which may have been built by King John.

RUFUS Portland, Dorset
(SY 697711) A
The present remains of a polygonal tower, built of Portland stone, stand upon the site of an earlier structure which may have been built as early as c.1100. A castle at Portland is mentioned by William of Malmesbury, the twelfth-century monk-historian. The tower is probably of the fifteenth century. The castle is also known as Bow and Arrow.

RUYTON-ELEVEN-TOWNS
Shropshire
(SJ 394222) A
Fragments of a stone tower, probably too small to have been a residential great tower, remain on this fourteenth-century castle site on a ridge of ground.

SAFFRON WALDEN Essex   †
(TL 538385) O
A late eleventh-century motte castle raised on a natural hill, Saffron Walden Castle received a substantial flintstone great tower of rectangular plan (almost square), about 38ft by 40ft, in the twelfth century. The tower is partly standing, though in ruins, and about one-third of its height has disappeared. Remaining are two storeys, with substantial round arched recesses in the western and southern walls. There was a central pillar which may have supported a pair of arcades whose other ends rested perhaps on wall corbels. The low addition at

Saffron Walden: the great tower of flint rubble

the north-west angle is a late eighteenth-century semaphore station. There was a forebuilding on the west wall of the great tower. The protruding wall ends on the south-east angle are part of the buttressing. The corner contained a spiral staircase.

ST BRIAVELS Gloucestershire
(SS 559046) C

An enclosure castle of the twelfth century, St Briavels received a square great tower probably in the time of Henry II, which is recorded as having finally collapsed in ruins in 1752. St Briavels still has its huge, twin-cylindrical towered gatehouse, built by Edward I, c.1292–3, at a cost of nearly £500. It can be seen from the road. The towers are supported at the bottom by spurs like those at Goodrich. St Briavels is situated within the Forest of Dean and in the thirteenth century it served as an arsenal for iron crossbow-bolts which were manufactured at the iron forges in the forest. In preparation for the siege of Bedford Castle in 1224, Henry III ordered miners from the Forest of Dean to assist in fashioning the stone missiles for the trebuchets and he may also have sent for supplies of crossbow-bolts from St Briavels.

ST CATHERINE'S Fowey, Cornwall
(SX 118508) DOE

This was a Henry VIII coastal fort, but not one of those erected in the 1538–43 invasion scare period, for it was built in the middle of Henry's reign, possibly c.1530.

ST MAWES Cornwall ††
(SW 842328) DOE

One of the major coastal fortresses built by Henry VIII between 1538–43, St Mawes was started in 1540. It was sited below the rising ground on the east side of the Carrick Roads, just north of Falmouth Bay, and it faced its 'sister' castle, Pendennis, built on high ground on the western side of the Roads. St Mawes has a cylindrical four-storeyed great tower, octagonal on the inner surface. Clustered about the great tower on three sides were built three semi-cylindrical bastions, also called lunettes, which were single-storeyed with parapets around the tops which were battlemented with wide gun embrasures. The plan was clover leaf described as an 'ace of clubs'. The fortress was built of local stone mingled with granite and freestone. Emerging from the great tower is a small cylindrical turret with a cupola.

Some statistics relating to the garrison and its armaments in the sixteenth and seventeenth centuries have been preserved and are cited by the DOE in its guide to St Mawes. These include the fact that the standard garrison was anything from sixteen to a hundred men, that in 1609 the armament included fourteen various guns of iron or brass. The castle was threatened in 1646 during the Civil War and surrendered without a single shot being fired. Thirteen pieces of ordnance were captured.

A plan of St Mawes appears on p.290.

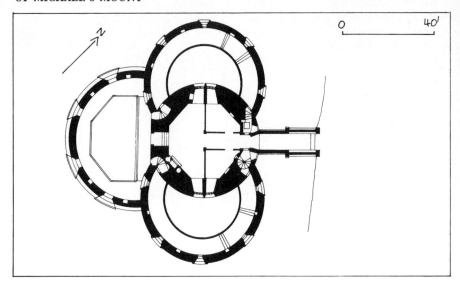

St Mawes: ground plan

ST MICHAEL'S MOUNT   †
off Marazion, Cornwall
(SW 515298) NT

There was a fort of some kind at St Michael's in the late twelfth century but no traces now exist. A Benedictine priory had already been established on the island in the previous century, in c.1044. For a long time the island appeared to be a bone of contention between Normandy and England. Sometime in the fifteenth century, when raids by French pirates against the island and against the nearby coast of Cornwall began to become too frequent for comfort, some military defences were developed. A castle was built on the top of the rock, about 200ft above sea level. It became a cluster of strong towers with battlemented parapets, including a platform for guns which were also housed in another gun battery part of the way down the path to the shore.

SALTWOOD Nr Hythe, Kent   ††
(TR 161359) O

At present this is the home of Lord Clark, OM, the eminent art historian. It was an enclosure surrounded by an oval curtain with open backed square flanking turrets and square-plan interior towers, adjoined to the east by a triangular bailey surrounded by

banking. The oval enclosure is thought to have been a motte, flattened possibly in the 1170s. It was surrounded by a moat. The inner enclosure was first raised by Henry of Essex in the 1150s–60s. He was disgraced and the castle reverted to the Crown. Further works were done in the fourteenth century. Buildings were raised in the oval enclosure, notably the Knight's Hall (c.1350), Thorpe's Tower, and the great tower itself was enlarged by Archbishop Courtenay of Canterbury (c.1381), having been started in the 1170s. The stone curtain was said to have been built round the triangular outer bailey by Henry Yevele, the celebrated designer of Queenborough, Cowling and possibly Nunney, who also designed Saltwood's magnificent twin-cylinder towered gatehouse (in c.1380).

Saltwood's moat was fed by a stream. This was dammed in order to keep the stream wide where it separated the oval enclosure from the rising ground nearby. The castle is in remarkably good condition and several original features can be seen.

SANDAL Nr Wakefield,   ††
West Yorkshire   (SE 337182) O

One of the most fascinating castle excavations undertaken in the present century has

290

been the uncovering and preservation of the substantial remains of Sandal Castle, on the south-east side of the River Calder, near Wakefield. The excavation project, which began in 1963 and took ten years, has been a brilliant *tour de force* in castle archaeology and history terms. Financed and organized by Wakefield Corporation, Wakefield Historical Society and the University of Leeds, with grants from the Carnegie UK Trust, this project has been directed with great skill and inspiration by Philip Mayes, now County Archaeologist for West Yorkshire, and by Dr L.A.S. Butler, of the Department of Archaeology, University of Leeds. It has been assisted in numerous ways on and off site throughout ten exciting years by people from local schools, societies and businesses and by private individuals. The project has revealed no less than the ruins of a complete medieval castle which had all but disappeared underneath 6 acres of accumulated earth and scrub of centuries of abandonment. The contrast between Sandal in 1963 and 1973 is well demonstrated in the two photographs on pp.294–5. It is a privilege to be able to write the first short summary of the story to appear in any book.

Sandal began as a motte castle of the twelfth century, probably c.1150, consisting of a motte about 45ft tall (with its own ditch) opposite a horseshoe-shaped bailey. Soon after 1200, the conversion of the castle to stone began, and it continued over a long period, to c.1280. Sandal was held first by the Warennes, earls of Surrey, but the 3rd earl died in c.1150, leaving his daughter as heir. She married (as her second husband) Hamelin Plantagenet, bastard half-brother of Henry II, who took on the earldom. He was the builder of Conisbrough in c.1180–90, and it was Hamelin who probably began the stone conversion at Sandal.

The excavations have been remarkable for many discoveries, but we have space only to record the most interesting:

1 The Public Record Office holds a drawing of Sandal, of 1565, executed in the stylized manner of the time, a mixture of accuracy with fantasy (see picture, p.292). The accuracy aspect is particularly germane to this castle, for the excavations uncovered some of the features depicted in the drawing. One was the remains of the lower level of a polygonal tower added in 1484–5 to the north-west corner of the great tower on

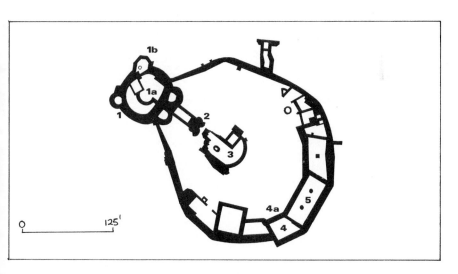

Sandal: ground plan of the castle after recent excavations. It follows the motte-and-bailey plan with later stone additions. 1=great tower; 1a=inner curved wall (part of inner turret?); 1b=new polygonal tower (*temp*. Richard III); 2=twin-cylinder tower structure; 3=barbican (shape similar to Goodrich and Lion Tower, London); 4=cellar with pantry over; 4a=base of pillar supporting staircase to great hall (see sixteenth-century picture of Sandal, p.292); 5=great hall

the motte. This had been built by Richard III on the site of a smaller semi-cylindrical tower that contained a well. The well was also investigated down to a depth of some 60ft by the team. In the drawing, the polygonal tower can be seen at extreme right, beside the trees. Another fragment discovered caused a great deal of excitement. Towards the top left of the drawing is a stairway up to a balcony leading into the great hall, which appears to be supported by a pillar with a conical 'dish' on top. The base of a pillar that matches the pillar in the drawing was uncovered beside the great hall in 1966, in the right position for it to have supported the stairway.

2   In the bailey of the stone castle, under several feet of earth, substantial traces of timber buildings of the earlier motte castle were found by the team. There were post-holes of a hall and of an adjoining kitchen. The hall was 38ft by 21ft, with narrow aisles about 4ft wide. In its last days before being submerged by earth dug out to create a ditch round a new barbican (see below at 4), the hall had housed a lead-smelting hearth.

3   Early in the thirteenth century the stone conversion began, probably, with the erection of the structure on the motte. This

appears to have been a cylindrical tower about 30ft in diameter, but which was not finished. Excavation revealed a little over half the cylinder (in the vertical plan) with a turn-back flight of steps. To the north-east of the half-cylinder, a wall projects towards the outer stonework on the motte. The suggestion is that there was a change of plan and that the cylindrical tower was abandoned. But it remains a mystery why the tower was left standing when a somewhat larger, irregularly cylindrical tower was built on the motte, about 84ft across, which had walls between 10–12ft thick except at the south-east where the arc was cut by a

chord in front of which was constructed the main gatehouse block (see 5 below). This later tower appears to have been a great tower, which had segmented chambers around its inside walls, and two clasping semi-cylindrical towers on its north and north-west sides. The north tower contained the well, and it was this tower that was rebuilt by Richard III as a polygonal tower. There is not much left of the great tower above ground storey, but the surviving stonework does permit a reliable interpretation, and this is being prepared in very considerable detail prior to publication of the full report of the excavations.

Sandal: before excavation began, 1963

4 One of the earliest buildings of the stone phase was the barbican, datable to the middle of the thirteenth century, perhaps a little before. Situated south-east of the gatehouse block from which it is separated by part of the ditching that surrounds the barbican (much of the ditching having been cut through sandstone and shales), the barbican stands as it were on an island which at some time received very fine ashlar revetting at base level along the south-west and west sides. The barbican is basically D-shaped (and in this respect reminds one of the barbican at Goodrich and the now vanished barbican, the Lion Tower, at the Tower of London, both of which are ante-dated by Sandal's); the entrance and exit were at north-east, through a guarded chamber out across a bridge, and at north-west, through a passage out across a bridge over the motte ditch to the great tower's gatehouse block. The masonry round the base of the barbican is of the highest quality, cut and beautifully shaped, comparable with much of the best contemporary ecclesiastical stonework. Similarly high-quality masonry is manifest round the bases of the gatehouse towers.

5 The gatehouse block consisted of a pair of wing walls running parallel and close down the motte slope out of the south-east of the great tower, and into a twin-cylindrical towered gateway flanking the end of the passage between the walls. A drawbridge provided access between the gatehouse and the barbican. Note particularly the very fine ashlar work round the splayed plinths of the remains of the towers. Only the lowest courses of the gatehouse block survive, but enough to confirm the sophisticated nature of the defensive arrangements for protecting the great tower which was, as in all great tower castles, the last refuge in the event of siege.

There were several other important buildings of stone within the overall perimeter of Sandal, which was enclosed by a substantial curtain wall whose ends 'fed' into the great tower at points more than half way up the motte. These have little more surviving than incomplete ground floor paving, varying heights of wall fragment, residual column bases, remnants of steps and so forth, but the remains are comprehensive enough to establish the existence of a semi-circular range of structures including

294

kitchen, larder, pantry, great hall and bailey gatehouse, all of the thirteenth century. The enclosing curtain also appears to have had some flanking towers, probably of square plan. In Richard III's time, in addition to the polygonal replacement tower, domestic buildings were added in the arc between the great hall and the gatehouse, and a bakehouse tower block on the western end of the earlier range.

The history of Sandal from the time of the stone conversion to the mid-seventeenth century was relatively uneventful. From c.1353 it was held by Edmund of Langley, Duke of York, fifth son of Edward III, and his successors until New Year's Eve in 1460. On that day, Richard Plantagenet, Duke of York, Protector of England, leader of the Yorkists and *de facto* heir to the feeble Henry VI, after spending Christmas in the castle, sallied forth into a skirmish with the Lancastrians outside nearby Wakefield, and was defeated and slain. The castle passed to his eldest son Edward, whom Warwick, the 'Kingmaker', made King

Edward IV a few weeks later, following the great Yorkist victory at Towton. The Crown held Sandal until 1566. Richard III used it as a key Crown stronghold, but when he was defeated and killed at Bosworth (1485), the victor, Henry VII, came into possession of it. Along with numerous other castles. Sandal was neglected. In 1558 it was transferred to the Duchy of Lancaster, and eight years later it was decided that it was 'especially to be meynteyned because it standith in a strong Contrie of men amongst whome (yf any rebellion shude happen, as God forbid) this castle must be the staie of it'. Notwithstanding this instruction, little was done to preserve it in usable condition, partly because Elizabeth I granted it out to a succession of private individuals who, it may be presumed, could not afford to maintain it and who certainly would not have succeeded in persuading the parsimonious queen to help out. By 1592, it was being described as 'very ruynous and in greater decay then th'other of our castles are'.

Sandal: the castle exposed after excavation, 1963-73

In 1642, Sandal was garrisoned by Royalists who built a stable block and a farriery on the ruins of Richard III's bakehouse block. Outwork defences were raised beyond the curtain. In 1645 it was twice besieged and the garrison surrendered after several weeks of bombardment in the second attack, in which the cannon fire appears to have been directed mainly at the great tower. The castle was then slighted. The site gradually became more and more derelict, covered over except for one or two standing-up wall fragments in the semi-circular range at the south. Some excavation work was done in the 1890s, and a plan was drawn (since shown to be considerably out in many respects). In 1957 Wakefield Corporation bought the site and the recent excavation project was conceived and put into operation soon afterwards (1964), producing the astonishing results, reports of which are already delighting the world of castle enthusiasts ('a sumptuous castle of almost Très Riches Heures sophistication' — Prof. Allen Brown). The site has been landscaped as a park around the outside of the castle precincts, and the park and castle are open to visitors. A model of the castle, as it is conjectured to have appeared in its heyday, is on show at Wakefield Museum.

Anyone who wants to study castles in any depth should put Sandal Castle at the top of his visiting list.

SAUVEY Withcote, Leicestershire (SK 787053) A

A very late motte castle was built here by King John in the early thirteenth century. The site was put in the path of a stream which was dammed to provide water for a wet moat around the castle. The king appears to have liked the site, and Sauvey was probably more residential and re-creational than military. There are records of money spent on fishponds at Sauvey in 1211. The castle remained in royal hands, though granted to the Count of Aumale for a few years. The castle began as a wooden one, and what stone was added is impossible to determine. After about 1260 it was allowed to decay, and the site was 'quarried' for other castles, including Rockingham, which received supplies of lead, stone and timber. The earthwork remains can be seen.

SCALEBY Nr Carlisle, Cumbria (NY 449624) P

Scaleby began as a pele-tower of the thirteenth century. This was enlarged to give it an extension on the eastern side consisting of a hall which is tunnel-vaulted at ground level. A licence to crenellate was granted to the castle's holder, Robert de Tilliol, and from this grew a fortified house with extra towers and a fourteenth-century gatehouse. Scaleby was garrisoned during the Bishops' War (1638-9) when an invasion from Scotland was feared. The castle has been restored and is occupied today. The original pele-tower is still standing but in a decaying state.

SCARBOROUGH North Yorkshire †† (TA 050893) DOE

The castle on the edge of the cliff at Scarborough was begun in the 1130s by Count William of Aumale who started work on a stone curtain and probably built the first stage of the great tower. The curtain, with the steep, natural slopes of the cliffs, formed a roughly triangular site. There had been a Roman signal station on the headland within the site area. In the 1150s Henry II seized Scarborough and improved the fortifications. He raised the great tower on Aumale's first work. It is now ruinous, but was an approximately 55ft square building and rose to over 100ft tall. It had pilaster buttresses, except on the south face, walls between 11-12ft thick, and 15ft thick on the west side. The tower stood on a battered plinth. It had a forebuilding on the south, about 40ft tall, 30ft long and 20ft wide, over a stone staircase some of whose steps remain (though the forebuilding has gone, like that at Hedingham). The tower was built of rough stone and mortar, faced with fine ashlar laid in beautiful courses. The windows were round headed at the top, tall and slim, in some places in pairs. Lower down they were wider.

Scarborough is notable for its barbican. This emerges westwards from a narrowing of the inner bailey in front of the great tower, the narrowing carried as a stone bridge over a ditch. The barbican is triangular and has an entrance/exit in a large twin-cylindrical turretted gateway, and this was probably built in the 1240s.

The castle was besieged on several occasions, including the revolt of 1536 known as the Pilgrimage of Grace, and twice during the Civil War. It even sustained damage from shells from German warships in World War I. Medieval records indicate considerable sums spent on repairs during its ownership by the kings, from Henry II to James I. On at least two occasions, estimates for repairs were given at £2,000 or so, but the work was not in fact done as suggested. King John spent that sum on the castle during his reign, and much of this was on the south and west curtain wall with its flanking towers.

SCOTNEY Nr Lamberhurst, Kent (TQ 689353) NT
The very small, cylindrical turret at Scotney, with machicolation and a conical roof on its top, standing half surrounded by water in a lake, is a famous ruin photographed for postcards, calendars and the like. It is part of a fourteenth-century moated castle connected to a seventeenth-century manor house, which is in ruins, both of which are in the grounds of a Georgian mansion owned by the National Trust.

SHERBORNE OLD CASTLE Dorset †
(ST 647167) DOE
The Old Castle is a rectangular stone enclosure with canted corners raised inside a ditch that has a bank outside. Plain rectangular towers were inserted in the four canted corners and one in the north wall which was a gateway. The south-west corner tower was a gate-tower. This enclosure was probably the early twelfth-century part, put up sometime between 1107–35. In that time it is possible also that the quadrangular bishop's palace consisting of a residential range round a courtyard was raised by the then holder, the bishop of Salisbury. At some time in the mid-twelfth-century, a small L-plan great tower was built into the south-west corner of the palace quadrangle. But there is doubt as to whether the castle was ever seriously intended to be more than a large residence with some attempt at fortification. The castle came into royal possession c.1183, and King John later spent a little over £100 on it, presumably on fortification.

The castle became the property of Sir Walter Raleigh towards the end of the 1590s. He carried out several alterations.

SHERIFF HUTTON North Yorkshire (SE 652661)
A very substantial, quadrangular fortified manor house which had four large towers on the angles of four storeys (one had five), and an interesting gatehouse of later (fifteenth-century) date, some of which is standing. The castle was built of reddish rubble with ashlar dressings and quoins. It was built by the powerful Neville family in c.1382, close to the site of a motte castle of the early twelfth century which was abandoned. It is now ruinous.

SHIRBURN Nr Watlington, Oxfordshire (SU 697960) C
This was a brick-built fortified manor house, begun in c.1380, with a section of dressed stone and chalk in the west front. It was quadrangular, with cylindrical towers on the corners and a gate-tower. Surrounded by a moat fed by local springs, the castle was greatly altered in the eighteenth and nineteenth centuries, incorporating much of the original brickwork.

SHOTWICK Nr Chester, Cheshire (SJ 350704) P
A motte castle that was enlarged in the twelfth and thirteenth centuries into a roughly hexagonal enclosure of stone with a great tower inside. The curtain had four rounded flanking turrets. There was also a gate-tower. The great tower was rectangular, with pilaster buttresses. The castle controlled a ford across the Dee. There is little of this castle left today, except for some earthworks.

SHRAWARDINE Nr Shrewsbury, Shropshire (SJ 400154) P
Shrawardine was a motte castle beside the Severn. Begun in the twelfth century, it was held by the Crown. Fragments of a shell wall on the motte, of rubble but with some ashlar dressing, and other stonework, are probably of Henry II's time. Henry and his sons, Richard I and John, all spent money on repairs. The castle was attacked and severely damaged by the Welsh, probably by

Llywelyn the Great (c.1196–1240), Prince of all Wales, who captured Shrewsbury in 1215. The Welsh returned the castle to the English and it is believed to have been repaired in c.1220. Shrawardine was razed to the ground in the Civil War.

SHREWSBURY Shropshire
(SJ 495128) O

Fifty-one houses were destroyed in a loop of the River Severn at Shrewsbury sometime in the years 1067–9 to make room for the motte castle built by Roger de Montgomery. Some of the woodwork was converted to stone in the twelfth century, and of this there are remains of the inner bailey wall and a gateway with a round-headed arch. Over the period c.1154–c.1350 several sums were spent on new works and repairs, though by no means all were specified. Some of this was spent on a stone curtain for the motte. A gatehouse was raised in the time of Henry III, possibly 1230s, and this may have been a twin-cylindrical towered type. A barbican was built in 1233–4. In c.1270 the tower on the motte collapsed, and it is thought that it was the original wooden great tower. There was a king's hall which received repairs in c.1287–9. Works were also carried out on the palisades on and off during the thirteenth century. By c.1350 the castle had become dilapidated.

SIZERGH Helsington, †
Nr Kendal, Cumbria
(SD 498878) NT

Sizergh is a roughly rectangular enclosure of three wings (there is no north-west wing) round a courtyard. The south-east wing consists of an entrance hall in the centre (which was a great hall in the fifteenth century), the north-east of domestic apartments and the south-west the pele-tower. The pele-tower is mid-fourteenth century, about 60ft by 39ft and 59ft tall. On the south side of the pele in the centre is a rectangular turret. This rises over 10ft higher than the pele itself, and is called the Deincourt Tower. At ground-floor level this tower has walls 7½–9½ft thick, and contained a dungeon, but was less thick higher up. Both towers are battlemented. The other two wings were added much later, about the sixteenth century.

Sizergh has belonged to the Strickland family since at least the fourteenth century. One of them, Sir Walter, committed himself to service of an almost feudal kind to the Earl of Salisbury whereby he undertook to provide a small army for the Earl's use in war — anywhere. The agreement documents have survived and they indicate the kind of dangers the kings faced in those times: powerful barons able to call up substantial military reserves at short notice.

SKIPSEA Nr Bridlington, ††
Humberside (TA 163551) A

This is one of the few motte castles where the motte is surrounded by its own ditch and rampart and also separated from its bailey, in this case by a marsh. There was a wooden causeway across the marsh. It was built in c.1086, and its motte is about 45ft tall with a flattened top nearly ¼ acre in area. The lake which surrounded much of the castle contained eels, then a staple fish diet, which produced revenue for the holders of the castle. The destruction of the castle was ordered by Henry III. Earthworks can still be seen.

SKIPTON North Yorkshire †
(SD 995519) O

This was initially an earthwork castle of c.1080, which late in the twelfth century received the beginnings of stonework. The twin-drum towered gatehouse, now restored and dominant among the much later buildings of the castle, is thought to stem from the late twelfth century or early thirteenth century. The castle was given several more towers in the thirteenth/ fourteenth centuries and the curtain walls were in places over 12ft thick. It was surrounded by a moat. The castle was besieged and severely damaged in the Civil War and has been renovated with additions.

SLEAFORD Lincolnshire
(TF 064455) A

A rectangular enclosure was erected here probably early in the twelfth century, perhaps by the bishop of Lincoln. It was surrounded on three sides by a moat and had an additional bailey. Fragments can be seen, to the north-west of the station.

SNODHILL Nr Dorstone,
Hereford & Worcester   (SO 322404) P
An early motte castle with an additional
bailey. Fragments of a rectangular (?) great
tower of c. 1200 have been found. The top of
the motte was enclosed by a polygonal shell
keep of sandstone rubble, dated to the
fourteenth century, with a gateway flanked
with solid cylindrical drum towers.

SOMERFORD Wiltshire
(ST 965831)
A twelfth-century motte castle with a low
mound. The mound was excavated earlier
this century and a stone wall fragment was
found which contained a doorway. The wall
was only about 2ft thick, which raised the
question of whether the wooden castle was
replaced by a stone castle or a more
residential and unfortified structure.

SOUTHAMPTON Hampshire   †
(SU 420110) A
A motte castle was built at Southampton
probably in the early twelfth century
(certainly by 1153 when the castle is
mentioned in a treaty). From the accession
of Henry II, Southampton Castle, because

of the extreme importance of its role *vis-à-vis*
Southampton Water, is continually mentioned in Exchequer records up to the
sixteenth century. Repairs and additions of
many kinds are noted, including references
to bridges, the king's house, castle quay and
so forth. Slates were brought from Dartmouth for buildings on the motte (*infra
motam*), which may indicate a shell keep on
the summit. Some of the wall round the
bailey survives today on Western Shore.
The castle is recorded as being in a ruinous
state in 1286, and although much money was
spent by the kings and others over the next
century, it seems to have remained in poor
shape. The town, although partly walled,
was attacked by the French several times,
and it seems that the castle was of little use in
helping to protect the important town and
its busy trading harbour.

Fresh refortification was carried out in
the time of Richard II, and this included a
cylindrical great tower raised on the motte
which may have been reduced in height
first. This would have entailed removing the
earlier buildings. The tower was built by
Henry Yevele at a cost of over £1,700. A
gatehouse, wall, barbican and other towers

Southampton: a c. 1900 postcard of Bar Gate, one of the gateways into the walled bailey of the medieval
castle

were added. Leland, writing in the 1540s, called the tower the 'Glorie' of the castle.

In the fifteenth and sixteenth centuries, decay set in again in some parts, though the great tower appears to have been kept in a condition fit enough for Elizabeth I to stay in it in c.1569. It was sold to a private buyer in the early seventeenth century and declined thereafter. Some of the castle walls are standing, and remains also of the water-gate, an eastern gate and other structures.

SOUTH MYMMS Hertfordshire   †
(TL 230026) A
This was a motte castle built by Geoffrey de Mandeville in c.1140–2. He may have had permission to do so from King Stephen (or from his rival, Matilda). It is an interesting site, and it was only recently investigated (1960–4 by Dr J.P.C. Kent). It stands on a low spur and consists of a bailey about 390ft by 350ft. The bank around it is about 20ft high. The motte in the north-west corner is about 27ft tall and has its own ditch. The motte base was a ring of clay and flint, about 4ft high, 20ft wide, 100ft across. There was a break in the ring for the entrance. Inside the ring was a 35ft square flint-based platform with slots for 9in-thick wooden beams laid round the square. Space was provided in the south of the square for an entrance. The superstructure erected on the base was battened inwards at a slope of about 80 degrees to give an inward-tapering tower of timber that may have been as high as about 60ft or so. The spaces for the entrance were covered by a timber-lined passage. The lower part of the tower was covered with chalk rubble. Numerous objects found suggest that the tower was occupied in some comfort. The tower was one of those where the motte was thrown up round the base, as at Lydford, being raised as the tower itself went up. The outside of the motte was revetted with timber planks, set vertically. (Barnet Historical Society Papers)

SOUTHSEA Portsmouth, Hampshire
(SZ 643980) O
This was a coastal fort built by Henry VIII as part of his coastal defence scheme of 1538–44 (chapter 16). It was erected in 1543–4, and its plan was a square great tower inside a curtain of lozenge shape, two opposite corners of which were chamfered and given rectangular projections. It had triangular-plan bastions.

Southsea came into use in 1545 when a French force invaded the Isle of Wight. It was held by a Royalist garrison in the Civil War, which surrendered without resistance when challenged by a Parliamentary force. Since the castle was close to Portsmouth Dockyard and harbour, it was garrisoned during both world wars. Today it houses a museum.

SPOFFORTH Nr Harrogate,   †
North Yorkshire   (SE 360511) DOE
A rectangular hall-tower range of thir-teenth-century beginnings with fourteenth- and fifteenth-century enlargements is what remains of Spofforth, which stands on a small plateau of rising ground. On the west side this ends in a rocky outcrop. The castle has been built against the rock. The present hall range may have been one wing of a larger structure round a courtyard.

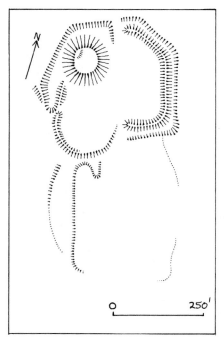

South Mymms (after J.P.C. Kent): plan of motte castle

Spofforth: (above) the hall-tower, whose east wall was built upon rock foundations; (left) perhaps this arch was inserted while the site supervisor was away on leave?

(above) Spofforth

The thirteenth-century part is the ground-floor undercroft to the later hall, whose eastern side is rock face, with a flight of stairs to it cut into the rock. A second stair flight is cut into rock further north, leading into the entrance passage and lobby. The fourteenth-century work is the two-storey chamber on the north side of the hall, which has a polygonal stair turret on the north-west corner. The fifteenth-century work included the upper storey of the hall part, namely the hall proper, which was a rebuilding job.

STAFFORD
(SJ 902222) A

There is a motte castle remnant in the southern part of the town, which is probably the one erected by William I, or with his leave, in c.1070. It was a motte partly within a bailey, the motte standing astride the bailey line. Sometime, c.1340s, a stone structure was erected on the older castle site. A licence to crenellate a castle was granted in 1348 to Ralph de Stafford. The principal building was a rectangular great tower, raised upon the motte. The walls were 7ft thick. The tower was demolished in the Civil War but the foundations with fragments of walling remained. In the last century it was partially reconstructed in the Gothic style.

STAMFORD Lincolnshire
(TF 027073) A

Originally a motte castle of the late eleventh century, Stamford motte received a shell keep, about 60ft across, before 1153, which may have been the tower surrendered to Henry of Anjou (later Henry II) in that year. The castle was considerably extended in several stages, and these included a hall with attached kitchens, cellars and chambers. Only fragments remain now, beside a car park.

302

STANSTED MOUNTFITCHET Essex
(TL 516249) A   †
An enclosure with bailey surrounded with
extensive ditching and ramparts. A small
tower was raised in the enclosure and other
stone fragments suggest additional buildings, including a (?) gate-tower. Docu-
mentation for this castle is meagre. It is
thought that the castle was dismantled in
King John's reign. The site is near the
railway station.

STAPLETON Hereford & Worcester
(SO 323656) O
This is an example of a natural hillock
adapted by scarping to form a motte castle.
The castle is mentioned in 1207. The
present ruins are those of a seventeenth-
century house built on the site, for which the
motte was levelled.

STOGURSEY Nr Bridgwater, Somerset
(ST 203426) A
Stogursey was an enclosure with several
baileys, raised at the end of the eleventh

century. A stone curtain and mural towers
were built in the twelfth century. The castle
was besieged in the 1220s. Some stonework
remains.

STOKESAY Shropshire   †
(SO 436817) O
This is one of the best-preserved medieval
fortified manor houses in England. The first
structure was a simple two storey twelfth-
century tower of rubble masonry with ashlar
quoins, roughly pentagonal in plan with a
projecting square wall turret on the north
angle. Today, the top of the tower carries a
seventeenth-century timber framed gallery
with gabled roofing, and this probably
replaces a similar hoarding of the late
Norman period, to judge from the put-log
holes. In the late thirteenth century, the
owner, the rich wool merchant, Lawrence of
Ludlow, built on to the tower's south wall a
long hall with solar, 52ft by 31ft internally
and without supporting aisles. At the south
end of the hall was added, in c.1290, a
multangular tower of three storeys with

303

battlemented parapet. This range of buildings formed one side of an enclosure of stone once surrounded by a moat. The stone curtain once reached to a height of about 30ft. In the curtain is a timber gatehouse of the seventeenth century.

SULGRAVE Northamptonshire
(SP 556452) A

A fortified enclosure of triangular shape was created, probably soon after the Conquest, on the site of a pre-Norman residence that was not fortified. A tower of stone was discovered in the earthworks in recent years. This was probably early twelfth century.

SUTTON VALENCE Nr Maidstone,
Kent (TQ 815491) DOE

A great tower was built here in the mid-to-late twelfth century, of limited size (36ft square), like Clitheroe. It had angle buttresses on the corners. The walls were about 8ft thick and contained small chambers and passages. Sometime after it was erected, a forebuilding was added, but there is evidence that it was demolished and replaced by a new staircase which was later encased by walls. The castle was abandoned in the 1200s. Fragments remain near the church (Arch. Cantiana, XXV, LXXI).

SWERFORD Nr Chipping Norton,
Oxfordshire (SP 373312) A

Earthworks of a motte castle of the eleventh century can still be seen here. Excavations revealed pottery of the mid-twelfth century. The castle was raised by Robert d'Oilly who had been granted leave by William I. This is the same d'Oilly who built Ascot d'Oilly.

SWINESHEAD Lincolnshire
(TF 243410) A

A motte castle of the twelfth century, mentioned in Pipe Roll for 1185–6. Earthworks can be seen near the remains of the medieval abbey.

TAMWORTH Staffordshire †
(SK 206037) O

There is still much to see of Tamworth. Most notable is its robust shell keep with a square tower projection, wrapped round the original tall motte which was raised in the eleventh century. One wing wall remains in part on the motte slope, and some of its masonry is set in the familiar Norman herringbone pattern (see p.62). The shell keep is an irregular polygon. The shell wall is thick enough to contain two flights of straight stairs which presumably opened into a now-vanished shell keep gate-tower. Today the shell is interrupted by the presence of a residential building of Tudor origin slotted into the circumference.

TATTERSHALL Lincolnshire ††
(TF 210575) NT

The great tower at Tattershall Castle, about 12 miles north-east of Sleaford on the A153, stands 100ft high from the ground to the tops of the four battlemented turrets that clasp the corners. It is just about all that remains of a remarkable fifteenth-century castle, erected on the site of an older fortified manor house and surrounded by a moat by Lord Cromwell, Treasurer of England from 1433 to 1443. But it dominates the countryside for miles around, and it is splendid proof of the fact that powerful lords had not given up building massive castles and that great towers were not out of date. Caister had just been completed and Ashby de la Zouch was yet to come.

Tattershall was built from red brick made of local clay from nearby Edlington Moor, and dressed with freestone from Willesford and limestone from Ancaster. Accounts for the building work at Tattershall survive and they show that nearly one million bricks were made for the tower and other buildings, and for the revetment round the 'platform' in the moat on which the castle stood. They also refer to the great tower as *Le Dongeon* a corruption of donjon, the alternative medieval word for great tower.

Lord Cromwell built a fortress tower, but he also intended that he should be able to enjoy living in it. Five storeys high (including the basement with its nearly 20ft-thick walls), it combined the military with the domestic. Large window openings and unguarded exterior doorways (at ground level) on the east wall fronting the inner enclosure ward looked vulnerable until one is close to the wall and looks upwards — to see at 80 ft or so a terrifying row of machicolations which were by no means just decorative, except round the four turrets. The windows on the other three sides looked out on to the moat, defensive in itself.

Cromwell built his castle over the years 1430–50 which span his time in office as Treasurer, one of the highest positions in the land. His castle was an aggressive symbol of his immense power, which was no less locally than it was throughout England. Once completed, he moved in and filled the tower and buildings with an army of servants and hangers-on, amounting to a hundred people. Then he died without heir, and Tattershall passed to the Crown and thence to the earls of Lincoln. Thereafter it fell into decay until it was rescued in 1910 by Lord Curzon (who also rescued Bodiam). Interestingly, Curzon had intervened to save parts of the derelict structure from being shipped abroad. The attempts to take the fragments out of the country aroused great public outcry and resulted in the passing of the Ancient Monuments Consolidation and Amendment Act by Parliament in 1913, an important landmark in the story of the state's involvement in helping to preserve ancient buildings.

TAUNTON Somerset   †
(ST 226247) O
An early Norman earthwork enclosure castle, raised on the south side of the River Tone and surrounded by a moat, received a rectangular stone great hall building inside its north-west perimeter in the very early 1100s. The castle belonged to the bishops of Winchester. Sometime in the second quarter of the twelfth century, further stone buildings were raised, including a great tower, rectangular in plan, with corner turrets, considered by local specialists to have been not dissimilar to the White Tower of London, though on a smaller scale. Of this great tower only the foundations remain. The dimensions were 63ft by 80ft and the walls were from 12–13ft thick.

Further improvements were undertaken in the early thirteenth century, including a constable's tower, about 50ft by 33ft, which still has a vaulted undercroft, and a major reconstruction of the great hall which is particularly well documented. There are details of accounts for building materials, including 6,800 board nails, 16,000 tie nails and 32,000 lath nails. The hall has survived to a considerable extent, but with some modifications, and is today a local-authority run building that houses the County Museum of Somerset. This has a major archaeological section. The hall bears scars from gun-fire during sieges by the Royalists in the Civil War. In 1662, the castle was slighted by government order, and the great tower was demolished. The great hall was the scene of part of Judge Jeffreys' notorious Bloody Assize, held after the collapse of the Duke of Monmouth's rebellion of 1685.

THERFIELD Hertfordshire
(TL 335373) A
A motte castle of the Anarchy of Stephen's reign, Therfield was dismantled after the accession of Henry II. Excavations in 1958 showed that the rampart round the bailey had been lined with clay and then clad with wooden palisading.

THETFORD Norfolk   ††
(TL 874828) A
Thetford has one of the tallest mottes in Britain, about 80ft high. The castle has been mentioned in chapter 3. The motte, of chalk rubble, was raised before 1086, on the site of an Iron Age fort. Thetford was an important castle, its site dominating the gently undulating area around, overlooking the River Ouse, and yet it does not appear to have had stonework additions. The surrounding double ditches and ramparts are impressive. The castle was owned for a time by the de Warenne family, but it was destroyed by Henry II in 1174. A second site, at the other end of the town, TL 862830, known as Red Castle, was an earthwork enclosure inside which stood an eleventh-century church. Some of the earthwork remains.

THIRLWALL Northumberland
(NY 660662) A
This rectangular tower-house with turrets on three corners and a larger angle tower on the eastern corner is now ruinous. The walls are in places over 9ft thick. The tower was built largely of stones quarried from a nearby section of Hadrian's Wall, near Greenhead. There is an iron yett in the entrance. The castle has been dated at about 1360.

305

THIRSK North Yorkshire
(SE 427820) A
A motte castle, probably of twelfth-century construction, that was held by the Mowbrays. The castle was yielded to Henry II in 1174–5, following the collapse of the revolt of his son, Prince Henry, whom the Mowbrays supported, and it was demolished. There are traces of the moat round part of the bailey site.

THORNBURY Nr Alveston, Avon
(ST 633907) O
Said to be the last major fortified manor house to be built in England as a serious fortification, Thornbury was raised in the early 1500s by Edward Stafford, Duke of Buckingham. It was basically a small quadrangle with corner towers (polygonal on south and west corners, square on the north and once also on the east). Attached to the west-south wall was a larger quadrangle consisting of two ranges of buildings, the fourth side open. These ranges were extensive, accommodating barracks for retainers (strictly forbidden by the Statute of Livery and Maintenance of 1504), and stables for horses for them and for the Buckingham family. The gatehouse in the western end of the smaller quadrangle is a twin semi-octagonal turret with a portcullis. Much of the walling is provided with gun-ports and loops. But it was never completed, for the Duke was arrested in 1521 by Henry VIII on a manufactured treason charge, executed, and his estates attainted. He was a direct descendant of the Plantagenets through Thomas of Woodstock, youngest son of Edward III.

TICKHILL South Yorkshire
(SK 594928) C
Tickhill was a motte castle, raised probably at the very end of the eleventh century by Robert de Belleme who was compelled to forfeit it to Henry I in 1102. The motte reached about 75ft high and was about 80ft in diameter on the top. The bailey was given a stone curtain early on, possibly c.1100, with an interesting gateway. On the motte was built an eleven-sided great tower, with pilaster buttresses on all angles. This unusual shaped tower was erected in c.1178–80 by Henry II at a cost of £120.

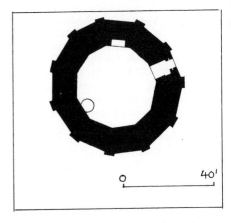

Tickhill: ground plan of the polygonal great tower, now only at foundation level

Tickhill was seized by Prince John when his brother Richard I was out of England fighting with the Third Crusade, but John was compelled to return it to the king three years later. John inherited the castle when he succeeded to the throne in 1199 and he lavished over £300 on it. John had a penchant for polygonal great towers (see Odiham).

The great tower has now gone but the motte remains. The foundations of the tower were excavated recently. The bailey wall survives for long stretches, and in its northern side can be seen (from the road) the square-plan gatehouse which has interesting features. Though part ruined, it has its walls, two shallow-rounded arches, a half-lozenge panel frieze across the front over the arch, and at second-storey height inside, on the west inner side an early Tudor fireplace. This projects out of the wall, but has no hearth or floor. The second storey was rebuilt in the sixteenth century.

TILBURY FORT Tilbury, Essex
(TQ 651754) DOE
Tilbury was one of the blockhouses of Henry VIII, erected as part of his coastal fortification scheme, c.1538–43. These blockhouses were simplified versions of the bigger and more sophisticated coastal forts like Deal. Tilbury was a D-ended bastion which guarded the approach to London where the Thames narrows and was crossed by a ferry. It was manned by nine men who

were paid 6d a day. The fort was enlarged in Elizabeth I's time and it was there that she made her famous call to the people of England to resist the Spaniards (1588) after the Armada had been scattered but while there was still great danger of a follow-up invasion from the continent.

A century later the fort was submerged in a massive redesign of the whole defensive area, which is outside the scope of this Gazetteer. There is nothing to see of the original Henrican fort, but the later work is open.

TINTAGEL Cornwall   †
(SX 048891) DOE

It is advisable, when considering Tintagel Castle, to forget any idea that it has anything to do with King Arthur, the legendary Celtic hero who has been developed (out of all proportion) from the practical and down-to-earth fifth/sixth century British cavalry leader of Roman descent who made a last ditch stand against the invading Saxons in the West Country. Tintagel Castle is not reliably documented before the twelfth century. That said, we are dealing with an interesting castle on a headland jutting into the sea. In the mid-twelfth century, the first structure, a narrow rectangular hall, was built on what was an isthmus between the headland and the mainland but which has been largely eroded by the sea, dividing the castle into two parts. It was raised by Reginald, Earl of Cornwall, who may also have built the twelfth-century chapel nearby. Little more than foundations survive of the hall.

About a century later, Richard, Earl of Cornwall, raised two stone-walled enclosures on the mainland part, with a castle main gate and a curtain round part of the headland and enclosing the hall. Evidently, a bridge was constructed to connect the two parts. In the fourteenth century Tintagel belonged to the Black Prince as Duke of Cornwall, and he rebuilt the great hall. Apparently, yet another hall was built over the remains of the previous two, in the late fourteenth/early fifteenth century. There are some ruins worth visiting.

TIVERTON Devon   †
(SS 954131) O

A quadrangular enclosure castle built by the Courtenay family, of pink sandstone, on the possible site of an earlier twelfth-century enclosure raised in the reign of Henry I. The quadrangle had towers on the corners (of which a cylindrical south-east and a square south-west remain) and it was surrounded by a double moat. The decayed gatehouse on the eastern side is also standing.

TONBRIDGE Kent   ††
(TQ 589466) O

'They came then to the castle at Tonbridge; inside . . . were the knights of Bishop Odo . . . determined to support him against the king [William Rufus]. But the Englishmen attacked and stormed the castle . . . .' Thus, the *Anglo-Saxon Chronicle* (trans. G.N Garmonsway), in an entry for 1088, mentions the motte castle at Tonbridge on the River Medway whose bailey was surrounded partly by water meadows. Some time in the twelfth century the motte received an oval shell keep, of walls 5ft thick, with buttressing on the south-east. Two wing walls ran down the motte sides. One eventually connected up with a massive gatehouse-tower; the other continued round a rough rectangle to form an enclosure.

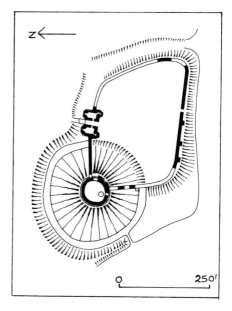

Tonbridge

buildings (most of which have vanished). The Tower had now become the greatest fortress in England, with the possible exception of Dover. While most succeeding monarchs carried out works of one kind and another, none were on the scale of Henry III's or Edward I's — indeed, they did not have to be, for, as a fortress it was already about as complete as it could be, while as a residence its supremacy over other royal palaces was beginning to decline. One work of Edward I's was the Lion Tower, which was a barbican, a D-shaped structure on the western extremity. This resembled the barbican at Goodrich (of slightly later date); and also the barbican recently excavated at Sandal, of earlier date.

Considering its history, the Tower is, on the whole, better documented than any other fortress. The Tower played a dominating role in the affairs of the kings and their governments for centuries. Apart from its use as a palace, a castle and a prison, it has housed the Royal Mint, the Royal Menagerie, the public records and even for a time the Royal Observatory. It has been a major arsenal, it has held the Crown Jewels for centuries, and it has long had one of the finest collections of armour in the world. Just outside the outer curtain is Tower Hill, scene of the beheading on a once permanent scaffold of many great and famous people, like Thomas More, Thomas Cromwell, John Dudley (Duke of Northumberland), Thomas Wentworth (Earl of Strafford) and Archbishop Laud. Inside the south-west corner of the inner curtain is Tower Green. There, a more private scaffold was from time to time erected, on which a sad roll of victims lost their heads, among them Anne Boleyn, second wife of Henry VIII, and Katherine Howard, his fifth wife, Margaret, Countess of Salisbury, last of the Plantagenets, and Lady Jane Grey.

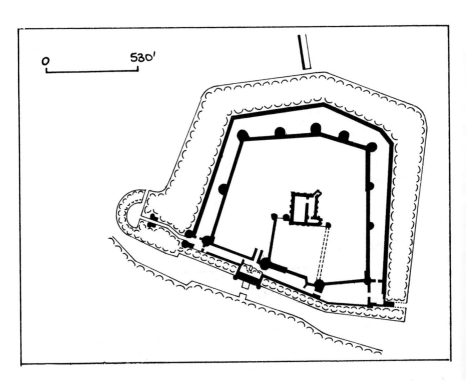

Tower of London: simplified ground plan, to show concentric scheme. In centre is the first stone building, the White Tower, c.1080. At extreme left are remains of foundations of the Lion Tower, a barbican of the thirteenth century similar to those at Goodrich and Sandal

310

The literature on the Tower of London is extensive, and in confining our discussion of the Tower to the briefest summary, we recommend the DOE's official guide (HMSO, 1980) and the *Tower and its Institutions* (HMSO, 1978).

TREAGO Hereford & Worcester
(SO 490239) P
A small square curtained enclosure with four angle towers of different sizes, this castle is difficult to date, though it appears to be of the later Middle Ages, with alterations of the seventeenth century.

TREMATON Saltash, Cornwall
(SX 410580)
Trematon was an early motte castle, mentioned in Domesday Book. It received a stone shell keep, probably in the twelfth century, and a stone curtain round the bailey that continued up the motte sides as two wing walls joining the shell. On the north-east side of the bailey is a gatehouse which began as a thirteenth century gateway. The later work shows signs of subsequent restoration.

The castle came into royal possession in the 1270s when Richard, Earl of Cornwall, bought it, The shell walls are about 10ft thick and rise to about 30ft for most of the circumference. There are indications of buildings ranged round the inside of the shell.

TROWBRIDGE Wiltshire
(ST 854579) A
An earthwork enclosure of the twelfth century was given stonework of some kind. The suggestion is of a small tower, possibly raised in the time of Stephen by Henry de Bohun. The moat of the castle is said to be partly defined in the curving main street (Fore Street) today.

TUTBURY Staffordshire †
(SK 209291) O
The motte castle at Tutbury stood on a natural hill of rock, overlooking the River Dove. Very little is known of its early history, but it appears to have been dismantled by Henry II in c.1175. After that it was neglected for more than a century. In the early 1300s, the site came into the possession of Thomas, Earl of Lancaster, Edward II's cousin, whose rebellious activities over a period of years were to involve a number of castles in England. He may have rebuilt a wooden gateway in stone. The castle later passed to John of Gaunt, Edward III's fourth son, who was Duke of Lancaster, and from him to Henry Bolingbroke, later Henry IV (1399–1413). Fifteenth-century improvements to the castle included a stone curtain with flanking towers, works that were spread intermittently over many years.

Tutbury was held for Charles I in the Civil War but was taken by Parliament and slighted. Today, it is largely in ruins. Parts of the curtain and some parts of the gatehouse stand, as well as fragments of other fifteenth-century buildings. There are also remains of much later additions.

TYNEMOUTH Nr Newcastle upon †
Tyne, Tyne & Wear (NZ 374695) DOE
Tynemouth Castle was integrated with Tynemouth Priory, so much so that every time there was warfare between England and Scotland, in which the castle played a role as a border fortress, the monks of the priory had to contribute towards the costs of garrisoning and provisioning the castle. On the whole the priory community suffered heavy financial losses on these occasions since they were seldom able to obtain assistance from the Crown.

The castle which began as an earthwork enclosure stood on a prominent headland with steep cliffs on three sides, on the north side of the mouth of the Tyne. Its late thirteenth-century curtain wall, with towers, surrounded the priory. There is a substantial gatehouse-tower with barbican built in the 1390s. The barbican was a tall passage protected at the entrance by two square turrets flanking the arch, and much of it remains today. The outer walls continue back to the rectangular-plan gatehouse-tower. There is a courtyard between the outer and inner gate. The gatehouse-tower has walls 5ft thick and rises three storeys. The first floor was the great hall, the second a great chamber above it. Adjacent to the tower at the south-east corner is a smaller tower structure containing the kitchen and two floors above.

311

UPNOR Nr Rochester, Kent   †
(TQ 758706) DOE

A blockhouse built in the years 1559–67 to defend the entrance to the Medway River and the growing ship-dock area of Chatham, Upnor was improved in the seventeenth century. When the Dutch navy under van Tromp sailed up the Medway in 1667, it was assailed by a barrage from the guns at Upnor Fort, until firing stopped because supplies of shot and gunpowder had run out. The Dutch sailed on and burned the English fleet at Chatham.

The basic design of Upnor Fort was a water-lapped rectangular turret on the river's edge with a triangular point below the surface. It is still much as it was in the sixteenth century.

WAKEFIELD West Yorkshire   †
(SE 327198) A

A motte castle with two baileys erected here may have remained an earthwork and timber castle for its entire existence. The castle is mentioned in a twelfth-century document, but excavations have revealed nothing of stone remains, apart from rubble used as hardcore for the motte itself. The motte is about 30ft tall, was surrounded by a moat, and the two baileys lay to the north-east of the motte, one behind the other. In the nineteenth century there were considerable intrusions upon the old site, which effectively spoiled much of it for excavating purposes. At the end of the century, Clarence Park, where the castle site lies, was opened as a public park. But some results have been obtained. Pottery of the twelfth century was found on the north edge of the motte where it leads into the ditch, in the 1953 excavations. Similar pottery was found a little to the north-east of the first cutting. Digs in the baileys produced charcoal and more pottery fragments. The castle has as a result been dated to the mid-twelfth century, c.1140–c.1150, a late date for a motte castle, and is suggested as one built during the 'Nineteen Long Winters' of Stephen's reign (1135–54). Brian Hope Taylor thinks it may have been one of the adulterine castles so often mentioned (cf. *Anglo-Saxon Chronicle* entry in chapter 3), and so rarely documented in any detail. The builder is also suggested — William, 3rd Earl de Warenne, or his successor as holder of the castle site, William of Blois, second son of Stephen. It seems the castle was never used, and may not even have been completed.

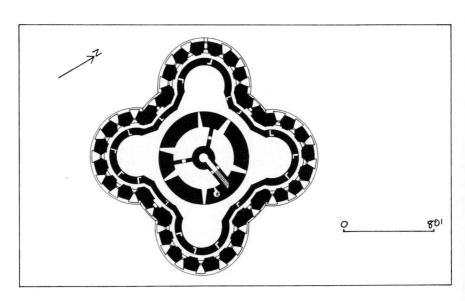

Walmer: ground floor of the centre tower with its bastions

WALLINGFORD Oxfordshire
(SU 610897) P
This appears to have been a very early motte castle, probably built in c.1071, and in the north-east corner of the old Anglo-Saxon *burh*. Eight buildings were knocked down to make space for the motte castle which was eventually to have three baileys. It guarded a useful ford across the Thames.

Wallingford was refortified during the Anarchy of Stephen's reign, and was held for Matilda, surviving at least three sieges. Money was spent on it by Henry II, Richard I and John who made his formal submission to Pope Innocent III there in 1213. Exactly when the stonework buildings were begun we do not know, but it may have been in the mid-twelfth century. It was at some time given a great tower though the size and shape are not known. In the period 1363–70, £500 was spent on general repairs to the castle, including the great tower.

It was a summer residence for young Henry VI from c.1428, was held by Francis, Viscount Lovell, friend of Richard III, and was visited by Henry VIII in 1518.

Wallingford was taken by Parliament in 1646. In 1652 it was demolished by order of the Commonwealth. The mound and some of the ditching remain in the grounds of Castle House.

WALMER Kent †
(TR 378501) DOE
One of the major Henrician fortresses of the 1538–43 coastal fortification programme, and known as one of the 'Three Castles which keep the Downs' (and protect the anchorage within the Goodwin Sands). The plan is quatrefoil, its round bastions surrounding a substantial cylindrical tower. These in turn were surrounded by a low curtain. Three tiers of guns were mounted, two in the bastions and the third on top of the tower. Considerable modifications have been made to the castle since the sixteenth century. Since the eighteenth century, Walmer has been the official residence of the Lord Warden of the Cinque Ports.

WALTON Nr Felixstowe, Suffolk
(TM 322358)
There was a castle here belonging to the Bigods, earls of Norfolk, in the mid-twelfth

century. Its plan is not definable, as the remnants have been undermined by the sea. The castle appears to have had a square tower, but this may have belonged to an earlier Roman fort on whose site the Norman castle was raised. Henry II appropriated the castle, along with others, from the Bigods in 1157. It was demolished after the revolt of Prince Henry in 1173–4, which Hugh Bigod had supported.

WAREHAM Dorset
(SY 920876) A
There was a castle at Wareham in the time of Henry I. Some form of mound, probably the remains of a fort of earlier times, was discovered (in 1910) to contain the remnants of a substantial great tower, about 80ft square, with pilaster buttresses. The bottom of the great tower was covered by gravel heaped up round the sides. The tower was built by Henry I. His elder brother, Robert, Duke of Normandy, who spent the first years of the reign, from 1100–06, attempting to seize Henry's throne, was finally defeated and imprisoned in one castle or another for twenty-eight years. For part of that time he was held at Wareham, but we do not know if the great tower was ready for his reception in 1106, though it appears to have been completed by 1119. The castle was taken by Robert, Earl of Gloucester, in c.1135 and apart from a few intervals, remained in baronial possession until its destruction during the Civil War. The mound is still in existence.

WARK Northumberland
(NT 824387) A
Wark started as a motte castle on the southern side of the Tweed. It was besieged and captured by David I, King of Scotland, and dismantled in 1138. Henry II recaptured it in c.1158 and fortified it afresh at a cost of £380. This work probably included the polygonal great tower on the old motte, of which a few traces survive. From the early fourteenth century Wark Castle was allowed to deteriorate.

WARKWORTH Northumberland †
(NU 248057) DOE
A late motte castle of the mid-twelfth century, built on a large scale, Warkworth

Warkworth: (above) the oriel, or chapel chamber, over the chapel in the great tower; (below) fishtail arrow slits in the eastern flanking tower which is called Grey Mare's Tail Tower

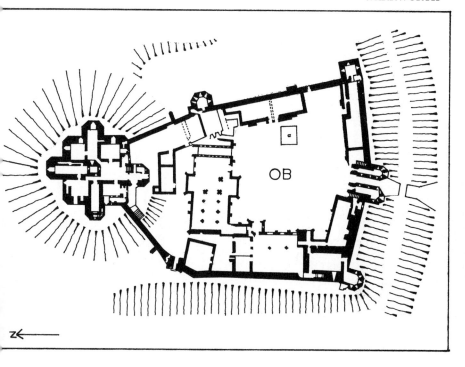

Warkworth: the great tower is at left. Some parts of the masonry of the east and west curtains of the outer bailey (OB) are probably of the twelfth century

stands on rising ground in a loop of the River Coquet. It may have been built in the 1140s by Henry, Earl of Northumberland, a son of David I of Scotland, or strengthened by him with the conversion of the bailey's wooden palisade into a stone curtain, and given a hall alongside the west curtain wall (which has a Norman fireplace in its south wall) which was later widened. There are some remains of this hall, which had a solar storey above. In 1173 the castle, which had reverted to the English Crown, was besieged and taken by William the Lion, King of Scotland, because it was 'feeble in wall and earthwork' (William had failed to take Alnwick, Carlisle or Newcastle in the same invasion).

Warkworth then passed into the holding of the Clavering family who built the first works of the great gateway at the south (later enlarged), raised a massive ashlar-clad curtain with flanking towers round the bailey in place of the earlier wood palisade and incorporating the twelfth century

stretches of curtain. One of the towers, Grey Mare's Tail Tower, is polygonal and was equipped with 16ft-long 'fan-tailed' crossbow loops. The motte also received a stone tower that can still be seen. This second great tower was built in c.1390 by Henry Percy, Earl of Northumberland, who had been granted the castle by Edward III.

Percy's great tower is the most unusual structure. It is multangular, on the following plan: a square has rectilinear projections from its four sides, the south projection slightly off centre; the corners of the square and of three projections (north, east and west) are canted, and on the south the canting of the southern projection is sharper, producing a semi-octagonal shape. Within this curious shape (the nearest thing to it being Castle Rushen in the Isle of Man) is a complete suite of apartments for private and public use. Its southern wall is joined to the north-east and north-west lengths of the massive curtain round the bailey, which are

315

in fact wing walls. The great tower stands on a splayed plinth. It has been altered since the end of the fourteenth century and refaced, but withal, it seems a powerful building, despite the insertion of large windows in the upper storeys. The apartments inside are grouped round a square lantern turret which rises from ground level right to the top. The lantern collected rain water and channelled it down to a tank in the basement where, by means of conduits, the water could be distributed to garderobes and basins. The tower has a square-plan watch turret projecting above the parapet line, in the centre.

These are the principal points of interest in Warkworth Castle. Its history is hardly less full. It was besieged in 1327 by the Scots, but not taken, it was attacked in the Percy rebellion against Henry IV (1403–5) and battered into surrender, and in 1644 it yielded to the armies of Scotland in the Civil War.

WARRINGTON Lancashire
(SJ 609876) A
An enclosure castle of earthworks beside marshes of the River Mersey. Excavations revealed artefacts of the late Norman period. Earthworks survive near the church.

WARWICK   ††
(SP 284047) O
Warwick Castle rises like a precipice above the River Avon. On this natural cliff William I founded a motte castle in 1068, on lands seized from a nearby Saxon convent. A wooden tower built on the motte was evidently still there in the reign of Henry II, by which time a polygonal shell keep had been raised round the motte top. Only fragments of the shell keep remain incorporated in the rebuilt shell of much later date.

Late in the fourteenth century, by which time some additional buildings like great hall and residential blocks had been put up in the bailey, the castle passed to Earl Beauchamp who initiated a fresh programme of works. These were substantially what can be seen today. They included restructuring the great hall and a range of other buildings on the south, a water-gate, and on the east front a high and stout defensive

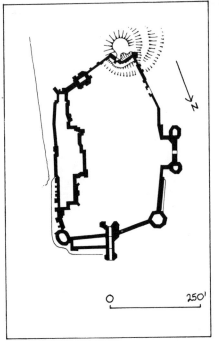

Warwick: the original motte is at the top. Caesar's Tower at the bottom left, with Guy's Tower at the bottom right

curtain leading north from a gatehouse to a very tall polygonal tower, known as Guy's Tower. The gatehouse is a remarkable building: a pair of towers above the doorway passage, which had portcullises. The towers are tall and battlemented. A barbican emerges eastwards, defended by gates at the outer end, with portcullises and murder-holes. Projecting from the south side of the gatehouse is a tall rectangular building leading to another tower. This latter tower is 133ft tall, six-storeys, trilobed (or six-lobed if the smaller bulges are counted) and capped by a two-fold system of battlements with machicolation all round below the battlements. It is called Caesar's Tower.

The castle is completed by curtain walling and further, much smaller, flanking towers along the north and west. The wall at west leads up the motte to the restored shell keep and down again southwards to the south range. The whole is thus a powerfully defended enclosure.

316

WATTLESBOROUGH Shropshire †
(SJ 355126) P

A great tower castle whose three-storeyed stone great tower appears to have been enclosed in wooden palisading. The tower, about 25ft square and built of dressed sandstone with pilaster buttresses on the corners, is probably of late twelfth-century origin. It has a spiral staircase in one corner turret. The top storey was originally a kind of platform behind the parapet, the roof rising up to this level, but in the fourteenth century it is thought the roof was lifted to the top storey. The castle gradually lost its military role and became part of a manor house. The remains of the great tower stand beside a farmhouse.

WEETING Nr Brandon, Norfolk †
(TL 778891) DOE

Weeting was a wet moated enclosure castle, in which there was a two-storeyed hall-type structure, with a square tower adjoining one end, three storeys high. It was a strongly fortified manor house. Some of the structures appear to be of late twelfth-century origin.

WELBOURNE Lincolnshire
(SK 968544)

Remains of an earthwork enclosure castle of the twelfth century can be seen.

WEOBLEY Hereford & Worcester
(SO 403153) A

An enclosure of earthworks that was captured in 1138 and mentioned in Pipe Rolls for 1186–7. The earthworks included double ditching. The later stonework is believed to have consisted of a quadrangle with corner and mid-wall towers, gateway and a great tower, but only the earthworks remain today. (RCHM, Herefordshire, III.)

WEST DERBY Nr Liverpool, Merseyside
(SJ 397933)

A simple motte castle with enclosing ditch was built here probably before 1086 by Roger of Poitou. It was granted in c.1115 to Stephen, Count of Blois. Its history and its form are almost unknown, but it is mentioned in Exchequer records for 1216, and was appropriated fifteen years later by the de Ferrers family. The Old Court House stands on the site.

WEST MALLING Kent †
(TQ 675570) O

An early and interesting medium-sized great tower (known as St Leonard's Tower) is about 60ft tall (but several feet taller originally). It was built in c.1100 of Kentish ragstone, and this is a very early date for a great tower. It is attributed to Bishop Gundulf (cf. Rochester) though this has been questioned. The tower is four storeyed, has corner pilaster buttresses (and one mid-wall), and a spiral staircase in the north-west corner. Remains of a curtain wall feed into the south-east corner.

WESTON TURVILLE Nr Aylesbury, Buckinghamshire
(SP 859104) P

Some remains of a motte castle built here probably in the twelfth century. They are in the grounds of Weston Turville Manor where, in the fourteenth century, a fortified manor house was erected by the de Moleyns family. That building was later dismantled, and the present manor built in the seventeenth century.

WHITCHURCH Buckinghamshire
(SP 799207) A

A twelfth-century motte castle here was given stonework later in the century. This may have been a stone great tower. In 1925, sites of drawbridges were discovered, which suggest a castle of some size. It is also called Bolebec Castle, and earthworks survive.

WHITCHURCH Shropshire †
(SJ 543415) A

A 15ft tall motte surrounded by a wide ditch is the remnant of Whitchurch Castle today. There are ramparts, some as high as 11ft. The castle was sited near a lake which provided protection on the east side.

WHITTINGTON Shropshire †
(SJ 325311) O

Today the principal structure of Whittington to be seen is the remnant of the twin-cylindrical towered gatehouse. The stonework was probably begun in the 1220s, for a licence to build upon the site of an earlier motte castle was granted by Henry III in 1220. This motte received a stone rectangular tower of which only the foundations remain. The castle was enclosed in a stone curtain in which the gatehouse was inserted, along with several other towers, mostly cylindrical. Three have survived. Outside the curtain was an extensive ditching system whose water levels from a nearby stream were controlled by means of drainage.

WHITWICK Leicestershire
(SK 436172) A
An oval-plan motte surrounded on three sides by a stream, this was less than 10ft high. The castle was held by the Earl of Leicester during the Anarchy of Stephen's reign. The mound is on rising ground near the church.

WHORLTON North Yorkshire
(NZ 481025) A
Situated near the county boundary between Yorkshire and Durham, Whorlton was an earthwork enclosure on a spur of land. It received stonework later. Today, the thirteenth-century stone gatehouse remains.

WIGMORE Nr Mortimer's Cross,
Hereford & Worcester   (SO 408693) P
A motte castle was raised here in c.1067 by William FitzOsbern, Earl of Hereford, and in 1086 it was held by Ralph de Mortimer. A sandstone rubble shell keep was built on the motte in the twelfth century, and a curtain wall with square and round towers was added, mostly, it appears, later. A square-plan gatehouse was also inserted in the curtain. There are traces of the shell keep to be seen today. Much reconstruction was done in the fourteenth century and also later, particularly when Edward IV and Richard III held the castle, between 1461–85, as they had been heirs to the Mortimer family who were of Plantagenet descent.

WILTON Bridstow, Hereford &
Worcester   (SO 590244) P
A structure of Stephen's time, possibly a motte castle, sited near the Wye, but few remains of that period can be seen. The remains visible today are thirteenth and fourteenth century, and are of an irregular quadrilateral curtain wall, with towers at each angle and an additional one in the east wall which may be part of a gatehouse. The castle was surrounded by a wet moat but this

has since been largely filled in. Further alterations were made in the sixteenth and seventeenth century.

WILTON Nr Salisbury, Wiltshire
A monastic structure at Wilton, probably of eleventh-century origin, was apparently altered to provide a fortified residence.

WINCHESTER Hampshire   ††
(SU 472296) O
At the time of the Conquest, Winchester was the capital of England. It had been certainly since the time of Alfred the Great (871–900), and the Conqueror had no plans to change this. In 1067 he built a castle there, 'hard (by) the south side of the west gate' of the Anglo-Saxon town, as Leland puts it. The new castle was erected on the rising ground there, and was a normal motte castle. The motte was probably a low one: a platform over 20ft high was found during recent excavations, and since then remains of timber structures have been detected beneath this, suggesting among other things that the motte had been revetted with timber planks. Some stonework was also found which replaced the timber revetting. The remains of a nave and apse of a chapel have also been found near the motte base, and the chapel has been dated c.1070 from the Anglo-Saxon style of building evident.

Winchester remained the capital of England until the end of the twelfth century. The royal exchequer was centred here, and Domesday Book was housed in the castle. The castle was the subject of an almost continuous programme of development over the years 1067 to at least the Tudor period. But nearly everything has disappeared or remains only in a fragmentary state, including a great tower, about 52ft square, with walls about 14ft thick, built in the time of Henry II or Richard I, a cylindrical tower said to have been raised on the motte in the reign of Henry III, and several other towers, curtain walling, apartments, etc. There is one exception, the splendid great hall built by Henry III between 1222–35.

Henry II favoured the castle and enjoyed it as a residence: records tell of a herb garden, of hedges round a new king's hall, of a special aviary for royal falcons and of a

Windsor

chapel for his daughter-in-law. Richard I stayed there in 1194. John spent a memorable Christmas there in 1206: 1,500 chickens, 5,000 eggs, 20 oxen, 100 sheep and 100 pigs were laid in for the festivities. The castle was captured by Louis of France in 1216 in the Magna Carta war. Henry III spent about £10,000 in restoring and improving it, making the castle a splendid residence. One new chapel was given floor tiles.

The great hall has been carefully tidied and restored in recent years, and can now be seen much as it must have been in the 1230s. Regarded by some specialists as second only to Westminster Hall, it has been in almost continuous use since its construction, and bears signs of minor modification over the centuries. It was used for law courts probably from the beginning, and was the scene of many notable trials.

WINDSOR Berkshire †
(SU 970770)
Windsor Castle's vast complex of palatial apartments, its huge and glorious chapel of St George, its towers, its enormous cylindrical shell keep, and its curtain wall with towers and gates, extending over half a mile in a rough figure-of-eight plan, is perhaps the nearest equivalent in Britain to the fairy-tale palace-castles depicted in *Les Très Riches Heures* du Duc de Berry. Though much has been added and altered since the end of the Middle Ages, notably by Henry

VIII, George III and George IV, it still resembles to a great extent the Windsor Castle seen by medieval visitors, official and private, travellers native and foreign. And by that time it had ceased to have any military significance, had already cost more than any other castle in the British Isles — over £50,000 was spent by Edward III alone, between c.1350 and c.1377 — and it had become the principal residence of the kings of England and Wales.

Windsor began very much more simply than that. It was a motte with two baileys (one on each side) — an aerial view today instantly reveals this plan under all the succeeding stonework. It was raised by the Conqueror in 1067 by scarping a mound out of a chalk cliff beside the Thames. It remained a wood and earth structure until Henry I began to convert the castle to stone by erecting a stone shell keep on the motte top (though there is a suggestion that this had already been done earlier). Henry II raised buildings in the upper bailey on a quadrangular plan like Old Sarum. Some of the stone was obtained from quarries at Totternhoe in Bedfordshire.

The shell was later refaced, probably in Henry II's time. Inside the shell, a large, slightly oval great tower was erected, with walls about 100ft in diameter, 5ft thick (later thickened), with pilaster buttresses some of the way up. The first height was about 35ft. The shell acted as a kind of surrounding base

319

for the great tower. Inside the tower, timber buildings were put up against the walls, leaving a square courtyard in the centre. This is much as it is today, and the two-storeyed, oak-framed buildings contain timberwork thought to have come from the Henry II structures. The tower has been much altered, and today stands nearly 65ft above the height of the old shell keep.

Henry II favoured Windsor and treated it as a royal home. He planted a herb garden and possibly a vineyard within its precincts. Henry III also favoured Windsor, and there is a record of an occasion on which he entertained the poor to a meal on Good Friday. Edward III's extensive improvements included the first chapel of St George and raising the height of the oval great tower. By the end of his reign, Windsor had become a palace and was no longer a real military structure.

Windsor was besieged in 1216, during the Magna Carta war.

WISBECH Cambridgeshire
(TF 462097) A
An earthwork castle was raised here early in the Conqueror's reign, possibly as part of William's campaign against Hereward the Wake (see also Ely) or perhaps just afterwards. Stonework was added much later. A few fragments are visible.

WOLVESEY Nr Winchester, Hampshire
(SU 484291) O
The ecclesiastical castle-palace at Wolvesey was begun in c.1100, and major works were added by Henry of Blois, Bishop of Winchester, c.1110–c.1139. It became a quadrangular castle — very early for this plan type — which also contained a square great tower and a great hall. The site has recently been excavated with great thoroughness. The rectangular great hall was erected along the east wall of the quadrangle in c.1130. This superseded an earlier hall of c.1110 on the western side, which thereafter was used as private apartments by the bishops of Winchester. The great tower is thought to have been erected in c.1138 as a defensive structure for the bishop during the Anarchy of Stephen's reign, and is the next building to the great hall. Some of the decorative treatment of the great hall is

similar to that at the monastery at Cluny where Henry of Blois had been a monk for a time. A square-plan gatehouse with central passage was inserted in the north wall of the quadrangle in c.1160–1170. Now in ruins.

WOODWALTON Cambridgeshire
(TL 211827) A
Although this castle is sometimes described as a motte castle, the raised ground was only a few feet above the earthworks surrounding it. The platform is about 135ft in diameter. It falls more sensibly into the enclosure class of early earthwork castle. The earthworks are now known as Castle Hill.

WORCESTER
(SO 847550)
There is nothing left of the motte castle raised at Worcester in c.1069, whose ditch encroached upon the cemetery of the cathedral priory. To begin with, the wooden castle was burned down in 1113. It was rebuilt, part in wood, part in stone, during the middle of the century, and a gateway of stone was added by King John in 1204. Interestingly, when King John was buried in 1216 in what became Worcester Cathedral, the monks asked the Great Council to return to them that part of the castle bailey which had once been church property, and this was granted. The castle lost its military importance. The motte was levelled in 1830.

WRESSLE Humberside
(SE 707316) P
The remains of this Percy family castle overlooking the River Derwent consist of two towers and part of a curtain of a quadrangular enclosure castle that had four towers at the corners, and a tower gatehouse. The castle was built in c.1380 by Sir Thomas Percy, brother of Henry Percy, Earl of Northumberland, and it was surrounded by a moat. Wressle was damaged in a siege by Parliament during the Civil War.

WYCOMBE Buckinghamshire
(SU 868934) A
A Norman earthwork castle with a motte of about 30ft in height. It was besieged during the Anarchy of Stephen's time. The remains are at Castle Hill.

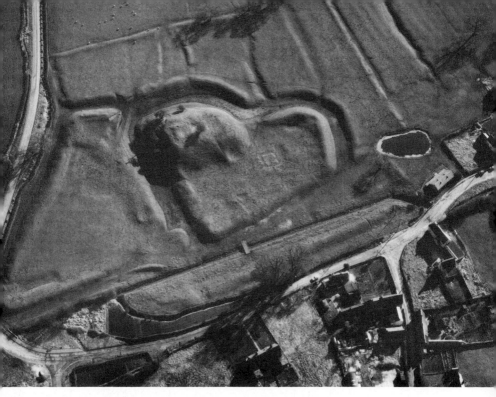

Yelden: an aerial view of the motte-and bailey remains

YANWATH Cumbria
(NY 508282)
A fourteenth-century pele-tower in good repair. Modifications were carried out in Tudor times.

YARMOUTH Isle of Wight   †
(SZ 354898) DOE
Yarmouth was built in 1545–7 after a French 'commando' raid on the Isle of Wight showed up considerable deficiencies in the island's defences. It was a 100ft square enclosure with sharp-pointed bastion projecting out of the south-east corner, right on the edge of the sea whose waters lapped the castle's north and west walls. It began as a two-storeyed tower, but has been modified over the years. When ready in 1547, the castle was equipped with three cannon and culverins and twelve smaller guns.

YELDEN Bedfordshire
(TL 014669)
A motte castle was raised here, possibly in the mid-twelfth century, by Lord Traylly.

The inner bailey was later enclosed by a stone wall with at least one flanking tower, traces of which were found in excavations.

YORK (BAILE HILL)
(SE 603513) A
The Conqueror built two motte castles in York, one on his first expedition to the north in 1068 and the second a year later. The first was on the west bank of the Ouse and the second on the east bank. In 1069, both were destroyed by the Vikings, and both were rebuilt. The second (eastern) castle eventually became York Castle, and later still Clifford's Tower (q.v.). The first castle was described in the fourteenth century as *vetus ballium* (Old Baile), and the remains of the motte that lie near Skeldergate Bridge are still called the Old Baile. The motte is the original thrown up in 1068 (the Vikings destroyed the tower), and excavations of 1968 revealed some steps cut in the slope. Traces of a square-plan building on the summit were also found.

Wales

ABER Bangor, Gwynedd
(SH 656727)
A motte remains of the castle built here by Hugh d'Avranches, Earl of Chester, in the last decade of the eleventh century. It overlooked the narrowest part of the Menai Straits to Anglesey. It is sometimes known as Bangor Castle.

ABER AFAN West Glamorgan
(SS 762901)
There was a motte castle here, which was attacked in 1153 at the end of the Anarchy in England. Possibly the attack was by the Welsh.

ABERCOWYN St Clears, Dyfed
(SN 297136)
Alternatively known as Castell Aber Taf or Castell Aber Carwy, this appears to have been a motte castle with an oval bailey, the motte astride the bailey. The motte is 25ft high, though much of it has been ploughed up. The bailey was near the river. Said to have been destroyed by the Welsh c.1116.

ABEREDW Nr Builth Wells, Powys
(SO 076474)
Aberedw was an enclosure castle with small towers. It was a royal castle of Llywelyn the Last, Prince of all Wales (c.1246–82). Llywelyn was defeated in north Wales by Edward I of England in 1282, escaped into mid-Wales and headed for Aberedw. But near Builth Wells he was ambushed and killed. The site was built over for railway construction in the nineteenth century.

ABEREINION Dyfed
(SN 687968)
Abereinion was a fortified mound enclosed

by a ditch, built by Rhys ap Gruffydd in the mid–twelfth century.

ABERGAVENNY Gwent †
(SO 299139)
The ruins of Abergavenny Castle stand on a spur of land at the southern end of the town, overlooking the junction of the rivers Usk and Gwenny. It was first a motte castle and then received stone additions. A square great tower was let into the mound on one side, and traces of this survive, together with remains of a curtain wall and two towers along it. The gatehouse and barbican are probably thirteenth-century structures.

Abergavenny was the scene of a deed of black treachery in the late twelfth century. The castle fell into Welsh hands in 1172 but was retaken by its owner, William de Braose, soon afterwards. Braose invited certain Welsh lords to dine with him, but when they were all seated and enjoying themselves, he gave a pre-arranged signal to troops who came into the dining hall and slaughtered the whole gathering.

ABERLLEINIOG Nr Llangoed,
Anglesey, Gwynedd (SH 617793)
Hugh d'Avranches, Earl of Chester, built the motte castle here, probably just after the end of the Conqueror's reign. It was attacked and burned by the Welsh under Gruffydd ap Cynan, Prince of Wales, in c.1095. The stonework was not added to the earthworks until the seventeenth century.

ABERLLYNFI Powys
(SO 171380)
An earthwork castle was built here in the twelfth century. It was captured in 1233, probably by the Welsh.

ABERRHEIDOL Nr Aberystwyth,
Dyfed (SN 585790) O

An earthwork enclosure about a mile to the south of Aberystwyth, where some of the timberwork has been deduced from post-holes and other imprints discovered in recent excavations. There is evidence of a motte formed out of the top of a spur emerging from the greater area of rising ground on which the castle stood. The castle was raised by the Norman lord, Gilbert FitzRichard, c.1110. It was attacked by the Welsh in 1116, and again in 1136 when it was burned down. It figures in the *Brut y Tywysogyon* (The Chronicle of the Princes [of Wales]), as having been burned (again) sometime between 1162 and 1164.

ABERYSTWYTH Dyfed ††
(SN 579815) A

Gilbert de Clare, a Norman lord, built an earthwork enclosure castle on a hill about

1½ miles south of the present town, at SN 585790, in c.1110. Traces of this can still be seen today (see Aberrheidol). It was attacked and burned by the Welsh in 1136, burned again in 1143, in 1162-4, and once more in 1208. Llywelyn the Great rebuilt it, and it disappears from the records. Nearly three-quarters of a century later, Edward I put in train the first phase of his great castle-building programme in Wales, and in 1277 work was begun on Flint, Rhuddlan, Builth and Aberystwyth. At Aberystwyth his brother, Edmund, arranged the construction of a substantial diamond-, or lozenge-, plan concentric castle of two curtain enclosures of stone (one inside the second), each curtain being on raised ground and supplied with flanking round towers on the angles, and each with a twin-towered gatehouse. The outer and smaller gatehouse led to a barbican: the inner was a substantial fortified residential gatehouse with D-ends

Aberystwyth: this concentric lozenge-plan Edwardian castle is now in only fragmentary form, but the aerial view considered in conjunction with the plan on p.324 does provide an overall idea of the castle's shape

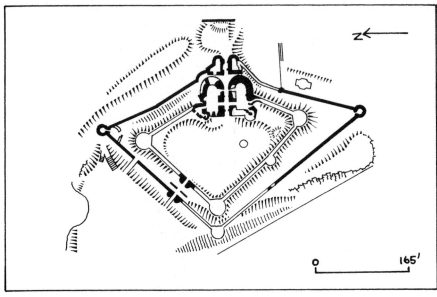

Aberystwyth: the bold lines indicate the masonry still visible (after C.J. Spurgeon)

to the east. It is thought a hall was built between this gatehouse and the south flanking tower of the inner curtain. There were additional gates at north-west in both curtains. Today much of the castle is in ruins, but there are stretches of curtain, some height in a few towers, and substantial remains of the great gate. There is thought to have been a third bailey to the north-west beyond the outer curtain, which has since been eroded by the sea.

For construction work, 120 masons and 120 carpenters were recruited from the West Country of England, transported by sea from Bristol to Carmarthen and finished their journey probably by land in 1277, having been joined by additional craftsmen and workers.

The building work started badly. Some years of what was probably 'jerry building' were followed by a sudden attack by Welsh patriots in 1282, who destroyed the castle. Master James of St George, who was working at Rhuddlan Castle at the time, was asked to go to Aberystwyth to 'construct' the castle, which probably meant 'rebuild' it. Master James put the work in the hands of his colleague, Master Giles of St George, and this went on for some years, ending, after

interruptions, c.1290, having cost nearly £4,500.

Aberystwyth was taken by Owain Glyndŵr in 1403 and he held it for five years. During that time he made a treaty with Charles VI of France and the document was said to have been sealed in the captured fortress. In 1409 Henry of Monmouth, eldest son of Henry IV, recaptured it, and thereafter it gradually decayed. In the Civil War Parliamentary forces besieged and took it, and in 1649 it was blown up. A visitor to the town in 1652 wrote that the ruins were 'confused heaps of unnecessary rubbish'.

AMROTH Earwere, Dyfed
(SN 170073) P
Amroth began as a motte castle built by Norman invaders early in the twelfth century. Sometime, probably in the fourteenth century, a stone enclosure with an interesting gateway was erected a few hundred yards away towards the sea, presumably within the original bailey.

BALA Gwynedd
(SH 928361)
A low level motte castle here was captured in 1202. It was near Lake Bala.

324

BASINGWERK Nr Holywell, Clwyd (SJ 220734)
A motte castle of the twelfth century. It was taken by Owain Gwynedd, Prince of all Wales, c.1166.

BEAUMARIS Anglesey, Gwynedd ††
(SH 607763) WO
Beaumaris is the last of the castles built by Edward I during and after his conquest of Wales. Its design, by Master James of St George, is almost perfectly concentric. It cost nearly £15,000 (over £2 million in today's terms); it took over thirty-five years to build and even then was not completed. At one time over 3,500 people were working on it, which is thought to be about 1 in 1,000 of the total population of England and Wales at the time — 1295. It was considered impregnable, but this was never put to the test. No shot appears to have been fired at Beaumaris in anger. And within twenty years of the last, but unfinished, building operations (c.1330), the castle was reported to be deteriorating: most of the timber work was in decay and some stonework was dilapidated.

Beaumaris is situated strategically in flat, marshy land on the south edge of the Isle of Anglesey. The castle is basically two concentric wings of walling with flanking towers and gatehouses. The inner ring, square in plan, with walls about 16ft thick and nearly 43ft high, has cylindrical towers on the four corners, D-end towers mid-wall on west and east, and on north and south, a substantial twin-cylindrical towered gatehouse mid-wall, the northern one completed, the southern one lacking its rear portions. None of the towers or gatehouses was completed to its full height. Both gatehouses were fitted with two suites of apartments, making them residential. Indeed, the gatehouses were the strongest parts of the castle, acting as great towers.

The outer ring, whose wall is 27ft tall and about half as thick as the inner walling, is octagonal in plan, has cylindrical flanking turrets all round from extreme south-west to extreme south-east, twelve in all. On the north-east side is an outer gateway and on the south-west, the sea gate, which abuts on to a dock for supply vessels to moor close to the castle. The whole castle is surrounded by a broad wet moat supplied by the waters of the Menai Straits.

The castle was built of grit and limestone rubble from a nearby quarry at Penmon. Both rings of wall and the towers and gatehouses were equipped with arrow slits

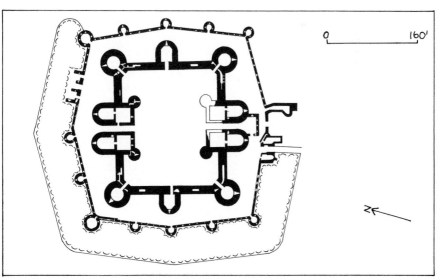

Beaumaris: the plan is almost perfectly concentric

325

Beaumaris: an aerial view of the concentric-plan castle that was never completed, and never had a shot fired at it in anger

all round, providing the maximum covering fire from all angles against attack from any direction. The southern gatehouse was further protected by a barbican.

BENTON Dyfed
(SN 005069) C
Small enclosure castle, with a cylindrical tower and a smaller cylindrical turret on one side, built in the thirteenth century. It has been merged in with later buildings. The cylindrical tower is still standing and is part-residential.

BLAENLLYNFI Cathedine, Powys
(SO 145229)
A stone castle built on a knoll below Llangorse Mountain, probably of the twelfth century. The knoll was surrounded by a ditch fed by local streams, and continued by an earthwork dam. The stonework is now fragmentary, but indicates a curtain walled enclosure with towers and with a gateway at east. The castle was destroyed in the 1230s by Llywelyn the Great, Prince of all Wales.

BLAENPORTH Aberporth, Dyfed
(SN 266488)
Otherwise called Castell Gwythian, it was a motte castle which today shows good traces of a stone shell keep on top. The motte may

have been raised by the de Clares c.1110. It was destroyed c.1153.

BLEDDFA Powys
(SO 209682) A
A motte castle, altered at some period, with fragments of a square tower with a mural staircase, which had been erected on the mound in the late twelfth century, discovered in recent excavations. The remnants are near the church.

BOUGHROOD Powys
(SO 132391) A
A recently excavated motte castle site on the side of the west road leading into the village. Masonry was found in the mound earth. This could mean either a stone tower which collapsed into the earth through insufficient foundations, or a tower built first and the earth heaped up round the basement level afterwards, like Aldingbourne and Lydford. The castle was mentioned in 1206.

BRECON Powys   †
(SO 043288) O
Brecon Castle remains stand in the grounds of the Castle Hotel in Brecon. It began as a motte castle erected at the end of the eleventh century. In the twelfth century a polygonal shell keep was built on the motte, and later on further buildings including a

hall and towers were added. Some of the stone for the shell keep and the other stone buildings was probably taken from the old Roman fort of Brecon Gaer nearby.

The castle was fought over on several occasions, held alternately by Welsh and English. In c.1380 Brecon became the property of Henry of Bolingbroke (later Henry IV) through marriage. Owain Glyndŵr tried to take it by storm in c.1404 but failed, and the constable was rewarded with an annuity for his stout defence of it.

BRONLLYS Nr Talgarth, Powys †
(SO 149346) WO
A twelfth-century motte castle with two baileys was given a cylindrical great tower c.1176. This is thought to have been after a fire in the 1170s, mentioned by Giraldus Cambrensis. The cylindrical tower is three storeys tall, the lower stage sloping slightly outwards. This was encircled by a curtain, and in the fourteenth century domestic buildings were added. Bronllys was captured in 1233 by the Welsh.

BUILTH Powys †
(SO 044510)
Builth was one of Edward I's ten new castles erected in Wales in the 1270s–80s as part of his scheme of conquest and government. There had already been a small castle on the site, a motte castle with double bailey and deep wet ditch of the end of the eleventh century, which received a polygonal stone shell keep in the mid-twelfth century, and was further fortified by King John, c.1208. In 1260 Builth was taken by Llywelyn the Last, Prince of all Wales, and destroyed. Edward was thus able to rebuild from scratch, and over five years, 1277–1282, he spent some £1,666. John FitzAdam of Radnor was *custos operacionum*. The principal works were a great hall, a kitchen block, a wet moat and a great tower. In 1278, the works are thought to have come under the general control of Master James of St George, and by 1280 the great tower, which may have been more like a shell keep since it had 'houses' within it, a stone curtain with six flanking turrets for the inner part of the castle and a gate-tower had been proceeded with, if not finished. Works ended in 1282, and the records seem to suggest that they

had petered out uncompleted, probably due to a shortage of money. In 1278, the master mason received 7½d a day and ordinary masons 2s a week, and about 140 men were on the payroll. Most of the stone was quarried locally, but freestone was waggoned over from Cusop and Clifford on Wye, while stone for burning for lime came from Llyswen (near Bronllys, another castle site).

Builth Castle was famous as the place near which Llywelyn the Last was ambushed and slain in 1282. It was severely damaged by Owain Glyndŵr in his campaigns of the early fifteenth century. Today, there is nothing to be seen except earthworks and a few foundations.

BWLCH Y DINAS Powys
(SO 179301)
A small enclosure castle with rectangular turrets raised in the twelfth century inside the remains of a hill-fort of (?) Iron Age times. The castle was given a rectangular great tower. Today the castle is ruinous.

CAEREINION Powys
(SJ 163055) A
Otherwise known as Twmpatch Garmon, Caereinion was a motte castle of Henry II's time, but built by a Welsh lord, presumably with Henry's leave, even though Montgomeryshire (now Powys) was Wales, not England. The castle was attacked in 1167 and burned.

CAERGWRLE Nr Mold, Clwyd
(SJ 307572) A
This ruined castle stands inside earthworks which are considered to have been of Iron Age origin. The stonework was an enclosure with half round and polygonal towers. It was taken in the 1281–3 war between Wales and Edward I.

CAERLEON Gwent
(ST 342905) P
A motte castle of steep sides erected in c.1086 on the outskirts of the site of the Roman fortress there. Giraldus Cambrensis (c.1180–90) mentions a vast tower on the motte, and remains of a tower foundation about 20ft by 30ft, and several feet thick were found in excavations. The tower may have

been built between 1158 and 1173. There was also a twin-towered barbican at the motte base, leading to the bailey, and the bailey wall had flanking towers, of which one has survived, and these may be of thirteenth-century origin.

Caerleon was attacked several times by the Welsh.

CAERNARVON Gwynedd   ††
(SH 477626) WO

It is no coincidence that the walls and towers of thirteenth-century Caernarvon Castle bear a strong superficial resemblance to the monumental fifth-century wall of the Byzantine Emperor, Theodosius II, that guarded the golden city of Constantinople on its western flank. Edward I commanded an army on the Seventh Crusade and all crusading armies spent time at the Byzantine capital on their way to Asia Minor. He would without doubt have been impressed by the high curtain interspersed with polygonal, round and square towers, with its banded masonry, that is, one kind of stonework interleaved here and there with a course or two of a different kind.

Caernarvon Castle was intended by Edward to be symbolic of his conquest and new government of Wales. There had once been a Norman motte castle on the northern edge of the Seiont River where it flows into the Menai Straits, and this had been captured and held by the Welsh for over a century. But the king chose to disregard its occupation, claiming that it had been English all the time, and he constructed his new hourglass-plan castle, with high curtain walls, polygonal flanking towers and great twin-towered gatehouses right round that castle. And because he wanted the defeated Welsh not only to accept English dominion but also to believe that they had been under English sovereignty for a good deal longer than the facts bore out, he chose to administer Wales from Caernarvon, just as previous Welsh rulers had — and just as the Romans had in the earliest centuries AD, for Segontium, the legionary fortress and town governing north Wales, was Caernarvon.

Edward's symbol had to be novel, vast, majestic and derived in some way from imperial Rome — hence its Roman/Byzantine appearance. Even the masonry was made to look like the walls of Constantinople, by dint of using limestone from the Penmon quarries in Anglesey, whose tiers of courses were interleaved every so often with darker brown sandstone courses, from quarries in Menai. But in reality the whole project must have been a great disappointment to him. Begun in 1283, it was never finished. Severe and extensive damage was

(opposite) Caernarvon: an aerial view of this Edwardian fortress which was built in conjunction with a fortified wall round the town

(below) Caernarvon: ground plan. The southern part from the Eagle Tower at left along to the north-east tower at right was built in the first stage, c.1283-c.1293

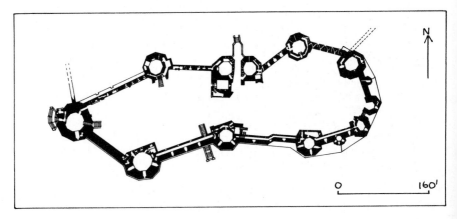

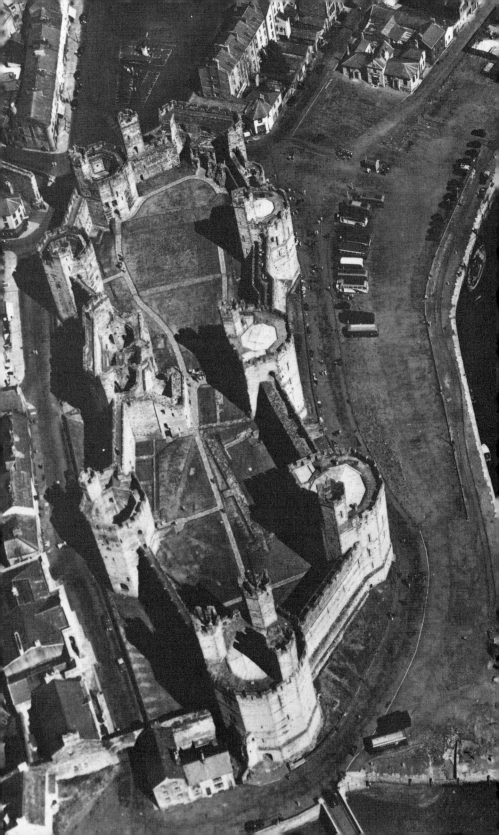

done in the attack by Madog ap Llywelyn in 1294–5. Edward had had to use press-gang methods to get English craftsmen and workers to come to the wilds of north-west Wales to build it, as he could not trust the native Welsh. By 1304 he had spent over £2 million (in today's figures) with less than half the work still to be done.

Despite this, the castle became the grandest of all his structures in Wales. The sophistication of its defences, once they were ready, has not ceased to astonish military historians. Below the battlemented parapet along the south side, upper and lower shooting galleries were constructed, with access to arrow slits in the curtain, which meant that a rain of missiles could be discharged against attackers from three levels and at several angles at once. To enter the lower courtyard by means of the King's Gate, a vast twin-towered fortress in itself, it would have been necessary to go across a drawbridge, though five doors and under six portcullises, turn right, and then across a second drawbridge. This progress would be subject to continual attack from defenders using arrow slits and spy-holes flanking all approaches at various levels, and in the gatehouse vaulting, a collection of murder-holes presented yet another obstacle.

Though Caernarvon is one of the most sophisticated castles in all Britain, it is nonetheless a simple figure-of-eight enclosure with curtain walls, towers and gatehouses. Its site on tidal waters meant it could be supplied by sea, like Harlech. There is a water-gate access to the huge polygonal Eagle Tower (at the west) with its three projecting turrets above the crenellations, so-called because the turrets once carried eagles of carved stone on the tops. The access led to a basement above which are three storeys of a residential kind. The masonry of the whole enclosure was tailored to fit the rock on which the castle was built, which explains its figure-of-eight plan. In the eastern half, a little higher than the west, was the original Norman motte, and this mound is the reason for the entrance through the Queen's Gate (a twin-polygonal towered gatehouse) being very high up, at first-storey level, reached by a ramp up to a drawbridge leading to it. The gatehouse sits across the slope of the motte, and sloping stonework continues to left and right of it.

The arrangement of the polygonal towers and gatehouses in the curtain, each one well equipped with loops at several levels, ensured maximum covering fire on every part of the castle, not only upon attackers outside trying to get in, but also upon them once they had entered the upper or lower bailey.

The building work fell into two main periods: the west, south and east curtain lengths with their towers and the Queen's Gate were raised mainly between 1283 and 1292, with top work to the Eagle Tower added afterwards, and the north side with the great King's Gate was built, though never completed, between 1296 and 1323. This second stage followed the assault in 1294–5 by Prince Madog ap Llywelyn.

Caernarvon Castle was part of a larger defensive arrangement incorporating the town which was enclosed inside a fortified wall with towers all round.

CAERPHILLY Mid Glamorgan ††
(ST 155870) WO
Caerphilly was the first concentric castle to be built from scratch in Britain. Its combination of land and water defences represented a level of military architectural sophistication unequalled anywhere in Europe. Despite several sieges and raids, long periods of neglect and, after the Civil War, serious attempts to demolish it, the great bulk of the castle has survived. Much has been restored with detailed care, and it is now one of the most spectacular military ruins in the world.

The position, some 7 miles north of Cardiff, appealed to the Romans who constructed a fort near the present castle site. Some time during the early Norman occupation of south Wales a castle of earth and timber was raised within the fort remains, but it is not clear whether this was a Norman or a Welsh work, for the hilly district around the castle was in Welsh hands right into the 1260s. In 1266 or 1267, after the war between Henry III of England and Simon de Montfort, Gilbert de Clare, Earl of Gloucester and Hertford and one of the richest barons of England who owned large tracts of Glamorgan, moved into the Caerphilly district. He began to construct a

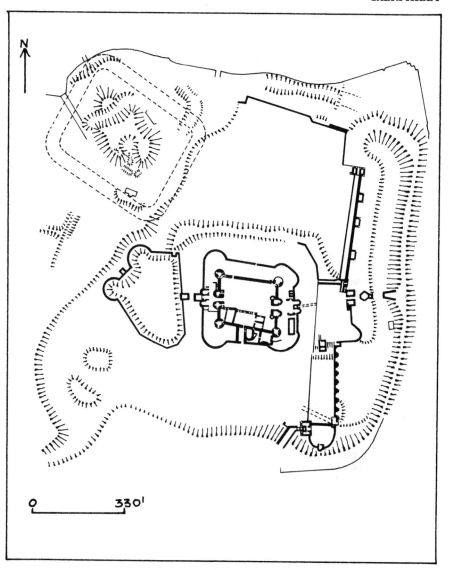

Caerphilly: general plan of the castle. At north-west is suggested site of Roman fort. At north-east is north lake, bordered on the east side by the north platform, and at south is south lake, bordered on east by south platform. Outer moat runs north to south in front of the platforms on east side. At west (centre) is western outwork separated from main castle block by inner moat. Main castle block is concentric in plan, with two twin-towered gatehouses on west and two on east. The inner enclosure wall of the block is of the first period, c.1268–71

stone castle, Kastell Kaerffili as it is called in *Brut y Tywysogyon*, in April 1268.

One of his motives for constructing a fortress here was to counter the activities of Llywelyn, Prince of Wales, who had been in alliance with Simon de Montfort and who, after the latter's defeat at Evesham, had come to an agreement with Henry III by which the prince was recognized as Prince of Wales. The English king realized, however, that Llywelyn constituted a danger to English holdings in south Wales, for it was his policy to recover the whole of Wales and govern it as an autonomous kingdom, a perfectly legitimate aspiration. Henry allowed de Clare to build Caerphilly and may even have given him some aid.

In the autumn of 1270, Llywelyn descended upon the embryo fortress and burnt it. By this time, considerable progress had been made on the inner part, much more than has been previously supposed because

the date for Llywelyn's first raid used to be taken as 1269. It seems likely that the entire inner quadrangle of walls with corner cylindrical towers and twin-cylindrical towered gatehouse in east and west wall had been largely completed, and that a start had also been made on the outer wall with its two gatehouses (also east and west). Work had also begun on the south defensive platform outside the outer wall. How much damage was done by Llywelyn is not absolutely clear, but the phrase used to describe the next stage of work after the attack — *reinceptum est* (taken up again) — suggests that work was resumed upon the construction actually standing, which would have been up to three years of work. And if the account that Llywelyn burnt the castle is taken literally, that must apply to wooden and not stone parts, such as wooden walling, scaffolding and so forth.

De Clare pressed on with the work and by

Caerphilly: an aerial view of this remarkable concentric castle of the later thirteenth century. The fracturing of the cylindrical (south-east) tower to the left of the gatehouse in the centre was probably the result of slighting at the end of the Civil War. The general arrangement of the water defences is clear. The north platform of the main dam is at the right bottom corner

the autumn of 1271 the castle had become almost completely concentric. Llywelyn attacked it again but this time was deflected, probably by the sheer extent of the fortifications. The prince called off the siege and a truce was arranged. Llywelyn is reported to have said he could have taken the castle in three days and laid it flat, but it seems an idle boast.

The third work stage began in about 1277, when the two outer gatehouses were finished and other buildings added. Thereafter, work seems to have been done at a desultory rate — at least, compared with the early feverish activity — and masons and carpenters were still busy in 1326. By that time the artificial lake surrounding the castle, the western hornwork which barred the approach to the west side, and the unique screen of curtain walls and platforms, fortified by projecting turrets and buttresses, running from south to north on the eastern front, were complete. So was the second lake separated from the inner one on the north side by a mole (see Chapter 8). The first lake may have been controllable by means of dam and sluice-gates by the time the third work stage began.

These drawn out later building works were not uninterrupted. In 1316 Caerphilly was besieged by Llywelyn Bren in a localized revolt against English rule and a drawbridge was burnt. Five years later the castle was broken into by barons and supporters quarrelling with its then owner, Hugh Despenser, favourite of Edward II. And five years after that, when Edward was on the run from his estranged wife Isabella and her paramour Roger Mortimer (see Nottingham Castle), he took refuge at Caerphilly. The queen caught up with his supporters there and invested the castle for several weeks (though Edward had already fled). The garrison surrendered in 1327, and the besiegers discovered that Edward had left half his treasure and clothes behind.

For a time Caerphilly remained in Despenser hands (though Hugh had been executed in 1326). It was threatened by Owain Glyndŵr in the early 1400s but does not appear to have been besieged. Perhaps it was yielded to him. Thereafter it was allowed to deteriorate. During the Civil War it played some part, but one difficult to determine in detail. Cromwell wanted it dismantled, and there are telling signs today of the effects of Parliamentary slighting, notably the 'leaning' south-east tower of the inner ward.

Caerphilly has received considerable restoration to its fabric, and its lakes have been re-flooded. The great hall was re-roofed, and its floors and windows were restored. The castle is in the care of the Welsh Office which has produced a new official handbook, the most authoritative work on the castle available anywhere.

CAERWENT Nr Chepstow, Gwent (ST 475917) WO
Caerwent is an ancient Roman site. It was a city of some size within a rectangular stonewall enclosure with bastions, banks and ditches. As such it is not part of this Gazetteer, but in the extreme south-east corner of the rectangle, in a space left when a section of the Roman wall was cleared away, a Norman motte was raised, probably between 1067 and 1070. Its summit is now about 7ft above the Roman bank. It was provided with extra ditching which, together with the Roman ditching already there, surrounded the motte. Nothing is known about its history, though it might be the same as Castell Gwent mentioned in about 1150.

CALDICOT Gwent †
(ST 487885) O
Beginning as a motte castle with two baileys, built beside a stream, probably in the early twelfth century, Caldicot developed in the late twelfth and early thirteenth centuries into a large stirrup-shaped stone enclosure castle of high walls, flanking towers, unusual gatehouse and a great tower erected on the motte in one corner. The great tower is cylindrical and made of local gritstone, described by Douglas Simpson as 'beautiful masonry'. It stands on a splayed plinth and has a mural staircase to the basement and spiral stairs upwards to the second floor, whence another mural stair continues to the top. The parapet was battlemented and the holes remain for the hoarding beams. The cylindrical plan is augmented with a bulging half-round turret which is solid except for the basement.

Caldicot's gatehouse, of the early fourteenth century and built of ashlar blocks, is rectangular with square garderobe turrets at each end. The longer sides of the rectangle are positioned lengthways in the curtain. The entrance passage has two portcullises and two pairs of folding doors. The gatehouse has handsome accommodation above the passage and was built as a residential structure. The fourteenth century saw additional buildings, including a postern tower of semi-hexagonal plan.

CAMLAIS Powys
(SN 956260) A

Also known as Cwm Camlais, this was a motte castle built on a natural rocky mound very high, over 1,000ft above sea level, on the edge of Mynyold Illtyd. The motte was given a cylindrical tower, of which the base remains.

CAMMAIS Dyfed
(SN 082401)

Alternatively called Nevern or Nanhyfer, Cammais was a motte castle which received a stone square-plan tower, among other buildings, in the late twelfth century. Money was allotted to be spent on Cammais in 1197, but it was probably diverted to Newport Castle in Dyfed instead.

CANDLESTON Nr Bridgend, †
Mid Glamorgan (SS 871772) O

This castle dates from the fourteenth century. It had a polygonal courtyard enclosing a square tower, and more domestic buildings were added later. The castle was held for a time by the Cantelupes, a powerful Norman family. It is now in a ruinous state. At one time the castle was held as a fortified residence by a tenant of Merthyr Mawr manor house nearby which was not fortified — a curious anomaly.

Cardiff: an impressive view of the twelve-sided shell keep built upon the eleventh-century motte. The stonework originated in the twelfth century but has been much altered and refurbished

CARDIFF South Glamorgan †† (ST 180767) O

When looking at the interesting castle at Cardiff, it is helpful to forget about the eighteenth- and nineteenth-century additions to this very old fortress. Basically, Cardiff began as a motte castle, raised by about 1080. The motte is a substantial one, over 40ft tall, sitting in a surrounding moat. On the summit was erected a twelve-sided shell keep, with one side having a projection that is tower-like. This was built in the twelfth century. Robert, Duke of Normandy, eldest son of William the Conqueror, was imprisoned here (c.1110–34) by his youngest brother, Henry I of England, and died in the castle. It is not known for certain whether the stone shell had been built by that time. If not, Robert will have been confined inside a wooden structure. Among the medieval additions were the Black Tower (1200s), below the motte and connected to the motte by a wing wall, an octagonal tower (c.1420s) on the south side of the shell keep and standing taller, and a substantial gatehouse linked to the Black Tower by a massive wall across the bailey.

The castle stands on the site of a Roman fort, with a stone curtain with flanking turrets. Later in the castle's history, apartments were raised in the bailey (inside the Roman fort area), including a range against the western wall, substantially remodelled in the eighteenth and nineteenth centuries. The octagonal turret on the shell keep is one of these additions.

Cardiff is a very good example in Wales of how an earth-and-timber motte castle was converted to a stone fortress (like Berkhamsted and Pickering). The castle was attacked several times by the Welsh.

CARDIGAN Dyfed Outside open (SN 177459 and SN 164464)

There is confusion over two castle sites here. The first was a Norman enclosure of c.1093 (at SN 164464) which was converted to stone by the Welsh who probably captured it, c.1170, and then sold it to King John in 1199. John and Henry III both spent money on it. Then in 1231 it was taken by Llywelyn the Great and destroyed. Cardigan town was recovered by the English in c.1240 and a castle was built near the older structure.

This may have included the curtain wall and flanking towers, and the cylindrical great tower. In 1254 the castle was in the custody of Edward, eldest son of Henry III and later Edward I. He made it the administrative centre of his new shire of Cardigan c.1279. Repairs were carried out in later reigns, including work on the roof of the 'great round tower' in the mid-fifteenth century.

CAREW Dyfed †† (SN 045037) O

Carew stands on a rock above the shore where the River Cleddau enters the sea. It began as an earthwork castle of the early twelfth century. This may have been the time when a rectangular gatehouse of rubble masonry was erected. Later in the century the gatehouse was altered to form a tower when the vaulted passage was blocked at the ends, and later still, probably in the thirteenth century, a square-plan curtain wall was built around the tower with a double line of defence on one side. The curtain had four large flanking towers of

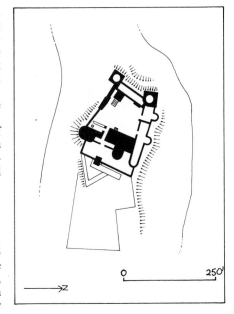

Carew: ground plan. The two spur-based cylindrical towers, at west, are among the oldest buildings, and they confirm the military aspects of the castle

335

Carew: a view from the south. Note spur-base tower at left

various shapes, two of which were cylindrical on spur bases, which today are massive and striking features (cf. Goodrich).

Carew was considerably altered in the fourteenth and fifteenth centuries, and converted more to a mansion, including a great hall with an imposing porch tower. There were further improvements in the sixteenth century in Tudor style, done chiefly by Sir John Perrott (see also Laugharne Castle). Some of the medieval work was also changed, notably the windows which were replaced by rows of wide, mullioned ones, particularly in the north front. Carew was besieged and badly damaged in the Civil War. It is an interesting ruin.

CARMARTHEN Dyfed
(SN 413420) A

Carmarthen began as a motte castle of the very early twelfth century (possibly even before). The motte was revetted for part of its height. It was Norman built, attacked several times by the Welsh during the century and was strengthened in 1181–3 for £170. In 1215 it fell to Llywelyn the Great, who probably damaged it beyond repair, for in the following decade it was to receive stonework for the first time. By 1275 it had an inner bailey with five towers, a great tower (actually described as *magna turris*), a hall, chapel, gate and curtain wall. Edward I made Carmarthen the centre for his administration of south-west Wales, and over the fourteenth and fifteenth centuries the castle was maintained in reasonable condition. Owain Glyndŵr captured the castle in c.1403 and held it for six years. Henry IV spent about £100 on the gate, converting it to the gateway which is one of the few remaining features that can be seen today.

CASTELL CARNDOCHAN Gwynedd
(SH 846306) A

A small Welsh-built castle of the mid-thirteenth century that commands the valley of Afon Lliw. It is a curtained enclosure with an integrated apsidal tower at the south-west end and a round turret on the north-east side. In the enclosure is a square-plan building, but this is too far ruined to speculate what it was.

CARREG CENNEN Nr Llandeilo, ††
Dyfed   (SN 668191) WO

This powerful courtyard castle clasped on the north-east and east sides by two outer

336

stone walled baileys with flanking solid turrets and gateway, stands on a 300ft high limestone crag overlooking the Towy Valley. The stonework was begun in the late thirteenth century, raised on the site of an earlier castle of Welsh origin but of which no structural details exist. This first work was the inner enclosure with a long range occupying the whole east wall and containing a hall, the northern twin-semi-octagonal towered gatehouse (of three storeys) and the cylindrical tower on the north-west corner, which had a gun-port inserted in the fifteenth century. The east range was three-storeyed for most of its length and contained hall, solar and kitchen on the middle (first) floor and a chapel on the top in what is called the chapel tower. The range was flanked by a square-plan, north-east corner tower with canted edges, three storeys tall. The gatehouse served in a defensive role as a great tower in as much as it was the last refuge in the event of assault. The passage through the ground floor had a portcullis at each end. In between was a gate, and there were several arrow slits along the walls of the passage between gate and portcullis. You could walk from the gatehouse at first-floor level to the north-west

and north-east towers through mural galleries, and at second-floor level above these galleries a wall-walk behind parapetting led round the whole enclosure.

The remains of the barbican show it to have been formidable. Projecting northwards from the gatehouse is the ruined Prison Tower, which was three-storeyed with thick walls. At right angles leading eastwards is an opening into a long narrow walled passage, extending beyond the easternmost part of the main castle block. This passage slopes on its easterly path downwards and the floor is a stepped ramp. Along its passage are deep pits which were crossed by movable bridges. It was thus difficult to get up to the Prison Tower entrance. At the east end the passage turns sharp right, emerging at a south access. The ground in front of the north wall of the barbican falls sharply away down the rock slope.

Carreg Cennen is much ruined, but the general layout of the castle and its sophisticated defences are clear. (Note the castle cave, reached by a door in the south-east corner of the inner enclosure.)

Very considerable damage was done to Carreg Cennen in the reign of Henry IV by

Carreg Cennen: a view of the ruins of this once great enclosure castle with flanking towers

Owain Glyndŵr, who destroyed most of the defences, costing over £500 to repair. It was finally rendered useless as a castle by the Yorkists in the Wars of the Roses. Five hundred men with 'bars, picks and crowbars of iron . . .' were engaged to 'breke and throw down the said castle' (*King's Works*).

CARREGHOFA Powys
(SJ 255222) A
An earthwork enclosure built c.1100 was captured in 1163 by the Welsh. It was retaken at the end of the century and repaired.

CASTELL-Y-BERE Abergynolwyn, ††
Gwynedd   (SH 667086) WO
This was a native Welsh castle raised on a spur of land in the shadow of Cadair Idris. It resembles the medieval German hill castles such as Staufen. It was begun probably in 1221 by Llywelyn the Great, Prince of all Wales (c.1196–1240), and consisted of an irregular curtained enclosure with flanking towers, one of them in the manner of a great tower, and a triangular barbican. The castle was not equipped with a drawbridge over the moat cut out of the rock, but had a fixed timber pontoon. The castle was formidable, nonetheless, because of its position. In April 1283, Bere was besieged and captured by

Edward I's forces. After the ending of hostilities between England and Wales, Bere was restored to use by Edward who spent over £260 on works over the years 1286–90. This work was mainly devoted to building a considerable stretch of tall curtain wall round the outside of the original castle. The castle appears to have been abandoned after c.1295. All the buildings are now ruined to their foundations.

CEFNLLYS Powys
(SO 089614) P
There was once a substantial castle here, inside a hill-fort. Fragments of a great tower were found in the north corner of the fort, and of a round tower in the south.

CHEPSTOW Gwent ††
(ST 533941) WO
Chepstow is a fascinating castle that offers the castle devotee a little of everything. Begun c.1068 as one of the very first stone castles in Britain, its building periods cover several centuries. Standing proudly and strategically on a natural limestone ridge whose north face falls in a steep vertical cliff into the River Wye, Chepstow was chosen by William FitzOsbern, whom the Conqueror had recently made Earl of Hereford,

Castell-y-Bere: a view of the ruins

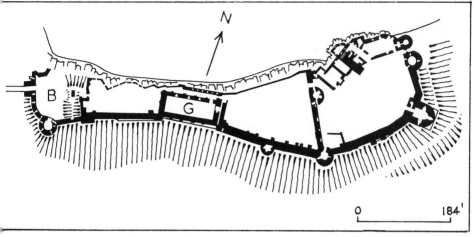

Chepstow: a castle of several periods, beginning with a great tower (G) c.1070; the barbican (B) was built in c.1225-45

as the site on which to erect the first stone great tower in Britain. It was a substantial quadrilateral two-storey building, about 100ft by 40ft, standing on a splayed plinth, with the ground scarped away from its south side. In the mid-thirteenth century, the top storey had an extra storey added at the west end which, towards the end of that century, was extended for the rest of the tower's length, to give a three-storeyed great tower, with cellar of unequal dimensions. Interestingly, different types of stone were used in the construction of the tower, notably old red sandstone, yellow sandstone and grey oolite rock.

The next stage was a thick curtain wall on the east side of the ridge, with cylindrical towers and a gate. This work was done by William the Marshal, Earl of Pembroke, c.1190–c.1220. It divided the central bailey from the lower bailey. Almost immediately after that, c.1225–1250, the great tower was heightened — proof that great towers were still needed in the thirteenth century, the upper (western) bailey was constructed and next to it the interesting barbican with cylindrical tower at south, the central bailey southern wall was raised, and the lower (eastern) bailey received its easterly curtain and a twin-cylindrical towered great gatehouse, three storeys high, with a prison in the northern tower containing only an airshaft. Between 1270 and the end of the century, the western gatehouse was built at the extreme west end of the barbican and various domestic buildings were erected in the lower bailey; and at the south-east corner of the lower bailey, a huge D-end tower was built (later called Martens Tower), named after Henry Marten, the regicide, who was imprisoned in it after the Restoration of Charles II, 63ft tall, with pyramidal spur bases, which was given gun-ports in the seventeenth century.

This is not a complete description, but it represents the principal features, and the visitor is particularly recommended to explore this castle.

Chepstow was well placed beside the Wye overlooking a harbour by means of which it could be provisioned by ships coming from Bristol. The castle was held for a few short periods by the Crown. It was never besieged in the Middle Ages though it was ready for defence, possessing several retaliatory siege engines, one of which was mounted on the great tower. It was, however, besieged twice in the Civil War while being held for the King. Much renovation was done in the seventeenth century to fit the castle out for guns and musketry, though more probably after the Civil War than before it, which suggests it may have been intended that Chepstow should be a prison for political

Chepstow: inside the great tower. The lower masonry, c.1067-70, is noticeably poorer than the higher levels of later date

offenders. Henry Marten, one of the men who signed the death warrant of Charles I and was branded as a regicide in Charles II's reign, spent twenty years in captivity in the tower, afterwards given his name. It had previously been called Bigod's Tower, as it was built during the time Chepstow was held by Roger Bigod III, Earl of Norfolk, in the late thirteenth century.

CHIRK Clwyd   †
(SJ 268380) NT
There was a motte castle here, of the mid-twelfth century. Nearby, in the 1280s,

the Mortimers started to build a lordship castle (see chapter 9), with a wide view across Cheshire to the Pennines. The fortress became a quadrangle with squat but substantial cylindrical corner towers and half-round towers on the mid-walls, which remain in the present more modern mansion. It is thought that the work went on into the 1320s, and was stopped when Roger Mortimer was disgraced.

In 1595 the castle was sold to Thomas Myddleton, later Lord Mayor of London, and his descendants still own it. It was besieged in the Civil War. Myddleton's son

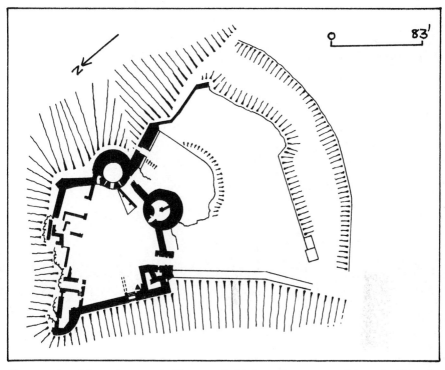

Cilgerran: plan of the enclosure castle. The two cylindrical mural towers at south are early thirteenth century. Note how they are sited bulging out of the curtain and that the walls outside are much thicker than inside

surrendered it rather than have it blown up by Parliamentary cannons. The transformation into a fine residence was done in the eighteenth century.

CILGERRAN Dyfed †
(SN 195431) WO

Built on a rocky promontory of great natural strength overlooking the Teifi River, with rock-cut ditches at the south end, Cilgerran began as a Norman enclosure castle with outer bailey in the early twelfth century. About a century later, a powerful stone castle was raised, using the Norman enclosure as an inner enclosure and giving it a stone wall, and raising another curtain round the old outer bailey. Cylindrical towers were built into the inner curtain c.1233 and a strong gate inserted. The outer enclosure was also strengthened but there is little to see of these. By the 1320s the castle was ruinous. Repairs were ordered in 1377,

one of Edward III's last acts, and probably enough was done to help it hold out against Owain Glyndŵr in the early fifteenth century.

CLYRO Powys
(SO 214436) P

Only fragments remain of this castle on a hillock which was surrounded by good ditching. It is not clear when the castle was first raised: early twelfth century seems possible.

COITY Nr Bridgend, Mid Glamorgan †
(SS 923816) WO

'Marry my daughter and you can have the castle of Coity without having to fight for it.' Thus in so many words said the Welsh Lord Morgan to a Norman knight, Payn de Turbeville, who had threatened to storm Coity sometime in the last years of the eleventh century, according to a legend. At

341

that time, however, Coity was but a circular earthwork enclosure, with good banks and ditches. A century elapsed before stonework was added there, and this was a curtain round the greater part of the inner bailey (surrounded for three-quarters of the circle by a moat). On the arc of the remaining part of the circle was built a rectangular great tower, some 40ft by 35ft, at the north-west. The ribbed vaults and other features internally are of much later (fourteenth-century) date. There were some more additions and alterations in Tudor times, including an abutting square turret, four storeys tall, on the north-east side of the great tower.

COLWYN Llansantffraid, Powys
(SO 108540) P
An enclosure castle with marked bank, possibly of early twelfth century beginnings, and said to have been rebuilt in c.1144. The earthworks stand in farm premises.

CONWY Gwynedd   ††
(SH 781777) WO
Conwy Castle is a fortress of superlatives. Described by Professor Allen Brown as one of the 'finest and noblest castles in Western

(above) Coity: the ruined curtain wall round the inner bailey

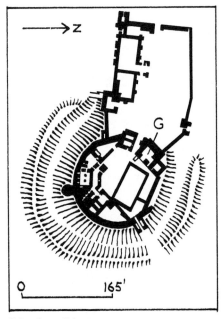

Coity: the wall in the lower half of the enclosure at left and the great tower at G are the oldest parts (late twelfth century) of this castle of several periods.

342

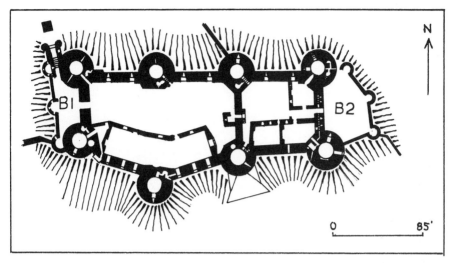

Conwy: ground plan. Despite the concentration of towers, the castle is basically a simple enclosure. B1 and B2 are barbicans

Europe and Latin Christendom', it was designed by Master James of St George and completed in very quick time — 1283–7. Over 1,500 men of one skill and another worked on the huge structure during the summer of 1285, and the work-force could hardly have been much less for the remaining building time. The bill came to nearly £20,000, or in our money, £2–3 million, the biggest sum spent on any castle in Wales between 1277 and 1304. And at the end of it, Edward I was presented with an almost perfect structure of high and thick curtain wall with eight huge cylindrical flanking towers, the most compact agglomerate of turretry in the British Isles.

Tailored to fit the rock site chosen for guarding the entrance to the River Conwy, the castle was a vast enclosure divided into an inner and an outer ward, separated by a thick wall at each end of which was one of the eight flanking towers. The towers themselves are massive, well over 30ft in diameter with walls up to 15ft thick. Reaching to over 70ft tall, they are like great towers, with several storeys equipped with rooms and staircases. This massive construction represented all that Edward I stood for — strength, terror, dominion, permanence, and it was hated by the Welsh for just those

things. Yet it was not besieged until the Civil War, perhaps because it really did seem too big to challenge, and within a generation the mighty fortress began to show signs of decay. Timber in the tower roofs was rotting away, and stonework was crumbling here and there.

In 1294, Prince Madog ap Llywelyn, a cousin of Llywelyn the Last, organized a rising against English rule in north Wales, and descending upon some of the Edwardian castles, wreaked a great deal of damage, particularly at Caernarvon (q.v.). The king marched rapidly to Wales, assembled a small force and set out to establish a base for operations in Conwy, leaving his commanders to marshal the main army for dealing with the revolt. He was no sooner inside the great castle than the waters of the river rose, effectively trapping him within and cutting off supplies. The king spent anxious days waiting for the waters to subside, his temper not at all improved by the deteriorating diet on which he and his men were compelled to subsist — salted meat, suspect water and coarse bread. Then at last the river went down and Edward emerged to deal with the revolt.

Conwy Castle was part of a walled town to which it was joined. The castle was used

343

Conwy: an interesting view of the 'agglomerate of turretry' that is the feature of this Edwardian castle

sporadically during the fourteenth century, and then gradually began to decay. In 1609 it was described in an official report as 'utterly decayed'. It was then sold — for £100!

CRICCIETH Gwynedd ††
(SH 500377) WO

Originally raised by the Welsh during the reign of Llywelyn the Great (c.1196–1240), Criccieth began as a roughly triangular curtain enclosure of grey stone upon a high peninsula. Nearly half its perimeter was protected by the steep slope of the cliff leading to the sea shore. Ditches and banks were cut and raised on the remaining sides which also had scarps. The enclosure was covered by a rectangular great tower at the south-west corner, let into the curtain, and by a second rectangular tower at the north corner, called the Engine Tower, also let in the curtain. Both towers commanded the slopes. The Engine Tower is so named because it was equipped to mount a siege engine on the top behind the protection of a parapet. The great tower, which has been compared (by personnel at the Royal Commission on Ancient & Historical Monuments in Wales) with the great tower at Dolwyddelan, was about 68ft by 40ft, and rose three storeys with battlemented parapet above. There was a simple gateway at the south corner. The great part of this work was

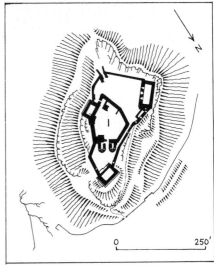

Criccieth: the outer walling and two rectangular towers at right are the first (Welsh) parts, of early to mid-thirteenth century. The inner ward (I) with north-east gatehouse is Edwardian

done in the first half of the thirteenth century.

In the years following the conquest of Wales by Edward I, c.1285–92, an inner enclosure of reddish stone was erected inside the older work. This was given a rectangular tower on the south-east called

344

Criccieth: the inner gatehouse on the north-east side of the English-built inner ward. It was a residential tower as well as protective gateway

the Leyburn Tower, named after the castle's constable in that period, possibly on the site of an earlier Welsh-built tower. The enclosure was also fortified by the insertion of a powerful twin-half-cylindrical towered gatehouse. Considerable repairs were carried out in Edward II's reign. Over £500 was spent on the castle between 1285 and 1326. It was captured by Owain Glyndŵr in 1404, and soon afterwards appears to have been badly damaged by fire, to judge from such charred timber discovered in excavations of the building ruins in the 1930s.

CRICKHOWELL Powys   †
(SO 217182) A
A motte castle of late date, probably early thirteenth century, which was given a stone shell keep on the summit, with possibly a gate at bailey level. A pair of conjoined towers (cylindrical and rectangular) in fragmentary state are close to the motte. The pair are like those at Brecon and Abergavenny.

CASTELL CRUGERYDD
Llanfihangel-nant-Melan, Powys
(SO 158593)
Otherwise known as Crug Eryr, this was a motte castle on the side of a high hill. It was mentioned by Giraldus Cambrensis towards the end of the twelfth century.

CYMARON Powys
(SO 152703)
A motte castle of the early twelfth century which was rebuilt c.1144 and appears to have been rebuilt again in 1195.

CYMMER Gwynedd
(SH 732195)
A castle was built here in 1116. It appears to have been destroyed in the same year.

DEGANNWY Gwynedd
(SH 781794)
A Welsh castle that began as a double motte castle of c.1090 (mentioned by Ordericus Vitalis). Two hillocks side by side were

345

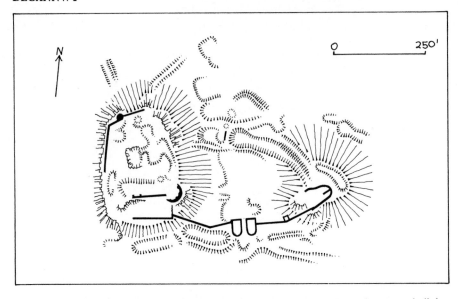

Degannwy: only fragments remain of this once formidable castle of the thirteenth century, built by Henry III and destroyed by Llywelyn the Last. There were powerful towers on the two hills (bottom left and right) Note also the remains of the twin-towered gateway. Degannwy combined natural geographical features with its stonework in a cohesive plan

made into a double motte castle, and linked by ramparts and ditching. This was taken by the Welsh in the twelfth century and was in the hands of Llywelyn the Great in c.1200. It was taken again by the English c.1210, refortified with timber by the Earl of Chester, but retaken by Llywelyn c.1213. It was attacked in 1241 by Henry III of England and taken. In 1257, Llywelyn the Last recaptured it and destroyed it. This chequered history has obscured the building details. It was the site itself that was of value to both sides. Certain buildings were raised, of which traces remain or evidence is available regarding their existence. These included a great tower on one of the hillocks, an enclosure with three towers on the other, and a twin D-ended towered gatehouse of the thirteenth century in between the two, on the saddle, so to speak.

The Exchequer records indicate that Henry III took much personal interest in the building work in the 1240s. In 1245 he camped nearby for two months to supervise operations. The great tower was probably started in 1247. The *History of the King's*

Works reckons that about £10,000 must have been spent in all, which is a very substantial sum. Henry gave the castle to his son Edward in 1254. Within twenty years it had been utterly destroyed by Llywelyn the Last, and only traces of the work can be seen today.

DENBIGH Clwyd ††
(SJ 051657) WO
There was a motte castle here of unknown date, but mentioned in Pipe Rolls at the end of the twelfth century. During Edward I's campaigns in Wales he encouraged some of his barons to build castles besides his own. Henry de Lacy, Earl of Lincoln, an enormously rich and powerful magnate, erected Denbigh Castle over the years 1282–1311, in two main periods: in 1282–6 the west and south curtain walls of an enclosure, with round flanking towers, were built, and 1286 onwards saw the completion of the enclosure with polygonal flanking towers and the insertion, in the north face, of a remarkable triangular complex of three polygonal towers to make a gatehouse.

The question has been asked: Did Master James of St George, then working at Caernarvon Castle (q.v.), advise de Lacy to complete his castle in this fashion? Inside the enclosure, domestic apartments were raised, including a great hall with a dais, and a barbican was added to the south postern tower, access being provided through an entrance in the curtain wall.

The great gatehouse has been described in chapter 7. It was by far the most imposing feature of the whole castle, and still dominates the ruins today, notwithstanding the disappearance of much of it.

Denbigh was, like Flint and Rhuddlan, associated with an adjoining town which was fortified with a thick wall, towers and gates. The castle was besieged during the Civil War, in an assault lasting nearly six months, from April to October 1646. The royalist garrison finally surrendered and the castle was used by Parliament as a prison for captured royalists.

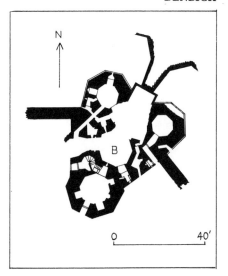

(above) Denbigh: the Great Gatehouse. B = octagonal hall with stone vaulting

(below) Denbigh: all that remains of the three-towered, triangular-plan gatehouse and its complex defensive mechanisms. There is some speculation that this gatehouse was similar to one at Pontefract

CASTELL DINAS BRAN Llangollen, Clwyd (SJ 223430) O

An early castle of Welsh construction, probably twelfth century, Dinas Bran was a stone walled enclosure, roughly rectangular, containing a square great tower. The curtain was flanked by a large D-ended tower, inserted in the thirteenth century. There was also a twin-towered gatehouse, likewise (?) thirteenth century. The castle was taken from the Welsh sometime in the Edwardian wars, between 1277 and 1282. The castle was also known as Crow Castle, the suggestion being that 'Crow' is an English rendering of 'Bran'. Its recorded history ends in 1282, though a suggestion has been put forward that Owain Glyndŵr attacked it c.1402.

CASTELL DINAS EMRYS Nr Beddgelert, Gwynedd (SH 606492) A

A Welsh-built castle consisting of the remains of a rectangular tower, erected on an earlier (?) Roman site. Dinas Emrys is in a district once rich in copper deposits, and the

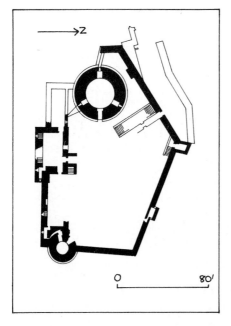

Dinefwr: plan of polygonal enclosure castle of thirteenth century, with the cylindrical great tower at top

castle was raised by Llywelyn the Great in the early thirteenth century to protect them.

CASTELL DINAS POWYS †
St Andrews Major, South Glamorgan (ST 152716)

Two structures are at this site. The first was an earthwork enclosure surrounded by a rubble reinforced bank on which a wooden palisade was set (whose post-holes have been found), with a ditch cut in rock. This is at ST 148722. There were additional banks and ditches outside associated with the enclosure. Nearby, the second castle (ST 152716) contained a square tower of late twelfth century date beside a rectangular enclosure of stone, with no towers but with a gateway, of later date. The curtain is of rubble, 20–30ft tall and 6ft thick. This contained buildings, including a hall and (?) a chapel on the south of the curtain near the west end.

DINEFWR Dyfed (SN 611217) C

A polygonal inner stone enclosure was raised on an earlier earthwork castle on the top of a cliff here in the late twelfth century or early thirteenth century. The curtain has been repaired at later dates. Inside the enclosure a cylindrical great tower was built at the east, between 1150 and 1250. The north side had a defensive moat cut out of the solid rock. There was also an outer enclosure. Domestic buildings were added in later periods, after the conquest of Wales by Edward I. Dinefwr was besieged in c.1402 by Owain Glyndŵr but not taken. Today, the remains stand in Dinefwr (Dynevor) Park. The 'summer house' cap on the great tower is a folly added in the eighteenth century.

DINGESTOW Gwent (SO 455104)

A motte castle by the River Trothiu, probably built c.1180.

DINHAM Gwent (ST 480923)

Parts of a small rectangular tower of (?) the thirteenth century, and traces of other stonework.

DINIERTH Llanbadarn Trefeglwys, Dyfed (SN 945624)

A motte castle of c.1110 was badly damaged

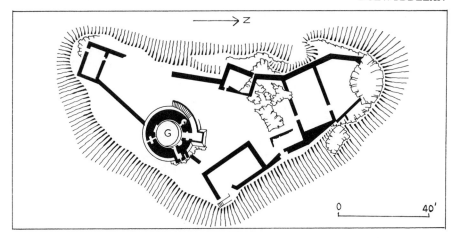

Dolbadarn: ground plan of castle. G = great tower

by Gruffyd ap Rhys c.1116, and again in 1136. The castle was destroyed c.1208. There is some masonry rubble on the motte surface but it is thought that the rubble is part of the motte's own construction material and not of any building thereon.

DOLBADARN Nr Llanberis, ††
Gwynedd   (SH 586598) WO
From its boomerang-shaped, rock-based platform between the Peris and Padarn lakes, Dolbadarn Castle commanded the entrance to the Llanberis Pass. The east side of the platform slopes down to the Padarn. The west side is protected by a sheer rock cliff down to a marsh. The castle site is peppered with rock crops where the platform was not flattened. The principal structure is a cylindrical great tower of mortared local slate and grit rubble, with splayed plinth, a curving outside stairway on the west arc, which may replace an earlier small forebuilding. The walls are 7–8ft thick with a spiral staircase within the north-west facing segment, the overall diameter is over 40ft, and the height at present some 40ft with three storeys, but once reached nearly 50ft. The tower forms part of the curtain round the site, which is interspersed with other buildings such as a south tower, a thick-walled west tower of which only the base remains and a rectangular hall at the north-west.

The whole castle was probably erected as one operation over several years by Llywelyn the Great in the early thirteenth century, though there is discussion as to whether the great tower and west tower were raised shortly after the other works.

In the campaign against Wales, 1281–3, Dolbadarn was abandoned after Llywelyn the Last's death and Edward I declined to rebuild it. Instead, it was used as a quarry for materials for other buildings. Timber was taken to Caernarvon in 1284.

DOLFORWYN Bettws Cedewain, Powys (SO 152950) A
A Welsh-built castle on a ridge site, with a stone curtain rectangular in plan, with no corner towers, but with one large cylindrical tower, the whole castle dated mid-thirteenth century (c.1270). It was probably raised by Llywelyn the Last, Prince of all Wales. Only traces of the curtain on the north and east are standing, but the overall plan can be detected. The castle fell to Edward I in 1278. It was a contemporary castle of Dolbadarn.

DOLWYDDELAN Gwynedd   ††
(SH 722523) WO
Built upon a rock ridge towering from the slopes of Moel Siabod, Dolwyddelan was built by Iorwerth Trwyndwn (the Flat-nosed) in the 1170s. Here, c.1173, was born Llywelyn ap Iorwerth, who was to become Llywelyn the Great, Prince of all Wales,

Dolbadarn: the cylindrical great tower of this Welsh-built castle. The square projection contained a chamber and garderobe

from c.1196 to 1240. The castle is surrounded by rock-cut ditches, and is protected on all sides by its fine position. The first building was a rectangular great tower, Welsh-built on Norman lines, about 44ft by 31ft, with its entrance at the first floor, and the approach to it covered by a forebuilding which had a drawbridge over a pit inside to deflect direct assault on the tower door. At first the tower was two-storeyed, and its third storey, battlements and new roofline are later works. The castle rock was skirted by a stone curtain whose two arms projected from either end of the great tower (northeast and south-west) along to two ends of a second rectangular tower which was of later date, c.1270, which was also two-storeyed, and about 50ft by 30ft, using part of the north and west curtain as two of its four walls.

Dolwyddelan was captured by the English in January 1283, after the death of Llywelyn the Last, and it was maintained.

DRYSLWYN Dyfed
(SN 554203) O
Dryslwyn was a Welsh-built castle of

uncertain origin, probably twelfth century. It stood on an isolated hill where there may have been an early Celtic hill-fort. A large earthwork enclosure contained three stonework enclosures in line, with the hall and chapel in the central one. There is little left to see.

The castle figured in an interesting siege in 1287. The holder, Rhys ap Maredudd, rose against the new English dominion in Carmarthenshire. Edward I responded by besieging the castle. One detachment led by Lord Stafford dug a tunnel in the hope of coming up under one of the towers, but the earth collapsed. Most of the detachment, including Lord Stafford, were asphyxiated. Some of those behind, however, dug through the fallen earth and eventually gained access to the chapel.

DYSERTH Clwyd
(SJ 060799) P
A castle was built near the present structure (which is not part of this Gazetteer) in c.1241–2 by the English. It had two baileys, the outer one with masonry for part of its circumference, the inner completely

350

Dolwyddelan: the rectangular great tower was probably raised by Owain Gwynedd, Prince of Wales

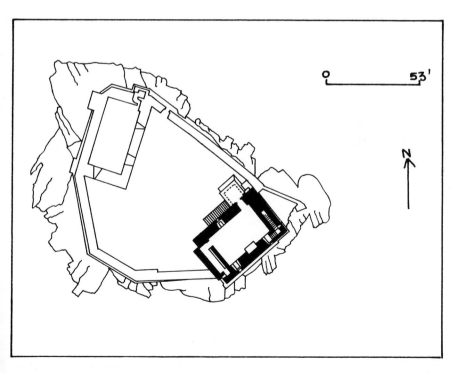

Dolwyddelan: the great tower at right was raised in the twelfth century. The remainder of the enclosure is thirteenth century

351

Ewloe: the great tower, known as the Welsh Tower, has an apsidal end at the east. The approach was via an exterior flight of steps which may have been protected by a screen

enclosed in stone, set well back from its moat. A twin-towered gatehouse and two further polygonal towers were inserted. The site was on rock near the church. It commanded an approach to the Vale of Clwyd. It was besieged by David ap Llywelyn, Prince of all Wales (1240–6), in 1245. It was captured in 1263 by David's nephew, Llywelyn the Last, Prince of all Wales (c.1246–82), who demolished it so thoroughly that 'not one stone was left upon another' (*Annales Cambriae*, cited by *The History of the King's Works*). The ruins have been used as a quarry, and practically nothing remains.

EWLOE Nr Hawarden, Clwyd   †
(SJ 288675) WO

A possible motte castle raised by Owain Gwynedd, Prince of all Wales (1137–70), in c.1150, which was converted to a stone castle in the very early 1200s by Llywelyn the Great. The earliest building was probably the substantial two-storeyed, D-shaped great tower, known as the Welsh Tower. This stands in the eastern (upper level) bailey of a two-bailey enclosure surrounded by extensive earthworks. The

tower had a forebuilding along its south wall. The inner bailey was partly enclosed by a stone curtain. The outer (lower) bailey, polygonal in plan with stone curtain, had a cylindrical two-storeyed West Tower at the extreme west end on a boss of rock. This outer work was probably by Llywelyn the Last, in the late 1250s. The castle is set upon a slope.

FLINT Clwyd   ††
(SJ 247733) WO

Flint was the first of the Edwardian castles to be built in Wales during the king's campaign there of 1277. It was planned, like Rhuddlan of the same time, to be associated with a fortified town nearby, and like Rhuddlan, it was given direct access to tidal waters, in this case the estuary of the Dee. It was not concentric — it really had no need to be: the basic part of it, a roughly rectangular stone enclosure with three substantial cylindrical corner towers, and on the fourth corner (separated by its own moat) a huge cylindrical great tower, was protected by the waters of the Dee. The south wall of the enclosure was also protected by a moat, in front of which

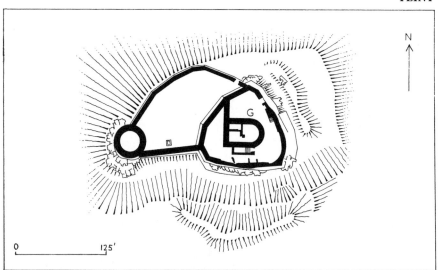

(above) Ewloe: plan of castle as it was c.1260. G = great tower, of c.1210. The enclosure and the cylindrical tower at left were built in the 1250s

(below) Flint: the remains of the great tower. The open space visible in the centre is the cylindrical room of the lower level

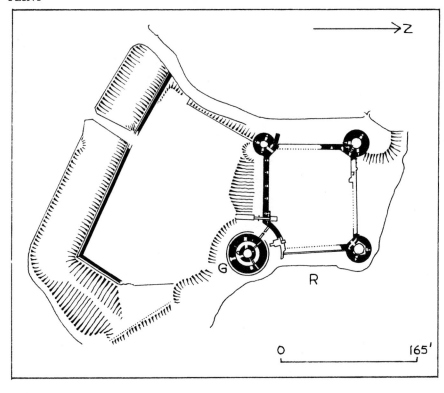

Flint: R = line of River Dee; G = great tower, with its own moat

was a walled outer bailey and beyond that a second and very large moat fed from the Dee.

The inner enclosure's three towers were placed on the corners, built into them, and where the segments of the cylinders 'fed' into the walls, the walls were mitred off for additional strength. The dominating feature of the castle, however, was the great tower. Cylindrical in plan, it was unusual. Its basement was a centre room around which was walling. On the other side of the wall was a circular wall gallery inside the outer wall; that is, the tower was concentric. Above the basement for two more storeys, the gallery space was partitioned off and provided with mural chambers and apartments. The centre core, however, remained hollow and changed from cylindrical to polygonal, was open to the sky and thus provided light for the rooms through indoor openings. There is doubt as to whether the

space in the centre core was used for rooms. Certainly the mural chambers included a chapel, kitchen, garderobes, residential rooms. This arrangement would in fact have made the tower somewhat cramped for prolonged residence, and it has been suggested that the tower was used for short stays, possibly as judge's lodgings.

If proof were needed that great towers had not gone out of fashion, Flint's great donjon is splendid evidence.

The work on Flint Castle was spread mainly over the nine years 1277–86, and cost a little over £6,000. The castle was involved in the Civil War when it changed hands several times, surrendering finally to Parliament in 1646. It was slighted so thoroughly that, as an eye witness stated six years afterwards, it was 'almost buried in its own ruins'. But there is enough left to see the general plan of the castle, notably of the great tower.

FONMON Penmark, South Glamorgan
(ST 047681)
Founded in c.1200, this was a stonework structure with two round towers and one square tower (presumably) flanking a stone curtain. The buildings were subsequently absorbed into a later seventeenth-century mansion. It was further modified in the eighteenth century. The square tower may have been a residential great tower.

GARN FADRYN Gwynedd
(SH 278352) A
A small fort inside an Iron Age fort, probably built c.1190.

GROSMONT Gwent   †
(SO 405244) WO
This is a very interestingly planned castle on the border between Wales and England. It is a compact enclosure of stone surrounded by a moat. It contained a rectangular hall tower, with a gatehouse building at the south-east corner and a rectangular building with D-ended tower at its west end at the north-west corner. A stone curtain with two semi-cylindrical flanking towers formed an arc to complete the enclosure. The earliest structure was the hall tower, built in c.1210, upon the site of an earlier earthwork castle,

probably of the end of the eleventh century. The hall is 96ft by 32ft, with pilaster buttresses on the corners and on three walls. It is likely that the great hall on the first floor was one long room, though there could have been a solar partitioned at one end. The gatehouse and the four-storeyed cylindrical towers are of c.1220–40, and were partly the work of Hubert de Burgh who held Grosmont. The gatehouse was three-storeyed with a very large passage about 16ft wide and 42ft long and it had a drawbridge out front. The northern building between the hall tower and the D-ended tower was raised in the fourteenth century.

Grosmont was attacked by the Welsh in a night raid in 1233, and it was besieged by Owain Glyndŵr in 1405.

HARLECH Gwynedd   ††
(SH 581312) WO
The second phase of Edward I's monumental fortress construction programme in the newly conquered Wales (in the 1280s) embraced four of the biggest castles in all Britain — Beaumaris, Caernarvon, Conwy and Harlech. Two of these, Beaumaris and Harlech, are concentric. While the former took over thirty-five years to build and was never finished, Harlech was

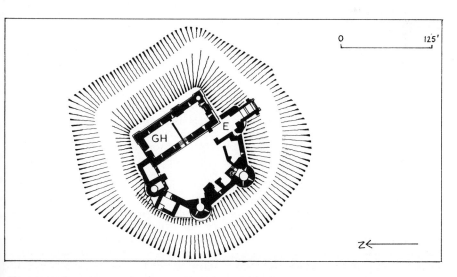

Grosmont: plan of buildings of the two main periods. GH = great hall with solar etc of c.1210; E = gatehouse of c.1220–40. Most of remaining curtain and angle towers are also c.1220–40

355

completed inside seven years, 1283–90. It rose up, a majestic, towering, white-grey edifice that cast, and still casts today, its shadow over the countryside for miles around, clearly visible across Tremadoc Bay at Criccieth, where an earlier Welsh castle was being modernized by the English at the same time.

Costing about £9,000 (nearly £2 million today), Harlech was designed and personally supervised by Master James of St George. It was one of his most splendid creations, and from 1290 to 1293 he was its constable, a well-paid job that gave him status as well as the time to superintend the other castles being built to his overall design, notably Beaumaris and Caernarvon. Harlech's design was relatively simple, and yet immensely formidable: an inner trapezium of high curtain with huge cylindrical towers on the corners and buildings ranged round the inside including a great hall, is surrounded by an outer and much lower wall enclosing a fighting platform. The south and east sides of the castle are further protected by a deep moat cut into the rock on which the castle stands, while the west side is sheer rock cliff

sloping to the sea of Tremadoc Bay (now marsh and dune, for the sea has receded) and the north is protected by a mass of rock obstacles. At the extreme north end of the west side are the remains of the sea gate. Along the stretch of rock in front of the outer west wall are traces of specially cut artificial platforms for siege engines. Along the north outer wall is a twin-cylinder turreted postern. On the eastern side there is an outer gateway (incomplete) which let out over a bridge (now a causeway) across the moat.

The dominant structure in the castle is the gatehouse, set in the east inner wall. This is a massive oblong great-tower-like structure, 80ft by 54ft, three-storeyed, with twin cylindrical towers out front that flank the entrance passage which was once further guarded by three portcullises and three sets of doors. The structure also projects inwards into the inner bailey, with two more cylindrical towers, one placed at each end of the west wall, both containing spiral staircases leading to the fine residential apartment suites above. The gatehouse walls were 9–12ft thick, equipped with arrow loops, and the passage has murder-holes in the ceiling, though as likely as not these were intended for drenching the wooden doors if they were set alight by intruders. Harlech's seeming impregnability was tested in 1294, when it was attacked by Welsh patriots led by Prince Madog ap Llywelyn, whose forces had wreaked great destruction at Caernarvon (q.v.). Thirty-seven men stationed along the parapets of the lower wall and the wall-walks of the inner curtain successfully beat off the Welsh assault. Then, unaccountably, this magnificent fortress was allowed to decay to an alarming extent. There were some repairs and modifications, but in the mid-fourteenth century phrases like 'weak and ruinous' were already being used to describe parts of it.

In the early 1400s, Owain Glyndŵr surrounded the castle and settled down to invest it. The structure proved too strong to take by storm, so the great Welshman decided to starve the garrison into surrender. For many months his forces controlled every road to the castle and watched every entrance. Inside, provisions began to run out, and there was no chance of revictualling, not even by sea, one of the main reasons for it having been sited on the coast in the first place. Then disease broke out and some of the defenders tried to escape across the countryside, presumably towards England, but they were caught and put to death. Finally, Owain himself came to the castle gate and demanded surrender, and the garrison filed out.

Owain moved in with his family and set up his headquarters. He may have held a second Parliament of Welshmen (the first had been at Machynlleth), and for four years he managed his remarkable campaign to free Wales from English rule. Then, in 1409, the English King, Henry IV, sent a strong force under Gilbert Talbot against Harlech and a short siege forced the Welsh to yield. Among those taken were Owain's wife and four children, but the elusive leader had already slipped away. The fall of Harlech marked the end of his career.

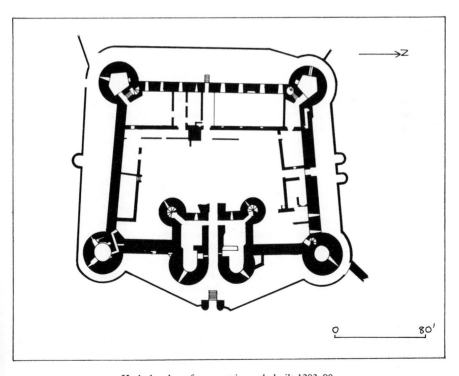

Harlech: plan of concentric castle built 1283–90

357

HAVERFORDWEST Dyfed   †
(SM 953157) O
Strategically placed upon a ridge about 80ft above the River Cleddau in the town of Haverfordwest, this castle has two enclosures. The inner enclosure contained two towers, one of which was residential, and so is classed as a great tower. This has an unusual plan. The stonework is local gritstone called Boulston, and some Nolton sandstone was also used, for dressings.

The castle may have begun as a stone structure, for no earthworks are in evidence. The dating is possibly early twelfth century for the beginnings. The curtain wall of probably late twelfth or early thirteenth century was 12ft wide, which is extraordinarily thick. The castle was attacked by Owain Glyndŵr, whose army was assisted by a force of some 3,000 Frenchmen, but the garrison held out.

HAWARDEN Clwyd
(SJ 319653) O
Hawarden was one of the four lordship castles (see chapter 9) in north Wales built or fortified at the instigation of Edward I (but at the lord's expense!) in the years leading up to the conquest of north Wales (c.1277–82). It had begun as a motte castle with two ditches, which received stonework in the early thirteenth century, and this earlier work included a cylindrical great tower on the motte, a hall and a simple curtain round the bailey. A small round tower was added as part of the Edwardian improvement, and a complex barbican in the fourteenth century.

Hawarden was besieged and taken in 1282 by Dafydd, brother of Llywelyn the Last, but when the latter was captured and executed, the castle was returned. In the Civil War, Hawarden was held for Charles I, fell to Parliament, was retaken by Royalists and taken again by Parliament. It was slighted by Cromwell in 1647–8. The castle is near the mansion known as Hawarden, the home of W.E. Gladstone, the Victorian Liberal Prime Minister.

HAY-ON-WYE Powys   †
(SO 229423) Partly A
There are two earthwork sites close to one another at this site, one a motte and one an enclosure. There is confusion over the two

until the thirteenth century. The enclosure castle was fortified in stone in the thirteenth-century with a curtain wall, a square tower (which may be sixteenth century) and a gateway. The castle changed hands between Welsh and English several times during the thirteenth century. From 1380 to 1421 it belonged to the House of Lancaster.

HEN DOMEN Powys   †
(SO 214980) A
The subject of considerable excavation in recent years, Hen Domen was a motte castle raised in the period 1070–4, probably by Robert of Montgomery, one of William the Conqueror's principal commanders who was given large tracts of land in Herefordshire, Worcestershire and the Severn area, and who led the invasion of central Wales. Hen Domen is a motte astride the line of its oval bailey. There was a wooden palisade around the base of the motte as well as a ditch. The motte was built by ramming down layers of earth and rubble dug from the surrounding ditch, the standard procedure for motte castles graphically illustrated in the picture of the building of Hastings Motte on the Bayeux Tapestry. Hen Domen has a double ditch around the castle, as at Berkhamsted. Access from the bailey to the motte top was by a flying wooden bridge stepped at intervals. Traces of further buildings were found. Hen Domen was also known as Old Montgomery (see p. 365).

HOLT Clwyd
(SJ 412537) A
There is little to see of this lordship castle built on the bank of the River Dee soon after 1282 by John de Warenne, Earl of Surrey, on land granted to him by Edward I. It was a single enclosure castle, roughly pentagonal in shape, with flanking round towers and with buildings against the sides of the curtain. It is probable that Warenne had the services of Master James of St George as building consultant. The castle was demolished in the late seventeenth century and the stonework was used in the construction of Eaton Hall in Cheshire.

HOLYWELL Clwyd
(SJ 186762)
A small motte castle was raised here in the

Hen Domen: known also as Old Montgomery, this motte castle of the eleventh century may have been used as an outpost for the new Montgomery Castle after the mid-thirteenth century

early thirteenth century. It is known as Castle Hill.

HUMPHREY'S Nr Llandyssul, Dyfed (SN 440477)
A motte castle of c.1110 founded by one Humphrey, a follower of Gilbert de Clare. It was raised on a spur of land in the Teifi Valley. The castle was destroyed by the Welsh c.1137 and rebuilt in 1151. It is alternatively called Castell Humphrey.

KENFIG Nr Port Talbot, Mid †
Glamorgan (SS 801827) A
Kenfig is an example in Wales of the variation on a motte castle found at Aldingbourne and Lydford in England, where the earth is heaped up round the basement storey of a great tower. This castle is at low level by the river. The great tower was built of local rubble with Sutton ashlar quoins, its basement having a vaulted ceiling, the basic dimensions of the tower being 46ft by 44ft

with walls about 11ft thick. The tower stood on a splayed plinth under the earth mould. The date is uncertain but was probably late twelfth century. The tower was enclosed by a narrow curtain wall. There was also an outer enclosure (or bailey), likewise walled with a gatehouse and this may have been of the thirteenth century.

Kenfig was attacked in 1232, and it was burned, possibly as the result of hostilities, in 1295. It is now in ruins.

KIDWELLY Dyfed ††
(SN 409070) WO
This well-preserved, almost concentric castle stands on a bluff beside the estuary of the Gwendraeth Fach River. Before any stonework was raised, Kidwelly had been an extensive Norman earthwork castle of c.1106, which consisted of a banked, roughly oblong site surrounded by ditching, with an oval site in the centre (which may have contained a motte) along the edge of the

359

Kidwelly: an aerial view of this interesting concentric-plan castle. Note powerful gatehouse at south end

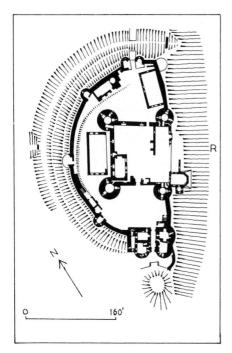

Kidwelly: the inner quadrangle is c.1275. The outer curtain, towers, gatehouses are predominantly early fourteenth century. R = Gwendraeth Fach River

scarp facing the river. The present town of Kidwelly spreads over into the original Norman earthworks, and is part walled from medieval times. There is a record that the castle was captured and burnt by the Welsh in 1215. It was attacked again in 1257 but not taken.

The first stonework is of the 1270s and consisted of an enclosure of a square curtain with cylindrical towers on the four corners. The towers had very thick walls. The south-west tower has five storeys. Adjoining this is a slightly later semi-octagonal chapel supported on a spur base, which is built into the slope of the bluff. The north-east tower flanked a postern which had gate and portcullis. The enclosure was surrounded on three sides by a second stone enclosure curtain with flanking half cylindrical towers, and at each end (north-east and south-west) is a gatehouse. This work, making the castle concentric on three sides, was carried out in the fourteenth century. The south-west gatehouse is substantial, of three storeys, with semi-cylindrical towers flanking the entrance. The south-east wall of the gatehouse bulges outwards to cover attack from the river and up the scarp. The gatehouse had spacious accommodation on the first floor.

Kidwelly was attacked by Owain Glyndŵr in the period 1403–7, when one of the gatehouses was burned.

KNIGHTON Powys
(SO 284722)
There are two early motte castle sites at Knighton, one in the town near the church, the other a quarter mile or so away near the river (SO 290722). The first named is thought to have lasted until the 1260s when it was captured, probably by the Welsh.

KNUCKLAS Beguildy, Powys †
(SO 250746)
A castle on a hill-site that was probably a hill-fort in much earlier times (Iron Age?), the principal medieval remains are a small square stone block with what appear to be round corner turrets, of about the thirteenth century.

LAMPETER Dyfed
(SN 579482)
Otherwise known as Llan Ystyffan, a motte castle was raised in what are now the grounds of St David's College, Lampeter. It was a Norman castle and was destroyed in 1136.

LAUGHARNE Dyfed †
(SN 302107) O
A castle of unknown shape was built here in the twelfth century. Subsequently, rebuilding took place, probably in the thirteenth century, and this included a cylindrical great tower, another tower and a gatehouse which may have been fourteenth century. There were two baileys, and the inner bailey was converted into a mansion in the sixteenth century by Sir John Perrott. The remaining medieval gatehouse is an interesting structure, four storeys tall, containing

Laugharne: the remains of the Tudor-period alterations to the thirteenth-century castle

an entrance arch of Perpendicular style which was probably added in the sixteenth century. The cylindrical tower has its battlements.

LLANBLETHIAN South Glamorgan
(SS 989742) O

Otherwise called St Quentin's Castle, this was a late thirteenth- or early fourteenth-century stone enclosure with flanking towers, one square, two cylindrical and a fine twin-towered gatehouse (now the principal feature of the remains of the castle). There appears to have been a great tower in the centre of the enclosure of early fourteenth-century or possibly late thirteenth-century date. Discovery of traces of a great tower of such date adds to the already considerable weight of evidence that great towers remained a feature of fortification or residence in British castles during the Middle Ages (see chapter 4).

LLANDAFF South Glamorgan
(ST 156780) C

A small, irregular, quadrilateral plan castle, of stone curtain with flanking towers and good gatehouse. Two towers (one square, one cylindrical) remain. Llandaff was a bishopric castle, and it is said to have been destroyed by Owain Glyndŵr in c.1402. It was modified in later centuries — for example mullioned and transomed windows were inserted at first-floor level in the western tower of the gatehouse in the late sixteenth century.

LLANDEILO TALYBONT West
Glamorgan   (SN 587027) A

A motte castle was raised here in the twelfth century near the river.

LLANDOVERY Dyfed †
(SN 767342) O

In the grounds of the Castle Hotel stand the remains of the castle founded by the Norman lord, Richard Fitzpons, in the early twelfth century. It was taken by the Welsh in 1116 and recovered by the family in c.1158, when it was strengthened. It changed hands several times up to the reign of Edward I of England. Llandovery began as a motte castle. Stonework was added in the twelfth century, including a D-end tower of some strength and a gatehouse.

LLANELLI Dyfed
(SN 501004)

Alternatively known as Carnwillion Castle, this motte castle has been almost submerged in the reservoir at Llanelli.

LLANFAIR DISCOED Caerwent,
Gwent   (ST 445924) A

A small square-plan enclosure with curtain, two cylindrical turrets and part of a square-plan gatehouse of the mid-thirteenth century. The castle has been added to in later years which has obscured much of the original work. No recorded history has yet been found.

LLANGADOG Dyfed
(SN 709276) A

A motte castle, 30ft tall, with a narrow ditch, was raised here in the twelfth century. The bailey is horseshoe-shaped, at one time bordered on one side of the River Sawdde. The castle was taken by the Welsh c.1209.

LLANGIBBY Llangybi Fawr, Gwent
(ST 364974) O

Also known as Tregrug Castle, and which is the subject of investigation and excavation at present, Llangibby stands on a high site and was only one single huge enclosure with a large gatehouse and a rectangular great tower. There were also four turrets on the walls, and a second (smaller) gateway. The castle was built in the fourteenth century. There are also references to an earlier earthwork structure at ST 369973 nearby.

LLANGWYNYD Mid Glamorgan
(SS 852887) P

A small castle of the (?) thirteenth century that may have been Welsh built. Traces of twin-towered gatehouse have been found.

LLANQUIAN South Glamorgan
(ST 019744)

There was once a stone revetted mound here. History unknown.

LLANSTEPHAN Dyfed ††
(SN 352102) WO

Llanstephan Castle was a double enclosure, the inner being in the north-east corner of the outer. The inner enclosure, or ward, was the first structure, a simple irregular polygon of stone with a gate-tower at the south-west, the whole standing on a ridge with all but one of its sides protected by natural scarping. The remaining side was given a ditch for protection. This early work was chiefly twelfth century, with early and mid-thirteenth-century completion. The outer enclosure was protected by a double ditch, which is earlier than the stonework. The enclosure was fortified with a stone curtain in the thirteenth century with flanking towers and a bastion at the eastern corner. Sometime in the late thirteenth century, the great gatehouse was erected in the southern side of the enclosure wall. It is a typical gatehouse of the later thirteenth century, not unlike Tonbridge, and much of it stands today. The gatehouse was later blocked at its entrance (in the last years of the fifteenth century) to convert the building into a residence.

Llanstephan was captured by Owain Glyndŵr in the early fifteenth century.

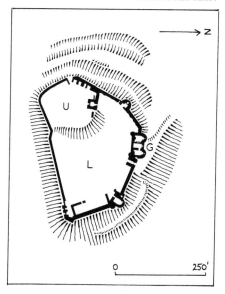

(above) Llanstephan: the curtain of the upper bailey (U) is end of twelfth century. The curtain of the lower bailey (L) with its towers is mainly thirteenth century. The gatehouse (G) is c.1280 and is similar to Tonbridge, Harlech, St Briavels, *inter alia*

(below) Llanstephan: the great gatehouse-tower, built in c.1280, became a residential as well as military building. This picture was taken before the latest restoration work by the Welsh Office, which included removal of the dense foliage

LLANTRISANT Gwent
(ST 047834) C

The origins of this castle appear to go back to the early thirteenth century, when it was constructed having two baileys, the inner smaller than the outer. The inner bailey contains fragments of wall and of a large cylindrical great tower thought to be mid-thirteenth-century construction. The fragments of the cylindrical flanking tower on the curtain wall suggest that the curtain had been a tall one.

LLAWHADEN Nr Narberth, Dyfed   †
(SN 073174) WO

Llawhaden was a fortified palace built by the bishops of St Davids. It was originally an earthwork enclosure of the twelfth century, about 150ft in diameter and surrounded by a dry moat, 70ft wide, and a bank. It was destroyed in c.1192 by Lord Rhys, satrap ruler of south-west Wales, and demolished. Soon afterwards, stonework was raised. This included a small cylindrical tower, 28ft in diameter, and a curtained wall, of irregular shape, but following the line of the earlier earthwork. This may have been done by the bishop of St Davids of the time. In the 1280s, Bishop Thomas Bek converted the castle into a palace, obliterating much of the earlier work, though there are remains of the cylindrical tower and traces of the curtain. The new work produced a courtyard surrounded by ranges of buildings, with two polygonal towers on two angles, and a gatehouse was erected in the late fourteenth century, the façade of which still stands to its full height.

LOUGHOR West Glamorgan   †
(SS 564980) A

Loughor consists today of a tower projecting from a curtain wall on a natural mound. The stonework is thirteenth/fourteenth century, raised on the twelfth-century motte castle site originated by the Normans and demolished in c.1150 by the Welsh. The castle was repaired and then demolished again in 1215. The castle is sited over the remains of a Roman fort.

LYCHEWEIN Dyfed
(SN 578148)

A castle at Lychewein was destroyed in 1206.

Manorbier: an aerial view of the enclosure castle with towers which was once the home of Giraldus Cambrensis

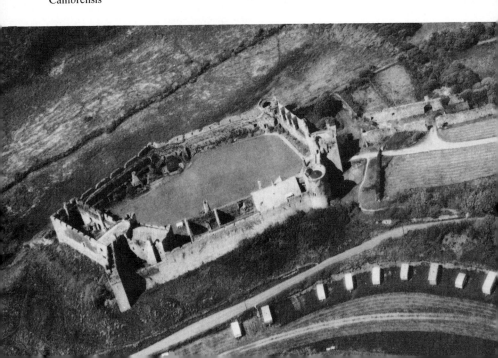

MACHEN Gwent
(ST 226887) P
A Welsh castle built in the thirteenth
century on a rocky ridge, of which little
remains. It had a cylindrical tower. The site
is in the neighbourhood of ancient lead
mines used by the Romans.

MANORBIER Nr Tenby, Dyfed   ††
(SS 064978) O
This was the birthplace in 1146 of Giraldus
Cambrensis (Gerald of Wales), the celebrated Welsh scholar who served Henry II,
Richard I and John. The castle began as an
earthwork of the late eleventh century, and
in the twelfth century it received a square
great tower of three storeys, with entrance at
first floor. Other stone buildings were
added, including a hall block, and by the
thirteenth century it consisted of two high
stone curtain enclosures in line, with
flanking towers (cylindrical in the case of the
outer enclosure), and with a strong square
gatehouse which may not have been completed until well into the thirteenth century.
The castle well was sunk to 30ft. Giraldus
described the castle as 'excellently well
defended by turrets and bulwarks'. Manorbier's residential features were pronounced, notably the state apartments in the
inner enclosure, the fish-pond and the park.
The castle is superbly sited on the coast, and
is in a remarkable state of preservation.

MEURIG Gwnnws Issa, Dyfed
(SN 702675) P
Also known as Castell Ystrad-Meurig, this is
one of the few Cardigan castles to have been
refortified with stone buildings and defences. The principal structure was a
substantial rectangular great tower, possibly 60ft square, date unknown but possibly
late twelfth century. There is a record of the
castle being destroyed in c.1208, but as there
are two castle sites in the neighbourhood, it
is not clear if the 1208 date refers to this great
tower. Only fragments remain.

MOLD Clwyd
(SJ 235644) A
A late motte castle which retained its
earthwork and timber structures right into
the thirteenth century.

MONMOUTH Gwent   †
(SO 507129) WO
An earthwork enclosure castle was built
here in the period 1067–71, probably by
William FitzOsbern. It stands on a bluff
overlooking the Wye and Monnow rivers. In
c.1120–30, a rectangular two-storey hall
tower like that at Chepstow was raised on the
motte, with a west wall over 10ft thick, and it
was built of sandstone rubble with ashlar
dressings. The tower has pilaster buttresses
and stands on a splayed plinth. A length of
curtain wall projected south-eastwards from
the south wall and this later became part of a
rectangular great hall, built c.1270.

The castle came into royal possession in
1399 when its owner, Henry Bolingbroke,
became Henry IV. Twelve years earlier, his
son, Henry of Monmouth (later Henry V
who was to win glory at Agincourt and
elsewhere in the early fifteenth century) had
been born in the castle gatehouse. The castle
was slighted at the end of the Civil War,
when the Round Tower, said to have stood
on the motte, was demolished.

MONTGOMERY Powys
(SO 221968) WO
This was a stone double enclosure castle
begun in the 1220s. It superseded Old
Montgomery Castle, known as Hen Domen
(p.358), an eleventh-century motte castle
that may have been used later as an outpost
for the new structure.

Montgomery was built upon a promontory of greenstone (limestone) running
roughly north to south, the northern end
protected by sheer rock cliffs. The first work
in stone was the inner ward at the north end,
raised between 1224 and 1235, and it
featured a D-ended flanking tower at north
and at south a twin-cylindrical towered
gatehouse whose later parts were solid. A
large D-ended tower projecting out of the
western wall, in which the castle well was
situated, was added sometime between 1280
and 1350. Various buildings were put up
within this enclosure in the fourteenth
century and in Tudor times.

At about the same time as the inner
enclosure was begun, a second enclosure of
wood was built adjoining the southern side.
This is the middle ward and it was separated

(above) Montgomery: the remnants of the thirteenth-century castle seen from the air before excavations began in 1963. (below) Excavations on the promontory exposed the two main enclosures (in line) separated by the west-east ditch

by a ditch cut from west to east which was crossed by a bridge from the south gatehouse of the inner ward. This second ward was converted to stone probably in the mid-thirteenth century, for there was added to it a twin-towered gatehouse of stone at the southern extremity which is dated to c.1250. The curtain walls were thick and were flanked by rounded turrets. Outside the south gatehouse was a rock-cut ditch which was crossed by a timber causeway. Evidence of the causeway was discovered in very recent excavation work.

The castle was slighted after the Civil War. It had belonged to the Herbert family who had erected a house within the enclosure, and this too was demolished. By the 1960s the ruins of Montgomery were almost entirely covered with earth and scrub. Then a major scheme of excavation was begun by the then Ministry of Works. By 1973 the two enclosures and various adjoinments had been revealed. Excavations are still in progress (see pictures of castle before 1963 and after 1973).

MORGRAIG South Glamorgan
(ST 160843) P
An irregular hexagonal curtain with horseshoe-shaped towers on four corners, nothing on the fifth, and one side of a large rectangular tower making up the bulk of the sixth side, built of local sandstone and limestone rubble, with limestone dressings. Built on an east-west ridge that was artificially enlarged to accommodate it, Morgraig was never completed and was probably allowed to decay as early as the mid-thirteenth century. Morgraig was a Welsh-built castle.

MORLAIS Merthyr Tydfil, Mid Glamorgan   (SO 048097) A
This was a thirteenth-century castle raised probably in the time of Edward I after his final conquest of Wales (1282–3). It appears to have been the cause of friction between two lords for it lay on a common boundary between their lands. Morlais contained a cylindrical great tower, a curtain enclosure with probably four flanking turrets, and extensive ditching. The ruins overlook the Taff Gorge. It is thought to have been begun by Gilbert de Clare, constructor of Caerphilly (among others).

NANTCRIBBA Powys   †
(SJ 237014) A
Traces of a stone curtain and towers, surrounded by a moat.

NARBERTH Dyfed
(SN 110144) P
This castle was a stone enclosure on a ridge at the south end of the town. It contained a cylindrical great tower, and the ruins of four out of five original round flanking towers can be seen. The stone castle was built in the thirteenth century, near the site of a Norman motte castle of c.1100, which had been destroyed by the Welsh in 1116.

NEATH West Glamorgan
(SS 753977) Exterior open
There was a motte castle here, of which no trace remains, founded by the Norman knight, Richard de Granville, c.1130. Nearby, in the 1180s, another motte castle was raised in a bend of the river which supplied the ditch with water, and which could isolate the motte from attackers. In the thirteenth century the motte was revetted with stonework and two towers were built on the north side towards the river. The existing wall round Neath town was brought within the castle grounds by enclosing it with a curtain. Between the western tower and the town wall a strong outer gatehouse was constructed, and about 4 yards of its staircase can be seen.

Neath was attacked in 1231 and 1258, and captured in 1321 and the buildings levelled. The whole castle was then remodelled and new buildings erected on a level about 2ft higher than earlier main ground level. The original round towers were modified to D-end towers.

NEWCASTLE Bridgend,   †
Mid Glamorgan   (SS 902801) WO
A stone enclosure castle of the mid-to-late twelfth century raised against a steep spur overlooking the Ogmore River, probably upon the site of an earlier earthwork castle of c.1106. The plan is polygonal of nine unequal sides, with two almost square-plan towers in the curtain, one at the west angle, one at the south. The second tower is nearly 30ft square and could be called a great tower, for it was residential (fireplaces, windows,

Newport: the centre tower in the frontage onto the river contains a hall above and the water-gate (see plan above) below. Small ships could enter the gateway at high tide

staircases) and rose to three storeys. But there were also other buildings in the enclosure for residential purposes. The entrance to the enclosure was adjacent to the south tower, through an elaborately decorated round-headed arch. The angles of the sides in the curtain have ashlar quoins.

NEWCASTLE EMLYN Dyfed †
(SN 311407) A

A fine site overlooking the Teifi River in this picturesque town, Newcastle Emlyn was raised as a quadrangle in the 1240s by the Welsh. The twin-polygonal towered gatehouse ruin is Welsh, but the second polygonal tower is thought to have been English built. The castle changed hands several times in the 1281–3 war between England and Wales. It was also held for Charles I in the Civil War but was captured and blown up.

NEWPORT Dyfed
(SN 057389) C

A castle built in the early thirteenth century, on a natural mound with a moat cut round it, Newport now has only ruins. A few traces of the curtain may be seen and the remains of three towers and a twin-towered gatehouse (of later date). The present mansion, of nineteenth-century origin, absorbed these medieval remains. There is a surviving dungeon of the thirteenth century.

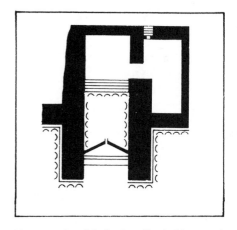

Newport: plan of the 'harbour' level of the central water gate tower at Newport. The double gates could be closed at low tide and thus keep out the rising river level

NEWPORT Gwent ††
(ST 312884) WO

A castle here is referred to as the new castle on the Usk by the Chronicler of the *Brut y Tywysogyon* for the year 1172. What is left at Newport today, however, is part of a later castle consisting of a long curtain wall facing the Usk, with three towers, the curtain once having been part of a quadrangle. The centre tower is a square gate-tower with an arched entrance. The river came up to this gate giving access to the castle: in other words, we have a specially designed water-gate that allowed the river to come into the ground floor of the tower at high tide, making a pool in which boats could draw up alongside a quay at the rear of the tower. The arch to the gateway had two strong portcullises. There was a chapel in the top of the gateway. Presumably the portcullises lifted up into the chapel (see Tonbridge). Flank-ing this gateway on either side are two polygonal towers in the curtain, supported on spur bases. There was a hall in the range between the gateway and the north polygon-al tower. There are remains of other parts, including some walling of the remainder of the quadrangle. Most of the building work is of the fifteenth century, much of it remod-elling of the earlier stonework which was probably mid-thirteenth century.

OGMORE Nr Bridgend, †
Mid Glamorgan (SS 882769) WO
Ogmore Castle is a stone-walled enclosure on an earlier earthwork site of c.1110, on the edge of the Ewenny River. It is entirely surrounded by a moat except for the north side which is bound by the river, and it guards an important ford, in which a unique

row of stepping stones leads from the outer bailey across the river. The earliest stone building was the rectangular great tower of the late twelfth century, constructed of boulders in brown mortar with roughly hewn quoins at the lower end, and better ashlar higher up. It was three storeys tall, with 6ft thick walls and measured about 44ft by 32ft, and was reached by an exposed staircase on the east side to the first floor. A gateway was built next to the great tower in the thirteenth century. Opposite the great tower was built, also in the twelfth century, a rectangular building with one storey, a kind of cellar, but its use is not clear. In the thirteenth century, the old earthwork ram-part line was roughly followed by the erection of a stone curtain to form a polygonal enclosure. At the north end of this was built a long rectangular two-storeyed hall with a solar. There were other buildings in the enclosure, and some in the outer bailey, including a court house of the fourteenth century.

OLD BEAUPRE Nr Cowbridge, †
South Glamorgan (ST 009721) WO
This castle is an Elizabethan quadrangular mansion (with extension at the south-east),

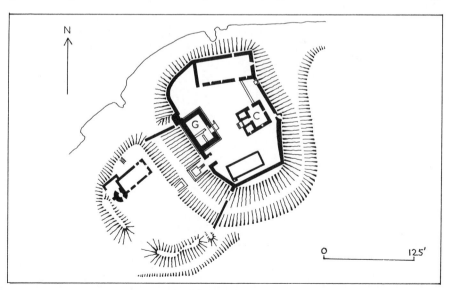

Ogmore: the great tower (G) and the cellar building (C) are twelfth century. The rest of the main enclosure is thirteenth century which incorporates stonework remains of an earlier strucure of the late thirteenth/early fourteenth century. The principal medieval remains include a gatehouse, incorporated in the south wing of the quadrangle and which may have led to other buildings now vanished, other segments of the same wing which are now part of the Elizabethan structure, and a block adjacent to and projecting north along the east wing. The differences in the periods of masonry can best be seen in the medieval gatehouse and the inner porch beside it to the west which is c.1600, where the porch joins the north wall of the south wing.

OXWICH West Glamorgan
(SS 498862)
A sixteenth-century manor house which incorporates fragments of an earlier structure, possibly of late fourteenth- or early fifteenth-century origin.

OYSTERMOUTH Nr Swansea, †
West Glamorgan   (SS 613883)
A castle of c.1099 on a natural rock hill site with bailey beside, overlooking Swansea Bay, was abandoned for a masonry enclosure of later date. The enclosure contained a rectangular tower of the late thirteenth century, and it received a twin-towered gatehouse at the other end. Today, the tower remains, with decorated windows, added in the fourteenth century, adjoining a second rectangular building and an attached gateway, which are in ruins.

PAINSCASTLE Powys †
(SO 167461) P but A
A substantial motte castle, raised in the 1130s by Sir Payn FitzJohn. Fragments of walling on the motte suggest a cylindrical tower, and there are remains of another stone tower in the bailey, work of the rebuilding in c.1230–1. It is recorded as having been captured in 1215.

PEMBROKE Dyfed ††
(SM 982016) O
This was one of the grandest of the earlier castles built in Wales. Its dominating

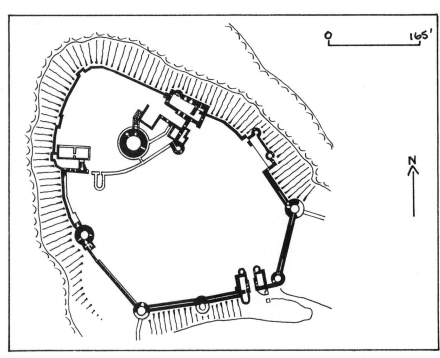

Pembroke: ground plan. Note the cylindrical great tower in upper bailey

Pembroke: the splendid great tower of c.1200, probably built by William the Marshal. The splayed plinth is exceptionally pronounced, as at Conisbrough

feature was, and still is, its cylindrical great tower (built in c.1200–10), massive, four-storeyed, over 53ft in diameter, rising from a splayed plinth to almost 80ft tall, with 15–16ft 6in thick walls (thickest where the spiral staircase ascends), and capped by a remarkable stone dome, over 4ft thick at the top.

Pembroke began as an oval earthwork enclosure erected by Arnulf de Montgomery in the 1090s. The enclosure was divided into two, an inner smaller bailey of triangular plan, two sides of which were cliffs overlooking the Pembroke River. This bailey was given a stone hall of trapezoid shape in the twelfth century and surrounded with stone walls. The third side of the triangle was a substantial curtain wall with flanking towers. The larger outer bailey was enclosed with a stone curtain and several cylindrical corner towers on the angles, plus a substantial twin-rectangular towered gate-house and a powerful postern tower. Part of the southern curtain wall along the outer bailey was of double thickness for extra defence.

The great tower contained no mural chambers. All the storeys were cylindrical inside. The parapet at the top of the fourth storey protected a wall-walk, and on the inside of that was a second wall with parapet top which at one time protected the dome and provided a second fighting platform. This parapet was severely damaged during the Civil War when the castle endured a prolonged siege by Cromwell.

Pembroke was held by William the Marshal who was Earl of Pembroke and one of King John's staunchest allies. It was at Pembroke also that Henry Tudor, later to become King Henry VII, was born in 1456.

PENCADER Llanfihangel-ar-Arth, Dyfed   (SN 445362)
A motte castle of the mid-twelfth century. The motte was 25ft tall.

PENCELLI Powys
(SO 095249) P
A motte castle of which not much is left following the raising of modern farm buildings. The motte was surrounded by a ditch. There are fragments of a tower which appears to have been about 50ft square. In

the thirteenth century it was given a twin-towered gatehouse. It was captured in 1215 and 1234, possibly by Llywelyn the Great.

PENCOED Nr Newport, Gwent
(ST 406894) P
The remains of a thirteenth-century tower and curtain are beside a sixteenth-century mansion.

PENHOW Nr Newport, Gwent   †
(ST 423908) O
Penhow is a small enclosure castle of irregular polygonal plan, with buildings round a tiny courtyard. The principal feature is a rectangular-plan tower, battlemented, three storeys tall, with walls 6ft thick. Its entrance used to be at first-floor level, but a doorway was inserted later in the ground floor. The tower has a mural staircase and two garderobes, one of which was later altered to lead into the great hall. The castle was probably begun in the early thirteenth century by the then holder of the land, Sir William St Maur, a name later

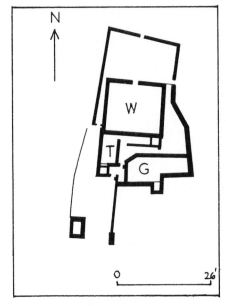

Penhow: late nineteenth-century plan of the castle. G = great hall; T = great tower (twelfth century); W = sixteenth-century wing added

The south-west tower of Pencoed Castle

adapted to Seymour. He was an ancestor of Edward Seymour, brother-in-law of Henry VIII and Protector during the reign of Henry's son, Edward VI. Alterations were carried out in the fifteenth century.

PENLLINE South Glamorgan
(SS 979761) C

Also spelled Penllyn. So little of the twelfth- and thirteenth-century buildings remain that it is difficult to determine its original shape, which is also obscured by a later mansion.

PENMAEN West Glamorgan
(SS 534880) A

Known also as Penmaen Burrows Motte, this was an earthwork enclosure castle which had stone rubble as part of its structure. Traces of a timber gateway have been found, approximately 20ft square. This was burned down and later replaced by an entrance formed by dry stone walls. There was also a timber watch-tower, about 17ft by 12ft, and again replaced by a dry stone structure of larger dimensions.

PENMARK Nr Fonmon, South Glamorgan
(ST 059689) P

A (?) thirteenth-century stone enclosure with cylindrical turrets and an outer bailey. There are a few fragments of wall and towers.

PENNARD West Glamorgan
(SS 544885) A

Occasionally spelt Penard, there was an enclosure of earth and timber on rock which was erected probably in the early twelfth century. Later in the century a stone rectangular hall was raised. The castle was further expanded into an enclosure with towers and gatehouse (probably of late thirteenth century), the buildings being mainly of light construction. It is thought that the stone hall replaced an earlier timber one.

PENRICE West Glamorgan
(SS 497885) O

An enclosure castle of c.1100 where remains of some wooden parts were found in excavations of about half a century ago. This

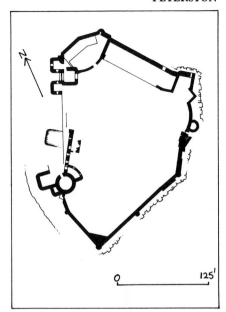

Penrice: plan of the enclosure castle of several periods. The cylindrical great tower at south-west is the oldest structure, of mid-thirteenth century

is sometimes called Old Penrice Castle, and the site is at SS 492879. A second (stone) castle was raised nearby in the mid-thirteenth century at SS 497885 and there are remains of a hall block and enclosure walls with small solid turrets, and a gatehouse of three towers bunched rather like those at Denbigh Castle. Later, a residential complex was built beside an earlier tower and stood as a separate fortified structure on higher ground within the enclosure.

PENTREFOELAS Clwyd
(SH 870522) A

A motte, with some traces of stone wall.

CASTELL PEN-YR-ALLT Dyfed
(SN 158420) P

Small earthwork enclosure, with ditching and some stone fragments.

PETERSTON South Glamorgan
(ST 084764) P

Traces of a square-plan tower.

373

PICTON Dyfed
(SN 011135) P
A motte castle built in the time of William II
(1087–1100) at the top of a stretch of rising
ground, with a (?) bailey to the north. This
was not converted to stone. About 150 years
later, c.mid-thirteenth century, a second
castle was built near the original site, which
presumably had decayed. The new castle
was a quadrangular enclosure with strong
corner towers and mid-wall towers, one of
which guarded the entrance in the east
curtain. The castle is still occupied, but has
been drastically altered over the centuries.

POWIS Nr Welshpool, Powys
(SJ 216064) 0
Powis Castle, today a graceful residence of
towers and battlements, mullioned windows and turrets, compressed together and
standing by the site of a thirteenth-century
castle, belies the original. The latter was
destroyed by Llywelyn the Last in the 1270s
because its owner had taken sides with the
English in the Prince's quarrel with Edward
I. The old castle had two baileys, with a
twin-towered gatehouse which has been
considerably modified.

PRESTATYN Clwyd
(SJ 073833) P
A low-level motte castle with a half-moon
bailey inside a larger rectangular enclosure,
Prestatyn received stonework in the twelfth
century. It was destroyed in 1167.

PRYSOR Gwynedd
(SH 758369) P
A motte castle, the motte partly revetted,
with some stone fragments. No date.

RADNOR Powys
(SO 212610) P
There appear to have been three castles of
some kind at various times in this area. The
reference SO 212610 is of New Radnor, of
which some evidence exists of strong
earthworks of the late twelfth century.
There may have been some stonework.

RAGLAN Gwent   ††
(SO 415083) WO
At first sight the great stone castle at Raglan
looks as if it was one of Edward I's
thirteenth-century fortresses for holding
down the Welsh. In fact it was not built until

the fifteenth century, though it stands on the
site of a Norman motte castle of c.1070, the
great Yellow Tower of Gwent actually
superimposed upon the motte. This early
castle survived, it seems, in some form or
other up to the early 1400s, and included a
lord's hall. In c.1430, the castle became the
property of Sir William ap Thomas, a Welsh
knight who had fought at Agincourt and
presumably made money in the wars in
France. And in the 1430s, Thomas started to
build the castle of unusual design whose
towering ruins still dominate the landscape
around Raglan.

The first building of this period was a
unique hexagonal-plan great tower, whose
foundations and lowest courses of walling
encase the old Norman motte. Known as the
Yellow Tower of Gwent, this interesting
structure has three storeys above the
basement (and had one more before it was
slighted after the Civil War, in 1646). It was
built over the years c.1430–c.1445, given
combined arrow-slit and gun-port openings
at ground-floor level, and was probably
equipped with a boldly projecting machicolated parapet round the top (like the later
gatehouse). The hexagonal tower tapered
outwards slightly from top downwards on
all six sides, and at ground level, the walls
were nearly 10ft thick. Each storey was one
main room, with chambers off where
needed, served by a spiral stair in the
walling. Around the outside of the basement
is the remnant of a low curtain wall, added in
c.1450–60, also hexagonal, with rounded
projecting corners which were turrets with
battlements, whose tops were approximately as tall as the gun-port/arrow-slit openings,
enabling defenders inside the tower to give
protected covering fire to other, more
exposed, defenders behind the battlements.
This tower stood completely surrounded by
its own wide and deep ditch, at first crossed
by means of two drawbridges with elaborate
mechanisms on the north-west face. When
the castle was enlarged in a second building
period, c.1450–69, a great gate was built,
approached from outside the castle, and the
drawbridges were abandoned. A new
approach from the great tower into the
newer parts was constructed in the form of a
three-storey forebuilding which led to a
bridge across the moat, and which joined

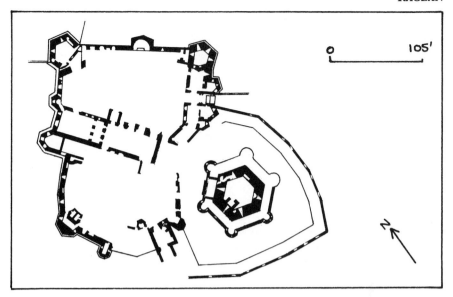

Raglan: outline plan of the castle. Note especially the unique hexagonal great tower (c. 1435-45) at right, sitting in its own moat. Nearly all the work spans from c. 1435 to c. 1525

with the parlour/dining room block on the north-east side of the new works.

These new works may be summarized as buildings round two courtyards, the north-east Pitched Court and the north-west Fountain Court. Incorporated in the new works were some structures of the first period, and the South Gate which was even earlier (see below). The principal building in the Pitched Court is the great gate, a twin-semi-hexagonal towered structure with a well-protected entrance covered by machicolation above, by portcullises and double doors, and gun-ports in the flanking towers. Originally, there was a drawbridge in front of the great gate. Immediately to the north-east is a further polygonal three-storeyed plus basement corner tower, the Closet Tower, built at much the same time, and also machicolated. This tower has fireplaces and garderobes, indicating its residential, in addition to defensive, role. Extending north-westwards from the Closet Tower is an Office Wing with polygonal mid-wall tower and leading to a second polygonal corner tower, the Kitchen Tower. The Office Wing was a more elaborate rebuild in the early sixteenth century upon the site of an earlier wing. The Kitchen Tower was machicolated and had three storeys, the walls of which stand, but the floors have gone. The Kitchen Tower is adjoined by a pantry and buttery range on two sides of an obtuse angle, and the latter leads into the great hall on the opposite side of the courtyard, and parallel with the Office Wing. The hall is the most complete part of the castle to survive, and is of more than one building period, starting in c.1460. The hall was given Tudor-style domestic window cases in the mid-sixteenth century, and the glass was reported to have been stained, with heraldic design. It is basically three-storeyed, and has backing on its south-west side, the remains of the chapel with long gallery above which extended in front of the buttery. The hall adjoined a parlour block on the south-east end, and this block was connected to the forebuilding structure of the great tower.

Fountain Court, so called from the marble fountain that once graced its court-yard, is an approximate rectangle with ranges of apartments along the three sides other than the chapel and long gallery side. In the south corner is the South Gate, an

almost square-plan structure (with a polygonal garderobe turret abutting on its south-east wall), With a bridge which once crossed an arm of the moat round the great tower. From the south outside, it is possible to see the shoot of the garderobe turret into the moat, down at water level. The base of the tower is of masonry that is out of place in relation to the fine quality stonework of the castle, and this is taken by some authorities to suggest that it is the remnant of an earlier stone tower (or gate), presumably of the motte castle period. The gate entrance was once protected by a portcullis and drawbridge.

In the sixteenth century, Raglan became the property of Charles Somerset, 1st Earl of Worcester, whose grandson, William Somerset, 3rd Earl of Worcester, rebuilt the hall and carried out the enlargements in the Pitched Court, including the Office Wing.

During the Civil War, Henry Somerset, 5th Earl of Worcester (later 1st Marquess), sided with the king and defended the castle against a siege by Parliament which began on the 3 June 1646. Worcester was exceedingly wealthy, and he financed the entire defence out of his own pocket, paying the wages of an army of 800 men. The castle endured devastating bombardment from mortar pieces for several weeks. On 19 August, Worcester surrendered to Fairfax. The fall of Raglan was the last major event of the First Civil War. Parliament ordered the castle to be slighted. It was no easy job. Two months of bombardment during the siege had failed to bring down the Yellow Tower of Gwent. The demolition gangs were hardly more successful in their efforts in dismantling it by pickaxing from the top downwards: the tower had to be undermined.

RHAYADER Powys
(SN 968680)
A motte castle built by the Welsh, known as Tower Mount, which confirms the motte and bailey character. It is dated late twelfth century.

RHUDDLAN Clwyd †† (SJ 024779) WO
A motte castle was raised here c.1070 which is mentioned in Domesday Book. It appears to have changed hands several times between Welsh and Normans. The mound can still be seen south of the later Edwardian concentric castle built by Master James of St George in 1277–82, and associated with the fortified town. This later castle is a roughly lozenge-shaped inner stone enclosure with cylindrical towers at north and south corners, and substantial twin-cylindrical towered gatehouses at east and west corners. This was surrounded by a larger polygonal stone curtain with flanking rectilinear turrets on every angle and occasionally mid-wall, some of them solid bastions. Three-quarters of the outer curtain was surrounded by a wide moat, the fourth quarter at the west by the River Clwyd. To provide a two-mile long, deep water channel wide enough to accommodate supply ships from the sea, the river was diverted, an operation taking three years and employing about seventy men working six days a week. The cost of the castle, which included the walls of the town, came to not far short of £10,000. The water channel of course rendered the construction works easier since building materials like stone, timber and lead (for roofing), could be brought from many sources by ship, such as timber from Delamere Forest.

Rhuddlan's building works were interrupted when the castle was attacked by Llywelyn the Last's forces, probably under the command of his brother Dafydd, and materials taken for the Welsh Prince's own uses. The castle otherwise survived throughout the Middle Ages and served as a centre of civil administration in north Wales. In the Civil War, Rhuddlan was held for the King, but surrendered to Parliament in 1646. Two years later, it was slighted.

Four kinds of stone were used in the construction of Rhuddlan Castle: dark, purple sandstone from a quarry near St Asaph; a lighter red stone from Cheshire, chiefly for windows; a yellow sandstone from the neighbourhood of Flint; and a grey limestone, also quarried locally.

RHYMNEY Gwent
(ST 210789) A
Remains of a motte castle about which nothing is known, except for a reference to a castle here in Exchequer records of 1184.

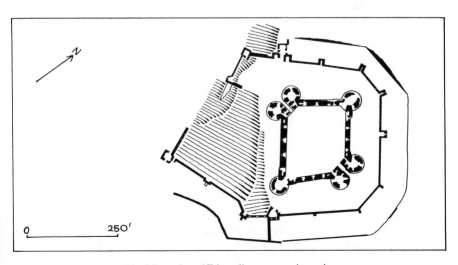

Rhuddlan: plan of Edwardian concentric castle

Rhuddlan: an aerial view of this Edwardian concentric castle of c.1277–82

ROCH Dyfed
(SM 880212) C
Built on a 'horn of a double upburst of
igneous rock' and consisting of a D-end
tower with lengthened sides, of the late
thirteenth century, surrounded by earthworks and a double ditch, Roch has been
considerably altered in later centuries. The
basic tower was residential — and still is.
The castle's moments of glory were during
the Civil War, when it changed hands
several times.

RUTHIN Clwyd   †
(SJ 124579) O
Now part of the Castle Hotel, Ruthin was
one of the new lordship castles ordered by
Edward I to be built between 1277 and the
1280s as part of his scheme of conquest and
annexation of Wales. This castle was in its
time formidable, but the bulk of its
structure has either disappeared or been
absorbed, and it is difficult to define its
shape. Its basic plan appears to have been
two stone enclosures, each with a twin-
towered gatehouse and flanking cylindrical
towers, three of which have survived in

some form. The castle stood on a red
sandstone ridge gently rising above the
Clwyd.

The building work began in the summer
of 1277. Then it seems the castle and the
lands about were granted to Dafydd,
brother of Llywelyn the Last, and records
are not clear as to what was done over the
next years or by whom. In 1283, by which
time Llywelyn had been slain and Dafydd
taken and executed, Ruthin reverted to
Edward, and it is possible that work was
continued. Master James of St George is
mentioned as being involved in some
undisclosed capacity. The reconstruction
work is considered tasteful and elegant, but
it is nonetheless unhelpful in assessing the
original form.

ST CLEARS Dyfed
(SN 280154) A
A motte castle near the river, of unknown
date but perhaps mid-twelfth century,
changed hands between Welsh and English
on at least three occasions between c.1153
and 1215, when it was destroyed.

378

ST DONAT'S Nr Llantwit, South Glamorgan (SS 934681) O
Now Atlantic College, an adult education centre, St Donat's was a formidable double enclosure castle of the late thirteenth century on a striking foreland site. The inner enclosure was flanked with towers, but the outer polygonal curtained enclosure was unflanked. Considerable alterations have been made in subsequent centuries.

ST FAGANS South Glamorgan †
(ST 120771) O
A small castle of two enclosures, one round and one rectangular. Little remains of the original work as it has been obscured by the sixteenth-century mansion built on its site. Received opinion is that there was a great tower of the thirteenth century where the remains of the mansion now stand. The site is part of the Welsh Folk Museum.

ST MELLONS South Glamorgan
(ST 227803)
Also referred to as Cae Castell, St Mellons is an earthwork enclosure castle which may date from the twelfth century.

SENNYBRIDGE Powys
(SN 919283) P
Probably a Welsh-built castle of the late twelfth/early thirteenth centuries, this consisted of a residential block of unclear shape, and a tower. The works appear not to have been finished.

SKENFRITH Gwent ††
(SO 457202) WO
A small but compact quadrilateral enclosure with corner cylindrical towers of great strength, surrounding a cylindrical great tower that has a semi-cylindrical buttress on its western side. The tower, of thirteenth-century construction, stands on an earlier low-level motte of the late eleventh century, which was raised with gravel from the moat, and it has a slightly splayed plinth. The tower is about 35ft in diameter and rose certainly to three storeys including the ground floor. There was no connection between the ground and first floor, except by trap-door. The entrance to the first floor was by timber staircase to an arched door. Access to the second storey was by spiral stair in the semi-cylindrical buttress.

Skenfrith: the cylindrical great tower. The projecting lobe at the right is the half-turret which once contained the staircase

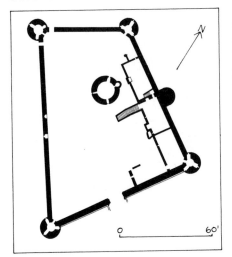

(above) Skenfrith: ground plan. The cylindrical great tower and the enclosure curtain are of c. 1220–40

(below) Swansea: some of the arcading on the parapet of the rectangular tower, of the fourteenth century

The quadrilateral has a strong curtain wall with a fifth cylinder tower of later date on the south face, and outside was a moat with its sides revetted in stone. The River Monnow on which the castle stands completed the water defences on the east side.

SWANSEA West Glamorgan   †
(SS 657931) A
There was a motte castle here, built by Henry Beaumont, Lord of Gower. It was attacked and burned in 1115–16. It was probably not rebuilt as a motte castle. Later, an enclosure castle with towers was built near the site. This appears also to have declined, and parts of it are incorporated in a third structure raised there, in the late thirteenth/early fourteenth centuries; for example, the outer walls of the south block are most probably the curtain of the previous bailey. To this was added in the fourteenth century the interesting arcaded parapet and a rounded-end tower bearing a corbelled offset (which can be seen today) with the wall as part of a new set of buildings unconnected with the castle.

SYCHARTH Nr Llangedwyn, Clwyd ††
(SJ 205259) A
A very interesting site. Today, a mound sits surrounded by a dished moat, the two being on rising ground. Excavations of 1962–3 revealed stone fragments and traces of burnt timber. There were foundations of what appears to have been a rectangular hall, and beside it, on the edge of the summit, another rectilinear building, which the archaeologists think was a latrine block. The charred timber suggests a stone and timber structure that was burned down. The date of the building may have been twelfth century. It appears that the site was occupied by Owain Glyndŵr in the very early fifteenth century, and if so, the hall may have been part of a residence. Was the structure attacked and burned down by the English? There is a record that it was destroyed in 1403.

TENBY Dyfed †
(SN 138005) A
Now in ruins, this interesting castle is sited on a headland overlooking what is now Tenby Harbour. It began as a late Norman tower-gate complex, a square tower with D-ended barbican. This was probably built after an earlier earthwork had been captured in 1153, as is recorded in the *Brut y Tywysogyon*. Later, further buildings were added, but the town nearby was likewise fortified with wall and flanking towers, one of which is a large cylindrical battlemented tower with five arched entrances in its walling, and in time the town was much better defended than the structures on the headland.

CASTELL TINBOETH Powys
(SO 090755) P
Some stone foundations of an enclosure and of a gateway of the (?) twelfth century.

TOMEN-Y-MUR Maentwrog, Gwynedd
(SH 705386) A
A motte castle, some 30ft tall and about 300ft round the base, sited inside the remains of a Roman earthwork fort. Remnants of masonry, including ashlar blocks, have been found on the motte site. William Rufus is thought to have built it c.1090. He is recorded as having encamped there on one of his expeditions against Wales.

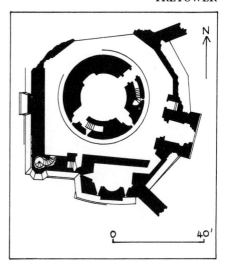

Tretower: ground plan. The great tower is the centre ring (first half of the thirteenth century). The outer range and curtain is largely earlier (mid-twelfth century)

TRETOWER Nr Crickhowell, Powys ††
(SO 184212) WO
Here is an early Norman motte castle of about 1100, which was converted to a stonework castle in the twelfth century, with additional work in the thirteenth century. The motte was revetted with stone because the water supply to the original moat was undermining it. Sometime in the twelfth century the motte summit was surrounded by a thick stone curtain within which buildings were ranged round the walls in the manner of a shell keep, and a strong square-plan gate-tower inserted in the wall at the east.

Then in the thirteenth century, probably 1220–30, the buildings were pulled down and in their place a cylindrical great tower was erected, with three storeys plus basement, and walls 9ft thick on a splayed plinth. The entrance was at first-floor level. On the first storey, now floorless, is a fireplace with sloping hood of ashlar on corbels supported by pillars. There are two mural staircases.

The castle is associated with a mansion of the late Middle Ages, which is not pertinent to this Gazetteer. It seems possible that the castle was taken by Llywelyn the Last in the 1260s and held for a while.

Tretower: the great tower was erected in the thirteenth century within the curtain wall of the earlier shell keep. The curtain was thickened to support a parapet with a wall-walk

UPTON Dyfed
(SN 020047) C
Once a thirteenth-century small enclosure castle, with hall, towers and gate, it has been absorbed by later works.

USK Gwent †
(SO 377010) O
An earthwork castle of c.1138 built by de Clare, which had a second structure of stone raised in its bailey during the reign of Henry II. A small square tower of rubble and ashlar quoins projects from a curtain of later date. Considerable improvements were made in the thirteenth and fourteenth centuries, but it was besieged and severely damaged by Owain Glyndŵr in c.1403–4. Repaired, it was held for Charles I in the Civil War but slighted by Parliament after the war. The well-preserved three-storeyed gatehouse, probably of fourteenth-century origin, is incorporated in Castle House at Usk.

WELSHPOOL Powys
(SJ 230074) A
Considerable confusion exists about the castle at Welshpool. Recent investigation has revealed that there was a motte castle here, and that it was captured by mining sometime in the twelfth century.

WEOBLEY West Glamorgan †
(SS 478927) WO
A small, compact enclosure castle consisting of an irregular square of buildings joined together, principally of thirteenth to fourteenth century construction. Weobley Castle is more in the manner of a fortified manor house, and is set on high ground overlooking the estuary of the River Loughor, on the north coast of the Gower Peninsula. Weobley was started towards the end of the thirteenth century, when a rectangular, almost square, tower — probably a great tower of three storeys — was raised in the south-west corner. This had a splayed plinth, walls 7ft thick and was entered at first-floor level (as is normal with great towers). On the north side of the earthwork enclosure, an interesting hall and kitchen block was erected at the same time.

The square consists of a variety of towers, or tower-like buildings of square, cylindrical, polygonal shape, which for the most part are still in remarkably good condition, though much of this is due to fifteenth- and sixteenth-century rebuildings. Note the polygonal garderobe tower on the north-east corner of the great tower, which had three storeys of latrines and also an interesting quatrefoil loop which provided light for the

382

middle storey garderobe. Weobley was damaged in an assault by forces of Owain Glyndŵr c.1403–4.

WHITCHURCH South Glamorgan
(ST 156804) C
Sometimes known as Treoda, a motte castle was built here probably in the early twelfth century. No stonework has been found.

WHITE CASTLE Nr Abergavenny, ††
Gwent (SO 380168) WO
White Castle appears to have been predominantly a military structure and little attempt was made to render it comfortable as a residence. It consisted of a central pear-shaped enclosure, flanked on the north-west and south-east by two outer enclosures, all three moated, the south and the central surrounded by one moat which also separated the two. The north enclosure has a curtain wall with flanking cylindrical towers and an outer gateway. This curtain is thirteenth century. The central enclosure

also has a stone curtain with cylindrical flanking towers, and a twin-cylindrical towered gatehouse at the north-west end. The towers and gatehouse are late thirteenth century but the curtain is earlier, c.1184–6, and cost £128. At about the same time, when the curtain was raised, there had been a square great tower built on the south-east arc of the original earthwork enclosure, whose foundations survive. At a later date, the tower was partly demolished to extend the curtain and join up the original two arcs. This was done when the flanking towers were inserted. Within the enclosure after the great tower was abandoned, various buildings were erected against the inside wall, including a hall, a solar and a kitchen and oven block.

The curtain walls of both outer and central enclosure and their towers were formidable, and the whole defence system was of considerable sophistication. White Castle is so-named because it was once coated with white plaster on the masonry, traces of which may still be seen.

WISTON Dyfed
(SN 022181) C
A motte castle, whose mound was 40ft tall and about 550ft round the base. It is possible that the mound was increased in height to take the polygonal shell keep with sloping plinth that was erected in the early twelfth century, and of which only a few feet in height remain. The mound was surrounded by a 10ft deep ditch, and the bailey attached was rectangular. Remains of a doorway into the shell keep can be seen. The castle was destroyed by Llywelyn the Great, Prince of all Wales (c.1196–1240)

WREXHAM Clwyd
(SJ 327487) A
A motte castle, also referred to as Erddig Castle, lying against Offa's Dyke on raised ground by the Clywedog River, was mentioned in Pipe Rolls in 1161. There were remains of masonry reported in 1912.

YSTRADFELLTE Powys
(SN 936145) P
Uncertain date for this, and only traces of stone fragments survive.

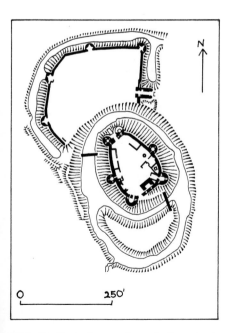

White Castle. the inner enclosure in the centre is largely twelfth century, but the gatehouse is thirteenth century, as are the round D-end towers

383

Scotland

ABERCORN Lothian
(NT 082792)
Once thought to have begun as a motte castle in the twelfth century, it is now believed that Abercorn rose from scratch in stonework, though its shape has not been determined. It belonged to the mighty Douglas family and featured in the power struggle between them and the king, James II, in the 1450s. It was besieged in 1455 by James, using cannon, mentioned specifically in Scottish Treasury accounts. It was probably destroyed, for a mansion was later raised on the site, using masonry from the older fortress. There is nothing to see of the older work.

ABERDOUR Fife   †
(NT 193854) SDD
Aberdour is a rambling assemblage of ruins of several periods. It was begun in the fourteenth century, sometime after the site had been granted by Robert Bruce to his great friend and nephew Thomas Randolph, Earl of Moray. After centuries of improvements and also changes of family ownership, it was burnt sometime towards the end of the seventeenth century and thereafter allowed to deteriorate, although an ornamental garden was erected in the courtyard to the south.

The castle started as a rhomboidal great tower, of which not much remains today beyond some walling. The tower is 52ft by 36ft with angle buttresses on two corners. The walls are almost 6ft thick. Unlike most great towers, the entrance was at ground (and not first) floor level. It has a spiral staircase in the wall thickness on the east corner. The tower was modified in the fifteenth century to enlarge the accommoda-

tion, and this entailed rebuilding the top part. It also included erecting a new square-plan staircase tower on the south-east corner adjacent to the part of the wall containing the original spiral staircase.

In the sixteenth century a fresh range of buildings was raised on the south-east, abutting at the top on the staircase tower. This range extends in a north-easterly direction and was added to in the seventeenth century, the principal building being a long rectangular structure with a square-plan tower on its extreme east corner.

Aberdour passed on to the famous Douglas family in the mid-fourteenth century. It belonged to the Regent Morton from about 1548 to his execution in 1581. It has been the subject of recent excavations.

ABERUCHIL Tayside
(NH 745212)
A seventeenth century L-plan tower-house in poor condition.

ABOYNE Grampian
(NO 523995) C
Aboyne was a motte castle raised in the thirteenth century which received stone additions, probably by the time of the War of Independence (c.1296-c.1307). The motte received a stone great tower. In the seventeenth century the great tower was drastically altered to a tower-house, and altered again in the nineteenth century into a mansion, which is now in a poor state.

ACHADUN Strathclyde,
(NM 804392)
Also spelled Achanduin, this very early castle was built for the bishops of Argyll. It

384

Aberdour: the castle from the north-east

Aberdour: some Scottish people still like to have turrets in their homes. This is a modern bungalow in Aberdour, a stone's throw from the castle. Others like it can be seen in many parts of Scotland, particularly north of the Forth.

was an irregular quadrilateral stone enclosure, the greater part of which has collapsed and is ruined. Part of the north-west wall stands to a maximum height of about 22ft and is 5–8ft thick. It dates from the early thirteenth century. The castle has a small rectangular turret projection in one corner, and a garderobe built into the curtain wall itself.

ACKERGILL Wick, Highland
(ND 352547)
A rectangular great tower of the end of the fifteenth century, approximately 48ft by 34ft, which has received later additions and restorations. Its history is not known.

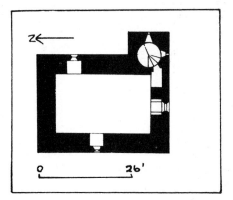

Affleck: Plan of first floor of tower-house. The main room was the Common Hall

AFFLECK Monikie, Tayside   ††
(NO 495388) SDD
This is a well-known L-plan tower-house of the late fifteenth century which is still in very good condition. It is built of local reddish sandstone rubble, with fine quality dressings on the angles, around windows, arrow loops and so on. It is four storeys to the parapet which has two square corner turrets and two small corner roundels. Though sparsely provided with windows, which at upper levels have iron grilles, and more liberally supplied with arrow loops, Affleck tower-house has elaborate internal appointments, including a chapel at the top storey (over the top of the wheel stair in the staircase tower), and a well-designed solar, also on the top floor, which has a remarkable

fireplace, a garderobe and several wall chambers which were probably bedrooms.

Affleck was — and still is — a fine residence. It was also a well-fortified one: the walls are 6–7ft thick; there are inverted keyhole gun-ports at lower levels, and there are battlemented caphouses acting as watch turrets at the top on two corners.

AIKET Strathclyde
(NS 388488)
This began as a rectangular tower-house of the sixteenth century.

AIRLIE Kirriemuir, Tayside
(NO 293522) O
On a promontory over the junction of the Isla and Melgund rivers stands the greatly renovated castle of Airlie, belonging as it has for centuries to the Ogilvy family. The first work began in c.1432 and was probably a large enclosure castle. There is a long stretch of wall of this surviving, about 120ft, 10ft thick and 35ft tall in places. In the wall is a gateway with a portcullis. The remainder of the original is no longer detectable, and a more modern mansion occupies part of the north area of the enclosure. The original ditch to the south of the long wall is still there. The old castle was burnt by the Duke of Argyll in 1640.

AIRTH Central
(NS 900868)
Airth Castle is basically fifteenth century, raised on an earlier castle site. The tower is 33ft by 28ft. In the sixteenth century a wing was added on the east wall of the tower, and a further north wing was joined to that at a point where a small rectangular stair turret abuts on the end of the east wing.

The castle was burned by James III before the Battle of Sauchieburn, in 1488, and is a ruin today.

ALDIE Tayside   †
(NT 050977)
Aldie has been well restored, both in the seventeenth century and in recent years and is no longer known as a castle. But its original purpose was as a fortified home, built in the late fifteenth century. The tower is four-storeyed with garret. The top part

has been rebuilt, and the original wing containing the staircase was removed and replaced by a lower structure. The tower has bartizans corbelled out at the corners, though these were added after the need for fortification, and so are decorative rather than military. Other additions of the seventeenth century, and later, converted the castle into a courtyard mansion.

ALDOURIE Highland
(NH 601372)
An early seventeenth-century tower-house which has been absorbed in later buildings.

ALLARDICE Arbuthnott, Grampian
(NO 817739) C
A seventeenth-century simple rectangular tower-house which has been considerably altered and expanded, Allardice now has a cluster of turrets and label moulding in the corbelling of the turrets and parapet. There is also an interesting old archway into the courtyard.

ALLOA Central
(NS 888925)
Once a massively tall tower of the fifteenth century, this was greatly altered in the seventeenth century, and new features included bigger windows and a Renaissance-style entrance.

ALMOND Tayside
(NS 956772) P
Almond Castle used to be known as the Castle of Haining. It was probably begun in the fifteenth century as an L-plan tower of four storeys plus a garret in the roof. Later additions were built on the north-east and south-east. The castle was once surrounded by a ditch fed by a nearby stream which has dried up. It is a ruin today.

AMISFIELD Dumfries and Galloway †
(NX 992837)
Amisfield Tower is a very tall tower-house of about 1600. In its way it embodies the Scottish anxiety to build tall and strong. Amisfield incorporates a variety of features that might almost be described as having been thrown together, and it remains in good condition, standing quite alone, its lower storey walls built of random rubble,

its higher levels of better ashlar work. It is five-storeyed to the main garret level, but one end rises for two further storeys as a narrow double caphouse. Scattered — for that is the appropriate word — around the top are bartizans and rectangular projections. Lower down on one corner is a roundel that stops at about 10ft from the ground. Its top end supports a square-plan chamber of two storeys with its own attic inside a gable roof. The basic dimensions of the tower are 30ft square and over 70ft tall.

The weird appearance of Amisfield's design is heightened by the different shades of colour of the stone used.

ARDBLAIR Central
(NO 163445)
An L-plan tower-house with courtyard, probably built in the sixteenth century, which has been little altered and is a substantial ruin.

ARDROSSAN Strathclyde
(NS 232422)
This is a courtyard castle sited on part of a rock detached from a larger promontory. Parts of a large gatehouse at the north-east survive. There are also remains of another tower at the south-west. The lower level of the gatehouse is the earliest work of the castle, probably late thirteenth century. There was major reconstruction in the fourteenth century when the gatehouse was rebuilt from the first floor upwards. In the fifteenth century, the gatehouse was converted into a gatehouse–tower and heightened, and fortified with gun-ports in the sixteenth century.

ARDTORNISH Morvern, Highland
(NM 692426) C
This was built in the fourteenth century. It was a rectangular great tower, of which only walling of the ground floor remains, some 9–10ft thick and several feet high. Ardtornish belonged to the Macdonalds, Lords of the Isles.

ARDVRECK Assynt, Highland
(NC 239236) C
Perched on a rocky promontory jutting into the north side of Loch Assynt, Ardvreck is now a ruin. It was raised in the sixteenth

century as a simple rectangular tower with a cylindrical staircase turret at the south-east corner, corbelled out on the upper storeys. The three chambers on the ground floor were vaulted. The tower had three storeys, and the windows in the top storey were served by a gable passage. Montrose was taken to Ardvreck Castle in 1650 and handed over to Parliament.

ARNAGE Ellon, Grampian
(NJ 935370) C
A mid-seventeenth-century Z-plan tower-house still in sound condition and which is being renovated. It was enlarged in the nineteenth century by the addition of a wing which obscured some of the original work.

ASLOUN Grampian
(NJ 543149)
Ruins of a late sixteenth-/early seventeenth-century Z-plan tower-house.

ASSYNT Highland
(NC 195250)
Vestiges of dry stone walling on this site, reaching 5ft in places, are almost the only remains of a fortress of uncertain shape recorded as having been given to Torquil McLoyd of Lewis c.1343. There is some retaining wall round the edge of the island.

AUCHEN Dumfries and Galloway   †
(NT 063035) A
Known also as Auchencass, this interesting castle was begun in the thirteenth century. It was partly demolished in the Wars of Independence, possibly in furtherance of Robert Bruce's policy of 'slighting' castles. It was rebuilt later in the fourteenth century as an irregularly shaped thick-walled quad-rangle castle with cylindrical corner turrets, whose lower levels are solid masonry. The quadrangle was surrounded by a deep and wide ditch, providing a formidable defence, though not really a concentric defence as has been suggested. The east wall of the quadrangle has a mural passage with a corbelled roof. There was a drain running from the castle into the moat. It is now in ruinous condition.

AUCHENHARVIE Strathclyde
(NS 363443)
A fifteenth-century great tower in ruins.

AUCHINDOUN Montlach, Grampian
(NJ 349374) C
A late fifteenth-century L-plan tower-house inside the limits of a prehistoric hill-fort, Auchindoun has ribbed vaulting in the remains of the great hall. It may have been designed by Robert Cochrane, who was the court mason and favourite of James III (1460–88), responsible (among other works) for the great hall at Stirling Castle. The castle has been in ruinous condition for some time, but restoration is in progress by the Scottish Development Department.

AUCHNESS Kirkmaiden, Dumfries and Galloway   (NX 107446)
A small rectangular tower-house of the sixteenth century, which rose to three storeys and a garret, Auchness has been absorbed into a farmhouse, with many alterations. Turrets have been added for decoration.

AUCHTERARDER Tayside
(NN 943133) C
A very early rectangular tower, possibly twelfth century, enclosed by a moat. Some fragments of the tower walls remain, to a height of about 16ft. The castle is reputed to have been associated with Malcolm III (1057–93), but if this is so, then it will only have been an earth and wood castle at the time. Nothing is known about its later structural history.

AULDEARN Highland
(NH 917556)
A castle of the time of William the Lion (1165–1214) is mentioned in an early charter (1187–8). Remains consist of a raised area enclosed by a rampart.

AULDTON Dumfries and Galloway
(NT 094058)
A twelfth-century motte in good preservation. It has remains of a ditch around the base. Nothing is known of its history.

AYR Strathclyde
(NS 335222)
Traces have been found of the late twelfth-century castle built here probably by William the Lion, King of Scotland. It began as an earthwork enclosure and

received stone additions. It was besieged in 1298 by the English, using siege engines sent to the site from Carlisle by sea (S. H. Cruden).

BALBEGNO Grampian
(NO 639729) P
Balbegno was built in the late 1560s on a roughly L-shape plan, and has considerable additions of the seventeenth, eighteenth and nineteenth centuries. The upper hall in the earlier tower part is notable for its ribbed vaulting.

BALBITHAN Grampian
(NJ 812189) O
Now called Balbithan House, this began as a sixteenth-century L-plan tower. It is occupied and open seasonally.

BALFLUIG Alford, Grampian
(NJ 586150) Open occasionally
An L-plan tower-house of the mid-sixteenth century which was ruinous for a long period. It has recently been restored and is occasionally open.

BALFOUR Tayside
(NO 337546)
A sixteenth-century round tower was built here, a shape rare in Scottish castles.

BALGONIE Markinch, Fife †
(NO 313007) C
A substantial castle of fifteenth-century beginnings standing on the south bank of the Leven, Balgonie is a gaunt, dilapidated structure as seen from a distance, but restoration work has been in progress for some while. The main rectangular great tower of four storeys plus garret was built of ashlar blocks and is complete to the roof. This was renovated very recently. Additional buildings were raised in the early seventeenth century by the 1st Earl of Leven and considerable remains of these are still standing.

BALINSHOE Tayside
(NO 417532)
A sixteenth-century tower-house, of which little original work remains.

BALLINDALLOCH Grampian
(NJ 179365)
A Z-plan tower-house of the late sixteenth and early seventeenth centuries, consider-

ably enlarged and modified since. Nearby is the remnant of a second Ballindalloch Castle, probably of the fifteenth century.

BALLONE Highland
(NH 929837)
A late sixteenth-century Z-plan castle, which was already in ruins by the mid-eighteenth century. The main central rectangular tower, lying north-south, rose three storeys with a garret above, and of the diagonally opposing towers one was cylindrical, the other square. In each angle a narrow staircase turret was inserted. The remaining two corners of the main block still have corner turrets. The present ruins are two storeys tall. Gun-ports were placed all round the tower-house at ground-floor level.

BALNAGOWN Highland
(NH 763752)
A fifteenth-century great tower castle that has been considerably modified.

BALQUHAIN Inverurie, Grampian
(NJ 731236)
A huge quadrilateral great tower was built here in the fifteenth century. It was destroyed in 1526 and rebuilt soon afterwards. The walls were very thick, with deep recesses and narrow window loops. A curtain wall enclosed the tower and also some outbuildings. Mary, Queen of Scots, is thought to have taken refuge here before the Battle of Corrichie in 1562. The castle was destroyed by the Duke of Cumberland in 1746.

BALTHAYOCK Tayside
(NO 174230)
A simple but impressive ruin of a fourteenth-century rectangular great tower, approximately 52ft by 37ft with thick walls.

BALVAIRD Tayside
(NO 169115) C
A fifteenth-century L-plan tower-house with a separate square-plan staircase tower in the angle. The tower-house is in ruinous condition, but several features are still visible, such as battlemented parapets, a rectangular caphouse on the wing tower with its own parapet and bartizan corners,

and part of the barmkin which had been added somewhat later than the tower's construction period. Balvaird has the remains of interesting plumbing arrangement: latrines were flushed out by means of a chute in the wall thickness, with an outlet at the bottom covered by a stone 'plug', called a 'grund-wa'-stane' (ground wall stone, cf. Corgarff).

BALVENIE Dufftown, Grampian   ††
(NJ 326408) SDD
This is an interesting castle of late thirteenth-century origin, which began as a substantial stone quadrilateral enclosure with walls basically 7ft thick, and probably up to 35ft high. There are remnants of a small latrine turret on the north corner, and of a larger square-plan tower on the west corner, and other buildings were raised inside. In the mid-sixteenth century, the eastern part was completely remodelled by the then owner, John Stewart, 4th Earl of Atholl, who constructed a range consisting of three storeys facing south-eastwards, with a cylindrical tower on the east corner, about 28ft in diameter, three storeys tall and which once had a 'pepper pot' roof. The tower has wide-mouthed gun-ports, as has the lower storey of the range.

The castle was an extensive building in the sixteenth century, about 150ft by 130ft in area, with buildings round three inside walls, and is today an equally extensive ruin. It stands on a platform surrounded on three sides by a 40ft-wide moat, the fourth side falling away as a steep cliff. The moat has stone facing. Balvenie once belonged to the Douglases. When the mighty family was brought low by James II in the 1450s, Balvenie became crown property, but the king gave it to John Stewart, 1st Earl of Atholl. It was occupied until the eighteenth century.

BALWEARIE Kirkcaldy, Fife
(NT 251904) A
Only ruins remain of this fifteenth-century tower-house inside an enclosing curtain wall. The tower was 43ft by about 28ft, with 6ft-thick walling. The masonry was ashlar, set in courses of 10–12in.

BANFF Grampian
(NJ 689641) C
There is very little to see here of the original stone enclosure castle that was raised in the twelfth or thirteenth century, apart from a stretch of wall about 140ft long, up to about 18ft high and up to 6½ft thick. A modern building covers the site and incorporates the wall.

BARCALDINE Strathclyde
(NM 908406) Open by appointment
Sited about 15 miles north of Oban with a fine view over Loch Creran towards Glencoe, Barcaldine was built to L-plan in 1601–9. The main tower block was 43ft by 27ft, with the walls varying between 4-6ft thick. The south-west wing was 23ft by 22ft. The tower-house rose three storeys plus attic (which has been rebuilt). It was allowed to decay, but in the final years of the last century it was restored and is occupied.

BARDOWIE Strathclyde   †
(NS 578737) O
This sixteenth-century tower-house has later additions, which are not castellar. The tower is four-storeyed, with walls 6½–8ft thick, and is built of rubble.

BARHOLM Kirkmabreck, Dumfries and Galloway (NX 521529) C
Situated high above the sea, Barholm is now a ruinous L-plan tower-house of three storeys plus garret with parapet, to which has been added a wing of greater height, containing the staircase. The tower wing is topped with a caphouse. Around the tower was built a curtain wall, about 10ft tall and about 3ft thick. Barholm was built in the late sixteenth and early seventeenth centuries.

BARJARG Dumfries and Galloway
(NX 878901)
A late sixteenth-century L-plan tower-house forms the eastern wing of a mansion built here in the early nineteenth century. It was built of red rubble and rises to four storeys plus attic, and has corbelled angle turrets on the corners of the parapet (which are probably of a later period).

BARR TOWER Strathclyde
(NS 502364)
A plain tower castle of the fifteenth and sixteenth centuries that has received modifications.

BARRA Bourtie, Grampian
(NJ 793258) Open by arrangement
This is a fortified stone rectangular building of the seventeenth century with a wing which joins the main block towards the south so that there are two angles. In the eighteenth century a second wing was added projecting eastwards from the north, and the three sides of a rectangle thus formed were completed by the building of a curtain wall across. The castle is occupied.

BASS OF INVERURIE Grampian †
(NJ 781206) A
A natural mound some 50ft tall was altered into a motte by scarping the sides and excavating a ditch round it. The work was probably done c.1180 by David, Earl of Huntingdon, brother of William the Lion, King of Scotland. The remains of an oak gangway up the south face of the motte were found in recent excavations. The motte is thought to have been given a shell keep of stone at a later date, but this has not yet been finally determined.

BAVELAW Penicuik, Lothian
(NT 167627) P
This (?) seventeenth-century L-plan tower-house build around an earlier structure, three storeys high with an attic, is equipped with gun-ports. A cylindrical turret projects from the north-east angle of the main tower block, and a rectilinear turret abuts on the southern edge. Bavelaw was a hunting lodge used by Mary, Queen of Scots, and by James VI, though they must have used the earlier building which was probably the main tower, or part of it.

BEDRULE Borders
(NT 598180)
Bedrule began as an oval stone wall enclosure on the bluff jutting westwards from the rising ground on the right bank of Rule Water. A gatehouse was inserted at the north-west and a cylindrical flanking tower on the south-east, with two further towers at west and south-west. The structure was built in the late thirteenth century and may have been put up by the English during the John Balliol – Edward I contention. Robert Bruce captured it during the War of Independence and gave it to his friend and counsellor, Sir James Douglas. It is a ruin.

BELDORNEY Grampian
(NJ 423369)
An altered Z-plan tower of the sixteenth century.

BEMERSYDE Mertoun, Borders
(NT 592333)
A modernized mansion which incorporates a sixteenth-century tower-house whose original height was five storeys. The walls of the tower are 10ft thick. Bemersyde has been held by the Haig family for centuries. By far its most celebrated occupant was Field Marshal Sir Douglas Haig, 1st Earl Haig of Bemersyde, Commander-in-Chief of the British Army in France, 1915–18.

BENHOLM Grampian
(NO 804704) C
An uncomplicated tower-house of the fifteenth century is intact but in a ruinous state. It is attached to a modern mansion.

BLACKNESS Nr Linlithgow, Lothian
(NT 055802) SDD ††
Once a very important Scottish fortress by virtue of its position by the waters of the Firth of Forth, Blackness is a fifteenth–sixteenth-century castle whose overall plan is very much like a ship. It is sited on a rocky outcrop at the sea end of a promontory. We say fifteenth/sixteenth century to cover its two distinct phases. The fifteenth century saw the erection of the rectangular great tower, which was given, probably in the seventeenth century, a cylindrical staircase corner turret on the north-east angle (reminiscent of Rochester, c.1230). The tower stands inside the 'ship-shape' courtyard of mainly sixteenth-century construction, which has another tower at one end, and a triangular tower-like bastion at the 'bow' end of the courtyard. The latter has a pit prison beneath the ground floor. Blackness was used as a prison for Covenanters in the 1660s.

BLAIR Tayside
(NN 866662) O
This palatial home of the dukes of Atholl is largely a late eighteenth-century reconstruction grafted upon the remains of an earlier and complex tower-house castle. The first building, of which some lower portions

of wall survive, was the Comyn Tower, built c.1270 of square plan. It is now called the Cummings Tower. It was subsequently enclosed in a barmkin along with further buildings including a lord's hall. The medieval castle was for a time the seat of the first earls of Atholl, who were royal Stewarts. It was occupied for a few weeks by Bonnie Prince Charlie, the Younger Pretender, during the Second Jacobite Rising, 1745–6. After the flight of the prince, Blair was taken over by the Hanoverian Government. The Duke of Atholl attempted to recover it by siege but was fought off. This was probably the last siege of any castle in Britain.

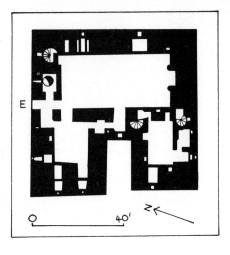

Borthwick : First-floor plan of tower. Note massive wall thickness. E = entrance

BLERVIE Grampian
(NJ 071572)
A well-preserved Z-plan tower-house of the seventeenth century.

BOGHALL Nr Biggar, Strathclyde
(NT 041369) C
A sixteenth-century tower-house, now ruined.

BONSHAW TOWER Annan, Dumfries and Galloway (NY 243721)
An unadorned late fifteenth-century small rectangular tower, 34ft by 25ft, three-storeyed to the wall head and with a roofed attic. The basement is vaulted. The tower is in fair condition.

BORTHWICK Lothian
(NT 369597) P Visible from road
Borthwick is one the greatest tower-houses in all Britain, possibly in west Europe, and certainly the most imposing tower-house built in Scotland in one operation. It has been in almost continuous occupation since its erection in 1430–2, and is today preserved and lovingly cared for by its present owner in the sort of uncomplicated magnificence that would have been understood and enjoyed by the first Lord Borthwick who was granted a licence to build it by James I in 1430.

The structure is built of large ashlar blocks. It is a rectangular tower with two wings projecting from the ends of one longer (west) side. The longer sides of the rectangular part are 71ft long, the shorter sides 45ft.

The wings are slightly dissimilar in dimension: the more northerly wing 32ft by 23ft, the southerly wing 28ft by 20ft. The walls of the tower–house are 10–14ft thick in most places, and this becomes particularly impressive when one looks at some of the window sills. The great hall takes up the whole of the first floor of the large rectangular part of the tower-house, and has a tall barrel vaulted roof. At the south end is a magnificent canopied fireplace 20ft high, flanked on either side by a deep window with stepped sills. From the hall four spiral staircases wind their separate ways to other parts of the tower–house, up to chambers and thence to the roof, and downwards to dungeons and cellars. A large kitchen opens off the great hall into the northerly wing, and the southerly wing contains a solar on the same floor. Next to the solar is a garderobe, whose chute discharged into a system of movable containers for subsequent emptying. The tower-house is 100ft tall and has machicolated parapets.

Borthwick Tower was enclosed in the early sixteenth century by a curtain wall with one large cylindrical corner tower flanking a gateway in the wall, just to the south-west of the southerly wing of the tower. The corner turret has gun-ports.

The great tower-house was bombarded by Cromwell in the war between England

and Scotland in 1650. The 9th Lord Borthwick, holder of the castle and a staunch royalist, refused to yield his fortress to Cromwell's forces after the great man's victory over the Scots at Dunbar. Cromwell formally demanded surrender in a letter which included the threat: '. . . if you necessitate me to bend my cannon against you, you may expect what I doubt you will not be pleased with . . .' Borthwick at first refused to yield, whereupon Cromwell's guns opened fire and fragmented the battlements and some wall stonework on the top part of the east main wall. Then Borthwick surrendered, and the great tower-house was spared further damage. The results of the bombardment can still be seen today. They mar the otherwise noble and tidy appearance of the castle's masonry. The walls proved too thick, however, for the cannon shot to damage the interior.

BOTHWELL Uddingston, Strathclyde (NS 688593) SDD ††

We have encountered this important thirteenth-century Scottish castle (with later additions) in chapter 14. As we have seen, it has been described in somewhat exaggerated terms by some authorities. One even referred to the quality of the polished ashlar masonry with which it was built as being beyond the capacity of Scottish craftsmen of the time, leaving the reader with the unanswered question, who built the castle? and an implication that the answer should be, French craftsmen. The great tower resembles in some points the colossal great tower at Coucy, built in c.1225–40. We may, however, discount this undervaluing of Scottish craft skills and accept that Bothwell was Scottish built, that its great tower was the first structure, raised in the 1270s at the latest, and that it belonged to the Moravia family (later Moray) who also owned Duffus.

The castle was raised on red sandstone rock upon the south bank of the Clyde. The masonry is red sandstone quarried nearby, finely cut and dressed. The great tower, or donjon, was over 65ft in diameter, rose to at least 80ft and had walls about 15ft thick. It had four storeys, a spiral stair in the wall thickness on the north-east side, and a mural passage at first-floor level leading out of the south-east side into a wing wall jutting out south-eastwards. This wall led to a cylindrical turret. This was just about all of the stonework completed by c.1290, though

Bothwell: general view from the south. The remains of the donjon can be seen at extreme left

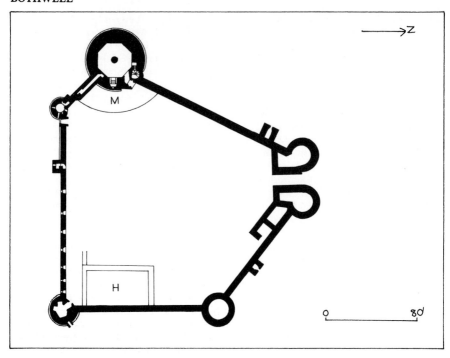

Bothwell: Plan shows main outline of the castle. Some of the walling and part of the turrets and other buildings are in ruins. At top is the great tower or donjon. The outer half of the tower was destroyed. M = separate moat for great tower. H = Hall

foundations have been discovered of parts of a planned curtain wall, a twin-towered gatehouse and other towers laid out to form a quadrilateral enclosure. These northerly structures were never completed, and indeed some may never have risen higher than a few feet above ground. We may assume, however, that it was intended to continue this building plan, and even that the curtain line was temporarily followed by wooden palisading. The positioning of wide ditches to north-east and east suggests at least that an area of some size was to be fortified. A ditch was also cut into the rock in front of the donjon, between the two wing walls.

In the 1290s, the castle fell into English hands during the Interregnum when Edward I of England attempted to rule Scotland after the deposition of John Balliol (1296). When Wallace's campaign to recover Scotland began in 1297, the Scots attacked Bothwell and captured it after a fourteen-month siege. In 1301 Edward I

recaptured it. To do so he employed a variety of artifices including a huge belfry of prefabricated parts made in Glasgow and moved eight miles in two days to Bothwell by thirty wagons. The Scots surrendered after a six-week siege. As likely as not the castle was held by the English for the next thirteen years, though it may have fallen to a second Scottish assault and been recovered again. But after Bruce's great victory at Bannockburn (1314), the castle reverted to Scotland and remained in Scottish hands until the 1330s. During that time it may have been dismantled under Bruce's policy of slighting castles likely to be useful to the English again.

In c.1331, during hostilities between Scotland and England, Bothwell was captured by the English and Edward III used it as a headquarters. Much restoration work was done to the great tower, and a hall was built on the eastern side of the quadrilateral, but possibly not completed. In 1337, Sir

Andrew de Moravia recovered the castle once more from the English and he dismantled it. The donjon was partially thrown down, so that half of it remained standing to almost its full height, the other half demolished, rendering the tower totally useless.

In the 1360s, the castle came into the possession of the Black Douglas family who rebuilt some of it, including the hall, a chapel and walling, and erected a new wall from east to west. Further work was done in the fifteenth and sixteenth centuries, but by then it was no longer a military structure, and its history from the end of the fourteenth century is not our concern.

BOYNE Boyndie, Grampian
(NJ 611656) O

The ruins of a courtyard castle of the late sixteenth century. Boyne was protected on three sides by Boyne Water and a dry ditch on the fourth. At each corner of the courtyard was a cylindrical tower, about 22ft in diameter. The connecting curtain wall was on average 5ft thick. Inside the courtyard ranges of domestic buildings were put up on three sides. The entrance consisted of a walled walkway covered by a pair of cylindrical towers.

BRAAL Highland
(ND 139601)

This is a rectangular tower of the late thirteenth or early fourteenth century, about 35ft by 37ft and rising today to the second storey only. The walls are 8–10ft thick. It is a simple structure with no vaulting. The entrance is at first-floor level at the south-west. The tower was surrounded by a wet ditch. The castle may have been built by a Norse lord in Caithness.

BRACO Ardoch, Tayside
(NN 823113)

A tall, square tower-house with projecting staircase tower, of the sixteenth century. This was given an extension on the south side absorbing the stair tower (seventeenth century) and a further extension of L-plan (eighteenth century), rendering the castle three sides of a square round a courtyard.

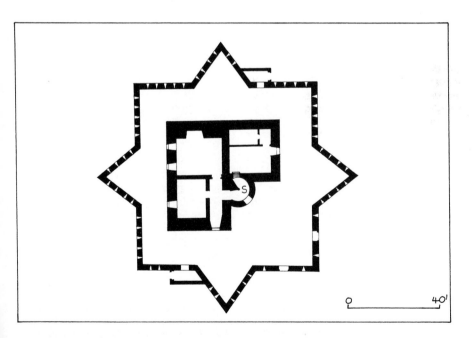

Braemar: ground plan (after Fenwick). Star-shaped enclosing wall is the mid-eighteenth century addition to the original L-plan tower-house. S = Stair twist in re-entrant

BRAEMAR Grampian †
(NO 156924) O
Not far from Balmoral (the Scottish home of the Royal Family), lies the castle of Braemar. It is basically an L-plan tower-house with some interesting additions. Begun c.1628, it was burned in 1689 and restored in 1748 to be used as a military base for the Hanoverian army after the Second Jacobite Rising of 1745–6. The corners of both wing ends were provided with cylindrical turrets corbelled out from second-storey level upwards, and these turrets were battlemented at the top. A large cylindrical staircase tower was inserted in the angle. And around the tower was raised a star-shaped barmkin, or stone curtain, battlemented and supplied with gun-ports all round (see also Corgarff). All this remains to be seen.

BRAIKIE Kinnell, Tayside
(NO 628508) P
An L-plan tower-house built by the Fraser family in 1581 (according to a date stone). It has been altered but little in the four centuries, and has the usual features of sixteenth- and seventeenth-century smaller Scottish tower-houses, such as crow-stepped gables, corbelled embrasures and iron yett at the entrance.

BREACACHADH Strathclyde
(NM 160589) A
A medieval great tower castle with curtain wall and other buildings, mainly of the fourteenth century, but which is now in ruins.

BRECHIN Tayside
(NO 598599) C
A fourteenth-century structure of uncertain shape, which has been incorporated in later buildings.

BRODICK Isle of Arran, Strathclyde
(NS 007379) O
Now built of red sandstone, Brodick began as a Viking fort, probably of the twelfth century. In the fourteenth century it was converted to an early stone L-plan tower-house. The north wing is all that remains of the original. The remainder of the structure is chiefly nineteenth-century work, de-signed by Gillespie Graham for the owner, the Duke of Hamilton.

BRODIE Forres, Grampian †
(NH 979578) O
Brodie Castle belongs to the Brodie family: the land on which it stands has done so since the twelfth century. The present structure is basically of the sixteenth and seventeenth centuries but was raised on an earlier castle site. It is an L-plan formed from a strong centre rectangular tower with a projection. The tower is four-storeyed to the parapet which rests on highly decorated corbelling, and there is a garret above, with crow-stepped gable. It is equipped with loops and gun-ports.

BROUGHTY Broughty Ferry, Tayside
(NO 465304) SDD
About two miles from Dundee, Broughty has been extensively altered. It started as a tower-house of the last years of the fifteenth century. It appears to have been allowed to decay, probably as a result of damage by the English in 1547, and more damage when it was retaken in 1550. In c.1603, Broughty was restored, but again damaged, this time in 1650. The actual shape of the castle in its earlier state is difficult to determine but its main tower block foundations are still visible. In 1855 the castle was purchased by the War Department and modified as a coastal fort. Parts of the east block are the only upright remains of the fifteenth–century castle.

BRUCE'S St Ninians, Central
(NS 857878) P
Not connected with the illustrious king of Scotland, this castle stood on a rocky spur. It was built of sandstone rubble and was of rectangular plan with walls nearly 10ft thick. It was begun in the fifteenth century. Only the ground and parts of the first storey remain.

BRUNSTON Lothian
(NT 201582) P
Brunston, or as it is also known, Brunstane, is a sixteenth-century courtyard plan castle, with a medium sized tower-house of earlier date on the south-east side, of two storeys and a garret. The castle was burnt down in

1547 and rebuilt in the 1560s, at which time it received the main part of the courtyard buildings.

BUITTLE Dumfries and Galloway
(NX 819616)
This is a thirteenth-century enclosure castle with cylindrical towers on the angles, now in ruins. There is an entrance at the north-west which appears to have led out through a twin-towered gateway to a drawbridge.

BURGIE Grampian
(NJ 094593)
A seventeenth-century Z-plan tower-house. One interesting feature is its groups, or batteries, of gun-ports which are set in threes in the walls.

BURLEIGH Milnathort, Tayside
(NO 129046) SDD
Close to the north edge of Loch Leven, the early sixteenth-century tower of Burleigh stands without roof and in ruins, about 32ft by 27ft in horizontal dimensions. A stretch of enclosure wall joins to a later sixteenth-century gatehouse which is in much better condition. This gatehouse has several interesting features, including gun-ports and shot holes, in a few of which the wooden sills are still in place.

BUSBIE Strathclyde
(NS 397390)
Ruins of a seventeenth-century tower-house.

CADZOW Hamilton, Strathclyde †
(NS 734537) O
There is thought to have been an early castle here in the twelfth century, used by David I and succeeding kings. It stood on a natural hill, overlooking the Avon, and was later surrounded by a formidable curtain and a wide ditch. Two round towers project into the ditch, one at each end of a stretch of the curtain that is less well protected. One tower has wide-mouth gun-ports, inserted in the sixteenth century, which cover the ditch, since the tower is hardly higher than the ditch. The other, now only fragmentary, presumably had gun-ports as well. The artillery-type fortifications (c.1542–4) are the work of the 2nd Earl of Arran.

CAERLAVEROCK Dumfries and †† Galloway (NY 026656) SDD
'Caerlaverock was so strong a castle that it feared no siege . . . it had but three sides round it, with a tower at each corner but one of them was a double one, so high, so long and so wide, that the gate was underneath it, well made and strong, with a drawbridge and a sufficiency of other defences. . .and it had good walls, and good ditches filled right up to the brim with water . . .' This description of the great concentric fortress of Caerlaverock comes from a translation of a contemporary French rhyming account of the siege of the castle in 1300 by Edward I, *Le Siege de Karlaverock*, and it is an apt summary of the castle's defensive features which are hardly less imposing to look at today. It was probably built c.1280–90, though there has been a suggestion that it was raised c.1290–1300 by the English during the struggle between Edward I and the Scots. Its position on the northern shore of the Solway Firth, with its huge twin-towered gatehouse pointing northwards, is taken to suggest it may have been constructed as an English bridgehead for the invasion of Scotland, and this is backed by the belief that it was designed by Master James of St George. But while it has 'St

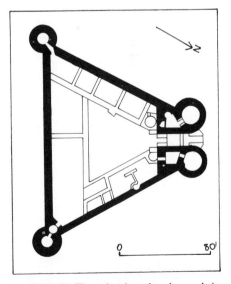

Caerlaverock: The only triangular-plan castle in the UK. The bold lines represent the earlier fortified walls and towers

397

Caerlaverock: (*above*) the formidable gatehouse of this unique triangular-plan castle. The machicolations are fifteenth-century: the original gatehouse stonework is thirteenth century

make-shift repairs at the rear of castle

Georgian' features, they do not seem enough for proof of his hand. It could equally well have been built by the Scots to defend the neighbourhood.

The castle was besieged very early in its history by Edward I, and it surrendered. The English held it for twelve years. The constable then changed sides and declared for Robert Bruce, and dismantled the castle in accord with the Scottish king's policy of rendering defenceless all military buildings which might prove useful to the English. Caerlaverock deteriorated, but it was rebuilt in the fifteenth century, carefully following the original design. The massive gatehouse was strengthened and altered internally to make it residential; in other words, it was changed into a Scottish tower-house, with the quarters protected from dangers at ground level. Gun-ports were inserted into the stonework for cannons and other small guns (see drawing), sometime near the end of the sixteenth century, and this may have helped the garrison defending it for the king against the Covenanters in 1640, for it held out for nearly three months under siege.

Caerlaverock's triangular plan is unusual but simple (see plan); an enclosure of three massive curtains covered by angle towers on two corners and the huge gatehouse on the third. It was made concentric by surrounding it with an inner moat, then ramparts of earth which in their earlier years were topped with palisading, then another moat and finally a higher ring of earthworks. Attackers had to cross two separate bridges before even reaching the daunting gatehouse, rendered more forbidding still (in the fifteenth century) by the addition of machicolated parapets and toughened stonework over and round the gateway.

Besieged several times, large parts of it demolished and then rebuilt, abandoned to the elements and then reoccupied and garrisoned for war, the castle has had its fill of usage. And then, in the 1630s, its owner, Lord Nithsdale, built a three-storeyed residential block against the inner face of the eastern wall, in Classical Renaissance style, quite out of character with its medieval features, recalling a similar incongruity at Berry Pomeroy in Devonshire (q.v.). Nonetheless much remains of its formidable defensive building work.

CAIRNBULG Rathen, Grampian
(NK 017639) C
Cairnbulg is situated on the right-hand bank of Philorth Water near Fraserburgh. It used to be called Philorth. It was raised in the mid-thirteenth century by the Comyn family, and was a rectangular tower, some 70ft tall, which had a smaller tower as a wing. Additions were made in later years, and it was converted largely to a mansion at the end of the last century. The old parts can be seen.

CAIRNS Midcalder, Lothian
(NT 090605) P
Cairns is in ruinous condition. It was a roughly L-plan tower-house of the fifteenth century. The main tower was 27ft by 23½ft, with walls from 4½–6ft thick, and it was three-storeyed to the parapet. The extension making it L-shaped was a wing about 18ft square. The staircase is in a rounded extension on the outer angle between the two towers.

CAIRSTON Nr Stromness, Orkneys
(HY 251129)
Cairston has also been known locally as Bloody Castle. It is probably of Norse origin and was built in the twelfth century. Now only in fragmentary state, and absorbed by farm buildings, the castle was a small square enclosure with a tower in the north-west angle. The castle was attacked in 1152.

CAISTEAL DUBH Pitlochry, Tayside
(NN 947589)
Caisteal Dubh means Black Castle. It is a ruin of a thirteenth-century rectangular stone enclosure which had cylindrical corner towers. The enclosure was about 110ft by 85ft. Some walling remains to a height of about 10ft. The castle is also known as Moulin Castle.

CAKEMUIR Nr Crichton, Lothian †
(NT 412590) O
Cakemuir belonged to the Wauchope family. Built in the sixteenth century as a rectangular tower-house, 30ft by 24½ft, four storeys tall with gun-loops along the top storey wall level, it has been added to since then, notably in the eighteenth century. The castle is in good condition.

the wall head of the rectangular central block consists of a band of false gun-barrel gargoyles. It is also provided with a 'luggie' between the vaulting of the hall and the chamber above, formed in the thickness of the wall which was attained from behind a window shutter. The 'spy' or 'eavesdropper' could slip into a cubicle by lifting a stone slab, replace it and listen to what was going on in the hall.

CASTLE GRANT Highland
(NJ 041302) C

An L-plan tower-house of the sixteenth century was absorbed by a new mansion of the 1740–70 period, on the banks of the Spey. It has been neglected for a long time and is ruinous.

CASTLE KENNEDY Stranraer,
Dumfries and Galloway
(NX 111605) Gardens open

Kennedy was built probably in the late fifteenth century. It was a rectangular tower block with square wing, well built with dressed quoins. The tower was burned in 1716, but the shell stands today. At the time it was the home of the 2nd Earl of Stair, subsequently a field-marshal in the British army.

CASTLE LACHLAN Strathclyde
(NS 005952) A

This is an interesting ruin. From the outside it appears to be a large rectangular tower-house. Its external dimensions are 70ft by 54ft and today it reaches over 40ft high. But inside it is in fact in two parts round an open inner courtyard. It belonged to the Maclachlans, but during the Second Jacobite Rising (1745–6) it was fired on by government warships. Apparently, the Maclachlans abandoned the castle and it has not been occupied since.

CASTLE LEOD Strathpeffer, Highland
(NH 486593)

Leod was an early seventeenth-century L-plan tower-house with bartizans at the angles and an open parapet. It has been modified and is in an excellent state. It can be seen on application.

CASTLE OF PARK Old Luce,
Dumfries and Galloway   †
(NX 188571) SDD

Castle of Park stands over the shore of Luce Bay. It was built c.1590 as a four-storey plus attic tower-house. It received two wings, one a two-storeyed block at the south-east and the other a single-storey building at the north-east, both in the eighteenth century, but these have since disappeared. The remaining tower building has been restored and can be seen from the outside.

CASTLE ROY Highland
(NJ 007219)

A very early stone castle, beginning as a quadrilateral stone enclosure surrounded by a ditch beside the River Spey. There is a square tower on the north-west of the quadrilateral and a small garderobe tower along the west wall, worked into the wall. Timber buildings were erected against the inside of the enclosure wall, as is shown by grooves in the stonework. The wall is about 7ft thick, and is now from 10–15ft high. The entrance was through a doorway in the north. Roy may be compared with Sween for interest, but it is not in such good repair.

CASTLE STALKER Creagan,
Strathclyde   (NM 921473) C

You can see this relic on a small island in Loch Laich from the road driving from Ballachulish down towards Oban. Acccess to Stalker has apparently always been by boat. The building was a rectangular tower-house, about 45ft by about 36ft with walls about 9ft thick. The ground storey contained a pit prison. The entrance was at first-floor level, originally reached by a wooden ladder or stairway, later converted to a stone stepway. Stalker was built in the mid-sixteenth century, fell into disrepair after the Second Jacobite Rising (1745–6) and was restored in the present century.

CASTLE STEWART Dumfries and
Galloway   (NX 379690)

A seventeenth-century courtyard castle which has a square great tower with rounded angles.

402

CASTLEMILK Glasgow, Strathclyde
(NS 609593)
There was a tower-house of the fifteenth century here, used by the Stewarts, but it has been absorbed by the present children's home.

CAWDOR Highland
(NH 847499) O
This palatial range of buildings belongs to the Earl of Cawdor, whose family has owned the castle since the sixteenth century. Before that it was the seat of the Calders, who were Thanes of Cawdor. There was an earlier stone building, possibly a house of the fourteenth century, on the site. This was, demolished. Some of the masonry went into the fifteenth-century tower. The fortified

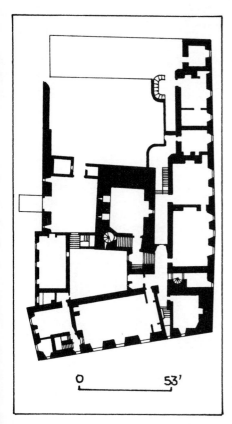

O   53'

Cawdor: Ground plan. Note original rectangular tower-house in centre, with thick walls and very limited window allowance

part of the castle is this central rectangular great tower built in 1454 following a licence to fortify his home granted to John Calder, Thane of Cawdor, by James II of Scotland. This licence allowed him to erect his castle '. . . with walls and ditches and [to] equip the summit with turrets and means of defence', but on the understanding that it was always to be open to the King and his successors. The tower which resulted was substantial, and the lower parts of it survive today, heightened by one of the Cawdors in the sixteenth century. The walls are between 8–11ft thick, and the basement is vaulted. In the fifteenth century it was enclosed by a deep ditch with drawbridge across. The entrance had an iron yett and was at first-floor level (which today has a large window in the space).

The later extensions and improvements were residential and are not relevant to this Gazetteer, but the castle is most certainly worth a visit not merely for the great tower, but also to see how a simple structure can have 'an expansive establishment built round it'.

CESSFORD Eckford, Borders
(NT 738238)
Once regarded as one of the strongest castles in Scotland, Cessford was a massive L-plan great tower of the early fifteenth century, with very thick walls and vaulted basement, and possibly vaulted all the way up in the smaller arm of the 'L'. The stone is local red freestone.

CLACKMANNAN Central   †
(NS 906919) SDD
A substantial L-plan tower-house, with additional buildings, stands on the summit of King's Seat Hill by Clackmannan. The oldest part is the north end of the L-plan, an oblong tower of the late fourteenth century. The 'L' wing was added in the fifteenth century and is five storeys tall, one storey higher than the original tower. The castle was once surrounded by a moat with a drawbridge across it. Note the machicolations and battlements round the parapets. The castle has a fine commanding view of the land beyond the town towards the Firth of Forth.

Claypotts: a Z-plan tower-house in remarkable condition. Note the clean cut gun-ports, the quoins along the square edges, and the masonry of the curved parts

CLAYPOTTS Nr Dundee, Tayside †† (NO 453318) SDD

Claypotts is a Z-plan castle, and it was built in the 1570s by John Strachan, lord of the lands of Claypotts, north-west of Broughty. The unusual fortress began as a rectangular gabled four-storeyed great tower-house of hard local stone. Cylindrical towers were grafted diagonally on to north-east and south-west corners, which rose to the same height as the bottom of the central tower's gable, thus forming a Z-plan (see plan). The towers were topped with overhanging square caphouses (inside which are garrets) and the towers were large enough to contain rooms all the way up. Each of the towers covers two surfaces of the centre building which in turn covers both towers. In theory it should have been impossible to approach the castle from any angle without being in the direct line of fire, which at ground level was administered through a series of wide-mouthed gun-ports a few feet up the walls on

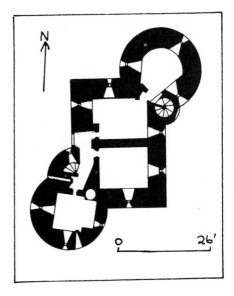

Claypotts: ground floor plan

404

every face. One shot-hole was put in the back of the kitchen fireplace, on the eastern side of the south-west tower. Another was put just outside the entrance door, at right angles and about 4ft up.

This compact defensive structure is one of several Z-plan castles built in Scotland in the sixteenth and seventeenth centuries (cf. Noltland, Kilcoy), and it is notable for its excellent state of preservation, its surviving roof and its unaltered construction. There were other buildings round it but these have vanished. The all-round defensiveness of Claypotts was never put to the test. Strachan seems to have been a law-abiding man and kept out of trouble, leaving his heirs not only an interesting castle but also a detailed will which listed his debts and assets before the bequests. In the 1620s Claypotts was sold to Sir William Graham of Claverhouse, whose great-grandson, John Graham, was to become famous through Scotland as Bonnie Dundee. John Graham, who became 1st Viscount Dundee, raised an army to help the cause of James II, driven off the English throne late in 1688 by English supporters of William of Orange. There were many supporters of James, however, in Scotland, to whom he was James VII, and when 'Dutch' William advanced into Scotland in 1689 to secure recognition as William III (II of Scotland), many Scots refused to accept him. War followed, and at Killiecrankie, near Pitlochry, Dundee commanded a Scottish army that defeated an army of William's under General Mackay. But in the moment of triumph Dundee was shot by a musketeer and died. Resistance to William collapsed soon afterwards, and Claypotts Castle was forfeited to the Crown. William III gave it to the Marquis of Douglas, and it has descended through the family to Lord Home who put it under the guardianship of the Scottish Development Department.

CLEISH Tayside
(NT 082979)
Restored in the 1840s, Cleish Castle is L-plan, was built of ashlar masonry in the sixteenth century. The main rectangular block of the tower-house is 40ft by 29ft and rose to five storeys. The two bottom levels are thought to have been built earlier than

the upper three, which may have been as late as the early seventeenth century. The outer angles are rounded.

CLONBEITH Strathclyde
(NS 338456)
A tower-house of plain rectangular plan, of the late sixteenth century.

CLUNIE Tayside
(NO 113440)
A simple L-plan tower-house, attributed to the bishops of Dunkeld between c.1485 and c.1515. Clunie is on an island which may be an artificial site.

CLUNY Highland
(NH 646943)
Fragments only of a medieval stone castle, probably of fourteenth century origin.

CLUNY CRICHTON Nr Banchory, Grampian   (NO 685997) P
This L-plan tower-house was built in the 1660s. It had a rectangular staircase tower set in the angle. The tower-house was three-storeyed with a garret. The entrance was protected by gun-ports.

COLLAIRNIE Dunboy, Fife
(NO 306171)
A fortified building which had ornamented shot-holes, Collairnie was once of L-plan within a stone barmkin. It was built in the sixteenth century. A tall wing was added in the 1580s with four storeys plus garret. The castle has been substantially mutilated, probably by time and exposure, and the main tower is now only one storey tall. It is used as a farm building, and thus may be missed when driving by. The wing contains painted ceilings, bearing the arms of several families associated with the castle and with Fife generally. The castle was probably built by the Barclays.

COLLISTON Arbroath, Tayside
(NO 613464)
A Z-plan castle of conventional shape, built in 1583 (though an alternative date of 1553 has been suggested), Colliston's main block is 45ft by 24ft, and has two diagonally opposite cylindrical towers. The castle's original entrance was guarded by two

shot-holes (Claypotts has one gun-port in a similar position), but a seventeenth-century modification moved the entrance into the middle of the main block (dated 1621). Further modifications were carried out in the eighteenth and nineteenth centuries which altered the castle into a residence without a military role.

COMLONGON Dumfries and Galloway
(NY 079689) C
This is a really splendid Scottish tower-house, of c. 1435, which dominates the north shores of the Solway Firth. It is one of three great fifteenth-century castles (the others are Borthwick and Elphinstone) at which the great tower predominates and which are perhaps the nearest equivalent in Scotland of the English (and Welsh) great tower. Comlongon is a seat of the earls of Mansfield (Murrays) and is in fine condition. It is occupied and not open. All the same, its exterior can be seen, and we may give a few details of its original interior arrangement.

The great tower is a massive structure of four storeys, the basement being vaulted and the others having timber floors. At the top of the tower is an over-sailing parapet upon multiple corbelling, the parapet being battlemented on three sides and provided with caphouses on two corners. The fourth side has a roofed gallery which is a later work. Inside, each floor consists of one main large room, with chambers, closets and stairs opening off into the tower's wall thicknesses. The first floor has the great hall. This has two fireplaces, one at each end. One fireplace is in an arched recess which was once a kitchen, and which is reached directly from the spiral staircase passing up and down the corner of the tower. The recess is now separated from the hall, but at one time probably had a screen with serving hatches.

The tower's storeys are reached by means of an unbroken spiral staircase from beside the entrance passage in the basement right to the parapet where it emerges into a turret. Like Borthwick, Comlongon's great tower was not provided with gun-ports or arrow loops. The massive strength of the tower itself was presumably reckoned sufficiently defensive.

COMRIE Tayside
(NN 787486) C
A castle of the Menzies clan, built in the fifteenth century, Comrie is now ruined.

CONTULLICH Highland
(NH 636705)
A stone fortress was built here in the eleventh century. Its shape is not known, for it was dismantled completely and the masonry used for a residence.

CONZIE Grampian
(NJ 095450)
A seventeenth-century castle, with little original work remaining.

CORGARFF Cock Bridge, Grampian †
(NJ 255087) SDD
A now derelict plain rectangular tower-house of the sixteenth century, about 35ft by 24ft, Corgarff was modified after the Second Jacobite Rising: a single-storeyed building was added to each short end, and the whole tower was enclosed inside a star-shaped barmkin with narrow vertical loops for guns. This provided a useful fortress for guarding crossings of the rivers Dee, Don and Avon by Cock Bridge.

Corgarff was the scene of an appalling crime in 1571. During a quarrel between the Forbes family, holding the castle, and the Gordons of Auchindoun, the 'ground wall stone' of the garderobe chute was removed by one of the Gordons and fire was inserted up the flue which set the castle alight (cf. Balvaird). Margaret Forbes and her family and servants were burned to death. Corgarff was burned again in 1689.

CORSBIE Legerwood, Borders
(NT 607438)
A rectangular plan fortress with walls about 6ft thick was raised on rising ground. The tower was about 40ft by 27ft, but is now in a decayed state.

CORSE Grampian
(NJ 549074)
A sixteenth–century L-plan tower-house built by the Forbes family. Patrick Forbes is quoted as saying, 'I will build me such a house as thieves will need to knock at ere they enter' (S. H. Cruden). This was after

the previous building there had been destroyed in a raid.

CORSINDAE Grampian
(NJ 685088)
Now called Corsindae House, the castle was a sixteenth-century L-plan tower. It has been absorbed.

CORTACHY Tayside
(NO 398595) O
This enclosure castle of the fifteenth century was considerably altered in the nineteenth century to include towers and turrets which were purely decorative. Originally more simple, the castle had four cylindrical flanking towers, and of this structure some of the curtain and three towers remain, absorbed in the newer work. The castle belonged, and still does, to the Ogilvys.

COULL Grampian
(NJ 512022)
Coull Castle was built in the 1230s. Its plan seems to have been roughly a pentagonal courtyard walled in stone. Remains of three flanking towers were discovered in excavations earlier this century, but the castle is in such poor state that it is not easy to determine its true shape. It was dismantled in c.1307 by Robert Bruce, following his policy of slighting castles.

COULTHALLEY Carnwarth,
Strathclyde   (NS 971481) O
This castle is mentioned in a late twelfth-century document, though we do not know its form. It was rebuilt c.1375, altered c.1415 and again c.1520. It emerged as an enclosure with three towers, one of them as part of the curtain wall. The castle was besieged in 1557 and rebuilt. Part of the rebuilding was an L-plan tower, but not much of the castle is left.

COVINGTON Strathclyde
(NS 975399)
Covington was an earthwork castle of the late twelfth century, or early thirteenth century, surrounded by a ditch. In the fifteenth century a rectangular four-storeyed tower-house was built on the site, with walls 10ft thick, some of which now reach as high as 45ft. The tower was built

with some skill. The corners are ashlar quoins, and the arrow loops are ashlar dressed at all levels.

COXTON TOWER Highland
(NJ 262607)
Coxton Tower was built in 1644. It has four storeys, is 23ft square, with walls 4½ft thick, and the principal entrance is on the south wall, 9ft above the ground. It has corbelled bartizans on two opposing corners and rectangular crenellated bartizans on the other two. The storeys are vaulted. The roof is unsound.

CRAIG Highland
(NH 632638) O
A rectangular tower of the sixteenth century, on the Black Isle. The tower is in ruins.

CRAIG Auchindoir, Grampian
(NJ 470248) O
Built c.1548 as an L-plan, three-storeyed (plus garret) castle with battlements, which was given ribbed vaulting and provided with wide-mouthed gun-ports at lower levels, Craig has been extensively altered and enlarged. S.H. Cruden states that there was originally an oratory over the entrance to the great hall (as at Towie Barclay). The castle was built by the Gordon family.

CRAIGCAFFIE Inch, Dumfries and
Galloway   (NX 088641)
A very small castle in good repair, consisting of a rectangular tower with vaulted ground floor and rising to three storeys plus attic. It is about 30ft by 19ft and hardly big enough for comfortable residence, one might suppose. There are fragments of some kind of courtyard. The tower-house well rises in the ground floor. The parapet is crenellated with rounded corner half-turrets. The tower-house was built in the 1570s.

CRAIGCROOK Nr Edinburgh, Lothian
(NT 210742)
This early seventeenth-century tower-house, whose three-storeyed main block is 60ft by 20ft and has wing towers (one square, one cylindrical and a rectilinear staircase tower), is incorporated in later renovations and additions.

CRAIGIE Strathclyde
(NS 409317) C

Most Scottish tower-houses were vertical rather than horizontal buildings, but there were some, generally of the earlier centuries, which were long, rectangular hall towers, constructed in the manner of Chepstow in Wales or Christchurch in Hampshire. One was Craigie, (but see also Skipness and Kindrochit). Craigie probably dates from the early 1200s, and the original long hall structure was incorporated in a later similar (?) fifteenth-century building. The earlier hall had a flush battlemented parapet round its wall tops. The embrasures were subsequently filled in and the walls carried on upwards and widened outwards to form a new hall tower, which was given rib-vaulting at the top. The ribs sprang from sculptured corbels set in the wall-walk of the first hall tower. The original entrance was a round-headed arch at ground-floor level on the northern long side.

The hall tower stood on a mound which was enclosed by a moat. There was a shot-hole near the entrance, inserted probably in the sixteenth century. The castle is largely ruined.

CRAIGIEVAR Alford, Grampian ††
(NJ 566095) NTS

This stepped L-plan castle is tall, substantial and formidable to look at. Built in c.1620–6, it has been described as being in the front rank of European architecture. Internally, it is luxuriously appointed, with a vaulted roof to the great hall bearing much decoration, including moulded plaster ceiling of which there are more in other main rooms, straight flights of stairs with landings, as well as spirals. And it has been changed but little since the 1620s. Moreover, it has been continuously occupied since its foundation.

Craigievar has seven storeys, and is topped with finely corbelled, well-proportioned cylindrical turrets with conical roofs. The re-entrant tower is surmounted by a pillar balustrade. The top half of the tower is well provided with windows but lower storeys have few, and these are mostly small. Palatial rather than military, it was fortified with ramparts and a courtyard wall with towers and an outer gateway. There

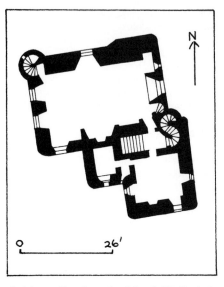

Craigievar: first-floor plan (after S. H. Cruden)

was only one way in — through a massive iron-studded door, past a yett and through a pair of equally stout doors.

The castle is in excellent condition, and standing high in the hills it has a fairy-tale appearance.

CRAIGMADDIE Strathclyde
(NS 575765) P

A sixteenth-century tower-house, of which only one storey remains. The dimensions are 28ft by 24ft and the walls were 5ft thick, presumably all the way to the parapet.

CRAIGMILLAR Liberton, ††
Edinburgh, Lothian (NT 285710) SDD

This is one of the most famous castles in Scottish history, chiefly because it was the place where the murder of Darnley, husband of Mary, Queen of Scots, was planned while the queen was actually staying there in 1566–7, so it is believed. It is also interesting by virtue of its plan, which is the result of four main periods of building.

The castle began in the late fourteenth century as a large L-plan tower-house, 53ft along the east-west axis on the north and 49ft on the north-south axis on the east. It has walls over 9ft thick, and is built with close texture rubble of red-grey sandstone, with long dressed quoins. The entrance is in the small extending wing from the south side of the tower which also contains a spiral staircase. Two floors above the entrance is a chamber generally thought to have been that occupied by Mary, Queen of Scots.

This great tower-house was fortified in the 1420s by a massive quadrangular enclosure wall on both sides of the south of the tower where a cliff forms a natural defence, and extending wide on the other three sides to form a courtyard, with rounded towers on the corners which were machicolated. The enclosure wall is 5ft thick and about 28ft tall. Ranges of buildings were erected along the inside of the east, south and west sectors of the enclosure. The entrance is in the north wall sector. Gun-ports were inserted in the north-east and the south-east corner towers. There are also gun-ports of later insertion in three of the four towers.

Extensions were added to the quadrangle in the sixteenth and seventeenth centuries, and there are remains of these to be seen, including kitchens and chapel. North of the quadrangle, a large outer courtyard enclosed in a curtain wall was created in the seventeenth century, or possibly in the late

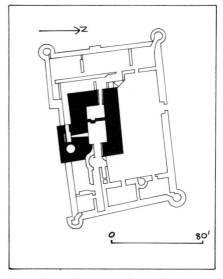

(*above*) Craigmillar: ground plan of inner court-yard. L-plan tower is late fourteenth/early fifteenth century, remainder is largely fifteenth century

(*below*) Craigmillar: an aerial view of this substantial castle

sixteenth century. On the east corner of this outer enclosure is a dovecot which has gun-ports.

Craigmillar was attacked and burned by the Earl of Hertford (later the Duke of Somerset) on behalf of Henry VIII in 1544. But it was restored in time for Mary, Queen of Scots, to reside there from 1566 to 1567, after the murder of her Italian secretary, David Rizzio by her husband Darnley. During her stay, a band of conspirators, Argyll, Huntly, Bothwell, 'Mr Secretary' Maitland (see Lennoxlove) and Gilbert Balfour (see Noltland) met and plotted to ensure that 'sic ane young fool and proud tirrane suld not reign nor bear reull over thame: and that . . . he sould be put off, by ane way or uther . . .', that is, Darnley was to be despatched.

CRAIGNETHAN Nr Lanark,   ††
Strathclyde (NS 816464) SDD
Craignethan stands on a rocky promontory overlooking the Clyde. It is an extensive castle and though in ruinous condition, it has numerous features of interest. A great deal of careful restoration work has been done by the Scottish Development Department.

Craignethan was built to incorporate defences using artillery, and these are of great interest. Basically, the castle consists of a western outer courtyard, of c.mid-sixteenth century, rectangular in plan with two square-plan corner towers, and surrounded on three sides by a curtain wall. On the east side the yard is protected by a ditch. In the west wall is a very fine battlemented gateway, defended at low level by business-like gun-ports. In the south-west corner was built a private house, about a century after the construction of the courtyard. This house is still standing and is called Andrew Ray's House. To the east of this courtyard is the older part of the castle, built in the main between 1525 and 1545. This consists of a second courtyard surrounded by a thick barmkin with two rectangular towers on the east, at north-east and south-east corners, a median tower on the north and a turret projection containing a wheel staircase on the south. On the west was built a huge stone structure, running from north to south across the ends of the barmkin, three storeys equivalent in height, with walls over 16ft

thick, with its ends turning at right angles inwards to meet the barmkin. This was equipped with gun-ports and battlements. This structure, described as a stone rampart, has now disappeared down to ground level. It edged the ditch separating the inner courtyard from the outer courtyard.

The principal feature of the inner courtyard was the substantial rectangular tower-house, much of which still stands. It is about 35ft tall, three-storeyed to the parapet, and built of rubble masonry. It is about 52ft by 65ft. Its west wall is about 12–13ft thick. The roof is missing but there is a wide parapet wall-walk. The tower has no gun-ports, but they were plentiful in the flanking towers along the barmkin. The south-east tower today shows gun-ports near the top which covered the slopes of the promontory at this point.

Craignethan was built by Sir James Hamilton, bastard son of the 1st Earl of Arran, and remained a Hamilton stronghold on and off throughout the sixteenth century. But because the Hamiltons backed Mary, Queen of Scots, against the forces of the Regent, and had also been implicated in the murder of two Regents, including the Good Earl of Moray, the castle was slighted by order of the governement in 1579.

CRAIGSTON Grampian
(NJ 762550) Open by arrangement
Built in 1604–7 (according to an inscription on a wall), Craigston belonged to John Urquhart, grandfather of the translator of François Rabelais' *Gargantua*, Sir Thomas Urquhart. It is a massive structure, with two wings at the front linked by an *arc de triomphe* over the entrance (see Fyvie). The castle contains a fine great hall, 30ft and nearly 21ft high.

CRAIL Fife
(NO 614075) O
Crail is on the north coast of the Forth Estuary. The site is practically bare, but there is a stretch of mortared wall about 16ft long, 4ft wide and 4ft high which may be the remains of a hall tower. The date is perhaps twelfth century.

CRATHES Banchory, Grampian   †
(NO 735968) NTS
An impressive tower-house castle, consider-

Craignethan: a reconstruction drawing of the castle as it was in the 1530s. The massive western rampart (which today is only a remnant a few feet above ground) served as a powerful protection to an already strong tower-house

ably restored and in fine condition, Crathes is well known for some interesting painted ceilings, notably in the Chamber of the Nine Muses. One end has a modern extension.

Crathes began as an L-plan tower-house in 1553. A date panel of 1596 suggests the completion of improvements rather than the end of the original building work, for a period of 43 years is long for a simple tower-house. Many of the alterations and improvements were done by masons from the Bell family. There have also been further alterations, including a three-storeyed east wing, another later wing, and some ornamental corbelled turrets. The original tower was equipped with a 'luggie', an iron yett by the door and a re-entrant tower for a staircase.

CRAWFORD Strathclyde
(NS 954214)
Crawford is mentioned in documents of c.1175-8. It was a motte castle which by that

time had probably received a stone curtain of rectilinear shape round the summit. Traces of a hall were found. But the remains there today are chiefly of a much later seventeenth-century structure which is not easy to define.

CRICHTON Nr Pathhead, Lothian
(NT 380612) SDD
Crichton Castle is a formidable structure of several periods, whose buildings are ranged round a square courtyard. It is among the largest castles of Scotland, and stands on a high site overlooking the River Tyne. From the top of the old tower-house it is possible to see Borthwick Castle, five miles away.

Crichton is now in ruins. It has little more than its walls, but it is nonetheless possible to trace the various building periods. The first structure was a plain rectangular tower-house of coursed rubble, which originally rose three storeys (but is now only two storeys tall), measuring 48ft by 35ft,

411

Crichton: an aerial view. The tower-house of the first building stage (fourteenth century) is at right, but now only a shell

Crichton: some interesting gun-ports in the parlour tower of c.1585 and remains of a corbelled projection stair turret. The tower adjoins the original rectangular tower-house

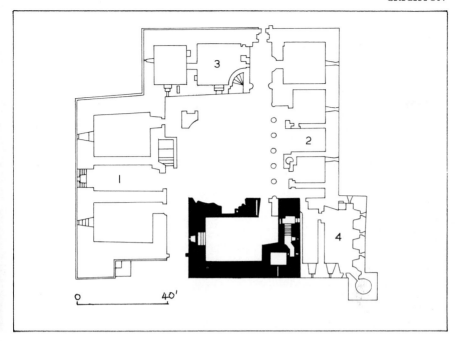

Crichton: (after S. H. Cruden). The bold lines indicate the original rectangular tower of the late fourteenth century. The other ranges were added later, in order of numbers

with walls about 8ft thick. This was built, probably by John de Crichton, towards the end of the fourteenth century. In the basement, which is vaulted, there is a prison cell in the north-east corner, with a kitchen above it. It appears that the tower-house was originally surrounded by a barmkin, later demolished and built over.

The second stage of Crichton's building story is the once massive gatehouse tower at south-west, built a few feet away from the tower-house and at right angles to it. This was erected probably in the 1440s by John de Crichton's son, William, who became Lord Chancellor, and who virtually managed Scotland during some of the minority years of James II. The gatehouse tower was a powerful structure, presenting a formidable front towards attackers. Entrance was through a passage in the centre of the ground floor, but this was blocked up in a later building period. The storey above the ground floor was principally taken up by a long hall right across. The walls of this

gatehouse are 6ft or so thick, and the rectangular dimensions of the block are 69ft by 38ft. The top storey of the building, which contained a second hall, carried a machicolated parapet outside, not unlike that at Borthwick.

The third stage, later in the fifteenth century, was a range of buildings on the north-east, at right angles to the original tower-house and projecting out beyond the north-east wall of the tower-house. This building, which was radically altered later still, was probably two-storeyed. The basement cellars remain in part. These were built upon later in the sixteenth century (see below). The fourth stage, built perhaps only a short while after the third, was a western range, three storeys high except for the south-west end which actually rises to six storeys. This range contained a variety of living rooms, cellars, offices and so on, and a postern gate on the north-west corner. The castle was besieged and captured in 1559 in the struggle between Protestant and Catho-

413

lic parties during the Scottish Reformation.

The last major stage, of c.1580–90, a century after the previous work, was not of military significance, but is interesting, nonetheless. The north range was heightened and developed, and given an arcade at ground level facing into the courtyard. Above this, the wall of the whole range was dressed with a spectacular diamonded façade (nail-head mason-work, as S.H. Cruden puts it) in the Italianate manner, like the Palazzo dei Diamanti at Ferrara. This was the work of Francis Stewart, Earl of Bothwell, a cousin of Mary, Queen of Scots' Bothwell, who had spent some time adventuring in Spain and Italy and who held the castle.

CROMARTY Highland
(NH 792671)

A motte castle of the twelfth century which received a stone tower in c.1470. The remainder of the structure was added in the seventeenth century, rendering the castle L-shaped (see Dunskeath).

CROOKSTON Glasgow, Strathclyde †
(NS 525627) NTS

This was a substantial rectangular tower-house castle whose origins go back to the late twelfth century. The tower-house is fifteenth century. Its plan was a rectangular tower with four rectangular corner towers (not unlike Hermitage, but much less pronounced). The walls were in part 12–15ft thick, and contained numerous passages and stair flights, garderobes and chambers. There is a noticeable shortage of defensive arrow loops or gun-ports, which has prompted the idea that Crookston was not a real fortress, despite its thick walls.

CRUGGLETON Dumfries and
Galloway (NX 484428)

Only fragments remain of this once important castle sited on a promontory, which began as a motte-and-bailey in the twelfth century. Traces of part of its original moat survive on the west, about 35ft wide. In the mid-thirteenth century, stonework was added, principally a walled enclosure, which appears to have been reinforced with flanking towers. Cruggleton belonged to the lords of Galloway, who ruled south-west Scotland as semi-independent princes during the Middle Ages.

CRUIVIE Nr Logie, Fife
(NO 419229)

A late fifteenth-century L-plan tower-house with what may have been an encircling ditch, Cruivie has some walls today rising to over 20ft.

CUBBIE ROO'S Isle of Wyre, Orkney †
(HY 442264) SDD

One of the earliest stone castles built in Scotland, Cubbie Roo's is a slightly rhomboid great tower of the mid-twelfth century. The walls are about 5ft thick, and the dimensions are about 25ft square. Today it reaches about 6ft tall. At a later date, a projection was added to the north-east corner, of which only traces remain. The tower is enclosed in an oval earthwork with ditching.

Cubbie Roo's was probably the castle (*steinkastala*) built in c.1145 by Kolbein Hruga, a Viking chief, which is mentioned as the 'fine stone castle . . . a safe stronghold' in the *Orkneyinga Saga* (translated). The origin of the castle's name is explained if it was built by Kolbein Hruga.

CULCREUCH Fintry, Central
(NS 620876) P

A rubble-built sixteenth-century tower-house is now part of a larger building. The tower is in a good state of repair.

DAIRSIE Fife
(NO 414160)

Two castles were built on this site. The first was probably a simple rectangular great tower of the fourteenth century. In the sixteenth century it was enlarged and converted to what appears to have been a Z-plan tower-house: the main tower has three storeys with cylindrical towers at diagonally opposite corners. The castle was occupied for a short period by Mary of Guise, wife of James V and mother of Mary, Queen of Scots. The castle is in poor condition, and little more than a shell of the tower remains.

DALCROSS Highland
(NH 779483)

A seventeenth-century L-plan tower-house in fine condition. It is occupied.

Crookston: an unusually narrow tower-house

DALHOUSIE Nr Cockpen, Lothian
(NT 323635) C
Dalhousie began as a fifteenth-century great tower-house in a courtyard enclosed by a tall, thick curtain wall. The tower is four-storeyed and L-shaped, and a staircase turret was added in the seventeenth century. Considerable alterations have been done since then. One of the entrances was protected by a drawbridge, whose lifting slots can still be seen clearly in the walling above. Dalhousie was occupied by Cromwell during his campaign in Scotland.

DALKEITH Lothian
(NT 333678) O
Dalkeith House is a palatial residence of about 1700. It incorporates part of the much earlier (fifteenth century) L-plan tower-house which was later encircled by a curtain wall. The castle belonged to the Douglases of Dalkeith, notably James Douglas, 4th Earl of Morton, Regent of Scotland, 1572–8.

DALQUHARRAN Strathclyde
(NS 273018) C
A fifteenth-century L-plan tower-house which is still occupied.

DARNAWAY Nr Forres, Grampian
(NH 994550) C
One of the homes of the earls of Moray from the fifteenth century, Darnaway Castle has few remains left of its original work. But one interesting survival is the great hall, about 90ft by 35ft, which had, and still has, an open oak roof. In the early years of the nineteenth century a substantial mansion was erected in front of the great hall.

DARNICK Nr Melrose, Borders   †
(NT 532343) O
Sir Walter Scott is said to have been so attached to Darnick when a boy that his friends called him 'Duke of Darnick'. Still in remarkably good condition, it is basically a T-shaped sixteenth-century tower-house built on an earlier site. The main rectangular tower has three storeys. The south wall has a square projecting turret with a caphouse, inside which is a staircase. Entrance to the castle was through the stair turret.

Darnick is built of rubble with freestone dressings. The larger windows are of much later date. The walls of the tower are up to 8ft or so thick, and the parapet is battlemented. There are later buildings attached to the tower.

DEAN Kilmarnock, Strathclyde
(NS 437394)
A straightforward fourteenth-century, high, rectangular tower-house which has had many additional buildings erected next to it, some of them in the fifteenth century, some of much later date, and all of them now restored. The tower is almost square, rises four storeys with battlemented parapet, and gabled garret above, bearing in one corner a small square turret. Though part of the present palatial structure, the tower has no communication with the rest of it. Beside the stonework is the remnant of a low motte. Dean belonged to the Boyds of Kilmarnock, the parvenu but ambitious family which dominated the young King James III during some of his minority years in the late 1460s.

DELGATIE Turriff, Grampian
(NJ 754505) O
Built in c.1570–80 on the site of an earlier castle of the (?) thirteenth century, whose main feature had been a four-storeyed rectangular great tower, Delgatie was L-plan, incorporating some of the original structure. Features of this late sixteenth-century structure, notably rib-vaulted rooms, resemble contemporary work at Towie Barclay, and the question arises, were the same builders at work on the two? The castle has survived remarkably well. A mansion was added to the tower in the seventeenth century.

DIRLETON Lothian   ††
(NT 516839) SDD
Dirleton began as an earth and timber castle built upon a craggy knoll at the eastern end of a low ridge by the de Vaux, a Norman family, encouraged to settle in Scotland by David I. Some time in the early thirteenth century, possibly c.1225 if the 'castellum de Dyrlton' mentioned for that date in *Liber St Marie de Dryburgh* is the stone castle of Dirleton, a cluster of towers was erected upon the earlier castle site. The principal

416

(*above*) Dirleton: the cluster of towers

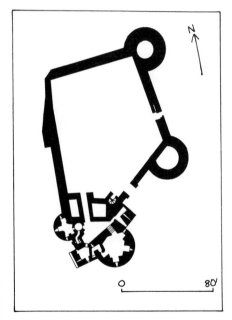

Dirleton: Ground-floor plan (after S. H. Cruden) Outline of the castle as it was in mid-to-late thirteenth century. The original two round towers at right are only at foundation stage

part of this cluster is the substantial cylindrical great tower, or donjon, facing south, about 37ft in diameter, on a splayed plinth, which rose three storeys, two of them vaulted, and polygonal in plan inside with a spiral staircase at the north-west corner. This donjon is not a complete cylinder: its north-west face was chamfered off to produce a straight side. To the west of the donjon and as a projection from it, is a square-plan tower. Emerging from the north-west of this is a walled passage into a second cylindrical tower of smaller size than the donjon. The cluster connected to a curtain which travelled north-east into another cylindrical tower (only the base of which remains below later work), and on the north side of that tower the curtain continued at a changed angle — northwards — to a second cylindrical tower, also reduced to traces at foundation level and now bearing later work on top. This thirteenth-century cluster and its extensions were complex, and the arrangements inside are best understood by reference to the SDD Guide Book.

In the fourteenth and fifteenth centuries considerable alterations and extensions were made, converting the castle into a more elaborate enclosure with ranges of buildings along the east, a more powerful gatehouse (remains of which can be seen) on the south-east, and a block on the north-east.

The cluster at the south presented, as it still does, a formidable front mass. Some of its lower rooms and prison pits are hewn out of the rock on which the castle stands. It was almost surrounded by ditching, most of this cut into the rock, some of which has since been filled in. Dirleton was besieged in 1298 by Edward I's orders and the garrison was compelled to surrender. For the next fifteen years the castle was held by the English, but it was retaken by Robert Bruce who may have ordered it to be slighted. This is a probable date for the damage done to the cylindrical tower on the south-east corner whose foundations survive underneath the fourteenth-century additions.

Dirleton was besieged in 1650 by General Lambert on behalf of Cromwell, since Royalists were using the castle (among others) as a refuge. A description of the attack survives in a contemporary letter. Evidently, 'the fourth shot of their [Lambert's] mortar-piece . . . beat down the Drawbridge into the moat . . .' Surrender followed.

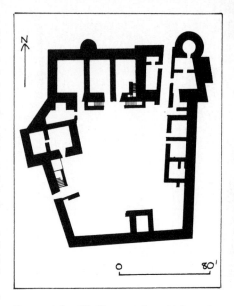

Doune: (after W. Simpson) Ground floor. The great gatehouse-tower is in the north-east corner

DOUNE Central
(NN 728011)

The name 'Doune' is reputed to be derived from *dun*, the ancient word for a fortified town, and there are traces of prehistoric earthworks around this splendid stone enclosure castle. It was built towards the end of the fourteenth century for one of the greatest men of Scottish history, Robert Stewart, Duke of Albany, Regent of Scotland from c.1396–1420 — the last fourteen years of which were the minority years of James I (1406–37). Much of it has been restored in the last and the present centuries.

Doune Castle is of unusual design even for Scottish castles. Basically, it is an irregular pentagonal stone enclosure with a powerful frontal range on the north side, and on the west a rectangular building which breaks the obtuse angle between two of the sides. The frontal mass consists of a thick-walled (8–10ft), roughly rectangular, block which is made up as follows: the eastern end is a substantial gatehouse tower, nearly 95ft tall now and probably several feet taller still in its heyday, shaped in plan like a rectangle with the two shorter sides tapering outwards; a bulging semi-cylindrical turret, five storeys tall, at the north-east, and adjacent to that a flat rectangular projection, similarly tall, solid and acting as a buttress. The entrance passes through the rectangle at a slant centrally at basement level into the open courtyard, and is protected by arrow loops in the passage walls. The gatehouse tower, which had a portcullis, is the strongest point of the castle. Above the entrance passage is the lord's hall, which has no access from the basement, but which is reached by a protected staircase inside the courtyard.

In the same frontal mass, west of the gatehouse tower, is the retainers' hall block with tall roof (restored) and parapet. Midway along the north wall is a projecting semi-cylindrical turret with open battlemented parapet of its own, providing a platform for covering fire against attack.

Behind the frontal mass, the castle tails off, as it were, into a quadrangle, whose curtain wall is about 40ft high and 7ft thick. The western rectangular building astride the join of two sides of the curtain is itself a substantial tower structure. This contains the remnants of the massive kitchen on the

Doune: an aerial view of the frontal mass, including the gatehouse-tower (at right), with the enclosure walls trailing behind

first floor, which is vaulted and has a remarkable fireplace about 18ft across, spanned by a segmental arch. This fireplace has a window in the wall between the arch and the back wall, and a drain in the floor. So substantial a kitchen is understandable for the scale of hospitality that the Regent Albany would feel obliged to extend. Above the kitchen are the royal apartments.

Albany died in 1420. His son, Murdoch, inherited the castle, along with much else, but he was put to death by James I in 1425, and Doune was taken over by the Crown, held for more than a century and then passed to the earls of Moray, relatives of the king, James VI, who still hold it. It was seized and garrisoned by the Jacobites in the Second Jacobite Rising in 1745 and used as a prison.

DOUNE OF INVERNOCHTY †
Strathdon, Grampian (NJ 351129)

A very fine Norman style motte castle was raised here with moat and encircling rampart. The summit of the mound, which is nearly 60ft tall, is surrounded by a low mortared stone wall, about 6ft thick, which was once much taller. The entrance is at the south end, with a square-plan tower nearby, inside the curtain. The shell of a rectangular building lies in the north segment. The rampart at the north extends as a dam, and by means of sluices controlled water from the River Don to fill the moat.

DROCHIL Newlands, Peebles, Borders (NT 162434) P
Drochil is a version of a Z-plan castle. It is a four-storeyed rectangular block of two rows of apartments separated by a corridor on each floor. On the north-east and the south-west are cylindrical towers about 26ft in diameter. The main block is 84ft by 69ft. The walls are 6–7ft thick. The towers are provided with wide-mouth gun-ports which cover the walls of the central block. But the block has no corresponding covering gun-ports. The doorway is largely unprotected. The castle is in poor condition. It was built during the 1570s by the Regent Morton who was executed in 1581.

DRONGAN Strathclyde
(NS 450178)
Fragments of a fifteenth-century great tower castle.

419

DRUM Nr Aberdeen, Grampian †
(NJ 796005) O
The castle at Drum is a fine surviving example of a late thirteenth-century great tower. It has rounded corners, walls about 12ft thick, and its original entrance was at first-floor level, as with many English great towers. It adjoins a mansion built in c.1620, which is still owned by the Irvine family whose ancestor, William Irvine, was armour bearer to Robert Bruce, and who was given the castle in the 1320s. The tower is over 70ft tall, has few window openings anywhere, and contains a spiral staircase from the first floor up to the battlemented parapet and wall-walk. S.H. Cruden states that the narrow and difficult way round the wall-walk was made easier to negotiate by the insertion of special footholds and that this feature is not repeated in any Scottish castle.

DRUMCOLTRAN Kirkgunzeon,
Dumfries and Galloway (NX 869683) O
A rectangular tower-house of the mid-sixteenth century, 34ft by 26½ft, three storeys tall, with gabled roof and a staircase wing. There is an overhanging parapet supported on corbels, and a narrow wall-walk behind. The tower stands amid farm buildings and can be seen at any time.

DRUMMINOR Nr Rhynie, Grampian †
(NJ 513264) O
Now only a fragment of its original size, this was begun between about 1440 and 1456 by the head of the Forbes family (who still own it). Curiously, the licence to fortify was granted *after* the structure was raised. The Forbes family were continually under attack by a rival family, the Gordons, and clearly needed a stronghold. But it was ultimately to no avail, for in 1571 it was sacked. It was a tower palace connected with buildings round a courtyard, and it has been restored with great care to attain something of its original shape and atmosphere. The staircase behind the entrance is said to be one of the widest in Aberdeenshire. The yett at the entrance was apparently stolen from the Gordons. The tower was four-storeyed, including the basement.

DRUMMOND Tayside (NN 844180)
The present mansion at Drummond in-
corporates the lower part of a fifteenth-century tower-house in its entrance gate. The original castle was destroyed by Cromwell in 1650.

DUART Isle of Mull, Strathclyde †
(NM 748354) O
Duart Castle has been extensively rebuilt. It stands high upon a rocky mound over the entrance to the Sound of Mull, and it belongs, as it did from the thirteenth to the eighteenth centuries, to the Clan Maclean. It began as an enclosure castle of late Norman construction, and its first stonework was a quadrilateral of walling, probably about 10ft thick all round. This has been greatly built upon and today much of the enclosing wall is 30ft tall. Adjacent to the enclosure was built a rectangular tower, about 63ft by 46ft, also of the late thirteenth century (or possibly early fourteenth), which has been considerably restored and modified.

DUCHRAY Central
(NS 480999) P
A rectangular tower, about 35ft by 21ft, with a cylindrical tower containing the staircase on the south-east corner. It was three-storeyed, the ground floor having a barrel vault roof. Erected in the late sixteenth century, it is in a remarkably good state of repair.

DUDHOPE Dundee, Tayside
(NO 395307) C
Predominantly an L-plan tower-house of the very early seventeenth century, Dudhope belonged to the Grahams of Claverhouse. The tower formed part of a courtyard castle, the remaining sides of which were high stone walls which have since disappeared. The tower began with three storeys, and a fourth was added later. The entrance was in the centre of the east front between a pair of squat cylindrical turrets.

Dudhope was owned by the celebrated Graham of Claverhouse, otherwise known as Bonnie Dundee, who commanded the Jacobite forces at Killiecrankie in 1689, but was killed at the moment of victory. The castle was used as army barracks for much of the last century.

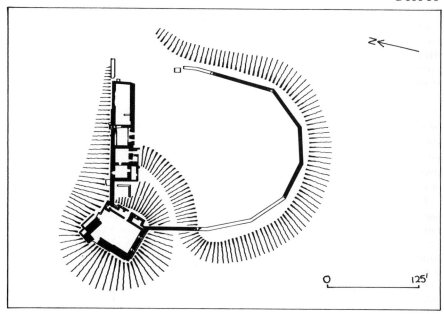

Duffus: the late thirteenth-century great tower at bottom left split and its north-west corner fell away. The range leading north is mainly fifteenth century

DUFFUS Elgin, Grampian ††
(NJ 175687) SDD

Duffus is one of the oldest and most interesting motte castles in Scotland that was later converted to stone. Founded by Freskin de Moravia, a Norman-Scottish baron in the reign of David I (1124–53), it began as a tall motte surrounded by a ditch and associated with a ditch-encircled bailey. The wooden tower and walling were completed probably by the mid-twelfth century, for David I stayed there in 1151. Duffus remained in the Moravia family's hands for some time. The name Moravia eventually became the much more famous Moray, and many of the Morays gave signal service to Scotland.

Duffus was held by a supporter of Edward I of England in his vain-glorious campaign to establish himself as king of Scotland, and it was burnt by Scottish patriots. It was rebuilt in c.1300, and it is thought this was the time when the motte was given a new stone great tower and the timber palisade round the bailey was replaced by a stone curtain. The stone great tower is rectangu-

lar, rising from a splayed plinth of ashlar. The stonework was of good quality, but the foundations were unstable. There are three storeys, about 67ft by 50ft exterior dimensions, with walls about 8ft thick. The staircase is a straight flight type in a projection to the south-east which is a thickening of the tower wall. Sometime later, the north-west corner of the great tower broke away from the rest of it and slid down the motte. The breakaway corner can still be seen today where it came to rest. This was due to the faulty foundations and the unstable condition of the motte soil, and indicates the risks involved in converting wooden motte towers to stone (see chapter 3).

In the fifteenth century further works were added, including a range of buildings (hall, cellars, etc.) along the north side of the bailey whose curtain wall joins into the great tower after crossing the ditch which was filled in. These are now in ruins, as is the great tower which shows traces of burning, probably in the attack on Duffus in 1452 by troops of the Earl of Moray.

421

DUMBARTON Strathclyde   ††
(NS 400745) SDD

Dumbarton Castle is built upon Dumbarton Rock, a volcanic neck of basalt jutting out into the Clyde. Its name is derived from Dun Breataun, fortress of the Britons, and it is probable that the earliest fortified structure on the rock was raised during the last years of Roman occupation of Britain in the fifth century AD. It became the capital of the ancient kingdom of Strathclyde, and it remained so until Strathclyde was absorbed into a united Scotland in c.1018. Nothing remains of the British fort, and indeed little of the medieval castle that followed it.

The medieval history of Dumbarton is one of continual change of holder: sometimes it was in firm control under the kings who appreciated its strategic value, or in the hands of the allies of the Crown; sometimes it was in the charge of the Lennox family, some of whose members held it against the kings. It was besieged several times, undoubtedly a difficult and hazardous operation in view of its geography.

The plan of the rock and the structures upon it (see plan) do not reveal the full extent of whatever medieval castle buildings were erected there, for the remains are too fragmentary. Certainly, dating is quite unreliable, even pointless. Buildings were raised upon the flat ground between the two rock mounts and on the incline to the river. Some wall lengths remain, and what is called the Portcullis Arch, dated to the (?) fourteenth century and thought to be the oldest stonework surviving. It was built to block access to the flat ground from the mounts. The portcullis groove is still discernible. The western mound contains on its summit the foundations of a cylindrical tower. The site of the governor's house at the south end of the rock contains traces of the wall of a medieval hall. From the seventeenth century, the castle was refortified with walling, batteries and gates, but these are beyond the scope of this book.

Dumbarton: the walls are delineated in bold lines

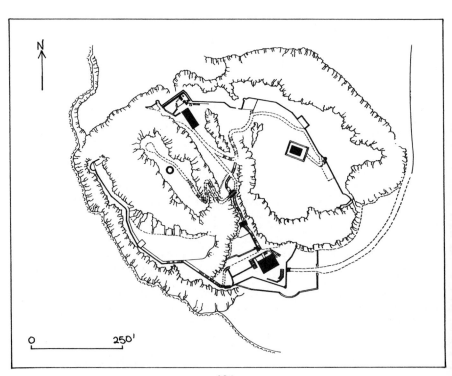

DUMFRIES
(NX 973765) O
There are some remains of a motte castle at the site of Dumfries Castle (D.F. Renn holds that these are the remains of two castles). The existing earthworks indicate a raised earth structure with associated ditching and a second mound 50 or 60 ft from the first. A castle existed in the 1180s, which was strengthened in 1263. The structure was refortified by the English-employed carpenter, Adam de Glasson, 1299–1302, which suggests it was taken from the Scots by the English.

DUNBAR Lothian
(NT 678793) O
Scene of several key struggles in Scottish history (notably the siege by England in 1339 which was relieved when supplies reached the Scottish defenders by sea, and the famous battle nearby in 1650 when Cromwell routed the Scots), Dunbar was dismantled in 1568 by the Regent Moray. Built of red freestone, it is now a jumble of ruins scattered over its high position 80ft above the sea. The castle plan was a stone enclosure with gatehouse, though the gatehouse was erected later than the walls, suggesting an earlier and simpler gate-tower. In the sixteenth century the masonry was given gun-ports. The castle may have been raised by the English in the very late thirteenth century.

DUNBEATH Highland
(ND 158282) C
Sited on a cliff, this elaborate building has absorbed the original fifteenth-century four-storeyed tower, which had walls about 5ft thick. The first additions were in the seventeenth century, when three corners were adorned with angle turrets of two storeys height. The castle was successfully besieged by Montrose in the Civil War.

DUNDARG Grampian
(NJ 895648) C
Dundarg ruins stand inside the site of an Iron Age fort on a promontory in Aberdour Bay. In the thirteenth century a castle of local red stone was raised here by the Comyn family, who were lords of Buchan. It was probably a simple enclosure castle. In 1308

Dundarg was besieged by Robert Bruce during his consolidation of power as King of Scotland. In 1334 it was rebuilt but almost immediately it was attacked, siege engines being used, as is recorded in a verse from Andrew Wyntoun's *Chronicle*:

> The wardane gert his wrichtis syne
> Set up richt stoutly ane ingyne.

Dundarg was rebuilt yet again. Among the features of which traces remain are an inner gatehouse, and a tower at the western end.

DUNDERAVE Inveraray, Strathclyde
(NN 143097)
Though this castle was built as the seat of Iain, chief of the MacNaughtons, in c.1590, there are charters relating to Dunderave going back to the fifteenth century. MacNaughton's castle was L-plan with a substantial cylindrical tower on one corner, something like Killochan. It was substantially restored by Sir Robert Lorimer (1864–1929).

DUNDEUGH Dumfries and Galloway
(NX 601880)
Little is known of this castle, and only a few fragments remain, enough to indicate that it had been a small L-plan tower-house, with walls only 3ft or so thick. The date is conjectured as sixteenth century.

DUNDONALD Strathclyde
(NS 363345) SDD
Dundonald is particularly interesting. A twin-D-end towered gatehouse was built for residential as well as military purposes by Walter Stewart, ancestor of Robert II of Scotland, sometime in the early thirteenth century. It stood on a hill at Dundonald and was part of a stone curtained enclosure. Robert II inherited the castle in 1371, appreciated its defensive position, and converted the original work which had been slighted in Robert Bruce's time, into a bigger, rectangular tower block, using its stone. This entailed blocking the passage through the gatehouse and altering the entrance arrangements, in effect turning the accommodation the other way round to face inwards. The king used the castle as a residence and died there in 1390. Much of

the tower still stands but is ruinous. The walls are over 7ft thick.

DUNGLASS Central
(NS 435736)
A fifteenth-century L-plan tower-house now in ruined condition.

DUNIVEG Islay, Strathclyde
(NR 406455)
Sited on a rock jutting into the sea, Duniveg (or Dunyvaig) now shows only foundations and fragments of wall somewhat buried by grass and heather. It was probably an enclosure of stone with an outer bailey. There are remains of a stone cylindrical tower, and foundations of a rectangular building. Duniveg is possibly a Viking fortress, but the dating is extremely uncertain. There are some fragments that have been ascribed to the 1500s, which suggests occupation in that century.

DUNNIDEER Grampian
(NJ 612281)
There was a first century BC vitrified fort within earlier earth outworks on Dunnideer Hill. In the early thirteenth century, a simple great tower was built using much of the ancient fort materials. Little remains of this castle, one of the earliest towers in Scotland. The basement had slits for windows and for arrow fire. The castle was mentioned in the Lindores Abbey Charters for c.1260 and belonged to the Balliol family.

DUNNOTTAR Grampian †
(NO 881838) O
Dunnottar is a rambling collection of ruins that were never an integrated castle. Some of the ruins have been restored. The site, on a promontory jutting into the North Sea, is surrounded by the sea except for a small, low-level isthmus connecting it to the mainland. The first structure was an earthwork and clay castle of the twelfth century (of which there is practically nothing left). Towards the end of the fourteenth century, William Keith, hereditary Great Marischal of Scotland, erected an early L-plan tower-house on the headland near the isthmus. This still stands to its full height but is roofless.

In the late sixteenth century, the castle was converted to a more palatial and residential structure. A quadrangular courtyard with ranges all round emerged. But one wall nearest the mainland was equipped with gun-ports, suggesting that the Keiths had not entirely neglected to defend the castle. It was as well, because Dunnottar was besieged by Montrose in 1645, and again in 1651, on the later occasion by the forces of Cromwell. It was slighted by the government after the collapse of the First Jacobite Rising. Considerable excavation and restoration work has been undertaken in the present century, notably by Viscountess Cowdray in the 1920s to help alleviate local unemployment. Several rooms in the quadrangle are now open.

DUNOLLIE Strathclyde
(NM 852315)
Dunollie is partly ruinous and partly in fair condition. It was the site of a fortress owned by the great Somerled, Lord of Argyll, who died in 1164 and was father of the founder of the MacDougall clan which still owns the castle. The principal structure is the four-storeyed rectangular tower-house (of the fifteenth century), which has a barrel vaulted basement. Associated with the tower are the remains of a later curtained enclosure which had buildings ranged along the inner walls. Only remnants of this work survive. There was also a second enclosure, of which only traces remain. A postern gateway in the first enclosure has a dog-tooth ornamented arch which suggests a much earlier period than the fifteenth century, probably late Norman of the twelfth/thirteenth centuries.

DUNOON Strathclyde †
(NS 175763) O
The earliest castle here was raised on an artificial mound in the late twelfth/early thirteenth centuries. It was a royal residence. Later, it was enlarged to consist of three cylindrical towers arranged in a triangular plan, but today it is in ruins.

DUNROBIN Golspie, Highland
(NC 850008) O
This amazing palace, largely the creation of the eighteenth and nineteenth centuries, is a superstructure upon an early fifteenth-

century great tower, with vaulted ceiling on each floor. The tower belonged to the earls of Sutherland (then Morays), and has remained in the family ever since. The first major enlargements were carried out in the seventeenth century when it was converted to a courtyard plan castle-mansion.

DUNSKEATH Migg, Highland
(NH 807689) A

Also spelled as Dunscath, this began as a low motte castle built by William the Lion (1165–1214) in c.1179. The surviving remains consist of two concentric semicircular ditches with ramparts.

DUNSKEY Port Patrick, Dumfries and Galloway (NX 004534)

Dunskey is on a promontory jutting into the sea. It is protected by a ditch separating it from the landward side. The tower-house is L-plan, with walls about 5ft thick, but it is roofless. Outside the tower are remains of enclosure walls built across the rocky site. The castle was erected in the sixteenth century, on the site of an earlier building which is said to have been burned down.

DUNSTAFFNAGE Nr Oban, ††
Strathclyde (NM 883344) SDD

This is a well-preserved, basically thirteenth-century, fortress on a rock on the south edge of Loch Etive which it commands. It is a quadrangular enclosure castle of stone with cylindrical projections on the corners which are embryo towers. The walls are about 10ft thick, and very interestingly, they can be seen to follow the contours of the rock on which they stand. The base of the south wall, for example, starts low down at the east and rises at an incline, so that the base at the west end is about 30ft above the ground outside. The walls are 60ft tall overall. The entrance is in the east corner about 20ft up, through a tall arched doorway, which is protected by a simple forework. Over the entrance passage is a tower which was added in the seventeenth century.

In the highest part of the castle, the north-west corner, there is another tower,

Dunstaffnage: this interesting thirteenth-century enclosure castle with towers rests upon rock foundations, notably along one side where the rock face actually represents a part of the wall, as at Spofforth (England)

larger than the seventeenth-century example, whose outer wall is curved, as it forms a corner tower to the enclosure. This projects square with one rounded corner into the courtyard, and is reached by a staircase outside into its ground floor several feet higher than the courtyard. Beneath the ground floor is a dark basement. The top storey is reached by the wall-walk behind the battlemented parapet. There are tower-like projections in the other two corners. Dunstaffnage was well provided with long, fishtail arrow slits, many of which were later modified to act as shot-holes. Its postern, however, was a natural one of great defensiveness.

The castle featured in several important periods of Scottish history. Alexander II and Alexander III used it during their campaigns against the Vikings in the western Islands. Edward I of England recognized its importance as a checkpoint to the approach to Glen Mor, and as a guard to the Sound of Mull. It was captured by Robert Bruce from the MacDougalls (owners also of Dunollie, q.v.), and who sided with Edward I. For a time it was held by the Campbells, Earls of Argyll. It is also traditionally on the site of an earlier building of the ancient kings of Dalriada, where the Stone of Destiny was kept until it was removed to Scone (whence it was stolen by Edward I of England and taken to Westminster).

DUNTREATH Central
(NS 536810) C

A quadrangular castle whose principal structure is a fifteenth-century rectangular tower-house, 47ft by 26ft, with walls about 4ft thick. Duntreath was given a gatehouse in the late sixteenth century.

DUNTROON Kilmartin, Strathclyde †
(NR 793955) O

This late thirteenth-century enclosure castle was raised on a promontory jutting into the northern side of Loch Crinan. The curtain wall is 24-28ft high and about 6ft thick, and the inner area is about 3,500sq ft. In the seventeenth century an L-plan tower-house was erected in the southern angle of the courtyard, possibly over the site of an earlier (demolished) tower. The castle was owned by the Campbells of Duntroon.

DUNTULM Kilmuir, Skye, Highland
(NG 409743)

A rectangular structure of the fifteenth century, some 82ft by 30ft, was raised on a site above the sea at the extreme north end of the island. In the seventeenth century a smaller tower was added. The castle is in poor condition.

DUNURE Strathclyde
(NS 252158) A

Dunure occupied a promontory overlooking the sea. It was a great tower castle of the thirteenth century, whose great tower was of irregular shape, possibly similar to Castle Sween. The basement was vaulted. A range of buildings was added in the fifteenth century. Only fragments remain of the castle today. Dunure was the scene of a frightful act: in 1570 the Earl of Cassilis seized the Abbot of Crossraguel Abbey and roasted him alive in order to get him to sign over the Crossraguel lands to him. The abbot survived to sue his tormentor and recover damages.

DUNVEGAN Skye, Highland †
(NG 247481) O

This romantic fortress is still occupied by the Macleod family whose ancestors erected it in the Middle Ages. The present structure is a nineteenth-century transformation of a castle that was begun in the fourteenth century.

Dunvegan stands on the top of a rock projecting into the sea. The first detectable building is the substantial great tower, 48ft by 35ft, which stands in the north-east and which has been embellished. The tower has 10ft-thick walls, and it is used today, among other things, to display many historic Scottish relics. One early feature of the castle still visible is the remnant of a sea gate which enabled the castle to receive supplies if the landward side was blockaded by enemies.

EARLSHALL Leuchars, Fife
(NO 465211)

Earlshall has been much restored by Sir Robert Lorimer. In its original shape of 1546, it was nearly Z-plan, but not quite. A rectangular tower block with thin walls had a cylindrical tower on the north-east corner (with its own spiral stair). Projecting southwards from the main block, and at the western end, was raised a square-plan tower whose southernmost walls at first and second storeys are considerably thicker (8ft and 7ft respectively). In the angle between this tower and the main block was built a rounded cornered staircase turret. The castle was later extended at the south to contain a courtyard at the other end of which was built, in the seventeenth century, a rectangular range, forming the third side of an enclosure. All this work became ruinous, and was not restored until the present century. It is occupied and is in excellent condition.

EDEN Grampian
(NJ 698588)
Ruins of a sixteenth-century Z-plan tower-house.

EDINAMPLE Central
(NN 625235)
A Z-plan castle of the early seventeenth-century, erected by the Campbells of Glenorchy. Edinample contains a notorious pit prison.

EDINBURGH Lothian   †
(NT 252736) SDD
Edinburgh is probably the most famous of all Scottish castles. The most prominent in a city of conspicuous buildings, its history is largely bound up with the story of Scotland. Its periods of construction span many centuries, beginning at least from the eleventh when Malcolm III erected a wooden fortress upon the huge rock mass that towers some 270ft above the valley that is now occupied by Waverley Station and Princes Street Gardens. The castle has been a palace, a treasury, the home of Scotland's records, a refuge for several Scottish kings during their minority years, and a prison.

The top of the rock is girt with a wall erected in several stages and inside that is the citadel which contains several buildings. The castle that can be seen today, however, bears small resemblance to the medieval castle, and only a few buildings of earlier than seventeenth-century date remain. Notable among these is the small chapel of St Margaret on the highest part of the castle. This is a fine Norman building of the early twelfth century, and is named after the wife of Malcolm III, Queen Margaret, who was

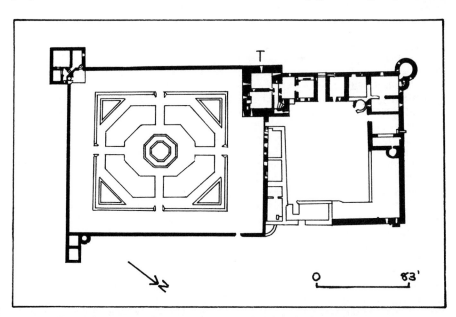

Edzell: ground plan T = the tower-house. At left is the famous Edzell garden

Edzell: the garden in front of the tower-house was first laid out in about 1604

canonized. It has been considerably altered and repaired over the centuries, but still retains some original features. Another early structure of which there are remnants is a tower that was L-shaped and which rose to about 60ft. It had a drawbridge. This is known as David's Tower, named after David II (1329–71) who built it probably between 1368 and 1371. Today, the ruins that include a vaulted chamber are submerged in the great Half-Moon Battery (or Great Half Bastion Round). This was built in the late sixteenth century by the Regent Morton, and later heightened. David's Tower had been largely destroyed in a siege of 1573.

Edinburgh Castle was besieged many times in the Middle Ages: for example, it was attacked and taken by Edward I of England in 1296, and recaptured by Robert Bruce's valiant nephew Thomas Randolph, Earl of Moray, in 1313. Moray destroyed the castle, but not the St Margaret Chapel.

EDZELL Nr Brechin, Tayside   †
(NO 585691) SDD

Edzell began as a substantial rectangular tower-house of the early sixteenth century with a square-plan projection out of the north-west corner to contain the stairs. Later in the century a quadrangle of buildings was raised beside it, anchored on the tower's north-west wall, and connected to it by an entrance hall. Finally, in the very first years of the 1600s, a spacious pleasaunce was added to the eastern side of the courtyard. This was a huge walled garden, with a square-plan bath-house tower on the south-east and a summer-house on the north-east corner. The garden is one of the most notable in any western European castle. As a fortress, Edzell had a peaceful history. Though fortified, it never sustained siege, but it was garrisoned for a while by troops of Cromwell in 1651–2. It was, however, vandalized by creditors and others after the Second Jacobite Rising.

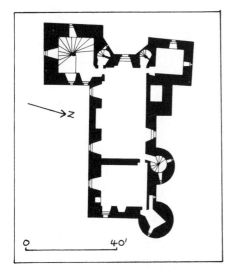

Elcho: first-floor plan showing 'haphazard placing and accretion of towers' (Cruden, p.161). Note the very wide ceremonial style staircase at top left

ELCHO Nr Perth, Tayside
(NO 164211) SDD

A massive five-storeyed, rectangular tower-house of the sixteenth century which is today in splendid condition after restoration. The castle is particularly fascinating for its tower attachments. This was a building propensity of many Scottish tower-house owners, alluded to by S.H. Cruden as the 'haphazard placing and accretion of towers', and is well demonstrated at Elcho. A substantial square-plan tower projects from the south-west corner of the block. It has walls 6–8ft thick. On the north long wall of the block are three more tower projections, west to east, one square and slightly tilted to north-east, one semi-cylindrical and one cylindrical (on the north-east corner). The castle windows are protected by iron grilles and the walls are equipped with gun-ports, most of them wide-mouthed. There is evidence that the tower-house was at one time enclosed inside a barmkin with a ditch outside.

ELGIN Grampian
(NJ 212628)
Mentioned as early as the 1220s, Elgin

Castle may have begun as a simple stone enclosure or great tower. A case has been put for its beginnings in the twelfth century. Very little remains of the building which is thought to have been derelict since the fifteenth century. The enclosure that can be detected was about 63ft by 32ft with rubble-built walls about 8ft thick.

ELLON Grampian
(NJ 960307)
A four-storeyed sixteenth-century tower-house that has undergone modification, so that its original shape is hard to determine.

ELPHINSTONE Lothian
(NT 390698)
Elphinstone is one of three massive, rectangular tower-houses of the early fifteenth century (Borthwick and Comlongon are the other two), which are regarded as the finest of their kind anywhere in Scotland.

Elphinstone was built in c.1440. The plan is rectangular, about 50ft by 35ft, with walls up to 9ft thick, the tower rising five storeys to the parapet, some 57ft from the ground, plus an attic storey above. Each storey has a

Elphinstone: elevation of tower-house

429

substantial main room. The lower two storeys are split by a wooden floor, but the upper ceiling is barrel vaulted. Above that is the great hall, vaulted but not split in two storeys. And above that are two more storeys, plus the attic. In the wall thickness is a virtual honeycomb of chambers, passages, staircases and cubicles. From the mezzanine storey to the lower half of the hall storey are three separate wheel stairs, and a straight flight up to the upper half and its many passages and chambers off. The flue of the fireplace in the great hall contains a chamber with a window looking over the hall. The chamber opens off a secret set of rooms in the north-west corner of the tower, which has an exclusive wheel stair from the hall. The tower is equipped with 'luggies'. The whole tower is amazingly short of window space, and has no gun-ports or shot-holes. And yet it presented a formidable appearance that did not belie its defensiveness.

ELSIESHIELS Lochmaben, Dumfries and Galloway (NY 069850)
A much modernized L-plan tower-house of the sixteenth century, three storeyed with attic, with a square stair-tower extension on the north wall of the tower. The stair tower is five-storeyed. The modern additions include bartizans on the south-east and south-west corners of the main block. Attached to the west wall is a Georgian mansion house.

ERCHLESS Kiltarlity, Highland.
(NH 410408)
This castle has been renovated and modernized but it was originally an L-plan tower-house of the period c.1590–c.1625.

ESSLEMONT Ellon, Grampian
(NJ 932297)
Two castles have occupied this site. The first, built in the fourteenth century, was destroyed by fire in the 1490s: marks of burning have been found. A licence to start again was granted in c.1500, though it is argued that the second structure did not begin until the late sixteenth century, probably 1570–90. This structure was a three-storeyed L-plan tower-house with a square-plan staircase turret in the angle. A

cylindrical tower at the east corner projects into the ditch. Some of the tower masonry appears to be of earlier date, presumably remains of the destroyed fourteenth-century building. The main tower block is 55ft by 42ft, and the walls are 6–7ft thick.

ETHIE Inverkeilor, Tayside
(NO 687468)
Basically an E-plan tower-house built in the fifteenth century, which has received considerable alterations that obscure the original shape. By the mid-sixteenth century, Ethie had grown into a courtyard castle with the main building on the south, and having a second yard on the northern end. It was enclosed by a moat which is now covered. The castle is well maintained and occupied.

EVELAW Westruther, Borders
(NT 661526)
A partly ruinous sixteenth-century tower-house, three-storeyed, and still whole to its parapet. The tower-house is L-plan, with rounded corners, corbelled out to square at the level of the eaves. Evelaw has wide-mouth splayed gun-ports in south and east walls. Another building has been raised against the tower-house, and this also has gun-ports.

EVELICK Kilspindie, Tayside
(NO 204257)
A four-storeyed L-plan tower-house of the early sixteenth century, Evelick is now derelict. There is a later building adjoining it, and this contains masonry that is thought to have come from another building of the original construction.

FAIRBURN TOWER Urray, Highland
(NH 469523)
A ruined tower-house of late sixteenth-/early seventeenth-century construction, the earlier part being the rectangular great tower with angle turrets. It was equipped with gun-ports in each wall. The castle was a Mackenzie stronghold.

FAIRLIE Largs, Strathclyde
(NS 213549)
This castle is in ruinous condition. It was a fifteenth-century rectangular tower, about 45ft by 29ft with a great hall on the first floor

served by a kitchen separated by screens, similar to Skelmorlie and Law in the neighbourhood. The first floor at Fairlie was reached by a spiral staircase at the ground floor next to the entrance. Fairlie was given a rounded angle turret at each corner.

FALKLAND Fife
(NO 254076) NTS
The present magnificent palace at Falkland was begun by James II (1437–60) in about 1458, and work was continued by his successors, notably James V. It was raised upon the remains of an earlier castle whose origins can be dated to the thirteenth century, but of which only a few fragments remain. Falkland is not within the scope of this work, but the palace is well worth a visit. Note some keyhole and wide-mouth gun-ports, inserted in the sixteenth century.

FALSIDE, Tranent, Lothian
(NT 377709) P
Falside began in the fifteenth century as a rectangular tower, 30ft by 39ft, with four storeys, the top storey of which was vaulted. This tower was badly damaged by the English after the Battle of Pinkie (1547). A few years later Falside was enlarged by adding an L-plan tower-house to the south wall of the original tower, to the same height.

FARNELL Tayside
(NO 624555) Open by arrangement
This is today a tidy, modern, three-storeyed building, with a semi-cylindrical projecting turret containing the entrance door and a staircase. It is a rebuild of a late thirteenth century castle. The first renovation was begun in the 1570s, and it was restored in the 1960s. Farnell has absorbed features of the thirteenth-century castle which had been a palace-fortress of the bishops of Brechin.

FAST Borders
(NT 595182)
A motte castle of the twelfth century, sometimes known as Castle Knowe. It was erected on the left bank of Rule Water only half a mile from Bedrule Castle. The mound was about 45ft tall in natural height, and about 10ft of extra height was added to it

before erecting the wooden great tower on the summit.

FATLIPS Minto, Borders
(NT 581208) O
This is one of two castles of this name in Scotland, and it stands in a commanding position. The basic structure is sixteenth century. Much restoration has been done. The original rectangular tower was 27ft by 32ft, and rose to four storeys with an additional garret. It was built of local whin-stone with freestone dressings. The castle contains a museum of interesting relics including a breech loading gun, a muzzle gun of the seventeenth century and outside a cannon of c.1637.

FATLIPS Symington, Strathclyde
(NS 968340)
There is very little to see of this sixteenth-century rectangular great tower built of coursed rubble. It was about 44ft by 28ft, with 5ft-thick walls, and the south-west corner was rounded. The tower contained a crosswall, reminiscent of English great towers. At present, some of the walling stands, but nowhere higher than about 5ft.

FEDDERATE Grampian
(NJ 897498)
Said to have been built in the thirteenth century, only some stone fragments remain.

FENTONS TOWER North Berwick, Lothian
(NT 543820)
A sixteenth-century rectangular tower-house with small area wing attached. The walls are about 4ft thick, hardly adequate as fortification.

FERNIE Monimail, Fife
(NO 316147)
A tall L-plan castle of the sixteenth century with many additions of the seventeenth century and later. It is in good condition and is used as a hotel.

FERNIEHURST Jedburgh, Borders
(NT 632179)
This castle is largely a sixteenth-century reconstruction of an earlier building. It consists of a long rectangular block of three

storeys, at one end of which are two wings, making the plan approximately T-shaped. One of the wings contains the principal staircase. The wings are provided with corner turrets corbelled out on the corners, with conical roof tops. The earlier building, whose remains are incorporated in the present structure, was seized by forces of Henry VIII during the 1547 war between Scotland and England, but they were driven out.

FETTERESSO Grampian
(NO 842855)
A rectangular block of the fifteenth century with a courtyard which had a second block added in the seventeenth century to make two sides of a quadrangle. Montrose burnt the eastern block in 1645 and it was rebuilt later in the century. The castle was further renovated in the nineteenth century, but is for the most part derelict today. The Old Pretender, James Edward, was proclaimed King James VIII of Scotland here in 1715.

FIDDES Grampian †
(NO 824812) O
A roughly L-plan castle of unusual shape, built at the end of the sixteenth century. It has a cylindrical staircase tower on the top edge of the lower arm of the 'L', and a second cylindrical tower on the bottom edge. A third cylindrical tower is corbelled out on the first floor and rises to the second floor, containing another staircase. This is in the middle of the other arm of the 'L'. Fiddes is provided with several gun-ports.

FINAVON Tayside
(NO 497565)
A seventeenth-century L-plan tower-house which has interesting double shot-holes.

FINDLATER Fordyce, Grampian
(NJ 542672)
Now in ruins, this was once a substantial castle on a high rock almost entirely encircled by the sea. It was reached across an isthmus. On the mainland a ditch provided extra protection. The castle appears to have had several towers and some curtain walling. The remains are scanty.

FINDOCHTY Grampian
(NJ 456674)
A sixteenth-century L-plan tower-house whose original work is ruined.

FINGASK Kilspindie, Tayside
(NO 228274)
The more modern structure here contains remains of a late sixteenth-century tower-house which was besieged during the Civil War (1642–6), and is recorded as having been dismantled in 1746 at the end of the Second Jacobite Rising.

FINLARIG Killin, Central
(NN 575338) O
A panel over the entrance dates this L-plan tower-house to 1609. It was raised on a mound of earth which indicates that an earlier castle had once been on the site, and this is lent support by traces of a moat. The tower-house, which reaches about 30ft high, is dilapidated. There are gun-ports in the walls. In the grounds of the castle is a stone tank, which was probably a water reservoir. But the first owners of Finlarig, the Breadalbanes, were a remarkably violent family, and local legend used to claim that the tank was a gallows: victims were pushed into it, their heads shoved through the drain and then chopped off.

FORDELL Dalgety, Fife
(NT 147853) O
Fordell was a Z-plan castle built in about 1580 on the site of an earlier fortified building. The plan is a main rectangular block (running east to west) with two wings containing staircases, one on the north-west edge and the other on the south-east. The wings were square towered, with a cylindrical turret corbelled out of the north-west wing. There were cylindrical turrets on the north-east and south-west corners as well. Though it is a small structure, its 5ft-thick walls indicate that it was a fortified residence. It has been modernized in recent years.

FORDYCE Grampian
(NJ 555638)
A three-storeyed tower-house of L-plan of the late sixteenth century, Fordyce has a tall semi-circular projection corbelled out from

the first-floor level upwards to the roof of the main rectangular block. The turrets and walls have shot-holes. A second tower extension was added later against one wall of the main block.

FORFAR Tayside
(NO 456508) O
There is nothing to see now of an early castle built here, probably in the twelfth century when it is first mentioned. It may have been a stone enclosure built upon an even earlier earthwork. There is evidence that remains were visible in the seventeenth century.

FORRES Grampian
(NJ 034587)
There is nothing now to see of what appears to have been a thirteenth-century castle here. The suggestion from excavation is that it was a rectangular enclosure castle of stone, with towers on the western side. Forres was destroyed and rebuilt more than once.

FOWLIS Tayside
(NO 321333)
Remains of a (?) fifteenth-century enclosure castle with thick walls, flanking towers and gateway with portcullis are incorporated in the later seventeenth-century four-storeyed tower block which has been enlarged by a more modern wing.

FRAOCH EILEAN Strathclyde
(NN 108252)
This began as a rectangular hall-tower of the twelfth or thirteenth century. The north wall was built thicker than the other three and it contains a straight staircase. Wooden buildings were raised at the same time, or even earlier. They were then all enclosed by a stone curtain with a gateway at the south, traces of which remain. In the 1600s, the hall-tower, which had been abandoned, was taken over and adapted to contain a house which was enlarged before the end of the century. The house was later abandoned. Today the hall-tower remains rise as tall as about 13ft.

FRENDRAUGHT Forgue, Grampian
(NJ 621419)
The present mansion contains fragments of a rectangular tower of the (?) fifteenth century.

FYVIE Grampian
(NJ 764323) C
This is a magnificent castle to look at today, one of Scotland's great fortress palaces. Its long rectangular block has a four-storeyed rectangular tower with garret and cylindrical corner bartizans on each end. In the centre is a massive gatehouse-like projection of twin semi-cylindrical towers, flanking a recess containing at ground level a doorway. This whole south front is about 150ft long, and has a formidable appearance, but in point of fact is not properly fortified. The work is a series of impositions on an earlier castle which may go back to the fourteenth century. The first mention of stonework at Fyvie is c.1390. The south-east tower (the Preston Tower) was raised in c.1390–1430, the south-west (the Meldrum) tower, sometime between c.1433 and c.1590. The

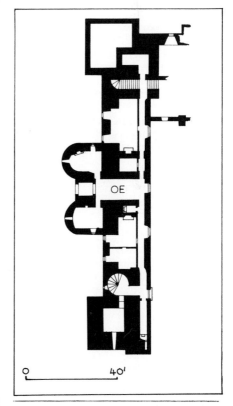

Fyvie: plan of the south facade at ground floor.
OE = old entrance

gatehouse is very late sixteenth century. Later still, additions were made, right up to the 1890s. One interesting feature is the wheel staircase which has wide sweep steps and a solid newel.

GALDENOCH Dumfries and Galloway (NW 973632)

This is now a ruin. It was an L-plan tower-house built between 1547 and 1570. It may have been three storeys tall, but the present height is about 20ft maximum.

GARDYNE Kirkden, Tayside (NO 574488)

Gardyne has been well maintained, and is still occupied. It began in 1568 as an L-plan tower-house with a rounded staircase turret bearing a rectangular caphouse (like Claypotts). The eastern end has a cylindrical turret on each corner. Later additions include a block on the north-west.

GARTH Coshieville, Tayside (NW 764503) C

Garth has been very well restored after a long period of decay. It is a square-plan tower-house about 60ft tall to the parapet, with walls 6ft thick and built of rough boulders. The tower was raised in the fourteenth century for Alexander Stewart, the 'Wolf of Badenoch', brother of Robert II of Scotland, who is thought to have died at Garth in 1396.

GIGHT Methlick, Grampian (NJ 826392) C

Built in the third quarter of the sixteenth century, Gight is a ruin. It was an L-plan tower-house which had ribbed vaulting (some remains today). The gun-loops are interesting: a crosslet (arrow slit in the shape of a cross) at the top of a slit and an oillet at the base, like Tillycairn and Towie Barclay and others.

The castle was built by the Gordon family, which, in the sixteenth and seventeenth centuries, had a reputation for violence. The burning of Corgarff Castle in 1571 is a terrible example (see Corgarff).

GLAMIS Tayside (NO 386480) O

This magnificent mansion of the earls of Strathmore and Kinghorne, one of the finest in Scotland, conceals a number of castle structures reaching back to the early fourteenth century. In 1376 Robert II granted the site, which probably contained a fortress of some kind, to John Lyon who constructed an L-plan tower-house. This had outer defences of barmkin wall and flanking towers, and the structures were surrounded by a moat which was later filled in. Remains of this castle are incorporated in the much later conversion to baronial mansion.

GLASCLUNE Tayside (NO 154470)

A sixteenth-century Z-plan tower-house.

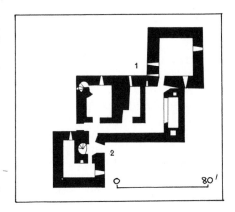

Glenbuchat: ground-floor plan of the c.1590 Z-plan tower-house

GLENBUCHAT Grampian (NJ 398149) SDD

An interesting late sixteenth-century castle on the Z-plan, with square towers at diagonally opposite corners of the main rectangular block. There is a staircase from first floor upwards in a half-cylindrical projection in the re-entrant between the north-east tower and the main block (1), and another exteriorly between the south-west tower and the main block (2). Both are supported by squinch arches and not corbelling. The entrance to the castle building is in the east wall of the south-west tower, and it had an outer door and an inner yett. The door could not be opened until the yett behind had opened. There was a staircase up from opposite this entrance to the first floor where, at right angles, access

434

was available to the spiral staircase in the cylindrical projection (2). The tower walls were equipped with gun-loops all round, providing for maximum covering fire against all directions of attack. The castle is standing with most of its walling, but it is roofless.

Glenbuchat belonged to the Gordon family who were powerful in Aberdeenshire. It was built in c.1590. One of its owners was John Gordon, a hero of both Jacobite Risings. Known as Old Glenbuchat, his devotion to the Pretenders cause was such that George II (of England, Scotland and Ireland) was haunted by him in his dreams and would wake up screaming 'De gread Glenbogged is goming', in his excruciating German accent.

GLENDEVON Central
(NN 976055)
A Z-plan tower-house developed from an earlier, possibly fifteenth-century, rectangular tower. It has been considerably modified since, and is today a hotel.

GLENGARNOCK Kilbirnie,
Strathclyde   (NS 310573)
This castle was based upon a square great tower integrated in a roughly polygonal stone curtained courtyard, which had other buildings against the inside of the curtain. It was begun in the fifteenth century. The tower was 45ft by 35ft with vaulted ground and first floors. The condition today is so bad that it is not possible to say what height the tower reached.

GRANDTULLY Nr Aberfeldy, Tayside
(NN 891515) C
Principally a late sixteenth-century Z-plan tower-house of three storeys, which has had a large modern house of the same building style erected on its north and east sides. The corner turrets are rectangular. This Z-plan is thought to have been raised upon the remains of a c.1400 square-plan tower-house, which itself was enlarged to L-plan in the early sixteenth century. There is a gatehouse containing oval gun-loops. Another noteworthy feature of seventeenth-century origin is the tall cylindrical stair turret sited not on a corner, nor in an angle,

but projecting out of one long side. This stair tower is six-storeyed with ogee roof.

GREENAN Strathclyde
(NS 312193)
A rectangular tower-house of the sixteenth century, with seventeenth-century additions.

GREENKNOWE TOWER Gordon,   †
Borders   (NT 639428) SDD
An interesting tower-house of L-plan, built in c.1581 (this date is etched on the doorway lintel), by the Seton of Touch family. It stands on rising ground once enclosed by marshy ground. The tower is 36ft by 22ft, with walls 5–7ft thick. The shorter wing is about 17ft by about 11ft and contains the spiral staircase. The entrance is in the angle, and is still guarded by its iron yett. On the first floor there is a second staircase in a turret staircase corbelled out over the angle. This leads to the three higher floors.

GUTHRIE Tayside
(NO 562505) Open occasionally
A modern mansion has been added to the older square-plan tower at Guthrie. The old tower is 40ft by 31ft, and the walls vary between 5–8ft. It was raised in the fifteenth century, and has had additions.

HAILES Nr East Linton, Lothian   †
(NT 575758) SDD
An early castle with a dramatic history, Hailes is today a ruin on the south bank of the Tyne. It is one of the few Scottish castles which still displays masonry of the thirteenth century. This is to be found in the lower part of the tower in the north range of buildings overlooking the river, which has a pit prison. In the fourteenth century, the castle was granted to the wild and dangerous Hepburns (who later became earls of Bothwell) who raised the height of this north tower and built additional structures, including a substantial square-plan tower at the west, and some lofty curtain walls, much of which can be seen though in a dilapidated state. The west tower also contains a pit prison, this one in the thickness of the wall. Later work included a chapel in the sixteenth century.

Hailes was besieged but not taken in c.1400 by the Percys from Northumberland in the Border hostilities with England. It was attacked c.1444, in 1544 during the 'Rough Wooing', and in 1650 by Cromwell, whose cannon reduced it.

HALLFOREST Kintore, Grampian
(NJ 777154)

A ruined rectangular tower, still over 60ft tall, with 7ft thick walls, Hallforest was built in the late thirteenth/early fourteenth century. It had six storeys (including attic) and measures 48ft by 30ft. Little remains of the tower which is said to have been built at the encouragement of Robert Bruce and granted in 1309 to Sir Robert Keith, Great Marischal of Scotland, who commanded a major wing at Bannockburn (1314). No staircase of stone appears to have been provided, which means that access to floors was by wooden ladder.

HARTHILL Oyne, Grampian
(NJ 686252) C

Harthill is now a roofless ruin of a Z-plan tower-house, with barmkin and gatehouse. It was built by the Keiths in c.1600. There is a stone slab with the date 1601, but doubt has been raised as to whether this relates to the original building work, or inserted at a later date of building. The plan was a rectangular tower with one square corner tower diagonally opposite a cylindrical corner tower. The masonry was provided with a limited number of gun-ports and the tower does not appear to have been designed for defence against anything except a frontal assault. No gun-ports were put in the barmkin.

HATTON Newtyle, Tayside
(NO 302411)

Lord Oliphant built a three-storeyed Z-plan tower-house with gable top here in the 1570s. The main tower is rectangular and has square towers on the north-east and south-west angles. The building was equipped with gun-ports all round at ground-floor level, providing defensive fire over every direction of assault.

HAWICK Borders †
(NT 499140) A

Hawick motte is an artificial mound of the twelfth century, about 25ft tall, which may have been subsequently reduced in height by several feet. A coin of Henry II was found in the earth round the motte, which confirmed the date for its erection. Today, it

Hawick: the small motte as it is today. The step-way is of course modern, but looks very much as it might have done in the twelfth century

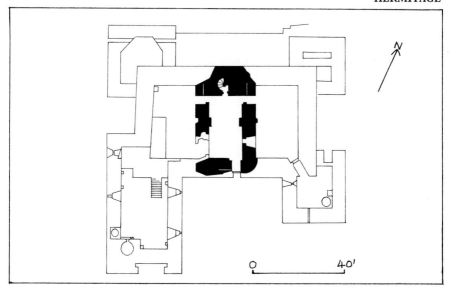

Hermitage: the bold area is the original tower-house of the fouteenth century. The rectangle immediately enclosing the original tower represents the first additional work, of the late fourteenth century

has a flight of stone steps to the top which vividly re-creates the appearance it probably had 800 years ago.

HAWTHORNDEN Lothian
(NT 286636)
Sited on a triangular promontory at the eastern end of a ravine above the North Esk, not far from Edinburgh, Hawthornden has a ruined fifteenth-century tower at the north which adjoins a seventeenth-century L-plan house. The tower was originally three-storeyed. Its owner, William Drummond, helped to organize the celebrations of the coronation of Charles I.

HELMSDALE Highland
(ND 027151)
Fragments remain here of a medieval castle of uncertain date, which was altered in the (?) fifteenth century into an L-plan tower-house.

HERMITAGE Borders   ††
(NY 497961) SDD
This is a massive tower-house castle of several periods of building. It has figured in many episodes of Scottish history, and for a

time was held by the wild and dangerous James Hepburn, Earl of Bothwell, whose liaison with Mary, Queen of Scots was the scandal of the sixteenth century in Scotland.
    The original structure was an early thirteenth-century rectangular enclosure of stone with walls about 5ft thick on three sides, and about 10ft thick on the north side where the spiral staircase was enclosed. This was more of a domestic structure, though there is evidence of ditching around it of early date. A castle at Hermitage is recorded as having been repaired at the end of the thirteenth century by order of Edward I of England. Whatever form it took, it appears to have changed hands a few times in the earlier decades of the fourteenth century. In 1338 it was captured by the Knight of Liddesdale, Sir William Douglas, from the English baron, Ralph Neville who held it by gift of Edward III. Later in the century it

(*overleaf*) Hermitage: the massive tower-house complex which for a while belonged to James Hepburn, Earl of Bothwell, paramour of Mary, Queen of Scots

was granted to William, 1st Earl of Douglas, nephew of Sir James Douglas (one of Robert Bruce's three trusted advisers). Hermitage was thereafter held by the Douglases to the end of the fifteenth century, and during that time developed from the simple stone enclosure into the huge structure it is today. First of all it was wrapped round by a much larger rectangular enclosure whose north and south (longer) walls are about 8ft thick and extend to about 75ft. In the south-west corner, the wall projected westwards into a wing in which the entrance was placed several feet above the ground. At the very end of the fourteenth century, projecting square towers of great strength were added to the corners of the rectangular mass. These towers are close together (they encased the corners of the mass), and on the east and west sides they are linked at the top by a continuous storey presenting the appearance of a huge stone wall with a great central pointed arch reaching to the top storey from the ground. There have been subsequent alterations, notably the provision of wide-mouth gun-ports in the 1540s.

HODDOM Dumfries and Galloway (NY 156729) C

An interesting variant on the L-plan, Hoddom's tower-house has cylindrical turrets on the corners. The walls of the main tower are up to 10ft thick, and rise to four storeys plus a garret. The building is on a strong site surrounded by a moat. It was built in the sixteenth century, incorporating some stonework of an earlier building.

HOLLOWS TOWER Canonbie, Dumfries and Galloway (NY 382786)

This is also known as Gilknockie. It is now roofless, but it was once well fortified. A rectangular tower-house of the sixteenth century, 23ft by 15ft, with walls 6ft thick, it rose to four storeys plus an attic, with a bold parapet. The tower was equipped with gun-ports on all sides, some of which are still in sound condition. The tower belonged to the wild, aggressive and lawless Armstrongs, who terrorized much of the Border district in the sixteenth century.

HUME Borders (NT 704414) O

This began as a medieval high-walled enclosure castle of the thirteenth century. Hume was extensively altered and enlarged in later centuries, and little remains today of the early buildings.

HUNTERSTON West Kilbride, †† Strathclyde (NS 193515) O

Basically a long rectangular block tower of two main periods. The first structure was a rectangular tower four storeys high. This was raised in the fifteenth century, and is about 24ft by 22ft with walls 4–5ft thick. The small square stair turret at the south-west corner was added in the seventeenth century, at the same time as the extension to the tower, slightly longer but of equal width. This new block contained the great banqueting hall. The tower (the first building) is battlemented, though the crenellations may have been altered. The castle itself was surrounded by a moat.

Hunterston was probably built on the site of a much earlier castle, an earthwork enclosure, which had been raised by the Hunter family (of Norman origin) in the twelfth century. It is in excellent condition.

HUNTINGTOWER Nr Perth, † Tayside (NO 084252) SDD

This is a fine tower-house beside the River Almond, made up from tower blocks of two periods. It began as a rectangular tower of the early fifteenth century which was renovated at the end of the century. It had an entrance in the south wall beside the east wall, which has since been filled in. This entrance led right through to an inner yard, and there was a door off to the west into the tower which rose to three storeys. The top can be seen, for the extra floors erected above at a later date are of different masonry work. This tower contained the great hall. The walls were plastered, and the ceilings were decorated with painted designs between and on the wooden ceiling joists.

In the late fifteenth/early sixteenth century, a second tower was built, rectangular, three-storeyed plus garret, with a square jamb, or out-tower, on the south-west corner one storey taller, and these works are still in good repair. The first floor of the western tower was given over to a great hall, which is reached by spiral staircase inside on the north-west corner, and outside by a flight of steps in through a door in the north wall. Sometime in the seventeenth century the space between the two towers was completed by adding walling up to three storeys plus garret.

Huntingtower is famous as the scene of the Ruthven raid of 1582, when William Ruthven, Earl of Gowrie, and the Earl of Mar, friends of boy King James VI, kidnapped him to get him away from the influence of their rivals, the Duke of Lennox and the Earl of Arran. In later years, the King ordered the name of the castle — then Ruthven — to be altered to Huntingtower.

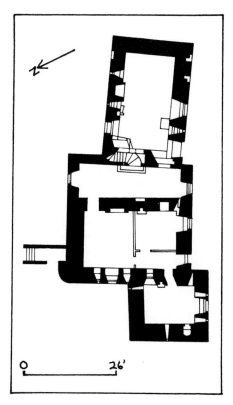

(*left*) Huntingtower: plan of ground floor (after SDD)

(*below*) Huntingtower: the south front of the castle. The fifteenth-century masonry is in the lower courses of the east tower-house

HUNTLY Grampian   ††
(NJ 532407) SDD

Huntly has been described as one of the noblest baronial ruins in Scotland. It is an apt description. This remarkable structure, a mixture of periods of building, was the fortified residence of one of the most powerful families in Scotland, the earls (and later marquises) of Huntly. Originally there had been a motte castle on the site, probably of the twelfth century — the mound and some ditching are still there. Parts of the wooden castle may have survived until the 1450s when in the confrontation between the king, James II, and the Douglases, Huntly was burned by the latter. Before this time, perhaps at the end of the fourteenth century, the first stonework was undertaken. It was a very substantial L-plan tower with walls over 8ft thick, but which has now vanished except for foundations. It had been placed among the earlier timber buildings in the castle, to the east of the motte.

After the 1453 fire, the 1st Earl of Huntly, who owned the castle, began to put up what was called the 'new werk' to the south of the 'auld werk' (the great tower). This is now in ruins but its shape is easy to determine — a rectangular block about 69ft by 33ft, four storeys tall, with walls about 8ft thick On the south-west corner is a boldly projecting cylindrical tower of five storeys equipped with gun-ports, and on the north-east corner is a smaller cylindrical tower. The whole block is fascinating. The top storey has oriel windows. The façade above and below the oriel window line has an inscription bearing the name of the 1st Marquis of Huntly and his wife. It may seem as if the block was not a defensive building, but its thick walls, particularly so at basement- and ground-floor level, its gun-ports, vaulted ground floor and iron yett in front of the door all belie this.

The structure is not all of one period, however. The basement is largely original

Huntly: the 'New Werk' of the last years of the late sixteenth and early seventeenth centuries

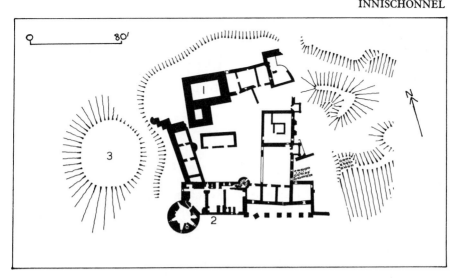

Huntly: (after SDD). 1. The 'Auld Werk' (fifteenth century). 2. 'New Werk' 3. Site of Norman Motte

fifteenth century. The storeys above are sixteenth century (some of the work 1550–4), and there was also rebuilding of those upper levels in the seventeenth century. The work was extensive and spread over many years. It was seriously interrupted in 1594 when the 5th Earl of Huntly foolishly joined a revolt against James VI. The revolt collapsed and Huntly paid for his folly by having his fine home blown up. But later he made his peace and was advanced by James to become 1st Marquis of Huntly. He celebrated this by rebuilding the castle, particularly the New Werk which had been severely damaged by the explosion. It was at this time that the inscriptions over the oriel range were put in, namely c.1606. The castle was occupied by Covenanters in 1639–40. The 2nd Marquis sided with Charles I and was executed in 1647.

INCHDREWER Grampian
(NJ 656607) C
A sixteenth-century L-plan tower-house which was destroyed by fire in 1713, following the murder of the owner, Lord Banff, an unpopular local laird. When it was restored later in the eighteenth century, the L-plan was enlarged and given a cylindrical staircase tower at the south end and ranges of

buildings to form a type of courtyard castle. Gun-ports were inserted. This castle was recently restored even more magnificently by the present owner, and has been described by Hubert Fenwick as resembling 'some knightly tower in an illuminated manuscript'.

INCHMURRIN Strathclyde
(NS 373863) A
This is an early tower-house castle which was built round a courtyard. The tower was probably raised in the fourteenth century. Remains of its wall are mainly 2ft or so thick.

INNERPEFFRAY Tayside
(NN 905179)
Remains of a towered castle of the seventeenth century.

INNISCHONNEL Strathclyde
(NM 977119)
Also spelled Inchconnell, this began as a rectangular stone enclosure of the early thirteenth century, which had pilaster buttresses like those at Sween. The castle was greatly altered in the fifteenth century, but it retained the older work, much of which can be seen. Additional buildings included a tower on the south-east and a

range of buildings adjoining, including a four-storey block. The castle was for a time the chief stronghold of the Campbells.

INVERGARRY Highland
(NM 315006)

An L-plan tower-house of the seventeenth century.

INVERLOCHY Nr Fort William, Highland (NN 120754) SDD

Old Inverlochy Castle was a c.1270–80 quadrilateral stone enclosure with four corner cylindrical towers. The north-west tower is larger than the other three, and is a donjon. The enclosure has an entrance at north and south, which have plain arches. Foundations of later barbicans in front of both gates have been found. There was a moat round three sides of the enclosure with a rampart behind that, and the fourth side was defended by the River Lochy, attainable by means of a water-gate, whose waters fed the moat. Although the castle is dilapidated, it has survived well. The cylindrical towers and the curtain stand 30ft high. Inverlochy commands the main route through Glen Môr into the Highlands.

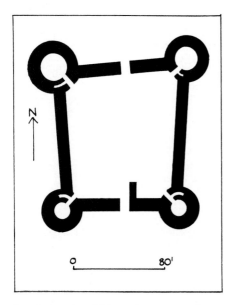

Inverlochy: plan of thirteenth-century enclosure with towers

INVERMARK Lochlee, Tayside
(NO 442804)

A tower-house of two major building periods, Invermark rose to four storeys plus a garret. The lower storeys were raised in the sixteenth century, and it is possible that the gun-ports in the basement level were inserted at this stage. Then in the seventeenth century the upper parts were completed. One of these was a cylindrical turret which has pistol-holes below a loop. The entrance to the castle is at first-floor level and is still guarded by an iron yett. Foundations of other buildings have been found to the south and east.

INVERNESS Highland
(NH 666451)

The first castle at Inverness was built in the twelfth century, possibly by David I. It guarded the routes to and from the Highlands. It was an earthwork structure which later received stonework, whose shape we are not able to determine. It had also had a hall built of timber boards, a *domus Scoticana*, for Alexander III. Its earthen outworks were also reinforced in 1263. The castle was captured by the Lord of the Isles in 1491 but retaken by James IV soon afterwards. It was severely damaged in Mary, Queen of Scots' reign, damaged again during the Civil War, and finally all but razed by the Young Pretender, Bonnie Prince Charlie, in 1746. The only remains are parts of the ancient curtain wall and some earthworks. It has been transformed by a variety of works dating from the eighteenth and nineteenth centuries and is used as a courthouse.

INVERQUHARITY Kirriemuir, Tayside (NO 411579)

A smaller tower-house of the fifteenth century, which began as an L-plan, though the smaller wing has gone. Inverquharity was built by the Ogilvy family. The main block is 45ft by 35ft with walls about 8ft thick, and it rises four storeys to the parapet behind which is a wall-walk and an attic storey. The disappeared east wing has been replaced by a later building. The castle remained empty for a long time but restoration work has been carried out recently. The second storey of the main block has the great hall of which the timber roofing is the original fifteenth-century work.

JEDBURGH Borders
(NT 647202)
A motte castle was built on a site at Castle Hill, probably by David I. The castle is mentioned in a mid-twelfth century charter. It was appropriated by Edward I in 1296, taken back by Wallace in 1297 and recaptured by Edward I in 1298. It was finally destroyed in c.1410 by the Regent Albany. In the 1820s, a building was erected over the site. This was originally designed as a prison and used as such for many years.

KAMES Bute, Strathclyde
(NS 063075) P
Originally a five-storeyed tower-house of the sixteenth century, Kames was rectangular in plan, about 36ft by 25ft, with walls over 5ft thick.

KEIRS Strathclyde
(NS 430080)
Fragments remain here of a stone castle of the thirteenth century. The castle was attacked by Wallace in 1297–8.

KEISS Highland
(ND 357616)
A Z-plan tower-house of the sixteenth century.

KELBURN Largs, Strathclyde
(NS 217567) Open by arrangement
This interesting castle is really in two parts. One is a four-storeyed, late sixteenth-century rectangular tower-house of Z-plan with cylindrical flanking towers on the south-west and north-east corners. In the early eighteenth century this was enlarged by the erection of a mansion house by the owner, David Boyle, 1st Earl of Glasgow. The site is said to have belonged to the Boyle family since the thirteenth century.

KELLIE Nr Arbroath, Tayside   †
(NO 608402) O
Kellie was raised on rock overlooking Elliot Water. It is a substantial L-plan tower of the seventeenth century, raised upon the site of a late twelfth-century castle built by the

Mowbrays. The tower-house has associated buildings around it.

KELLIE Pittenweem, Fife   †
(NO 520052) NTS
Owned by the Oliphants, and later the Lorimer family, Kellie is huge. Three towers are joined to a main block, the plan roughly in the shape of a 'T'. The north tower was built in the fifteenth century, the east tower was added in the sixteenth and the two were joined by the substantial main block in the seventeenth, with a south tower. There is evidence of the north tower having been raised over earlier remains and it is conjectured that the first 10ft or so of wall above the ground is of fourteenth-century origin.

KENMURE Dumfries and Galloway
(NX 635764)
Kenmure had been deteriorating for a long time until the 1960s, when it was taken in hand for restoration. Basically it was an L-plan tower-house of the sixteenth century which was burnt down at the end of the century. In the seventeenth century it was rebuilt, and extended into a courtyard castle of two adjacent ranges (south and west), reaching to three storeys plus attic. It fell into decay again, and was abandoned until the nineteenth century when some remodelling altered its character. Then it was left again, until the 1960s.

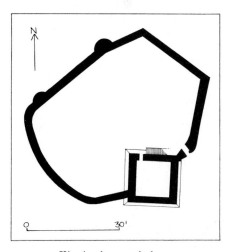

Kiessimul: ground plan

KIESSIMUL Isle of Barra, Western ††
Isles (NL 665979) O

Described in the chapter on Scottish Castles, Kiessimul is a late twelfth/early thirteenth century enclosure castle of irregular shape, following the contour of the rock on which it stands, with a square-plan tower in the south-to-south-west wall. It is the westernmost castle in Scotland, and was probably used as a stronghold in the national struggle against the Vikings in the first half of the thirteenth century. Eventually, the castle came into the ownership of the MacNeils, descendants of whom still hold it today, and who have restored it.

KILBURNIE
(NS 304541)

Now known as Kilburnie House, this began as a fifteenth-century castle of towers and curtain wall which received considerable modifications over the centuries.

KILCHURN Strathclyde †
(NN 133276) SDD

Sited on a peninsula in Loch Awe, Kilchurn Castle stands, a splendid ruin, among reeds and marshes. It began as a five-storey, square tower at the east, which was built in the mid-fifteenth century by Colin Campbell of Glenorchy, 1st Earl of Breadalbane. Additions were constructed during the sixteenth century, and by the end of the seventeenth the buildings were grouped round a courtyard. Kilchurn then seems to have been abandoned in the mid-eighteenth century, and is a gaunt shadow of obvious former splendour. Work has been done to secure some of its dangerous remains and the ruins may be seen from the grounds.

KILCONQUHAR Fife
(NO 493027)

A much altered L-plan tower-house of the sixteenth century.

KILCOY Killearnan, Highland
(NH 576512)

An interesting Z-plan castle of seventeenth-century construction, which has been restored. Its extension towers (at north-west and south-east) are cylindrical, the latter smaller than the former. Unlike Claypotts, which it resembles in plan, the ground floor

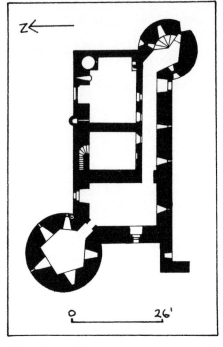

Kilcoy: Ground-floor plan of early seventeenth century Z-plan tower-house

has apartments separated from one main wall by a corridor. Kilcoy has vertical and horizontal gun-loops. The castle belonged to the Mackenzies of Kintail.

KILDRUMMY Nr Alford, Grampian ††
(NJ 455164) SDD

A remarkable early thirteenth-century castle, Kildrummy superseded a twelfth-century motte castle and was put up in the reign of Alexander II (1214–49), who was married to the daughter of Enguerrand of Coucy, constructor of Coucy, the most formidable great tower in France. Built of red sandstone, Kildrummy was a substantial enclosure castle, roughly seven sided — one of the longer sides of a rectangle pushed out to form a multangular curtain with a large twin-cylindrical towered gatehouse at the apex (south-east). Each of the four corners of the rectangle had towers: D-shaped at south and east; cylindrical at north and a much larger cylindrical great tower at west. A range of buildings was erected along

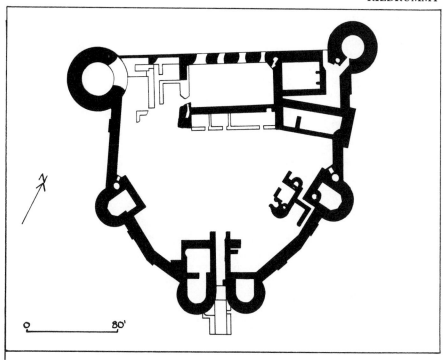

Kildrummy: bold lines indicate the main works of the thirteenth century

Kildrummy: the gatehouse remains (*at front*) resemble the plan of the gatehouse at Harlech

the inner face of the north-west curtain, and the whole was surrounded by banks and ditches. This interesting structure is now ruinous, though there is something left of the towers, the range and the gatehouse. The chapel straddled the east wall of the enclosure at an oblique angle; the twin towered gatehouse is considered to have been of later construction, probably at the close of the thirteenth century. The great tower is now only visible above ground for a few feet, but it apparently rose five storeys, each of them vaulted (like Coucy). The first floor had a gallery in the wall thickness with arrow loops all round the outside. The gatehouse, recently excavated and carefully examined, was guarded by a barbican, probably of fifteenth-century building. This has a deep pit which was traversed by a drawbridge. The gatehouse appears to have been burned at some time.

Kildrummy was held by Sir Nigel Bruce in 1306 when it was besieged by the English under the Earl of Gloucester. He beat off every assault until his garrison's blacksmith, Osbourne, set the castle on fire (in return for a promise of a substantial sum in gold by the English). It may be that the signs of burning discovered at the gatehouse stem from this act of treachery. The castle was besieged again in 1335, and again in 1361, on the second occasion by David II who kept it for several years.

KILHENZIE Strathclyde
(NS 308082) O
This rectangular tower-house of the sixteenth century has been much restored. It is open seasonally.

KILLOCHAN Strathclyde
(NS 227003) C
Said to be one of the finest fortified houses in southern Scotland and today in very good repair, Killochan is a late sixteenth-century, roughly L-plan tower-house, whose main block is five storeys tall. Straight flights of stairs with landings were constructed in the stair tower in the re-entrant angle.

KILMARONOCK Strathclyde
(NS 455877)
Kilmaronock is today derelict. It was a rectangular great tower about 45ft by 40ft

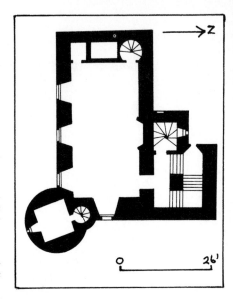

Killochan: first-floor plan (after Renwick) of late sixteenth century stepped L-plan towerhouse with straight flights of stairs

and five storeys tall. Built in the late fifteenth century, it has ashler dressings.

KILRAVOCK Croy, Highland
(NM 814494) Open by arrangement
A small rectangular great tower, 39ft by 31ft, was built here in c.1460. In the seventeenth century it received a square-plan stair tower on the south-west corner and a rectangular structure extended from that to make half a quadrangle. It has been added to in later times. The original works can be seen.

KINCARDINE Tayside
(NO 671751) C
This is a very early Scottish castle. Probably of twelfth-century, certainly of thirteenth-century origin, it was a simple enclosure castle of curtain wall on a natural hill, which was surrounded by marsh land. There were rectangular gate towers on the south wall. There was also an outer wall with battered plinth.

Kincardine was a royal castle for a time. John Balliol (1292–6) is thought to have drafted his abdication document there. Only fragments remain.

KINCLAVEN Tayside †
(NO 158377) O
A ruined rectangular enclosure of stone, with projecting square corner towers, whose curtain was 7ft thick, overlooking the junction of the Tay and Isla rivers. The stonework is probably twelfth century, though it has been attributed to Malcolm III (1057–93). Only fragments remain. Kinclaven had been a royal castle in the early thirteenth century. In 1297–8, it was taken and destroyed by Wallace.

KINDROCHIT Nr Braemar, Grampian
(NO 151913) O
An impressive ruin, this fourteenth-century castle began as a royal hunting lodge in the reign of Robert II (1371–90). The King then granted the site to his friend, Malcolm Drummond, who in the 1390s erected a substantial hall tower of horizontal rather than vertical shape, about 100ft by 30ft. Evidently, as shown from excavations in the present century, the hall tower was erected across the remains of the hunting lodge which had had a basement storey. The earlier building appeared also to have had rectangular turrets on the corners. The Drummond hall tower was among the largest of this type of tower built in Scotland.

KINGENCLEUCH Strathclyde
(NS 503256)
A borderline castle, that is, a house built as a castle but not well fortified. It was a four-storeyed L-plan tower-house with ashlar dressings. The walls were less than a yard thick. The north-west wall stands to about 23ft with a crow-step gable above. The ground-floor chamber was vaulted.

KINKELL Highland
(NH 554543)
A sixteenth-/seventeenth-century tower-house built on the 'E' plan. It has been greatly restored.

KINNAIRD Fraserburgh, Grampian
(NJ 999675)
An interesting sixteenth-century tall, rectangular tower-house, with cylindrical bartizans at the angles and square bartizans in the straight sides. The tower is 60ft tall, measures 39ft by 27ft, and was raised in the 1570s. In the 1780s, it was converted for use as a lighthouse which it is today.

KINNAIRD Nr Brechin Tayside
(NO 634571) C
Kinnaird's first buildings were destroyed by fire in 1452. By the end of the fifteenth century, the castle had been rebuilt, with a substantial rectangular tower as the core. Considerable improvements were made in the sixteenth and seventeenth centuries, and more changes later still, but parts of the walls of the earlier building have been incorporated. The castle has been owned by the Carnegie family since the seventeenth century.

KINNAIRD Perth, Tayside
(NO 241289)
An early sixteenth-century, rectangular tower-house, five storeys tall, which later received a two-storey extension. The tower-house was enclosed inside a curtain wall. The castle is in good repair and is occupied. One feature of interest is that the staircase to the first floor is a straight flight inside the tower wall, and not the more usual wheel stair.

KINNAIRDY Marnock, Grampian
(NJ 609498)
This is a structure of several periods and features. It began as a twelfth-century motte castle, possibly contemporary with Duffus. A stone tower was raised on the motte which was partly encased within the stonework. Something of this can be seen today. A curtain wall was built with a tall arched entrance at the north-west. At a later date, possibly c.1420, a six-storey tower with crenellated parapet round its roof was built in the north corner of the enclosure. In the eighteenth century the two highest storeys of the tall tower were pulled down and a gabled attic substituted. By that time Kinnairdy had become a palatial mansion and no longer a castle.

KIRKCUDBRIGHT Dumfries and Galloway (NX 677509) A
Only some earthworks and stone foundations remain of this thirteenth-century castle. It is thought to have been built by the English during the early years of the war

between John Balliol, King of Scotland (1292–6) and Edward I of England. The castle appears to have been a rectangular stone enclosure, comprehensively protected by ditching and banks. The curtain walls were between 7–9ft thick. There were cylindrical towers on the corners, about 36ft in diameter. The entrance was guarded by two flanking cylindrical towers.

KNOCKHALL Foveran, Grampian
(NJ 994265)
A three-storeyed L-plan tower-house of the mid-sixteenth century, Knockhall was rebuilt in the seventeenth century, and severely damaged by fire in 1734 (recorded as accidental). A cylindrical tower built on the south-east of the tower-house has collapsed. The castle is a ruin.

LAURISTON Nr Edinburgh, Lothian
(NT 203760) O
A nineteenth-century mansion has been grafted round the late sixteenth-century tower-house built here, near the southern side of the Firth of Forth. The original tower-house was a rectangular structure, 40ft by 24ft with a central projecting tower on the north side which contained the staircase. The castle was the birthplace of John Law, the financier who established the National Bank of France in the eighteenth century, which collapsed, bringing ruin to the economy of France.

LAW West Kilbride, Strathclyde
(NS 211484)
This rectangular tower of c.1460, now roofless, but whose walls are intact, has four storeys and a garret.

LENNOXLOVE Lothian   †
(NT 514720) Open by arrangement
This used to be known as Lethington as it belonged to the famous Maitlands of Lethington (William Maitland was 'Mr Secretary' Maitland, the Protestant statesman in the time of Mary, Queen of Scots). It began as an L-plan tower in the early fifteenth century, built of rubble, the main block 55ft by 38ft, and the wing 23ft by 31ft. The walls were 8–10ft thick. The parapet was altered in the sixteenth century. There were more alterations in the seventeenth

century and in more modern times. The tower survives in good condition, and among the original features of interest are dungeons and two iron yetts.

LESLIE Grampian   †
(NJ 599248) O
Built in 1661, Leslie Castle is often said to be the last fortified tower-house built in Scotland. This claim can, however, be countered by later dates for others, such as Lethendy in Tayside (1678) and Cluny Crichton (1667). It was a stepped L-plan tower-house with a square stair tower in the angle. The staircase was given straight flights. Gun-ports were inserted, one of which covered the entrance to the tower. The castle was built upon the site of a previous structure and the traces of moat round part of it belong to that earlier building. It is in ruins.

LETHENDY Cromdale, Highland
(NJ 084274)
A sixteenth-century L-plan tower-house, now in poor state, that had at least three storeys. The castle was taken over by supporters of James VII (James II of England, 1685–8) during the campaign between James and his son-in-law, William of Orange (William III).

LETHENDY Tayside
(NO 140417)
Lethendy Tower is thought to be one of the very last tower-houses to be built in Scotland (c.1678), though argument has been made for an earlier building date, perhaps very late sixteenth century. It was a three storey, L-plan tower-house with attic. Despite extensive alterations, the original form can be seen.

LIBERTON Nr Edinburgh, Lothian   †
(NT 265696) O
The rectangular tower-house, 35ft by 26ft, with four storeys beneath its parapet and a garret in the roof, was raised here in the fifteenth century. The parapet encloses an interesting wall-walk. There are few windows or loops in the tower walls.

LICKLYHEAD Insch, Grampian
(NJ 627236) Open by arrangement
An L-plan tower-house which has a panel

bearing the date 1629, but which is possibly of the late sixteenth century. It has been much altered. A tall roundel staircase turret rises in one corner, corbelled out only a few feet above the ground. The tower is three storeys to the wall head, with garret above.

LINLITHGOW Lothian ††
(NT 003774) O

Sited on a mound overlooking Linlithgow Loch, Linlithgow is today a ruin of a great palace-cum-castle. It is roofless, but has most of its walling, giving the visitor a good idea of its impressive size and architecture. The fabric is of several building periods, from the 1400s to the 1600s. Its defensive features hinge chiefly upon thick outer walls and tall corner towers which are almost great towers.

The origins of Linlithgow are obscure, but an enclosure with turrets made of 'great logs not split too small' was erected upon the mound by Edward I's orders in c.1302–3, under the supervision of Master James of St George, towards the end of the great builder's life. The works cost over £1,400. We say the early history is obscure because a stonework relic of a stone church at Linlithgow, dated to mid-twelfth century, was found within the precincts of the enclosure. The enclosure is also recorded as having surrounded other earlier buildings,

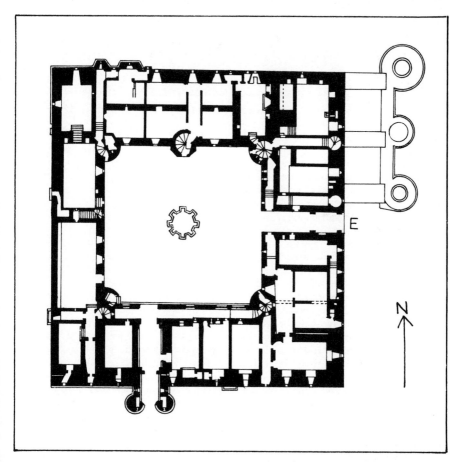

Linlithgow: ground-floor plan. E = Old Entrie. The great hall is over the east range which contains the old entrance. The extension at the extreme north-east is the outer great bulwark (Utter Gret Bulwerke, a forebuilding which is now ruinous)

Linlithgow: the castle-palace from the loch. The Old Entrie is in the centre of the façade

including a royal manor house, thought to date from David I (1124–53), and which was used by subsequent Scottish kings. The 1302–3 works at Linlithgow are notable for the men failing to be given their money properly. When the English king requested these men to join the building gangs at Dunfermline across the Forth, they refused, saying they would rather leave the country. Similar defaults with wage payments occurred at Edward's works at St Andrews, resulting in a strike.

The enclosure at Linlithgow was besieged in 1303 but seems to have withstood it. But in 1313 it was taken by the Scots and the military role came to an end for at least a century, during which time the manor house deteriorated.

In 1425, James I of Scotland decided to build a fortified palace on the site at Linlithgow, and over the next decade over £4,500 was spent. The structure that rose was a fine mix of the best contemporary residential appointments with up-to-date fortifications. The palace was based upon a square courtyard plan with buildings on four sides. The works were spread over

many years, and here we have space to draw attention to only one or two major features.

The eastern side of the palace contains, on the first floor, the Lyon Chalmer (or Great Hall). This is a remarkable structure, running the entire length of the side from the north-east corner tower to the south-east corner tower. It had a hammer-beam roof over the main floor space, and a stone barrel vault over the fireplace at the south. The hall was lit by high clerestory windows. At the north end was a massive stone screen with serving hatches opening into the kitchens in the north-east corner tower. Entrance was via a wheel stair leading up from the courtyard below but there had also been a stairway. The fireplace is in three sections, and with its embellishments, is reckoned the finest surviving in Scotland. This great hall was built in c.1430. The northern side was reconstructed in the 1620s, and the resulting range, known as the New Wark, is an interesting building of five storeys with wheel stair tower on the west, and a polygonal wheel stair tower in the mid-wall position.

Other notable features to look for are the

Old Entrie, a round-head arch into the passage through the eastern side range beneath the great hall with guardroom and prison flanking one side of the passage. This passage had portcullises. The outside of the entrance passage also has a rounded arch with a carved heraldic panel of the royal arms mounted on the wall face above. There had been a drawbridge, massive oak doors and an iron yett.

Mary, Queen of Scots, was born in the palace on 8 December 1542, scarcely a week before her father, James V, died, broken by the news of the defeat of the Scottish army at Solway Moss. Her son, James VI, stayed often at Linlithgow, and even presided over a meeting of the Scottish Parliament there in 1585. The palace was accidentally set on fire during the Second Jacobite Rising in 1746 by troops of the Duke of Cumberland and it was gutted.

LITTLE CUMBRAE Bute, Strathclyde (NS 152513) P

There was a fortress on this site dating back to the fourteenth century, which was probably owned by the Crown (Robert II). This was considerably enlarged so that by the sixteenth century it had a rectangular great tower 41ft by 29ft, rising to about 46ft to the parapet. The walls are 6–7ft thick, and in the north-west corner a kitchen was arranged partly in the wall thickness of the first floor. Wide-mouthed gun-ports were inserted low in the front façade.

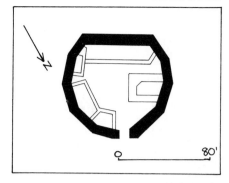

Loch Doon: this is the late thirteenth- /early fourteenth-century simple enclosure castle that was moved from its original site, stone by stone, to a new site in the present century. The buildings in outline were later than the enclosure

LOCH DOON Strathclyde †
(NX 484950) SDD

If you can build a castle in stone, you can also take it down and re-erect it elsewhere. This was done with Loch Doon, a late thirteenth-century enclosure castle of stone, erected originally upon an island in Loch Doon. The plan of the castle is polygonal, with the longest side about 60ft long, facing south-south-west. The polygon is completed by ten further uneven sides and at north an arched entrance (see plan). The walling is up to 28ft tall, averages 8ft thick and is splayed outwards at the base all round, except for the entrance which is about 9ft wide and has a pointed arch, with two gates. The entrance is not complete.

This was the stonework that was moved piece by piece from the island to the west shore of the loch in 1934–5, when the water level in the loch was raised to service a hydro-electric scheme. The castle was shifted with the greatest skill and care by the Ministry of Works (now the Scottish Development Department); every stone was numbered in advance.

The original castle received buildings inside the enclosure at the time of construction and further buildings later, notably a sixteenth-century range. This later work was not moved in the 1930s. The castle now to be seen on the shore is much as it was in c.1300.

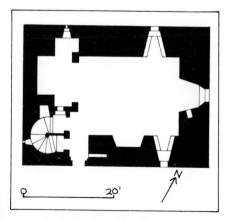

Little Cumbrae: first-floor plan

LOCHINDORB Grampian
(NH 974353)

A very interesting early thirteenth-century stone quadrilateral enclosure castle raised on an island on the Moray–Nairn border, with slightly projecting small cylindrical towers on the angles, Lochindorb resembles Inverlochy in plan. There are substantial remains to be seen. The southern end has an extra courtyard inside an outer wall which has its own gateway with portcullis, but curiously no access to the main enclosure. Presumably the outer yard was a later work. The main enclosure walls are noticeably thin.

Lochindorb was Scottish built, probably by the Comyn family, but it seems to have been held for a time by Edward I of England in the first years of the fourteenth century. One point of interest is the masonry — large blocks of hard stone brought to a level course every 6ft or so by flat pinnings.

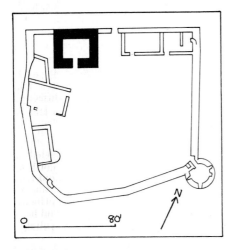

Loch Leven: the fourteenth century tower-house (bold lines) along the north curtain of the later, mainly sixteenth-century enclosure

LOCH LEVEN Tayside †
(NO 138018) SDD

One of the earliest tower-houses in Scotland, Loch Leven Castle stands on an island in the loch, and was begun in the early fourteenth century. It is a simple building, an almost square-plan tower, some 36ft by

31ft, rising to five storeys, the lowest two of which are vaulted, with walls about 8ft thick. The bulging parapet has corbelled roundels on three corners. The principal entrance to the tower was at the second floor on the east wall, leading into the great hall, and a spiral staircase in the wall thickness goes down to the first floor which was also accessible from the basement by a similar stair. Today, the entrance to the castle is in the basement, through a converted window opening. The tower stands in the length of a stone barmkin which was built in the sixteenth century, and which joins the tower on either end of the north face. Loch Leven is, of course, famous for having been the place where Mary, Queen of Scots was imprisoned from June 1567 to May 1568, when she escaped.

LOCHMABEN Nr Dumfries, †
Dumfries and Galloway
(NY 088811) O

Lochmaben began in the late twelfth century and appears to have been an earthwork enclosure with extensive ditch and rampart defences. Some time in the 1290s it was given a wooden tower. This may have been the tower upon which the head of Robert Cunynghame, castellan of Caerlaverock, was impaled in 1299 by the English. It is attributed as a stronghold of the Bruce family, and Robert Bruce's father had for a while been on Edward I's side in his conflict with the Scots, probably because he wanted the Scottish throne which John Balliol had abdicated, and which Edward had assumed.

Some time in the early fourteenth century, Lochmaben received the first stonework, an enclosure curtain, rectangular in plan. Supports for the bridge from the enclosure across the inner moat have survived. The enclosure walls are not in good condition, though parts are still standing high.

LOCH MABERRY Kirkcowan,
Dumfries and Galloway   (NX 285751)

An island site that has the remains of a substantial dry stone wall, between 6–7ft thick, and as tall as 7ft in some places, surrounding it. Traces of buildings inside the enclosure remain, and there are entrances on east and west sides. Much doubt surrounds the origin of this structure, and its history is unknown.

LOCHNAW Dumfries and Galloway
(NW 993632) C
Fragments of a rectangular tower-house of large dimensions, about 120ft by 56ft, are all that can be seen of the castle built here at the end of the fourteenth century.

LOCHRANZA Isle of Arran, Bute, †
Strathclyde (NR 933507) SDD
There are substantial remains of this castle which stands on the edge of a promontory jutting into Lochranza, at the north end of the Isle of Arran. These are of two main periods, and it is difficult to separate the two completely, for the later period, the sixteenth century, saw a reconstruction of the earlier, late thirteenth-/early fourteenth-century work, using the older masonry and to some extent, the older lay-out. In the first period, Lochranza was given a rectangular hall tower of two storeys, the greater part of which remains, with a small square-plan tower (having small rooms and long arrow loops in the wall face) projecting from one corner. The seventeenth-century reconstruction work included heightening the tower and rearranging the interior.

LOCHWOOD Johnstone, Dumfries and Galloway (NY 084968)
There was a motte castle here, thought to be of the twelfth century, with some evidence of a terraced bailey edged with palisades. In the fifteenth century the Johnstone clan erected near the motte 'a fair, large tower' (as a description of 1547 gave it). The tower was rectangular with a stretch of wall extending beyond the north end against which other buildings were raised. The north wall of the tower was about 9ft thick, but the other three were only 6ft. The tower contained a pit prison. Little remains of this fortress today.

LUFFNESS Aberlady, Lothian †
(NT 475804) O
The three-storey house at Luffness which overlooks Aberlady Bay was raised in the sixteenth century on the site of a much earlier structure. The castle stood inside a strong arrangement of fortifications.

MACDUFF'S Wemyss, Fife
(NT 344971) P
Not much remains of this castle which does not have any connection with Shakespeare's character Macduff, a Scottish lord in his play *Macbeth*. It began as a late fourteenth-century rectangular tower-house whose entrance was in the middle of the west wall. Much later, in the sixteenth century, a range of buildings was built on to the south wall of the tower, and at the end of the range was another rectangular tower, with a rounded projecting turret on the north-east corner, containing the staircase. Some outer walling was looped for guns. The original entrance in the older rectangular tower was blocked up, probably in the sixteenth century.

MACLELLAN'S Kirkcudbright,
Dumfries and Galloway †
(NX 682510) Open by arrangement
MacLellan's Castle is another 'borderline' castle. Basically L-plan, built in 1582, it has an extra small square tower at one corner. The tower-house is four-storeyed with a double height garret. It was built from the stones of an older convent of the Greyfriars that stood on the site, and which had become derelict as a result of the Reformation. Features that put MacLellan's into the defendable castle category include minimum window space in the lower storeys, no direct access between the basement and the hall, staircase access upstairs independent of lower storeys, and a spyhole (which doubtless could be used as a shot-hole) in the back of an inglenook in the great hall.

MAINS East Kilbride, Strathclyde
(NS 627560) C
Mains is in good repair. A late fifteenth-/early sixteenth-century tower-house, built of ashlar, about 38ft by 27ft, is surrounded by ditching. It stands on an artificial mound which may have been an earlier motte castle. There were probably several other buildings ranged around it.

MAINS Tayside
(NO 411330)
A rectangular tower-house of the sixteenth century, in good condition, which has rounded parapets with wide-mouthed gunports.

MAUCHLINE Strathclyde
(NS 498273)
A fifteenth-century tower-house, which has ribbed vaulting.

MAYBOLE Strathclyde
(NS 301100) C
This was a property of the notorious Cassilis family (see Dunure Castle) and it was built in the late sixteenth or possibly early seventeenth century. It was an L-plan tower-house of four storeys plus garret. The tower was given corbelled circular turrets on the angles. The castle has been greatly restored and altered, and today, it is the office of the Cassilis and Culzean estates.

MEARNS Strathclyde
(NS 552553)
Mearns Tower was built in the mid-fifteenth century. A licence to 'surround and fortify it [the castle] with wall and ditches, to strengthen by iron gates and to erect on the top of it all warlike apparatus necessary for its defence' was granted to Lord Maxwell in 1449. The result was a rectangular great tower, four storeys tall, 40ft by 30ft, with walls 10ft thick, built of rubble masonry. The entrance was inserted at first-floor level, with a spiral staircase to the top. The tower has been restored and converted into a church hall. There are also remains of an enclosing barmkin.

MEGGERNIE Tayside
(NN 554460) C
A sixteenth-century, simple, square tower with rectangular corner turrets, five storeys tall, attached to a later hunting lodge. It was owned in the eighteenth century by James Menzies who introduced the larch tree into Scotland from Austria.

MEGGINCH Inchture, Tayside
(NO 242246)
A late fifteenth-century L-plan tower-house with gun-ports, Megginch became part of a larger and less fortified structure in the seventeenth century. It has been restored and the gardens are open.

MELGUND Nr Aberlemno, Tayside
(NO 546563)
A ruined castle of the mid-sixteenth century which began as a rectangular tower-house more typical of the great Scottish fifteenth-century tower-houses. The tower is four-storeyed plus attic, with gun-ports at lower storey levels. A tall staircase tower was built on the west end, rising higher than the main tower.

MENSTRIE Central
(NS 849967) O
The birthplace of Sir William Alexander, founder of Nova Scotia, Menstrie is a late sixteenth-century L-plan tower-house that was enlarged by the adding of a second wing and joining with a curtain wall the two wings to form a quadrangle. The castle deteriorated, and by the 1950s, only the two wings survived in any reasonable state. It was proposed to demolish the castle altogether, but after a considerable and sustained public protest, the local authority stepped in and rescued it, and together with the National Trust for Scotland, restored it.

MENZIES Weem, Tayside
(NN 837496)
Also called Castle Menzies, this seat of the Clan Menzies is Z-plan and dates from the second half of the sixteenth century (1571–7). The diagonally opposite corner towers of Menzies are massive constructions, described by S.H. Cruden as 'no less commodious than many an isolated tower house of the same period'. The castle is indeed a substantial fortified residence of formidable appearance. The central block is three-storeyed, with a substantial attic as a fourth, and with a wide squat bartizan on the two free corners. The diagonally opposed towers which are four-storeyed plus attic, also have these squat bartizans. There are gun-ports by the entrance. The masonry is in excellent condition. Some renovation has been carried out, including the insertion of new, larger windows.

MERCHISTON Edinburgh, Lothian †
(NT 242718) O
Still in fine condition, Merchiston tower-house, built in the fifteenth century, rises five storeys and has walls 6ft thick. Its entrance is on the second floor. The castle received alterations in later years including several sash windows which gave the tower

much more interior light. Merchiston was originally enclosed by a curtain wall. It was attacked in 1572 by troops loyal to Mary, Queen of Scots (by then a prisoner of Elizabeth I of England). It was also the family home of the Napiers, notably John Napier, Lord of Merchiston (1550–1617), the inventor of logarithms, who was born there.

METHVEN Tayside
(NO 042260)
A considerably modified rectangular tower-house castle of the seventeenth century, it is five-storeyed.

MEY Nr John O'Groats, Highland
(ND 290739) C
Originally a Z-plan castle of the late sixteenth century (or possibly early seventeenth century), with later alterations. It has now been completely restored and is the home of Queen Elizabeth the Queen Mother.

MIDHOPE Lothian
(NT 072786) O
The remains of this late sixteenth-century rectangular tower-house, five-storeys tall with an attic, are situated in the grounds of Hopetoun House. In the seventeenth century two extensions, one storey lower, were added to the east end, as well as an interesting gateway of ashlar, standing at right angles to the castle.

MIDMAR Grampian
(NJ 704052) C
This is one of the Z-plan castles which was given diagonally opposite smaller towers of different shapes, the north-west tower square plan, the south-east cylindrical. The main block has a passage way along east and north on the ground floor. There is a half-cylindrical staircase turret in the southern re-entrant between the main block and the cylindrical tower. The north-west tower has straight flights of stairs inside, and is adorned with capped roundels on the corners. No gun-ports were fitted.

Midmar was built by the Bell family of masons (who also worked at Crathes) between c.1570 and 1575. The original structure was badly damaged in the 1590s

and reconstructed. The castle belonged to the Gordon family who were powerful in north-east Scotland.

MIGVIE Grampian
(NJ 436066)
Remains of a thirteenth-century enclosure castle.

MINGARY Ardnamurchan, ††
Highland (NM 503631) O
Described in the chapter on Scottish castles, Mingary is an irregular hexagonal enclosure castle with rounded angles, begun in the thirteenth century. It received additions and alterations in later centuries, including buildings erected inside the enclosure, even a barrack block of the eighteenth century. It is thought to have been used as a prison for Covenanters in the seventeenth century.

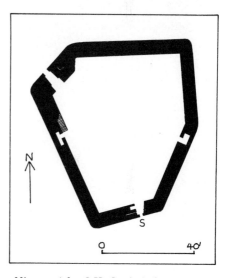

Mingary: (after S.H. Cruden). S = sea gate

MONIACK Highland
(NH 552436)
Originally an L-plan tower-house of the mid-seventeenth century, Moniack (or Moniac) has been modernized.

MONTQUHANIE Fife
(NO 348212)
Remains of a sixteenth-century rectangular tower-house.

457

Mote of Urr: an aerial view

MORTON Dumfries and Galloway
(NX 891992) SDD

An interesting rectangular hall tower, with a cylindrical turret projecting from one corner, Morton is similar to Rait. It is almost complete to the parapet but has no roof or floors. The principal entrance was through an arch at first-floor level at one end into the main hall. The ground floor is an undercroft. There were other buildings in the castle complex, including a twin-towered gatehouse set in an enclosing curtain. The castle stands high on a promontory overlooking Morton Loch. It was begun in the fourteenth century, but is now roofless.

MOTE OF ANNAN Dumfries and †
Galloway (NY 192668)

A motte castle of the early twelfth century on the east side of the River Annan, which is mentioned in a document of 1124. The motte was raised to about 50ft tall, and a ditch was cut to separate it from its bailey. The site has been altered.

MOTE OF URR Dumfries and
Galloway
(NX 815649) O
Excavated in the early 1950s by Dr Brian
Hope-Taylor (see Abinger motte, Surrey),
the Mote of Urr is a motte castle of the
mid-twelfth century, perhaps c.1130–50,
which was surfaced with clay. The castle was
destroyed in 1174 and later rebuilt, with an
additional few feet of earth and rubble upon
the summit and a new timber tower. The
wooden palisade encircling the motte summit is thought to have had turrets projecting
inwards.

MOY Highland
(NM 617247)
A ruined tower-house of the sixteenth
century.

MUCHALLS Grampian   †
(NO 891918) O
Built in the 1620s round a courtyard,
Muchalls has two sides and part of the third
as a tall range of apartments, the square
closed by a high wall for the rest of the third
and the whole of the fourth side. There is a
vault with barrel roof in a tower structure on
the south side and this may be the remains of
what is thought to have been a thirteenth- or
fourteenth-century castle on the site.
Muchalls was burned by the Duke of
Cumberland in 1746, during the Second
Jacobite Rising, but was later rebuilt.

MUGDOCK Central   †
(NS 550772) A
Fragments of a fourteenth-century courtyard plan castle are still to be seen on this
site. It has later additions. The walls are
massive and part of the gatehouse is
standing.

MUNESS Unst, Shetland Islands
(HP 629013) SDD
A late sixteenth-century Z-plan tower-
house with cylindrical corner towers,
Muness is built of local rubble. It was very
well provided with shot-holes of dumb-bell
and quatrefoil design. The rectangular
tower block has a straight flight of stairs in
the wall thickness. Some of the shot-holes in
the external wall were served by a protected
passage in the wall. The tower-house was

four-storeyed, but the topmost has all but
disappeared.

MURTHLY Nr Stanley, Tayside
(NO 072399) C
Sited on the south side of the Tay, and today
enveloped in woodland, Murthly was begun
probably in the late fifteenth century, and
the earliest building may have been the
surviving, tall, slim, 14ft-square tower,
with slightly projecting stair turret at the
south-east. The tower was at the south-west
angle of a later courtyard with western
range, built in the late sixteenth century,
and this acquired subsequent additions
during the next two hundred years. In the
nineteenth century a substantial mansion
was built adjacent to this earlier part.

MYRES Auchtermuchty, Fife
(NO 242109)
The greater part of this castle is of modern
building upon a small sixteenth-century
three-storeyed house (plus attic), consisting
of a central rectangular block 32ft by 24ft,
with two towers projecting from opposing
corners, with a most interesting corbelled
out square-plan turret at the top levels of the
north-east angle.

NAIRN Highland
(NH 885566)
There is nothing left now to see of a castle of
uncertain shape built here in the late twelfth
century. The north and west sides appear to
have been enclosed by ditching and ramparts.

NEIDPATH Nr Peebles, Borders
(NT 236404) C
This massive L-plan tower-house, built at
the end of the fourteenth century on a rocky
slope leading down to the Tweed, is in
remarkably good exterior condition. Its
plan is interesting: both arms of the 'L' are
parallelograms, not rectangles; the corners
are rounded, not squared. The top two
storeys of the four have been remodelled.
There are other buildings of later date,
chiefly of the sixteenth century, including
an interesting gateway with a round-headed
arch in the east wall of a range of buildings.
The walls of the tower-house are 10ft thick
in places.

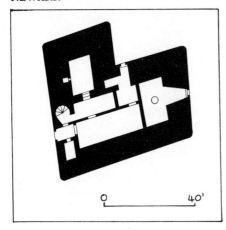

Neidpath: basement plan. The basement is vaulted

Although the castle has the most formidable appearance, its only siege experience appears to have been in the time of Cromwell.

NEWARK Borders
(NT 421293) C
Newark tower-house was a Douglas-held castle built on a mound c.1423/4. It was a rectangular tower-house with end gables, surrounded by a barmkin. Keyhole gunports were added in the tower walls in the later part of the fifteenth century. After the Battle of Philiphaugh in 1645, at which Montrose was defeated by the Covenanters but escaped, many of his followers were taken and put to death in the courtyard of the castle. Newark is a ruin today, but well preserved.

NEWARK Strathclyde
(NS 329744) SDD
Newark forms three sides of a square, and is chiefly of sixteenth- and seventeenth-century construction. But its oldest part is the fifteenth-century rectangular great tower, one of whose walls is substantially thicker than the others and contains a wheel staircase all the way up. The entrance to the castle is through a rectangular gate-tower opposite the great tower. This entrance has a round-headed arch. The castle is in fine restored condition and has several corner turrets with conical roof caps.

NEWARK Strathclyde
(NS 322173)
A sixteenth-century tower-house, 32ft by 27ft, on rising ground once surrounded by a moat (now filled), Newark rises to four storeys with a battlemented parapet enclosing a garret. Additions in the seventeenth century included another tower built on to the western wall, which has five storeys. In the nineteenth century the castle was further renovated.

NEWTON Tayside
(NO 172452)
A seventeenth-century Z-plan castle built upon the ruins of a sixteenth-century mansion that was later destroyed by fire. Masonry from the first building appears to have been used for foundations and lower walls for the second.

NEWTON Strathclyde
(NS 339223)
Only ruins remain of the fifteenth-century castle of towers and curtain walling.

NIDDRY Kirkliston, Lothian
(NT 095743) C
Niddry, a tall, massive tower of L-plan shape, was built in the early sixteenth century on a rocky mound near Kirkliston. It was given a curtain wall of which traces can still be seen on the western side. The tower is four storeys high to the parapet, though the top storey was added in the seventeenth century. The tower walls are 7–8ft thick.
Mary, Queen of Scots, was brought to Niddry by Lord Seton on the evening of her escape from Loch Leven in 1568.

NOLTLAND Isle of Westray, Orkney
(HY 429488) SDD
Founded in the 1560s by Gilbert Balfour (who was party to the murder of Cardinal Beaton in 1546), Noltland is one of the earliest of the Z-plan castles. Noltland has square-plan towers on diagonally opposite corners of a long rectangular main tower block. The tower-house was extremely well fortified. Both main block and corner towers are fitted with tiers of gun-ports, wide-mouthed and both square and round cornered, enough to give covering fire in all

Noltland: bristling with gun-ports, Noltland was one of the most heavily fortified tower-houses in Scotland

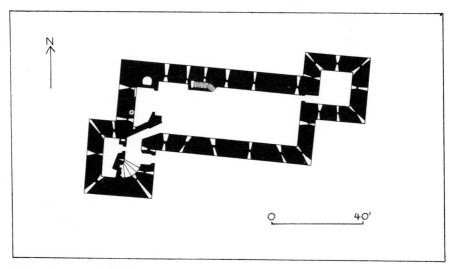

Noltland: ground floor of the sixteenth century, powerfully fortified, Z-plan castle. Note the proliferation of gun-ports of this one floor level

directions — some seventy gun-ports in all. The south-west angle tower was not completed. In almost every respect the castle's military features overwhelmed the domestic: even the great hall on the first floor had windows on only one side. And the solar was effectively separated from the hall by a thick wall with a stout door. The walls of the tower-house are basically 6–7ft thick.

Gilbert Balfour was also involved in the murder of the Earl of Darnley, second husband of Mary, Queen of Scots, in 1567, and the castle at Noltland was a hideout for him and his followers.

OLD DUNDAS Dalmeny, Lothian
(NT 117767) P
Old Dundas has the distinction of being the earliest Scottish castle for which a proper licence to crenellate was issued, in 1424: 'to build a tower . . . of Dundas in the manner of a castle with the kernels, etc., usual in a fortalice of this sort according to the manner of the Kingdom of Scotland . . . ' And to bear this out it has to this day an impressive crenellated parapet round the top of its L-plan and its second wing on the north-west angle. The crenellation is thought to be of the sixteenth century but this may be too late an estimate. Its entrance is protected by a yett, and its walls are in places 10ft thick. Old Dundas has been altered internally. It was once used as a distillery.

OLD SLAINS Grampian
(NK 053300) C
The sole remains of the castle of Old Slains are the ruins of a fourteenth-century tower-house and some vestiges of barmkin to the south. The castle was built by the Hay family, the chief of which became Hereditary High Constable of Scotland.

OLD WICK Highland
(ND 369488) O
Old Wick stands on a promontory of rock. Three of the four sides are protected by cliffs. The fourth was defended by a ditch. The castle began as a rectangular great tower of the late thirteenth or early fourteenth century, with four storeys, walls up to 7ft thick, and measuring about 32ft by 23ft. The walls still stand to a maximum height of 40ft. There was no entrance on the ground

floor, and that storey is lit only by a few loops. The entrance was in the first storey and was reached by an outside staircase which was probably made of wood, since no traces of a stone flight of steps have been detected.

Old Wick is thought by some authorities to have been of Viking origin. Today, the castle is a ruin.

OLIVER'S Tweedsmuir, Borders
(NT 099250) A
Considerable doubts surround this castle site. Fragments of a fortress on a low hill have been found. The site was protected on one side by a long slope falling 200ft to the Tweed Valley. On its other sides it appears to have been protected by two lines of ditch and scarp. A castle at Oliver is mentioned in a document of c.1200. Is this ruin the same castle?

ORCHARDTON Nr Castle Douglas, Dumfries and Galloway †
(NX 817551) SDD
This is one of the very few cylindrical tower-houses built in Scotland. It was raised in the mid-fifteenth century by John Caryns (or Cairns), Provost of Lincluden. The internal arrangements of the tower are much the same as those of a rectangular tower-house of the same period: in Orchardton's case the basement is vaulted; entrance to the tower is at first-floor level by means of a stairway outside; the internal plan of the basement is rectangular but the plans of the first, second and top storeys are circular. The tower walls are basically 6ft thick, the tower's spiral staircase is in the wall thickness. The top of the tower had a gabled caphouse resting on a corbelled parapet. It is 33ft tall from the ground to the parapet. Nothing is known of the history of the tower.

PEEL OF LUMPHANAN Grampian ††
(NJ 576037) SDD
Lumphanan was the site of the battle where the great Scottish king, Macbeth (1040–57) was killed, having lost to Malcolm Ceanmor who became Malcolm III (1057–93). A motte castle was built here in the twelfth century. The mound is over 30ft tall, and was surrounded by a ditch about 50ft wide,

Orchardton: a mid-fifteenth century small tower-house. The quarters inside were extremely cramped, and living in it for any length of time would have been oppressive

banked, and enclosed by another ditch. In the late twelfth or early thirteenth century a shell keep was raised on the motte, whose wall was about a yard thick. Against the curtain of the shell was built a hall, about 50ft by 12ft, possibly after the raising of the curtain. The castle is now ruinous. There has been further excavation in recent years, and it was established that the original height of the mound had been artificially raised in the thirteenth century, presumably to support the shell keep.

PENKHILL Girvan, Strathclyde
(NX 232985) C
A sixteenth-century tower-house which has been modernized.

PITCAPLE Grampian
(NJ 727260) O
A Z-plan castle of c.1570, renovated in the 1830s, Pitcaple's main building is four storeys tall with two round towers on diagonally opposite corners. The tower on

the west corner contains the staircase and is smaller than the east tower. High walling was added to form a sort of courtyard, and the whole was provided with ditching, though there are no signs of it now. There are grounds for believing that the central block is earlier than 1570, possibly by a century or more. In the nineteenth century an extra block was added.

PITCRUVIE Fife
(NO 414046)
Little remains of the original sixteenth-century tower-house.

PITCULLO Leuchars, Fife
(NO 413193)
A small late sixteenth-century three-storey tower-house, basically L-plan, with a cylindrical staircase tower centrally placed along the northern long wall. A second staircase was provided in the south-west corner of the wing. There is a surviving undercroft at the east end, vaulted, and now used as a dining

463

room. Another tower, of rectangular plan, was added later and juts out of the south and east corner. The castle was restored after World War II.

PITFICHIE Monymusk, Grampian
(NJ 677166)
A late sixteenth-/early seventeenth-century half Z-plan rectangular tower with one cylindrical corner turret, which today has no roof and is derelict.

PITHEAVLIS Tayside
(NO 103228)
An early sixteenth-century rectangular tower with a square projecting tower at south-west and two corner turrets. The tower is provided with gun-ports.

PITSLIGO Grampian
(NJ 937670) O
Pitsligo Castle is largely in ruins. There is an outer shell of a tower of the early fifteenth century, about 52ft by 37ft, with 10ft-thick walls, rising to the second storey. The third storey was demolished c.1700. In the sixteenth century the tower was absorbed into a quadrangular-plan mansion. The castle was surrounded by a ditch. The tower appears to have had one large room on each floor, possibly the normal arrangement found in many earlier and smaller English and Welsh great towers, viz. basement kitchen, ground-floor dining hall (with screened off solar for the owner and his wife) and room for family guests on top.

PITTEADIE Kinghorn, Kirkcaldy, Fife
(NT 257891) A
This ruinous castle stands about 1½ miles north of Kinghorn. It began as a rectangular tower-house of the late fifteenth century, about 33ft by 27ft, with four storeys and a caphouse on top of one corner. There are signs of alterations of later date, but the whole is in a very poor state.

PITTULIE Pitsligo, Grampian
(NJ 945670)
The ruins of a seventeenth-century rectangular tower block about 70ft by 24ft with walls 3ft thick. The block had a square tower in the north-west corner, which still stands to roof height.

PLEAN TOWER St Ninians, Central
(NS 849869) A
Only fragments remain here of a rectangular tower-house built in the fifteenth century. It appears to have had a courtyard partly bounded by a range of buildings, of later date.

PLUNTON Dumfries and Galloway
(NX 605507)
An L-plan tower-house, of only 21ft by 15ft, with a staircase turret at the west angle, Plunton was three-storeyed with an attic, but is now roofless and decaying.

PORTENCROSS West Kilbride,
Strathclyde (NS 175489)
This ruinous castle on the coast of the Clyde began as a rectangular tower of three storeys and a garret. The walls were massively built and most of them remain today. A wing tower of one storey extra in height, with a vaulted ground floor, was added to one long side. The vaulted storey incorporated a kitchen and a second kitchen was provided at first-floor level. The tower had two entrances and two stairs, the staircase beginning from the ground floor being straight, the first-floor case ascending as a spiral. From ground level it was possible to climb to the battlements without disturbing the occupants of the hall in the main tower block. The castle, which was begun in the fourteenth century, was given by Robert Bruce to the Boyd family of Kilmarnock. It guarded a crossing to Bute.

POWRIE Tayside
(NO 421346)
A fifteenth-century great tower castle with barmkin wall and other buildings, of which little remains.

PRONCY Dornoch, Highland
(NH 771925)
A small rectangular tower, about 20ft by 12ft, with walls about 5ft thick, was built on a motte here probably in the fourteenth century. There are few remains to be seen.

RAIT Nairn, Highland
(NM 894525) C
Rait Castle is complete to the top of the walls. It was an unusual rectangular hall-

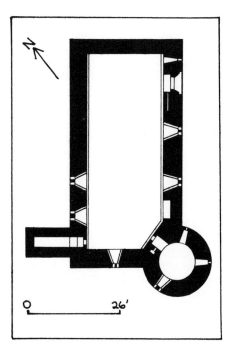

tower of the early fourteenth century whose larger horizontal dimension was greater than the height: 54ft by 22ft by 36ft tall to the wall top. Entrance to the tower was at the end of the first-floor level, protected by a portcullis, and at the south corner of the other end was built a cylindrical tower. On the west corner is an 8ft-wide garderobe tower, about 12ft long. The walls of the hall and the cylinder tower are about 6ft thick, except the north-east end which is about 18in thinner. The castle is being restored at present.

RAVENSCRAIG Kirkcaldy, Fife   ††
(NT 290924) SDD
The disposition of Ravenscraig's buildings and fortifications is outlined in chapter 13. It

(*left*) Rait: first-floor plan

(*below*) Ravenscraig (Fife): elevation facing the sea

465

was the first castle in Britain to be designed specifically for defence by guns. It was intended by James II of Scotland, who initiated the work in the year of his death, 1460, to be a coastal fortress to guard against attack from the waters of the Firth of Forth. The building work accounts for the years 1460–3 have largely survived. It was equipped to store gunpowder and armaments in spacious and well-protected cellars, in addition to its remarkable offensive gunfire capability.

RAVENSCRAIG Grampian
(NK 095488)
A fifteenth-century L-plan tower-house, which has interesting gun-loops. They are positioned at ground level and are for the most part long slits with shorter crosslets near the top and circular openings at the bottom. The castle was licensed in c.1490 (S.H. Cruden).

RED CASTLE (of LUNAN) †
Inverkeilor, Tayside (NO 687510) A
There was a fortified house raised on a promontory and partly surrounded by ditches in the twelfth century. It was used by William the Lion (1165–1214) as a hunting lodge. Fragments of a thirteenth-century, high curtain wall (6ft thick) and of a fifteenth-century rectangular tower remain. The castle was besieged in 1579 and is thought to have remained ruinous ever since.

RED CASTLE Highland
(NH 584495)
Situated on the south coast of the Black Isle this castle has also been known as Ederdover. There are at present the roofless remains of a sixteenth-century L-plan tower-house, with a staircase in the re-entrant. Two angle turrets on the western wing are of some age. This structure occupies the site of an older twelfth-century castle which may have been built by William the Lion in c.1180.

RENFREW Strathclyde
(NS 513674)
A fortification is mentioned in a mid-twelfth-century manuscript (c.1163–5). Its shape is unknown. It was replaced by a stone castle in the thirteenth century, which in turn was demolished in c.1777 and replaced by a mansion, also demolished (1924) according to the Ordnance Survey at Edinburgh.

REPENTANCE Annandale, Dumfries and Galloway (NY 155722)
Repentance Tower was constructed by John Maxwell, Lord Herries, in the mid-sixteenth century. It was on a square plan, with three main storeys to the parapet, and built of coursed rubble. It was equipped with more gun-ports and shot-holes than windows. It has been repaired and is in fine condition.

ROSSEND Burntisland, Fife
(NT 228858) C
An ecclesiastical castle at first, built by the abbots of Dunfermline in the thirteenth century. In the sixteenth century it was converted to a T-plan tower-house, incorporating some original stonework at lower levels. It has been restored and so its original shape is not definable. The castle was taken by Cromwell in 1650.

ROSSLYN Lasswade, Lothian †
(NT 275627) C
Rosslyn Castle, also spelt Roslin, stands on a strong position on a peninsula created by the River Esk, which provides protection on three sides. Owned by the St Clair family, Princes (and later Earls) of Orkney, the 2nd Earl erected a tower-house on the site in the 1390s. It was added to in later generations, but is now derelict, due chiefly to the artillery, first, of the Earl of Hertford in the 1540s and, second, that of Cromwell in the late 1640s. Extensions were added in the later seventeenth century.

ROSYTH Nr Dunfermline, Fife †
(NT 108821) SDD on application
The castle lies in the Royal Naval Dockyard at Rosyth. It consists of a rectangular enclosure of sixteenth-/seventeenth-century origin, inside which at the north-east angle is an earlier (fifteenth-century) tower-house. The tower-house, which was freestanding, is about 41ft by 48ft, three storeys tall, with walls about 10ft thick. It was built with ashlar facing, and the ground and first floors were vaulted. There is a small wing at the south-east with the staircase.

ROTHESAY Bute, Strathclyde ††
(NS 088646) SDD
The castle probably began as a low-level earth platform surrounded by a broad wet ditch, erected in the twelfth century. Then, sometime in the thirteenth century the motte was crowned with a huge and tall circular stone curtain of sandstone some 150ft in diameter, making it an enormous shell keep. It is one of the few shell keeps in Scotland. It was battlemented right round the top, but when part of the curtain was later heightened, the battlements were sealed up and used as the base for the extra wall height which was raised on top of them. This preservation of the original parapet is interesting because the merlons (the solid vertical projections) had loopholes for archers to watch through while they reloaded their weapons before darting in front of the embrasures to fire a rapid shot and then step back again.

Early in the thirteenth century, four stout cylindrical towers were added to the outside of the shell, equidistantly round the circumference, and between the west and east towers a simple but tall square-plan gateway was inserted which was considerably altered and enlarged by James IV in the early 1500s.

There were other buildings inside the enclosure. The ruins of the shell, the gateway and the towers are clear today.

In 1230 Rothesay was besieged by Vikings from the Western Islands and Scandinavia under a chief called Uspak, whose men succeeded in breaking through the wall under the protection of a penthouse by hacking away at the stonework with axes, for the stone and the mortar were soft. The castle fell again to the Vikings, this time under their king, Haakon of Norway, in 1263, but a few weeks later Haakon and his forces were decisively defeated by Alexander III at the great Battle of Largs.

When the Stewarts became kings of Scotland in the fourteenth century, Rothesay passed into royal hands. James IV altered the gateway and expanded it into a great gatehouse tower which was known as 'le dungeoun'.

ROWALLAN Strathclyde
(NS 435424) SDD
A sixteenth-/seventeenth-century mansion of thin walls that was built as a castle. The plan was approximately L-shaped, with two ranges of buildings at right angles, the 'square' being completed by curtain walling

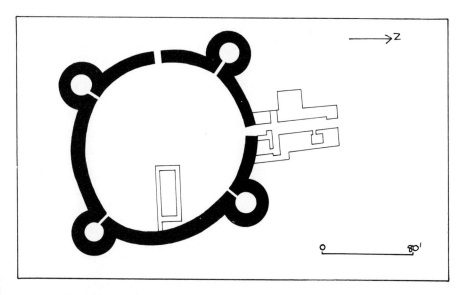

Rothesay: one of the few shell keeps in Scotland. The shell wall was built in the late twelfth century and the round turrets added in the thirteenth

467

Rothesay: it was attacked by the Vikings in the thirteenth century

and a further tower. In the south front there is a twin-cylindrical towered gatehouse approached up a flight of stairs. The gatehouse has a passage nearly 20ft long leading into the courtyard formed by the 'square'. The two ranges have their own spiral staircases. The gatehouse has a very formidable look, but is in fact a showpiece: the walls are less than a yard thick. The whole structure, the west range of which is equipped with dumb-bell gun-ports at ground level, was built upon the remains of an earlier mid-thirteenth century rectangular great tower castle. The original great tower was 35ft by 28ft and probably rose to three storeys.

ROXBURGH Borders
(NT 713337) O

Roxburgh was once a major Border fortress. The most famous event in its history was also one of the most disastrous for Scotland. King James II was killed by an exploding cannon when he was besieging it in 1460.

But by that time there had been a castle at Roxburgh for three centuries.

A motte castle was raised on the north side of the Teviot early in the twelfth century (a castle is mentioned in a charter of c.1128). One early building appears to have been a chapel, another a tower, but nothing remains of either. Whether the motte castle was built by a Scot or a Norman is not known, but from 1175 to 1189 it was held by Henry II of England. During Edward I's campaigns in southern Scotland at the end of the thirteenth century, Roxburgh was garrisoned, and presumably played an important role by virtue of its position. In 1314 it was captured by the Scots after an attack by night and, according to the Lanercost chronicler, was pulled down to the ground. If this is correct, it was no more than was intended in the policy of Robert Bruce to slight castles that could be of use again to the English. In 1335–7, it was taken and rebuilt by Edward III, and this work included a small pele-tower of wood, the

468

prefabricated parts for which were transported by sea from Newcastle to Berwick and then by river (or land) to Roxburgh. The castle was retaken in 1342 by David II but lost again after the Battle of Neville's Cross in 1346. In Richard II's reign, a gatehouse was built and other fortifications undertaken, including heightening of existing towers, a great wall 30ft tall, with towers, the works costing about £2,000.

In 1436, James I of Scotland besieged Roxburgh but failed to capture it. His son, James II, also besieged the castle in July 1460, but was killed in August when one of his cannons exploded beside him. But a few days later the castle fell and once more the Scots destroyed it.

In the 1540s, Roxburgh fell into English hands again, and it was partially rebuilt. But it did not last, and by the 1550s it was once more in ruins, in which state it is today. Fragments remain of some of the towers and of the Richard II gatehouse, and there are stretches of the curtain wall (also *temp.* Richard II) as high in places as 13ft.

RUSKO (Rusco) Dumfries and Galloway
(NX 584604)
A sixteenth-century rectangular tower-house, still three storeys plus attic in height. The tower is about 38ft by 29ft, and the walls 6–8ft thick. Its parapet is battlemented. A two-storey wing on the north, added in the seventeenth century, is ruinous but the castle is being restored.

RUTHERGLEN Strathclyde
(NS 614617)
The site of this once important castle in the Glasgow area has been built over. It was taken by the English during the War of Scottish Independence, besieged by Robert Bruce but did not fall until his brother, Edward Bruce, attacked and took it in c.1313.

The castle was besieged again, in the war between Mary, Queen of Scots, and the Regent, James, Earl of Moray, to whom it fell in 1568.

SADDELL Mull of Kintyre, Strathclyde
(NR 789315) C
An interesting tower-house built between

1508 and 1512 which stands among some later buildings that are not of concern to us here. The tower is in a decayed state, but it has four storeys plus garret, a battlemented parapet with open angle turrets, with a caphouse on one side. The entrance is on the ground floor. The tower-house was enclosed by a barmkin over 4ft thick and about 12ft tall, some of which remains today. For a time the castle belonged to the bishops of Argyll, and later became a Campbell possession.

ST ANDREWS Fife ††
(NO 513169) SDD
This interesting archiepiscopal fortress stands on a rock promontory on the north-east of the ancient city, which has the oldest university in Scotland (1412). The first stonework was erected in the late twelfth century, and was the inner part of the Fore-Tower on the south (inland) side of the promontory. The Fore-Tower cannot have stood alone, for it was too small to serve any purpose other than as a gateway, and it may be presumed that the tower was flanked on either side by wooden palisading that might have followed the lines of the present ruins of the later stonework enclosure. Timber buildings were doubtless raised inside. The castle was protected by a deep ditch on the south side.

In c.1336, the Fore-Tower was enlarged by a projection southwards of the same width, and one line of similar walling projected northwards. This tower was demolished a year later when Andrew Moray slighted the castle. Towards the end of the fourteenth century, Bishop Traill embarked on a major building programme, which included erecting a substantial curtain round the whole enclosure with two new towers (the Sea Tower at north-west and the Kitchen Tower at north-east), and repairing the Fore-Tower. Much of the west and south-west curtain is still standing. Traill is said to have died in his castle. It was also the place where Bishop Wardlaw of St Andrews taught the boy king, James I, before he was captured by pirates and delivered, a prisoner, to England in 1406. It was Wardlaw who founded the university. The castle later became a favourite residence of the Crown: James III was probably born there in 1451.

St Andrews: inside the Fore-Tower. The different masonry periods are apparent

The next building phase was in the first half of the sixteenth century, when the south-east and south-west corners were given cylindrical towers, which were destroyed in the 1546–7 siege. The siege of 1546–7 resulted when Cardinal Beaton, Archbishop of St Andrews, was murdered in the castle by Protestant infiltrators during the religious strife of the mid-sixteenth century in Scotland. The Protestants captured the castle and held it for a year against Catholic forces under Mary of Guise, mother of Mary, Queen of Scots. The Catholic siege was fierce and sustained, and extensive damage was done to the stonework. It was during this siege that the attackers sank a mine through the rock on which the castle stood, tunnelling towards the Fore-Tower. The defenders got to know of the attempt, calculated the direction the tunnel was taking, and sank a counter-mine, just outside the Fore-Tower, hoping to join up with the besiegers' tunnel and fight them off. The mine and the counter-mine, cut in the living rock, have survived to this day.

The former is about 7ft tall and about 6ft wide and slants downwards to pass under the ditch. The counter-mine is much the same size, and it reached the head of the besiegers' mine nearly 40ft out from the Fore-Tower (see p.74). Visitors may traverse the tunnels. They are lit and there are railings. The castle fell after nearly a year, and among the Protestant prisoners taken was John Knox, later to become the champion of the Scottish Reformation and virtual founder of the Scottish Presbyterian Church. He was sent to serve as a galley slave in the French fleet and spent two years chained to an oar.

The castle was patched up by Beaton's successor, Hamilton, who added the front range of buildings to the west of the Fore-Tower.

SALTCOATS Lothian
(NT 486818)
A late sixteenth-century courtyard castle, as it were, whose principal structure was a 72ft by 23ft building with two projecting angle

470

towers at the western end. The castle is partly ruinous and much walling is missing.

SANQUHAR Dumfries and Galloway
(NS 785092)
Sanquhar is now in ruins. Begun by the Crichton family in the fifteenth century, it was a rectangular courtyard castle with a substantial frontal mass (like Doune), with a tall tower at the south corner, which has been restored. The site was protected naturally on north-west, south and east sides by a cut-ditch of which little remains, and which is flanked by a rampart. The quadrangle had a range of buildings on each inner side, of varying periods, beginning in the fifteenth century. The curtain wall at the north may be the oldest part (early 1400s). There are remains of associated buildings in front of the rectangular enclosure, dating chiefly from the seventeenth century.

SAUCHIE Alloa, Central
(NS 896957) P
A square-plan tower of the fifteenth century is the principal feature of this courtyard

castle. The tower was build of ashlar and is still in good condition. There are three storeys to the parapet which has a bartizan on one edge. Buildings were added later.

SCALLOWAY Nr Lerwick, Shetland †
(HU 405393) SDD
Scalloway is a four-storeyed tower-house of the end of the sixteenth century. Today its garret and roof are missing. Its plan is rectangular with the north-east corner bulging into a cylindrical stair turret from first storey upwards, and its south-west provided with a large square-plan tower containing straight flights of stairs to the top. There is also a secondary spiral staircase in a curved projection in the angle between the main block and the south-west tower, on the north side, also from first floor upwards. Fortification was provided by the insertion of shot-holes in window breasts (many have since been blocked), and by gun-ports, especially in the south-west stair tower. The ground floor of the stair tower has a vaulted chamber under the stairs, and this was a

Scalloway: the tower-house was built c.1600, but in a style more pertinent to the fifteenth century

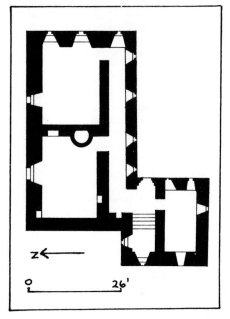

Scalloway: ground-floor plan. This is an early example of a Scottish tower house having straight flights of stairs

guard room, equipped with platforms and gun-ports.

Scalloway was built by Patrick Stewart, Earl of Orkney, a man of violent and cruel disposition who is said to have used the blood of his victims as liquid with which to mix the mortar for his castle — almost certainly a myth. Animal blood, however, might well have been used. The castle was allowed to deteriorate for a long time, but was restored by the Office of Works (now the SDD).

SCHIVAS Tarves, Grampian
(NJ 897368)
A sixteenth-century L-plan tower-house incorporated now in a more modern mansion. It is notable for its ornamental shot-holes designed mainly for pistols but which could be used for muskets.

SCOTSTARVIT TOWER Nr Cupar,
Fife †
(NO 370113) SDD
A fine tower-house of L-plan design, built between 1550 and 1579. It was the home at

one time of Sir John Scot, brother-in-law of the poet William Drummond, who wrote a book called *Scot of Scotstarvit's Staggering State of Scots Statesmen* (later described by Carlyle as a 'homily on life's nothingness enforced by examples'). The tower is six-storeyed, including mezzanine (between ground and first floors) and attic (surrounded by parapet). The very small wing of the 'L' contains the spiral stair all the way up, and the wing was topped with a caphouse of conical stone. The six storeys contained six rooms of equal floor area, one above the other. The tower is notable for the scarcity of windows.

SELKIRK Borders
(NT 470281)
A large natural mound north of Loch Haining formed the basis of an early twelfth-century motte castle which was later given stone buildings, probably by Edward I, in the very late thirteenth century. The mound received a pele-tower. The surrounding ditch was about 40ft wide on average. The castle was taken by the Scots in 1301–2.

SKELBO Dornoch, Highland
(NH 792952)
Now a ruin, Skelbo appears to have begun as a rectangular great tower in the fourteenth century, enclosed inside a barmkin. Some of the barmkin has been rebuilt in later style. The tower is 43ft by 29ft, with walls about 5ft thick, and much of this is still standing. It is clear that the tower was repaired for use in much later times. There are remains of other buildings within the barmkin.

SKELMORLIE Largs, Strathclyde
(NS 195658)
A rectangular tower-house of c.1500 with additions of the 1630s which included a smaller tower. It was renovated in the nineteenth century and converted into a mansion. In the original tower part, the kitchen was divided from the dining hall by a screened passage.

(*opposite*) Scotstarvit: the tower house

472

SKIPNESS Kintyre, Strathclyde †
(NR 907577) SDD
Skipness is an enclosure castle of thirteenth-century origin, which has been considerably modified over the centuries. Today, it is a ruin in fair condition, basically a stone quadrangle with a tower-house of L-plan in one corner. The masonry of the earliest work is of good quality.

The first structure was a rectangular stone hall-house. This was enclosed by a timber palisade upon an encircling rampart. Near-by, and at more or less the same time, a chapel was built, and it was dedicated to St Columba. Towards the end of the thirteenth century, the hall-house was reduced and absorbed in some new building work and the palisade was converted to stone. These buildings included a larger hall and some towers, one of which, in the north-east corner, used part of the original hall-house's east wall. This tower was later developed into an L-plan tower-house, whose remaining shell rises to four storeys to the parapet. The stonework enclosure received an arched entrance gate on the south wall, equipped with a portcullis, which faces the sea. A second arch was inserted in the north wall later. Note the quality of the early masonry, the ashlar cross-loops in the west curtain, and the interesting siting near the sea.

SMAILHOLM Borders †
(NT 637346) SDD
This four-storey rectangular tower-house stands on a spur which was enclosed by ditch and by stone walling. Three sides of the spur are rock cliff. The tower walls are nearly 10ft thick and the tower reaches nearly 60ft. The building is chiefly seventeenth-century work. Smailholm was a favourite castle of Sir Walter Scott. It is a ruin.

SORBIE TOWER Dumfries and
Galloway   (NX 451470)
This L-plan tower-house of the sixteenth century was abandoned after the Second Jacobite Rising (1745–6). The main block is 40ft by 24ft, and probably rose to four storeys.

SORN Strathclyde
(NS 548269)
A fifteenth-century great tower and curtain wall castle of rectangular plan, which has been restored and modified.

SPEDLIN'S TOWER Lochmaben,
Dumfries and Galloway
(NT 097875)
This is an interesting ruin of a once splendid rectangular tower-house. It began as a three-storeyed tower (including basement) with a pit prison of dimensions of only 7ft 7in by 2ft 6in. In the seventeenth century, the tower was considerably modified by adding two further storeys, the top of which was surrounded by a parapet, at each end of which was inserted a round corbelled turret with 'pepper-pot' roof. The roof of Spedlin's was unusual: it was a double one with two gables in between which ran a horizontal stretch. The horizontal stretch roofed a central corridor in the storey below, which had rooms off both sides. The tower is now without its roofs, but the stonework is in good condition considering its age.

STANE Strathclyde
(NS 338399)
A sixteenth-century tower-house.

STAPLETON TOWER Dornock,
Dumfries and Galloway
(NY 235689)
This is a rectangular tower, about 43ft by 27ft and over 40ft tall to the parapet. It was built in the sixteenth century but is now a shell. It abuts upon a much more modern house.

STIRLING Central ††
(NS 790941) SDD
Perhaps more than any other castle, Stirling represented Scotland's military resistance to English aggression in the Middle Ages. In the War of Independence it was constantly being attacked, its buildings destroyed and then rebuilt. In 1296, it was seized by Edward I of England. A year later, Wallace recovered it, along with many others, but lost it again in 1298. In 1299, the Scots took it again and this time held it until 1304, the year of the great siege by Edward I which was planned with some care. For three months the garrison resisted everything the old warrior could hurl against it, including a battery of siege engines weighted down with

474

lead stripped from neighbouring church roofs, under the general control of Master James of St George. These engines hurled Greek fire, stone balls and possibly even some sort of gunpowder mixture (see chapter 6). At the end of July the garrison surrendered. The English held the castle for ten years but it was yielded to the Scots after their great victory nearby at Bannockburn, in 1314, and it was then dismantled, remaining a ruin, militarily speaking, for some years.

The structure that endured so many changes of hands and so much battering was basically a timber and earthwork castle tailored to the great basalt rock some 250ft high at Stirling, which commanded the main route into the Highlands. Some kind of fort was built there late in the eleventh century. Alexander I (1107–24) built a chapel, and died there. David I stayed there on many occasions and his grandson, William the Lion, died there in 1214. But of the buildings of these years, even up to the fourteenth century, nothing remains. And the complex of stone structures and walls that graces the huge rock today stem from the fifteenth century and later.

Stirling became a more permanent Crown residence under the Stewart dynasty. The oldest surviving stone buildings, though doubtless not the first to be erected, are the gatehouse with its square centre block containing the entrance passage and two narrower side entrances, the block flanked by substantial cylindrical towers which once had roof caps but which were replaced in the eighteenth century by crenellations, and, for a different role, the great hall.

The great hall was designed and built by Robert Cochrane, favourite of James III (1460–88), and was one of the first and certainly the finest of the fifteenth-century Renaissance buildings erected anywhere in the British Isles. James III may also have erected curtain walls and towers. James IV began the great Palace Block with its rich carving on the north and south faces, and this was continued by his son, James V. In c.1594, James VI rebuilt a much earlier chapel, probably of c.1470–80.

Stirling was the place of baptism in 1566 of the infant who was to become James VI a year later when his mother, Mary, Queen of

Scots, was forced to abdicate. The baby James was crowned there, aged only thirteen months. The Earl of Gowrie who organized the Raid of Ruthven in 1581 was executed beneath the walls of Stirling. The castle was besieged by Monk in 1651. It was attacked also by Bonnie Prince Charlie on his sensational advance through Scotland in the Second Jacobite Rising in 1745–6.

STRANRAER Dumfries and Galloway
(NX 061608) C
Stranraer Castle is in poor condition. It is in the middle of the town and was used as the town gaol from the seventeenth to the nineteenth century. It began as an L-plan tower-house of the sixteenth century whose main block is 35ft by 28ft. It was heightened in the seventeenth century and given a caphouse with wall-walk.

STRATHAVEN Strathclyde
(NS 703444) P
A substantial rectangular tower, 70ft by 38ft, with a four-storeyed round tower extension. There is little of this fortress standing. It was originally a castle of the great Douglas family.

STRATHENDRY Leslie, Fife
(NO 225019)
Now incorporated in a modern mansion, the military part of Strathendry was a sixteenth-century tower-house, about 39ft by 26ft. The tower-house, now restored, has a staircase turret projecting from the north wall.

STROME Loch Carron, Highland   †
(NG 862354) NTS
A rectangular hall tower, about 100ft by 30ft, now in ruins. It has a crosswall. The highest part of the tower is about 20ft tall, but much of the tower has crumbled away. Strome was a fortress of the Lords of the Isles. It was begun in the fifteenth century.

STRUTHERS Fife
(NO 377097)
A sixteenth-century L-plan tower-house incorporating some earlier work. Major alterations were carried out in the eight-eenth century. The castle is now in ruinous condition.

SUNDRUM Colyton, Strathclyde
(NS 411212)

The original part of what is now a hotel is an early rectangular tower of (?) fourteenth-century construction which has walls about 10ft thick.

SWEEN Knapdale, Strathclyde ††
(NR 713789) SDD

Castle Sween, as it is generally known, stands on the rocky coast of Knapdale, halfway down on the western side. Described in the chapter on Scottish Castles, it is a quadrilateral stone enclosure (or possibly great tower) erected probably towards the end of the eleventh century, or very early twelfth century. It may have been built by a family called McSwine, which could be a mixed Scottish-Viking name, the 'Swine' part being a rendering of Sweyn. It is thought to have been sacked in 1645 or 1647 by Alastair 'Colkitto' MacDonald, a one-time ally of Montrose, during the Civil War. For its age, Castle Sween is a remarkably well preserved ruin.

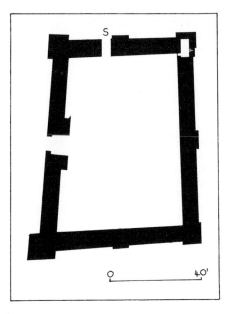

Sween: plan of the earliest wall. S = sea gate

Sween: probably the oldest stone great tower in Scotland. It is distinctly Norman in character

TANTALLON North Berwick, †† Lothian (NT 596850) SDD
This is a fascinating castle that makes the most of its coastal site on the Firth of Forth. A promontory with north-west, north-east and south-east sides juts into the Firth and consists of sheer rock cliffs about 100ft tall falling straight down to the sea. On the fourth (south-western) side, a ditch about 20 ft wide cut into the rock in the shape of an arc, straddles the promontory, effectively sealing off the rough rectangle site from the mainland. Inside the ditch, set back (south-eastwards) about 30ft or so, is a massive battlemented curtain wall of dressed red freestone, some 50ft tall, and 12ft or so thick. The variations in the face-work of the curtain are thought to be due to different masons at work at the same time. In the curtain is a central mid-tower containing the entrance, and remains of end towers at north-west and south-east extremities. The ruins of all three towers rise to nearly 80ft. The north-west (Douglas) tower had six storeys above the basement which was a pit prison. It was cylindrical, but today only a short segment remains. The south-east tower (known as the East tower) rose to five storeys, originally with wooden floors but later given stone vaulting. A cylindrical

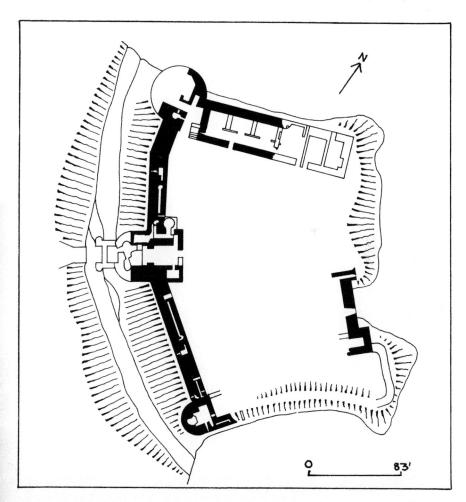

Tantallon: ground plan. The bold lines are the parts built in the fourteenth century section of the height remains to the second storey, but above that only parts of two sides survive to the top. The mid-tower, gatehouse tower, is 42ft square, had four storeys of residential accommodation above the room containing the portcullis mechanism, and consisted at front of a pair of square-plan wings up to second storey, flanking the entrance, which then changed to cylindrical turrets on corbelling. The tower contained a drawbridge mechanism, and this was protected by a barbican projecting into the ditch.

This structure, together with a two-hall (one above the other) block at north attached to the Douglas Tower and a sea-gate protecting the castle interior on the north-east side, was erected in the fourteenth century. Additions and alterations followed in the fifteenth and sixteenth centuries, but by 1400 the great bulk of the castle had already been raised.

In considering Tantallon's history, it is as well to disregard the legend about it in Sir Walter Scott's *Marmion*. Tantallon be-longed to the earls of Fife in the fourteenth century but probably the great stonework frontal wall with towers had not been built when it passed in c. 1360 to William, 1st Earl of Douglas, of the Black Douglas family. It later passed to the Red Douglas family (cousins of the former). One of its holders was Archibald 'Bell-the-Cat' Douglas, 5th Earl of Angus. He was besieged in Tantallon by James IV in 1491 who used both crossbows and culverins (small cannons). His grandson, Archibald, 6th Earl of Angus, who married the widow of James IV, (Margaret Tudor, sister of Henry VIII of England), plotted continually against Scotland's interests, and was deprived of his titles and estates by James V in 1526. Soon afterwards, Tantallon, held by Angus's brother, was besieged by the king whose troops marched to the siege chanting the refrain, 'Ding Doun, Tantallon! Ding Doun, Tantallon!' But the king failed to take the castle, despite the employment of 'two great cannones . . . two double falkons and four quarter falkons'.

Tantallon: the east wing of the enclosure that straddles the rock jutting into the sea

Tantallon was surrendered to James in 1529 after Angus had fled to England. It stayed in Crown hands until 1543 when Angus returned, his estates restored to him — and promptly began plotting against the Regent of Scotland, the Earl of Arran. Its history thereafter was a chequered one, and it appears in numerous documents. The variations of the spelling of Tantallon are quaint: Temptalloun (1548), Thomptalloun (1581) Tymptallon (1657).

In 1651 Tantallon was attacked by General Monck on behalf of Cromwell, and it was surrendered after twelve days of bombardment. Afterwards it fell into decay.

TARBERT Kilcalmonell, Strathclyde † (NR 868690) O
An interesting agglomeration of ruins beside the sea, about which little is known. Even the dating is open to much question. The castle appears to have been begun in the thirteenth century, when a plain rectangular tower was built on one side of an irregularly shaped curtain. A further tower was raised in the fifteenth century in the wall of a second, outer enclosure, which may be of the same period. There are traces of projecting turrets in the enclosure walls. Tarbert was equipped with inverted keyhole gun-ports which were probably inserted in the sixteenth century.

TARINGZEAN Strathclyde (NS 556205)
A much restored and altered tower-house which was begun in the fifteenth century.

TERPERSIE Alford, Grampian (NJ 546202) C
This was one of the first Z-plan castles in Scotland (S.H. Cruden suggests it is the earliest). It was raised in 1561 and was smaller than the majority of those that followed. Terpersie was a rectangular tower block, 28ft by 18ft, with small cylindrical towers on diagonally opposite corners, 17ft in diameter. The cylindrical towers were equipped with gun-ports and pistol holes. Today the castle is ruinous.

THIRLESTANE Ettrick, Borders (NT 280154)
Thirlestane Tower is today little more than a

length of rubble built wall, about 43ft long, with indications that the ground floor was vaulted. It stands on a rocky platform and was built in the sixteenth century.

THIRLESTANE Lauder, Borders (NT 533479) C
This is a splendid building of interesting design. It began as a fourteenth-century structure, sometimes known as the Old Fort of Lauder, which was extended in the sixteenth century by the then owners, the celebrated Maitlands (see also Lennoxlove). The major work, however, was done by John Maitland, Duke of Lauderdale (the last of the five men who ruled Britain under Charles II from 1666–73, whose initials formed the word CABAL — Clifford, Arlington, Buckingham, Ashley, Lauderdale). He employed the well-known architect, William Bruce, who took the original shell of the tower-house, about 108ft by 22ft contained by massive cylindrical towers with curved lobes extended at the corners, the longer sides of the tower divided by semi-cylindrical towers, three on each wall, and crowned the whole building with a tower bearing an ogee roof. Parapets,

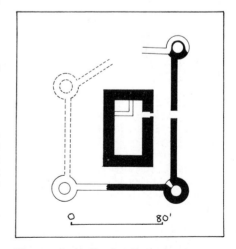

Threave: the 'artillery' wall runs from north to south between the cylindrical turrets and then at right angles from south to west. The space in the east wall indicates the position of the gatehouse. The great tower is in the centre

479

Threave: the powerfully built Douglas stronghold was further strengthened by an artillery wall with turrets

caphouses, conical turrets, fine windows were all added to make it even more sumptuous. By this time, however, it was no longer a fortress.

THREAVE Nr Castle Douglas, ††
Dumfries and Galloway
(NX 739623) SDD

Threave stands on an islet in the Dee, and even as a ruin it is a mighty and forbidding structure. It is a massive great tower partly enclosed by a powerful 'artillery' wall which today has the remains of three cylindrical corner turrets. The castle has been the subject of major investigation in the 1970s, and the results are interesting.

The first building was the great tower: today, 61ft by 40ft, four-storeyed and rising to over 70ft to the remnants of the battlements, with walls nearly 10ft thick. It was built by Archibald 'the Grim', 3rd Earl of Douglas, Lord of Galloway, in about 1370, and it was a defensive structure as well as a building intended to impress.

During the reign of James II (1437–60), the earls of Douglas were locked in a deadly quarrel with the king who was determined to break their power once and for all. In 1454, perhaps a year or two earlier, Threave great tower was reinforced by the erection of an 'artillery' wall along the east and south sides which faced the mainland. The wall was 18ft

480

tall (the remains are less high today), and it was provided with vertical loops with embrasures for hand-guns and for cross-bows (both types of weapon were often used together in the fifteenth century), and its towers were equipped with two types of gun-port, inverted keyholes and dumb-bells. There was a gatehouse in the middle of the eastern wall. The wall used to be dated c.1514, but the recent work puts it squarely into the mid-fifteenth century, and makes it the earliest 'artillery' wall in Britain.

Additionally, the excavations revealed the existence of buildings and facilities of the mid-fifteenth century (such as blacksmith's shop, carpenter's workshop and lead smelt-ing hearth) that suggest the castle's com-munity in its isolated site was self-supporting. Threave was besieged in 1455 by James II using the latest available cannons and bombards, including Mons Meg (p.122), and eventually taken.

TIBBERS Dumfries and Galloway
(NX 863982) O
Not much of this castle remains. It was one of the castles built by the English towards the end of the thirteenth century, during Edward I's attempts to take over Scotland after the demise of King John Balliol. It was a simple quadrangular curtain enclosure of stone with a cylindrical tower on each corner, of which one was a flanking tower for an entrance in the walling. There was a second flanking tower on the other side of the entrance. In front of this side of the enclosure are a rock-cut ditch and bank. The enclosure walls were between 7–9ft thick. Of these structures, enough stretches of masonry remain to indicate the plan, which resembles that of Inverlochy.

TILLYCAIRN Grampian
(NJ 665114)
A castle ruin of mid-sixteenth-century L-plan construction. The main tower was 41ft by 37ft, and probably rose to four storeys. The staircase wing, circular in plan, was one storey taller. Tillycairn has some interesting gun-ports; crosslet top and oillet bottom loops, one of which covered the door in the re-entrant; wide-mouth ports all round; and pistol shot-holes in the roundels.

TILQUHILLY Nr Banchory, Grampian
(NO 721941) C
Tilquhilly is a Z-plan castle, and was built in c.1576, almost contemporary with Claypotts (q.v.). One end tower was square plan, the other rectangular. The towers had been well provided with gun-loops. The castle is massive looking, but has lost its fortified appearance.

TIMPENDEAN TOWER Borders
(NT 635226)
The remains of this rectangular tower-house of the late sixteenth century consist of walls, two opposites reaching to gable height. The tower is 29ft by 24ft. It was equipped with wide-mouth gun-ports.

TIORAM Moidart, Highland   †
(NM 662724)
Tioram stands on an island in Loch Moidart, high on a rock making the castle stand well clear of the water. It is a stone enclosure, approximately five-sided, whose angles (like Mingary's) are rounded. It occupies the whole summit of the rock on which it stands. Buildings were erected inside, which are now ruined.

TORCASTLE Highland
(NN 133786)
Fragments remain of a very early medieval castle here, dated by some to the eleventh century. It is more probable that Tor was built in the twelfth.

TOLQUHON Tarves, Grampian   ††
(NJ 874286) SDD
Tolquhon belonged to the Forbes family. It is a castle of two main building periods, (?) late fifteenth century and 1584–9. The first period saw the construction of the 'auld tour' (old tower), also known as Preston's Tower (the site of the castle had belonged to a family called Preston). This tower is now ruined: only the vaulted basement and parts of the first floor remain. The walls are 7–9ft thick and contained mural staircases.

In 1584, William Forbes enlarged the castle by building round the 'auld tour' a substantial irregular quadrangular enclo-sure with ranges of buildings along the inside of three walls. On the north-west corner he erected a cylindrical tower some

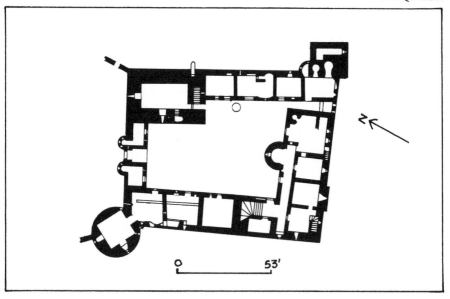

Tolquhon: ground floor. The 'Auld Tour' is at top left

Tolquhon: the gatehouse. Note the triple opening gun-ports

26ft in diameter, and on the south-east corner a tower about 20ft square. The ranges contain well-appointed apartments on two levels, including a great dining hall, a long gallery and a laird's private room. On the inward face of the south range a semi-cylindrical tower contains a spiral staircase in the upper half.

Tolquhon was equipped with wide-mouth gun-ports, notably in the masonry of the two semi-cylindrical towers on the north face which flank the entrance (which has a small round-headed arch). Behind the two semi-cylinders are guardrooms (at ground-floor level). Both the corner towers were equipped with gun-ports, each to cover two sides of the quadrangle. Some of the gun-ports are ornamented. The parapet of the 'auld tour' had been machicolated. We have here a fine residence that is amply provided with fortification.

Near the gatehouse is a tablet of stone containing the terse inscription — 'Al this warke. excep the auld tour. was begun be William Forbes 15 Aprile. 1584. and endit be him. 20 October. 1589.'

TORTHORWALD Dumfries and Galloway   (NY 033782)
Torthorwald is now a shell of a tower-house, which was part of a stone curtain enclosure. The ruin, which had two vaulted storeys, rises to about 60ft tall, and is partly shored up by more modern building works. The castle is of mid-fourteenth-century construction, but was raised upon the site of an earlier earthwork castle. The site has remains of considerable ramparts and ditches.

TORWOOD Dunipace, Central
(NS 835843)
An L-plan tower-house whose main block is now roofless. It was built in the 1560s (a date panel of 1566 has been found), and the ground floor was vaulted. The tower is three-storeyed, with a wing tower containing the staircase. In front of the angle is a courtyard with other domestic buildings.

TOWARD Strathclyde
(NS 118678) P
The ruins of a fifteenth-century tower of four storeys and a later courtyard can be seen

here. The castle was besieged and taken by the Argyll Campbells in 1646. It is being restored.

TOWIE BARCLAY Turriff,   †
Grampian   (NJ 744439) O
A later sixteenth-century L-plan tower-house which has the unusual feature of a rib-vaulted great hall, reached by a spiral staircase within the tower wall thickness. Above the entrance to the hall is a small oratory reached by another mural staircase that rises unseen over the doorway. In the late eighteenth century, Towie Barclay was altered, the most substantial change being the removal of two storeys of the tower. It has been further restored and is now open.

TROCHRIE Tayside
(NN 978402)
A seventeenth-century Z-plan tower-house, now in ruins.

TULLIALAN Nr Dunfermline, Fife   †
(NS 926887) O
An early fourteenth-century hall-house with a remarkable undercroft, rib vaulted from central piers. The hall received additions, including a strong curtain wall round most of the central structure. Tullialan is built on a natural rock outcrop, and was partly protected by a deep ditch. Note a hooded fireplace with sconces, considered by S.H. Cruden to be unusual for four-teenth-century Scottish castles.

TULLIBOLE Tayside
(NO 053005) O
Finely restored after World War II, Tullibole was begun in the first years of the seventeenth century, on the site of an earlier building which is mentioned in fourteenth-century documents. This was probably an unfortified structure. The newer castle was fortified with turrets and gun-ports. Two interesting features are a 'luggie', a seven-teenth-century form of room 'bugging', and a shot-hole beside the main entrance door.

TULLOCH Highland
(NH 547603)
A much-restored castle which originated in the thirteenth century as a simple rectangu-lar tower.

TURNBERRY Strathclyde
(NS 196072) C
Raised on a promontory to the south of Maiden's Bay, Turnberry began as a cylindrical great tower castle of the thirteenth century. It is thought to have been the childhood home of Robert Bruce, for the castle belonged to his father. The remnants are fragmentary and much interfered with by later building work. The great tower was probably surrounded by a stone curtain which in turn was enclosed by a moat.

UDNY Grampian
(NJ 882268) C
This five-storeyed rectangular tower, with rounded corners like Drum Castle was built in the fifteenth and sixteenth centuries. It is thought that originally the tower rose only to three storeys in height, and that the extra two floors were added in the sixteenth century. Two of the original storeys have

vaulted ceilings and very thick walls. In the nineteenth century a new mansion was built on to the tower, but this has since been demolished, leaving the ancient tower much as it was, with restorations of the last decade or so.

URQUHART Drumnadrochit,   ††
Loch Ness, Highland   (NH 531286) SDD
Urquhart stands on a sandstone promontory jutting into Loch Ness from the north-west, overlooking Urquhart Bay which is in the form of a 'kink' in the straightish shore of the loch. The castle site was defended from attack from the landward side by a ditch up to about 100ft wide and 15–17ft deep, and this was crossed by a bridge with high walls on either side of the path, broken in the middle by a drawbridge. This bridge led out from a massive twin-cylindrical towered gatehouse in the length of the high stone curtain wall that skirted the west side of the

Urquhart: a model of what the castle probably looked like in the seventeenth century

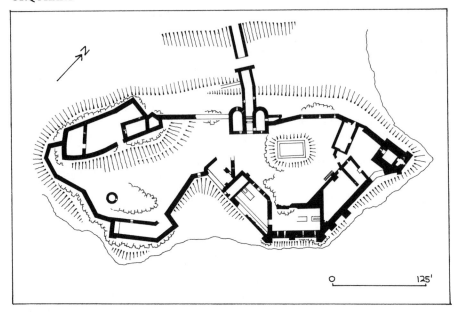

Urquhart: plan of the buildings, as they probably were in the late seventeenth century. The great tower of the sixteenth century is at extreme right

castle. The curtain followed the contour of the irregular rocky ground of the promontory, and it survives in part, though not to its full height. At the north end of the curtain is the ruined shell of the great tower which has its south wall missing, and which is built of rubble with freestone dressings. Its walls are 10–12ft thick, and it rises to four storeys. The period of the tower seems to have been three-fold: the basement is fourteenth-century, the next storeys, sixteenth century (probably rebuilding of older work destroyed), and the top, seventeenth century. Gun-ports were inserted in the sixteenth century.

To the south of the great tower is a semi-hexagonal plan range of buildings skirting the top of the promontory containing the great chamber, hall and kitchen, now all ruined. The southern end of this range forms one side of an inverted V-shaped inlet for the loch water, and a landing place. At the apex of the 'V' is a water gate, built in a length of curtain that continues along the promontory and round to join up with an irregularly shaped, polygonal, thick stone walled enclosure which skirts the top of a natural mound. This mound was once a Norman-style motte, which centuries earlier had been the base for an Iron Age vitrified fort. The curtain continues north-eastwards out of the polygonal enclosure to join up with the western gatehouse, thus completing the circuit of a substantial enclosure castle with buildings whose ground plan is roughly in the shape of a figure-of-eight, like Prudhoe. The motte enclosure (a kind of shell keep) remains to about 18ft tall, and contained buildings inside, of which traces can be seen.

The beginnings of Urquhart as a motte castle were probably mid-twelfth century. It passed to the powerful Durward family, and thence to the Comyn family. Edward I of England put it under English control, but it was retaken by the Scots in 1303, changed hands twice more, and in 1313 became the property of Randolph, Earl of Moray, one of Bruce's three greatest friends and counsellors. Thereafter it had a turbulent history in the struggle between the kings and the Lords of the Isles.

486

VAYNE Tayside
(NO 494599)
An interesting Z-plan castle of the sixteenth century. One diagonally placed tower is square plan, the other is round.

WALLACE'S Gamrie, Grampian
(NJ 773605)
There are fragments of walling on Ha' Hill in Glen Minonie which are of thirteenth-century date. They are thought to be remnants of a simple tower or enclosure which may have been used by William Wallace during his war against Edward I, c.1297–1305. Wallace was helped by Anthony de Moravia who was operating in and around Morayshire.

WAUGHTON Prestonkirk, Lothian
(NT 567808)
A terrace of rock supported an L-plan tower-house here, of which a wing remains.

WEMYSS Fife
(NT 329951)
A fifteenth-century tower-house built on the 'E' plan. This has been considerably altered, enlarged, altered again and reduced in size during its history, and now looks magnificent in its palatial glory.

WESTER KAMES Strathclyde
(NS 062681)
A much-restored rectangular tower-house of the sixteenth century.

WESTHALL Oyne, Grampian
(NJ 673266)
A much modified seventeenth-century L-plan tower-house with cylindrical staircase tower projecting in the angle. A second cylindrical tower containing another staircase was added later, and there were further alterations in the nineteenth century. The tower-house was enclosed by a barmkin.

WHITTINGHAME Lothian
(NT 602732)
An L-plan tower of possibly fourteenth-, or more probably fifteenth-, century beginnings, which was added to in the seventeenth century. The castle has been restored.

WIGTOWN Dumfries and Galloway
(NX 437550)
Fragmentary remains of an early thirteenth-century enclosure castle of stone, circular in plan and about half an acre in area. The enclosure is partly surrounded by a ditch and the remainder by the sea, as it stands on the shore. The castle was destroyed by Robert Bruce.

YESTER Lothian
(NT 556667) C
Yester Castle is one of the older fortresses of Scotland, whose remains now stand in the grounds of Yester House, on a peninsula into Hopes Water, two miles from Gifford. The first work was a motte castle, perhaps of the twelfth century. In the middle of the thirteenth century, a rectangular great tower was erected partly in the side of the motte. This had an undercroft, some 37ft by 13ft, with a high pointed barrel vaulted ceiling. The undercroft has survived and is now known as 'Goblin Ha'' because its origin was surrounded in mystery. 'Ha'' is Scottish for 'hall'. The great tower was later reduced in height when alterations were made in the layout, probably in the fifteenth century, to include a substantial enclosure curtain between 6–8ft thick. Part of the curtain survives, one length being nearly 70ft. A range of buildings was erected in the fourteenth century of which there are some remains.

Glossary

apse circular or polygonal recess or end of a chapel or tower

arcading row of arches supported on columns

arrow-loop or slit long, usually narrow and vertical opening in a wall, or in a merlon, through which arrows were shot. Round or triangular ends were for crossbows, as were horizontal cross-slits, sometimes called crosslets. These gave greater side-to-side range

ashlar blocks of smooth, squared stone of any kind

bailey or ward courtyard within walls of a castle

ballista siege engine in the form of a large bow for shooting missiles, usually iron bolts

barbican outward continuation of a gateway or entrance, erected to defend it, often in the form of a walled passage without roof

barmkin outer defensive walling (generally Scottish)

barrel vault semi-circular roof of stone, or timber

bartizan small turret corbelled out from corner or flank of a tower or wall

bastion another word for tower or turret projecting from a wall length or at the junction of two walls

batter sloping, or splayed, part of a wall, particularly of a great tower or an enclosing curtain

battlements (or crenellation) The parapet of a tower or wall with indentations, or openings (embrasures or crenelles) alternating with solid projections (merlons)

belfry tall, moveable wooden tower on wheels, used in sieges

berm horizontal space between a curtain or tower and its moat

billet one of a row of rectangular blocks raised as ornament in Norman architecture

brattice *see* hoarding

buttress projecting pillar on wall added to strengthen it

caphouse small chamber at top of spiral staircase in a tower or turret, leading to the open wall-walk on the roof

chevron moulding moulding in the form of inverted 'V', a Norman feature

clunch hard chalk used as building material. Often plastered with limewash for durability

corbel stone bracket projecting from a wall or a corner

counterscarp outer slope or wall of a ditch. *See* scarp

crenellation *see* battlements

cross-wall internal dividing wall in tower

crowsteps step gabled end to roof

curtain general term for castle walling, inner or outer, enclosing a courtyard. Sited between towers or tower and gatehouse, giving appearance of being hung between, from which 'curtain'

dog-legged with right-angled bends (passages, etc)

donjon alternative word for great tower

drawbridge wooden bridge which could be raised and lowered, stied in front of tower or gatehouse, across ditch

dressing carved or smoothed stonework around openings and along edges

embrasure *see* battlements

forebuilding structure on outside wall of a great tower protecting the entrance and all, or part, of the approaching staircase(s). Some forebuildings contained chambers and chapels over the stairs

freestone soft, easily worked stone

gallery long, narrow passage or room

garderobe latrine

groin junction of two curved surfaces in a vault

gun-loop or gun-port opening in wall for gun

hoarding covered wooden gallery affixed to the top of the outside of a tower or curtain, to defend the castle. It was supported on wooden beams inserted into put-log holes. The floor was slatted to allow defenders to drop missiles or liquids on to besiegers below

light window pane or window division

lintel horizontal beam of stone, or wood, across an opening at its top

machicolation projecting part of a stone or brick parapet with holes in the floor, as in hoarding

mangonel stone-throwing machine worked by torsion

mantlet mobile wooden protective shield on wheels

merlon *see* battlements

murder-holes openings in roof of gateway or part of gatehouse over entrance passage, popularly thought to be used for dropping missiles or shooting weapons at besiegers, but more probably for rapid water

discharge over wooden parts, such as gates, set on fire by besiegers
newel centre support for a spiral stair
offset ledge in wall followed by reduced thickness of wall
oriel window projecting curved or polygonal window
oubliette dungeon or pit under the floor, reached by a trap-door, used for incarcerating prisoners (Scottish pit prison)
pilaster buttress buttress with projection, on corner or mid-wall
portcullis wood and iron grille-pattern gate which was raised and lowered in grooves by ropes or chains in or in front of or behind an entrance
postern small gateway, usually in side or rear flanks of a castle, used as a getaway
put-log beam inserted into special hole in a great tower or gatehouse or curtain to support hoarding, or as scaffolding for building or repairs
quatrefoil four lobed
quoin corner stones
re-entrant angle that points inward (opposite to salient)
relieving arch arch built in wall to relieve thrust on another opening
revet face with a layer of stone, stone slabs, etc, for more strength. Some earth mottes were revetted with stone
rib vaulting arched roof with ribs of raised moulding at the groins
rubble uncut stone, or only roughly shaped stone, for walling
scarp inner wall or slope of ditch or moat (*see* counterscarp)
segmental less than a semi-circle (for example, segmental arch)
shot-hole hole for firearms, generally smaller than a gun-port
six-foil six lobed
slight damage or destroy a castle to render it unfit for use or occupation as fortress
solar lord's parlour or private quarters, sometimes adjacent to a great hall, sometimes over it
squinch-arch arched support for angle turret that does not reach ground
stepped recessed in a series of ledges
trebuchet stone throwing engine worked by counterweight
trefoil three lobed
voussoir wedge-shaped stone forming part of an arch
wall-walk path along top of wall, protected by parapet
ward *see* bailey
wing-wall wall descending slope of motte

Bibliography

An enormous amount of literature and reference material was studied in researching this book. It was a uniquely rich and rewarding experience. The lists include every county archaeological journal and every other learned journal studied, but not the individual volume and page numbers. It was my aim to examine every volume that carried any reference to castles individually or generally, in many cases going back to the last century. The lists also include almost every book on castles in the English language written between 1880 and 1980. A considerable number of more general works were consulted, embracing the political, military and social history of England, Wales and Scotland of the periods concerned, together with works relating to similar fields in the medieval history of western Europe. The majority of these are listed. Numerous medieval works and records were consulted (mostly in translation), and these too are listed.

Extensive work was done in the record departments of the Department of Environment, Welsh Office and Scottish Development Department, the Ordnance Survey (England and Wales, and Scotland), Royal Commission on Historical Monuments, Royal Commission on Ancient and Historical Monuments in Wales, Royal Commission on Ancient and Historical Monuments of Scotland, Public Record Office, Scottish Record Office, and in numerous city and university libraries. To everyone associated with these august institutions who helped — and there were many — my very deep gratitude.

Numerous local authorities, public bodies and private individuals (as castle owners) have produced valuable booklets, and I have read as many of these as were available. The unique series of DoE, Welsh Office and Scottish Development Department official handbooks have been carefully studied in their most recent editions.

493

Medieval sources (*translations or later editions*)

Anglo-Saxon Chronicle (tr Garmonsway, Everyman, 1954)
Annales Cambriae (c.444–1288, Rolls series, 1860)
Annales Monastici (c.AD 1–1432, ed Luard, Rolls series, 1864–9)
Brut y Tywysogyon: Red Book of Hergest version. (ed Jones, University of Wales Press, 1973)
Chartulary of Lindores (c.1195–1479, ed Dowden, Edinburgh, 1903)
Chronica: Roger of Hovedon (c.732–1201, ed Stubbs, Rolls series, 1868–71)
Chronica Gentis Scotorum: John Fordun (to 1383, ed Skene, Edinburgh, 1871–2)
Chronica Majora: Matthew Paris (to 1259, ed Luard, Rolls series, 1872–83)
Chronicle of Lanercost (1272–1346, trans 1913)
Chronicle of Melrose (tr Stevenson, London, 1856)
Chronicles of reigns of Stephen, Henry II and Richard I (ed Howlett, Rolls series, 1884–9)
Chronicon Anglicanum: Ralph de Coggeshall (1066–1223, ed Stevenson, Rolls series, 1875)
Chronicon ex Chronicis: Florence of Worcester (c.450–1117, ed Thorpe, London, 1849)
Chronicon Richardi Divisiensis de tempore regis Richardi primi: Richard of Devizes (ed Appleby, 1963)
Domesday Book (Public Record Office)
Flores Historiarum: Roger of Wendover (to 1235, ed Cox, 1841)
Ecclesiastical History of Ordericus Vitalis (c.AD 1–1141, ed Chibnall, 1969)
Gesta Normannorum Ducum: William of Jumièges (c.1028–70, ed Marx, Paris, 1914)
Gesta Regis Henrici Secundi (1169–92, ed Stubbs, Rolls series, 1867)
Gesta Regum Anglorum: William of Malmesbury (c.449–1127, ed Stubbs, Rolls series, 1887–9)
Gesta Stephani (tr K. Potter, London, 1955)
Giraldus Cambrensis Opera: Gerald of Wales (tr Everyman, 1908)
Histoire de Guillaume le Conquerant: William of Poitiers (ed Foreville, Paris, 1962)
Historia Anglorum: Henry of Huntingdon (55 BC–AD 1154, ed Arnold, Rolls series, 1879)
Historia Novella: William of Malmesbury (1125–42, tr K. Potter, London, 1955)

Historia Rerum Anglicanum: William of Newburgh (ed Howlett, Rolls, 1884–9)

Historical Collections of Walter of Coventry (to 1225, ed Stubbs, Rolls series, 1872–3)

Historical Works of Gervase of Canterbury (to c.1210, ed Stubbs, Rolls series, 1879–80)

Historical Works of Symeon of Durham (tr Stevenson, London, 1853–8)

Historie and Chronicles of Scotland: Robert Lindsay of Pitscottie (1437–1575, ed Mackay, 1899–1911)

Itinerary: John Leland (ed Toulmin Smith, 1904)

Itinerary in Wales: John Leland (ed Toulmin Smith, 1906)

Liber Eliensis (Ely; ed for Royal Historical Society, 1962)

Liber Landavensis (Llandaff; ed Evans & Rhys, Oxford, 1893)

Liber St Marie de Dryburgh (ed 1847)

Metrical Chronicle of Robert of Gloucester (to 1270, ed Wright, Rolls series, 1887)

Monasticon Anglicanum: William Dugdale (Caley's edition, 1846)

Opera Historica: Ralph de Diceto (ed Stubbs, Rolls series, 1876)

Original Chronicle of Andrew de Wyntoun (ed Amours, Edinburgh, 1902–14)

Textus Roffensis (Rochester; to c.1150, ed Hearne, 1720)

see also records such as:
Exchequer records, including Pipe Rolls: Issue Rolls, Memoranda Rolls, Calendar of Ancient Correspondence Concerning Wales (Board of Celtic Studies, 1955), Calendar of Patent Rolls (1232–1509, Public Record Office), Calendar of Liberate Rolls (John & Henry III, HMSO), Calendar of Close Rolls (1272–1485, HMSO), Register of Great Seal of Scotland (1306–1668), Register of Privy Seal of Scotland (from 1488), Scottish Rolls (1296–1516), Exchequer Rolls of Scotland (1264–1600, ed 1878–1908), Acts of the Parliament of Scotland (1124–1707), Calendar of Documents relating to Scotland (1108–1509, ed 1881–8).

More recent works
Books
Anderson, William *Castles of Europe* (Elek, 1970)
Armitage, Ella S. *Early Norman Castles of the British Isles* (1912)
Ashdown, Charles *British Castles* (A. & C. Black, 1911)

495

Ashurst, J. and Dimes, F. *Stone in Building* (Architectural Press, 1978)

Barrow, G.W.S. *Feudal Britain* (Edward Arnold, 1956)

Braun, Hugh *The English Castle* (Batsford, 1947)

Brown, Prof R. Allen *English Castles* (Batsford 1976)

—— *The Normans and the Norman Conquest* (Constable, 1969)

Burke, John *Life in the Castle in Mediaeval England* (Batsford, 1978)

Clark, G.T. *Mediaeval Military Architecture in England* (London, 1884) 2 vols

Cruden, S.H. *The Scottish Castle* (Nelson, 1960)

Dickinson, W.C. *Source Book of Scottish History* (Edinburgh, 1952–4)

Fedden and Thompson *Crusader Castles* (John Murray, 1957)

Fenwick, Hubert *Scotland's Castles* (Hale, 1976)

Graham, Frank *Castles of Northumberland* (F. Graham, 1976)

Harvey, John *English Mediaeval Architects: a biographical dictionary* (1954)

History of the King's Works Vols i, ii, iii. (HMSO, 1963 onwards)

Keen, Maurice *Pelican History of Mediaeval Europe* (Penguin, 1969)

Kinross, John *Discovering Castles in England and Wales* (Shire Publications, 1973)

Knoop, D. and Jones, G.P. *The Mediaeval Mason* (Manchester University Press, 1933)

Lloyd, Sir Edward J. *History of Wales From the Earliest Times to the Edwardian Conquest* (1939) 2 vols

MacGibbon, D. and Ross, T. *The Castellated and Domestic Architecture of Scotland* (1887-92) 5 vols

McKenzie, W.M. *The Mediaeval Castle in Scotland* (1927)

McKisack, May *The Fourteenth Century* (OUP, 1959)

Morris, J.E. *Welsh Wars of Edward I* (1901)

Oman, Sir Charles *Castles* (Great Western Railway, 1926)

—— *A History of the Art of War in the Middle Ages* (Cornell University Press, ed. Beeley, 1960)

O'Neil, B.J. *Castles* (HMSO)

Parker, J.H. *Domestic Architecture of the Middle Ages* (1859)

Poole, A. Lane *From Domesday Book to Magna Carta* (OUP, 1955)

Powicke, Sir Maurice *King Henry III and the Lord Edward* (OUP, 1947) 2 vols

—— *Loss of Normandy* (1913)

Renn, D.F. *Norman Castles in Britain* (J. Baker, 1973)

Ritchie, R.L. Grahame *Normans in Scotland* (Edinburgh, 1954)

Round, J.H. *Geoffrey de Mandeville* (1892)
Simpson, Prof. W. Douglas *Castles in Britain* (London, 1966)
—— *Castles in England and Wales* (Batsford, 1969)
Somerset Fry, Plantagenet *British Mediaeval Castles* (David & Charles, 1974)
Sorrell, Alan *British Castles* (Batsford, 1973)
Southern, R.W. *Making of the Middle Ages* (Hutchinson, 1953)
Stenton, Sir Frank *Bayeux Tapestry* (London, 1965)
—— *English Society in the Early Middle Ages* (Penguin, 1951)
Stevenson, J. (ed). *Documents Illustrative of the History of Scotland, 1286–1306* (Edinburgh, 1870)
Thompson, A. Hamilton *Military Architecture in England during the Middle Ages* (OUP, 1912)
Toy, Sidney *Castles of Great Britain* (London, 1953)
Tuchman, Barbara W. *A Distant Mirror* (Macmillan, 1979)
Viollet le Duc, E. *Military Architecture* (trans, Oxford, 1879)

See also: the county inventories published by the Royal Commission on Historical Monuments (England), RCAM (Wales), RCAHM (Scotland), including Anglesey, Caernarvonshire, Cambridgeshire (all vols, 1959–72), Carmarthenshire, Denbighshire, Dorset (all vols, 1952–75), Essex (all vols, 1916–23), Flintshire, Herefordshire (all vols, 1931–4), Hertfordshire (1910), Huntingdonshire (1926), Merionethshire, Montgomeryshire, Northamptonshire (1976), Oxfordshire (1967), Pembrokeshire and Radnorshire.

See also: Victoria County Histories of all counties concerned.

Booklets and papers
Bailey, Helen *Borthwick Castle*
Borg, Alan *Arms and Armour in Britain* (HMSO, 1979)
Boxall, O.N. *Bickleigh Castle*
Bradfer-Lawrence, H.L. *Castle Rising* (1954)
Busby, J.H. *Eye Castle: an historical note*
Cane, Hugh (following Hugh Braun) *Bungay Castle* (1958)
Clarke, David *Colchester Castle* (1974 ed)
Fox, Levi *Leicester Castle* (1970)
Greenshields, Margaret *The Siege of Bedford Castle* (1954)
Hassell, Jane and Baker, David *Bedford Town Origins* (1975)
Hilton, John *Tonbridge Castle: occasional paper series*
Holland, N. *New Buckenham Castle*

Hope-Taylor, Dr Brian *Excavations at Lowe Hill* (Wakefield Historical Society, 1953)
Hunt, T.J. *Taunton Castle*
Jackson, George *Bolton Castle* (1976)
Kent, J.P.C. *Excavations at the motte and bailey castle at South Mymms (1960–67)* (1968)
Lorimer, H. *Kellie Castle, Fife* (National Trust of Scotland, 1971)
Majendie, M. *Hedingham Castle*
Mayes, Philip *Sandal Castle* (Wakefield, 1973)
Morley, Beric *Henry VIII and the Development of Coastal Defence* (HMSO, 1976)
Renn, D.F. *Three Shell Keeps* (HMSO, 1969)
Ridgway, Maurice *Beeston Castle*
Sandal Castle Excavations (Wakefield Hist. Soc. for Joint Excavation Committee, 1964, 1965, 1966, 1967, 4 booklets)
Simpson, W. Douglas *Doune Castle* (1973)
Spurgeon, C.J. *Aberystwyth Castle*
Taylor, Dr A.J. *Castle Building in 13th century Wales and Savoy* (British Academy, 1977)
Whitehead, John *Pontefract Castle* (Var. papers, 1979–80)
Yorkshire Castles (HMSO, 1968)

See also: Broughton Castle, 1977; Caister Castle, 1977; Croft Castle (National Trust) 1975; Dudley Castle; Hunterston Castle, 1975; Lincoln Castle; Muncaster Castle; Rayleigh Mount (NT) 1965; Saltwood Castle, 1975; Sizergh Castle (NT); Tattershall Castle (NT), 1974

Official handbooks (Dept. of Environment for England, Welsh Office, Scottish Development Dept.)

Acton Burnell, Ashby de la Zouch, Baconsthorpe, Barnard, Berkhamsted, Berwick-on-Tweed, Bolsover, Brough, Carisbrooke, Carlisle, Castle Rising, Christchurch, Clifford's Tower, Conisbrough, Dartmouth, Deal & Walmer, Donnington, Dover, Dunstanburgh, Eynsford, Farleigh Hungerford, Farnham, Framlingham, Goodrich, Helmsley, Hylton, Kenilworth, Kirby Muxlow, Launceston, Longthorpe, Lydford, Middleham, Norham, Nunney, Okehampton, Old Beaupre, Old Sarum, Old Wardour, Orford, Pendennis & St Mawes, Pevensey, Peveril, Pickering, Portchester, Portland, Restormel, Richmond, Rochester, Scarborough, Spofforth, Tintagel, Totnes, Tower of London, Warkworth, Yarmouth.

Beaumaris, Bridgend, Caernarvon, Caerphilly, Carreg Cennen, Chepstow, Coity, Conwy, Criccieth, Denbigh, Dilbadarn, Dolwyddelan, Ewlow, Flint, Grosmont, Harlech, Kidwelly, Llanstephan, Llawhaden, Monmouth, Newcastle, Ogmore, Raglan, Rhuddlan, Skenfrith, Tretower, White, Weobley.

Aberdour, Affleck, Balvenie, Bothwell, Caerlaverock, Carsluith, Castle Campbell, Claypotts, Craigmillar, Craignethan, Crichton, Dirleton, Dumbarton, Duffus, Edinburgh, Edzell, Greenknowe, Hermitage, Huntingtower, Huntly, Kildrummy & Glenbuchat, Linlithgow Palace, Loch Leven, Noltland, Orchardton, Ravenscraig, Rothesay, St Andrews, Scalloway, Scotstarvit, Stirling, Tantallon, Tolquhon, Urquhart.

Special articles

'Additions and Corrections to Lists published in 1963 and 1967', Hogg, A.H. and King, D.J.C. *Archaeologia Cambrensis*, cxix (1970)

'Early Ordnance in Europe', Clephan R. *Archaeologia Aeliana*, xxv (1904)

'Early Castles in Wales and the Marches', Hogg, A.H. and King, D.J.C. *Archaeologia Cambrensis*, cxii (1963)

'Excavations at Castle Acre', *Château Gaillard*, viii (1976)

'Fulk Nerra Castles', *Bulletin Monumental*, t. 132 (1974)

'An Historian's approach to the origin of the Castle in England', Brown, R. Allen. *Archaeological Journal*, cxxvi (1969)

'List of Castles: 1154–1216', Brown, R. Allen. *English Historical Review*, lxxiv (1959)

'Masonry Castles in Wales and the Marches', Hogg, A.H. and King, D.J.C. *Archaeologia Cambrensis*, cxvi (1967)

'Moats and Mottes', Roberts, B.K. *Mediaeval Archaeology*, viii (1964)

'Mottes: a classification', Renn, D.F. *Antiquity*, xxxiii (1959)

Norman Motte at Abinger, Surrey, and its wooden castle, Hope-Taylor, Brian. *Recent Archaeological Excavations in Britain*. (1956)

'Origins of the Castle in England', Davidson, B.K. *Archaeological Journal*, cxxiv (1967)

'Ringworks of England and Wales', Alcock, L. and King, D.J.C. *Château Gaillard*, iii (1966)

'Royal Castle Building in England: 1154–1216', Brown, R. Allen. *English Historical Review*, lxx (1955)

'Sandal Castle, Wakefield', Mayes, P. *Château Gaillard*, vii (1974)

Academic journals, county archaeological journals, etc.
Antiquaries Journal
Antiquity
Archaeologia
Archaeologia Aeliana
Archaeologia Cambrensis
Archaeologia Cantiana
Archaeologia Scotica
Archaeological Bulletin for the British Isles
Archaeological Excavations, 1961–76
Archaeological Journal
Archaeological Reports, since 1956 (DoE)
Archaeological Review
Archaeology in Wales
Archéologie Médiévale (1973–4)
Archéologique du Comité des Travaux Historiques, Bulletin d'
Ayrshire Archaeological & Nat. Hist. Soc., Transactions

Bedfordshire Arch. Journal
Bedfordshire Hist. Record Soc., Trans
Berkshire Arch. Jnl
Birmingham & Warwickshire Arch. Soc., Trans
Board of Celtic Studies, Bulletin of
Bristol & Gloucestershire Arch. Soc., Trans
British Archaeological Association, Journal of the (JBAA)
Brycheiniog (Brecon)
Bulletin Monumental, France, 1974

Caernarvon Hist. Soc., Trans
Cambridge Antiquarian Soc., Proceedings
Cambridgeshire & Huntingdonshire Arch. Soc., Trans
Cardiganshire Antiquarian Soc., Trans
Carmarthen Antiquarian Soc., Trans
Ceredigion
Château Gaillard
Chester Arch. Soc. Jnl
Chester & North Wales Arch. Soc., Trans
Cornish Archaeology
Cumberland & Westmorland Antiquarian Soc.
Cymmrodorion Soc., Trans

Denbighshire Hist. Soc., Trans
Derbyshire Arch. Jnl
Devon Arch. Soc., Procs
Devon & Cornwall Notes & Queries
Devonshire Association, Trans
Dorset Natural History and Arch. Soc., Procs
Dumfriesshire & Galloway Nat. Hist. Soc., Trans
Durham & Northumberland Architectural and Arch. Soc.

East Anglian Hist. and Archaeology
East Herts Arch. Soc., Trans
East Lothian Antiquarian Jnl
East Midland Arch. Bulletin
East Riding Archaeologist
English Historical Review
Essex Arch. and Hist. Soc., Trans

Field Guide, West Cornwall
Flintshire Hist. Soc. Jnl

Glasgow Arch. Soc., Trans
Gloucestershire Historical Studies

Hampshire Field Club, Procs
Hertfordshire Archaeology
Historical Society of Lancashire and Cheshire, Trans

Institute of Archaeology, Bulletin of
Isle of Wight Nat. Hist. Soc., Procs

Lancashire & Cheshire Antiquarian Soc., Trans
Leicestershire Arch. & Hist.Soc., Trans
Lincolnshire History & Archaeology
London Archaeologist
London & Middlesex Arch. Soc., Trans

Mediaeval Archaeology
Merioneth History Society Jnl
Monmouthshire Antiquary

Nat. Hist. Soc. of Northumbria, Trans

Norfolk Archaeology
Northamptonshire Archaeology
Northamptonshire Nat. Hist. Soc. and Field Club
North Staffordshire Jnl of Field Studies
Nottingham Mediaeval Studies

Orkney Antiquarian Soc., Procs
Oxoniensia

Post-Mediaeval Archaeology

Radnorshire Society, Trans

Scottish Historical Review
Shropshire Arch. & Nat. Hist. Soc., Trans
Société des Antiquaires de Normandie, Bulletin de, liii (1955–6)
Society of Antiquaries of Scotland, Trans
Somersetshire Arch. & Nat. Hist, Soc., Procs
South Staffordshire Arch. & Hist. Soc., Trans
Staffordshire Archaeology
Suffolk Institute of Archaeology, Procs
Surrey Archaeological Collections
Surtees Society
Sussex Archaeological Collections

Thoroton Society of Nottinghamshire, Trans

West Wales Historical Records
Wiltshire Arch. & Nat. Hist. Magazine
Woolhope Field Club (Herefordshire), Trans
Worcestershire Arch. Soc., Trans

Yorkshire Archaeological Journal

Grateful acknowledgment is made to the following for permission to reproduce photographs, listed under page numbers:

Committee for Aerial Photography, University of Cambridge: 135, 139, 191, 198, 204, 214, 321, 323, 359, 364, 366 (both), 378, 458, 480
Aerofilms: 294
HMSO: 95
Paul Procter: 213, 228, 232, 267, 314
Scottish Development Department: 74 (bottom), 143, 385 (top), 409, 411, 428, 441, 442, 447, 452, 461, 471, 473, 483, 485
Ronald Faux: 126, 385
Pontefract Museum: 277
Wakefield Corporation: 295
Royal Commission on Ancient and Historical Monuments of Wales: 334, 336, 340, 342, 345, 347, 353, 361, 363, 368, 379, 380
A.F. Kersting: 40-1, 55, 85, 108, 112-13, 130, 135, 224-5, 302-3, 438-9
E. Lumb: 160
J. Cozens, South Hams Photography: 155
Adrian Robinson: 382
Acknowledgment is made to the Institute of Geological Sciences for the specially drawn map on p. 65. The notes that accompany it were kindly supplied by Francis Dimes, BSc, FGS, of the Royal Geological Museum.

Index

Castles listed in the index are those mentioned in the introductory chapters, pp. 7-169. Page numbers for their entries in the Gazetteer are given when they are of particular importance or having special points of interest. Entries in *italic* type relate to illustrations. Abbreviations are: C = Count; D = Duke; E = Earl; M = Marquis or Marquess; Q = Queen